Balanced Presentation of Fundamentals

Excellence in Business
Communication
SIXTH EDITION

John V. Thill
Courtland L. Bovée

ISBN: 0-13-141965-X

Business Communication Today Custom One-Color Option

The Core

$40.⁰⁰!

for the core nine chapters

- Net price to bookstore

Optional Chapters

$5.⁰⁰!

each additional chapter

- Net price to bookstore

Contact your local PH Rep for more information on the custom/core option.

Business Communication Essentials

Second Edition

Courtland L. Bovée

Professor of Business Communication
C. Allen Paul Distinguished Chair
Grossmont College

John V. Thill

Chief Executive Officer
Communication Specialists of America

PEARSON
Prentice
Hall

Upper Saddle River, New Jersey 07458

Library of Congress Cataloging-in-Publication Data
Bovée, Courtland L.
   Business communication essentials/Courtland L. Bovée, John V. Thill.—2nd ed.
     p. cm.
   Includes bibliographical references and index.
   ISBN 0-13-147245-3
     1. Business communication. 2. Business writing. 3. Business presentations. I. Thill,
John V. II. Title.

HF5718. B659 2005
651.7—dc22   2004018995

Acquisitions Editor: David Parker
VP/Editorial Director: Jeff Shelstad
Assistant Editor: Melissa Yu
Editorial Assistant: Denise Vaughn
Media Project Manager: Nancy Welcher
Marketing Manager: Anke Braun
Marketing Assistant: Patrick Danzuso
Senior Managing Editor (Production): Judy Leale
Production Editor: Theresa Festa
Permissions Supervisor: Charles Morris
Manufacturing Buyer: Diane Peirano
Design Manager: Maria Lange
Art Director: Janet Slowik
Interior Design: Karen Quigley
Cover Design: Janet Slowik
Cover Photo: Adri Berger / Stone / Getty Images, Inc.
Art Studio: ElectraGraphics, Inc.
Manager, Print Production: Christy Mahon
Full-Service: Carlisle Communications, Ltd.
Composition/Full-Service Project Management: Carlisle Communications, Ltd.
Printer/Binder: Courier/Kendallville/Phoenix Color

Credits and acknowledgments borrowed from other sources and reproduced, with permission,
in this textbook appear on page AC-1 and AC-2.

Pearson Prentice Hall™ is a trademark of Pearson Education, Inc.
Pearson® is a registered trademark of Pearson plc
Prentice Hall® is a registered trademark of Pearson Education, Inc.

Pearson Education LTD.
Pearson Education Singapore, Pte. Ltd
Pearson Education, Canada, Ltd
Pearson Education–Japan

Pearson Education Australia PTY, Limited
Pearson Education North Asia Ltd
Pearson Educación de Mexico, S.A. de C.V.
Pearson Education Malaysia, Pte. Ltd

1 0 9 8 7 6 5 4 3 2

ISBN 0-13-147245-3

Contents in Brief

Contents

Unit 2: The Three-Step Writing Process 51

Learn How the Blending of Text with Technology Creates a Total Teaching and Learning Solution

Experienced instructors know that teaching is more effective—and more efficient—when it integrates all elements of the learning experience, from content to teaching approach to pedagogy. This imperative grows every year, too, with the increasing complexity of business and the growing pervasiveness of communication technology.

Responding to this challenge, *Business Communication Essentials* integrates a text, a workbook, and a Handbook of Grammar, Mechanics, and Usage, providing an all-in-one package for a course covering the essentials of business communication. The blending of this text with technology, such as its "Document Makeovers" that are presented in an engaging multimedia environment, OneKey Learning Modules, and interactive website, make the text the most effective teaching and learning tool you'll find for a business communication course.

The book also includes numerous real-world examples and document critiques and features the most extensive end-of-chapter activities available, including questions, extensive worksheet exercises, assignments, and cases.

A unique three-level approach for learning grammar and mechanics identifies students' weaknesses and helps strengthen their skills using a variety of print and electronic resources.

Business Communication Essentials' integrated learning system is designed to help students develop employable skills more quickly and more effectively than they can with any other book. Each of the 14 chapters implements this learning system in four important ways:

1. Previewing Essentials
Each chapter's learning objectives provide a clear overview of the key concepts students are expected to master.

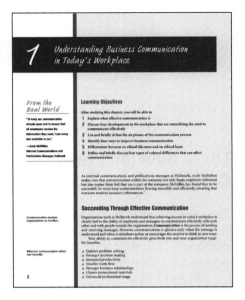

2. Developing Essentials
The chapter's textual material develops, explains, and elaborates on concepts with a highly organized, concise presentation that enables students to grasp concepts quickly and easily. A three-step graphic of the writing process appears throughout the book to give students a standard way to write business messages.

Planning	Writing	Completing
Analyze Study your purpose, lay out your writing schedule, and then profile your audience.	**Organize** Define your main idea, limit the scope, group your points, and choose the direct or indirect approach.	**Revise** Evaluate content and review readability, editing, and rewriting for conciseness and clarity.
Investigate Gather information through formal or informal research methods.	**Compose** Control your style through level of formality and conversational tone. Choose your words carefully so that you can create effective sentences and paragraphs.	**Produce** Use effective design elements and suitable delivery methods.
Adapt Choose the right channel and medium; then establish a good relationship with your audience.		**Proofread** Review for errors in layout, spelling, and mechanics.
1	**2**	**3**

3. Enhancing Essentials
Student learning is enhanced and strengthened by the chapters' real-life examples and annotated model documents. Plus, student interest is piqued and then maintained by a striking selection of exhibits and by a state-of-the-art design in a full-color book.

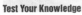

4. Reinforcing Essentials

Chapter material is reinforced not only with margin notes and a chapter summary but also with end-of-chapter exercises, assignments, and cases that have been logically sorted into categories such as "Test Your Knowledge," "Apply Your Knowledge," "Practice Your Knowledge," and "Expand Your Knowledge." In addition, the extensive "Improve Your Grammar, Mechanics, and Usage" section in each chapter helps students polish their English skills. Students can visit the OneKey website and do "Document Makeovers" to polish their skills.

Test Your Knowledge

1. What benefits does effective communication give you and your organization?

2. How is technology changing communication in the workplace?

...nication?

...diversity have on communication?

Expand Your Knowledge

Exploring the Best of the Web

Check Out These Resources at the Business Writer's Free Library   www.mapnp.org/library/commskls/cmm_writ.htm The Business Writer's Free Library is a terrific resource for business communication material. Categories of information include basic composition skills, basic writing skills, correspondence, reference material, and general resources and advice. Log on and read about the most common errors in English, become a word detective, ask Miss Grammar, review samples of common forms of correspondence, fine-tune your interpersonal skills, join a newsgroup, and more. Follow the links and improve your effectiveness as a business communicator.

Exercises

1. What are some st... uncooperative aud...
2. What is the value...
3. Why is bad etiquet...

Exploring the Web on Your Own

Review these chapter-related websites on your own to learn more about achieving communication success in the workplace.

1. Netiquette Ho... index.html. Lea... nication at this...
2. The Informatio... provided by Res... www.vts.rdn.ac... Internet skills... cation"). Lear... Internet, figure...

Apply Your Knowledge

1. Why do you think communication is the lifeblood of business organizations? Explain briefly.

...ion process help you conduct business more

...Vietnamese subculture is strongly established.
...member of the human resources
...prove communication between management
...ring?

Practice Your Knowledge

Activities

For live links to all websites discussed in this chapter, visit this text's website at www.prenhall.com/bovee. Just log on, select Chapter 1, and click on "Featured Websites." Locate the name of the page or the URL related to the material in the text.

1. **Analyze This Document**   Your boss wants to send a brief e-mail message welcoming employees recently transferred to your department from your Hong Kong branch. They all speak English, but your boss asks you to review her message for clarity. What would you suggest your boss change in the following e-mail message—and why? Would you consider this message to be audience centered? Why or why not?

I wanted to welcome you ASAP to our little family here in the states. It's high time we shook hands in person and not just across the sea. I'm pleased as punch about getting to know you all, and I for one will do my level best to sell you on America.

Business Communication Essentials is the centerpiece of a comprehensive package that includes a remarkable assembly of resources to support teaching and promote learning. With its heavy emphasis on exercises to improve grammar, punctuation, style, usage, and writing skills, this text offers students—especially those who lack proficiency in business English—the tools they need to succeed in today's workplace.

An All-in-One Text/Workbook with Business English Exercises

Get Excellent Results with These Business English Exercises

In each of this book's 14 chapters, students are taken step by step through the essential elements of English grammar, mechanics, and usage. Space is allocated for students to write their answers, and instructors can have students submit their answers if they choose. The "Improve Your Grammar, Mechanics, and Usage" section includes activities on three levels of difficulty:

Level 1. Self-Assessment

These 15 self-assessment exercises help students identify specific areas of weakness and overcome them by studying the basics presented in the Handbook of Grammar, Mechanics, and Usage that appears near the end of the book.

Level 1: Self-Assessment—Nouns

Use the following self-assessment exercises to improve your knowledge of and power over English grammar, mechanics, and usage. Review all of Section 1.1 in the Handbook of Grammar, Mechanics, and Usage that appears at the end of this book. Answers to these exercises appear on page xxx.

In items 1–5, underline the common nouns and circle the proper nouns.

1. Give the balance sheet to Melissa.

2. We'd like to order 50 more satchels for Craigmont Stores, and 3 each for the other stores on our list.

3. Tarnower Corporation donates a portion of its profits to charity every year.

4. Which aluminum bolts are packaged?

5. Please send the Joneseses a dozen of the following: stopwatches, canteens, headbands, and wristbands.

In items 6–10, underline the subjects and circle the objects.

6. The technician has already repaired the machine for the client.

Level 2. Workplace Applications

These 15 real-world exercises contain common errors in grammar, punctuation, capitalization, abbreviation, number style, word division, and vocabulary that students learn to recognize and correct.

Level 2: Workplace Applications

The following items contain numerous errors in grammar, capitalization, punctuation, abbreviation, number style, word division, and vocabulary. Rewrite each sentence in the space provided, correcting all errors. Write C in the space after any sentence that is already correct.

1. If a broken down unproductive guy like Carl can get a raise; why can't a take charge guy like me get one?

Level 3: Document Critique

The following document contains errors in grammar, capitalization, punctuation, abbreviation, number style, word division, and vocabulary. Correct all errors using standard proofreading marks (see Appendix C).

Level 3. Document Critique

Students are given a document that contains numerous errors and they are asked to correct the errors by using standard proofreading marks, which are presented in Appendix C.

In addition, students are given numerous exercises throughout the book to help them improve their writing skills. This text provides students with workplace-focused writing instruction that emphasizes real, on-the-job situations. This approach helps students become more effective communicators and thus more successful in business.

Peak Performance Grammar and Mechanics

Peak Performance Grammar and Mechanics

To improve your skill with nouns and pronouns, visit www.prenhall.com/onekey, click "Peak Performance Grammar and Mechanics," click "Grammar Basics," and then click "Nouns and Pronouns." Take the Pretest to determine whether you have any weak areas. Then review those areas in the Refresher Course. Take the Follow-Up Test to check your grasp of nouns and pronouns. For an extra challenge or advanced practice, take the Advanced Test. Finally, for additional reinforcement in nouns, go to the "Improve Your Grammar, Mechanics, and Usage" section that follows, and complete the "Level I: Self-Assessment" exercises.

In each chapter, students are directed to the OneKey website to improve their skills with mechanics and specific parts of speech by using the "Peak Performance Grammar and Mechanics" module. Students can take the pretest to determine whether they have any weak areas; then they can review those areas in the module's refresher course. Students can also take a follow-up test. For an extra challenge or advanced practice, students can take the advanced test.

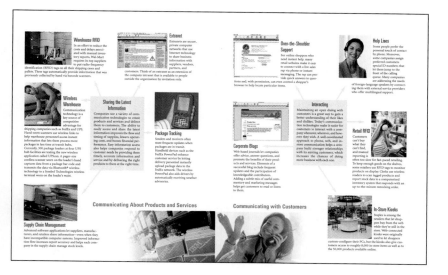

New Technology in This Edition

Integrated Approach to Technology

Students are introduced to the pervasive role of communication technology in a special four-page photo essay in Chapter 1, "Powerful Tools for Communicating Effectively." Colorful photos and informative text illustrate e-mail, instant messaging, wireless networks, web-based meetings, videoconferencing and telepresence, intranets, Internet videophones, flexible workstations, electronic wall displays, corporate blogs, and online workspaces. This overview helps students quickly grasp how technology is helping businesspeople communicate effectively. Then throughout the text, vital technologies such as e-mail and instant messaging—which have rapidly become the media of choice for many business communicators—are woven into the content presentation.

Document Makeovers

In each chapter of the book, an assignment overview directs students to the OneKey website, where interactive exercises help them apply chapter concepts to an actual business document. "Document Makeovers" offer students an appealing opportunity to use new technology to refine and reinforce their writing skills in a dynamic multimedia environment.

Document Makeover

Improve This Memo

To practice correcting drafts of actual documents, visit www.prenhall.com/onekey on the web. Click "Document Makeovers," then click Chapter 1. You will find a memo that contains problems and errors relating to what you've learned in this chapter about improving business communication. Use the Final Draft decision tool to create an improved version of this memo. Check the message for ethical communication, an audience-centered approach, and intercultural sensitivity.

Explore More of the Features That Are the Hallmark of All Bovée/Thill Business Communication Textbooks

Emphasis on Process and Product

The authors have organized the text into a process of three easy-to-follow steps, offering students a practical strategy for writing business messages. The three-step process comprises

- planning business messages
- writing business messages
- completing business messages

To complement the text's focus on process, the authors have provided numerous sample documents throughout the book so that students can refer to a variety of effective messages—including letters, memos, e-mail, instant messages, business reports, and employment messages.

Sample Documents

Students can examine numerous sample documents, many collected by the authors in their consulting work at well-known companies. These documents include marginal annotations to help students understand how to apply the principles being discussed. Many documents are also accompanied by a three-step-writing-process graphic that gives students important insights into the issues the writer considered when planning, writing, and completing the document. In addition, pairs of ineffective and effective drafts help students recognize the best writing techniques.

Documents to Analyze

This text/workbook provides a wide selection of documents that students can critique and revise. Documents include letters, memos, e-mail messages, graphic aids, a letter of application, and a résumé. Hands-on experience in analyzing and improving sample documents will help students revise their own business messages. "Document Critiques" are also part of the activities in the "Improve Your Grammar, Mechanics, and Usage" section, providing students with even more opportunities for analyzing and revising actual business messages.

Questions and Exercises

The end-of-chapter questions are divided into two types:

- Test Your Knowledge (10 review questions)
- Apply Your Knowledge (5 application questions)

These questions are designed to get students thinking about the concepts explained in the chapter and may prompt students to stretch their learning beyond the chapter content. Instructors can use these questions for class discussion, in-class assignments, student teamwork, homework, or extra-credit assignments.

Dozens of exercises give students practical assignments like those they will most often face at work. Each exercise is labeled by type, such as "Analyze This Document," "Team," "Ethical Choices," "Internet," and so on.

Pointers

A boxed insert appears near many sample documents, giving students a concise list of writing pointers. Students will also find these pointers handy when they are on the job and need to refresh their memory about effective writing techniques.

Cases

Nearly all companies featured in this text's cases are real. Both interesting and functional, these cases give students a chance to flex their communication muscles while dealing with all types and sizes of organizations, both domestic and international. Labels indicate those cases that focus on team, e-mail, web skills, or instant messages. In Chapters 6 to 9, because instant messaging is rapidly becoming the preferred communication tool for many businesspeople, instant messaging cases have been included, a first for a business communication text.

Business Communication Notebook

This feature, placed near the end of each chapter, centers on one of four themes: ethics, technology, intercultural communication, and workplace skills. To enrich their learning, students are referred to a website related to the subject of the feature. In addition, three "Applications for Success" discussion questions are included.

Real-World Chapter Openers

Each chapter opens with a quote, "From the Real World," that gives a communication expert's insights into an important aspect of business communication.

Focus on Teams

Communicating effectively through teamwork is covered extensively in Chapter 2. Also, teamwork activities are identified and labeled in the end-of-chapter "Practice Your Knowledge" section. Students can complete exercises, solve cases, and work on other assignments that help them prepare for the widespread use of teams in business today.

Internet Exercises

Students become acquainted with the wealth of business communication information on the web by participating in the end-of-chapter "Expand Your Knowledge" activities. Students are encouraged to visit the "Best of the Web" sites and complete the "Best of the Web" exercises. Plus, they are encouraged to explore the web on their own by visiting other chapter-related websites.

Video Cases

The video cases are introduced with a synopsis. Exercises ask students to react to the videos by responding to questions, making decisions, and taking the initiative to solve real business communication problems.

Teach with an Unparalleled Supplements Package

OneKey Online Courses

OneKey offers the best teaching and learning online resources, all in one place. OneKey is all instructors need to plan and administer their course. OneKey is all students need for anytime, anywhere access to online course material. Conveniently organized by textbook chapter, these compiled resources help save time and help students reinforce and apply what they have learned. OneKey is designed for convenience, simplicity, and success. OneKey is available in three course management platforms: Blackboard, CourseCompass, and WebCT.

For the Student

- **Peak Performance Grammar Tool**—for self-paced grammar skills development
- **Document Makeovers**—allow students to practice their revision skills and concept application in dynamic, on-line business documents
- **Learning Modules**—include section reviews, learning activities, and pretests and posttests
- **Student PowerPoints**—are easy-to-print black and white PowerPoints
- **Research Navigator**—four exclusive databases of reliable source content to help students understand the research process and complete assignments

Instructor's Resource Center

The Instructor's Resource Center, available on CD, at www.prenhall.com, or in your OneKey online course, provides presentation and other classroom resources. Instructors can collect the materials, edit them to create powerful class lectures, and upload them to an online course management system.

Using the Instructor's Resource Center on CD-ROM, instructors can easily create custom presentations. Desired files can be exported to the instructor's hard drive for use in classroom presentations and online courses.

With the Instructor's Resource Center, you will find the following faculty resources:

- **PowerPoints.** Two PowerPoint packages are available with this text. The first is a fully developed, noninteractive set of instructor's PowerPoints. The second is an enhanced, interactive version of the first with video clips and web links in each chapter. Both versions contain teaching notes.
- **TestGen Test-Generating Software.** The printed test bank contains approximately 100 questions per chapter including multiple-choice, true/false, fill-in, and essay questions. (*Print version also available.*)
- **Instructor's Manual.** This is an instructor's tool kit. Among its many teaching aids, this manual provides a section on cooperative learning, as well as suggested exercise solutions, fully formatted solutions for every case in the chapters on writing brief messages, and a grammar pretest and posttest. (*Print version also available.*)
- **Test Item File** (Word file)

Transparencies

A set of color transparencies is available to instructors upon request. The acetates highlight text concepts and supply facts and information to help bring concepts alive in the classroom and enhance the classroom experience. (*In print only*)

Companion Website

The text website www.prenhall.com/bovee features chapter quizzes and student PowerPoints, which are available for review or can be conveniently printed three-to-a-page for in-class note taking. The website also includes the English-Spanish Audio Glossary of Business Terms; the Handbook of Grammar, Mechanics and Usage Practice Sessions; and the Business Communication Study Hall, which allows students to brush up on several aspects of business communication—grammar, writing skills, critical thinking, report writing, résumés, and PowerPoint development.

Video Cases

Videos are included on topics such as ethics, technology, intercultural communication, and globalization.

Authors' E-Mail Hotline for Faculty

hotline@leadingtexts.com

Many Thanks

We owe a debt of gratitude to the people at Prentice Hall who worked with us and provided significant support for the development of this book. We thank David Parker, our editor, Theresa Festa, our production editor, and Denise Vaughn, editorial assistant. Special words of appreciation are due to Jackie Estrada and Gail Olson and to the following people who reviewed and provided helpful feedback in the development of this book's content. Thank you to the following professors who participated in review activities:

Faridah Awang
Eastern Kentucky University

Michele Taylor
Ogeechee Technical College

Pashia Hogan
Northeast State Tech Community College

Darlynn Fink
Clarion University of Pennsylvania

Linda Nitsch
Chadron State College

Christy L. Kinnion
Lenior Community College

Irene Joanette Gallio
Western Nevada Community College

W. Dees Stallings
Park University

Fran Kranz
Oakland University

Helen Grattan
Des Moines Area Community College

Ruth Hopkins Zajdel
Ohio University Chillicothe

Cynthia Herrera
Orlando Culinary Academy

Yvonne Block
College of Lake County

Ruth Levy
Westchester Community College

Rebecca Hsiao
East Los Angeles College

Matthew Gainous
Ogeechee Technical College

Diane Paul
TVI Community College

Deborah Kitchin
City College of San Francisco

Nancy Goehring
Monterey Pennisula College

Brian Wilson
College of Marin

Kate Ferguson Marsters
Gannon University

Business Communication Foundations

Unit 1

1 Understanding Business Communication in Today's Workplace

Learning Objectives

After studying this chapter, you will be able to

1 Explain what effective communication is

2 Discuss four developments in the workplace that are intensifying the need to communicate effectively

3 List and briefly define the six phases of the communication process

4 Identify four ways to improve business communication

5 Differentiate between an ethical dilemma and an ethical lapse

6 Define and briefly discuss four types of cultural differences that can affect communication

As internal communications and publications manager at Hallmark, Andy McMillen makes sure that communication within the company not only keeps employees informed but also makes them feel they are a part of the company. McMillen has found that to be successful, he must keep communication flowing smoothly and efficiently, ensuring that everyone receives necessary information.[1]

Succeeding Through Effective Communication

Communication enables organizations to function.

Organizations such as Hallmark understand that achieving success in today's workplace is closely tied to the ability of employees and managers to communicate effectively with each other and with people outside the organization. **Communication** is the process of sending and receiving messages. However, communication is *effective* only when the message is understood and when it stimulates action or encourages the receiver to think in new ways.

Your ability to communicate effectively gives both you and your organization tangible benefits:

Effective communication offers real benefits.

- Quicker problem solving
- Stronger decision making
- Increased productivity
- Steadier work flow
- Stronger business relationships
- Clearer promotional materials
- Enhanced professional image

2

- Improved response from colleagues, employees, supervisors, investors, customers, and other stakeholders

People aren't "born" writers or speakers. The more they write and speak, the more their skills improve. This course teaches you how to create effective messages and helps you improve your communication skills through practice in an environment that provides honest, constructive criticism. Working hard in this course will not only improve your writing skills, it will help you avoid making costly mistakes on the job.

No matter what career you pursue, this course will help you discover how to collaborate in teams, listen well, master nonverbal communication, and participate in productive meetings. You'll learn about communicating across cultures and through the Internet. You'll learn a three-step process for writing business messages, and you'll get specific tips for writing messages, whether in the form of letters, memos, e-mail messages, instant messaging* (an alternative to e-mail that allows two or more people to transmit messages instantaneously), reports, or oral presentations. You'll learn how to write effective résumés and job application letters and how to handle employment interviews. Plus, this text offers a superb collection of communication examples that include comments to guide you through your own communication efforts.

Before we get to all these topics, consider some of the communication challenges you'll be facing in today's workplace as you communicate in an organizational setting.

Adapting to the Changing Workplace

Good communication skills are more vital today than ever before because people need to adapt to a workplace that is constantly changing. (See the photo essay on "Powerful Tools for Communicating Efficiently" on pages 4–7.) Effective communication will help you meet challenges such as advances in technology, the need to access vast amounts of information, the growth of globalization and workforce diversity, and the increasing use of teams in the workplace.

- **Communicating amid advancing technology.** The Internet, e-mail, instant messaging (IM), voice mail, faxes, pagers, and other wireless devices have revolutionized the way people communicate. These tools increase the speed, frequency, and reach of our communication (see Figure 1.1 on page 8). People from opposite ends of the world can work together seamlessly, 24 hours a day, whether they are at the office, in a car, in an airport, in a hotel, or at home. Technology reveals your communication skill with every e-mail, phone conversation, or videoconference.[2] Today, you have to think not only about what you're going to say and how you're going to say it but also about which technological tools you will use.

- **Communicating in the age of information.** In today's workplace, you must know how to find, evaluate, process, and communicate information effectively and efficiently. Plus, you must be able to use what information you receive to make strong, speedy decisions. Unfortunately, people are so inundated with information, they tend to ignore messages they see as less important. Your challenge is to get your audience's attention so that they will read and act on your message.

- **Communicating globally and within a culturally diverse workforce.** More and more businesses are crossing national boundaries to compete on a global scale. Over 2 million North Americans now work for multinational employers, and the number of foreign companies with plants in the United States is increasing.[3] Plus, the U.S. workforce includes growing numbers of people with diverse ethnic backgrounds. To communicate effectively, you must understand other backgrounds, personalities, and perceptions.

- **Communicating in team-based organizations.** Traditional management style is changing in today's fast-paced, e-commerce environment.[4] Successful companies no

(continued on page 8)

In this course, you will learn how to create effective business messages.

Effective communication helps us adapt to change.

*While instant messaging and text messaging perform a similar function, and some people use the terms interchangeably, instant messaging is generally considered a computer-to-computer activity while text messaging is a phone-to-phone or computer-to-phone function.

Powerful Tools for Communicating Effectively

The tools of business communication evolve with every new generation of digital technology. Selecting the right tool for each situation can enhance your business communication in many ways. In today's flexible office settings, communication technology helps people keep in touch and stay productive. When co-workers in different cities need to collaborate, they can meet and share ideas without costly travel. Manufacturers use communication technology to keep track of parts, orders, and shipments—and to keep customers well-informed. Those same customers can also communicate with companies in many ways at any time of day or night.

Flexible Workstations

Many professionals have abandoned desktop PCs for laptops they can carry home, on travel, and to meetings. Back at their desks, a docking station transforms the laptop into a full-featured PC with network connection. Workers without permanent desks sometimes share PCs that automatically reconfigure themselves to access each user's e-mail and files.

Wireless Networks

Laptop PCs with wireless access cards let workers stay connected to the network from practically anywhere within the office—any desk, any conference room. This technology offers high-speed Internet access within range of a wireless access point.

Follow-Me Phone Service

To be reachable without juggling multiple forwarding numbers, some people have follow-me phone service. Callers use one number to reach the person anywhere—at the office, a remote site, a home office. The system automatically forwards calls to a list of preprogrammed numbers and transfers unanswered calls to voice mail.

Redefining the Office

Technology makes it easier for people to stay connected with co-workers and retrieve needed information. Some maintain that connection without having a permanent office, a desktop PC, or even a big filing cabinet. For example, Sun Microsystems lets staff members choose to work either at the main office or at remote offices called "drop-in centers." Many Sun facilities have specially equipped "iWork" areas that can quickly reconfigure phone and computer connections to meet individual requirements.

Electronic Presentations

Combining a color projector with a laptop or personal digital assistant (PDA) running the right software lets people give informative business presentations that are enhanced with sound, animation, and even website hyperlinks. Having everything in electronic form also makes it easy to customize a presentation or to make last-minute changes.

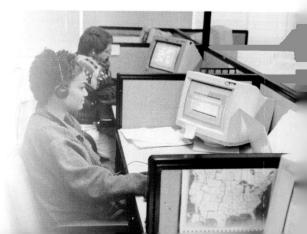

Communicating in the Office

Intranets

Businesses use Internet technologies to create an intranet, a private computer network that simplifies information sharing within the company. Intranets can handle company e-mail, instant messaging (IM), websites, and even Internet phone connections. To ensure the security of company communication and information, intranets are shielded from the public Internet.

Wall Displays

Teams commonly solve problems by brainstorming at a whiteboard. Wall displays take this concept one step further, letting participants transmit words and diagrams to distant colleagues via the corporate intranet. Users can even share the virtual pen to make changes and additions from more than one location.

Web-Based Meetings

Workers can actively participate in web-based meetings by logging on from a desktop PC, laptop, or cell phone. Websites such as WebEx help users integrate voice, text, and video, and let them share applications such as Microsoft PowerPoint and Microsoft Word in a single browser window.

Internet Videophone

Person-to-person video calling has long been possible through popular instant messaging programs. Internet videophone services do even more, letting multiple users participate in a videoconference without the expense and complexity of a full-fledged videoconferencing system. Some services are flexible enough to include telecommuters who have broadband Internet connections.

Collaborating

Working in teams is essential in almost every business. Teamwork can become complicated, however, when team members work in different parts of the company, in different time zones, or even for different companies. Technology helps bridge the distance by making it possible to brainstorm, attend virtual meetings, and share files from widely separated locations. Communication technology also helps companies save money on costly business travel without losing most of the benefits of face-to-face collaboration.

Shared Workspace

Online workspaces such as eRoom and Groove make it easy for far-flung team members to access shared files anywhere, any time. Accessible through a browser, the workspace contains a collection of folders and has built-in intelligence to control which team members can read, edit, and save specific files.

Communicating Remotely

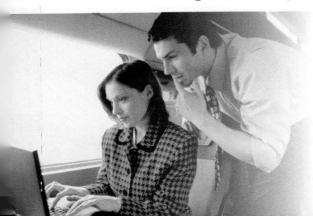

Videoconferencing and Telepresence

Less costly than travel, videoconferencing provides many of the same benefits as an in-person meeting. Advanced systems include telepresence and robot surrogates, which use computers to "place" participants in the room virtually, letting them see and hear everyone while being seen and heard themselves. Such realistic interaction makes meetings more productive.

Warehouse RFID

In an effort to reduce the costs and delays associated with manual inventory reports, Wal-Mart requires its top suppliers to put radio-frequency identification (RFID) tags on all their shipping cases and pallets. These tags automatically provide information that was previously collected by hand via barcode scanners.

Extranet

Extranets are secure, private computer networks that use Internet technology to share business information with suppliers, vendors, partners, and customers. Think of an extranet as an extension of the company intranet that is available to people outside the organization by invitation only.

Wireless Warehouse

Communication technology is a key source of competitive advantage for shipping companies such as FedEx and UPS. Hand-worn scanners use wireless links to help warehouse personnel access instant information that lets them process more packages in less time at transit hubs. Currently, 300 package loaders at four UPS hub facilities are testing the new wireless application called UPScan. A pager-size cordless scanner worn on the loader's hand captures data from a package bar code and transmits the data via Bluetooth® wireless technology to a Symbol Technologies wireless terminal worn on the loader's waist.

Sharing the Latest Information

Companies use a variety of communication technologies to create products and services and deliver them to customers. The ability to easily access and share the latest information improves the flow and timing of supplies, lowers operating costs, and boosts financial performance. Easy information access also helps companies respond to customer needs by providing them timely, accurate information and service and by delivering the right products to them at the right time.

Package Tracking

Senders and receivers often want frequent updates when packages are in transit. Handheld devices such as the FedEx PowerPad enhance customer service by letting delivery personnel instantly upload package data to the FedEx network. The wireless PowerPad also aids drivers by automatically receiving weather advisories.

Communicating About Products and Services

Supply Chain Management

Advanced software applications let suppliers, manufacturers, and retailers share information—even when they have incompatible computer systems. Improved information flow increases report accuracy and helps each company in the supply chain manage stock levels.

Over-the-Shoulder Support

For online shoppers who need instant help, many retail websites make it easy to connect with a live sales rep via phone or instant messaging. The rep can provide quick answers to questions and, with permission, can even control a shopper's browser to help locate particular items.

Help Lines

Some people prefer the personal touch of contact by phone. Moreover, some companies assign preferred customers special ID numbers that let them jump to the front of the calling queue. Many companies are addressing the needs of foreign-language speakers by connecting them with external service providers who offer multilingual support.

Corporate Blogs

Web-based journals let companies offer advice, answer questions, and promote the benefits of their products and services. Elements of a successful blog include frequent updates and the participation of knowledgeable contributors. Adding a subtle mix of useful commentary and marketing messages helps get customers to read or listen to them.

Interacting

Maintaining an open dialog with customers is a great way to gain a better understanding of their likes and dislikes. Today's communication technologies make it easier for customers to interact with a company whenever, wherever, and however they wish. A well-coordinated approach to phone, web, and in-store communication helps a company build stronger relationships with its existing customers, which increases the chances of doing more business with each one.

Retail RFID

Customers can't buy what they can't find, and manual reporting is often too slow for fast-paced retailing. To keep enough goods on the shelves, some retailers use RFID tags to monitor products on display. Clerks use wireless readers to scan tagged products and report stock data to a computerized inventory system that responds with an up-to-the-minute restocking order.

Communicating with Customers

In-Store Kiosks

Staples is among the retailers that let shoppers buy from the web while they're still in the store. Web-connected kiosks were originally used to let shoppers custom-configure their PCs, but the kiosks also give customers access to roughly 8,000 in-store items as well as to the 50,000 products available online.

FIGURE 1.1   Technology and Communication: Effective E-Mail

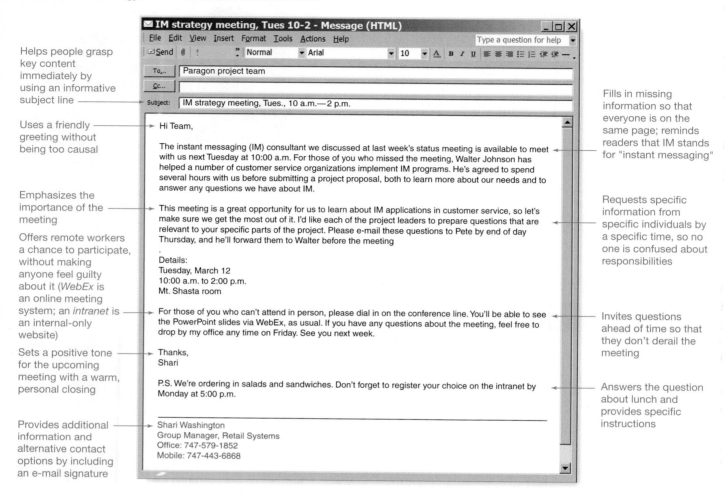

Helps people grasp key content immediately by using an informative subject line

Uses a friendly greeting without being too causal

Emphasizes the importance of the meeting

Offers remote workers a chance to participate, without making anyone feel guilty about it (*WebEx* is an online meeting system; an *intranet* is an internal-only website)

Sets a positive tone for the upcoming meeting with a warm, personal closing

Provides additional information and alternative contact options by including an e-mail signature

Fills in missing information so that everyone is on the same page; reminds readers that IM stands for "instant messaging"

Requests specific information from specific individuals by a specific time, so no one is confused about responsibilities

Invites questions ahead of time so that they don't derail the meeting

Answers the question about lunch and provides specific instructions

---

longer limit decisions to a few managers at the top of a formal hierarchy. Instead, organizations use teams and work groups to collaborate and make fast decisions. As Chapter 2 discusses in detail, before you can function in a team-based organization, you must understand how groups interact. You must be a good listener and correctly interpret all the nonverbal cues you receive from others. Such interaction requires a basic understanding of the communication process in organizational settings.

Understanding the Communication Process

Effective communication doesn't occur haphazardly in organizations. Nor does it happen all at once. Communication is a dynamic, two-way process that can be broken down into six phases (see Figure 1.2):

The communication process has six steps.

1. **The sender has an idea.** You conceive an idea and want to share it.
2. **The sender encodes the idea.** You decide on the message's form (word, facial expression, gesture), length, organization, tone, and style—all of which depend on your idea, your audience, and your personal style or mood.
3. **The sender transmits the message.** You select a **communication channel** (verbal or nonverbal, spoken or written) and a **medium** (telephone, letter, memo, e-mail, instant message, report, face-to-face exchange). This choice depends on your message, your audience's location, your need for speed, and the formality required.

FIGURE 1.2 The Communication Process

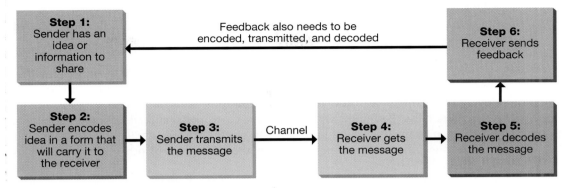

4. **The receiver gets the message.** Your audience must receive the message. If you send a letter, your receiver has to read it before understanding it. If you're giving a speech, your audience has to be able to hear you, and they have to be paying attention.
5. **The receiver decodes the message.** Your receiver must absorb, understand, and mentally store your message. If all goes well, the receiver interprets your message correctly, assigning the same meaning to your words as you intended.
6. **The receiver sends feedback.** After decoding your message, the receiver responds in some way and signals that response to you. This **feedback** enables you to evaluate the effectiveness of your message: If your audience doesn't understand what you mean, you can tell by the response and refine your message.

As Figure 1.2 illustrates, the communication process is repeated until both parties have finished expressing themselves.[5] To communicate effectively, don't cram too much information into one message. Instead, limit the content of your message to a specific subject, and use this repeated back-and-forth exchange to provide additional information or details in subsequent messages.

Improving Business Communication

In the coming chapters, you'll find real-life examples of both good and bad communication, with explanations of what's good or bad about them. After a while you'll begin to see a pattern. You'll notice that four themes keep surfacing: (1) committing to ethical communication, (2) adopting an audience-centered approach, (3) improving your intercultural sensitivity, and (4) improving your workplace sensitivity. Close attention to these themes will help you improve your business communication.

You can improve your business communication by
- Committing to ethical communication
- Adopting an audience-centered approach
- Improving your intercultural sensitivity
- Improving your workplace sensitivity

Committing to Ethical Communication

Ethics refers to the principles of conduct that govern a person or a group. Unethical people say or do whatever it takes to achieve an end. Ethical people are generally trustworthy, fair, and impartial, respecting the rights of others and concerned about the impact of their actions on society. Former Supreme Court Justice Potter Stewart defined ethics as "knowing the difference between what you have a right to do and what is the right thing to do."[6]

Ethical communication includes all relevant information, is true in every sense, and is not deceptive in any way. By contrast, unethical communication can include falsehoods and misleading information (or exclude important information). Some examples of unethical communication include:[7]

For business communication to be effective, it must be ethical.

- **Plagiarism.** Stealing someone else's words or work and claiming it as your own
- **Selective misquoting.** Deliberately omitting damaging or unflattering comments to paint a better (but untruthful) picture of you or your company

Avoid unethical practices when preparing your business messages.

- **Misrepresenting numbers.** Increasing or decreasing numbers, exaggerating, altering statistics, or omitting numerical data
- **Distorting visuals.** Making a product look bigger or changing the scale of graphs and charts to exaggerate or conceal differences

An ethical message is accurate and sincere. It avoids language that manipulates, discriminates, or exaggerates. To communicate ethically, do not hide negative information behind an optimistic attitude, don't state opinions as facts, and be sure to portray graphic data fairly. Be honest with employers, co-workers, and clients, and never seek personal gain by making others look better or worse than they are. Don't allow personal preferences to influence your perception or the perception of others. In short, act in good faith.

On the surface, such ethical practices appear fairly easy to recognize. But deciding what is ethical can be quite complex.

Recognizing Ethical Choices

Every company has responsibilities to various groups: customers, employees, shareholders, suppliers, neighbors, the community, and the nation. Unfortunately, what's right for one group may be wrong for another.[8] Moreover, as you attempt to satisfy the needs of one group, you may be presented with an option that seems right on the surface but that somehow feels wrong. When people must choose between conflicting loyalties and weigh difficult trade-offs, they are facing a dilemma.

When choosing between two ethical alternatives, you are facing an ethical dilemma.

An **ethical dilemma** involves choosing between alternatives that aren't clear-cut (perhaps two conflicting alternatives are both ethical and valid, or perhaps the alternatives lie somewhere in the vast gray area between right and wrong). Suppose you are president of a company that's losing money. You have a duty to your shareholders to try to cut your losses and a duty to your employees to be fair and honest. After looking at various options, you conclude that you'll have to lay off 500 people immediately. You suspect you may have to lay off another 100 people later on, but right now you need those 100 workers to finish a project. What do you tell them? If you confess that their jobs are shaky, many of them may quit just when you need them most. However, if you tell them that the future is rosy, you'll be stretching the truth.

When choosing an alternative that is unethical or illegal, you are experiencing an ethical lapse.

Unlike a dilemma, an **ethical lapse** is making a clearly unethical or illegal choice. Suppose you have decided to change jobs and have discreetly landed an interview with your boss's largest competitor. You get along well with the interviewer, who is impressed enough with you to offer you a position on the spot. Not only is the new position a step up from your current job, but the pay is double what you're getting now. You accept the job and agree to start next month. Then as you're shaking hands with the interviewer, she asks you to bring along profiles of your current company's 10 largest customers when you report for work. Do you comply with her request? How do you decide between what's ethical and what is not?

Making Ethical Choices

For ethical guidance, first look to the law.

One place to look for guidance is the law. If saying or writing something is clearly illegal, you have no dilemma: You obey the law. However, even though legal considerations will resolve some ethical questions, you'll often have to rely on your own judgment and principles. One guideline: If your intent is honest, your message is ethical, even though it may be factually incorrect. However, if your intent is to mislead or manipulate your audience, the message is unethical, regardless of whether it is true. You might look at the consequences of your message and opt for the solution that provides the greatest good to the greatest number of people—a solution that you can live with.[9] You might ask yourself:[10]

To help make an ethical decision, you can ask yourself four questions.

- **Is this message legal?** Does it violate civil law or company policy?
- **Is this message balanced?** Does it do the most good and the least harm? Is it fair to all concerned in the short term as well as the long term? Does it promote positive, win-win relationships? Did you weigh all sides before drawing a conclusion?

■ **Is it a message you can live with?** Does it make you feel good about yourself? Does it make you proud? Would you feel good about your message if a newspaper published it? If your family knew about it?

■ **Is this message feasible?** Can it work in the real world? Have you considered your position in the company? Your company's competition? Its financial and political strength? The likely costs or risks of your message? The time available?

One way to help you make your messages ethical is to consider your audience: What does your audience need? What will help your audience the most?

Adopting an Audience-Centered Approach

Adopting an **audience-centered approach** means focusing on and caring about the members of your audience, making every effort to get your message across in a way that is meaningful to them (see Figure 1.3). To create an effective message, you need to learn as much as possible about the biases, education, age, status, and background of your audience.

An effective business message focuses on its audience.

FIGURE 1.3   An Audience-Centered Letter

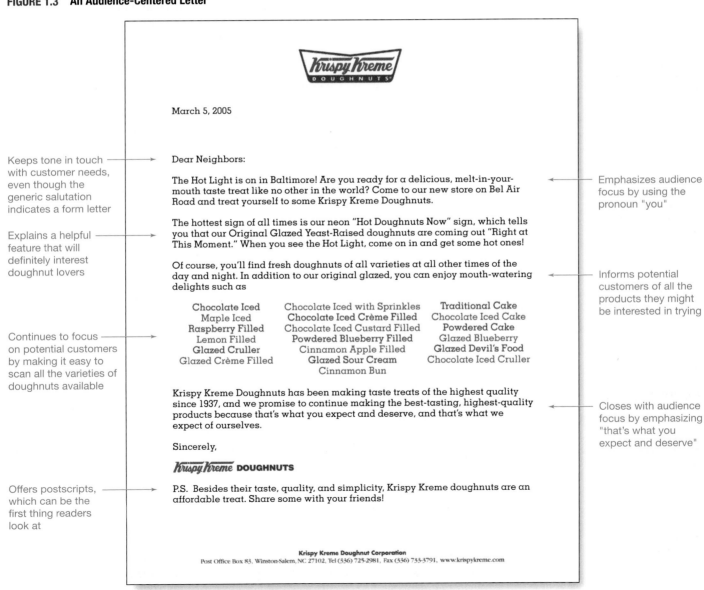

Keeps tone in touch with customer needs, even though the generic salutation indicates a form letter

Explains a helpful feature that will definitely interest doughnut lovers

Continues to focus on potential customers by making it easy to scan all the varieties of doughnuts available

Offers postscripts, which can be the first thing readers look at

Emphasizes audience focus by using the pronoun "you"

Informs potential customers of all the products they might be interested in trying

Closes with audience focus by emphasizing "that's what you expect and deserve"

When you address strangers, try to find out more about them; if that's impossible, try to project yourself into their position by using your common sense and imagination. By writing and speaking from your audience's point of view, you can help them understand and accept your message—an approach that is discussed in more detail in Chapter 3, "Planning Business Messages." Audience focus takes on special importance when you're communicating with someone from another culture. You will improve your business communication tremendously by becoming more sensitive to the differences that exist between people from various cultures.

Improving Your Intercultural Sensitivity

Effective business communicators take cultural differences into account.

To communicate more effectively, be aware of and sensitive to cultural differences. **Culture** is a shared system of symbols, beliefs, attitudes, values, expectations, and norms for behavior. Members of a culture have similar assumptions about how people should think, behave, and communicate, and they all tend to act on those assumptions in much the same way.

Yet, from group to group, cultures differ widely. When you write to or speak with someone from another culture, you encode your message using the assumptions of your own culture. However, the members of your audience decode your message using the assumptions of their culture, so your intended meaning may be misunderstood.[11]

For example, when Japanese auto manufacturer Mazda opened a plant in the United States, officials passed out company baseball caps and told U.S. employees that they could wear the caps at work, along with their mandatory company uniform (blue pants and khaki shirts). The employees assumed that the caps were a *voluntary* accessory, and many decided not to wear them. This decision upset Japanese managers, who regarded this behavior as a sign of disrespect. Managers believed that employees who really cared about the company would *want* to wear the caps. However, U.S. employees resented being told what they should *want* to do.[12]

Improve your cultural sensitivity by
- Recognizing cultural differences
- Overcoming the tendency to stereotype
- Polishing your written intercultural communication skills
- Polishing your oral intercultural communication skills

You can improve your ability to communicate effectively across cultures by recognizing such cultural differences, by overcoming your tendency to judge others based on your own standards, by polishing your written intercultural skills, and by polishing your oral intercultural skills.

Recognizing Cultural Differences

Problems arise when we assume, wrongly, that other people's attitudes and lives are like ours. A graduate of one intercultural training program said, "I used to think it was enough to treat people the way I wanted to be treated. But [after taking the course] . . . I realized you have to treat people the way *they* want to be treated."[13] You can improve intercultural sensitivity by recognizing and accommodating cultural differences in such areas as context, ethics, social customs, and nonverbal communication.

Cultural differences exist in areas such as context, ethics, social customs, and nonverbal communication.

Context   **Cultural context** is the pattern of physical cues, environmental stimuli, and implicit understanding that conveys meaning between two members of the same culture (see Figure 1.4). In a **high-context culture** such as in South Korea or Taiwan, people rely less on verbal communication and more on the context of nonverbal actions and environmental setting to convey meaning. A Chinese speaker expects the audience to *discover* the essence of a message and uses indirectness and metaphor to provide a web of meaning.[14] In high-context cultures, the rules of everyday life are rarely explicit; instead, as individuals grow up, they learn how to recognize situational cues (such as gestures and tone of voice) and how to respond as expected.[15]

To communicate with one another, members of different cultures rely on the context of physical cues, environmental stimuli, and implicit understanding to different degrees.

To communicate in high-context cultures, members rely less on words and more on context.

On the other hand, in a **low-context culture** such as in the United States or Germany, people rely more on verbal communication and less on circumstances and cues to convey meaning. An English speaker feels responsible for transmitting the meaning of the message and often places sentences in chronological sequence to establish a cause-and-effect pattern.[16] In low-context cultures, rules and expectations are usually spelled out through explicit statements such as "Please wait until I'm finished" or "You're welcome to browse."[17]

To communicate in low-context cultures, members rely more on words and less on context.

FIGURE 1.4 How Cultural Context Affects Business Communication

In Low-Context Companies	In High-Context Companies
Executive offices are separate with controlled access.	Executive offices are shared and open to all.
Workers rely on detailed background information.	Workers do not expect or want detailed information.
Information is highly centralized and controlled.	Information is shared with everyone.
Objective data are valued over subjective relationships.	Subjective relationships are valued over objective data.
Business and social relationships are discrete.	Business and social relationships overlap.
Competence is valued as much as position and status.	Position and status are valued much more than competence.
Meetings have fixed agendas and plenty of advance notice.	Meetings are often called on short notice, and key people always accept.

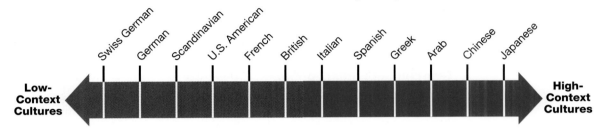

Contextual differences are apparent in the way cultures approach problem solving, negotiations, and decision making. For example, in lower-context cultures such as Germany, businesspeople want to make decisions as quickly and efficiently as possible. However, in higher-context cultures such as Greece, businesspeople consider it a mark of good faith to spend time on each little point before reaching a decision.

Ethics   Legal and ethical behaviors are also affected by cultural context. For example, because members of low-context cultures value the written word, they consider written agreements binding. They also tend to view laws with flexibility. However, members of high-context cultures put less emphasis on the written word and consider personal pledges more important than contracts. Plus, they tend to adhere more strictly to the law.[18]

> Members of different cultures have different views of what is ethical and even legal.

Legal systems differ from culture to culture. In the United Kingdom and the United States, someone is presumed innocent until proved guilty, a principle rooted in English common law. However, in Mexico and Turkey, someone is presumed guilty until proved innocent, a principle rooted in the Napoleonic code.[19] These distinctions are particularly important if your firm must communicate about a legal dispute in another country.

Making ethical choices can be difficult within your own culture. But trying to make these choices across cultures can seem incredibly complicated. When communicating across cultures, keep your messages ethical by applying four basic principles:[20]

- **Actively seek mutual ground.** Both parties must be flexible and avoid insisting that an interaction take place strictly in terms of one culture or another.

> Four principles will help you keep your intercultural messages ethical.

- **Send and receive messages without judgment.** Both parties must recognize that values vary from culture to culture, and they must find a way to trust each other.

- **Send messages that are honest.** Both parties must see a situation as it is—not as they would like it to be. They must be fully aware of their personal and cultural biases.

- **Show respect for cultural differences.** Both parties must understand and acknowledge the other's needs and preserve each other's dignity by communicating without deception.

Social Customs   In any culture, the rules of social etiquette may be formal or informal. Formal social rules are specifically taught "rights" and "wrongs" of how to behave in common social situations (such as table manners at meals). When formal rules are violated, people can explain why they feel upset. However, informal social rules are usually learned by watching how people behave and then imitating that behavior, so these rules are more difficult to identify (such as how males and females are supposed to behave, or when it's appropriate to use a person's first name). When informal rules are violated, people often feel uncomfortable without knowing exactly why.[21]

> Whether formal or informal, the rules governing social customs differ from culture to culture.

Differences in social values are apparent in the way various cultures define manners, think about time, recognize status, and value wealth. For example, the predominant U.S. view is that money solves many problems, that material comfort is a sign of superiority and is earned by individual effort, and that people who work hard are better than those who don't. But other cultures condemn materialism, some prize communal effort above that of the individual, and some value a more carefree lifestyle.

Nonverbal Communication   The simplest hand gestures change meaning from culture to culture, so interpreting nonverbal elements according to your own culture can be dangerous. Differences in nonverbal communication are apparent in body language and in the varying attitudes toward personal space. For example, Canadian and U.S. businesspeople usually stand about five feet apart during a conversation. However, this distance is uncomfortably close for people from Germany or Japan and uncomfortably far for Arabs and Latin Americans. (See more on nonverbal communication in Chapter 2.)

Overcoming Ethnocentrism

Being aware of cultural differences is only the first step in improving your intercultural communication. To communicate across cultures successfully, you must be able to overcome our human tendency to judge others by one's own standards. When communicating across cultures, your effectiveness depends on maintaining an open mind. Unfortunately, many people lapse into **ethnocentrism**, the belief that one's own cultural background is superior to all others. They lose sight of the possibility that their words and actions can be misunderstood, and they forget that they are likely to misinterpret the actions of others.

When you first begin to investigate the culture of another group, you may attempt to understand the common tendencies of that group's members by **stereotyping**—predicting individuals' behavior or character on the basis of their membership in a particular group or class. For example, Japanese visitors often stereotype Americans as people who walk fast, are wasteful in utilizing space, speak directly, ask too many questions in the classroom, don't respect professors, are disrespectful of age and status, lack discipline, and are extravagant.[22]

Stereotyping maybe useful in the beginning, but your next step is to move beyond the stereotypes to relationships with real people. Unfortunately, when ethnocentric people stereotype, they tend to do so on the basis of limited, general, or inaccurate evidence. They frequently develop biased attitudes toward a group, and they fail to move beyond that initial step.[23] So instead of talking with Abdul Karhum, unique human being, ethnocentric people are talking to "an Arab." They may believe that all Arabs are, say, hagglers, so Abdul Karhum's personal qualities cannot alter such preconceptions. His every action is forced to fit the preconceived image, even if that image is wrong.

To overcome ethnocentrism, follow a few simple suggestions:

- **Acknowledge distinctions.** Don't ignore the differences between another person's culture and your own.
- **Avoid assumptions.** Don't assume that others will act the same way you do, that they will operate from the same assumptions, or that they will use language and symbols the same way you do.
- **Avoid judgments.** When people act differently, don't conclude that they are in error, that their way is invalid, or that their customs are inferior to your own.

Too often, both parties in an intercultural exchange are guilty of ethnocentrism and prejudice. Little wonder, then, that misunderstandings arise when communicating across cultures.

Polishing Your Written Intercultural Skills

The letter in Figure 1.5 communicates across culture quite effectively. To help you prepare effective written communications for multicultural audiences, remember these tips:[24]

- **Use plain English.** Use short, precise words that say exactly what you mean.
- **Be clear.** Rely on specific terms and concrete examples to explain your points.

Ethnocentrism blocks effective communication because it closes the mind to new information.

Stereotyping can be useful, but only as a first step in learning about another culture.

Eight tips will help you improve your written intercultural skills.

FIGURE 1.5   Effective Intercultural Letter

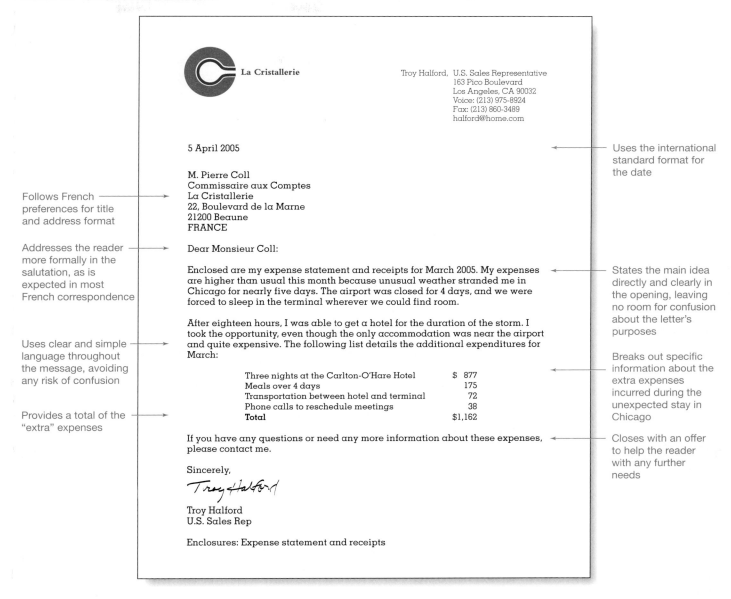

Follows French preferences for title and address format

Addresses the reader more formally in the salutation, as is expected in most French correspondence

Uses clear and simple language throughout the message, avoiding any risk of confusion

Provides a total of the "extra" expenses

Uses the international standard format for the date

States the main idea directly and clearly in the opening, leaving no room for confusion about the letter's purposes

Breaks out specific information about the extra expenses incurred during the unexpected stay in Chicago

Closes with an offer to help the reader with any further needs

Letter content:

La Cristallerie

Troy Halford, U.S. Sales Representative
163 Pico Boulevard
Los Angeles, CA 90032
Voice: (213) 975-8924
Fax: (213) 860-3489
halford@home.com

5 April 2005

M. Pierre Coll
Commissaire aux Comptes
La Cristallerie
22, Boulevard de la Marne
21200 Beaune
FRANCE

Dear Monsieur Coll:

Enclosed are my expense statement and receipts for March 2005. My expenses are higher than usual this month because unusual weather stranded me in Chicago for nearly five days. The airport was closed for 4 days, and we were forced to sleep in the terminal wherever we could find room.

After eighteen hours, I was able to get a hotel for the duration of the storm. I took the opportunity, even though the only accommodation was near the airport and quite expensive. The following list details the additional expenditures for March:

Three nights at the Carlton-O'Hare Hotel	$ 877
Meals over 4 days	175
Transportation between hotel and terminal	72
Phone calls to reschedule meetings	38
Total	$1,162

If you have any questions or need any more information about these expenses, please contact me.

Sincerely,

Troy Halford

Troy Halford
U.S. Sales Rep

Enclosures: Expense statement and receipts

- **Address international correspondence properly.** The order and layout of address information vary from country to country, so follow the conventions that appear in the company's letterhead.
- **Cite numbers carefully.** Use figures (27) instead of spelling them out (twenty-seven).
- **Avoid slang, idioms, jargon, and abbreviations.** Acronyms (such as CAD/CAM) and unfamiliar product names may also lead to confusion.
- **Be brief.** Construct sentences that are short and simple.
- **Use short paragraphs.** Each paragraph should stick to one topic.
- **Use transitional elements.** Help readers follow your train of thought.

Polishing Your Oral Intercultural Skills

When speaking in English to people who speak English as a second language, you may find these tips helpful:

- **Try to eliminate noise.** Pronounce words clearly, stop at distinct punctuation points, and make one point at a time.

Twelve tips will help you improve your oral intercultural skills.

- **Look for feedback.** Be alert to signs of confusion in your listener. Realize that nods and smiles don't necessarily mean understanding. If the other person's body language seems at odds with the message, take time to clarify the meaning.

- **Speak slowly and rephrase your sentence when necessary.** If someone doesn't seem to understand you, choose simpler words; don't just repeat the sentence in a louder voice.

- **Clarify your true intent with repetition and examples.** Try to be aware of unintentional meanings that may be read into your message.

- **Don't talk down to the other person.** Try not to overenunciate, and don't "blame" the listener for not understanding. Say, "Am I going too fast?" rather than "Is this too difficult for you?"

- **Use objective, accurate language.** Avoid throwing around adjectives such as *fantastic* and *fabulous,* which people from other cultures might consider unreal and overly dramatic.

- **Learn foreign phrases.** Learn common greetings and a few simple phrases in the other person's native language. Key phrases are usually listed in travel books and in a separate section of most travel dictionaries.

- **Listen carefully and patiently.** Let other people finish what they have to say. If you interrupt, you may miss something important. You'll also show a lack of respect. If you do not understand a comment, ask the person to repeat it.

- **Adapt your conversation style to the other person's.** For instance, if the other person appears to be direct and straightforward, follow suit.

- **Check frequently for comprehension.** Make one point at a time and pause to check on comprehension before moving on.

- **Clarify what will happen next.** At the end of a conversation, be sure that you and the other person agree on what has been said and decided. If appropriate, follow up by writing a letter or a memo summarizing the conversation and thanking the person for meeting with you.

- **Observe body language.** Be alert to roving eyes, glazed looks, and other facial expressions that signal the listener is lost or confused.

In short, take advantage of the other person's presence to make sure that your message is getting across and that you understand his or her message too.

Improving Your Workplace Sensitivity

Today's culturally diverse workforce is made up of men and women from various nations, ethnic backgrounds, age groups, and races.

The U.S. workforce includes immigrants and people from a variety of ethnic backgrounds (such as African Americans, Hispanic Americans, and Asian Americans) who often bring their own languages and cultural customs to the workplace. Today's workforce is made up of more and more people who differ in race, gender, age, culture, family structure, reli-

Document Makeover

Improve This Memo

To practice correcting drafts of actual documents, visit **www.prenhall.com/onekey** on the web. Click "Document Makeovers," then click Chapter 1. You will find a memo that contains problems and errors relating to what you've learned in this chapter about improving business communication. Use the Final Draft decision tool to create an improved version of this memo. Check the message for ethical communication, an audience-centered approach, and intercultural sensitivity.

gion, and educational background. Such **cultural diversity** affects how business messages are conceived, planned, sent, received, and interpreted in the workplace. To communicate more effectively with people at work, learn all you can about the cultures of the people around you. Read books and articles about these cultures, and talk to people who have done business with members of these cultures. However, don't expect to understand another culture completely. No matter how much you study German culture, for example, you'll never be a German or share the experiences of having grown up in Germany.

The trick is to learn useful general information while remaining aware of and open to variations and individual differences. You can communicate more effectively if you heed the following tips from successful intercultural businesspeople:[25]

Fifteen tips help you communicate effectively in a culturally diverse workforce.

- **Assume differences until similarity is proved.** Don't assume that others are more similar to you than they actually are.
- **Take responsibility for communication.** Don't assume it's the other person's job to communicate with you.
- **Withhold judgment.** Learn to listen to the whole story and accept differences in others without judging them.
- **Show respect.** Learn how respect is communicated in various cultures (through gestures, eye contact, and so on).
- **Empathize.** Before sending a message, put yourself in the receiver's shoes. Imagine the receiver's feelings and point of view.
- **Tolerate ambiguity.** Learn to control your frustration when placed in an unfamiliar or confusing situation.
- **Look beyond the superficial.** Don't be distracted by things such as dress, appearance, or environmental discomforts.
- **Be patient and persistent.** If you want to communicate with someone from another culture, don't give up easily.
- **Recognize your own cultural biases.** Learn to identify when your assumptions are different from the other person's.
- **Be flexible.** Be prepared to change your habits and attitudes when communicating with someone from another culture.
- **Emphasize common ground.** Look for similarities from which to work.
- **Send clear messages.** Make both your verbal and nonverbal signals clear and consistent.
- **Deal with the individual.** Communicate with each person as an individual, not as a stereotypical representative of another group.
- **Learn when to be direct.** Investigate each culture so that you'll know when to send your message in a straightforward manner and when to be indirect.
- **Treat your interpretation as a working hypothesis.** Once you think you understand a foreign culture, carefully assess the feedback provided by recipients of your communication to see if it confirms your hypothesis.

This advice will help you communicate with anybody, regardless of culture.

Reviewing Key Points

This chapter highlights the importance of making business communication effective by ensuring that it stimulates action and encourages audiences to think in new ways. It explains how effective communication helps you adapt to today's changing workplace. Amid today's advancing technology, selecting the proper communication tool enables you not only to reach your audiences but also to help them better understand your messages. In today's age of information, getting your audience's attention prevents people from overlooking vital information that you pass on. With today's global marketplace and diverse workforce, understanding other backgrounds, personalities, and perceptions enables you to communicate clearly with people from other cultures. And since today's companies are committed to working in teams, knowing how to listen to colleagues and to recognize the meaning behind their nonverbal signals helps you collaborate with the others in your work groups.

This chapter also describes the six steps in the communication process. And it cautions you not to pack too much information into each message you send. It explains the four ways to improve your business communication: by committing to ethical communication, adopting an audience-centered approach, improving your intercultural sensitivity, and improving your workplace sensitivity.

The next chapter discusses communicating in teams. It explains how to listen to others by overcoming the common barriers to good listening. It also talks about how to understand nonverbal communication. Finally, it helps you put this new information to work when planning and participating in meetings and when using telephones and voice mail.

Test Your Knowledge

1. What benefits does effective communication give you and your organization?

2. How is technology changing communication in the workplace?

3. How can information overload affect communication?

4. What effects do globalization and workforce diversity have on communication?

5. How are teams changing business communication?

6. In which phases of the communication process are messages encoded and decoded?

7. Define ethics, and explain what ethical communication encompasses.

8. Why should communicators take an audience-centered approach to communication?

9. In what four general areas can you expect to observe cultural differences?

10. What is the trick for communicating effectively in a diverse workplace?

Apply Your Knowledge

1. Why do you think communication is the lifeblood of business organizations? Explain briefly.

2. How does your understanding of the communication process help you conduct business more effectively?

3. Your company has relocated to a U.S. city where a Vietnamese subculture is strongly established. Many employees will be from this subculture. As a member of the human resources department, what suggestions can you make to improve communication between management and the Vietnamese Americans your company is hiring?

4. Do you think that written or spoken messages would be more susceptible to cultural misunderstanding? Why?

5. **Ethical Choices**   Because of your excellent communication skills, your boss always asks you to write his reports for him. But when the CEO compliments him on his logical organization and clear writing style, your boss responds as if he'd written all those reports himself. What kind of ethical choice does this represent? What can you do in this situation? Briefly explain your solution and your reasoning.

Practice Your Knowledge

Activities

For live links to all websites discussed in this chapter, visit this text's website at www.prenhall.com/bovee. Just log on, select Chapter 1, and click on "Featured Websites." Locate the name of the page or the URL related to the material in the text.

1. **Analyze This Document**   Your boss wants to send a brief e-mail message welcoming employees recently transferred to your department from your Hong Kong branch. They all speak English, but your boss asks you to review her message for clarity. What would you suggest your boss change in the following e-mail message—and why? Would you consider this message to be audience centered? Why or why not?

   > I wanted to welcome you ASAP to our little family here in the states. It's high time we shook hands in person and not just across the sea. I'm pleased as punch about getting to know you all, and I for one will do my level best to sell you on America.

2. **Ethical Choices**   In less than a page, explain why you think each of the following is or is not ethical.
   a. Deemphasizing negative test results in a report on your product idea
   b. Taking a computer home to finish a work-related assignment
   c. Telling an associate and close friend that she'd better pay more attention to her work responsibilities or management will fire her
   d. Recommending the purchase of excess equipment to use up your allocated funds before the end of the fiscal year so that your budget won't be cut next year

3. **The Changing Workplace: Always in Touch**   Technological devices such as faxes, cellular phones, e-mail, instant messaging (IM), and voice mail are making business-people easily accessible at any time of day or night, at work, and at home. What kind of impact might frequent intrusions have on their professional and personal lives? Please explain your answer in less than a page.

4. **Internet**   As a manufacturer of aerospace, energy, and environmental equipment, Lockheed Martin has developed a code of ethics that it expects employees to abide by. Visit Lockheed Martin's website at www. lockheedmartin.com/data/assets/7856.pdf, and review the company's six important virtues and the code of ethics. In a brief paragraph, describe three specific examples of things you could do that would violate these provisions. Now scroll down and study the list of "Warning Signs" of ethics violations and take the "Quick Quiz." In another brief paragraph, describe how you could use this advice to avoid ethical problems as you write business letters, memos, and reports. Submit both paragraphs to your instructor.

5. **Ethical Choices**   Your boss often uses you as a sounding board for her ideas. Now she seems to want you to act as an unofficial messenger. You are to pass her ideas along to the staff, without mentioning her involvement. Then she wants you to inform her of what staff members say, without telling them you're going to repeat their responses. What questions should you ask yourself as you consider the ethical implications of this situation? Write a short paragraph explaining the ethical choice you will make in this situation.[26]

6. **Self-Introduction**   Write a paragraph or prepare a two-minute oral presentation introducing yourself to your instructor and your class. Include such things as your background, interests, achievements, and goals.

7. **Teamwork**   Your boss has asked your work group to research and report on corporate child-care facilities. Of course, you'll want to know who (besides your boss) will be reading your report. Working with two team members, list four or five other

things you'll want to know about the situation and about your audience before starting your research. Briefly explain why each of the items on your list is important.

8. **Communication Process: Analyzing Miscommunication**   Use the six phases of the communication process to analyze a miscommunication you've recently had with a co-worker, supervisor, classmate, teacher, friend, or family member. What idea were you trying to share? How did you encode and transmit it? Did the receiver get the message? Did the receiver correctly decode the message? How do you know? Based on your analysis, what do you think prevented your successful communication in this instance?

9. **Ethical Choices**   Your team has been given the critical assignment of selecting the site for your company's new plant. After months of negotiations with landowners, numerous cost calculations, and investments in ecological, social, and community impact studies, your team is about to recommend building the new plant on the Lansing River site. Now, just 15 minutes before your team's big presentation to top management, you discover a possible mistake in your calculations: Site-purchase costs appear to be $50,000 more than you calculated, nearly 10 percent over budget. You don't have time to recheck all your figures, so you're tempted to just go ahead with your recommendation and ignore any discrepancies. You're worried that management won't approve this purchase if you can't present a clean, unqualified solution. You also know that many projects run over their original estimates, so you can probably work the extra cost into the budget later. On your way to the meeting room, you make your final decision.

   Your task: In a few paragraphs, explain the decision you made.

10. **Intercultural Sensitivity: Recognizing Differences**   Your boss represents a Canadian toy company that's negotiating to buy miniature truck wheels from a manufacturer in Osaka, Japan. In the first meeting, he explains that your company expects to control the design of the wheels as well as the materials that are used to make them. The manufacturer's representative looks down and says softly, "Perhaps that will be difficult." Your boss presses for agreement, and to emphasize your company's willingness to buy, he shows the prepared contract he's brought with him. However, the manufacturer seems increasingly vague and uninterested.

   Your task: What cultural differences may be interfering with effective communication in this situation? Explain briefly in an e-mail message to your instructor.

11. **Teamwork**   Working with two other students, prepare a list of 10 examples of slang (in your own language) that would probably be misinterpreted or misunderstood during a business conversation with someone from another culture. Next to each example, suggest other words you might use to convey the same message. Do the alternatives mean *exactly* the same as the original slang or idiom?

12. **Intercultural Communication: Studying Cultures**   Choose a specific country, such as India, Portugal, Bolivia, Thailand, or Nigeria, with which you are not familiar. Research the culture and write a brief summary of what a U.S. businessperson would need to know about concepts of personal space and rules of social behavior in order to conduct business successfully in that country.

13. **Multicultural Workforce: Bridging Differences**   Differences in gender, age, and physical abilities contribute to the diversity of today's workforce. Working with a classmate, role-play a conversation in which
   a. A woman is being interviewed for a job by a male personnel manager
   b. An older person is being interviewed for a job by a younger personnel manager
   c. A person using a wheelchair is being interviewed for a job by a person who can walk

   How did differences between the applicant and the interviewer shape the communication? What can you do to improve communication in such situations?

14. Intercultural Sensitivity: Understanding Attitudes   You are assistant to the director of marketing for a telecommunications firm based in Germany. You're accompanying your boss to negotiate with an official in Guangzhou, China, who's in charge of selecting a new telephone system for the city. Your boss insists that the specifications be spelled out in detail in the contract. However, the Chinese negotiator argues that in developing a long-term business relationship, such minor details are unimportant.

Your task: What can you suggest that your boss do or say to break this intercultural deadlock and obtain the contract so that both parties are comfortable? Outline your ideas in a brief e-mail message to your instructor.

Expand Your Knowledge

Exploring the Best of the Web

Check Out These Resources at the Business Writer's Free Library   www.mapnp.org/library/commskls/cmm_writ.htm The Business Writer's Free Library is a terrific resource for business communication material. Categories of information include basic composition skills, basic writing skills, correspondence, reference material, and general resources and advice. Log on and read about the most common errors in English, become a word detective, ask Miss Grammar, review samples of common forms of correspondence, fine-tune your interpersonal skills, join a newsgroup, and more. Follow the links and improve your effectiveness as a business communicator.

Exercises

1. What are some strategies for communicating with an uncooperative audience?
2. What is the value of diversity in the workplace?
3. Why is bad etiquette bad for business?

Exploring the Web on Your Own

Review these chapter-related websites on your own to learn more about achieving communication success in the workplace.

1. Netiquette Home Page, www.albion.com/netiquette. Learn the do's and don'ts of online communication at this site, then take the Netiquette Quiz.
2. The Information and Communication Technology tutorial provided by Resource Discovery Network in Great Britain, www.vts.rdn.ac.uk/, offers a free tutorial to improve your Internet skills (look under "Internet for Further Education"). Learn helpful techniques for searching the Internet, figure out what you can trust and what you can't, and find out how to use the Internet in your work.
3. 101 Best Web Sites for Writers, at www.writersdigest.com, points the way to great search engines and general reference sites. While aimed primarily at professional writers, the list has something to offer all business communicators. The site list is updated every year, so be sure to select the current year's list.

Learn Interactively

Interactive Study Guide

Go to the Companion Website at www.prenhall. com/bovee. For Chapter 1, take advantage of the interactive "Study Guide" to test your knowledge of the chapter. Get instant feedback on whether you need additional studying. Also, visit this site's "Study Hall," where you'll find an abundance of valuable resources that will help you succeed in this course.

Peak Performance Grammar and Mechanics

To improve your skill with nouns and pronouns, visit www.prenhall.com/onekey, click "Peak Performance Grammar and Mechanics," click "Grammar Basics," and then click "Nouns and Pronouns." Take the Pretest to determine whether you have any weak areas. Then review those areas in the Refresher Course. Take the Follow-Up Test to check your grasp of nouns and pronouns. For an extra challenge or advanced practice, take the Advanced Test. Finally, for additional reinforcement in nouns, go to the "Improve Your Grammar, Mechanics, and Usage" section that follows, and complete the "Level I: Self-Assessment" exercises.

Improve Your Grammar, Mechanics, and Usage

Level 1: Self-Assessment—Nouns

Use the following self-assessment exercises to improve your knowledge of and power over English grammar, mechanics, and usage. Review all of Section 1.1 in the Handbook of Grammar, Mechanics, and Usage that appears at the end of this book. Answers to these exercises appear on page AK–1.

In items 1–5, underline the common nouns and circle the proper nouns.

1. Give the balance sheet to Melissa.

2. We'd like to order 50 more satchels for Craigmont Stores, and 3 each for the other stores on our list.

3. Tarnower Corporation donates a portion of its profits to charity every year.

4. Which aluminum bolts are packaged?

5. Please send the Joneseses a dozen of the following: stopwatches, canteens, headbands, and wristbands.

In items 6–10, underline the subjects and circle the objects.

6. The technician has already repaired the machine for the client.

7. An attorney will talk to the group about incorporation.

8. After her vacation, the buyer prepared a third-quarter budget.

9. The new flat monitors are serving our department very well.

10. Accuracy overrides speed in importance.

In items 11–15, underline inappropriate noun plurals and possessives, and write the correct form in the space provided:

11. _____ Make sure that all copys include the new addresses.

12. _____ Ask Jennings to collect all employee's donations for the Red Cross drive.

13. _____ Charlie now has two son-in-laws to help him with his two online business's.

14. _____ Avoid using too many parenthesises when writing your reports.

15. _____ Follow President Nesses rules about what constitutes a weeks work.

Level 2: Workplace Applications

The following items contain numerous errors in grammar, capitalization, punctuation, abbreviation, number style, word division, and vocabulary. Rewrite each sentence in the space provided, correcting all errors. Write *C* in the space after any sentence that is already correct.

1. If a broken down unproductive guy like Carl can get a raise; why can't a take charge guy like me get one?

2. Visit our website and sign up for "On Your Toes", our free newsletter that keeps you informed of promotions, discounts and about Internet-only specials.

3. As of March, 2005, the Board of Directors have 9 members including: three women, one African-American, and one American of Hispanic descent.

4. As one of the nearly 3,000,000 New York Life policyholders eligible to vote, we urge you to approve the new investment advisory agreement.

5. Gerrald Higgins, vice president for marketing, told us reporters that Capital One provides financial services to one-fourth of homes in the United States.

6. Our Customer Relations associates work with people everyday to answer questions, provide assistance, and helping solve problems.

7. If anyone breaches the lease, its likely that the landlord will file legal action against them to collect on the remainder of they're lease.

8. A IRA is one of the most common plans for the self-employed because of it's ease of setting up and administering.

9. My advise to you is, to put you're mission statement on your web cite.

10. According to Karen Smiths' report small-business owners do'nt recognize the full effect that layoffs and terminations are liable to have on the motivation of surviving employees'.

11. To exacerbate the processing of your US tax return, use the mailing label and bar coded envelope that comes with your tax package.

12. The NASE have implemented a exciting array of programs that make it more easy for legislative opinions and concerns to be voiced by you.

13. Keep in mind the old saying "When we laugh the world laugh with us, when you cry you cry alone."

14. Albert Edmunds and me are Owners of the real estate firm of Edmunds & Cale, which have recently opened a new office in San Diego co.

15. The memo inferred that the economic downturn will have a greater affect on the company's bottom line then we previously assumed, this was the worse news we could of gotten.

Level 3: Document Critique

The following document contains errors in grammar, capitalization, punctuation, abbreviation, number style, word division, and vocabulary. Correct all errors using standard proofreading marks (see Appendix C).

MEMO

TO: All Employees

FROM: R. Smith, Personnel Director

DATE: December 28, 2005

SUBJECT: Time Cards

After reviewing our Current Method of keeping track of employee hours; we have concluded that time cards leave a lot to be desired. So starting Monday, we have a new system, a time clock. You just have to punch in and punch out; whenever you will come and go from your work area's.

The new system may take a little while to get used to, but should be helpful to those of us who are making a new years resolution to be more punctual.

Happy New Year to all!

eg

Test Your Intercultural Knowledge

Never take anything for granted when you're doing business in a foreign country. All sorts of assumptions that are valid in one place can cause you problems elsewhere if you fail to consider that customs may vary. Here are several true stories about businesspeople who blundered by overlooking some simple but important cultural differences. Can you spot the wrong assumptions that led these people astray?

1. You're tired of the discussion and you want to move on to a new topic. You ask your Australian business associate, "Can we table this for a while?" To your dismay, your colleague keeps right on discussing just what you want to put aside. Are Australians that inconsiderate?

2. You finally made the long trip overseas to meet the new German director of your division. Despite slow traffic, you arrive only four minutes late. His door is shut, so you knock on it and walk in. The chair is too far away from the desk, so you pick it up and move it closer. Then you lean over the desk, stick out your hand, and say, "Good morning, Hans, it's nice to meet you." Of course, you're baffled by his chilly reaction. Why?

3. Your meeting went better than you'd ever expected. In fact, you found the Japanese representative for your new advertising agency to be very agreeable; she said yes to just about everything. When you share your enthusiasm with your boss, he doesn't appear very excited. Why?

4. You've finally closed the deal, after exhausting both your patience and your company's travel budget. Now, two weeks later, your Chinese customers are asking for special considerations that change the terms of the agreement. How could they do this? Why are they doing it? And, most important, what should you do?

In each case the problems have resulted from inaccurate assumptions. Here are the explanations of what went wrong:

1. To "table" something in Australia means to bring it forward for discussion. This is the opposite of what Americans usually mean. The English that's spoken in Australia is closer to British than to American English. If you are doing business in Australia, become familiar with the local vocabulary. Note the tendency to shorten just about any word whenever possible, and adding "ie" to it is a form of familiar slang: for example, *brolly* (umbrella) and *lollie* (candy). And yes, it's true: "G'day" is the standard greeting. Use it.

2. You've just broken four rules of German polite behavior: punctuality, privacy, personal space, and proper greetings. In time-conscious Germany, you should never arrive even a few minutes late. Also, Germans like their privacy and space, and they adhere to formal greetings of "Frau" and "Herr," even if the business association has lasted for years.

3. The word *yes* may not always mean "yes" in the Western sense. Japanese people may say *yes* to confirm they have heard or understood something but not necessarily to indicate that they agree with it. You'll seldom get a direct no. Some of the ways that Japanese people say *no* indirectly include "It will be difficult," "I will ask my supervisor," " I'm not sure," "We will think about it," and "I see."

4. For most U.S. businesspeople, the contract represents the end of the negotiation. For Chinese businesspeople, however, it's just the beginning. Once a deal is made, Chinese negotiators view their counterparts as trustworthy partners who can be relied on for special favors—such as new terms in the contract.

Applications for Success

Learn how to improve your cultural savvy and gain an international competitive advantage. Visit Cultural Savvy (www.culturalsavvy.com) by Joyce Millet & Associates and read the country reports and cultural tips. Follow the site's links to interviews, profiles, articles, books, and more.

Answer the following questions:

1. Why should you avoid humor when communicating with people of a different culture?
2. Every culture has its own business protocol. What should you know about a culture's business protocol before you transact business with that culture?
3. What are some examples of cultural gift-giving taboos?

2 Communicating in Teams and Mastering Listening and Nonverbal Communication Skills

Learning Objectives

After studying this chapter, you will be able to

1 Explain how teams contribute to an organization's decision-making process

2 Outline four elements that are necessary to plan a productive meeting

3 Explain four ways to increase productivity during meetings

4 List and briefly explain the five phases of the listening process

5 Discuss three barriers to effective listening and some strategies for overcoming them

6 List several of the techniques for improving the way you answer phone calls, make phone calls, and use voice mail

7 Identify six categories of nonverbal communication

As director of human relations for 3M, Virginia Johnson relies heavily on effective communication among team members and between teams and upper management. To succeed, says Johnson, you need to develop an effective team and know how to get team members to collaborate, using good listening, nonverbal communication, and meeting skills.

Working in Teams

A **team** is a unit of two or more people who work together to achieve a goal. Team members share a mission and the responsibility for working to achieve it.[1] Teams are important in today's workplace. At their best, teams offer an extremely useful forum for making key decisions. Teams help the organizations succeed by[2]

Team members have a shared mission and are collectively responsible for their work.

Teams contribute to an organization's performance.

- **Increasing information and knowledge.** By aggregating the resources of several individuals, teams bring more information and expertise to the decision-making process.
- **Increasing the diversity of views.** Team members bring a variety of perspectives to decision-making tasks.
- **Increasing the acceptance of a solution.** Because team members share in making a decision, they are more likely to support that decision enthusiastically and encourage others to accept it.
- **Increasing performance levels.** Working in teams can unleash vast amounts of creativity and energy in workers who share a sense of purpose and mutual accountability. Teams also contribute to performance levels by filling the individual worker's need to

belong to a group, reducing employee boredom, increasing feelings of dignity and self-worth, and reducing tension between workers.

At their worst, teams are unproductive and frustrating, and they waste everyone's time. Team members must be careful to avoid the following:

Teams are unproductive when
- Members feel pressured to conform and agree to unwise decisions
- Group members' personal motives interfere with the group's efforts
- Some team members don't contribute
- The cost of coordinating a team runs high

- **Groupthink.** When belonging to a team is more important to members than making the right decision, that team may develop **groupthink,** the willingness of individuals to set aside their personal opinions and go along with everyone else, even if everyone else is wrong. Groupthink not only leads to poor decisions and ill-advised actions but can even induce people to act unethically.
- **Hidden agendas.** Some team members can have private motives that affect the group's interaction. Sam might want to prove that he's more powerful than Laura, Laura might be trying to share the risks of making a decision, and Don might be looking for a chance to postpone doing "real" work. Each person's hidden agenda can detract from a team's effectiveness.
- **Free riders.** Some team members don't contribute their fair share to the group's activities because they aren't being held individually accountable for their work. The free-ride attitude can cause certain tasks to go unfulfilled.
- **High coordination costs.** Aligning schedules, arranging meetings, and coordinating individual parts of a project can eat up a lot of time and money.

Effective teams
- Understand their purpose
- Communicate openly and honestly
- Build consensus
- Think creatively
- Stay focused
- Resolve conflict

Effective teams have a clear sense of purpose, communicate openly and honestly, reach decisions by consensus, think creatively, remain focused, and resolve conflict effectively. [3] The purpose of developing an effective team is to get members to collaborate on necessary tasks, and much of that collaboration takes place in meetings.

Preparing, Conducting, and Attending Meetings

A great deal of the oral communication that takes place in the workplace happens in small-group meetings. Unfortunately, too many meetings are unproductive. Some managers have recently reported that little more than half their meetings were actually productive and that a quarter of them could have been handled by a phone call or a memo. [4] To ensure productivity, take great care when planning, conducting, and attending meetings, and make sure to follow up.

Preparing for Team Meetings

The best preparation for a meeting is having a specific goal that would be best handled in a face-to-face situation.

Before you call a meeting, be sure that one is truly needed. Perhaps you could accomplish your purpose more effectively in a memo or through individual conversations. Team members who work in different locations may interact electronically through **virtual meetings,** conferencing online or over the phone. Some of these people may work together for months or years and never meet face to face. At times, technology replaces meetings entirely, such as when team members use e-mail or instant messaging to interact over the course of several hours or days.

If you do require the interaction of a group, be sure to bring the right people together in the right place for just enough time to accomplish your goals. The key to productive meetings is careful planning of purpose, participants, location, and agenda:

Productive meetings have the right purpose, include the right people, take place at the right location and time, and have a clear agenda.

- **Decide on your purpose.** Most meetings are one of two types: In *informational meetings,* participants share information and sometimes coordinate action. Briefings may come from each participant or from the leader. In *decision-making meetings,* participants persuade, analyze, and solve problems. They are often involved in brainstorming sessions and debates.

An effective agenda tells participants
- What must be done
- What issues are important
- What information is necessary for discussion
- Who is attending
- When and where the meeting is being held
- The order in which business will be handled

- **Select participants.** Try to invite only those people whose presence is essential. If the session is purely informational and one person will be doing most of the talking, you can include a relatively large group. However, if you're trying to solve a problem, develop a plan, or reach a decision, try to limit participation to between 6 and 12 people. [5]

- **Choose an appropriate location.** Decide where you'll hold the meeting, and reserve the location. For work sessions, morning meetings are usually more productive than afternoon sessions. Also, consider the seating arrangements. Are rows of chairs suitable, or do you need a conference table? Plus, pay attention to room temperature, lighting, ventilation, acoustics, and refreshments.

- **Set and follow an agenda.** Meeting agendas help prepare the participants. Although small, informal meetings may not require a formal agenda, even they benefit if you prepare at least a list of matters to be discussed. Distribute the agenda to participants several days before the meeting so that they know what to expect and can come prepared to respond to the issues at hand.

A typical agenda format (shown in Figure 2.1) may seem stiff and formal, but it helps you to start and end your meetings on time and to stay on track. Doing so sends a signal of good organization and allows attendees to meet other commitments.

An effective agenda answers three key questions: (1) What do we need to do in this meeting to accomplish our goals? (2) What issues will be of greatest importance to all the participants? (3) What information must be available in order to discuss these issues? [6] Agendas also include the names of the participants, the time, the place, and the order of business. Make sure agenda items are specific, in order to help all attendees prepare in advance with facts and figures.

Conducting and Attending Meetings

The success of any meeting depends largely on the effectiveness of its leader. If the leader is prepared and has selected participants carefully, the meeting will generally be productive.

Keep the Meeting on Track

Don't be so rigid that you cut off discussion too quickly.

A good meeting is a cross-flow of discussion and debate, not a series of dialogues between individual members and the leader. Good leaders occasionally guide, mediate, probe, stimulate, and summarize, but mostly they let others thrash out their ideas. That's why it's important for leaders to avoid being so domineering that they close off suggestions. Of course, they must also avoid being so passive that they lose control of the group. A meeting leader is responsible for

- **Keeping the meeting moving along.** If the discussion lags, call on those who haven't been heard.

Document Makeover

Improve This E-Mail Message

To practice correcting drafts of actual documents, visit www.prenhall.com/onekey on the web. Click "Document Makeovers," then click Chapter 2. You will find an e-mail message that contains problems and errors relating to what you've learned in this chapter about communicating in teams. Use the "Final Draft" decision tool to create an improved version of this e-mail message. Check the message for clarity, relevance of topics to meeting participants, and a collaborative tone.

FIGURE 2.1 Typical Meeting Agenda

AGENDA

PLANNING COMMITTEE MEETING

Monday, October 21, 2005
10:00 A.M. to 11:00 A.M.

Executive Conference Room

		Person	Proposed Time
I.	Call to Order		
II.	Roll Call		
III.	Approval of Agenda		
IV.	Approval of Minutes from Previous Meeting		
V.	Chairperson's Report on Site Selection Progress		
VI.	Subcommittee Reports	Person	Proposed Time
	a. New Markets	Alan	5 minutes
	b. New Products	Jennifer	5 minutes
	c. Finance	Craig	5 minutes
VII.	Old Business—Pricing Policy for New Products	Terry	10 minutes
VIII.	New Business		
	a. Carson and Canfield Data on New Product Sales	Sarah	10 minutes
	b. Restructuring of Product Territories Due to New Product Introductions	Edith	10 minutes
IX.	Announcements		
X.	Adjournment		

- **Pacing the presentation and discussion.** Limit the time spent on each agenda item so that you'll be able to cover them all.
- **Summarizing meeting achievements.** As time begins to run out, interrupt the discussion and summarize what has been accomplished; however, don't be too rigid. Allow enough time for all the main ideas to be heard, and give people a chance to raise related issues.

Follow Parliamentary Procedure

One way you can improve the productivity of a meeting is by using **parliamentary procedure**, a time-tested method for planning and running effective meetings. The most common guide to such procedure is *Robert's Rules of Order* (also available are less technical guides based on "Robert's Rules"). Decide how strictly you want to adhere to parliamentary procedure: For small groups you may be quite flexible, but for larger groups you'll

Robert's Rules of Order is the most common guide to parliamentary procedure.

want to use a more formal approach. Used correctly, parliamentary procedure can help teams conduct business efficiently, protect individual rights, maintain order, preserve a spirit of harmony, and accomplish team and organizational goals.[7]

Encourage Participation

The best meetings are those in which everyone participates, so don't let one or two people dominate your meeting while others doodle on their notepads. To draw out the shy types, ask for their input on issues that particularly pertain to them. You might say something like, "Roberto, you've done a lot of work in this area. What do you think?" For the overly talkative, simply say that time is limited and others need to be heard from. As you move through your agenda, stop at the end of each item, summarize what you understand to be the feelings of the group, and state the important points made during the discussion.

If you're a meeting participant, try to contribute to both the subject of the meeting and the smooth interaction of the participants. Use your listening skills and powers of observation to size up the interpersonal dynamics of the people; then adapt your behavior to help the group achieve its goals. Speak up if you have something useful to say, but don't monopolize the discussion.

Close Effectively

At the conclusion of the meeting, tie up the loose ends. Either summarize the general conclusion of the discussion or list the actions to be taken. Wrapping things up ensures that all participants agree on the outcome, and it gives people a chance to clear up any misunderstandings. Before the meeting breaks up, briefly review who has agreed to do what by what date.

Following Up

As soon as possible after the meeting, make sure all participants receive a copy of the minutes or notes, showing recommended actions, schedules, and responsibilities. Generally, the secretary who attends the meeting prepares a set of minutes for distribution to all attendees and other interested parties (see Figure 2.2). An informal meeting may not require minutes. Instead, attendees simply make their own notes on their copies of the agenda. Follow-up is then their responsibility, although the meeting leader may need to remind them to do so through an e-mail or a phone call.

Just as follow-up is the responsibility of team members, so is each person's ability to listen. Successful meetings depend on careful preparation, strong leadership, active participation, and diligent follow-up. But without effective listening skills on the part of every team member, meetings could not take place.

Listening to Others

Your ability to listen effectively is directly related to your success in meetings, conversations, phone calls, and other group relationships. Unfortunately, most of us listen at or below a 25 percent efficiency rate: We remember only about half of what's said in a 10-minute conversation, and we forget half of that within 48 hours.[8] In addition, when questioned about material we've just heard, we are likely to get the facts mixed up. That's because although we listen to words, we don't necessarily hear their meaning. [9]

The Listening Process

By understanding the process of listening, you begin to understand why oral messages are so often lost. Listening involves five related activities, which usually occur in sequence:[10]

FIGURE 2.2   Typical Meeting Minutes

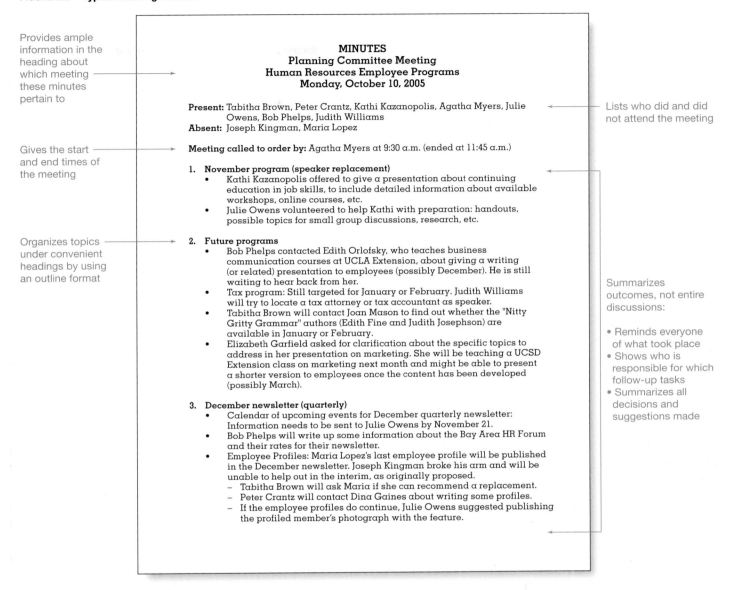

Provides ample information in the heading about which meeting these minutes pertain to

Gives the start and end times of the meeting

Organizes topics under convenient headings by using an outline format

MINUTES
Planning Committee Meeting
Human Resources Employee Programs
Monday, October 10, 2005

Present: Tabitha Brown, Peter Crantz, Kathi Kazanopolis, Agatha Myers, Julie Owens, Bob Phelps, Judith Williams
Absent: Joseph Kingman, Maria Lopez

Meeting called to order by: Agatha Myers at 9:30 a.m. (ended at 11:45 a.m.)

1. **November program (speaker replacement)**
   - Kathi Kazanopolis offered to give a presentation about continuing education in job skills, to include detailed information about available workshops, online courses, etc.
   - Julie Owens volunteered to help Kathi with preparation: handouts, possible topics for small group discussions, research, etc.

2. **Future programs**
   - Bob Phelps contacted Edith Orlofsky, who teaches business communication courses at UCLA Extension, about giving a writing (or related) presentation to employees (possibly December). He is still waiting to hear back from her.
   - Tax program: Still targeted for January or February. Judith Williams will try to locate a tax attorney or tax accountant as speaker.
   - Tabitha Brown will contact Joan Mason to find out whether the "Nitty Gritty Grammar" authors (Edith Fine and Judith Josephson) are available in January or February.
   - Elizabeth Garfield asked for clarification about the specific topics to address in her presentation on marketing. She will be teaching a UCSD Extension class on marketing next month and might be able to present a shorter version to employees once the content has been developed (possibly March).

3. **December newsletter (quarterly)**
   - Calendar of upcoming events for December quarterly newsletter: Information needs to be sent to Julie Owens by November 21.
   - Bob Phelps will write up some information about the Bay Area HR Forum and their rates for their newsletter.
   - Employee Profiles: Maria Lopez's last employee profile will be published in the December newsletter. Joseph Kingman broke his arm and will be unable to help out in the interim, as originally proposed.
     – Tabitha Brown will ask Maria if she can recommend a replacement.
     – Peter Crantz will contact Dina Gaines about writing some profiles.
     – If the employee profiles do continue, Julie Owens suggested publishing the profiled member's photograph with the feature.

Lists who did and did not attend the meeting

Summarizes outcomes, not entire discussions:

- Reminds everyone of what took place
- Shows who is responsible for which follow-up tasks
- Summarizes all decisions and suggestions made

■ **Receiving.** Physically hearing the message and taking note of it. Physical reception can be blocked by noise, impaired hearing, or inattention.

■ **Interpreting.** Assigning meaning to sounds according to your own values, beliefs, ideas, expectations, roles, needs, and personal history. The speaker's frame of reference may be quite different from yours, so you may need to determine what the speaker really means.

■ **Remembering.** Storing a message for future reference. As you listen, you retain what you hear by taking notes or by making a mental outline of the speaker's key points.

■ **Evaluating.** Applying critical thinking skills to weigh the speaker's remarks. You separate fact from opinion and evaluate the quality of the evidence.

■ **Responding.** Reacting once you've evaluated the speaker's message. If you're communicating one on one or in a small group, the initial response generally takes the form of verbal feedback. If you're one of many in an audience, your initial response may take the form of applause, laughter, or silence. Later on, you may act on what you have heard.

Listening involves five steps.

Obstacles to Effective Listening

A large part of becoming a good listener is the ability to recognize and overcome a variety of physical and mental barriers, including

- **Prejudgment.** To function in life, people must operate on some basic assumptions. However, these assumptions can be incorrect or inappropriate in new situations. Moreover, some people listen defensively, viewing every comment as a personal attack, so they distort messages by tuning out anything that doesn't confirm their assumptions.

- **Self-centeredness.** Some people tend to take control of conversations, rather than listen. If a speaker mentions a problem, self-centered listeners eagerly relate their own problems, trivializing the speaker's concerns by pointing out that their own difficulties are much worse. No matter what the subject, these people know more than the speaker does, and they're determined to prove it.

- **Selective listening.** When you listen selectively (also called *out-listening*), you let your mind wander to things such as whether you brought your dry-cleaning ticket to work. You tune out until you hear something that gets your attention. Thus, you don't remember what the speaker *actually* said; you remember what you *think* the speaker *probably* said. [11]

One reason people's minds tend to wander is that they think faster than they speak. Most people speak at about 120 to 150 words per minute. However, studies indicate that, depending on the subject and the individual, people can process information at 500 to 800 words per minute. [12] This disparity between rate of speech and rate of thought can be used to pull one's thoughts together, but some listeners let their minds wander and just tune out.

Strategies for Effective Listening

Effective listening strengthens organizational relationships, enhances product delivery, alerts the organization to innovation from both internal and external sources, and allows the organization to manage growing diversity both in the workforce and in the customers it serves. [13] Good listening gives you an edge and increases your impact when you speak (see Table 2.1). However, effective listening requires a conscious effort and a willing mind. To improve your listening skills, heed the following tips:

- **Find areas of interest.** Look beyond the speaker's style by asking yourself what the speaker knows that you don't.

- **Judge content, not delivery.** Evaluate and criticize the content, not the speaker. Review the key points. Do they make sense? Are the concepts supported by facts?

- **Keep quiet.** Don't interrupt. Depersonalize your listening so that you decrease the emotional impact of what's being said and are better able to hold your rebuttal until you've heard the total message.

- **Listen for ideas.** Listen for concepts and key ideas as well as for facts, and know the difference between fact and principle, idea and example, and evidence and argument.

- **Take careful notes.** Take meaningful notes that are brief and to the point.

- **Work at listening.** Look for unspoken messages. Often the speaker's tone of voice or expressions will reveal more than the words themselves. Provide feedback. Let the speaker know you're with him or her. Maintain eye contact. Provide appropriate facial expressions.

- **Block out competing thoughts.** Fight distractions by closing doors, turning off radios or televisions, and moving closer to the speaker.

- **Paraphrase the speaker's ideas.** Paraphrase or summarize when the speaker reaches a stopping point.

Table 2.1	Distinguishing Effective Listeners from Ineffective Listeners	
Effective Listeners		**Ineffective Listeners**
Listen actively		Listen passively
Take careful and complete notes		Take no notes or ineffective notes
Make frequent eye contact with the speaker (depends on culture to some extent)		Make little or no eye contact
Stay focused on the speaker and the content		Allow their mind to wander; are easily distracted
Mentally paraphrase key points to maintain attention level and ensure comprehension		Fail to paraphrase
Adjust listening style to the situation		Listen with the same style, regardless of the situation
Give the speaker nonverbal cues (such as nodding to show agreement or raising eyebrows to show surprise or skepticism)		Fail to give the speaker nonverbal feedback
Save questions or points of disagreement until an appropriate time		Interrupt whenever they disagree or don't understand
Overlook stylistic differences and focus on the speaker's message		Are distracted by or unduly influenced by stylistic differences; are judgmental
Make distinctions between main points and supporting details		Unable to distinguish main points from details
Look for opportunities to learn		Assume they already know everything that's important to know

■ **Stay open-minded.** Keep an open mind by asking questions that clarify understanding; reserve judgment until the speaker has finished.

■ **Capitalize on the fact that thought is faster than speech.** Stay ahead of the speaker by anticipating what will be said next and by thinking about what's already been said.

Listening to what someone is saying is crucial to business success, whether you're conversing with someone face to face, listening to a speaker during a meeting, or having a conversation over the phone. But telephone conversations and voice mail involve more than simply listening.

Using Telephones and Voice Mail

Just as important as how you plan, conduct, and participate in meetings is how you communicate using the telephone and voice mail. In fact, some experts estimate that 95 percent of most companies' daily contacts come via the telephone. [14]

Telephones and voice mail are essential for organizations to conduct business effectively.

When using the telephone and voice mail, your communication loses a great deal of the nonverbal richness that accompanies face-to-face conversations. Even so, your attitude and tone of voice can convey your confidence and professionalism effectively. Your voice and attitude can impress others with your eagerness to help, your willingness to listen, and your ability to communicate clearly.

Receiving Telephone Calls Effectively

When people call your place of business, they want to know, first, that they will reach someone who can help them and, second, that doing so will be quick and easy. They don't want to be passed from department to department. They don't want to hold while their party finishes up with someone else. And they don't want to get stuck talking with someone who lacks the knowledge or the ability to get them the information or the action they need.

If you answer the phone for someone who is unable to take the call right away, note the caller's name, telephone number, and a brief but accurate message—assuring the caller that the appropriate person will get the message and return the call. Likewise, if you will be away from your telephone for any length of time, forward your calls so that anyone calling you won't have to be transferred again and again. [15]

To be as effective as possible when receiving calls, observe the following helpful tips: [16]

- **Answer promptly and with a smile.** Answer within two or three rings. Also, answering with a smile makes you sound friendly and positive. Speak clearly, and don't rush your greeting. Speak slowly enough for people to understand what you're saying.

- **Identify yourself.** Announce the company name, the department, and your own name. Keep your manner friendly and professional so that the conversation begins pleasantly and positively, building an instant relationship with your caller.

- **Establish the needs of your caller.** Immediately ask, "How may I help you?" If you know the caller's name, use it to affirm a sense of warmth and personal interest. Also, use continuity expressions to show that you're listening (e.g., "Oh yes," "I see," or "That's right."). Keep focused on the subject at hand, and don't interrupt with pointless questions.

- **Be positive.** If you can, answer callers' questions promptly and efficiently. If you can't help, tell them what you can do for them. Explain that you will find the necessary information. Avoid conveying a lack of confidence; that is, don't use vague phrases, such as "I'm really not sure whether . . . " or "It may be that . . . "

- **Take complete, accurate messages.** Obtain as much information as you can so that you know how to process the call. Repeat names, telephone and fax numbers, e-mail addresses, and dates to make sure you have them right. Always take a return number, even if the caller assures you it is known. And don't forget to write neatly so that whoever gets your message can read it.

- **Give reasons for your actions.** If you absolutely must put a caller on hold briefly or transfer the call, explain to the caller what you are doing and why. Don't leave callers on hold for long periods of time. If it's necessary to hunt for information or to take another call, offer to call back.

Making Effective Telephone Calls

The key to making effective telephone calls is planning. Know precisely why you're calling and exactly what you need from the person you're calling. Before you make the call, gather all the materials you may need to refer to, and briefly outline or jot down notes about what you're going to say. To be as effective as possible when making phone calls, keep in mind the following tips:[17]

- **Be ready before you call.** Anticipate the conversation and plan ahead how you will handle any possible outcomes. Make an outline or notes and have them in front of you, along with a pad for taking notes. Also make sure you have at your fingertips any other necessary materials: account numbers, catalogs, electronic files, a list of contacts, a sales report, cost figures, and so on.

- **Schedule the call.** Decide ahead of time when you will call. Consider your own readiness, the time of day, and whether your contact is located in a different time zone. Don't call people first thing in the morning when they are answering mail and starting their day. Likewise, don't call anyone last thing at night when they're heading out of the office.

- **Eliminate distractions.** Don't call from a noisy pay phone or from an area where background noise will interfere with your concentration and your ability to hear and be heard. Similarly, don't tap a pencil or make other noises that might be picked up and amplified over the phone wires.

- **Make a clear, comprehensive introduction.** Immediately identify the person you're calling, give your own name and organization, briefly describe the reason for your call, and greet the person. This opening starts the call on a positive note. Keep your tone friendly, and always ask, "Is this a good time to talk briefly, or should I call you back?"

- **Don't take up too much time.** Avoid talking too slowly, spending too much time in small talk, or complaining about how difficult it is to get in touch with this person. Speak quickly and clearly, and get right to the point of the call.
- **Maintain audience focus throughout the call.** Ask questions and give clear answers so that both of you understand the call and can decide together what action is needed.
- **Close in a friendly, positive manner.** Double-check all vital information by summarizing what you've discussed. Check to see that you both agree on any action that either party will take. Thank the other person for his or her time, and if you promise to phone back, make sure you do so.

Using Voice Mail Effectively

Much more than a glorified answering machine, voice mail lets you send, store, and retrieve verbal messages. Actually, voice mail is just a part of what is now called *voice processing*, which can include an automatic attendant, automatic call distribution, e-mail and paging integration, call forwarding, call screening, and many other features.[18]

Voice mail can be used to replace short memos and phone calls that need no response. It is most effective for short, unambiguous messages. Like e-mail, it solves time-zone difficulties and reduces a substantial amount of interoffice paperwork.[19]

Before recording your outgoing greeting for your own voice mail system, organize your thoughts.[20] You want your message to be accurate and concise. The following tips may also help you make your voice mail greeting more effective:[21]

Seven tips will help you record a more effective voice mail greeting.

- **Be brief.** Your message should not take longer than 30 seconds.
- **Be accurate.** Specifically state what callers should do.
- **Sound professional.** Make sure your voice is businesslike but cheerful. Never eat, drink, chew gum, or suck candy while recording a message. Speak slowly. Don't say names or phone numbers so fast that they can't be understood.
- **Keep your callers in mind.** Encourage callers to leave detailed messages. Also remind them to leave a phone number (especially frequent callers who may assume you have it handy).
- **Make options logical and helpful.** Limit options to three or four. Make one of the options an easy way to reach a live operator without bouncing helplessly from one menu option to another. When describing options, state the action first and then the key to press.
- **Keep your personal greeting current.** Update your greetings to reflect your schedule and leave special announcements. Don't forget to change your message when you go on vacation or plan to be away from your desk for an extended period of time.
- **Respond promptly.** Check your voice mail messages regularly and return all necessary calls within 24 hours.

When you leave a message on someone else's voice mail system, think about your message in advance, and plan it carefully. Remember the following tips:[22]

Six tips will help you leave more effective voice mail messages.

- **Keep the message simple.** Save the complicated details to give in person. Leave your name, number, and purpose for calling. Designate a specific time when you can be reached (or arrange to call the person back at a specific time). Give just enough detail to get your message across so that the receiver can evaluate whether to call you back. Don't forget to repeat your name and phone number at the end of the message.
- **Sound professional.** Give your message a headline so that the listener can quickly judge its priority. Speak clearly, slowly, and loudly. Remember to smile while recording, so that your tone will be pleasant. Avoid background noise as much as possible, and before using a cell phone, consider the effect of a bad connection or interruption.
- **Avoid personal messages.** Remember, someone else may be in the room when your message is played back.

- **Replay your message before leaving the system.** Use this option whenever it is available, in order to listen to your message objectively and make sure it is clear.
- **Don't leave multiple, repetitious messages.** Rather than a series of messages with the same information, simply leave one detailed message and follow that up with a fax or an e-mail.
- **Never hide behind voice mail.** Don't use it to escape unpleasant encounters, and make sure to give praise in person.[23]

When using telephones and voice mail, the way you sound is important—your tone and your attitude shape the way other people perceive you and your message. Such factors go beyond the words you use. Although sound, tone, and attitude are nonverbal, these factors communicate an important message to your receivers. Your ability to use and interpret nonverbal communication is just as important as all the other skills discussed so far.

Understanding Nonverbal Communication

The most basic form of communication is **nonverbal communication:** all the cues, gestures, facial expressions, spatial relationships, and attitudes toward time that enable people to communicate without words. Nonverbal communication differs from verbal methods in terms of intent and spontaneity. You generally think about verbal messages, if only for a moment. However, when you communicate nonverbally, you sometimes do so unconsciously—you don't mean to raise an eyebrow or to blush.

The Importance of Nonverbal Communication

Nonverbal communication is more reliable and more efficient than verbal communication.

Actions actually do speak louder than words. In fact, most people can deceive others much more easily with words than they can with their bodies. Words are relatively easy to control; body language, facial expressions, and vocal characteristics are not. By paying attention to a person's nonverbal cues, you can detect deception or affirm a speaker's honesty.

Also, nonverbal communication is efficient. When you have a conscious purpose, you can often achieve it more economically with a gesture than with words. A wave of the hand, a pat on the back, a wink—all are streamlined expressions of thought. Even so, nonverbal communication usually blends with speech, carrying part of the message to augment, reinforce, and clarify the spoken word.

The Types of Nonverbal Communication

The thousands of forms of nonverbal communication can be grouped into some general categories. Just remember, the interpretation of these nonverbal signals varies from culture to culture (see Figure 2.3). Just compare a few gestures, and you can see many differences from culture to culture:[24]

- Canadian listeners nod to signal agreement.
- Greek listeners nod slightly upward to signal no.
- Japanese listeners nod to indicate only that they have understood.
- German listeners toss their head back to beckon someone closer.
- Indian listeners toss their head to signal yes.
- British listeners stare at the speaker, blinking their eyes to indicate understanding.
- People in the United States are taught that it's impolite to stare.

Facial Expression

The face and eyes command particular attention as sources of nonverbal messages.

Your face is the primary site for expressing your emotions; it reveals both the type and the intensity of your feelings.[25] Your eyes are especially effective for indicating attention and interest, influencing others, regulating interaction, and establishing dominance. In fact,

FIGURE 2.3   Avoiding Nonverbal Mishaps

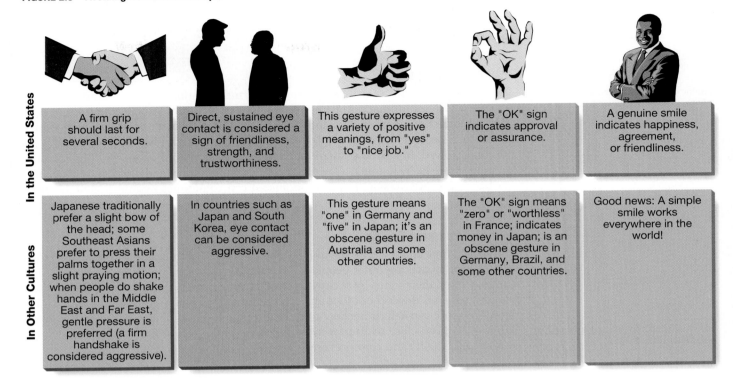

In the United States	A firm grip should last for several seconds.	Direct, sustained eye contact is considered a sign of friendliness, strength, and trustworthiness.	This gesture expresses a variety of positive meanings, from "yes" to "nice job."	The "OK" sign indicates approval or assurance.	A genuine smile indicates happiness, agreement, or friendliness.
In Other Cultures	Japanese traditionally prefer a slight bow of the head; some Southeast Asians prefer to press their palms together in a slight praying motion; when people do shake hands in the Middle East and Far East, gentle pressure is preferred (a firm handshake is considered aggressive).	In countries such as Japan and South Korea, eye contact can be considered aggressive.	This gesture means "one" in Germany and "five" in Japan; it's an obscene gesture in Australia and some other countries.	The "OK" sign means "zero" or "worthless" in France; indicates money in Japan; is an obscene gesture in Germany, Brazil, and some other countries.	Good news: A simple smile works everywhere in the world!

eye contact is so important in the United States that even when your words send a positive message, averting your gaze can lead your audience to perceive a negative one.[26] Some people try to manipulate their facial expressions to simulate an emotion they do not feel or to mask their true feelings.

Gesture and Posture

By moving your body, you can express both specific and general messages, some voluntary and some involuntary. Many gestures—a wave of the hand, for example—have a specific and intentional meaning, such as "hello" or "good-bye." Other types of body movement are unintentional and express a more general message. Slouching, leaning forward, fidgeting, and walking briskly are all unconscious signals that reveal whether you feel confident or nervous, friendly or hostile, assertive or passive, powerful or powerless.

Body language reveals a lot about a person's emotions and attitudes.

Vocal Characteristics

Like body language, your voice carries both intentional and unintentional messages. Consider the sentence "What have you been up to?" If you repeat that question four or five times, changing your tone of voice and stressing various words, you can intentionally convey quite different messages. However, your vocal characteristics also reveal many things you're unaware of. Your tone and volume, your accent and speaking pace, and all the little *um*'s and *ah*'s that creep into your speech say a lot about who you are, your relationship with the audience, and the emotions underlying your words.

Your tone of voice carries meaning, whether intentional or not.

Personal Appearance

People respond to others on the basis of their physical appearance. Because you see yourself as others see you, their expectations are often a self-fulfilling prophecy—that is, when people think you're capable and attractive, you feel good about yourself, and that feeling affects your behavior, which in turn affects other people's perceptions of you. Although

Physical appearance and personal style contribute to one's identity.

body type and facial features impose limitations, most people are able to control their attractiveness to some degree. Grooming, clothing, accessories, "style"—all modify a person's appearance. If your goal is to make a good impression, adopt the style of the people you want to impress.

Touching Behavior

Touch is an important vehicle for conveying warmth, comfort, and reassurance. Perhaps because it implies intimacy, touching behavior is governed in various circumstances by relatively strict customs that establish who may touch whom and how. The accepted norms vary, depending on the gender, age, relative status, and cultural background of the persons involved. In business situations, touching suggests dominance, so a higher-status person is more likely to touch a lower-status person than the other way around. Touching has become controversial, however, because it can sometimes be interpreted as sexual harassment.

Use of Time and Space

Like touch, time and space can be used to assert authority. Some people demonstrate their importance by making other people wait; others show respect by being on time. People can also assert their status by occupying the best space. In U.S. companies, the chief executive usually has the corner office and the prettiest view. Apart from serving as a symbol of status, space can determine how comfortable people feel talking with each other. When others stand too close or too far away, we are likely to feel ill at ease. Again, attitudes toward punctuality and comfort zones vary from culture to culture.

Ways to Improve Your Nonverbal Communication

When communicating orally, pay attention to your nonverbal cues, and avoid giving others conflicting signals.[27] You can improve your nonverbal communication by following these tips:

- Avoid giving conflicting signals.
- Be as honest as possible in communicating your emotions.
- Smile genuinely. Faking a smile is obvious to observers.
- Maintain the eye contact your audience expects.
- Be aware of your posture and of the gestures you use.
- Try to use appropriate vocal signals while minimizing unintentional messages.
- Imitate the appearance of the people you want to impress.
- Respect your audience's comfort zone.
- Adopt a handshake that matches your personality and intention.
- Be aware of varying attitudes toward time.
- Use touch only when appropriate.
- Be aware that people may give false nonverbal cues.

Keep in mind that few gestures convey meaning in and of themselves; they must be interpreted in clusters, and they should reinforce your words, not replace them. You'll have plenty of practice with nonverbal communication in meetings, whether you are leading or participating.

Reviewing Key Points

This chapter explains the importance of working in teams. Effective teams are able to accomplish their goals because members collaborate on the necessary tasks.

The chapter points out that for a team to be effective, its members require good listening skills. It discusses the listening process, the barriers to good listening, and effective listening strategies, such as focusing on areas of interest, not interrupting, blocking out competing thoughts, and keeping an open mind. This chapter also describes how understanding nonverbal communication can help you be a more effective team member.

The chapter offers fundamental methods for planning and participating in productive meetings. And finally, it gives you basic techniques for using telephones and voice mail effectively.

The next section introduces the three-step writing process and gives you three full chapters of practice. These three chapters deal with the fundamentals of planning, writing, and completing messages. They cover design, audience analysis, organization, style, and tone—among other topics. You will learn the basic skills required to compose messages that are clear, interesting, concise, diplomatic, and convincing.

Test Your Knowledge

1. In what four ways do organizations benefit from team decision making?

2. What four things must effective teams avoid?

3. What is the purpose of using parliamentary procedure?

4. What questions should an agenda answer?

5. What activities make up the listening process?

6. Name the three main barriers to effective listening.

7. Of the ten strategies listed to help you listen effectively, list and explain five.

8. Explain why your attitude and tone of voice are so important when using the telephone and voice mail.

9. In what six ways can an individual communicate nonverbally?

10. Of the dozen tips listed to improve nonverbal communication, list and explain five.

Apply Your Knowledge

1. Whenever your boss asks for feedback, she blasts anyone offering criticism, which causes people to agree with everything she says. You want to talk to her about it, but what should you say? List some of the points you want to make when you discuss this issue with your boss.

2. At your last department meeting, three people monopolized the entire discussion. What might you do at the next meeting to encourage other department members to voluntarily participate?

3. Chester never seems to be paying attention during weekly team meetings. He has never contributed to the discussion, and you've never even seen him take notes. He says he wants to support the team but that he finds it difficult to focus during routine meetings. List some ideas you could give him that might improve his listening skills.

4. How can nonverbal communication help you run a meeting? For example, how can it help you call a meeting to order, emphasize important topics, show approval, express reservations, regulate the flow of conversation, and invite a colleague to continue with a comment?

5. **Ethical Choices** As team leader, you've just received a voice mail message from Tanya Moore, asking to lead next week's meeting. She's been with the company for six weeks and with your team for three. From what you've already observed, she's opinionated (a bit of a know-it-all), and she tends to discourage the more reserved team members from speaking up.

You can't allow her to run next week's meeting, and without improvement in her attitude toward others, she may never be ready to lead. You consider three options for explaining your view of her position: (1) leaving her a friendly voice mail message, (2) meeting with her, or (3) sending her a friendly e-mail message. What should you do? Explain your choice.

Practice Your Knowledge

Activities

For live links to all websites discussed in this chapter, visit this text's website at www. prenhall.com/bovee. Just log on, select Chapter 2, and click on "Featured Websites." Locate the page or the URL related to the material in the text.

1. **Analyze This Document** A project leader has made notes about covering the following items at the quarterly budget meeting. Prepare a formal agenda by putting these items into a logical order and rewriting them, where necessary, to give phrases a more consistent sound:

   Budget Committee Meeting to be held on December 12, 2005, at 9:30 A.M.
   - I will call the meeting to order.
   - Site director's report: A closer look at cost overruns on Greentree site.
   - The group will review and approve the minutes from last quarter's meeting.
   - I will ask the finance director to report on actual vs. projected quarterly revenues and expenses.
   - I will distribute copies of the overall divisional budget and announce the date of the next budget meeting.
   - Discussion: How can we do a better job of anticipating and preventing cost overruns?
   - Meeting will take place in Conference Room 3.
   - What additional budget issues must be considered during this quarter?

2. **Teamwork** With a classmate, attend a local community or campus meeting where you can observe group discussion. Take notes individually during the meeting and then work together to answer the following questions:
   a. What is your evaluation of this meeting? In your answer, consider (1) the leader's ability to clearly state the meeting's goals, (2) the leader's ability to engage members in a meaningful discussion, and (3) the group's listening skills.
   b. How well did the individual participants listen? How could you tell?
   c. Compare the notes you took during the meeting with those of your classmate. What differences do you notice? How do you account for these differences?

3. Team Communication   Every month, each employee in your department is expected to give a brief oral presentation on the status of his or her project. However, your department has recently hired an employee with a severe speech impediment that prevents people from understanding most of what he has to say.

Your task: As assistant department manager, how will you resolve this dilemma? Please explain.

4. Meeting Productivity: Analyzing Agendas   Obtain a copy of the agenda from a recent campus or work meeting. Does this agenda show a start time or end time? Is it specific enough that you, as an outsider, would be able to understand what was to be discussed? If not, how would you improve the agenda?

5. Listening Skills: Overcoming Barriers   Identify some of your bad listening habits and make a list of some ways you could correct them. For the next 30 days, review your list and jot down any improvements you've noticed as a result of your effort.

6. Listening Skills: Self-Assessment   How good are your listening skills? Rate yourself on each of the following elements of good listening; then examine your ratings to identify where you are strongest and where you can improve, using the tips in this chapter.

Elements of Listening	Always	Frequently	Occasionally	Never
1. I look for areas of interest when people speak.	_____	_____	_____	_____
2. I focus on content rather than delivery.	_____	_____	_____	_____
3. I wait to respond until I understand the content.	_____	_____	_____	_____
4. I listen for ideas and themes, not isolated facts.	_____	_____	_____	_____
5. I take notes only when needed.	_____	_____	_____	_____
6. I really concentrate on what speakers are saying.	_____	_____	_____	_____
7. I stay focused even when the ideas are complex.	_____	_____	_____	_____
8. I keep an open mind despite emotionally charged language.	_____	_____	_____	_____

7. Telephones and Voice Mail   You are interested in the hiring policies of companies in your area. You want information about how often entry positions need to be filled, what sort of qualifications are required for these positions, and what range of pay is offered. Plan out your phone call. Think about what you will say (1) to reach the person who can help you, (2) to gain the information you need, (3) to leave a voice mail message. Once you've planned out your approach, call three companies in your area, and briefly summarize the results of these calls.

8. Nonverbal Communication: Analyzing Written Messages   Select a business letter and envelope that you have received at work or at home. Analyze their appearance. What nonverbal messages do they send? Are these messages consistent with the content of the letter? If not, what could the sender have done to make the nonverbal communication consistent with the verbal communication?

9. Nonverbal Communication: Analyzing Body Language   Describe what the following body movements suggest when they are exhibited by someone during a conversation. How do such movements influence your interpretation of spoken words?

- **a.** Shifting one's body continuously while seated
- **b.** Twirling and playing with one's hair
- **c.** Sitting in a sprawled position
- **d.** Rolling one's eyes
- **e.** Extending a weak handshake

Expand Your Knowledge

Exploring the Best of the Web

Making Meetings Work   www.3m.com/meetingnetwork
The 3M Meeting Network contains a wide selection of articles on planning meetings, designing activities to build teamwork, and making better presentations. Click on "Articles and Advice," find the appropriate articles, and then answer the following questions:

Exercises

1. How can you know if a meeting should be held or not?
2. How can good leaders show they trust the group's ability to perform successfully?
3. What are the advantages and disadvantages of "open space" meetings, which take place without formal agendas or facilitation?

Exploring the Web on Your Own

Review these chapter-related websites on your own to learn more about achieving communication success in the workplace.

1. CRInfo, www.crinfo.org, is a website dedicated to providing support for conflict resolution.
2. The Center for Collaborative Organizations, www.workteams.unt.edu, has many links, articles, and research reports on the subject matter of teams.
3. Symbols.com, www.symbols.com, offers a graphical search engine that explains the meaning of 2,500 graphical symbols. Find out what that unusual symbol on a foreign-language website means, or verify that the symbols you plan to use don't convey some inappropriate nonverbal meaning. The Word Index feature lets you see the graphical symbols associated with thousands of words and ideas.

Learn Interactively

Interactive Study Guide

Go to the Companion Website at www.prenhall.com/bovee. For Chapter 2, take advantage of the interactive "Study Guide" to test your knowledge of the chapter. Get instant feedback on whether you need additional studying. Also, visit this site's "Study Hall," where you'll find an abundance of valuable resources that will help you succeed in this course.

Peak Performance Grammar and Mechanics

In Chapter 1 you were referred to the Peak Performance Grammar and Mechanics activities on the web at www.prenhall.com/onekey to improve your skill with nouns and pronouns. For additional reinforcement in pronouns, go to the "Improve Your Grammar, Mechanics, and Usage" section that follows, and complete the "Level I: Self-Assessment" exercises.

Improve Your Grammar, Mechanics, And Usage

Level 1: Self-Assessment—Pronouns

Review Section 1.2 in the Handbook of Grammar, Mechanics, and Usage, and then look at the following 15 items.

In items 1–5, replace the underlined nouns with the correct pronouns:

1. _____ To <u>which retailer</u> will you send your merchandise?

2. _____ Have you given <u>John and Nancy</u> a list of parts?

3. _____ <u>The main office</u> sent the invoice to <u>Mr. and Mrs. Litvak</u> on December 5.

4. _____ The company settled <u>the company's</u> accounts before the end of the year.

5. _____ <u>Which person's</u> umbrella is this?

In items 6–15, write the correct pronouns in the spaces provided:

6. The sales staff is preparing guidelines for _____ (*their, its*) clients.

7. Few of the sales representatives turn in _____ (*their, its*) reports on time.

8. The board of directors has chosen _____ (*their, its*) officers.

9. Gomez and Archer have told _____ (*his, their*) clients about the new program.

10. Each manager plans to expand _____ (*his, their, his or her*) sphere of control next year.

11. Has everyone supplied _____ (*his, their, his or her*) Social Security number?

12. After giving every employee_____ (*his, their, a*) raise, George told _____ (*them, they, all*) about the increased work load.

13. Bob and Tim have opposite ideas about how to achieve company goals. _____ (*Who, Whom*) do you think will win the debate?

14. City Securities has just announced _____ (*who, whom*) it will hire as CEO.

15. Either of the new products would readily find _____ (*their, its*) niche in the marketplace.

Level 2: Workplace Applications

The following items contain numerous errors in grammar, capitalization, punctuation, abbreviation, number style, word division, and vocabulary. Rewrite each sentence in the space provided, correcting all errors. Write *C* in the space after any sentence that is already correct.

1. Anita Doig from Data Providers will outline their data interpretations as it relates to industry trends, additionally Miss Doig will be asked to comment on how their data should be utilized.

2. You're order for 2000 mylar bags has been received by us; please be advised that orders of less than 5000 bags only get a 20 percent discount.

3. Just between you and I, the new 'customer centric' philosophy seems pretty confusing.

4. Whether dealing with a catastrophe, or with the many problems that afflict a great city on a daily basis; Mr. Giuliani has relied on a systematic methodical approach that can work for any manager, in any sized business.

5. Among the specialties of Product Marketers International is promotional efforts for clients, including presence on the Internet, radio, and on television.

6. An overview of a typical marketing plan will be covered in the introduction to this report, to give you an idea of what's in it.

7. Subsidiary rights sales can be a discreet source of income and compliment your overall sales.

8. Special events ranging from author breakfasts and luncheons to awards programs and reception's offers a great way to make industry contacts.

9. We will show you how not only to meet the challenges of information rich material but also the challenges of electronic distance learning.

10. To site just one problem, the reason that the market is in such a state of confusion is the appalling lack of standards whether for hardware, software or for metadata.

11. Two leading business consultants Doug Smith and Carla McNeil will share their insights on how specialty stores can effectively compete in a world of Corporate Superstores.

12. One of the big questions we need to address are "How does buying effect inventory levels"?

13. The closing of many industry digital entities have greatly affected the perception of e-books as a viable platform.

14. A competent, motivated, and enthusiastic staff can be a managers' most important asset in a competitive marketplace.

15. Come by the Technology Lounge where you can log on to computers and plug into laptops and check out demos of sponsor's websites.

Level 3: Document Critique

The following document contains errors in grammar, capitalization, punctuation, abbreviation, number style, and vocabulary. Correct all errors using standard proofreading marks (see Handbook of Grammar, Mechanics, and Usage (see Appendix C).

Date: Thurs, 14 November 2005 11:07:33 -0800

From: rick glissmeyer <rickg@aol.com>

To: richard herman <rcherman@ddc.com>

CC:

BCC:

Attached:

Subject: Please supply shipping costs

Dear Richard:

As you requested heres the complete order for seed mixes required by Roberta Mcdonald in

Vancouver:

* Fifty-lb. 80/20 canary seed mix @ $15.45

* 50 lbs. soak seed @ $20.25

* Total order: $305.70

The seeds are to be shipped to:

Roberta C. McDonald

1725 w. Third Av.

Vancuover, BC, V5M-5R6

We will mail our check, as soon as you reply with the amount of shipping costs. Roberta

says "her flock's getting ready for breeding," and she needs the soak seed by the end of

this month.

Thanks for your Quick Srevice

Rick Glissmeyer

What You Should Know About Videoconferencing Versus Face-to-Face Meetings

Ever since AT&T unveiled a videophone at the 1964 World's Fair, two-way TV has been touted as the next revolution in communication. Videoconferencing has always been a good idea. But its high costs and technical complexity had put off widespread acceptance—until now.

Today's videoconferencing equipment is better, faster, and more user friendly. System quality makes participants feel like they are in the same room (referred to as telepresence). Furthermore, the costs of installing videoconferencing systems have dropped dramatically in the last few years. Installations range in price from $10,000 for a portable TV-monitor unit to $250,000 for a fully outfitted conference room with a giant screen and remote-control video camera. In some cases, the time and cost savings from reduced corporate travel could pay for these systems in less than one year.

Spurred by such cost savings, a heightened fear of flying, canceled flights, and long airport delays following the September 11, 2001, terrorist attacks, sales of videoconferencing equipment are soon expected to top $40 billion. Companies that have considered videoconferencing for years are now being pressured by customers and suppliers to install such services. In fact, the hottest first-class seat is no longer on an airplane—instead, it's in front of a videoconferencing camera.

Will videoconferencing make face-to-face meetings obsolete? Probably not. You still need to seal important deals with personal handshakes—especially when conflicts or emotions are involved or when a relationship requires personal interaction to flourish. But videoconferencing will likely change the way people meet. For instance, lower-priority meetings and even details of merger talks could take place without participants leaving their hometown offices. "There's been far too much traveling around the country for 30-minute meetings," says one corporate executive. "It's foolish to have 15 people from different places fly thousands of miles to sit opposite each other at a conference table . . . It doesn't make any sense. It never made any sense." As one frequent business traveler put it, with videoconferencing, "there is no reason to get on a plane unless you absolutely need to."

Applications for Success

Hone your videoconferencing skills. Videoconferencing Presentation Techniques (www.coe.tamu.edu/~kmurphy/ classes/telecom98f/webpages/stewartogier/home.htm) offers tips to help you succeed. You are assistant to the director of communications at Taylor & Green, a law firm with branches in San Francisco and San Diego, California. The partners have asked your boss to investigate whether the firm should purchase all the equipment necessary for videoconferencing. To begin, your boss asks you to examine the general pros and cons:

Do the following:

1. Summarize your own opinion about whether videoconferencing is appropriate for all the types of meetings that your firm conducts. Are there any meetings that would not be right for videoconferencing?
2. Make a list of videoconferencing's advantages and disadvantages for Taylor & Green.
3. Based on the results of your examination (and assuming that money is no object), make your own recommendation to your boss either to purchase the equipment or not.

The Three-Step
Writing Process

Unit 2

3

Planning Business Messages

To compete for attention, business messages must be purposeful, audience centered, and concise.

Learning Objectives

After studying this chapter, you will be able to

1   Describe the three-step writing process
2   List four questions that can help you test the purpose of your message
3   Discuss six ways to satisfy your audience's information needs
4   Identify six elements to consider when choosing a channel and medium
5   Specify six ways to establish a good relationship with your audience
6   Explain how to use the "you" attitude when writing messages
7   Give examples of bias-free language and explain its importance

After launching Home Depot in 1979, co-founders Bernie Marcus and Arthur Blank worked hard to help managers communicate effectively with employees, customers, and suppliers. Today, Home Depot stocks 40,000 to 50,000 products in each store, employs 200,000 workers, uses 25,000 suppliers, and has millions of customers, which means that communicating face-to face with their various audiences is no longer an option for Home Depot managers. Instead they must make the best use of the available channels and media to make their messages effective.[1]

Understanding the Three-Step Writing Process

Like Home Depot's managers, you'll face a variety of communication assignments in your career, both oral and written. Some of your tasks will be routine, needing little more than jotting down a few sentences; others will be more complex, requiring reflection, research, and careful document preparation. Whatever the situation, you can make your messages more effective by making them

- **Purposeful.** Business messages provide information, solve a problem, or request the resources necessary to accomplish a goal. Every message has a specific purpose.
- **Audience centered.** Business messages help audiences understand issues, collaborate on tasks, or take action. Each message considers the audience's needs, background, and viewpoint.

■ **Concise.** Business messages respect everyone's time by presenting information clearly and efficiently. Every message should be as short as it can be without detracting from the subject.

One of the best ways to create effective business messages is to follow a systematic writing process.

What Is the Three-Step Process?

The writing process outlined in Figure 3.1 on page 54 can help you write more effective messages. As the figure shows, this process may be viewed as three simple steps: planning, writing, and completing business messages.

The three-step writing process covers planning, writing, and completing business messages.

Planning Business Messages

First, think about the fundamentals of your message. Clarify your purpose in communicating, and analyze audience members so that you can tailor your message to their needs and expectations. Gather the information that will inform, persuade, or motivate your audience. Then adapt your message by selecting the channel and medium that will suit both your needs and those of your audience. Finally, establish a good relationship with your audience. Planning business messages is the focus of this chapter.

Writing Business Messages

Once you've planned your message, the next step is to organize your ideas and compose your first draft. In this stage, you commit your thoughts to words, create sentences and paragraphs, and select illustrations and details to support your main idea. Writing business messages is discussed in Chapter 4.

Completing Business Messages

After writing your first draft, it's time to step back to review the content and organization for overall style, structure, and readability. You'll want to revise and rewrite until your message comes across clearly and effectively; then edit your message for details such as grammar, punctuation, and format. The next task is to produce your message, putting it into the form that your audience will receive. The last step is to proof the final document for typos, spelling errors, and other mechanical problems. Completing business messages is discussed in Chapter 5.

How Does the Three-Step Process Work?

Because so many of today's business messages are composed under pressure, allocating your time among these three steps can be a challenge. But whether you have 30 minutes or two days, try using roughly half of your time for planning—for deciding on your purpose, getting to know your audience, and immersing yourself in your subject matter. Devote less than a quarter of your time to actually writing your document. Then use more than a quarter of your time for completing the project (so that you don't shortchange important final steps such as revising and proofing).[2]

Try to budget your time for each step.

Home Depot's managers understand that there is no right or best way to write all business messages. As you work through the writing process presented in Chapters 3, 4, and 5, try not to view it as a list of how-to directives but as a way to understand the various tasks involved in effective business writing.[3] Effective communicators complete all three steps, although they may not necessarily complete them in 1-2-3 order. Some jump back and forth from one step to another; some compose quickly and then revise; others revise as they go along. But for the sake of organization, we'll start with planning, the first step of the writing process.

The order of the three steps is flexible.

FIGURE 3.1   The Three-Step Writing Process

Planning	Writing	Completing
Analyze Study your purpose, lay out your writing schedule, and then profile your audience.	**Organize** Define your main idea, limit the scope, group your points, and choose the direct or indirect approach.	**Revise** Evaluate content and review readability, editing, and rewriting for conciseness and clarity.
Investigate Gather information through formal or informal research methods.	**Compose** Control your style through level of formality and conversational tone. Choose your words carefully so that you can create effective sentences and paragraphs.	**Produce** Use effective design elements and suitable delivery methods.
Adapt Choose the right channel and medium; then establish a good relationship with your audience.		**Proofread** Review for errors in layout, spelling, and mechanics.
1	**2**	**3**

Analyzing the Situation and Identifying Your Audience

When planning a business message, the first thing you need to think about is your purpose. For a business message to be effective, its purpose and its audience must complement each other.

Define Your Purpose

Business messages have both a general and a specific purpose.

All business messages have a **general purpose**: to inform, to persuade, or to collaborate with your audience. Business messages also have a **specific purpose**. To help you define the specific purpose of your message, ask yourself what you hope to accomplish with your message and what your audience should do or think after receiving your message. Before proceeding, consider whether your purpose is worth pursuing at this time. Ask yourself these questions:

- **Is my purpose realistic?** If your purpose involves a radical shift in action or attitude, go slowly. Consider proposing the first step and using your message as the beginning of a learning process.
- **Is this the right time?** If an organization is undergoing changes of some sort, you may want to defer your message until things stabilize and people can concentrate on your ideas.
- **Is the right person delivering this message?** Although you may have done all the work, having your boss deliver your message could get better results because of his or her higher status.
- **Is my purpose acceptable to the organization?** Even though you want to fire off an angry reply to an abusive letter attacking your company, your supervisors might prefer that you regain the customer's goodwill. Your response must reflect the organization's priorities.

Once you are satisfied that you have a legitimate purpose in communicating, take a good look at your intended audience.

FIGURE 3.2 Audience Analysis Helps You Plan Your Message

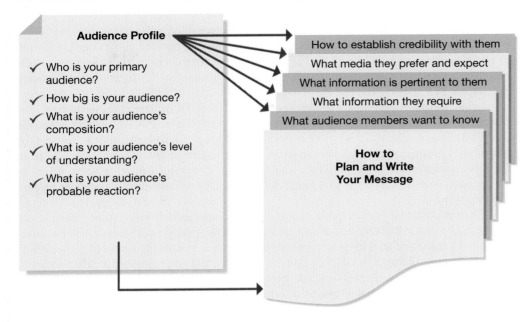

Develop an Audience Profile

Who are your audience members? What are their attitudes? What do they need to know? And why should they care about your message? The answers to such questions will indicate which material you'll need to cover and how to cover it (see Figure 3.2).

To satisfy your audience's information needs, begin by identifying your primary audience. If you can reach the decision makers or opinion molders in your audience, other audience members will fall into place. Key people are usually the ones with the most organizational clout. However, occasionally a person of relatively low status may have influence in a particular area.

Remember to determine the size of your audience. A report for a large audience requires a more formal style, organization, and format than one directed to three or four people in your department. Also, be sure to respond to the particular concerns of key individuals. The head of marketing would need different facts than the head of production or finance would need.

Try to define your audience's composition. Look for common interests that tie audience members together across differences in culture, education, status, or attitude. Include evidence that touches on everyone's area of interest. To be understood across cultural barriers, consider how audience members think and learn, as well as what style they expect.[4]

It's important to gauge your audience's level of understanding. If audience members share your general background, they'll understand your material without difficulty. If not, you must educate them. Include only enough information to accomplish your objective, gearing your coverage to your primary audience (the key decision makers).

Do your best to project your audience's expectations and preferences. Will members of your audience expect complete details, or will a summary of the main points suffice? Do they want an e-mail or will they expect a formal memo? Should the message be a short 1- to 2-page memo or a comprehensive 10- to 15-page report?

Remember to estimate your audience's probable reaction. If you expect a favorable response, you can state conclusions and recommendations up front and offer minimal supporting evidence. If you expect skepticism, you can introduce conclusions gradually, with more proof. Chapter 4 discusses how audience reaction affects message organization.

Ask yourself some key questions about your audience.

Profile your audience by
- Identifying key decision makers
- Determining audience size
- Looking for common interests
- Estimating audience understanding
- Satisfying audience expectations
- Predicting audience reactions

Investigating the Topic

Before you compose your message, you'll most likely need to gather some information to communicate to your audience. When writing long, formal reports, you'll conduct formal research to locate and analyze all the information relevant to your purpose and your audience. Formal techniques for finding, evaluating, and processing information are discussed in Chapter 11.

For many messages, you may need to collect information only informally.

Other kinds of business messages require less formal information gathering. For example, you may simply try to consider others' viewpoints. Put yourself in someone else's position to consider what that person or group might be thinking, feeling, or planning. Or your company's files may be a good source of the information you need for a particular memo or e-mail message. Consider company annual reports, financial statements, news releases, memos, marketing reports, and customer surveys for helpful information.

Chatting with supervisors, colleagues, or customers can help you gather information. At the least, fellow workers and customers may know what your audience will be interested in. Conducting telephone or personal interviews is a convenient way to gather information. And don't forget to ask your audience for input. If you're unsure of what audience members need from your message, ask them through casual conversation (face-to-face or over the phone), informal surveys, or unofficial interviews.

Include any additional information that might be helpful, even though the requester didn't specifically ask for it.

In addition, try to think of information needs that your audience may not even be aware of. In some cases, you may be able to tell your audience something they consider important but wouldn't have thought to ask. Although adding information of this sort lengthens your message, doing so creates goodwill.

Be careful when deciding what information to include in your messages. Make sure your information is

- **Complete.** One good way to test the thoroughness of your message is to use the journalistic approach: Check to see whether your message answers *who, what, when, where, why,* and *how.*

- **Accurate.** Your organization is legally bound by any promises you make, so be sure your company can follow through. Check with the appropriate people *before* you make the commitment. Also, review all mathematical or financial calculations, check all dates and schedules, and examine your own assumptions and conclusions.

- **Ethical.** Messages can be unethical simply because information is omitted. You need to include enough detail to avoid misleading your audience. Include as much information as you believe best fits your definition of complete, and then offer to provide more upon request.

- **Pertinent.** Choose and emphasize the points that affect your audience the most. Whereas engineers may be interested in customer reaction to product design, shipping managers might want to know when customers receive the product. For an unknown audience, use your common sense to identify points of particular interest. Factors such as job, location, income, or education can give you a clue.

Adapting Your Message to Your Audience and Purpose

By now you know why you're writing, you know the audience you're writing to, and you have most of the information you need. But before actually beginning to write your message, you need to figure out how to make it serve both your audience and your purpose. To adapt your message, you need to select a channel and a medium that fit your purpose and satisfy your audience's expectations. In addition, you need to establish a good relationship with your audience.

Select the Best Channel and Medium

Selecting the best channel and medium for your message can make the difference between effective and ineffective communication.[5] You must choose between the oral and written channels, and you must consider all the media within each one.

The *oral channel* includes media such as face-to-face conversation, telephone calls, speeches, presentations, and meetings. The chief advantage of oral communication is the opportunity it provides for immediate feedback. Your choice between a face-to-face conversation and a telephone call would depend on audience location, message importance, and your need for the sort of nonverbal feedback that only body language can reveal.

The *written channel* includes media that range from the scribbled notes people use to jog their own memories to formal reports that rival magazines in graphic quality. The most common written media are letters, memos, and reports (see Appendix A for business document formats). Written messages have one big advantage: They let you plan and control the message.

In addition to the traditional forms of oral and written media, both channels have electronic forms. Oral media also include voice mail, audiotape and videotape, teleconferencing and videoconferencing, closed-circuit television, and many more. Written media also include instant messaging, e-mail, faxing, computer conferencing (with groupware), websites, and more.

The trick to choosing the best channel and medium is to select the tool that does the best overall job in each situation (see Table 3.1). To choose the channel and medium that will best match your purpose and audience, consider the following elements:

- **Message style and tone.** You wouldn't write a report with the same level of informality that you might use in an e-mail message. To emphasize the formality of your message, use a more formal medium, such as a memo or a letter.
- **Possibility for feedback.** Various media offer various levels of feedback. The more feedback possible, the richer the medium. Face-to-face conversation is richest because it provides immediate verbal and nonverbal feedback. On the other hand, unaddressed documents such as fliers are leanest because they offer no feedback at all. Use leaner media (notes, memos, letters) for simple, routine messages; use richer media (meetings, videos) for complex, nonroutine messages; and use phone calls, e-mail, and voice mail for messages in between.
- **Audience perception.** To emphasize the confidentiality of a message, use voice mail rather than a fax, send a letter rather than a memo, or plan on a private conversation rather than a meeting. To instill an emotional commitment, consider videotape or a videoconference, unless you require immediate feedback, in which case a face-to-face conversation is best.[6]
- **Time.** If your message is urgent, you'll probably use the phone, send a fax, or send your message by next-day mail.
- **Cost.** You wouldn't think twice about telephoning an important customer overseas if you just discovered your company had erroneously sent the wrong shipment. But you'd probably choose to fax or e-mail a routine order acknowledgment to your customer in Australia.
- **Audience expectation.** Consider which media your audience expects or prefers.[7] You expect your college to deliver your diploma by hand at graduation or in the mail, not by fax. Moreover, culture influences channel preference. People in the United States and Germany prefer written messages, whereas people in Japan prefer oral ones.[8]

Establish a Good Relationship with Your Audience

Once you've chosen an appropriate channel and medium, you're still not ready to start writing. Effective communicators do more than simply convey information. They make sure that they establish a good relationship with their audience.

Different types of messages require different communication channels and media.

In general, use an oral channel if your purpose is to get immediate feedback from your audience.

A written channel increases the sender's control but eliminates the possibility of immediate feedback.

When choosing channel and medium, consider six elements.

Table 3.1	Choosing the Best Channel and Medium

Use Written Channels When

- You need no immediate feedback
- Your message is detailed, complex, or requires careful planning
- You need a permanent, verifiable record
- Your audience is large and geographically dispersed
- You want to minimize the distortion that can occur when messages pass orally from person to person
- Immediate interaction with the audience is either unimportant or undesirable
- Your message has no emotional component

Use Oral Channels When

- You want immediate feedback from the audience
- Your message is relatively simple and easy to accept
- You need no permanent record
- You can assemble your audience conveniently and economically
- You want to encourage interaction to solve a problem or reach a group decision
- You want to read the audience's body language or hear the tone of their response
- Your message has an emotional component

Use Electronic Forms When

- You need speed
- You're physically separated from your audience
- Time zones differ
- You must reach a dispersed audience personally

To establish a good relationship, be yourself.

To give the right impression in your message, think carefully about who you are and who your audience is. Then do your best to be yourself. Since a good relationship is based on sincerity, respect, and courtesy, show yours by using the "you" attitude, emphasizing the positive, establishing your credibility, being polite, using bias-free language, and projecting the company's image (see Figure 3.3).

Use the "You" Attitude

Express your message in terms of the audience's interests and needs.

To project your audience-centered approach, plan to adopt a **"you" attitude**—that is, speak and write in terms of your audience's wishes, interests, hopes, and preferences. On the simplest level, you replace terms that refer to yourself and your company with terms that refer to your audience. Plan to use *you* and *yours* instead of *I, me, mine, we, us,* and *ours*:

Instead of This	**Use This**
To help us process this order, we must ask for another copy of the requisition.	So that your order can be filled promptly, please send another copy of the requisition.
We are pleased to announce our new flight schedule from Atlanta to New York, which is any hour on the hour.	Now you can take a plane from Atlanta to New York any hour on the hour.

Don't overdo the "you" attitude.

However, using *you* and *yours* requires finesse. If you overdo it, you're likely to create some rather awkward sentences, and you run the risk of sounding like a high-pressure

FIGURE 3.3   Establishing a Good Relationship in Business Messages

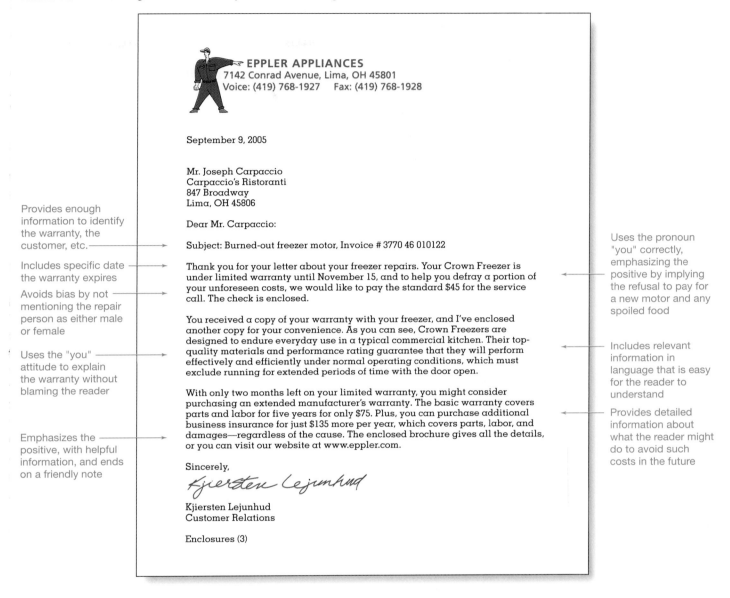

Provides enough information to identify the warranty, the customer, etc.

Includes specific date the warranty expires

Avoids bias by not mentioning the repair person as either male or female

Uses the "you" attitude to explain the warranty without blaming the reader

Emphasizes the positive, with helpful information, and ends on a friendly note

Uses the pronoun "you" correctly, emphasizing the positive by implying the refusal to pay for a new motor and any spoiled food

Includes relevant information in language that is easy for the reader to understand

Provides detailed information about what the reader might do to avoid such costs in the future

---

carnival barker.[9] The "you" attitude is not intended to be manipulative or insincere. You can use *you* 25 times in a single page and still ignore your audience's true concerns. It's the thought and sincerity that count, not the pronoun. If you're talking to a retailer, try to think like a retailer; if you're writing to a dissatisfied customer, imagine how you would feel at the other end of the transaction. The important thing when you're planning your message is your attitude toward audience members and your appreciation of their position.

In fact, on some occasions you'll do better to avoid using *you*. For instance, using *you* in a way that sounds dictatorial is impolite. Or, when someone makes a mistake, plan to minimize ill will by pointing out the error impersonally. You might say, "We have a problem," instead of "You caused a problem."

Be sure to consider the attitudes and policies of your organization and those of other cultures. In some cultures, it is improper to single out one person's achievements because the whole team is responsible for the outcome; using the pronoun *we* or *our* is more appropriate. Similarly, some companies have a tradition of avoiding references to *you* and *I* in their memos and formal reports. If you work for a company that expects a

Avoid using *you* and *yours* when doing so

■ Makes you sound dictatorial
■ Makes someone else feel guilty
■ Goes against your organization's style

formal, impersonal style, confine your use of personal pronouns to informal letters and memos.

Emphasize the Positive

Explain what you have done, what you can do, and what you will do—not what you haven't done, can't do, or won't do.

Another way of establishing a good relationship with your audience is to emphasize the positive side of your message.[10] Plan out how you'll stress what is or will be instead of what isn't or won't be. Most information, even bad news, has some redeeming feature. If you can make your audience aware of that feature, your message will be more acceptable.

Instead of This	Use This
It is impossible to repair your vacuum cleaner today.	Your vacuum cleaner will be ready by Tuesday.
We apologize for inconveniencing you during our remodeling.	The renovations now under way will help us serve you better.

Show audience members how they will benefit from complying with your message.

If you're trying to persuade your audience to buy a product, pay a bill, or perform a service for you, plan to emphasize audience benefits by pointing out what's in it for them. Don't focus on why *you* want them to do something. An individual who sees the possibility for personal benefit is more likely to respond positively to your appeal.

Instead of Saying	Say
Please buy this book so that I can make my sales quota.	The plot of this novel will keep you in suspense to the last page.
We need your contribution to the Boys and Girls Club.	You can help a child make friends and build self-confidence through your donation to the Boys and Girls Club.

In general, plan to state your message without using words that might hurt or offend your audience. Substitute mild terms (euphemisms) for those that have unpleasant connotations. You can be honest without being harsh:

Instead of This	Use This
cheap merchandise	bargain prices
toilet paper	bathroom tissue
elderly	senior citizen

On the other hand, don't carry euphemisms to extremes. If you're too subtle, people won't know what you're talking about. You won't be helping your audience by "derecruiting" workers to the "mobility pool" instead of telling them that they have six weeks to find another job.

Establish Your Credibility

People are more likely to react positively to your message when they have confidence in you.

If you're unknown to your audience members, you'll have to earn their confidence before you can win them to your point of view. You want people to trust that your word is dependable and that you know what you're doing. Your **credibility** (or believability) is based on how reliable you are and how much trust you evoke in others.

If you're communicating with a familiar group, your credibility has probably already been established, so you can get right down to business. But if audience members are complete strangers, or worse, if they start off with doubts about you, plan to devote the initial portion of your message to gaining credibility.

Try to show an understanding of your audience's situation. Call attention to the things you have in common. If your audience shares your professional background, you might say, "As a fellow engineer [or lawyer, doctor, teacher, or whatever], I'm sure you can appreciate this situation." Also, plan to use technical or professional terms that identify you as a peer.

During the planning step, decide whether you'll explain your credentials. Your title or the name of your organization might be enough to impress your audience with your abilities. Or you might mention the name of someone who carries some weight with your audience ("Professor Goldberg suggested that I contact you") or quote a recognized authority on your subject. Just be careful not to sound pompous.

Avoid exaggerating your claims. A mail-order catalog promised: "You'll be absolutely amazed at the incredible blooms on this healthy plant." Terms such as *amazing, incredible, extraordinary, sensational,* and *revolutionary* exceed the limits of believability, unless they're supported with some sort of proof. Similarly, plan to support compliments with specific points. Don't appear to be currying favor with compliments that are overblown and insincere.

To enhance your credibility
- Show that you understand the other person's situation
- Explain your own credentials or ally yourself with a credible source
- Back up your claims with evidence, not exaggerations
- Use words that express confidence
- Believe in yourself and your message

Instead of This	Use This
My deepest heartfelt thanks for the excellent job you did. It's hard these days to find workers like you. You are just fantastic! I can't stress enough how happy you have made us with your outstanding performance.	Thanks for the fantastic job you did filling in for Gladys at the convention with just an hour's notice. Despite the difficult circumstances, you managed to attract several new orders with your demonstration of the new line of coffeemakers. Your dedication and sales ability are truly appreciated.

Be sure that the information you provide is of the highest quality. Support your points with evidence that can be confirmed through observation, research, experimentation, or measurement.

Finally, avoid revealing any lack of confidence. Try not to undermine your credibility with vague sentiments or by using words such as *if, hope,* and *trust.* If you lack faith in yourself, you're likely to communicate an uncertain attitude that undermines your credibility.

Instead of This	Use This
We hope this recommendation will be helpful.	We're glad to make this recommendation.
If you'd like to order, mail us the reply card.	To order, mail the reply card.

The key to being believable is to believe in yourself. If you are convinced that your message is sound, plan to state your case with authority so that your audience has no doubts.

Be Polite

Being polite is another good way to earn your audience's respect. Plan out how to be courteous to members of your audience so that you show consideration for their needs and feelings. Express yourself with kindness and tact. Venting your emotions rarely improves the situation and can jeopardize your audience's goodwill. Instead, plan to be gentle when expressing yourself:

Try to express the facts in a kind and thoughtful manner.

Instead of This	Use This
You really fouled things up with that last computer run.	Let's go over what went wrong with the last computer run so that the next run goes smoothly.
You've been sitting on my order for two weeks, and we need it now!	We are eager to receive our order. When can we expect delivery?

Table 3.2	Tips for Overcoming Bias in Language	
Examples	**Unacceptable**	**Preferable**
Gender Bias		
Using words containing "man"	Man-made	Artificial, synthetic, manufactured, constructed
	Businessman	Executive, business manager, businessperson
	Salesman	Sales representative, salesperson, clerk, sales agent
	Foreman	Supervisor
Using female-gender words	Authoress, actress, stewardess	Author, actor, cabin attendant
Using special designations	Woman doctor, male nurse	Doctor, nurse
Using "he" to refer to "everyone"	The average worker. . . he	The average worker. . . he or she
Identifying roles with gender	The typical executive spends four hours of his day in meetings.	Most executives spend four hours a day in meetings.
	the nurse/teacher. . . she	nurses/teachers. . . they
Identifying women by marital status	Phil Donahue and Marlo Phil Donahue and Ms. Thomas	Phil Donahue and Marlo Thomas Mr. Donahue and Ms. Thomas
Racial/Ethnic Bias		
Assigning stereotypes	My black assistant speaks more articulately than I do.	My assistant speaks more articulately than I do.
	Jim Wong is an unusually tall Asian.	Jim Wong is tall.
Identifying people by race or ethnicity	Mario M. Cuomo, Italian American politician and ex-governor of New York	Mario M. Cuomo, politician and ex-governor of New York
Age Bias		
Including age when irrelevant	Mary Kirazy, 58, has just joined our trust department.	Mary Kirazy has just joined our trust department.
Disability Bias		
Putting the disability before the person	Crippled workers face many barriers on the job.	Workers with physical disabilities face many barriers on the job.
	An epileptic, Tracy has no trouble doing her job.	Tracy's epilepsy has no effect on her job performance.

In general, written communication requires more tact than oral communication. When you're speaking, your words are softened by your tone of voice and facial expression. Plus, you can adjust your approach according to the feedback you get. But written communication is stark and self-contained. If you hurt a person's feelings in writing, you can't soothe them right away.

Use Bias-Free Language

Avoid biased language that might offend your audience.

Bias-free language avoids unethical, embarrassing blunders in language related to gender, race, ethnicity, age, and disability. Good communicators plan how to correct biased language (see Table 3.2). To keep your messages bias-free avoid the following:

■ **Gender bias.** Avoid sexist language by using the same label for everyone (don't use *chairperson* for a woman and then use *chairman* for a man). Reword sentences to use *they* or to use no pronoun at all. Remember, the preferred title for women in business

Document Makeover

Improve This Letter

To practice correcting drafts of actual documents, visit www.prenhall.com/onekey on the web. Click "Document Makeovers," then click Chapter 3. You will find a letter that contains problems and errors relating to what you've learned in this chapter about planning business messages. Use the Final Draft decision tool to create an improved version of this letter. Check the message for use of the "you" attitude, a positive emphasis, politeness, bias-free language, and an image consistent with your company's style.

is *Ms.*, unless the individual asks to be addressed as *Miss* or *Mrs.* or has some other title, such as *Dr.*

- **Racial and ethnic bias.** The central principle is to avoid language suggesting that members of a racial or an ethnic group have stereotypical characteristics. The best solution is to avoid identifying people by race or ethnic origin unless such a label is relevant.
- **Age bias.** As with gender, race, and ethnic background, mention the age of a person only when it is relevant. When referring to older people, avoid such stereotyped adjectives as *spry* and *frail*.
- **Disability bias.** No painless label exists for people with a physical, mental, sensory, or emotional impairment. Avoid mentioning a disability unless it is pertinent. However, if you must refer to someone's disability, avoid terms such as *handicapped, crippled,* or *retarded.* Put the person first and the disability second.[11]

Project the Company's Image

Even though establishing a good relationship with the audience is your main goal, plan out how to project the right image for your company. When you communicate with outsiders, on even the most routine matter, you serve as the spokesperson for your organization. The impression you make can enhance or damage the reputation of the entire company. Thus you must plan to subordinate your own views and personality, at least to some extent, to the interests and style of your company.

Subordinate your own style to that of the company.

Reviewing Key Points

This chapter introduces the three-step writing process: planning, writing, and completing business messages. It discusses how the process works and how to schedule your time for each step, which may not occur in order. The majority of this chapter covers the first step of the three-step writing process: planning.

This chapter emphasizes the importance of defining both a general and a specific purpose, and it provides four questions to ask when deciding whether to pursue your purpose or put it aside. It helps you learn how to develop a profile of your audience by identifying the primary audience, determining audience size, determining audience composition, gauging your audience's level of understanding, projecting your audience's expectations and preferences, and estimating your audience's probable reaction. Finally, the chapter explains how to adapt messages to your audience and your purpose by selecting the best channel and medium and by establishing a good audience relationship.

The next chapter focuses on the second step of the writing process: writing business messages. It discusses how to organize your message by defining the main idea, limiting the scope, grouping your points, and choosing the direct or indirect approach. Then it explains how to compose your message. You will learn about controlling your style and tone, selecting the best words, creating effective sentences, and developing coherent paragraphs.

Test Your Knowledge

1. What are the three steps in the writing process?

2. What two types of purposes do all business messages have?

3. What do you need to know in order to develop an audience profile?

4. What are four methods of informal information gathering?

5. When including information in your message, what four conditions must you satisfy?

6. What are the main advantages of oral communication? Of written media?

7. What six elements must you consider when choosing a channel and medium?

8. What is the "you" attitude, and how does it differ from an "I" attitude?

9. Why is it important to establish your credibility when communicating with an audience of strangers?

10. How does using bias-free language help communicators establish a good relationship with their audiences?

Apply Your Knowledge

1. Some writers argue that planning messages wastes time because they inevitably change their plans as they go along. How would you respond to this argument? Briefly explain.

2. As a member of the public relations department, what medium would you recommend using to inform the local community that your toxic-waste cleanup program has been successful? Why?

3. When composing business messages, how can you be yourself and project your company's image at the same time?

4. Considering how fast and easy it is, should e-mail replace meetings and other face-to-face communication in your company? Why or why not?

5. **Ethical Choices**   The company president has asked you to draft a memo for her signature to the board of directors, informing them that sales in the new line of gourmet fruit jams have far exceeded anyone's expectations. As a member of the purchasing department, you happen to know that sales of moderately priced jams have declined quite a bit (many customers have switched to the more expensive jams). You were not directed to add that tidbit of information. Should you write the memo and limit your information to the expensive gourmet jams? Or should you include the information about the decline in moderately priced jams? Please explain.

Practice Your Knowledge

Exercises for Perfecting Your Writing

Specific Purpose   For each of the following communication tasks, state a specific purpose (if you have trouble, try beginning with "I want to . . . ").

1. A report to your boss, the store manager, about the outdated items in the warehouse

2. A memo to clients about your booth at the upcoming trade show

3. A letter to a customer who hasn't made a payment for three months

4. A memo to employees about the office's high water bills

5. A phone call to a supplier checking on an overdue parts shipment

6. A report to future users of the computer program you have chosen to handle the company's mailing list

Audience Profile   For each communication task below, write brief answers to three questions: (1) Who is my audience? (2) What is my audience's general attitude toward my subject? (3) What does my audience need to know?

7. A final-notice collection letter from an appliance manufacturer to an appliance dealer, sent 10 days before initiating legal collection procedures

8. An unsolicited sales letter asking readers to purchase computer disks at near-wholesale prices

9. An advertisement for peanut butter

10. Fliers to be attached to doorknobs in the neighborhood, announcing reduced rates for chimney lining or repairs

11. A cover letter sent along with your résumé to a potential employer

12. A request (to the seller) for a price adjustment on a piano that incurred $150 in damage during delivery to a banquet room in the hotel you manage

Media and Purpose   List three messages you have received lately (such as direct-mail promotions, letters, e-mail messages, phone solicitations, and lectures). For each message, determine the general and the specific purpose; then answer the questions listed.

Message #1:

13. General purpose:

14. Specific purpose:

15. Was the message well timed?

16. Did the sender choose an appropriate medium for the message?

17. Did the appropriate person deliver the message?

18. Was the sender's purpose realistic?

Message #2:

19. General purpose:

20. Specific purpose:

21. Was the message well timed?

22. Did the sender choose an appropriate medium for the message?

23. Did the appropriate person deliver the message?

24. Was the sender's purpose realistic?

Message #3:

25. General purpose:

26. Specific purpose:

27. Was the message well timed?

28. Did the sender choose an appropriate medium for the message?

29. Did the appropriate person deliver the message?

30. Was the sender's purpose realistic?

The "You" Attitude   Rewrite the following sentences to reflect your audience's viewpoint.

31. We request that you use the order form supplied in the back of our catalog.

32. We insist that you always bring your credit card to the store.

33. We want to get rid of all our 15-inch monitors to make room in our warehouse for the 19-inch screens. Thus we are offering a 25 percent discount on all sales this week.

34. I am applying for the position of bookkeeper in your office. I feel that my grades prove that I am bright and capable, and I think I can do a good job for you.

35. As requested, we are sending the refund for $25.

Emphasizing the Positive   Revise these sentences to be positive rather than negative.

36. To avoid the loss of your credit rating, please remit payment within 10 days.

37. We don't make refunds on returned merchandise that is soiled.

38. Because we are temporarily out of Baby Cry dolls, we won't be able to ship your order for 10 days.

39. You failed to specify the color of the blouse that you ordered.

40. You should have realized that waterbeds will freeze in unheated houses during winter. Therefore, our guarantee does not cover the valve damage and you must pay the $9.50 valve-replacement fee (plus postage).

Emphasizing the Positive Revise the following sentences to replace unflattering terms (in italics) with euphemisms:

41. The new boss is_____ (*stubborn*) when it comes to doing things by the book.

42. When you say we've doubled our profit level, you are _____ (*wrong*).

43. Just be careful not to make any _____ (*stupid*) choices this week.

44. Jim Riley is _____ (*incompetent*) for that kind of promotion.

45. Glen monopolizes every meeting by being _____ (*a loudmouth*).

Courteous Communication Revise the following sentences to make them more courteous:

46. You claim that you mailed your check last Thursday, but we have not received it.

47. It is not our policy to exchange sale items, especially after they have been worn.

48. You neglected to sign the enclosed contract.

49. I received your letter, in which you assert that our shipment was three days late.

50. We are sorry you are dissatisfied.

51. You failed to enclose your instructions for your new will.

52. We request that you send us the bond by registered mail.

53. Apparently you overlooked our terms for extending this contract.

54. We have been very patient about the postage machine we ordered.

55. We are at a loss to understand why the work has been delayed.

Bias-Free Language   Rewrite each of the following sentences to eliminate bias:

56. For an Indian, Maggie certainly is outgoing.

57. He needs a wheelchair, but he doesn't let his handicap affect his job performance.

58. A pilot must have the ability to stay calm under pressure, and then he must be trained to cope with any problem that arises.

59. Candidate Renata Parsons, married and the mother of a teenager, will attend the debate.

60. Senior citizen Sam Nugent is still an active salesman.

Activities

For live links to all websites discussed in this chapter, visit this text's website at www. prenhall.com/bovee. Just log on, select Chapter 3, and click on "Featured Websites." Locate the page or the URL related to the material in the text.

1. **Analyze This Document**   Read the following document, then (1) analyze the strengths and weaknesses of each sentence, and (2) revise the document so that it follows this chapter's guidelines.

   I am a new publisher with some really great books to sell. I saw your announcement in *Publishers Weekly* about the bookseller's show you're having this summer, and I think it's a great idea. Count me in, folks! I would like to get some space to show my books. I thought it would be a neat thing if I could do some airbrushing on T-shirts live to help promote my hot new title, *T-Shirt Art.* Before I got into publishing, I was an airbrush artist, and I could demonstrate my techniques. I've done hundreds of advertising illustrations and have been a sign painter all my life, so I'll also be promoting my other book, hot off the presses, *How to Make Money in the Sign Painting Business.*

   I will be starting my PR campaign about May 2005 with ads in *PW* and some art trade papers, so my books should be well known by the time the show comes around in August. In case you would like to use my appearance there as part of your publicity, I have enclosed a biography and photo of myself.

   P.S. Please let me know what it costs for booth space as soon as possible so that I can figure out whether I can afford to attend. Being a new publisher is mighty expensive!

2. **Message Planning Skills: Self-Assessment**   How good are you at planning business messages? Use the following chart to rate yourself on each of the following elements of planning an audience-centered business message. Then examine your ratings to identify where you are strongest and where you can improve.

Element of Planning	Always	Frequently	Occasionally	Never
1. I start by defining my purpose.	_____	_____	_____	_____
2. I analyze my audience before writing a message.	_____	_____	_____	_____
3. I investigate what my audience wants to know.	_____	_____	_____	_____
4. I check that my information is accurate, ethical, and pertinent.	_____	_____	_____	_____
5. I consider my audience and purpose when selecting media.	_____	_____	_____	_____
6. I adopt the "you" attitude in my messages.	_____	_____	_____	_____
7. I emphasize the positive aspects of my message.	_____	_____	_____	_____
8. I establish my credibility with audiences of strangers.	_____	_____	_____	_____
9. I express myself politely and tactfully.	_____	_____	_____	_____
10. I use bias-free language.	_____	_____	_____	_____
11. I am careful to project my company's image.	_____	_____	_____	_____

Expand Your Knowledge

Exploring the Best of the Web

Instant Insights into Instant Messaging   Wondering what all the fuss is about instant messaging (IM)? Haven't had a chance to use ICQ, AIM, or one of the other popular IM services? Learn the basics of IM at www.howstuffworks.com/instant-messaging.htm, and you'll be ready to use IM on the job.

Exercises

1. What are the key advantages of IM?
2. What is the difference between a chat room and IM?
3. Is IM a secure way to communicate?

Exploring the Web on Your Own

Review these chapter-related websites on your own to learn more about achieving communication success in the workplace:

1. Learn more about the writing process, English grammar, style and usage, words, and active writing at the Writing Center, http://writing2.richmond.edu/writing/wweb.html.
2. See how to put phone text messaging to work in business applications at Text.It, www.text.it (click on Text for Business).
3. Discover how e-mail works and how to improve your e-mail communications by following the steps at About Internet for Beginners—Harness E-Mail, www.learnthenet.com/english/section/email.html.

Learn Interactively

Interactive Study Guide

Go to the Companion Website at www.prenhall.com/bovee. For Chapter 3, take advantage of the interactive "Study Guide" to test your knowledge of the chapter. Get instant feedback on whether you need additional studying. Also, visit this site's "Study Hall," where you'll find an abundance of valuable resources that will help you succeed in this course.

Peak Performance Grammar and Mechanics

To improve your skill with Verbs, visit www.prenhall.com/onekey, click "Peak Performance Grammar and Mechanics," click "Grammar Basics," and then click "Verbs." Take the Pretest to determine whether you have any weak areas. Then review those areas in the Refresher Course. Take the Follow-Up Test to check your grasp of verbs. For an extra challenge or advanced practice, take the Advanced Test. Finally, for additional reinforcement in verbs, go to the "Improve Your Grammar, Mechanics, and Usage" section that follows, and complete the "Level I: Self-Assessment" exercises.

Improve Your Grammar, Mechanics, and Usage

Level 1: Self-Assessment—Verbs

Review Section 1.3 in the Handbook of Grammar, Mechanics, and Usage, and then complete the following 15 items.

In items 1–5, provide the verb form called for in the following exercises:

1. I _____ (present perfect, *become*) the resident expert on repairing the copy machine.

2. She _____ (past, *know*) how to conduct an audit when she came to work for us.

3. Since Joan was promoted, she _____ (past perfect, *move*) all the files to her office.

4. Next week, call John to tell him what you _____ (future, *do*) to help him set up the seminar.

5. By the time you finish the analysis, he _____ (future perfect, *return*) from his vacation.

For items 6–10, rewrite the sentences so that they use active voice instead of passive:

6. The report will be written by Leslie Cartwright.

7. The transaction was never recorded by anyone.

8. Have you been notified by the claims department of your rights?

9. We are dependent on their services for our operation.

10. The damaged equipment was returned by the customer before we even located a repair facility.

In items 11–15, circle the correct verb form provided in parentheses:

11. Everyone upstairs (*receive/receives*) mail before we do.

12. Neither the main office nor the branches (*is/are*) blameless.

13. C&B sales (*is/are*) listed in the directory.

14. When measuring shelves, 7 inches (*is/are*) significant.

15. About 90 percent of the employees (*plan/plans*) to come to the company picnic.

Level 2: Workplace Applications

The following items contain numerous errors in grammar, capitalization, punctuation, abbreviation, number style, word division, and vocabulary. Rewrite each sentence in the space provided, correcting all errors. Write *C* in the space after any sentence that is already correct.

1. Cut two inches off trunk and place in a water stand, and fill with water.

2. The newly-elected officers of the Board are: John Rogers, president, Robin Doig, vice-president, and Mary Sturhann, secretary.

3. Employees were stunned when they are notified that the trainee got promoted to Manager only after her 4th week with the company.

4. Seeking reliable data on U.S. publishers, *Literary Marketplace* is by far the best source.

5. Who did you wish to speak to?

6. The keynote address will be delivered by Seth Goodwin, who is the author of six popular books on marketing, has written two novels, and writes a column for "Fortune" magazine.

7. Often the reputation of an entire company depend on one employee that officially represents that company to the public.

8. The executive director, along with his staff, are working quickly to determine who should receive the Award.

9. Him and his co-workers, the top bowling team in the tournament, will represent our Company in the league finals on saturday.

10. Listening on the extension, details of the embezzlement plot were overheard by the Security Chief.

11. The acceptance of visa cards are in response to our customer's demand for a more efficient and convenient way of paying for parking here at San Diego International airport.

12. The human resources dept. interviewed dozens of people, they are seeking the better candidate for the opening.

13. Libraries' can be a challenging; yet lucrative market if you learn how to work the "system" to gain maximum visibility for you're products and services.

14. Either a supermarket or a discount art gallery are scheduled to open in the Mall.

15. I have told my supervisor that whomever shares my office with me cannot wear perfume, use spray deodorant, or other scented products.

Level 3: Document Critique

The following document may contain errors in grammar, capitalization, punctuation, abbreviation, number style, vocabulary, and spelling. You will also find errors relating to topics in this chapter. Concentrate on using the "you" attitude, emphasizing the positive, being polite, and using bias-free language as you improve this memo. Correct all errors using standard proofreading marks (see Appendix C).

MEMO

To: Blockbuster mngrs.

From: Tom Dooley, deputy chairmen, Viacom, Inc.

in care of Blockbuster Entertainment Group

Corporate headquarters, Renaissance Tower

1201 Elm street; Dallas TX 75270

Date   May 8 2005

Sub: Recent Cash Flow and consumer response—Survey

Now that our stores have been re-organized with your hard work and cooperation, we hope revenues will rise to new heights; if we re-emphasize video rentals as Blockbusters core business and reduce the visibility of our sideline retail products. Just in case though, we want to be certain that these changes are having the postive affect on our cash flow that we all except and look forward to.

To help us make that determination, respond to the following survey questions and fax them back. Answer concisely; but use extra paper if necessary—for details and explanations.

When you finsih the survey it will help headquarters improve service to you; but also, help us all improve service to our customers. Return your survay before before May 15 to my attention. Then blockbuster hopefully can thrive in a marketplace, that critics say we cannot conquer. Blockbuster must choose wisely and serve it's customers well in a difficult video-rental business environment.

Times are very tough but if we work hard at it its possible we might make Blockbuster 'the man on the streets favorite 'place to go to rent videos!'

Caution! E-Mail Can Bite

Gone are the days when memos were dictated, typed, revised, retyped, photocopied, and circulated by interoffice "snail" mail. Today, e-mail messages are created, sent, received, and forwarded in the blink of an eye, and at the stroke of a key. But this quick and efficient method of communication can cause a great deal of trouble for companies.

One of the greatest features—and dangers—of e-mail is that people tend to treat it far more informally than other forms of business communication. They think of e-mail as casual conversation and routinely make unguarded comments. Moreover, they are led to believe that "deleting" e-mail destroys it permanently. But that's a dangerous misunderstanding of technology.

Even after you delete an e-mail message, it can still exist on the system's hard drive and backup storage devices at both the sender's and the recipient's location. Deleting files only signals the computer that the space required to store the message is no longer needed. The space is so marked, but the data that occupy that space continue to exist until the computer overwrites it with new data. Thus, deleted messages are recoverable—even though doing so is an involved and expensive process—and they can be used as court evidence against you and your company. Embarrassing e-mail has played a big role in corporate battles. In the high-profile court battle between the U.S. Justice Department and Microsoft, for instance, e-mail emerged as the star witness.

So how can companies guard against potential e-mail embarrassment and resulting litigation? Besides restricting the use of e-mail by employees, monitoring employees' e-mail, developing company e-mail policies, and reprimanding or terminating offenders, companies can train their employees to treat e-mail as any other form of written communication. Perhaps one of the best ways to ensure that employee messages won't come back to haunt the company is to teach employees that e-mail messages are at least as permanent as letters and memos—if not more so.

To make sure that you use e-mail effectively, efficiently, and safely, follow these guidelines:

- Don't send large files (including large attachments) without prior notice.
- Proofread every message.
- Respect other people's electronic space by sending messages only when necessary.
- Respond to messages quickly.
- Avoid overusing the label "urgent."
- Be careful about using the "reply all" button.
- Remember that e-mail isn't always private.

Applications for Success

Improve your e-mail skills by visiting The Art of Writing E-Mail (www.net-market.com/email.htm). Whether you're working for a company or for yourself, be sure to give your e-mail messages as much consideration as you give more formal types of communication.

Answer the following questions:

1. Why do you think that most people treat e-mail so casually?
2. What kinds of things do you think a company should address in an e-mail policy?
3. Do you think that companies have the right to monitor employees' e-mail? Please explain.

4 Writing Business Messages

From the Real World

"My college professor said to take what you know, close your eyes, and pretend you're running home and opening the door and saying, 'Hey, Mom, guess what?' The next words will be your first line."

—Julie Galle
Writer/Producer, weather.com

Learning Objectives

After studying this chapter, you will be able to

1 Illustrate why good organization is important to both you and your audience

2 List the four activities required to organize business messages effectively

3 Summarize five features of an effective outline

4 Identify three factors you must consider before choosing a direct or an indirect approach

5 Explain four things you should avoid to achieve a conversational tone in business messages

6 Describe five techniques for selecting the best words when writing business messages

7 Discuss three measures you can take to help you create more effective sentences

8 List four methods of establishing transitions to make paragraphs coherent

Julie Galle is writer/producer for the official website of the Weather Channel, weather.com. Whether writing a short news item about a flood in Missouri or a lengthy report on the effects of global warming, Galle must organize and compose her messages so that members of her audience can easily understand the information, believe it, and quickly apply it to their own lives. Galle limits the scope of her articles and carefully organizes them. Although short news stories may require only the briefest notes of a few facts, Galle prepares outlines for long pieces. For non-news items and long reports, she usually writes three drafts: for style, for covering meteorological points, and for proofing grammar and punctuation.[1]

Organizing Your Message

Misinterpreted messages waste time, lead to poor decision making, and shatter business relationships. So you can see how valuable clear writing and good organization can be.[2] Successful communicators like Julie Galle rely on good organization to make their messages meaningful.[3]

What exactly makes a particular organization "good"? Although the definition of good organization varies from country to country, in the United States and Canada it generally means creating a linear message that proceeds point by point. Consider Figure 4.1 on page 82. The poorly written draft displays weak organization, but the organization is much improved in the revised version. Before you begin to write, think about what you're going to say and how you're going to say it.

What does good organization do for you? First and foremost, it saves you time. Your draft goes more quickly because you're not putting ideas in the wrong places or composing material you don't need. In addition, you can use your organizational plan to get some advance input from your audience, making sure you're on the right track before spending hours working on your draft. And, if you're project is large and complex, you can even use your organization plan to divide the writing job among co-workers.

In addition to helping you, good organization helps your audience:

- **Good organization helps your audience understand your message.** By making your main point clear at the outset, and by stating your needs precisely, your well-organized message will satisfy your audience's need for information.

- **Good organization helps your audience accept your message.** Even when your message is logical, you need to select and organize your points in a diplomatic way. Softening refusals and leaving a good impression enhances credibility and adds authority to your messages.

- **Good organization saves your audience time.** Audience members receive only the information they need, and because that information is relevant, brief, and logically placed, your audience can follow your thought pattern without a struggle.

When writing messages at weather.com, Julie Galle achieves good organization by defining the main idea, limiting the scope, grouping supporting points, and establishing their sequence by selecting either a direct or an indirect approach.

Define the Main Idea

In addition to having a general purpose and a specific purpose, all business messages can be boiled down to one **main idea**—one central point that sums up everything. The rest of your message supports, explains, or demonstrates this point. Your main idea is not the same as your topic. The broad subject of your message is the **topic**, and your main idea makes a statement about that topic.

Your main idea may be obvious when you're preparing a brief message with simple facts that have little emotional impact on your audience. If you're responding to a request for information, your main idea may be simply, "Here is what you wanted." However, defining your main idea is more complicated when you're trying to persuade someone or when you have disappointing information to convey. In these situations, try to define a main idea that will establish a good relationship between you and your audience. For example, you may choose a main idea that highlights a common interest you share with your audience or that emphasizes a point that you and your audience can agree on.

In longer documents and presentations, you'll need to unify a mass of material, so you'll need to define a main idea that encompasses all the individual points you want to make. For tough assignments like these, you may want to take special measures to define your main idea.

Limit the Scope

The scope of your message (its length and detail) must match your main idea. Whether your audience expects a one-page memo or a one-hour speech, you must develop your main idea within that framework. If you lack the time and space to develop your main idea fully, or if your main idea won't fill up the time and space allotted, you'll need to redefine the main idea of your message.

As you adjust your message to fit the time or space available, don't change the number of major points. Regardless of how long the message will be, stick with three or four major points—five at the very most. According to communication researchers, that's all your audience will remember.[4] Instead of introducing additional points, you can more fully develop complex issues by supporting your points with a variety of evidence.

Good organization saves time, strengthens relationships, and improves efficiency.

Good organization helps audience members understand your message, accept your message, and save time.

To organize a message
- Define your main idea
- Limit the scope
- Group your points
- Choose the direct or indirect approach

The topic is the broad subject; the main idea makes a statement about the topic.

Gear your main idea to the length of the message.

Deal with three or four major points (not more than five), regardless of message length.

FIGURE 4.1   Letter with Improved Organization

Ineffective

General Nutrition Corporation has been doing business with ComputerTime since I was hired six years ago. Your building was smaller then, and it was located on the corner of Federal Avenue and 2nd N.W. Jared Mallory, our controller, was one of your first customers. I still remember the day. It was the biggest check I'd ever written. Of course, over the years, I've gotten used to larger purchases.

Our department now has 15 employees. As accountants, we need to have our computers working so that we can do our jobs. The CD-RW drive we bought for my assistant, Suzanne, has been a problem. We've taken it in for repairs three times in three months to the authorized service center, and Suzanne is very careful with the machine and hasn't abused it. She does like playing interactive adventure games on lunch breaks. Anyway, it still doesn't work right, and she's tired of hauling it back and forth. We're all putting in longer hours because it is our busy season, and none of us has a lot of spare time.

This is the first time we've returned anything to your store, and I hope you'll agree that we deserve a better deal.

Sincerely,

Jill Saun

Jill Saunders

— Takes too long to get to the point

— Includes irrelevant material

— Gets ideas mixed up

— Leaves out necessary information

Pointers for Good Organization
- Get to the point right away, and make the subject and purpose clear.
- Include only information that is related to the subject and purpose.
- Group ideas and present them in a logical way.
- Include all necessary information.

Effective

GNC LiveWell.

September 13, 2005

Customer Service
ComputerTime
556 Seventh Avenue
Mason City, Iowa 50401

Dear Customer Service Representative:

States purpose clearly →

Can you please exchange the faulty CD-RW drive that GNC purchased from you. We bought an Olympic Systems, Model PRS-2, CD-RW drive from your store on November 15, 2004, during your pre-Christmas sale, when it was marked down to $199.95. We didn't use the unit until January, because it was bought for my assistant, who unexpectedly took six weeks' leave from mid-November through December. You can imagine her frustration when she first tried using it and it didn't work.

In January, we took the drive to the authorized service center and were assured that the problem was merely a loose connection. The service representative fixed the drive, but in April we had to have it fixed again—another loose connection. For the next three months, the drive worked reasonably well, although the response time was occasionally slow. Two months ago, the drive stopped working again. Once more, the service representative blamed a loose connection and made the repair. Although the drive is working now, it isn't working very well. The response time is still slow, and the motor seems to drag sometimes.

States precisely what adjustment is being requested →

What is your policy on exchanging unsatisfactory merchandise? Although all the repairs have been relatively minor and have been covered by the one-year warranty, we are not satisfied with the drive. We would like to exchange it for a similar model from another manufacturer. If the new drive costs more than the old one, we will pay the difference, even though we generally look for equipment with substantial business discounts.

Includes all necessary information and no irrelevant facts →

GNC has done business with your store for six years and until now has always been satisfied with your merchandise. We are counting on you to live up to your reputation for standing behind your products. Please let us hear from you soon.

Sincerely,

Jill Saunders

Jill Saunders

— Explains the situation so that the reader will understand the problem

— Presents ideas logically

— Motivates action from the reader in the close

General Nutrition Corporation, 300 Sixth Avenue, Pittsburgh, PA 15222
Tel: (412) 288-4600

If your message is brief (four minutes or one page), you'll have only a minute or a paragraph each for the introduction, conclusion, and major points. Because the amount of evidence you can present is limited, your main idea will have to be both easy to understand and easy to accept. However, if you're delivering a long message (say, a 60-minute presentation or a 20-page report), you can develop the major points in considerable detail. You can spend about 10 minutes or 10 paragraphs (more than three pages of double-spaced, typewritten text) on each of your key points, and you'll still have room for your introduction and conclusion.

Group Your Points in an Outline

Once you have narrowed the scope of your message, you must provide supporting details in the most logical and effective way. Constructing an outline of your message is a great way to visualize how your major points and supporting details will fit together. Whether you use the outlining features provided with word-processing software or simply jot down three or four points on the back of an envelope, your outline will keep you on track and help you cover the important information. You're no doubt familiar with the basic outline format (see Figure 4.2):

> An outline or a schematic diagram will help you visualize the relationship among parts of a message.

- Outlines use numbers (or letters and numbers) to identify each point.
- Outlines indent points to show which ideas are of equal status.
- Outlines divide a topic into at least two parts.
- Outlines restrict each subdivision to one category.
- Outlines ensure that each group of ideas is separate and distinct.

When outlining your message, begin with your main idea. To help you establish the goals and general strategy of your message, the main idea summarizes two things: (1) what you want audience members to do or think and (2) why they should do so. Everything in your message must either support the main idea or explain its implications.

> The main idea states the action you want your audience to take and why.

Next, you state the major supporting points. Try to identify between three and five major points that support and clarify your message in more concrete terms. If you come up with more, go back and look for opportunities to combine some of your ideas.

> Major supporting points clarify your main idea.

Finally, illustrate your major supporting points with evidence—the flesh and blood that helps your audience understand and remember your message. In a long, complex message, you may need to carry the outline down several levels. Just remember that every level is a step along the chain from the abstract to the concrete, from the general to the specific. The lowest level contains the individual facts and figures that make up your evidence.

FIGURE 4.2   Common Outline Forms

ALPHANUMERIC OUTLINE

I. First Major Point
  A. First subpoint
  B. Second subpoint
    1. Evidence
    2. Evidence
      a. Detail
      b. Detail
    3. Evidence
  C. Third subpoint
II. Second Major Point
  A. First subpoint
    1. Evidence
    2. Evidence
  B. Second subpoint

DECIMAL OUTLINE

I.0 First Major Point
  1.1 First subpoint
  1.2 Second subpoint
    1.2.1 Evidence
    1.2.2 Evidence
      1.2.2.1 Detail
      1.2.2.2 Detail
    1.2.3 Evidence
  2.0 Third subpoint
2.0 Second Major Point
  2.1 First subpoint
    2.1.1 Evidence
    2.1.2 Evidence
  2.2 Second subpoint

Choose Between the Direct and Indirect Approaches

Once you've defined your ideas and outlined your message, you choose the basic approach you'll use to present your points. When addressing a U.S. or Canadian audience with few cultural differences, you have two basic options:

■ **Direct approach (deductive).** The main idea comes first (a recommendation, conclusion, or request), followed by the evidence. Use this approach when your audience will be neutral about your message or pleased to hear from you.

■ **Indirect approach (inductive).** The evidence comes first, and the main idea comes later. Use this approach when your audience may be displeased about or may resist what you have to say.

Before you can choose one of these approaches, you must have a good idea of how your audience is likely to react to your purpose and message. The direct approach is generally fine when audience members will be receptive—if they are eager, interested, pleased, or even neutral. But you may have better results with the indirect approach if audience members are likely to resist your message—if they are displeased, uninterested, or unwilling (see Figure 4.3).

Bear in mind, however, that each message is unique. No simple formula will solve all your communication problems. Sometimes you'll want to get directly to the point, even if your message is unpleasant. Also, the direct approach may be better for long messages, regardless of your audience's attitude, because delaying the main idea could cause confusion and frustration. So before choosing a direct or an indirect approach, consider all relevant factors, including:

■ **Audience reaction:** Positive, neutral, or negative
■ **Message length:** Short memos and letters (discussed in Unit 3) or long reports, proposals, and presentations (discussed in Unit 4)

FIGURE 4.3 **Audience Reaction Affects Organizational Approach**

	Direct approach	Indirect approach	
Audience Reaction	Eager/interested/ pleased/neutral	Displeased	Uninterested/unwilling
Message Opening	Start with the main idea, the request, or the good news.	Start with a neutral statement that acts as a transition to the reasons for the bad news.	Start with a statement or question that captures attention.
Message Body	Provide necessary details.	Give reasons to justify a negative answer. State or imply the bad news, and make a positive suggestion.	Arouse the audience's interest in the subject. Build the audience's desire to comply.
Message Close	Close with a cordial comment, a reference to the good news, or a statement about the specific action desired.	Close cordially.	Request action.

Use direct order if the audience's reaction is likely to be positive and indirect order if it is likely to be negative.

Audience reaction can range from eager to unwilling.

Choice of approach depends on audience reaction, message length, and message type.

Just remember, your first priority is to make your message clear. In the following discussions, note how style, tone, word, sentence, and paragraph issues all play an important role in getting your message across, regardless of message type.

Composing Your Message

Once you've completed the planning process and organized your message, you're ready to begin composing your first draft. If your schedule permits, put aside your outline for a day or two. Then review it with a fresh eye, looking for opportunities to improve the flow of ideas. Once you begin writing, you may discover as you go along that you can improve on your outline. Feel free to rearrange, delete, and add ideas, as long as you don't lose sight of your purpose.

As you compose your first draft, try to let your creativity flow. Don't try to draft and edit at the same time or worry about getting everything perfect. Just put down your ideas as quickly as you can. You'll have time to revise and refine the material later. Once you have all your thoughts and ideas jotted down, begin shaping your message. Start by paying attention to your style and tone. Try to select words that match the tone you want to achieve. Next, create effective sentences and develop coherent paragraphs. The following sections discuss each of these elements.

Composition is the process of drafting your message; polishing it is a later step.

Control Your Style and Tone

Style is the way you use words to achieve a certain **tone,** or overall impression. You can vary your style—your sentence structure and vocabulary—to sound forceful or objective, personal or formal, colorful or dry. The right choice depends on the nature of your message and your relationship with your audience.

When composing your message, you can vary the style to create a tone that suits the occasion.

Use a Conversational Tone

Most business messages aim for a conversational tone, using plain language that sounds businesslike without being stuffy, stiff, wordy, or full of jargon. Compare the three versions of the letter in Table 4.1. The first is too formal and stuffy for today's audiences, whereas the third is too casual for any audience other than close associates or friends. The second message demonstrates the conversational tone used in most business communication. To achieve a conversational tone in your messages, try to avoid obsolete and pompous language, intimacy, humor, and preaching or bragging:

To achieve a warm but businesslike tone

- Don't use obsolete language
- Don't be too familiar
- Use humor only with great care
- Don't preach or brag

Avoid Obsolete Language   Business language used to be much more formal than it is today, and some out-of-date phrases still remain. You can avoid using such language if you ask yourself, "Would I say this if I were talking with someone face to face?"

Obsolete	Up to Date
in due course	today, tomorrow (or a specific time)
permit me to say that	(omit—permission is not necessary)
we are in receipt of	we have received
pursuant to	(omit)
In closing, I'd like to say	(omit)
we wish to inform you	(omit—just say it)
attached please find	enclosed is
please be advised that	(omit)

Table 4.1   Formal, Conversational, and Informal Tones

Formal tone	Conversational Tone	Informal tone
Reserved for the most formal occasions	**Preferred for most business communication**	**Reserved for communication with friends and close associates**
Dear Ms. Navarro:	Dear Ms. Navarro:	Hi Gabriella:
Enclosed please find the information that was requested during our telephone communication of May 14. As was mentioned at that time, Midville Hospital has significantly more doctors of exceptional quality than any other health facility in the state.	Here's the information you requested during our phone conversation on Friday. As I mentioned, Midville Hospital has the best doctors and more of them than any other hospital in the state.	How's it going? Just sending along the information you asked for. As I said on Friday, Midville Hospital has more and better doctors than any other hospital in the state.
As you were also informed, our organization has quite an impressive network of doctors and other health-care professionals with offices located throughout the state. In the event that you should need a specialist, our professionals will be able to make an appropriate recommendation.	In addition, we have a vast network of doctors and other health professionals with offices throughout the state. If you need a specialist, they can refer you to the right one.	We also have a large group of doctors and other health professionals with offices close to you at work or at home. Need a specialist? They'll refer you to the right one.
You would be entitled to utilize the numerous programs that we provide to assist you and your family in achieving the highest level of health possible. We are especially proud of our health hotline, which allows you to speak with a registered nurse 24 hours a day, seven days a week.	You and your family can also participate in numerous health programs, such as smoking-cessation classes, health fairs, nutritional guidance, and a 24-hour hotline whose registered nurse can answer your questions seven days a week.	You and your family can get and stay healthy, thanks to our health fairs and numerous classes to improve your overall fitness. We even have a health hotline where you can get answers to your health questions all day, every day.
In the event that you have questions or would like additional information, you may certainly contact me during regular business hours.	If you would like more information, please call anytime between 9:00 and 5:00, Monday through Friday.	Just give me a ring if you want to know more. Any time from 9:00 to 5:00 should do the trick.
Most sincerely yours,	Sincerely,	Take care,
Samuel G. Berenz	Samuel G. Berenz	Sam

Avoid Intimacy   Don't mention anything about anyone's personal life unless you know the individual very well. Avoid phrases that imply intimacy, such as "just between you and me" and "as you and I are well aware." Be careful about sounding too folksy or chatty; such a familiar tone may be seen as an attempt to seem like an old friend when, in fact, you're not.

Avoid Humor   Using humor can backfire, especially if you don't know your audience very well. What seems humorous to you may be deadly serious to others. Plus, what's funny today may not be in a week or a month. Moreover, when you're communicating across cultures, chances are slim that your audience will appreciate your humor or even realize that you're trying to be funny.[5]

Avoid Preaching and Bragging   Few things are more irritating than people who think that they know everything and that others know nothing. If you must tell your audience something obvious, place the information in the middle of a paragraph, where it will sound like a casual comment rather than a major revelation. Also, avoid bragging about your accomplishments or about the size or profitability of your organization (unless your audience is a part of your organization).

Use Plain English

Plain English is a way of writing and arranging technical materials so that your audience can understand your meaning. Because it's close to the way people normally speak, plain English is easily understood by people with an eighth- or ninth-grade education. If you've ever tried to make sense of an overwritten or murky passage in a legal document or credit agreement, you can understand why governments and corporations today are endorsing the plain-English movement.[6]

> Plain English is close to spoken English and can be easily understood.

Instead of This	Write This
The applicability of the general information and administrative procedures set forth below accordingly will vary depending on the investor and the record-keeping system established for a shareholder's investment in the Fund. Participants in 401(k) and other plans should first consult with the appropriate persons at their employer or refer to the plan materials before following any of the procedures below.	If you are investing through a large retirement plan or other special program, follow the instructions in your program material.

Plain English lacks the precision necessary for scientific research, intense feeling, and personal insight, but it is invaluable in general business messages. Even though it's intended for audiences who speak English as their primary language, plain English can also help you simplify the messages you prepare for audiences who speak English only as a second or even third language. For example, by choosing words that have only one interpretation, you will surely communicate more clearly with your intercultural audience.[7]

Select the Best Words

To compose effective messages, you must choose your words carefully.[8] Good business writing is learned by imitation and practice. As you read business journals, newspapers, and even novels, make a note of the words you think are effective and keep them in a file. Then look through them before you draft your next letter or report. Try using some of these words in your document. You may be surprised how they can strengthen your writing.

First, pay close attention to correctness. Using words correctly is important. If you make grammatical or usage errors, you lose credibility with your audience, and grammatical errors are distracting. If you have doubts about what is correct, look up the answer. Check the Handbook of Grammar, Mechanics, and Usage at the end of this text, or consult any number of special reference books and resources available in libraries, in bookstores, and on the Internet. Most authorities agree on the basic conventions.

> Correctness is the first consideration when choosing words.

Just as important as selecting the correct word is selecting the most suitable word for the job at hand. Word effectiveness is generally more difficult to achieve than correctness, particularly in written communication. Writers such as Julie Galle have to work at their craft to write messages that are clear, concise, and accurate. They do their best to find the words that communicate effectively.

> Effectiveness is the second consideration when choosing words.

Blend Abstract and Concrete Words

An **abstract word** expresses a concept, quality, or characteristic. Abstractions are usually broad, encompassing a category of ideas. They are often intellectual, academic, or philosophical. *Love, honor, progress, tradition,* and *beauty* are abstractions.

A **concrete word** stands for something you can touch or see. Concrete terms are anchored in the tangible, material world. *Chair, table, horse, rose, kick, kiss, red, green,* and *two* are concrete words; they are direct, clear, and exact.

Don't assume that concrete words are better than abstract words because they are more precise. For example, try to rewrite this sentence without using the underlined abstract words:

> We hold these <u>truths</u> to be <u>self-evident</u>, that all men are <u>created</u> <u>equal</u>, that they are <u>endowed</u> by their <u>Creator</u> with certain <u>unalienable</u> <u>Rights</u>, that among these are <u>Life</u>, <u>Liberty</u>, and the <u>Pursuit of Happiness</u>.

As you can see, the Declaration of Independence needs abstractions, and so do business messages. Abstractions permit us to rise above the common and tangible. They allow us to refer to concepts such as *morale, productivity, profits, quality, motivation,* and *guarantees.*

In business communication, use concrete, specific terms whenever possible; use abstractions only when necessary.

Even though they're indispensable, abstractions can be troublesome. They tend to be fuzzy and subject to many interpretations. They also tend to be boring. It isn't always easy to get excited about ideas, especially if they're unrelated to concrete experience. The best way to minimize such problems is to blend abstract terms with concrete ones, the general with the specific. State the concept, then pin it down with details expressed in more concrete terms. Instead of referring to a *sizable loss,* talk about a *loss of $32 million.* Save the abstractions for ideas that cannot be expressed any other way.

Choose Strong Words

Good business communicators choose strong words.

Choose words that express your thoughts most clearly, specifically, and dynamically (see Table 4.2 for a few examples of strong words). Nouns and verbs are the most concrete, so use them as much as you can. Adjectives and adverbs have obvious roles, but use them sparingly—they often evoke subjective judgments. Verbs are especially powerful, telling what's happening in the sentence, so make them dynamic and specific; for example, replace *rise* or *fall* with *soar* or *plummet.*

Choose Familiar Words

For effective messages, choose familiar words.

You'll communicate best with words that are familiar to your readers. Avoid using pompous language that contains big words, overly complicated phrases, and trite expressions. However, when trying to choose familiar words, remember that words familiar to one reader might be unfamiliar to another (Table 4.2).

Avoid Clichés

To make a good impression, avoid clichés.

Although familiar words are generally the best choice, beware of terms and phrases so common that they have become virtually meaningless. Because clichés are used so often, readers tend to slide right by them to whatever is coming next. Most people use these phrases not because they think it makes their message more vivid and inviting but because they don't know how to express themselves otherwise (see Table 4.2).[9]

Avoid Jargon

Be careful when using jargon.

Handle technical or professional terms with care. As Julie Galle puts it, meteorological terminology and jargon can add precision and authority to a weather message, but many people don't understand the jargon. When deciding whether to use technical jargon, let your audience's knowledge guide you. For example, when addressing a group of engineers or scientists, it's probably fine to refer to *meteorological effects on microwave propagation;* otherwise, refer to the *effects of weather on radio waves.*

Create Effective Sentences

In English, word order is important when constructing sentences.

In English, words don't make much sense until they're combined in a sentence to express a complete thought. Thus the words *Jill, receptionist, the, smiles,* and *at* can be organized into "Jill smiles at the receptionist." Now that you've constructed the sentence, you can

Table 4.2	Selecting the Most Effective Words	

Avoid Weak Phrases	Use Strong Terms
Wealthy businessperson	Tycoon
Business prosperity	Boom
Hard times	Slump

Avoid Unfamiliar Words	Use Familiar Words
Ascertain	Find out, learn
Consummate	Close, bring about
Peruse	Read, study
Circumvent	Avoid
Increment	Growth, increase
Unequivocal	Certain

Avoid Clichés	Use Plain Language
Scrape the bottom of the barrel	Strain shrinking resources
An uphill battle	A challenge
Writing on the wall	Prediction
Call the shots	Be in charge
Take by storm	Attack
Cost an arm and a leg	Expensive
A new ballgame	Fresh start
Worst nightmare	Strong competitor; disaster
Fall through the cracks	Be overlooked

begin exploring the possibilities for improvement, looking at how well each word performs its particular function. Nouns and noun equivalents are the topics (or subjects) that you're communicating about. Verbs and related words (or predicates) make statements about those subjects. In a complicated sentence, adjectives and adverbs modify the nouns and verbs, and various connectors hold the words together. You can make your sentences more effective by using all four types of sentences, emphasizing key thoughts through sentence style, and selecting active or passive voice.

Use All Four Types of Sentences

Sentences come in four basic types: simple, compound, complex, and compound-complex. A **simple sentence** has one main clause (a single subject and a single predicate), although it may be expanded by nouns and pronouns serving as objects of the action and by modifying phrases. Here's a typical example (with the subject underlined once and the predicate verb underlined twice):

> <u>Profits</u> <u>have increased</u> in the past year.

A **compound sentence** has two main clauses that express two or more independent but related thoughts of equal importance, usually joined by *and, but,* or *or.* In effect, a compound sentence is a merger of two or more simple sentences (independent clauses) that are related. For example:

> Wage <u>rates</u> <u>have declined</u> by 5 percent, and employee <u>turnover</u> <u>has been</u> high.

You can choose from four types of sentences:
- Simple
- Compound
- Complex
- Compound-complex

The independent clauses in a compound sentence are always separated by a comma or by a semicolon (in which case the conjunction—*and, but, or*—is dropped).

A **complex sentence** expresses one main thought (the independent clause) and one or more subordinate thoughts (dependent clauses) related to it, often separated by a comma. The subordinate thought, which comes first in the following sentence, could not stand alone:

> Although you may question Gerald's conclusions, <u>you</u> <u>must admit</u> that his research is thorough.

A **compound-complex sentence** has two main clauses, at least one of which contains a subordinate clause:

> <u>Profits</u> <u>have increased</u> in the past year, and although you may question Gerald's conclusions, <u>you</u> <u>must admit</u> that his research is thorough.

To make your writing as effective as possible, balance all four sentence types. If you use too many simple sentences, you won't be able to properly express the relationships among your ideas. If you use too many long, compound sentences, your writing will sound monotonous. On the other hand, an uninterrupted series of complex or compound-complex sentences is hard to follow.

Emphasize Key Thoughts with Sentence Style

Sentence style varies from culture to culture. In English, try to make your sentences grammatically correct, efficient, readable, interesting, and appropriate for your audience. For most business audiences, clarity and efficiency take precedence over literary style, so strive for straightforward simplicity. In every message, some ideas are more important than others. You can emphasize these key ideas through your sentence style.

Emphasize important ideas by

- Using sentence type to reflect the relationship between ideas
- Giving important ideas more space
- Making important ideas the subject of the sentence
- Putting important ideas at the beginning or at the end of the sentence

Reflect Relationships with Sentence Type   One obvious technique for emphasizing key ideas is to choose the type of sentence to match the relationship of the ideas you want to express. If you have two ideas of equal importance, express them as two simple sentences or as one compound sentence. However, if one of the ideas is less important than the other, place it in a dependent clause to form a complex sentence. By making the first thought subordinate to the second, you establish a cause-and-effect relationship:

> Because the chemical products division is the strongest in the company, its management techniques should be adopted by the other divisions.

Allocate More Space to the Important Ideas   Another way to emphasize key ideas is to give important points the most space. When you want to call attention to a thought, use extra words to describe it. Consider this sentence:

> The chairperson of the board called for a vote of the shareholders.

To emphasize the importance of the chairperson, you might describe her more fully:

> Having considerable experience in corporate takeover battles, the chairperson of the board called for a vote of the shareholders.

You can increase the emphasis even more by adding a separate, short sentence to augment the first:

> The chairperson of the board called for a vote of the shareholders. She has considerable experience in corporate takeover battles.

Make Important Ideas the Subject   You can also call attention to a thought by making it the subject of the sentence. In the following example, the emphasis is on the person:

> *I* can write letters much more quickly using a computer.

However, by changing the subject, the computer takes center stage:

> The *computer* enables me to write letters much more quickly.

Place Important Ideas First or Last   Another way to emphasize an idea is to place it at either the beginning or the end of a sentence:

> **Less Emphatic:** We are cutting the *price* to stimulate demand.

> **More Emphatic:** To stimulate demand, we are cutting the *price.*

In complex sentences, the placement of the dependent clause hinges on the relationship between the ideas expressed. If you want to emphasize the idea, put the dependent clause at the end of the sentence (the most emphatic position) or at the beginning (the second most emphatic position). If you want to downplay the idea, bury the dependent clause within the sentence.

> **Most Emphatic:** The electronic parts are manufactured in Mexico, *which has lower wage rates than the United States.*

> **Emphatic:** *Because wage rates are lower there,* the electronic parts are manufactured in Mexico.

> **Least Emphatic:** Mexico, *which has lower wage rates,* was selected as the production point for the electronic parts.

Techniques like these give you a great deal of control over the way your audience interprets what you have to say.

> The most emphatic position in a sentence is at the end. The second most emphatic position is at the beginning.

Choose Active or Passive Voice

Your choice of active or passive voice also affects the tone of your message. You're using **active voice** when the subject (the "actor") comes before the verb and the object (the "acted upon") follows the verb: "John rented the office." You're using **passive voice** when the object comes before the verb and the subject follows the verb: "The office was rented by John." As you can see, the passive voice combines a form of the verb *to be* (was) with the past participle of the main verb (rented).

Active sentences generally sound less formal and usually make it easier for the reader to figure out who performed the action. Passive voice de-emphasizes the subject and implies action done by something or someone. For examples of when to use active voice, see Table 4.3.

Table 4.3	Choosing Active or Passive Voice
Avoid Passive Voice in General	**Use Active Voice in General**
The new procedure was developed by the operations team.	The operations team developed the new procedure.
Legal problems are created by this contract.	This contract creates legal problems.
Reception preparations have been undertaken by our PR people for the new CEO's arrival.	Our PR people have undertaken reception preparations for the new CEO's arrival.
Sometimes Avoid Active Voice	**Sometimes Use Passive Voice**
You lost the shipment.	The shipment was lost.
I am analyzing the production line to determine the problem.	The production line is being analyzed to determine the problem.
We have established criteria to evaluate capital expenditures.	Criteria have been established to evaluate capital expenditures.

Active sentences are stronger than passive ones.

Using the active voice produces shorter, stronger sentences and makes your writing more vigorous, concise, and generally easier to understand.[10] Using the passive voice, while not wrong grammatically, is cumbersome, wordy, and often unnecessarily vague, and it can make sentences longer. Nevertheless, using the passive voice makes sense in some situations because it can help you focus on your audience and demonstrate the "you" attitude:

Use passive sentences to soften bad news, to put yourself in the background, or to create an impersonal tone.

- When you want to be diplomatic about pointing out a problem or error of some kind (the passive version seems less like an accusation)
- When you want to point out what's being done without taking or attributing either the credit or the blame (the passive version leaves the actor completely out of the sentence)
- When you want to avoid personal pronouns in order to create an objective tone (the passive version may be used in a formal report, for example)

For examples of when to use passive voice, see Table 4.3.

Develop Coherent Paragraphs

A paragraph contains sentences that pertain to a single thought.

A *paragraph* is a cluster of sentences all related to the same general topic. It is a unit of thought, separated from other units by skipping a line or indenting the first line. A series of paragraphs makes up an entire composition. Each paragraph is an important part of the whole, a key link in the train of thought. As you compose your message, think about the paragraphs and their relationship to one another.

Adapt Paragraph Length

Paragraphs vary widely in length and form. You can communicate effectively in one short paragraph or in pages of lengthy paragraphs, depending on your purpose, your audience, and your message. The typical paragraph contains three basic elements: a topic sentence, related sentences that develop the topic, and transitional words and phrases.

Use Development Techniques

Five ways to develop paragraphs:
- Illustration
- Comparison or contrast
- Cause and effect
- Classification
- Problem and solution

Paragraphs can be developed in many ways. Five of the most common techniques are illustration, comparison or contrast, cause and effect, classification, and problem and solution. Your choice of technique depends on your subject, your intended audience, and your purpose:

- **Illustration.** Giving examples that demonstrate the general idea
- **Comparison or contrast.** Using similarities or differences to develop the topic
- **Cause and effect.** Focusing on the reasons for something
- **Classification.** Showing how a general idea is broken into specific categories
- **Problem and solution.** Presenting a problem and then discussing the solution

Table 4.4 presents samples of each method; however, in practice, you'll often combine two or more methods of development in a single paragraph. To add interest, you might begin by using illustration, shift to comparison or contrast, and then shift to problem and solution. However, before settling for the first approach that comes to mind, consider the alternatives. Think through various methods before committing yourself. If you fall into the easy habit of repeating the same old paragraph pattern time after time, your writing will be boring.

Achieve Unity and Coherence

The topic sentence
- Reveals the subject of the paragraph
- Indicates how the subject will be developed

Every properly constructed paragraph is *unified*—it deals with a single topic. The sentence that introduces this topic is called the **topic sentence**. In business, the topic sentence is generally explicit, rather than implied, and is often the first sentence in the paragraph. The topic sentence gives readers a summary of the general idea that will be covered in the rest of the paragraph.

Paragraphs are developed through a series of related sentences that provide details about the topic sentence.

The sentences that explain the topic sentence round out the paragraph. These related sentences must all have a bearing on the general subject and must provide enough specific

Table 4.4	Methods of Paragraph Development
Technique	**Example**
Illustration	Some of our most popular products are available through local distributors. For example, Everett & Lemmings carries our frozen soups and entrees. The J.B. Green Company carries our complete line of seasonings, as well as the frozen soups. Wilmont Foods, also a major distributor, now carries our new line of frozen desserts.
Comparison or Contrast	In previous years, when the company was small, the recruiting function could be handled informally. The need for new employees was limited, and each manager could comfortably screen and hire her or his own staff. Today, however, Gambit Products must undertake a major recruiting effort. Our successful bid on the Owens contract means that we will be doubling our labor force over the next six months. To hire that many people without disrupting our ongoing activities, we will create a separate recruiting group within the human resources department.
Cause and Effect	The heavy-duty fabric of your Wanderer tent probably broke down for one of two reasons: (1) a sharp object punctured the fabric, and without reinforcement, the hole was enlarged by the stress of erecting the tent daily for a week, or (2) the fibers gradually rotted because the tent was folded and stored while still wet.
Classification	Successful candidates for our supervisor trainee program generally come from one of several groups. The largest group, by far, consists of recent graduates of accredited data-processing programs. The next largest group comes from within our own company, as we try to promote promising clerical workers to positions of greater responsibility. Finally, we do occasionally accept candidates with outstanding supervisory experience in related industries.
Problem and Solution	Selling handmade toys by mail is a challenge because consumers are accustomed to buying heavily advertised toys from major chains. However, if we develop an appealing catalog, we can compete on the basis of product novelty and quality. In addition, we can provide craftsmanship at a competitive price: a rocking horse of birch, with a hand-knit tail and mane; a music box with the child's name painted on the top; a real Indian teepee, made by Native American artisans.

details to make the topic clear. These developmental sentences are all more specific than the topic sentence. Each one provides another piece of evidence to demonstrate the general truth of the main thought. Also, each sentence is clearly related to the general idea being developed; the relation between the sentences and the idea is what gives the paragraph its unity. A paragraph is well developed when it contains enough information to make the topic sentence convincing and interesting.

In addition to being unified and well developed, effective paragraphs are *coherent;* that is, they are arranged in a logical order so that the audience can understand the train of thought. When you complete a paragraph, your readers automatically assume that you've finished with a particular idea. You achieve coherence by using transitions to show the relationship between paragraphs and among sentences within paragraphs. **Transitions** are words or phrases that tie ideas together and show how one thought is related to another. They help readers understand the connections you're trying to make. You can establish transitions in various ways:

> Because each paragraph covers a single idea, use transitional words and phrases to show readers how paragraphs relate to each other.

- Use connecting words: *and, but, or, nevertheless, however, in addition,* and so on.
- Echo a word or phrase from a previous paragraph or sentence: "A system should be established for monitoring inventory levels. *This system* will provide . . ."
- Use a pronoun that refers to a noun used previously: "Ms. Arthur is the leading candidate for the president's position. *She* has excellent qualifications."
- Use words that are frequently paired: "The machine has a *minimum* output of. . . . Its *maximum* output is . . ."

Here is a list of transitions frequently used to move readers smoothly between sentences and paragraphs:

Additional detail: moreover, furthermore, in addition, besides, first, second, third, finally

Document Makeover

Improve This Letter

To practice correcting drafts of actual documents, visit www.prenhall.com/onekey on the web. Click "Document Makeovers," then click Chapter 4. You will find a letter that contains problems and errors relating to what you've learned in this chapter about writing business messages. Use the Final Draft decision tool to create an improved version of this letter. Check the message for appropriate choice of approach, a conversational tone, correct use of active voice, and logical paragraphs.

Causal relationship:	therefore, because, accordingly, thus, consequently, hence, as a result, so
Comparison:	similarly, here again, likewise, in comparison, still
Contrast:	yet, conversely, whereas, nevertheless, on the other hand, however, but, nonetheless
Condition:	although, if
Illustration:	for example, in particular, in this case, for instance
Time sequence:	formerly, after, when, meanwhile, sometimes
Intensification:	indeed, in fact, in any event
Summary:	in brief, in short, to sum up
Repetition:	that is, in other words, as I mentioned earlier

Although transitional words and phrases are useful, they're not sufficient in themselves to overcome poor organization. Your goal is first to put your ideas in a strong framework and then to use transitions to link them together even more strongly.

You can use transitions inside paragraphs, between paragraphs, and between major sections.

Consider using a transition device whenever it might help the reader understand your ideas and follow you from point to point. You can use transitions inside paragraphs to tie related points together and between paragraphs to ease the shift from one distinct thought to another. In longer reports, transitions that link major sections or chapters are often complete paragraphs that summarize the ideas presented in the section just ending and serve as mini-introductions to the information that will be covered in the next section. Here's an example:

> Given the nature of this product, the alternatives are limited. As the previous section indicates, we can stop making it altogether, improve it, or continue with the current model. Each of these alternatives has advantages and disadvantages, which are discussed in the following section.

Reviewing Key Points

This chapter discusses the second step in the three-step writing process: writing business messages. It explains how to organize your message by defining the main idea, limiting the scope of the message, grouping your points into an outline, and choosing between a direct and an indirect approach.

This chapter helps you compose your message. It explains how to control your style by using a conversational tone and plain English. It also explains how to select the best words by blending abstract and concrete words, choosing words that are strong and familiar, and avoiding clichés and jargon. The chapter shows you how to create effective sentences, using all four types, selecting active or passive voice, and emphasizing key thoughts. Finally, this chapter explains how to develop coherent paragraphs by adapting paragraph length, using five development techniques, and achieving both unity and coherence.

The next chapter focuses on the last step of the writing process: completing business messages. It discusses how to revise your messages for conciseness and clarity. It covers how to produce your message by choosing the right design elements, making those design elements effective, and using computers to improve your finished documents. In addition, you will learn how to proofread your business messages—what to look for and how to adapt the process.

Test Your Knowledge

1. How does good organization help you write more effective messages?

2. How does good organization help your audience?

3. What four actions help you organize messages more effectively?

4. What three elements do you consider when choosing between a direct and an indirect approach?

5. What should you avoid to achieve a conversational tone?

6. How does an abstract word differ from a concrete word?

7. In what three situations should you use passive voice?

8. How can you use sentence style to emphasize key thoughts?

9. What is the purpose of the topic sentence?

10. What functions do transitions serve?

Apply Your Knowledge

1. Who does good organization help more, you or your audience? Please explain.

2. Some people feel that making an outline for a business message is a waste of time. Do you agree or disagree? Please explain.

3. Would you use a direct or an indirect approach to ask employees to work overtime to meet an important deadline? Please explain.

4. Which approach would you use to let your boss know that you'll be out half a day this week to attend your father's funeral—direct or indirect? Why?

5. **Ethical Choices**   Do you think that using an indirect approach to overcome audience resistance is manipulative? Discuss the ethical issues in your answer.

Practice Your Knowledge

Exercises for Perfecting Your Writing

Message Organization: Choosing the Approach   Indicate whether the direct or the indirect approach would be best in each of the following situations. Write *direct* or *indirect* in the space provided.

1. _____   A letter asking when next year's automobiles will be put on sale locally

2. _____   A letter from a recent college graduate requesting a letter of recommendation from a former instructor

3. _____   A letter turning down a job applicant

4. _____   An announcement that because of high air-conditioning costs, the plant temperature will be held at 78 degrees during the summer

5. _____   A final request to settle a delinquent debt

Message Organization: Drafting Persuasive Messages   If you were trying to persuade people to take the following actions, how would you organize your argument? Write *direct* or *indirect* in the space provided.

6. _____   You want your boss to approve your plan for hiring two new people.

7. _____   You want to be hired for a job.

8. _____   You want to be granted a business loan.

9. _____   You want to collect a small amount from a regular customer whose account is slightly past due.

10. _____   You want to collect a large amount from a customer whose account is seriously past due.

Message Composition: Selecting Words   In the following sentences, replace vague phrases (underlined) with concrete phrases. Make up any details you might need.

11. We will be opening our new facility <u>sometime this spring</u>.

12. You can now purchase our new Leaf-Away yard and lawn blower <u>at a substantial savings</u>.

13. After the reception, we were surprised that <u>such a large number attended</u>.

14. The new production line has been operating <u>with increased efficiency</u> on every run.

15. Over the holiday, we hired a crew to <u>expand the work area</u>.

Message Composition: Selecting Words   In the following sentences, replace weak terms (in italics) with words that are stronger:

16. The two reporters _____ (*ran after*) every lead enthusiastically.

17. Even large fashion houses have to match staff size to the normal _____ (*seasonal ups and downs*).

18. The _____ (*bright*) colors in that ad are keeping customers from seeing what we have to sell.

19. Health costs _____ (*suddenly rise*) when management forgets to emphasize safety issues.

20. Once we solved the zoning issue, new business construction _____ (*moved forward*), and the district has been flourishing ever since.

Message Composition: Selecting Words   Rewrite these sentences to replace the clichés with fresh, personal expressions:

21. Being a jack-of-all-trades, Dave worked well in his new selling job.

22. Moving Leslie into the accounting department, where she was literally a fish out of water, was like putting a square peg into a round hole, if you get my drift.

23. I knew she was at death's door, but I thought the doctor would pull her through.

24. Movies aren't really my cup of tea; as far as I am concerned, they can't hold a candle to a good book.

25. It's a dog-eat-dog world out there in the rat race of the asphalt jungle.

Message Composition: Selecting Words   In the following sentences, replace long, complicated words with short, simple ones:

26. Management _____ (*inaugurated*) the recycling policy six months ago.

27. I'll miss working with you when my internship _____ (*terminates*).

28. You can convey the same meaning without _____ (*utilizing*) the same words.

29. No one _____ (*anticipated*) that Mr. Hughes would retire so soon.

30. When Julian asked for my _____ (*assistance*), I grabbed the chance to learn more about accounting.

31. You'll never be promoted unless you _____ (*endeavor*) to be more patient.

32. I have to wait until payday to _____ (*ascertain*) whether I got the raise or not.

33. On your way back from lunch, don't forget to _____ (*procure*) more photocopy paper.

34. We'll send you an invoice when we _____ (*consummate*) the job.

35. Please _____ (*advise*) me when you're ready to begin the test.

36. John will send you a copy, once he's inserted all the _____ (*alterations*) you've requested.

37. The contract was _____ (*forwarded*) to you for your signature on July 19.

38. Grand Tree _____ (*fabricates*) office furniture that is both durable and attractive.

39. I understand from your letter that you expect a full refund, _____ (*nevertheless*) your warranty expired more than a year ago.

40. I have received _____ (*substantial*) support on this project from Claire Devon and Randy Smith.

Message Composition: Selecting Words   Rewrite the following sentences, replacing obsolete phrases with up-to-date versions. Write *none* if you think there is no appropriate substitute.

41. I have completed the form and returned it to my insurance company, as per your instructions.

42. Attached herewith is a copy of our new contract for your records.

43. Even though it will increase the price of the fence, we have decided to use the redwood in lieu of the cedar.

44. Saunders & Saunders has received your request for the Greenwood file, and in reply I wish to state that we will send you copies of Mr. Greenwood's documents only after Judge Taylor makes her ruling and orders us to do so.

45. Please be advised that your account with National Bank has been compromised, and we advise you to close it as soon as possible.

Message Composition: Creating Sentences   Rewrite each sentence so that it is active rather than passive:

46. The raw data are submitted to the data processing division by the sales representative each Friday.

47. High profits are publicized by management.

48. The policies announced in the directive were implemented by the staff.

49. Our computers are serviced by the Santee Company.

50. The employees were represented by Janet Hogan.

Message Organization: Transitional Elements   Add transitional elements to the following sentences to improve the flow of ideas. (Note: You may need to eliminate or add some words to smooth out your sentences.)

51. Steve Case saw infinite possibilities in cyberspace. Steve Case was determined to turn his vision into reality. The techies scoffed at his strategy of building a simple Internet service for ordinary people. Case doggedly pursued his dream. He analyzed other online services. He assessed the needs of his customers. He responded to their desires for an easier way to access information over the Internet. In 1992, Steve Case named his company America Online (AOL). Critics predicted the company's demise. By the end of the century, AOL was a profitable powerhouse.

52. Facing some of the toughest competitors in the world, Harley-Davidson had to make some changes. The company introduced new products. Harley's management team set out to rebuild the company's production process. New products were coming to market and the company was turning a profit. Harley's quality standards were not on par with those of its foreign competitors. Harley's costs were still among the highest in the industry. Harley made a U-turn and restructured the company's organizational structure. Harley's efforts have paid off.

53. Whether you're indulging in a doughnut in New York or California, Krispy Kreme wants you to enjoy the same delicious taste with every bite. The company maintains consistent product quality by carefully controlling every step of the production process. Krispy Kreme tests all raw ingredients against established quality standards. Every delivery of wheat flour is sampled and measured for its moisture content and protein levels. Krispy Kreme blends the ingredients. Krispy Kreme tests the doughnut mix for quality. Krispy Kreme delivers the mix to its stores. Krispy Kreme knows that it takes more than a quality mix to produce perfect doughnuts all the time. The company supplies its stores with everything they need to produce premium doughnuts—mix, icings, fillings, equipment—you name it.

Activities

For live links to all websites discussed in this chapter, visit this text's website at www.prenhall.com/bovee. Just log on, select Chapter 4, and click on "Featured Websites." Locate the page or the URL related to the material in the text.

1. **Analyze This Document**   A writer is working on an insurance information brochure and is having trouble grouping the ideas logically into an outline. Prepare the outline, paying attention to appropriate subordination of ideas. If necessary, rewrite phrases to give them a more consistent sound.

Accident Protection Insurance Plan
- Coverage is only pennies a day
- Benefit is $100,000 for accidental death on common carrier
- Benefit is $100 a day for hospitalization as result of motor vehicle or common carrier accident
- Benefit is $20,000 for accidental death in motor vehicle accident
- Individual coverage is only $17.85 per quarter; family coverage is just $26.85 per quarter
- No physical exam or health questions
- Convenient payment—billed quarterly
- Guaranteed acceptance for all applicants
- No individual rate increases
- Free, no-obligation examination period
- Cash paid in addition to any other insurance carried
- Covers accidental death when riding as fare-paying passenger on public transportation, including buses, trains, jets, ships, trolleys, subways, or any other common carrier
- Covers accidental death in motor vehicle accidents occurring while driving or riding in or on automobile, truck, camper, motor home, or nonmotorized bicycle

2. Teamwork   Working with four other students, divide the following five topics and write one paragraph on your selected topic. Be sure one student writes a paragraph using the illustration technique, one using the comparison-or-contrast technique, one using a discussion of cause and effect, one using the classification technique, and one using a discussion of problem and solution. Then exchange paragraphs within the team and pick out the main idea and general purpose of the paragraph one of your teammates wrote. Was everyone able to correctly identify the main idea and purpose? If not, suggest how the paragraph might be rewritten for clarity.

    a. Types of cameras (or dogs or automobiles) available for sale
    b. Advantages and disadvantages of eating at fast-food restaurants
    c. Finding that first full-time job
    d. Good qualities of my car (or house, or apartment, or neighborhood)
    e. How to make a favorite dessert (or barbecue a steak or make coffee)

Expand Your Knowledge

Exploring the Best of the Web

Compose a Better Business Message   At Purdue University's Online Writing Lab (OWL), owl.english. purdue.edu, you'll find tools to help you improve your business messages. For advice on composing written messages, for help with grammar, and for referrals to other information sources, you'll be wise to visit this site. Purdue's OWL offers online services and an introduction to Internet search tools. You can also download a variety of handouts on writing skills. Check out the resources at the OWL homepage, then answer the following questions:

Exercises

1. Explain why positive wording in a message is more effective than negative wording. Why should you be concerned about the position of good news or bad news in your written message?

2. What six factors of tone should you consider when conveying your message to your audience?

3. What points should you include in the close of your business message? Why?

Exploring the Web on Your Own

Review these chapter-related websites on your own to learn more about writing business messages.

1. Write it right by paying attention to these writing tips, grammar pointers, style suggestions, and reference sources at www.webgrammar.com.

2. Can't find the right word to use when writing about specialized topics? Check out one of the hundreds of subject-area glossaries available at www.glossarist.com.

3. Maximize your e-mail effectiveness by visiting A Beginner's Guide to Effective E-Mail, www.webfoot. com/advice/email.top.html.

Learn Interactively

Interactive Study Guide

Go to the Companion Website at www.prenhall.com/bovee. For Chapter 4, take advantage of the interactive "Study Guide" to test your knowledge of the chapter. Get instant feedback on whether you need additional studying. Also, visit this site's "Study Hall," where you'll find an abundance of valuable resources that will help you succeed in this course.

Peak Performance Grammar and Mechanics

To improve your skill with adjectives and adverbs, visit www. prenhall.com/onekey, click "Peak Performance Grammar

and Mechanics," click "Grammar Basics," and then click "Adjectives and Adverbs." Take the Pretest to determine whether you have any weak areas. Then review those areas in the Refresher Course. Take the Follow-Up Test to check your grasp of adjectives and adverbs. For an extra challenge or advanced practice, take the Advanced Test. Finally, for additional reinforcement in adjectives, go to the "Improve Your Grammar, Mechanics, and Usage" section that follows, and complete the "Level I: Self-Assessment" exercises.

Improve Your Grammar, Mechanics, and Usage

Level 1: Self-Assessment—Adjectives

Review Sections 1.4 in the Handbook of Grammar, Mechanics, and Usage, and then look at the following 15 items.

In items 1–5, fill in the appropriate form of the adjective that appears in parentheses:

1. Of the two products, this one has the _____ (*great*) potential.

2. The _____ (*perfect*) solution is *d*.

3. Here is the _____ (*interesting*) of all the ideas I have heard so far.

4. Our service is _____ (*good*) than theirs.

5. The _____ (*hard*) part of my job is firing people.

In items 6–10, insert hyphens wherever required:

6. A highly placed source revealed Dotson's last ditch efforts to cover up the mistake.

7. Please send an extra large dust cover for my photocopier.

8. A top secret document was taken from the president's office last night.

9. A 30 year old person should know better.

10. If I write a large scale report, I want to know that it will be read by upper level management.

In items 11–15, insert required commas between adjectives:

11. The two companies are engaged in an all-out no-holds-barred struggle for dominance.

12. A tiny metal shaving is responsible for the problem.

13. She came to the office with a bruised swollen knee.

14. A chipped cracked sheet of glass is useless to us.

15. You'll receive our usual cheerful prompt service.

Level 2: Workplace Applications

The following items contain numerous errors in grammar, capitalization, punctuation, abbreviation, number style, word division, and vocabulary. Rewrite each sentence in the space provided, correcting all errors. Write *C* in the space after any sentence that is already correct.

1. Its time that you learned the skills one needs to work with suppliers and vendors to get what you want and need.

2. Easy flexible wireless calling plans start for as little as $19 dollars a month.

3. There's several criteria used to select customer's to receive this offer.

4. PetFood Warehouse officially became PETsMART, Jim left the co. due to health reasons.

5. First quarter sales gains are evident in both the grocery store sector (up 1.03%) and the restaurant sector (up 3.17 per cent) according to Food Institute estimates.

6. Whatever your challenge, learning stronger "negotiating" tactics and strategies will improve the way people work and the results that comes from their efforts.

7. To meet the increasing demand for Penta bottled-drinking-water, production capacity is being expanded by Bio-Hydration Research Lab by 80 percent.

8. Seminars begin at 9 A.M. and wrap up at 4:00 P.M.

9. Temple, Texas-based McLane Co. a subsidiary of Wal-Mart has bought a facility in Northfield, Minn that it will use to distribute products to customers such as convenience stores, stores that sell items at a discount, and mass merchants.

10. The British Retail Consortium are releasing the 3rd edition of its Technical Standards on Apr. 22, reported The New York Times.

11. The reason SkillPath is the fastest growing training company in the world is because of our commitment to providing clients with the highest-quality learning experiences possible.

12. According to professor Charles Noussair of the economics department of Purdue University, opinion surveys "Capture the respondent in the role of a voter, not in the role of a consumer".

13. The Study found that people, exposed to Purina banner ads, were almost 50 percent more likely to volunteer Purina as the first Dog Food brand that came to mind.

14. In a consent decree with the food and drug administration, E'Ola International a dietary supplement maker agreed not to sell any more products containing the drug, ephedrine.

15. Dennis Dickson is looking for a company both to make and distribute plaidberries under an exclusive license, plaidberries is blackberries that are mixed with extracts and they are used as a filling.

Level 3: Document Critique

The following document may contain errors in grammar, capitalization, punctuation, abbreviation, number style, vocabulary, and spelling. You will also find errors relating to topics in this chapter. Concentrate on using the "you" attitude, emphasizing the positive, being polite, and using bias-free language as you improve this memo. Correct all errors using standard proofreading marks (see Appendix C).

Burdette's

• Special Sizes •

For Special Ladies and Gentlemen

820 10th Avenue South, Seattle, WA 98134 • (206) 777-1234 • Fax: (206) 777-1235 • www.burdettes.com

10/19/02

Mrs. Bruce Crandall

1597 Church Street

Grants Pass, Oreg. 97526

Dear Mrs. Crandall,

Order no. 89-97526-277

We were so happy to recieve your order—We know you'll be enjoying the dress you've selected from our fall catalog. We feel its a popular number because its so versitile and flatters our heavier customers. We think you'll get alot of use out of it on your trip to San Francisco.

Unfortunately, you forgot to indicate what size you need. We can't ship your dress until you tell us your size. Plus, if you don't mail in the postage paid card that we've enclosed for you to use very soon we can't be guaranteeing that your attractive new dress will arrive in time for your trip!

Sincerely,

Beating Writer's Block: Nine Workable Ideas to Get Words Flowing

Putting words on a page or on screen can be a real struggle. Some people get stuck so often that they develop a mental block. If you get writer's block, here are some ways to get those words flowing again:

■ **Use positive self-talk.** Stop worrying about how well or easily you write, and stop thinking of writing as difficult, time-consuming, or complicated. Tell yourself that you're capable and that you can do the job. Also, recall past examples of your writing that were successful.

■ **Know your purpose.** Be specific about what you want to accomplish with this particular piece of writing. Without a clear purpose, writing can indeed be impossible.

■ **Visualize your audience.** Picture audience backgrounds, interests, subject knowledge, and vocabulary (including the technical jargon they use). Such visualization can help you choose an appropriate style and tone for your writing.

■ **Create a productive environment.** Write in a place that's for writing only, and make that place pleasant. Set up "writing appointments." Scheduling a session from nine-thirty to noon is less intimidating than an indefinite session. Also, keep your mind fresh with scheduled breaks.

■ **Make an outline or a list.** Even if you don't create a formal outline, at least jot down a few notes about how your ideas fit together. As you go along, you can revise your notes, as long as you end up with a plan that gives direction and coherence.

■ **Just start.** Put aside all worries, fears, distractions—anything that gives you an excuse to postpone writing. Then start putting down any thoughts you have about your topic. Don't worry about whether these ideas can actually be used; just let your mind range freely.

■ **Write the middle first.** Start wherever your interest is greatest and your ideas are most developed. You can follow new directions, but note ideas to revisit later. When you finish one section, choose another without worrying about sequence. Just get your thoughts down.

■ **Push obstacles aside.** If you get stuck at some point, don't worry. Move past the thought, sentence, or paragraph, and come back to it later. Prime the pump simply by writing or talking about why you're stuck: "I'm stuck because . . ." Also try brainstorming. Before you know it, you'll be writing about your topic.

■ **Read a newspaper or magazine.** Try reading an article that uses a style similar to yours. Choose one you'll enjoy so that you'll read it more closely.

■ **Work on nontext segments.** Work on a different part of the project, such as formatting or creating graphics or verifying facts and references.

Remember, when deadlines loom, don't freeze in panic. Concentrate on the major ideas first, and save the details for later, after you have something on the page. If you keep things in perspective, you'll succeed.

Applications for Success

Learn more about beating writer's block. Visit Writer's Block at www.geocities.com/zigguratzen. Another way to overcome writer's block is to limit the scope of your message. Suppose you are preparing to recommend that top management install a new heating system (using the cogeneration process). The following information is in your files.

■ History of the development of the cogeneration heating process
■ Scientific credentials of the developers of the process
■ Risks assumed in using this process
■ Your plan for installing the equipment in your building
■ Stories about its successful use in comparable facilities
■ Specifications of the equipment that would be installed
■ Plans for disposing of the old heating equipment
■ Costs of installing and running the new equipment
■ Advantages and disadvantages of using the new process
■ Detailed 10-year cost projections
■ Estimates of the time needed to phase in the new system
■ Alternative systems that management might wish to consider

Do the following:

1. Limit the scope of this message by eliminating any topics that aren't essential.
2. Arrange the remaining topics so that your report will give top managers a clear understanding of the heating system and a balanced, concise justification for installing it.
3. List the ways you procrastinate, and discuss what you can do to break these habits.
4. Analyze your own writing experiences. What negative self-talk do you use? What might you do to overcome this tendency?

107

5

Completing Business Messages

Learning Objectives

After studying this chapter, you will be able to

1 List the main tasks involved in completing a business message

2 Identify nine techniques for improving the clarity of your writing

3 Discuss four methods for making your writing more concise

4 Explain how four design elements affect your document's appearance

5 Clarify the types of errors you look for when proofreading

6 Describe seven ways to improve your proofreading process

As corporate communications manager at Turner Broadcasting System (TBS), Adrianne Proeller writes speeches and statements for TBS president R. E. (Ted) Turner, and she writes letters, memos, speeches, press releases, executive biographies, corporate fact sheets, company histories, and sample questions and answers for corporate executives before media interviews. Proeller has enough public relations duties to keep her busy during frequent 10-hour days. She understands the importance of revising a document for the second or third time, weeding out weak verbs, simplifying complicated sentences, and eliminating unnecessary facts. She revises everything she writes, a task that she says "just comes with the territory." Proeller has to be certain that her memos and press releases are clear and accurate.[1]

Revising Your Message

Successful businesspeople such as Adrianne Proeller care very much about saying precisely the right thing in precisely the right way. Look back at the diagram of the three-step writing process (Figure 3.1 on page 54). You can see that completing your message consists of three tasks: revising, producing, and proofreading your message.

Although the tendency is to separate revision from composition, revision occurs throughout the writing process. You revise as you go along; then you revise again after you've completed the first draft. Ideally, you should let your draft age a day or two before you begin the revision process, so that you can approach the material with a fresh eye. Then read through the document quickly to evaluate its overall effectiveness (its content, organization, style, and tone) before you begin revising for finer points such as clarity and conciseness.

Revision takes place during and after preparing the first draft.

In your first pass, spend a few extra moments on the beginning and ending of the message. These are the sections that have the greatest impact on the audience. Be sure that the opening of a letter or memo is relevant, interesting, and geared to the reader's probable reaction. In longer messages, check to see that the first few paragraphs establish the subject, purpose, and organization of the material. Review the conclusion to be sure that it summarizes the main idea and leaves the audience with a positive impression.

The beginning and end of a message have the greatest impact on readers.

As you revise your messages, you'll find yourself rewriting sentences, passages, and even whole sections to improve their effectiveness. Of course, you're probably also facing a deadline, so try to stick to the schedule you set during the planning stage of the project. Do your best to revise and rewrite thoroughly but also economically. Look closely at the revised message in Figure 5.1. It has been edited using the proofreading marks shown in Appendix C. As you can see, the revisions provide the requested information in a more organized fashion, in a friendlier style, and with clearer mechanics.

Sometimes you'll find that you can solve the most difficult problem in a sentence simply by removing it. When you come upon a troublesome element, ask yourself, "Do I need it at all?" You may find that the element was causing a problem because it was trying to do an unnecessary job.[2] Of course, before you delete anything, keep copies of your previous versions. Professional communicators such as TBS's Adrianne Proeller know how important it is to keep a paper trail for future reference.

Solve some problems by deleting them.

Rewrite and Edit for Clarity

Once you've reviewed your message for overall effectiveness, you'll want to make sure that your message is clear. Perhaps a sentence is so cluttered that the reader can't unravel it, or it's constructed in a way that the reader can interpret it in several ways. Perhaps pronouns or tenses switch midsentence so that the reader loses track of who is talking or when an event took place. Perhaps sentence B does not logically follow sentence A. Or perhaps an important word is used incorrectly.[3]

Clarity avoids confusion.

Break Up Overly Long Sentences

Don't connect too many clauses with *and*. If you find yourself stuck in a long sentence, you're probably trying to make the sentence do more than it can reasonably do, such as express two dissimilar thoughts. You can often clarify your writing style by separating a string into individual sentences. Try not to take compound sentences too far:

In many cases, the parts of a compound sentence should be separated into two sentences.

Unacceptable	Preferable
The magazine will be published January 1, and I'd better meet the deadline if I want my article included.	The magazine will be published January 1. I'd better meet the deadline if I want my article included.

Rewrite Hedging Sentences

Sometimes you have to write *may* or *seems* to avoid stating a judgment as a fact. Nevertheless, when you have too many such hedges, you aren't really saying anything. Avoid overqualifying your sentences:

Don't be afraid to present your opinions without qualification.

Unacceptable	Preferable
I believe that Mr. Johnson's employment record seems to show that he may be capable of handling the position.	Mr. Johnson's employment record shows that he is capable of handling the position.

Impose Parallelism

When you have two or more similar (parallel) ideas to express, use the same grammatical pattern for each related idea—parallel construction. Repeating the pattern makes your

When you use the same grammatical pattern to express two or more ideas, you show that they are comparable thoughts.

FIGURE 5.1   Effective Edited Letter (Excerpt)

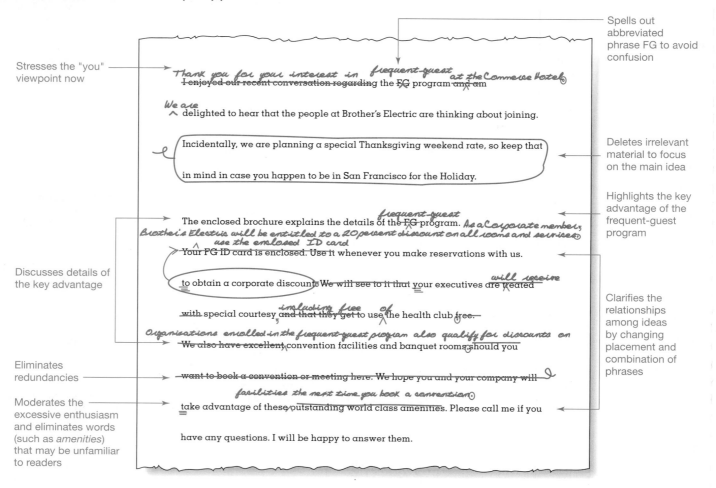

message more readable: It tells readers that the ideas are comparable, and it adds rhythm. Parallelism can be achieved by repeating the pattern in words, phrases, clauses, or entire sentences.

Unacceptable	Preferable
Miss Simms had been drenched with rain, bombarded with telephone calls, and her boss shouted at her.	Miss Sims had been drenched with rain, bombarded with telephone calls, and shouted at by her boss.
Ms. Reynolds dictated the letter, and next she signed it and left the office.	Ms. Reynolds dictated the letter, signed it, and left the office.
To waste time and missing deadlines are bad habits.	Wasting time and missing deadlines are bad habits.
Interviews are a matter of acting confident and to stay relaxed.	Interviews are a matter of acting confident and staying relaxed.

Correct Dangling Modifiers

Make sure that modifier phrases are really related to the subject of the sentence.

Sometimes a modifier is not just an adjective or an adverb but an entire phrase modifying a noun or a verb. Be careful not to leave this type of modifier dangling with no connection to the subject of the sentence. The first unacceptable example in the following group implies that the red sports car has both an office and the legs to walk there. The second example shows one frequent cause of dangling modifiers: passive construction. Avoid placing modifiers close to the wrong nouns and verbs:

Unacceptable	Preferable
Walking to the office, a red sports car passed her.	A red sports car passed her while she was walking to the office.
Working as fast as possible, the budget was soon ready.	Working as fast as possible, the committee soon had the budget ready.
After a three-week slump, we increased sales.	After a three-week slump, sales increased.

Reword Long Noun Sequences

When nouns are strung together as modifiers, the resulting sentence is hard to read. You can clarify such a sentence by putting some of the nouns in a modifying phrase. Although you add a few more words, your audience won't have to work as hard to understand the sentence. Avoid stringing too many nouns together:

Stringing together a series of nouns may save a little space, but it causes confusion.

Unacceptable	Preferable
The aluminum window sash installation company will give us an estimate on Friday.	The company that installs aluminum window sashes will give us an estimate on Friday.

Replace Camouflaged Verbs

Watch for word endings such as *ion, tion, ing, ment, ant, ent, ence, ance,* and *ency*. Most of them change verbs into nouns and adjectives. Get rid of them:

Turning verbs into nouns or adjectives weakens your writing style.

Unacceptable	Preferable
The manager undertook implementation of the rules.	The manager implemented the rules.
Verification of the shipments occurs weekly.	Shipments are verified weekly.

Also try not to transform verbs into nouns (writing "we performed an analysis of" rather than "we analyzed"). To prune and enliven your messages, use verbs instead of noun phrases:

Unacceptable	Preferable
reach a conclusion about	conclude
make a discovery of	discover
give consideration to	consider

Clarify Sentence Structure

Keep the subject and predicate of a sentence as close together as possible. When subject and predicate are far apart, readers have to read the sentence twice to figure out who did what. Try not to separate subject and predicate:

Subject and predicate should be placed as close together as possible, as should modifiers and the words they modify.

Unacceptable	Preferable
A 10 percent decline in market share, which resulted from quality problems and an aggressive sales campaign by Armitage, the market leader in the Northeast, was the major problem in 2004.	The major problem in 2004 was a 10 percent loss of market share, which resulted from both quality problems and an aggressive sales campaign by Armitage, the market leader in the Northeast.

Similarly, adjectives, adverbs, and prepositional phrases usually make the most sense when they're placed as close as possible to the words they modify:

Unacceptable	Preferable
Our antique desk is suitable for busy executives with thick legs and large drawers.	With its thick legs and large drawers, our antique desk is suitable for busy executives.

Clarify Awkward References

Be specific in your references.

To save words, business writers sometimes use expressions such as *the above-mentioned, as mentioned above, the aforementioned, the former, the latter,* and *respectively.* These words cause readers to jump from point to point, which hinders effective communication. Use specific references, even if you must add a few more words:

Unacceptable	Preferable
The Law Office and the Accounting Office distribute computer supplies for legal secretaries and beginning accountants, respectively.	The Law Office distributes computer supplies for legal secretaries; the Accounting Office distributes those for beginning accountants.

Moderate Your Enthusiasm

Business writing shouldn't be gushy.

An occasional adjective or adverb intensifies and emphasizes your meaning, but too many can ruin your writing. Try not to display too much enthusiasm:

Unacceptable	Preferable
We are extremely pleased to offer you a position on our staff of exceptionally skilled and highly educated employees. The work offers extraordinary challenges and a very large salary.	We are pleased to offer you a position on our staff of skilled and well-educated employees. The work offers challenges and an attractive salary.

Rewrite and Edit for Conciseness

Conciseness means efficiency.

Many business documents today are swollen with words and phrases that don't increase the message's effectiveness. In fact, a majority of executives responding to one survey complained that most written messages are too long.[4] Because executives are more likely to read documents that efficiently say what needs to be said, it's especially important to weed out unnecessary material. As you rewrite and edit your messages, concentrate on how each word contributes to an effective sentence and how that sentence develops a coherent paragraph.

Most first drafts can be cut by 50 percent.[5] When you rewrite and edit for clarity, you eliminate much of the excess. But rewriting and editing for conciseness means examining every word you put on paper. You eliminate every word that serves no function, replace every long word that could be a short word, and remove every adverb that adds nothing to the meaning already carried in the verb.

To test whether every word counts, try removing phrases or words that don't appear to be essential. If the meaning is unchanged, leave those elements out. For instance, *very* can be a useful word to achieve emphasis, but more often it's clutter. There's no need to call someone "very methodical." The person is either methodical or not. As you begin your editing task, simplify, prune, and strive for order.

Delete Unnecessary Words and Phrases

Some combinations of words have one-word equivalents that are more efficient. Avoid using wordy phrases:

Be on the lookout for inefficient phrases and excessive or confusing relative pronouns and articles.

Unacceptable	Preferable
for the sum of	for
in the event that	if
on the occasion of	on
prior to the start of	before
in the near future	soon
have the capability of	can
at this point in time	now
due to the fact that	because
in view of the fact that	because
until such time as	when
with reference to	about

In addition, avoid the clutter of too many or poorly placed relative pronouns (*who, that, which*). Even articles can be excessive (mostly too many *the*'s):

Unacceptable	Preferable
Cars that are sold after January will not have a six-month warranty.	Cars sold after January will not have a six-month warranty.
Employees who are driving to work should park in the underground garage.	Employees driving to work should park in the underground garage.

However, well-placed relative pronouns and articles prevent confusion. Make sure to use enough relative pronouns to be clear:

Unacceptable	Preferable
The project manager told the engineers last week the specifications were changed.	The project manager told the engineers last week *that* the specifications were changed.
	The project manager told the engineers *that* last week the specifications were changed.

Shorten Long Words and Phrases

Short words are generally more vivid and easier to read than long ones are. The idea is to use short, simple words, *not* simple concepts.[6] Try to get rid of overly long words:

Short words and infinitives are generally more vivid than long words and phrases, and they improve the readability of a document.

Unacceptable	Preferable
During the preceding year, the company accelerated productive operations.	Last year the company sped up operations.
The action was predicated on the assumption that the company was operating at a financial deficit.	The action was based on the belief that the company was losing money.

Also, by using infinitives in place of some phrases, you not only shorten your sentences but also make them clearer. Be careful to use infinitives rather than wordy phrases:

Unacceptable	Preferable
If you want success as a writer, you must work hard.	To be a successful writer, you must work hard.
He went to the library for the purpose of studying.	He went to the library to study.
The employer increased salaries so that she could improve morale.	The employer increased salaries to improve morale.

Eliminate Redundancies

Remove unneeded repetition.

In some word combinations, the words tend to say the same thing. For instance, "visible to the eye" is redundant because *visible* is enough; nothing can be visible to the ear. Try not to repeat meanings:

Unacceptable	Preferable
absolutely complete	complete
basic fundamentals	fundamentals
follows after	follows
reduce down	reduce
free and clear	free
refer back	refer
repeat again	repeat
collect together	collect
future plans	plans
return back	return
important essentials	essentials
midway between	between
end result	result
actual truth	truth
final outcome	outcome
uniquely unusual	unique
surrounded on all sides	surrounded

In addition, avoid using double modifiers with the same meaning.

Unacceptable	Preferable
modern, up-to-date equipment	modern equipment

Recast "It Is/There Are" Starters

Avoid starting sentences with *it* and *there*.

If you start a sentence with an indefinite pronoun (an expletive) such as *it* or *there*, odds are that the sentence could be shorter. Make sure that your sentences start with something other than *it* or *there*:

Unacceptable	Preferable
It would be appreciated if you would sign the lease today.	Please sign the lease today.
There are five employees in this division who were late to work today.	Five employees in this division were late to work today.

Producing Your Message

Once you have revised and refined your message from start to finish, you are ready to produce it. You want to give your message an attractive, contemporary appearance by designing your document carefully. Also, make sure that your design allows for added elements such as graphics or hypertext.

Before you can proofread your final version, you must produce it in some readable form.

Select the Right Design Elements

The way you package your ideas has a lot to do with how successful your communication will be. The first thing your readers notice about your message is its appearance. If your document looks tired and out of date, it will give that impression to your readers—even if your ideas are innovative. Good looks can help you get your message across, especially to busy readers.

Design affects the impression your message makes.

When designing your message, balancing graphics and text is important. Consider the memo in Figure 5.2. The bar chart in this memo is centered to give a formal impression, and the color used in the graphic is balanced by the letterhead logo.

You can use a variety of design elements, such as white space, margin and line justification, typefaces, and type styles to make your message look professional, interesting, and up to date. But be careful—too many design elements will confuse your audience. If you will be designing a lot of documents that contain a variety of elements, you would be wise to take a course in page layout or to at least read further about effective design techniques.

White Space

White space is the part of a document that is free of text or artwork. It provides visual contrast for your readers, and perhaps even more important, it gives their eyes a resting point. White space includes the open area surrounding headings and margin areas, the vertical space between columns, the space created by ragged line endings, the paragraph indents or extra space between unindented paragraphs, and the horizontal space between lines of text.

White space is free of text and artwork.

Margins and Line Justification

Margins define the space around your text and between text columns. They're influenced by the way you place lines of type, which can be set (1) justified (flush on the left and flush on the right), (2) flush left with a ragged right margin, (3) flush right with a ragged left margin, or (4) centered.

Margins frame your text.

Justified type "darkens" your message's appearance, because the uniform line lengths lack the white space created by ragged margins. It also tends to make your message look more like a form letter and less like a customized message. Justified type is often considered more difficult to read, because large gaps can appear between words and because more words are hyphenated at the end of lines. Excessive hyphenation is distracting and hard to follow. Even so, many magazines and newspapers use justified type because it accommodates more text.

Flush-left, ragged-right type "lightens" your message's appearance. It gives a document an informal, contemporary feeling of openness. Spacing between words is the same, and only long words that fall at the ends of lines are hyphenated.

Flush-left, ragged-right type gives your message an open feeling.

FIGURE 5.2   The Importance of Appearance

Adds to a professional appearance with colorful letterhead

Uses white space and paragraph headings effectively to make the document easy to skim

Balances graphics, text, and color to create a polished appearance and to lend credibility to the message

Draws attention to important points with colorful graphics

Centered type lends a formal tone to your message. However, centering long blocks of type slows reading because your audience has to search for the beginning of each line. The same problem is true of flush-right, ragged-left type. These two approaches are not usually used for long passages of text.

Typefaces

Typeface refers to the physical design of letters, numbers, and other text characters. Most computers offer innumerable choices of fonts or typefaces. Each typeface influences the tone of your message, making it look authoritative, friendly, expensive, classy, casual, and so on. Choose fonts that are appropriate for your message.

Serif typefaces are commonly used for text.

Serif typefaces have small crosslines (called serifs) at the ends of each letter stroke (see Table 5.1). Serif faces such as Times Roman (packaged with most laser printers) are commonly used for text; they can look busy and cluttered when set in large sizes for head-

Table 5.1	Common Typefaces	
Sample Serif Typeface	**Sample Sans Serif Typeface**	
Times Roman is often used for text.	Helvetica is often used for headings.	
TIMES ROMAN IS HARDER TO READ IN ALL CAPS.	HELVETICA IS A CLEANER FACE, EVEN IN ALL CAPS.	

ings or other display treatments. Typefaces with rounded serifs can look friendly; those with squared serifs can look official.

Sans serif typefaces have no serifs. Faces such as Helvetica (packaged with most laser printers) are ideal for display treatments that use larger type. Sans serif faces can be difficult to read in long blocks of text. They look best when surrounded by plenty of white space—as in headings or in widely spaced lines of text.

Sans serif typefaces are commonly used for headings.

Limit the number of typefaces in a single document.[7] In general, use no more than two typefaces on a page. Many great-looking documents are based on a single sans serif typeface for heads and subheads, with a second serif typeface for text and captions. Using too many typefaces clutters the document and reduces your audience's comprehension.

Type Styles

Type style refers to any modification that lends contrast or emphasis to type. Most computers offer underlining, boldface, italic, and other highlighting and decorative styles. Using boldface type for subheads breaks up long expanses of text. Just remember that too much boldfacing will darken the appearance of your message and make it look heavy. You can set isolated words in boldface type in the middle of a text block to draw more attention to them. However, if you boldface too many words, you might create a "checkerboard" appearance in a paragraph.

Use italic type for emphasis. Although italics are sometimes used when irony or humor is intended, quotation marks are usually best for that purpose. Italics can also be used to set off a quote and are often used in captions. Boldfaced type and italics are most effective when reserved for key words—those words that help readers understand the main point of the text.

As a general rule, don't use any style that slows your audience's progress through your message. For instance, using underlining or all-uppercase letters can interfere with your reader's ability to recognize the shapes of words and thus slow their progress. Other styles that slow readers include type that is in boldface or italic and type that is shadowed or outlined. So use such styles judiciously.

Avoid using type styles that slow your readers down.

Make sure the size of your type is proportionate to the importance of your message and the space allotted. Small type in a sea of white space appears lost. Large type squeezed into a small area is hard to read and visually cramped. For most business messages, use a type size of 10 to 12 points (a point is approximately 1/72 of an inch).

Make Design Elements Effective

Simply selecting the right design elements for your message doesn't guarantee that your design will be effective. You need to make all design elements work together. Effective document design guides your readers through your message, so be sure to focus on being consistent, maintaining balance, showing restraint, being detail-oriented, and using whatever technological tools you can (see Table 5.2).

For effective design, pay attention to
- Consistency
- Balance
- Restraint
- Detail

Avoid last-minute compromises. Don't reduce type size or white space to squeeze in text. On the other hand, avoid increasing type size or white space to fill space. If you've planned your message so that your purpose, your audience, and your message are clear, you can design your document to be effective.[8] Start by thinking about your medium (press release, magazine or newsletter article, brochure, direct-mail package, slide presentation, formal report, business letter, or internal memo). Once you've decided on a

Table 5.2	Five Pointers for Making Design Elements Effective
Pointer	**What to Do**
Be consistent throughout a message	Keep margins, typeface, type size, and spacing consistent from document to document (and sometimes even from message to message). Also be consistent when using recurring design elements, such as vertical lines, columns, and borders.
Balance all visual elements	Create a pleasing design by balancing the space devoted to text, artwork, and white space.
Use the best technology available	Word-processing and desktop publishing programs help you combine text and graphics for a professional, inviting appearance. They add a first-class finish with attractive typefaces and color graphics. They also let you manage document style with formatting commands that you can save and apply as needed—to ensure consistency from section to section and from document to document. Technology can turn a plain piece of text into a dazzling, persuasive document.
Strive for simplicity in design	Don't clutter your message with too many design elements, too much highlighting, or too many decorative touches.
Pay attention to design details	When headings and subheadings appear at the bottom of a column or a page, readers can be offended because the promised information doesn't appear until the next column or page. Plus, narrow columns with too much space between words can be distracting.

medium for your message, try to make it look as interesting as you can while making it as easy as possible to read and understand.

Use Computers to Improve Your Documents

Technology offers many ways to get text, graphics, sound, and even hypertext links into your document. Whether you're composing your message, adding graphics, or revising your first draft, technology helps you do so more efficiently, and it helps you produce more professional-looking results. So it is important that you learn how to use technology, including computers, word-processing software, graphics software, printers, scanners, and so on.

The most common means for creating printed documents is word-processing software.

Word processors give you the ability to delete and move text easily, with features such as automatic list numbering, page numbering, and dating. Such software saves you time and reduces mistakes by allowing you to use *boilerplates*—any standard block of text used in various documents without being changed. You also have the ability to combine multiple documents into one by using your word processor's *file merge* capability.

When it's time to revise and polish your message, your word processor helps you add, delete, and move text with functions such as *cut and paste* (taking a block of text out of one section of a document and pasting it in somewhere else) and *search and replace* (tracking down words or phrases and changing them if you need to). In addition, the AutoCorrect feature allows you to store words you commonly misspell or mistype, along with their correct spelling. So if you frequently type *teh* instead of *the*, AutoCorrect will automatically correct your typo for you. Finally, software tools such as revision marks keep track of proposed editing changes electronically and provide a history of a document's revisions. The revisions appear in a different font color than the original text, giving you a chance to review changes before accepting or rejecting them.

Spell checkers, grammar checkers, and computerized thesauruses can all help with the revision process, but they can't take the place of good writing and editing skills.

Spelling and grammar checkers have their limitations.

Three advanced software functions can help bring out the best in your documents: a *spell checker*, a *thesaurus*, and a *grammar checker*. Just don't rely on grammar or spell checkers to do all your revision work. For example, spell checkers cannot tell the difference between *their* and *there*. Moreover, some of the "errors" they do detect may actually be proper names, technical words, words that you misspelled on purpose, or simply words that weren't included in the spell checker's dictionary. Grammar checkers are even more limited, so it's up to you to decide whether each flagged item should be corrected or left alone, and it's up to you to find the errors that your spell and grammar checkers have overlooked.[9]

With the recent advances in computer technology, it's becoming easier and easier to illustrate and enliven your text. The software for creating business visuals falls into two basic groups: *Presentation software* helps you create overhead transparencies and computerized slide shows (presentations are discussed in Chapter 12); *graphics software* ranges from products that can create simple diagrams and flowcharts (see Chapter 11) to comprehensive tools used by artists and graphic designers. You can create your pictures from scratch, use *clip art* (collections of uncopyrighted images), or scan in drawings or photographs. Adding sound bites to your documents is an exciting new way to get your message across. Plus, you can use hypertext markup language (HTML) to insert hyperlinks into your message.

> You can use graphics software to add visual elements to your message.

Proofreading Your Message

Most readers view attention to detail as a sign of your professionalism. Whether you're writing a one-paragraph memo or a 500-page report, if you let mechanical errors slip through, your readers wonder whether you're unreliable in more important ways. Adrianne Proeller of TBS says, "When I get a college résumé and I see a typo on it, I instantly disregard that résumé."

> Your credibility is affected by your attention to the details of mechanics and form.

What to Look For When Proofreading

To ensure that your message is letter perfect, proofread it. Give some attention to your overall format. Have you followed accepted conventions and company guidelines for laying out the document on the page (margin width, number of columns, page numbering)? Have you included all the traditional elements that belong in documents of the type you're creating? Have you been consistent in handling heading styles, exhibits titles, source notes, and other details? (To resolve questions about format and layout, see Appendix A.)

Check your document for correct grammar, usage, and punctuation (for a quick review, see the Handbook of Grammar, Mechanics, and Usage at the end of this textbook). Also look for common spelling errors and typos. Check for missing material: a missing source note, exhibit, or paragraph. Look for design errors; for example, make sure that all headings and text appear in the right typeface.

> The types of details to look for when proofreading include language errors, missing material, design errors, and typographical errors.

One or two special elements may appear in the wrong type style (boldface or underlined instead of italic). Columns within tables and exhibits on a page might be misaligned. Graphic characters such as ampersands and percent signs may appear when they should be spelled out, and numerical symbols might be incorrect. Look closely at the type to spot problems such as extra spacing between lines or between words, crowded type, a short line of type ending a paragraph at the top of a new page, a heading that's been left hanging at the bottom of a page, or incorrect hyphenation. For a quick reminder of what to look for when proofreading, see Table 5.3.

How to Adapt the Proofreading Process

How many and what sorts of errors you catch when proofreading depend on how much time you have and what type of document you are preparing. The more routine your document, the less time you'll need to spend proofreading it. Routine documents have fewer elements to check. Moreover, the more often you prepare one type of document, the more you'll know about what sorts of errors to look for. Longer, more complex documents can have many more components that need checking.

For complicated documents, you may feel pressed for enough time to do a good proofreading job. But back in step one of the writing process (look back at Figure 3.1 on page 54), you planned how you would approach this message, and you allotted a certain amount of time for each task. Try to stick to your schedule. You want to do your best to create a perfect document, but you also want to meet your deadline and turn your work

> Even when you're pressed for time, try to maintain the schedule you laid out during the planning step of the writing process.

Table 5.3	Proofreading Tips

Look for Writing Errors

☑ Typographical mistakes

☑ Misspelled words

☑ Grammatical errors

☑ Punctuation mistakes

Look for Missing Elements

☑ Missing text sections

☑ Missing exhibits (drawings, tables, photographs, charts, graphs, and so on)

☑ Missing source notes, copyright notices, or other reference items

Look for Design and Formatting Mistakes

☑ Incorrect or inconsistent font selections

☑ Column sizing, spacing, and alignment

☑ Margins

☑ Special characters

☑ Clumsy line and page breaks

☑ Page numbers

☑ Page headers and footers

☑ Adherence to company standards

in promptly. As with every task in the writing process, practice helps—you become not only more familiar with what errors to look for but also more skilled in identifying those errors.

Proofreading may require patience, but it adds credibility to your document. To help make your proofreading more effective and ensure that your document is error free, remember the following pointers:

■ **Multiple passes.** Go through the document several times, focusing on a different aspect each time. The first pass might be to look for omissions and errors in content. The second pass could be for layout, spacing, and other aesthetic features. A final pass might be to check for typographical, grammatical, and spelling errors.

■ **Perceptual tricks.** Your brain has been trained to ignore typos. Try (1) reading each page from the bottom to the top (starting at the last word in each line), (2) placing your finger under each word and reading it silently, (3) making a slit in a sheet of paper that reveals only one line at a time, and (4) reading the document aloud and pronouncing each word carefully.

■ **Impartial reviews.** Have a friend or colleague proofread the document for you. Others are likely to catch mistakes that you continually fail to notice. (All of us have blind spots when it comes to reviewing our own work.)

■ **Distance.** If you have time, set the document aside and proofread it the next day.

■ **Vigilance.** Avoid reading large amounts of material in one sitting, and try not to proofread when you're tired.

■ **Focus.** Concentrate on what you're doing. Try to block out distractions, and focus as completely as possible on your proofreading task.

■ **Caution.** Take your time. Quick proofreading is not careful proofreading.

Document Makeover

Improve This Letter

To practice correcting drafts of actual documents, visit www.prenhall.com/onekey on the web. Click "Document Makeovers," then click Chapter 5. You will find a letter that contains problems and errors relating to what you've learned in this chapter about completing business messages. Use the Final Draft decision tool to create an improved version of this letter. Check the message for clarity, conciseness, appropriate design, and accuracy.

Reviewing Key Points

This chapter discusses the third step in the three-step writing process: completing business messages by revising, producing, and proofreading them. The chapter explains nine techniques for improving the clarity of your message and four techniques for improving message conciseness.

In this chapter, you learn how to produce your message. You learn how to select the right design elements and ensure the effectiveness of those elements. You also learn the value of using technology to improve your documents. Finally, the chapter explains what to look for when proofreading and how to adapt the proofreading process to be more effective.

The next section focuses on brief business correspondence. Chapter 6 introduces you to message forms, such as letters, memos, e-mail messages, and instant messaging—giving you tips on how to improve message readability. Chapters 7, 8, and 9 discuss the types of business messages that can be sent by letter, memo, e-mail, and instant messaging—including routine messages, bad-news messages, and persuasive messages.

Test Your Knowledge

1. What are the three main tasks involved in completing a business message?

2. What is a hedging sentence, and how can you correct one?

3. What is parallel construction, and why is it important?

4. Why is it a good idea to use verbs instead of noun phrases?

5. What are some ways you can make your message more concise?

6. What are design elements?

7. How do readers benefit from white space?

8. How can you make design elements more effective?

9. What computer tools can you use when revising messages?

10. Why is proofreading an important part of the writing process?

Apply Your Knowledge

1. Why should you let your draft "age" a day before you begin the revision process?

2. Why is it important that your business messages be clear?

3. Why is it important that your business messages be concise?

4. How does design contribute to a document's overall effectiveness?

5. Ethical Choices You have been asked to write a document explaining how your customers can appeal a decision made in the company's favor during a dispute. What are the ethical implications of using hard-to-read type styles such as underlining and all capitals in your message?

Practice Your Knowledge

Exercises for Perfecting Your Writing

Revising Messages: Clarity Break these sentences into shorter ones by adding more periods:

1. The next time you write something, check your average sentence length in a 100-word passage, and if your sentences average more than 16 to 20 words, see whether you can break up some of the sentences.

2. Don't do what the village blacksmith did when he instructed his apprentice as follows: "When I take the shoe out of the fire, I'll lay it on the anvil, and when I nod my head, you hit it with the hammer." The apprentice did just as he was told, and now he's the village blacksmith.

3. Unfortunately, no gadget will produce excellent writing, but using a yardstick like the Fog Index gives us some guideposts to follow for making writing easier to read because its two factors remind us to use short sentences and simple words.

4. Know the flexibility of the written word and its power to convey an idea, and know how to make your words behave so that your readers will understand.

Revising Messages: Conciseness   Cross out unnecessary words in the following:

5. The board cannot act without a consensus of opinion.

6. To surpass our competitors, we need new innovations both in products and in company operations.

7. George McClannahan has wanted to be head of engineering a long period of time, and now he has finally gotten the promotion.

8. Don't pay more than you have to, you can get our new fragrance for a price of just $50.

Revising Messages: Conciseness   Revise the following sentences, using shorter, simpler words:

9. The antiquated calculator is ineffectual for solving sophisticated problems.

10. It is imperative that the pay increments be terminated before an inordinate deficit is accumulated.

11. There was unanimity among the executives that Ms. Jackson's idiosyncrasies were cause for a mandatory meeting with the company's personnel director.

12. The impending liquidation of the company's assets was cause for jubilation among the company's competitors.

Revising Messages: Conciseness   Use infinitives as substitutes for the overly long phrases in these sentences:

13. For living, I require money.

14. They did not find sufficient evidence for believing in the future.

15. Bringing about the destruction of a dream is tragic.

Revising Messages: Conciseness Condense these sentences to as few words as possible:

16. We are of the conviction that writing is important.

17. In all probability, we're likely to have a price increase.

18. Our goals include making a determination about that in the near future.

19. When all is said and done at the conclusion of this experiment, I'd like to summarize the final windup.

Revising Messages: Modifiers Remove all the unnecessary modifiers from these sentences:

20. Tremendously high pay increases were given to the extraordinarily skilled and extremely conscientious employees.

21. The union's proposals were highly inflationary, extremely demanding, and exceptionally bold.

Revising Messages: Hedging Rewrite these sentences so that they no longer contain any hedging:

22. It would appear that someone apparently entered illegally.

23. It may be possible that sometime in the near future the situation is likely to improve.

24. Your report seems to suggest that we might be losing money.

25. I believe Nancy apparently has somewhat greater influence over employees in the word-processing department.

Revising Messages: Indefinite Starters   Rewrite these sentences to eliminate the indefinite starters:

26. There are several examples here to show that Elaine can't hold a position very long.

27. It would be greatly appreciated if every employee would make a generous contribution to Mildred Cook's retirement party.

28. It has been learned in Washington today from generally reliable sources that an important announcement will be made shortly by the White House.

29. There is a rule that states that we cannot work overtime without permission.

Revising Messages: Parallelism   Present the ideas in these sentences in parallel form:

30. Mr. Hill is expected to lecture three days a week, to counsel two days a week, and must write for publication in his spare time.

31. She knows not only accounting, but she also reads Latin.

32. Both applicants had families, college degrees, and were in their thirties, with considerable accounting experience but few social connections.

33. This book was exciting, well written, and held my interest.

Revising Messages: Awkward Pointers Revise the following sentences to delete the awkward pointers:

34. The vice president in charge of sales and the production manager are responsible for the keys to 34A and 35A, respectively.

35. The keys to 34A and 35A are in executive hands, with the former belonging to the vice president in charge of sales and the latter belonging to the production manager.

36. The keys to 34A and 35A have been given to the production manager, with the aforementioned keys being gold embossed.

37. A laser printer and a dot-matrix printer were delivered to John and Megan, respectively.

Revising Messages: Dangling Modifiers Rewrite these sentences to clarify the dangling modifiers:

38. Running down the railroad tracks in a cloud of smoke, we watched the countryside glide by.

39. Lying on the shelf, Ruby saw the seashell.

40. Based on the information, I think we should buy the property.

41. Being cluttered and filthy, Sandy took the whole afternoon to clean up her desk.

Revising Messages: Noun Sequences   Rewrite the following sentences to eliminate the long strings of nouns:

42. The focus of the meeting was a discussion of the bank interest rate deregulation issue.

43. Following the government task force report recommendations, we are revising our job applicant evaluation procedures.

44. The production department quality assurance program components include employee training, supplier cooperation, and computerized detection equipment.

45. The supermarket warehouse inventory reduction plan will be implemented next month.

Revising Messages: Sentence Structure   Rearrange the following sentences to bring the subjects closer to their verbs:

46. Trudy, when she first saw the bull pawing the ground, ran.

47. It was Terri who, according to Ted, who is probably the worst gossip in the office (Tom excepted), mailed the wrong order.

48. William Oberstreet, in his book *Investment Capital Reconsidered,* writes of the mistakes that bankers through the decades have made.

49. Judy Schimmel, after passing up several sensible investment opportunities, despite the warnings of her friends and family, invested her inheritance in a jojoba plantation.

Revising Messages: Camouflaged Verbs   Rewrite each sentence so that the verbs are no longer camouflaged:

50. Adaptation to the new rules was performed easily by the employees.

51. The assessor will make a determination of the tax due.

52. Verification of the identity of the employees must be made daily.

53. The board of directors made a recommendation that Mr. Ronson be assigned to a new division.

Activities

For live links to all websites discussed in this chapter, visit this text's website at www.prenhall.com/bovee. Just log on, select Chapter 5, and click on "Featured Websites." Locate the page or the URL related to the material in the text.

1. **Analyze This Document**   Read the following document, then (1) analyze the strengths and weaknesses of each sentence, and (2) revise it so that it follows the guidelines in Chapters 3 through 5.

   I have so many questions I would like to ask you: Did you encounter any unforeseen costs when you were first starting up your franchise? Did you have trouble fitting into the franchise mold? How much say did you have in the location of your store? In its size? How long did it take you to start making a profit? How many hours a week do you work? Do you have any costs that are not covered by the franchise fee? How do you calculate royalty and advertising fees? How much say do you have in choosing suppliers? Do Subway's advertising programs satisfy your needs? How much did Subway help you in the beginning?

   As a potential franchisee, I am investigating Subway operations. Can you help me answer some of these questions? With your experience, you can provide the kind of information I need. Can you help me? I would be so grateful. You can reach me at (918) 555-9983, day or evening. My cell phone is (918) 555-8838.

   Please let me hear from you soon; I hope to make my franchise decision fairly quickly.

2. **Internet**   Visit the stock market page of Bloomberg's website at www.bloomberg.com, and evaluate the use of design in presenting the latest news. What design improvements can you suggest to enhance readability of the information posted on this page?

3. **Proofreading Messages: E-Mail**   Proofread the following e-mail message and revise it to correct any problems you find:

> Our final company orrientation of the year will be held on Dec. 20. In preparation for this sesssion, please order 20 copies of the Policy handbook, the confindentiality agreenemt, the employee benefits Manual, please let me know if you anticipate any delays in obtaining these materials.

Expand Your Knowledge

Exploring the Best of the Web

Write it Right: Tips to Help You Rethink and Revise   Are you sure that readers perceive your written message as you intended? If you want help revising a message that you're completing, use the Paradigm Online Writing Assistant (POWA). With this interactive writer's guide, you can select topics to get tips on how to edit your work, reshape your thoughts, and rewrite for clarity. Read discussions about perfecting your writing skills, and for practice, complete one of the many online activities provided to reinforce what you've learned. Or select the Forum to talk about writing. At POWA's website, www.powa.org, you'll learn how to improve the final draft of your message. Explore POWA's advice then answer the following questions:

Exercises

1. Why is it better to write out ideas in a rough format and later reread your message to revise its content? When revising your message, what questions can you ask about your writing?
2. Name the four elements of the "writing context." Imagine that you're the reader of your message. What questions might you ask?
3. When you revise a written message, what is the purpose of "tightening"? What is one way to tighten your writing as you complete a message?

Exploring the Web on Your Own

Review these chapter-related websites on your own to learn more about writing business messages.

1. Produce flawless messages by reviewing the material at the Guide to Grammar and Writing, ccc.commnet.edu/grammar.
2. Troubled by those tricky word choices that bother every writer? Not sure if "alternate" or "alternative" is the right choice? Visit the Grammar Slammer at englishplus.com/grammar and click on "Common Mistakes and Choices" for advice on dozens of common word choice dilemmas.
3. Learn the basics of page layout in Microsoft Word to make sure your documents are designed effectively. Visit office.microsoft.com, click on Assistance, find the link to browse assistance for Word, then click through the pages of advice on document formatting.

Learn Interactively

Interactive Study Guide

Go to the Companion Website at www.prenhall.com/bovee. For Chapter 5, take advantage of the interactive "Study Guide" to test your knowledge of the chapter. Get instant feedback on whether you need additional studying. Also, visit this site's "Study Hall," where you'll find an abundance of valuable resources that will help you succeed in this course.

Peak Performance Grammar and Mechanics

In Chapter 4 you were referred to the Peak Performance Grammar and Mechanics activities on the web at www.prenhall.com/onekey to improve your skill with adjectives and adverbs. For additional reinforcement in adverbs, go to the "Improve Your Grammar, Mechanics, and Usage" section that follows, and complete the "Level I: Self-Assessment" exercises.

Improve Your Grammar, Mechanics, and Usage

Level 1: Self-Assessment—Adverbs

Review Section 1.5 in the Handbook of Grammar, Mechanics, and Usage, and then look at the following 15 items.

In items 1–5, select the correct word (in italics), and write it in the space provided:

1. Their performance has been _____ (*good/well*).

2. I _____ (*sure/surely*) do not know how to help you.

3. He feels _____ (*sick/sickly*) again today.

4. Customs dogs are chosen because they smell _____ (*good/well*).

5. The redecorated offices look _____ (*good/well*).

In items 6–10, provide the correct form of the adverb in parentheses:

6. Which of the two programs computes (*fast*) _____?

7. Kate has held five jobs over 13 years, and she was (*recently*)_____ employed by Graphicon.

8. Could they be (*happily*) _____ employed than they are now?

9. Of the two we have in stock, this model is the (*well*) _____ designed.

10. Of all the arguments I've ever heard, yours is the (*logically*) _____ reasoned.

In items 10–15, rewrite the sentences to correct double negatives.

11. He doesn't seem to have none.

12. That machine is scarcely never used.

13. They can't get no replacement parts until Thursday.

14. It wasn't no different from the first event we promoted.

15. We've looked for it, and it doesn't seem to be nowhere.

Level 2: Workplace Applications

The following items contain numerous errors in grammar, capitalization, punctuation, abbreviation, number style, word division, and vocabulary. Rewrite each sentence in the space provided, correcting all errors. Write *C* in the space after any sentence that is already correct.

1. All too often, whomever leaves the most out of his cost estimate is the one who wins the bid - if you can call it winning.

2. CEO, Dennis Kozlowski, called the plan to break up Tyco a 'mistake', considering the sluggish economy, spending cutbacks, and jitters on wall street over corporate accounting.

3. Shoppers were disinterested in the Web initially because many hyped services, offered no real cost or convenience advantages over offline stores.

4. Different jobs and different customers call for different pricing, estimating, and negotiating strategies.

5. Get to know the customer and their expectations, get the customer to talk about their primary use for you're product.

6. To homeowners, who feel they have found a competent contractor who has they're best interest's at heart, price will not matter nearly as much.

7. If I was you, I would of avoided investing in large conglomerates in light of the collapse of energy trader, Enron Corp., over accounting irregularities.

8. Outdoor goods retailer REI has had significant, success with in-store kiosks that let customers choose between several types of merchandise.

9. To people in some areas of cyberspace "Advertising" is a four letter word but "Marketing" is perfectly acceptable.

10. In any business effort, making money requires planning. Strategic marketing, a good product, good customer service, considerable shrewdness—and much hard work.

11. Investors must decide weather to put their capitol into bonds or CDs.

12. Running at full capacity, millions of Nike shoes are being produced by manufacturing plants every day.

13. Metropolis' stationary has a picture of the Empire state building on it.

14. Starbucks are planning to add fruit drinks to their menu in states throughout the south.

15. Credit ratings ain't what they used to be.

Level 3: Document Critique

The following document may contain errors in grammar, punctuation, capitalization, abbreviation, number style, vocabulary, and spelling. You will also find errors relating to topics in this chapter. For example, look for long words and phrases, redundancies, dangling modifiers, camouflaged verbs, or ways to impose parallelism as you improve this memo. Correct all errors using standard proofreading marks (see Appendix C).

MEMORANDUM

TO: Metro power Employees

FROM: sUSANNAH bEECH, hR aDMINISTRATOR

SUBJECT: Ways to improve your response to technology failures

date: 22 September 2005

Dear Metro Employees:

THere is always a chance of racing toward a deadline and suddenly having equipment fall. The following includes a few proposed suggestions to help you stave off, and cope with, technical equipment and system failures:

- Stay cool. There are many technical failures so they are commonplace in business; and it is likely that your bosses and co-workers will understand that you're having a prolbem and why.

- Practice preventive maintenance: Use cleaning cloths and sprays regularly, liquids and foods should be kept away from keyboards and printers; and you should make sure systems are shut down when you leave at night.

- It is important for faster repair asistance to promptly report computer failures to Bart Stone assistant director of information services ext. 2238, who will get to your poblem as soon as it is humanly possible for him to do so but you must keep in mind that there are many people demanding his focused attention at any given time;

- If you suspect that a problem may be developing, don't wait until the crucial last moment to call for assistance.

- When a last-minute technical failure of equipment threatens to disrupt your composure you might want to consider taking a walk to calm down.

The last suggeston is perhaps the most important to keep your career on track. Lost tempers; taking out your feelings in violent outbursts, and rude language are threatening to co-workers and could result in a reprimand or other disciplinary action. By calling technical support lines for help, your equipment can stay in good working order and your temper will stay calm.

The timely implemention of repairs is important, so ask your supervisor for a list of support numbers to keep handy. Then, the next time you experience a technology giltch in your equipment or systems, there are going to be quite a few numbers handy for you to call to help you handle it as just another aspect of your business regeem.

Sincerely,

Susannah Beech

Human Resources administrator

Improving Your Writing for the Web

The web is unlike any other medium you may be required to write for. People visit the web because they want to get information efficiently. So you need to grab a reader's attention and make your main points immediately. In addition to incorporating the business-writing skills discussed in this textbook, you must modify the structure and style of your writing for this medium.

Before beginning to write for the web, understand what web users need and expect. Most are impatient, and because their time is limited, they tend to scan text rather than read it, moving between sites instead of spending a lot of time on a single webpage. This skim-and-scan style demands extreme brevity. Moreover, reading on a computer monitor is more difficult than reading from the printed page, and written information on a webpage can take up multiple screens, forcing readers to scroll through the document. Although most readers move through a printed document in a fairly linear path from beginning to end, web users move about a document and its related screens in any order they please.

A webpage has no beginning, middle, or end. Readers usually access a website from another site's link. Once readers arrive, getting an overview of a website could take hours, requiring readers to click on every page of the site. Plus, cyber content is constantly changing, so readers find it nearly impossible to quantify or gauge the depth of a site's material. In addition, links to other websites can increase the scope of a document to the entire cyberworld.

Successful web writers help their readers along by breaking information into smaller screen-sized chunks that may be accessed in any order. *Hyperlinks* are the in-text tags that allow readers to click on a screen element and be instantly transported to information somewhere else. Using hyperlinks, web writers can create three-dimensional documents that are minutely tailored to the needs of various members of their audience.

The following pointers summarize the ways that you can improve your web writing:

1. **Develop a well-organized hyperlink structure:**
   - Plan your navigation first.
   - Let readers decide how they will access the information on your site—how much they will read, in what order, and when.
   - Provide a search engine in your document.
   - Make your structure obvious with a hyperlinked site map or a table of contents at the top or bottom of your page.

2. **Modify your message style:**
   - Use a lighter, less-formal writing style.
   - Avoid clever, humorous, or jargon-filled phrases that could be misunderstood by readers from other cultures.
   - Modify your messages for global audiences, perhaps localizing material so that it reflects your customers' native language, norms, weights, measures, time, currency, and so on—making your site and material appear as if they were originally developed in the local region.

3. **Modify your message format:**
   - Break information into independent chunks (self-contained, readable pages of information) and connect the chunks with hyperlinks.
   - Don't repeat information; instead, link your reader to the page where that information already resides.
   - Don't burden others with unwanted detail. Place specific details on subsequent pages.
   - Try to keep longer pieces to a maximum of three scrollable screens, if possible.
   - Avoid randomly breaking a single, linear article (even a lengthy one) into a series of pages once you've determined its concept cannot be further subdivided.
   - Include a downloadable, printable version of longer documents for offline reading.
   - Adopt an inverted pyramid style so that readers can quickly see your topic, main idea, and conclusion.
   - Put your most important concept in the first 50 words, in case search engines pick up those words to describe your site.

4. **Help readers skim text for the information they need:**
   - Write shorter sentences and paragraphs to ease the reading process and to fit in narrow columns.
   - Cut traditional print by about 40 percent and try to keep chunks to 75 words or less.
     - ✓ Tighten your writing by avoiding passive voice, needless prepositional phrases, and wordiness.
     - ✓ Avoid tightening your prose to the point that it's choppy and abrupt.
     - ✓ Delete superfluous details, and stick to what's relevant.
   - Use bulleted and numbered lists.

- Use boldface, color, and other typographical elements conservatively.
- Write informative headings that stand on their own and are consistent in their wording.
- Write concise summaries and descriptions that are informative and crystal clear.

5. **Write effective links and place them strategically:**
   - Use a combination of textual and graphical hyperlinks, but don't overdo graphics, since they slow down document loading time.
   - Avoid self-referential terms such as "click here" or "follow this link."
   - Use absolute directions.
   - Write informative hyperlinks so that the content of subsequent pages is obvious.
   - Place your links strategically and carefully.

6. **Establish your credibility (important because anyone can post material on a website):**
   - Include your name and the name of your sponsor (if applicable) on every webpage.
   - Provide contact information (at least an e-mail address) so that readers can get in touch with you or your sponsor easily.
   - Include posting and revision dates for your information.
   - Make sure your content is error free.

Applications for Success

Writing for the Web (www.useit.com/papers/webwriting) offers you a huge amount of information on web writing. Visit this site and access research on how users read on the web, the official Sun Microsystems guidelines booklet, and links to other web-writing sites.

Do the following:

1. Select any webpage and critique the headings. Do they make sense on their own? Do they include hyperlinks? Does the designer use color or boldface effectively? What changes, if any, would you recommend?

2. Select any webpage and critique the effectiveness of the written hyperlinks. Does the designer use self-referential terms or absolute directions? Is the writing concise? Are linked words embedded in a sentence or paragraph to provide the reader with context? Are the hyperlinks placed effectively?

3. Select a short article from any print magazine or newspaper. Now rewrite the article in a format suitable for the web using the techniques discussed in this workshop. Focus on writing only one webpage. Include some hyperlinks on that page and in your article (but don't take the time to develop material for the linked page).

Brief Business Correspondence

6

Working with Letters, Memos, E-Mail, and Instant Messages

From the Real World

"Our goal is to demonstrate understanding, knowledge, professionalism, and efficiency. Accomplishing this goal takes careful planning—not only with regard to the words we use but also with regard to the form we use to convey those words. If consumers are writing to you in short grunts, you don't want to write back sounding like a novel."

—— Jeff Hagen
Director of Consumer Services
General Mills

Understanding the differences among letters, memos, e-mail, and instant messages is important.

Learning Objectives

After studying this chapter, you will be able to

1 Explain the difference between internal and external communication

2 Discuss how letters, memos, and e-mail messages differ in format

3 Summarize four techniques you can use to improve message readability

4 Distinguish between descriptive and informative headings

5 Describe four methods you can use to improve the readability of e-mail messages

6 Define e-mail etiquette and give examples

7 Name the three business message categories that determine your writing strategy

At General Mills, Jeff Hagen manages a staff of 65 full-time employees who respond to between 700,000 and 1 million contacts from consumers every year—in whatever medium consumers choose. The ability to respond to consumers in their own language is the key to Hagen's success. For instance, e-mail is typically brief and sometimes irreverent, so Hagen encourages his team to write responses that are professional but not stuffy. Hitting just the right balance is a tough line to walk, he admits. In business you need to know when to use a casual tone and when to be formal. Just as important, you need to know when to mail a letter, send a memo, or transmit an e-mail message.[1]

Using Letters, Memos, E-Mail, and Instant Messages

Although a lot of business communication is oral (taking place in face-to-face conversations, in meetings, during phone conversations, and in voice mail), a significant amount of your time will be spent writing letters, memos, and e-mail messages. Getting written information to the people who need it and receiving written information from the people who have it are easier if you understand the differences among letters, memos, and e-mail messages.

First, think about whether your message is internal or external and then whether it requires a formal format or a less formal one. Once you know which form to use, you'll want to do everything you can to improve the readability of your message. Finally, if you know what categories of messages are sent in letters, memos, and e-mail, you can adopt the appropriate writing strategy.

Internal or External Communication

Internal communication refers to the exchange of information and ideas within an organization. As an employee, you are in a position to observe things that your supervisors and co-workers cannot see: a customer's first reaction to a product display, a supplier's brief hesitation before agreeing to a delivery date, an odd whirring noise in a piece of equipment, or a slowdown in the flow of customers. Managers and co-workers need these little gems of information to do their jobs. If you don't pass that information along, nobody will—because nobody else knows.

You use memos and e-mail for the routine, day-to-day communication within the organization. Internal communication helps you do your job. It helps employees develop a clear sense of the organization's mission, identify potential problems, and react quickly to ever-changing circumstances.

Just as internal communication carries information throughout the organization, **external communication** carries it into and out of the organization. Companies constantly exchange messages with customers, vendors, distributors, competitors, investors, journalists, and community representatives. Sometimes this external communication is carefully orchestrated; at other times it occurs informally as part of routine business operations.

In addition to conveying a particular message, letters perform an important public relations function. Therefore, you use letters most frequently for external communication with outsiders. Even so, you may also use e-mail for external communication (1) in response to e-mail messages that you receive, (2) when the purpose of your message is informal, and (3) when your audience accepts e-mail as appropriate. External communication helps employees create a favorable impression of their company, plan for and respond to crises, and gather useful information (such as feedback from customers and other stakeholders).

Format Differences

Most letters, memos, and e-mail messages are relatively brief, generally less than two pages long (often less than a page for e-mail). Instant messages are even shorter. Letters are the most formal of the three. Memos and e-mail are less formal, and instant messages are the least formal of all. For in-depth format information, see Appendix A: Format and Layout of Business Documents. When trying to distinguish between these types of documents, keep the following format differences in mind.

Letters

Although the format for a letter depends on the traditions of the organization, it does have some generally accepted characteristics. For example, consider the letter in Figure 6.1. Montana's Save the Wolves Foundation seeks to raise funds for relocating wolves from other states into selected wilderness areas of Montana. The foundation tries to educate the public and garner support, so it communicates externally. Figure 6.1 is a letter from the foundation to representatives of the mass media. Comments in the left margin point out format elements.

Most business letters appear on letterhead stationery, which includes the company's name and address and other contact information. The first thing to appear after the letterhead is the date. Next comes the inside address, which identifies the person receiving the letter. And after that comes the salutation, usually in the form of *Dear Mr.* or *Ms. Last Name.* The message comes next, often running several paragraphs and sometimes running over to a second page. After the message is the complimentary close, usually *Sincerely* or *Cordially.* And last comes the signature block: space for the signature, followed by the sender's printed name and title.

Memos

Being less formal than letters, most memos begin with a title, such as *Memo, Memorandum,* or *Interoffice Correspondence.* They use *To, From, Date,* and *Subject* headings

---

Internal communication is the way employees exchange information within an organization.

Use memos and e-mail for internal communication.

External communication is the way employees exchange information with the world outside the organization.

Use letters and e-mail for external communication.

Different media have varying levels of formality:
- *Formal = letters*
- *Less formal = memos, e-mail messages*
- *Least formal = instant messages*

Letters have elements such as
- *Letterhead*
- *Date*
- *Inside address*
- *Salutation*
- *Complimentary close*
- *Signature block*

Memos have elements such as
- *Title*
- *"To, From, Date, Subject" heading*

FIGURE 6.1   A Typical Letter

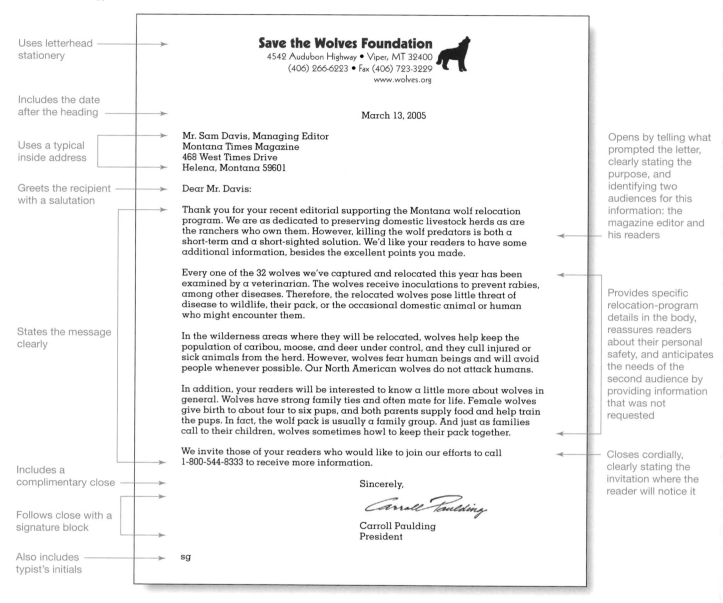

Uses letterhead stationery

Includes the date after the heading

Uses a typical inside address

Greets the recipient with a salutation

States the message clearly

Includes a complimentary close

Follows close with a signature block

Also includes typist's initials

Opens by telling what prompted the letter, clearly stating the purpose, and identifying two audiences for this information: the magazine editor and his readers

Provides specific relocation-program details in the body, reassures readers about their personal safety, and anticipates the needs of the second audience by providing information that was not requested

Closes cordially, clearly stating the invitation where the reader will notice it

---

Save the Wolves Foundation
4542 Audubon Highway • Viper, MT 32400
(406) 266-6223 • Fax (406) 723-3229
www.wolves.org

March 13, 2005

Mr. Sam Davis, Managing Editor
Montana Times Magazine
468 West Times Drive
Helena, Montana 59601

Dear Mr. Davis:

Thank you for your recent editorial supporting the Montana wolf relocation program. We are as dedicated to preserving domestic livestock herds as are the ranchers who own them. However, killing the wolf predators is both a short-term and a short-sighted solution. We'd like your readers to have some additional information, besides the excellent points you made.

Every one of the 32 wolves we've captured and relocated this year has been examined by a veterinarian. The wolves receive inoculations to prevent rabies, among other diseases. Therefore, the relocated wolves pose little threat of disease to wildlife, their pack, or the occasional domestic animal or human who might encounter them.

In the wilderness areas where they will be relocated, wolves help keep the population of caribou, moose, and deer under control, and they cull injured or sick animals from the herd. However, wolves fear human beings and will avoid people whenever possible. Our North American wolves do not attack humans.

In addition, your readers will be interested to know a little more about wolves in general. Wolves have strong family ties and often mate for life. Female wolves give birth to about four to six pups, and both parents supply food and help train the pups. In fact, the wolf pack is usually a family group. And just as families call to their children, wolves sometimes howl to keep their pack together.

We invite those of your readers who would like to join our efforts to call 1-800-544-8333 to receive more information.

Sincerely,

Carroll Paulding

Carroll Paulding
President

sg

---

to emphasize the needs of the readers (who usually have time only to skim messages). Figure 6.2 is a typical memo at Carnival Corporation (responding to a request for data on passenger capacity). The comments in the left margin point out typical memo format elements.

The Carnival writer might have chosen to respond using e-mail; however, the data being provided are clearest in table form, and tabular material comes out more reliably in print. Also, if you need to document all correspondence on a particular issue, printed memos provide paper trails that e-mail messages do not.

In general, memos lack a salutation. Good memos discuss only one topic and use a conversational tone. Memos generally have no complimentary close or signature. Because of their open construction and informal method of delivery (either interoffice mail or e-mail), memos are less private than letters.

E-Mail Messages

Like memos, e-mail messages also have a heading. The particulars of the heading depend on the e-mail program you use, but most include *To, From,* and *Subject* information, at

FIGURE 6.2   A Typical Memo

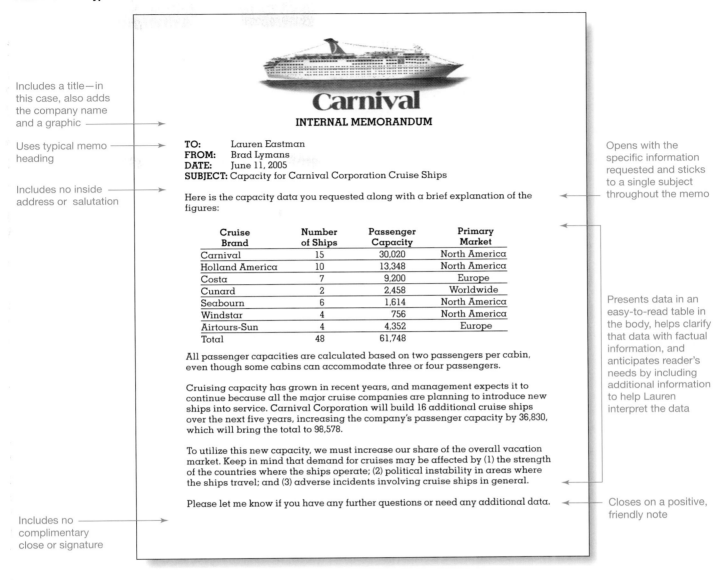

Includes a title—in this case, also adds the company name and a graphic

Uses typical memo heading

Includes no inside address or salutation

Opens with the specific information requested and sticks to a single subject throughout the memo

Presents data in an easy-to-read table in the body, helps clarify that data with factual information, and anticipates reader's needs by including additional information to help Lauren interpret the data

Closes on a positive, friendly note

Includes no complimentary close or signature

Carnival
INTERNAL MEMORANDUM

TO: Lauren Eastman
FROM: Brad Lymans
DATE: June 11, 2005
SUBJECT: Capacity for Carnival Corporation Cruise Ships

Here is the capacity data you requested along with a brief explanation of the figures:

Cruise Brand	Number of Ships	Passenger Capacity	Primary Market
Carnival	15	30,020	North America
Holland America	10	13,348	North America
Costa	7	9,200	Europe
Cunard	2	2,458	Worldwide
Seabourn	6	1,614	North America
Windstar	4	756	North America
Airtours-Sun	4	4,352	Europe
Total	48	61,748	

All passenger capacities are calculated based on two passengers per cabin, even though some cabins can accommodate three or four passengers.

Cruising capacity has grown in recent years, and management expects it to continue because all the major cruise companies are planning to introduce new ships into service. Carnival Corporation will build 16 additional cruise ships over the next five years, increasing the company's passenger capacity by 36,830, which will bring the total to 98,578.

To utilize this new capacity, we must increase our share of the overall vacation market. Keep in mind that demand for cruises may be affected by (1) the strength of the countries where the ships operate; (2) political instability in areas where the ships travel; and (3) adverse incidents involving cruise ships in general.

Please let me know if you have any further questions or need any additional data.

the very least. The heading information is brief; the *To* and *From* lines sometimes show no names or titles, just e-mail addresses. The heading also often includes information about copies and attachments. The date is automatically inserted into the document by the program. Figure 6.3 is a typical e-mail message (a request for capacity data at Carnival Corporation). The comments in the left margin point out typical e-mail format elements.

For e-mail messages, a salutation is optional; however, as you will see later in this chapter, using a greeting is highly recommended. After the salutation comes the message, followed by the complimentary close and the typed name of the sender. Because the information in the header is often extremely brief, you may want to include contact information after your name, especially if the e-mail is going outside the company.

E-mail messages have elements such as

- Heading (often brief, including information about copies and attachments)
- Salutation (optional but highly recommended)
- Complimentary closing (optional but highly recommended)
- Typed name of sender
- Contact information (optional but recommended)

Instant Messages

As speedy as e-mail can be, it sometimes isn't fast enough. Instant messaging (IM) lets you know who on your list of contacts is online at the very moment you are. Then you can send multiple messages back and forth in real time, without having to click through all the reply and send steps that e-mail requires. The format is informal, just a small window

FIGURE 6.3   A Typical E-Mail Message

Uses a typical e-mail heading that lets the reader know the purpose of the message with an informative subject line

Uses an informal salutation for e-mail to peers

Includes a brief complimentary close and a typed name

Includes contact information in case e-mail is forwarded to someone else

Always provides information on To, From, and Subject

Opens by stating the specific request for information

Communicates one clear and concise objective, in the body, and clearly states what is expected of Brad

Closes cordially, making a statement about the specific action requested

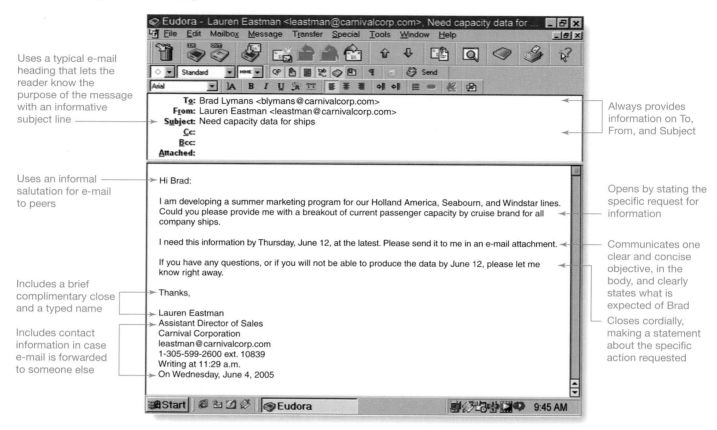

on your computer screen, which displays your entire conversation—your messages and your contact's responses (see Figure 6.4).

Instant messaging is a recent entry into the corporate communication scene, but it may soon surpass e-mail as the more commonly used tool for communicating with business associates and customers. Businesses use IM to replace in-person meetings and phone calls, to supplement online meetings, and to interact with customers. The benefits of IM in the workplace are numerous. It allows rapid response to urgent messages, costs less than both phone calls and e-mail, can mimic conversation more closely than e-mail, and is available on a wide range of devices from PCs to phones to personal digital assistants. To learn more about how IM works, check out http://computer.howstuffworks. com/instant-messaging.htm. For the latest on the business applications of IM, log on to www.instantmessagingplanet.com.

Electronic messages have a reputation for speed and informality, but you'll want to write your e-mail and instant messages carefully. Appearance, organization, and style are just as important for electronic messages as for any other type of business message. In fact, you can take several steps to improve readability and help your audience accept your short business messages.

Improving Readability in Short Business Messages

Several techniques improve your message's readability.

Most business writers know that busy readers seldom read every word of a message on their first pass. Instead, they typically skim a message, reading only certain sections carefully to assess the value of the document. If they determine that the document contains valuable information or requires a response, they will read it more carefully when time permits. You can adopt a number of techniques to make your message easier to skim:

FIGURE 6.4   A Typical Instant Message

varying sentence length, using shorter paragraphs, using lists and bullets, and adding effective headings and subheadings.

Vary Sentence Length

Although good business writers use short sentences most of the time, too many short sentences in a row can make your writing choppy. To increase interest, use a variety of both short and long sentences:

Using a variety of long, medium, and short sentences makes your message more interesting.

- Long sentences are well suited for grouping or combining ideas, listing points, and summarizing or previewing information.
- Medium-length sentences (those with about 20 words) are useful for showing the relationships among ideas.
- Short sentences emphasize important information.

Document Makeover

Improve This Letter

To practice correcting drafts of actual documents, visit www.prenhall.com/onekey on the web. Click "Document Makeovers," then click Chapter 6. You will find a letter that contains problems and errors relating to what you've learned in this chapter about formatting business messages and readability. Use the Final Draft decision tool to create an improved version of this letter. Check the message for proper format and readability issues, such as sentence length and bulleted lists.

Most good business writing has an average sentence length of 20 words or fewer. (Varying sentence length can create translation problems for international readers, so stick to short sentences for audiences abroad.)[2]

Keep Paragraphs Short

Short paragraphs are easier to read than long ones.

Most business readers are put off by large blocks of text. Unless you break up your thoughts somehow, you'll end up with a three-page paragraph that's guaranteed to intimidate even the most dedicated reader. Short paragraphs (of 100 words or fewer) are easier to read than long ones, and they make your writing look inviting.

As you write your message, try to use a variety of paragraph lengths, but be careful to use one-sentence paragraphs only occasionally and only for emphasis. When you want to package a big idea in short paragraphs, break the idea into subtopics and treat each subtopic in a separate paragraph—being careful to provide plenty of transitional elements.

Use Lists and Bullets

Lists help you focus your reader's attention on important points.

Set off important ideas in a **list**—a series of words, names, or items. Lists can show the sequence of your ideas, heighten visual impact, and help readers find your key points. In addition, lists simplify complex subjects, ease the skimming process for busy readers, and give the reader a breather.

You can separate list items with numbers, letters, or bullets (a general term for any kind of graphical element that precedes each item). Bullets are generally preferred over numbers or letters, unless the sequence of events is critical (if the steps in a process must be completed in a specific order, for example).

Introduce lists clearly.

When using lists, introduce them clearly so that people know what they're about to read. One way to introduce a list is to make it a part of the introductory sentence:

The board of directors met to discuss the revised annual budget. To keep expenses in line with declining sales, the directors voted to

- Cut everyone's salary by 10 percent
- Close the employee cafeteria
- Reduce travel expenses

If necessary, add further discussion after the lists to complete your thought. Another way to introduce a list is to use a complete introductory sentence, followed by a colon:

To accomplish our mission, our team will follow three steps:

1. Find out how many employees would use on-site day care facilities.

2. Determine how much space the day care center would require.

3. Estimate the cost of converting conference rooms for the on-site facility.

The items in a list should be in parallel form. If one list item begins with a verb, all list items should begin with a verb. If one is a noun phrase, all should be noun phrases:

Make sure list items are parallel in structure.

Avoid Nonparallel List Items	Use Parallel List Items
■ Improve our bottom line	■ Improving our bottom line
■ Identification of new foreign markets for our products	■ Identifying new foreign markets for our products
■ Global market strategies	■ Developing our global market strategies
■ Issues regarding pricing and packaging size	■ Resolving pricing and packaging issues

For additional discussion of parallelism see "Rewrite and Edit for Clarity" in Chapter 5 on page 109.

Add Headings and Subheadings

A **heading** is a brief title that cues readers in to the content of the section that follows. Headings and subheadings serve several important functions:

Headings and subheadings help readers decipher the content of your message.

- **Organization.** Headings show your reader at a glance how the document is organized. They are labels that group related paragraphs together, organizing your material into short sections.

- **Attention.** Informative, inviting, and in some cases intriguing, headings grab the reader's attention, make the copy easier to read, and help readers find the parts they need to read—or skip.

- **Connection.** Using headings and subheadings visually indicates shifts from one idea to the next, helping readers see the relationship between subordinate and main ideas.

Headings fall into two categories. **Descriptive headings** ("Cost Considerations") identify a topic but do little more. **Informative headings** ("A New Way to Cut Costs") put your reader right into the context of your message. Informative headings guide readers to think in a certain way about the topic. They also help guide your work as a writer. However, informative headings are more difficult to create. A well-written informative heading is self-contained; readers can read your headings and subheadings and understand them without reading the rest of the document. Keep your headings brief, and use parallel construction as you would for an outline, a list, or a series of words.

Informative headings help your readers understand how to think about your subject matter.

Improving Readability in E-Mail Messages

E-mail can be as informal and casual as a conversation between old friends. But it can also emulate "snail mail" by using conventional business language, a respectful style, and a more formal format—using a traditional greeting, formalized headings, and a formal closing and signature.[3] As with any business communication, how formal you make your message depends on your audience and your purpose.

Be sure to use correct spelling and proper grammar for your e-mail, indeed for all your electronic messages. Some e-mail old-timers insist that spelling, grammar, capitalization, and punctuation can take a backseat in cyberspace.[4] But in business communication, electronic messages need to be as clear and as easy to understand as possible. To improve e-mail readability even more, be sure to make your subject lines informative, make your message easy to follow, personalize your messages, and observe basic e-mail etiquette.

You can improve e-mail readability by
- *Writing informative subject lines*
- *Making messages visually easy to follow*
- *Personalizing your messages*
- *Observing basic e-mail etiquette*

Make Subject Lines Informative

To capture your audience's attention, make your subject line informative (good advice for memos as well as e-mail messages). Do more than just describe or classify message content. Build interest with key words, quotations, directions, or questions:[5]

Ineffective Subject Line	Effective Subject Line
July sales figures	Send figures for July sales
Tomorrow's meeting	Bring consultant's report to Friday's meeting
Marketing report	Need budget for marketing report
Employee parking	Revised resurfacing schedule for parking lot
Status report	Warehouse remodeling is on schedule

If you are exchanging multiple e-mails with someone on the same topic, be sure to periodically modify the subject line of your message to reflect the revised message content. Most e-mail programs will copy the subject line when you click the Reply button. Multiple messages in your e-mail electronic files with the same subject line can be confusing. Moreover, they may have absolutely nothing to do with the original topic. Modifying the subject line with each new response will prevent reader confusion and can make it easier to locate a message at a later date.

Make Your E-Mail Messages Easy to Follow

Avoid lines that run off screen or wrap oddly by using the Enter key to limit lines to 80 characters (60 if e-mail will be forwarded). Avoid styled text (boldface, italics), unless your receiver's system can read it.[6] Write short, focused, logically organized paragraphs. And try to limit e-mail to one screen; otherwise, write like a reporter—starting with the "headline" and adding detail in descending order of importance.[7] That way you'll be sure to get your point across as early as possible, in case your reader doesn't have the time or interest to finish reading your message.

Personalize E-Mail Messages

Adding a salutation to your e-mail message makes it more personal. Naturally, whether you use a formal greeting (*Dear Professor Ingersol*) or a more casual one (*Hi Marty*) depends on your audience and your purpose. Your complimentary closing and signature also personalize your e-mail message. In most cases, use simple closings, such as *Thanks* or *Regards,* rather than more traditional business closings such as *Sincerely yours.* However, you may want to use a more formal closing for international e-mail.

For your signature, you can simply type your name on a separate line. Or you may want to use a *signature file,* a short identifier that can include your name, company, postal address, fax number, other e-mail addresses, and so on. You can also use a digital copy of your handwritten signature, which is becoming acceptable as legal proof in business transactions, especially when accompanied by the date stamp that is automatically inserted by your e-mail program.

Observe Basic E-Mail Etiquette

The best business communicators know how to communicate quickly and courteously. They know how to refrain from putting into writing anything that could come back to haunt them, and they know how important it is to proofread e-mail messages before sending them. Following basic e-mail etiquette means being courteous, brief, and careful.

Be Courteous

Common courtesy is an important consideration when sending e-mail. Because e-mail creates a false sense of intimacy, it is tempting to write less carefully than you would when composing a memo or letter. However, you should always think about how your messages affect your various audiences; that includes thinking about more than just message content.

Being courteous pertains to more than just what you write; it also pertains to how you go about writing.

- **Compose your message offline.** Consider drafting your message in a word processor and then cutting and pasting it into your e-mail. This way, you'll conserve network resources and save significant Internet connection charges.
- **Send only necessary messages.** Do your best not to add to your audience's information overload.
- **Know who your audience is.** Before clicking on the Send button, double-check your addressees to make sure you've included everyone necessary and no one else.
- **Know your audience's culture.** Don't assume that your audience reads and understands your language. Make sure you know the culture and language of your readers before you begin to write.
- **Be clear about time.** In international e-mail, be sure to use a 24-hour military time format (say 18:00 instead of 6:00 p.m.). Also, indicate the appropriate time zone—Eastern Standard Time (EST), Pacific Daylight Time (PDT), and so on.
- **Respect your audience's schedule.** Identify messages that require no response by including words such as "for your information only" in your subject line or opening comments. Moreover, don't waste time sending jokes or chain letters.
- **Don't flame.** A negative e-mail message containing insensitive, insulting, or critical comments is called a *flame*. If you're upset about something or angry with someone, compose yourself before composing your e-mail.
- **Use the priority feature with care.** Many e-mail programs allow you to assign a priority to your message, such as *high, normal,* or *low.* Make sure the priority assigned to your message matches its urgency.

Be Brief

Make sure that you craft tight, meaningful messages. Cover only what is necessary. Identify the issue, add the relevant facts, suggest a resolution, offer possible obstacles, present a timetable for response, and ask for agreement.

Avoid wasting readers' time.

- **Narrow your scope.** Stick to one purpose. If you find yourself with two or three purposes, write separate e-mails. This narrow scope not only helps your readers focus on your message but also facilitates filing and forwarding.
- **Write short messages.** Short, direct messages have a much better chance of being understood and acted on than long, roundabout ones. However, don't edit your e-mail messages so much that your readers cannot understand them.
- **Rely on short sentences.** Long sentences are particularly hard to read on a computer screen. Whenever possible, break up long sentences into short, concise ones. If you need to write longer sentences now and then, make sure they are logically and clearly written.

Be Careful

E-mail's speed is its greatest benefit and can also be its greatest drawback. When we sit down at the keyboard, our mind-set is typically to empty our e-mail box and move on to other business. E-mail prompts such quick responses that we forget to organize our thoughts. Successful e-mail is written carefully.

Write your e-mail carefully, but also be careful about addressing your e-mail messages and replying to e-mail messages.

- **Be sure you hit the right reply button.** When you receive an e-mail message, it may be addressed to you alone or to dozens of others. It may be "copied" to others or "blind copied" to recipients you don't know about. Make sure you hit the correct reply button so that only intended recipients receive your message.

- **When you choose to "reply to all," do so wisely.** Even though the original e-mail sender may think it's a good idea to update everyone on the team, not all team members may need to see every recipient's reply.

- **Understand the use of the cc and bcc fields.** When you add addresses to the cc (courtesy copy) field, make sure that you want all recipients to see who is receiving a copy of your message. Otherwise, use the bcc (blind courtesy copy) field.

- **Slow down.** Every word matters. Even though the fast pace of technology encourages us to respond to others instantaneously, take your time and proceed at your own comfortable pace. The other party will wait.

- **Reread your message.** Avoid sending important e-mail messages immediately after you write them. Ideally, reread them the next morning and make changes.

- **Edit e-mail carefully.** Double-check your e-mail message before sending it. Proofread every e-mail message for completeness, content, fluency, punctuation, and grammar. Finally, make sure that promised documents are indeed attached.

- **Be aware of the permanence of e-mail.** Even after you delete an e-mail message, it can still exist on hard drives and storage devices, both yours and your receiver's. Deleted messages can be not only recovered but also used as court evidence against you. Therefore, send only necessary e-mail messages that have been prepared responsibly.

Understanding the Categories of Brief Messages

Message categories dictate how you approach the opening, body, and close of your short business message.

Whether you send letters, memos, or e-mail messages, all your messages have three parts: the opening, the body, and the close. How you handle these three parts depends on the type of message you're sending: (1) routine, good-news, and goodwill; (2) bad-news; or (3) persuasive.

Routine, Good-News, and Goodwill Messages

The most straightforward business messages are routine, good-news, and goodwill messages. Your readers will most likely be pleased to hear from you, or at the very least, they will be neutral. In the opening, state your main idea directly. The body of your message provides all necessary details. The close is cordial, emphasizing your good news or making a statement about the specific action desired. (Look again at Figures 6.1 on page 142, 6.2 on page 143, and 6.3 on page 144. The comments in the right-hand margins point out how the opening, body, and close are handled in these routine messages.) Routine, good-news, and goodwill messages are discussed in greater detail in Chapter 7.

Bad-News Messages

Successful communicators take a little extra care with their bad-news messages. If your audience will be disappointed, it may be best to use the indirect approach—putting the evidence first and the main idea later. Open with a neutral statement that acts as a transition to the reasons for the bad news. In the body, give the reasons that justify a negative answer before stating or implying the bad news. Your close must always be cordial. Bad-news messages are discussed further in Chapter 8.

Persuasive Messages

An indirect approach is also useful when you know that your audience will resist your message (will be uninterested in your request or unwilling to comply without extra coaxing). Before you can persuade people to do something, you must capture their attention. In the opening, mention a possible benefit, referring to a problem that the recipient might have, posing a question, or mentioning an interesting statistic. In the body, build interest in the subject and arouse your readers' desire to comply. Once you have them thinking, you can introduce your main idea. The close is cordial and requests the desired action. Persuasive messages are discussed at greater length in Chapter 9.

Reviewing Key Points

This chapter introduces the forms and uses of business letters, memos, e-mail messages, and instant messages (IM). The chapter explains when to send a letter, a memo, an e-mail, or an instant message, based on whether the message is intended for internal or external communication and whether the message form suits the formality of the situation.

This chapter helps you improve the overall readability of short business messages, by using sentences of varying length, short paragraphs, lists and bullets, and headings and subheadings. It explains how to improve e-mail readability by making your subject line informative, personalizing your message, making your message easy to follow, and observing basic e-mail etiquette. Finally, the chapter introduces you to the categories of business messages: routine, good-news, and goodwill messages; bad-news messages; and persuasive messages.

The next chapter focuses on routine, good-news, and goodwill messages. You learn how to apply the three-step writing process to routine messages. The chapter explains the strategies for writing routine requests, routine replies, and other positive messages. Finally, the chapter introduces you to specific types of messages that fall into this category.

Test Your Knowledge

1. Which message forms are used for internal communication? Why?

2. Which message forms are used for external communication? Why?

3. What format elements make letters more formal than memos and e-mail?

4. How can you increase the readability of your short business messages?

5. What functions do headings serve?

6. How can you increase the readability of your e-mail messages?

7. How do you use the subject line in an e-mail?

8. In what ways can you be courteous when preparing your e-mail messages?

9. Besides wording the content of your e-mail message, what other steps should you take to be careful?

10. What three message categories affect your short business messages? How?

Apply Your Knowledge

1. Why do you think good internal communication improves employee attitudes and performance? Explain briefly.

2. What do you think is important about matching the formality of your message to the formality of the situation and audience expectations?

3. Does it matter whether you personalize your e-mail messages? Please explain.

4. Is it ever okay to use an indirect approach when writing e-mail? How can you put off the bad news when you have to state your purpose in the subject line? Explain.

5. Ethical Choices   Your boss wants you to send a message to the production staff, thanking all six members for their hard work and overtime to get the new manufacturing line set up and running on schedule. Your boss has been working a lot of overtime herself; she's been under a lot of pressure, and it's beginning to show. She wants to send the thank-you message by e-mail and asks you to work on the wording. You think each member of the production staff should receive a formal letter to keep for future promotions or other jobs. You know your boss won't like being interrupted about an issue that she thinks is off her desk, and you know how valuable her time is.
   a. Should you draft the letter and produce six copies so that you don't have to bother your boss?
   b. Should you simply draft the e-mail message as requested to save everyone time?
   c. Should you discuss the issue with your boss, regardless of taking her away from the tasks she so desperately needs to get done?

Practice Your Knowledge

Exercises for Perfecting Your Writing

Form and Audience   Barbara Marquardt is in charge of public relations for a cruise line that operates out of Miami. She is shocked to read a letter in a local newspaper from a disgruntled passenger, complaining about the service and entertainment on a recent cruise. Marquardt will have to respond to these publicized criticisms in some way.

1. What audiences will she need to consider in her response?

2. For each of these audiences, should Marquardt send her message via letter, memo, or e-mail?

Teamwork   Your team has been studying a new method for testing the durability of your company's electric hand tools. Now your team needs to summarize the findings in three separate reports: (a) one for company administrators who will decide whether to purchase the new testing equipment needed for this new method, (b) one for company engineers who design and develop the hand tools, and (c) one for the trainers from the test equipment company, who will be showing your workers how to use the new testing equipment. Your team leader emphasizes that all three reports need to reach receivers so that your team can receive responses in less than a month. Working with at least two other students, answer the following questions for each of the three reports:

3. Should your team send the report by letter, memo, or e-mail?
   a. Administrators
   b. Engineers
   c. Trainers

4. Should the language be formal or conversational?
    a. Administrators
    b. Engineers
    c. Trainers

Using Bullets   Rewrite the following paragraph using a bulleted list:

5. With our alarm system, you'll have a 24-hour security guard who signals the police when there is any indication of an intruder. You'll also appreciate the computerized scanning device that determines exactly where and when the intrusion occurred. No need to worry about electrical failure, either, thanks to our backup response unit.[8]

Keeping Paragraphs Short   Using proofreading marks, indicate where to break the following paragraph into shorter paragraphs:

6. Donner Corporation faced a major transformation, growing from a small, single-product company to a large, broadly based corporation in just three years. This changeover involved much more than simply adding on to the plant and hiring more people, because the quality of the existing staff and products was not good enough for a first-rate operation. The task therefore required both physical expansion and quality improvement. The physical expansion alone represented a major undertaking. The investment in facilities required $18 million. Over a three-year period, the organization spent more on the new plant and equipment than it had spent in the past 17 years of its operation. To raise its competitive capability, the company had to develop new programs and organizational units and, at the same time, expand and upgrade its existing operations. It also needed to double the size of its staff by recruiting high-caliber people from many fields. This staffing had to be accomplished in an increasingly competitive labor market and without benefit of an experienced human resources department.

Varying Sentence Length   Using proofreading marks, revise the following paragraph to vary the length of the sentences and to shorten the paragraph so that readers find it more readable:

7. Although major league baseball remains popular, more people are attending minor league baseball games because they can spend less on admission, snacks, and parking and still enjoy the excitement of America's pastime. Connecticut, for example, has three AA minor league teams, including the New Haven Ravens, who are affiliated with the St. Louis Cardinals; the Norwich Navigators, who are affiliated with the New York Yankees; and the New Britain Rock Cats, who are affiliated with the Minnesota Twins. These teams play in relatively small stadiums, so fans are close enough to see and hear everything, from the swing of the bat connecting with the ball to the thud of the ball landing in the outfielder's glove. Best of all, the cost of a family outing to see rising stars play in a local minor league game is just a fraction of what the family would spend to attend a major league game in a much larger, more crowded stadium.

Making Subject Lines Informative   Use your imagination to make the following subject lines more informative:

8. New budget figures

9. Your opinion on our current marketing brochure

10. Production schedule

Activities

For live links to all websites discussed in this chapter, visit this text's website at www.prenhall.com/bovee. Just log on, select Chapter 6, and click on "Featured Websites." Locate the page or the URL related to the material in the text.

1. **Analyze This Document**   Read the following document, then (1) analyze the strengths and weaknesses of each sentence, and (2) revise it so that it follows the guidelines in Chapters 3 through 6.

   Dear Ms. Giraud:

   Enclosed herewith please find the manuscript for your book, *Careers in Woolgathering*. After perusing the first two chapters of your 1,500-page manuscript, I was forced to conclude that the subject matter, handicrafts and artwork using wool fibers, is not coincident with the publishing program of Framingham Press, which to this date has issued only works on business endeavors, avoiding all other topics completely.

   Although our firm is unable to consider your impressive work at the present time, I have taken the liberty of recording some comments on some of the pages. I am of the opinion that any feedback that a writer can obtain from those well versed in the publishing realm can only serve to improve the writer's authorial skills.

   In view of the fact that your residence is in the Boston area, might I suggest that you secure an appointment with someone of high editorial stature at the Cambridge Heritage Press, which I believe might have something of an interest in works of the nature you have produced.

   Wishing you the best of luck in your literary endeavors, I remain

   Arthur J. Cogswell

   Editor

2. **Analyze This Document**   Read the following document, then (1) analyze the strengths and weaknesses of each sentence, and (2) revise it so that it follows the guidelines in Chapters 3 through 6.

   For delicious, air-popped popcorn, please read the following instructions: The popper is designed to pop 1/2 cup of popcorn kernels at one time. Never add more than 1/2 cup. A half cup of corn will produce three to four quarts of popcorn. More batches may be made separately after completion of the first batch. Popcorn is popped by hot air. Oil or shortening is not needed for popping corn. Add only popcorn kernels to the popping chamber. Standard grades of popcorn are recommended for use. Premium or gourmet-type popping corns may be used. Ingredients such as oil, shortening, butter, margarine, or salt should never be added to the popping chamber. The popper, with popping chute in position, may be preheated for two minutes before adding the corn. Turn the popper off before adding the corn. Use electricity safely and wisely. Observe safety precautions when using the popper. Do not touch the popper when it is hot. The popper should not be left unattended when it is plugged into an outlet. Do not use the popper if it or its cord has been damaged. Do not use the popper if it is not working properly. Before using the first time, wash the chute and butter/measuring cup in hot soapy water. Use a dishcloth or sponge. Wipe the outside of the popper base. Use a damp cloth. Dry the base. Do not immerse the popper base in water or other liquid. Replace the chute and butter/measuring cup. The popper is ready to use.

3. Planning a Memo: Learn While You Earn—Memo Announcing Burger King's Educational Benefits

Herb Schervish, owner of a Burger King store in Detroit's downtown Renaissance Center, is worried about employee turnover. He needs to keep 50 people on the payroll to operate the outlet, but recruiting and retaining those people is tough. The average employee leaves after about seven months, so Schervish has to hire and train 90 people a year just to maintain a 50-person crew. At a cost of $1,500 per hire, the price tag for all that turnover is approximately $60,000 a year.

Schervish knows that a lot of his best employees quit because they think that flipping burgers is a dead-end job. But what if it weren't a dead end job? What if a person could really get someplace flipping burgers? What if Schervish offered to pay his employees' way through college if they remained with the store? Would that keep them behind the counter?

He's decided to give educational incentives a try. Employees who choose to participate will continue to earn their usual salary, but they will also get free books and college tuition, keyed to the number of hours they work each week. Those who work from 10 to 15 hours a week can take one free course at nearby Wayne County Community College; those who work 16 to 25 hours can take two courses; and those who work 26 to 40 hours can take three courses. The program is open to all employees, regardless of how long they have worked for Burger King, but no one is obligated to participate.

If you were Herb Schervish, or if you worked for him, how would you plan and write a memo announcing the new educational incentives? The purpose is clear (to inform employees about the new offer), the audience has already been defined (all Renaissance Center Burger King employees), and the medium has been chosen (a written memo). Now use the following questions to continue your planning, choosing the best answer for each one. Then, creating sentences of your own, draft the memo based on what you've learned from this planning exercise.

a. Which sentence best expresses the memo's main idea?
  1. Turnover at the Renaissance Center Burger King costs approximately $60,000 a year.
  2. Flipping burgers doesn't have to be a dead-end job.
  3. The Renaissance Center Burger King is offering its employees an exciting new educational program.
  4. The new educational incentive program is open to all employees, no matter how long they've worked for Burger King.

b. Which of these sentences will help you establish a good relationship with your audience?
  1. We are hoping that many of you will take advantage of the new program because it will reduce our turnover.
  2. Employees need not attend college to continue working for us.
  3. We hope that you will find the program useful.
  4. Now you can earn free college tuition while you work at Burger King.

c. What must the body of your message accomplish? (Choose all that apply.)
  1. Tell employees how to take advantage of the educational offer.
  2. Explain how working hours relate to tuition payments.

3. Describe how Mr. Schervish came up with his idea.
4. Influence employees to attend college.

   d. Which of the following methods will be best for conveying the relationship between hours worked and tuition paid?
      1. A two-column table with the headings: "Those Who Work" (listing hours per week) and "May Take" (listing number of courses paid for).
      2. A paragraph explaining the connection between hours worked and courses paid for.
      3. A bulleted list with parallel entries such as, "If you work 10-15 hours, you'll get one free course; If you work 16-25 hours, you'll get two free courses"; etc.
      4. A paragraph suggesting that details can be obtained from Mr. Schervish's office for those interested in taking advantage of the program.

   e. To close the memo, which of the following sentences is the best choice?
      1. We hope you'll take advantage of this offer, since doing so will help us reduce our turnover problem.
      2. You don't have to take college courses to continue working for us.
      3. I'll be happy to answer any questions you might have about how working for Burger King can help you earn free college tuition; just ask me.
      4. If you're thinking of quitting, this may give you second thoughts.

Now imagine that you are Herb Schervish and draft your own memo in your own words.

4. Revising a Memo: Break-Time Blues—Memo Requesting a New Employee Procedure The following memo contains numerous errors related to what you've learned about planning and writing business messages. First, list the flaws you find in this version. Then follow the steps below to plan and write a better memo:

MEMO

TO: Billing Department

FROM: Felicia August, Sr. Supervisor

DATE: December 28, 2005

SUBJECT: Compliance with new break procedure

Some of you may not like the rules about break times; however, we determined that keeping track of employees while they took breaks at times they determined rather than regular breaks at prescribed times was not working as well as we would have liked it to work. The new rules are not going to be an option. If you do not follow the new rules, you could be docked from your pay for hours when you turned up missing, since your direct supervisor will not be able to tell whether you were on a "break" or not and will assume that you have walked away from your job. We cannot be responsible for any errors that result from your inattentiveness to the new rules. I have already heard complaints from some of you and I hope this memo will end this issue once and for all. The decision has already been made.

Starting Monday, January 1, you will all be required to take a regular 15-minute break in the morning and again in the afternoon, and a regular thirty-minute lunch at the times specified by your supervisor, NOT when you think you need a break or when you "get around to it."

There will be no exceptions to this new rule!

   a. Describe the flaws you discovered in this memorandum:
   b. Develop a plan for rewriting the memo. Use the following steps to organize your efforts before you begin writing:
      1. Determine the purpose
      2. Identify and analyze your audience
      3. Define the main idea
      4. Outline the major supporting points
      5. Choose between a direct and an indirect approach

   c. Now rewrite the memo. Don't forget to leave ample time for revision of your own work before you turn it in.

5. Revising a Memo: Moving Day—Memo Informing Employees about an Office Relocation From what you've learned about planning and writing business messages, you should be able to identify numerous errors made by the writer of the following memo. List them below, then plan and write a better memo, following the guidelines given.

MEMORANDUM

TO: All Office Personnel

FROM: David Burke, Manager

DATE: September 27, 2005

SUBJECT: Get Ready

We are hoping to be back at work soon, with everything running smoothly, same production schedule and no late projects or missed deadlines. So you need to clean out your desk, put your stuff in boxes, and clean off the walls. You can put the items you had up on your walls in boxes, also.

We have provided boxes. The move will happen this weekend. We'll be in our new offices when you arrive on Monday.

We will not be responsible for personal belongings during the move.

nd

   a. Describe the flaws you discovered in this memorandum:
   b. Develop a plan for rewriting the memo. Use the following steps to organize your efforts before you begin writing:

1. Determine the purpose
2. Identify and analyze your audience
3. Define the main idea
4. Outline the major supporting points
5. Choose between direct and indirect approaches

c. Now rewrite the memo. Don't forget to leave ample time for revision of your own work before you turn it in.

Expand Your Knowledge

Exploring the Best of the Web

Improve Your Use of E-Mail   You've probably used e-mail for personal communication, but writing business e-mail can be both risky and daunting. Before you begin, brush up your skills with Mary Houten-Kemp's Everything E-Mail website at http://everythingemail.net/email_help_tips.html. You'll learn "Netiquette" (network etiquette) standards for some of the more advanced applications of e-mail. You'll also find simple technical advice on how to make your messages readable in all types of e-mail programs, how to attach documents, and how to include URLs (website addresses) as links that your readers can follow. Also, tips on style and usage help you convey a professional image, free of blunders that might offend business e-mail veterans.

Exercises

1. When is it okay to promote your business in an e-mail discussion group? If you break this rule, what do you think might happen?
2. What's wrong with using common e-mail jargon and abbreviations in business e-mail, such as BTW (by the way) or IMHO (in my humble opinion)?

3. What is an *autoresponder?* If you're operating a website, how might it improve the effectiveness of your e-mail communication? Can you think of situations in which it might work against your business interests?

Exploring the Web on Your Own

Review these chapter-related websites on your own to learn more about writing business messages.

1. Become fluent in your e-mail usage, from basic set-up to advanced techniques, by taking the tutorial at http://www.webteacher.org/home-windows/index.html. On the homepage, click "Communicating," then select "E-mail."
2. Master e-mail's unique challenges by studying suggestions for developing clear content, using special cues, and creating context at A Beginner's Guide to Effective E-Mail, www.webfoot.com/advice/email.top.html.
3. Gain more insight into the parts of a memo and their effective use by reading the handbook notes at www.ecf.utoronto.ca/%7ewriting/handbook-memo.html.

Learn Interactively

Interactive Study Guide

Go to the Companion Website at www.prenhall.com/bovee. For Chapter 6, take advantage of the interactive "Study Guide" to test your knowledge of the chapter. Get instant feedback on whether you need additional studying. Also, visit this site's "Study Hall," where you'll find an abundance of valuable resources that will help you succeed in this course.

Peak Performance Grammar and Mechanics

To improve your skill with prepositions, conjunctions, and articles, visit www.prenhall.com/onekey, click "Peak Performance Grammar and Mechanics," click "Grammar Basics," and then click "prepositions, conjunctions, and articles." Take the Pretest to determine whether you have any weak areas. Then review those areas in the Refresher Course. Take the Follow-Up Test to check your grasp of prepositions, conjunctions, and articles. For an extra challenge or advanced practice, take the Advanced Test. Finally, for additional reinforcement in prepositions, conjunctions, and articles, go to the "Improve Your Grammar, Mechanics, and Usage" section that follows, and complete the "Level 1: Self-Assessment" exercises.

CASES

Apply each step in Figure 3.1 on page 54 to the following cases, as assigned by your instructor:

E-MAIL SKILLS 1. No exaggeration: Short e-mail describing internship duties

You've been laboring all summer at an internship, learning how business is conducted. You've done work nobody else wanted to do, but that's okay. Even the smallest tasks can make a good impression on your future résumé.

This morning, your supervisor asks you to write a description of the job you've been doing. "Include everything, even the filing," she suggests, "and address it to me in an e-mail message."

She says a future boss might assign such a task prior to a performance review. "You can practice describing your work without exaggeration—or too much modesty," she says, smiling.

Your task: Using good techniques for short messages and relying on your real-life work experience, write an e-mail that will impress your supervisor.

WEB SKILLS 2. Satisfaction guaranteed: Letter from L.L. Bean granting a claim

One of the nicest things about working in customer service for sporting goods and clothing retailer L.L. Bean is that company policy guarantees satisfaction, "no questions asked." This means you always get to say yes to angry customers who want a refund.

In your hand is a package from Arvin Bummel (212 North Star, Traverse City, MI 49684). You open it to find (a) one pair of wool covert twill trousers, stiff and shrunken, (b) a Maine guide shirt (regular), also two sizes smaller than it should be, and (c) an angry letter from Mr. Bummel saying the clothes were ruined the first time he washed them.

You're not surprised, since they all clearly say, "Dry Clean Only."

Your task: Write a letter to Mr. Bummel granting him a refund, to be credited to his MasterCard. Visit the L.L. Bean website, www.llbean.com, to verify current prices and to find suggestions for washable clothing he might want to try. But remember not to blame him in your letter; an L.L. Bean customer is always right.

TEAM SKILLS 3. Measuring suppliers: Memo requesting reviews at Microsoft

Microsoft evaluates employees regularly to determine their performance—so why not do the same with the independent contractors the company hires to perform key functions? Nearly every department uses outside providers these days—a practice called *outsourcing*. So if there's a gap between what Microsoft expects from contractors and what the contractors actually deliver, shouldn't Microsoft tell them how they can improve their performance?

You've been discussing these questions all morning in a meeting with other members of the Employee Services Group. Your boss is convinced that regular reviews of independent contractors are essential.

"It's all about improving clarity in terms of goals and expectations," he says, adding that if contractors receive constructive feedback, Microsoft can develop good relationships with them instead of having to look for new service suppliers all the time.

Your boss assigns your team the task of informing all Microsoft departments that they'll be required to evaluate subcontractors every six months, beginning immediately. The goal of the review is to determine the performance of independent contractors so that Microsoft can (1) give them constructive feedback and continue a strong relationship or (2) end the relationship if service is substandard. Departments will need to rate each contractor on a scale of 1 (poor) to 5 (excellent) for each of several factors that your group is going to determine. Departments will be sending their reports to Roxanna Frost, group program manager for Microsoft's Executive Management and Development Group.

Your task: Working as a team with your classmates, develop a list of factors that will help you rate the overall service of independent contractors. You'll need to consider "cost," "quality of work," "innovation," "delivery," and other factors similar to those you'd encounter in a job performance review. Then compose a memo to all Microsoft department managers: explain the new review requirements and include your list of factors to be rated on the 1-to-5 scale.[9]

4. Pizza promises: Message from an unknown parent, VF Corporation

The human relations director at VF Corporation is grinning at you. "We can't let them go on in ignorance, and I know just what will get their attention."

As his assistant, you're listening to your boss defeat a problem. A spot survey taken yesterday showed that none of the 40,000 line workers at VF's subsidiaries recognized the corporate parent's name. They didn't even know they had a parent company. They're working in factories that make Lee, Wrangler, and other clothing brands, and those are the only names they know.

Your task: You're to write an e-mail message to be sent to all 40,000 employees, explaining that tomorrow, 15,000 pizzas will be delivered to their factories at lunchtime, compliments of their corporate parent, VF Corporation.[10]

5. Wakeboard mania: Letter from Performance Ski & Surf inquiring about availability

Your boss, Bill Porter, owner of Performance Ski & Surf in Orlando, Florida, hasn't seen a sport this popular since in-line skating took off.

"I hope these kids don't get hurt trying to imitate the pros," Porter says. You're both admiring a picture of professional wakeboarder Dean Lavelle catching air as he trails behind a boat on nearby Lake Butler. He's 15 feet in the air, with the short, stubby fiberglass board strapped to his feet—only he's upside down. His grimace shows the flip isn't as easy as it looks.

"Don't worry," you say, admiring Lavelle's skill. "Extreme sports are hot. Think of snowboarding. I guarantee, you'll see wakeboarding at the Olympics soon."

"Well, meanwhile, we've got to keep these Wake Techs, Neptunes, and Full Tilts in stock," Porter replies. "They're outselling traditional water skis 20 to 1."

Your task: Draft a letter Porter can send to manufacturers to inquire about availability throughout Florida's busy winter season. It's summer now and you're well stocked, but when other states' summer ends, your sales will only increase.

6. Nap time: Memo announcing new sleeping room at Phidias & Associates

"We're going to do what?" you ask in astonishment. But your boss is standing over your desk and he isn't smiling. Jonas T. Phidias is senior partner of Phidias & Associates, a San Francisco architectural firm, and he's completely serious.

"A nap room," he says somewhat impatiently. "We've hired a subcontractor to convert those two back offices that we haven't been using. You know what pressures our people are under to handle the stress of long hours and still be cre-

ative. Well, we'll soon be offering them the opportunity to rejuvenate with a quick, creative nap."

From his snappish tone, you realize that your response wasn't what he had expected. Quickly you compose yourself. As you think about it, his idea makes a lot of sense. You've felt the need yourself—after working late on a rush job, you've wondered how you're supposed to be creatively inspired when you can barely get your eyes to focus. "Why, naps could be great!" you finally manage.

"Yes," he interrupts before you can go on. "Thomas Edison knew the creative value of a quick nap. I've just read *The Art of Napping* by William A. Anthony, and the benefits of a nap room are too great to ignore."

"Other companies are proving that naps can improve employees' mental function sufficiently to affect the bottom line. I've decided that no matter what they think of it, Phidias & Associates employees are going to take naps during working hours. Draft a memo to tell them of my decision, and I want no arguments from them!" he instructs as he strides away.

Your task: As Phidias's assistant, write a straightforward memo informing employees that the new "nap room" will be ready for their convenience in approximately three weeks, and that they will be expected to make good use of it. Try to keep humor out of your memo, since it will be sent from Jonas T. Phidias.

7. Environmental planning: E-mail announcing a committee meeting

You've probably worked as a volunteer on a committee or with team members for class assignments. You know how hard it is to get a diverse group of individuals together for a productive meeting. Maybe you've tried different locations—one member's home, or a table at the library. This time you're going to suggest a local restaurant.

The committee you're leading is a volunteer group planning a trash-clearing project at an area park. Your meeting goal is to brainstorm ways to encourage public participation in this environmental event, to be held next Earth Day.

Your task: Develop a short e-mail message telling committee members about the meeting. Include time, date, duration, and location (choose a place you know). Mention the meeting goal to encourage attendance.

8. Mercedes merchandise: Letter announcing exclusive online gift shop

Mercedes-Benz owners take their accessories seriously, which is why you get angry letters when they buy fake Mercedes merchandise produced by "sweatshop entrepreneurs," as your boss calls them. Too often, these unauthorized imitations fall apart, and it's Mercedes' high-class image that suffers.

That's why Mercedes started producing and promoting its own high-quality accessories, from T-shirts and toddler's jumpers to travel alarm clocks. First the company hired top-of-the-line manufacturers and designers to produce a glossy, full-color catalog of "Mercedes-Benz Personal and Automotive Accessories." Now the catalog has moved online.

At **www.mbusi.com/miva/merchant.mv**, homepage for the Mercedes manufacturing plant in Tuscaloosa, Alabama, shoppers can follow links to the online gift shop. But first they need to know it exists.

Your task: As assistant for Steve Beaty, vice president of accessories marketing, you're to draft an informative letter to Mercedes owners telling them about the online gift shop. Visit the website to learn more about it, then write the letter using a style you think suits the car manufacturer's image.

■E-MAIL SKILLS 9. Bolga boo-boo: E-mail to Getrade (Ghana) Ltd. from Pier 1 Imports

When you were hired as an assistant buyer for Pier 1 Imports, you thought it would be an exciting introduction to the import-export business—the job you've always dreamed about. What a romantic way to earn a living—traveling overseas, buying products, and then shipping them back to the United States for sale. But now you've learned some of the realities of the job, and your romantic ideas are fading.

For example, Pier 1 sent a buyer to Accra, Ghana, to find local handicrafts to satisfy your customers' unquenchable thirst for African art. So far the local entrepreneurs are having trouble meeting the demand from large-quantity buyers like Pier 1 (and your rival, Cost Plus). A good example of what's been going wrong is the shipment that just arrived from Getrade (Ghana) Ltd., one of your best Ghanaian suppliers. You sympathize with Ladi Nylander, chairman and managing director of Getrade, who is trying hard to adapt to the specific tastes of his U.S. buyers. He's hiring local artisans to carve, shape, and weave all sorts of artifacts—often from designs provided by Pier 1.

Pier 1 customers love bowl-shaped Bolga baskets, traditionally woven by the Fra-fra people of northern Ghana. You

can't keep the baskets in stock, so this was to be a huge shipment—3,000 Bolga baskets. Your order requested 1,000 green, 1,000 yellow, and 1,000 magenta baskets in the traditional shape.

However, when the order came in, you found 3,000 mixed-color, flat Bolga baskets. Your overseas buyer reported that the Body Shop had ordered baskets similar to yours but with mixed-color patterns and a flatter shape. Pier 1 may have received the Body Shop's order by mistake.

Your task: As assistant buyer, you need to send an e-mail message to Nylander at **Nylander@Getrade.co.za**, informing him of the error in your order. You can mention that your order and the Body Shop's may have been mixed up, a mistake that should be relatively easy to fix.

■INSTANT MESSAGES 10. Yes, we do purple: Instant message from Lands' End

When clothing retailer Lands' End offered its 2,500 telephone service representatives the chance to train on its new instant messaging system, "Lands' End Live," you jumped at the opportunity. As it turned out, so many volunteered for the new training that the company had to give preference to a few hundred who'd been on the job longest. You were one of the lucky ones.

Now you've had months of practice answering messages like the one you just received from a customer named Alicia. She wants to know if she can have a red Polartec Aircore-200 Scarf custom monogrammed—not in the standard, contrasting wheat-colored thread, but in radiant purple as a gift for her husband, whose favorite colors are red and purple. According to Alicia, her husband says, "Red & purple are feng shui symbols of wealth & prosperity."

On its website, Lands' End promises to fulfill nonstandard monogram requests "if technical limitations allow." You've done a quick check and yes, her husband can have his initials in bright purple on the red background.

Your task: Write the instant message reply to Alicia, telling her the good news.[11]

Improve Your Grammar, Mechanics, and Usage

Level 1: Self-Assessment—Prepositions and Conjunctions

Review Sections 1.6.1 and 1.6.2 in the Handbook of Grammar, Mechanics, and Usage, and then look at the following items.

Rewrite items 1–5, deleting unnecessary words and prepositions, and adding required prepositions:

1. Where was your argument leading to?

2. I wish he would get off of the phone.

3. This is a project into which you can sink your teeth.

4. U.S. Mercantile must become aware and sensitive to its customers' concerns.

5. We are responsible for aircraft safety in the air, the hangars, and the runways.

In items 6–10, write the correct preposition in the blank:

6. Dr. Namaguchi will be talking _____ the marketing class, but she has no time for questions.

7. Matters like this are decided after thorough discussion _____ all seven department managers.

8. We can't wait _____ their decision much longer.

9. Their computer is similar _____ ours.

10. This model is different _____ the one we ordered.

In items 11–15, rewrite the sentences in the space provided to make phrases parallel:

11. She is active in not only a civic group but also in an athletic organization.

12. That is either a mistake or was an intentional omission.

13. The question is whether to set up a booth at the convention or be hosting a hospitality suite.

14. We are doing better in both overall sales and in profits.

15. She had neither the preferred educational background, nor did she have suitable experience.

Level 2: Workplace Applications

The following items contain numerous errors in grammar, capitalization, punctuation, abbreviation, number style, word division, and vocabulary. Rewrite each sentence in the space provided, correcting all errors. Write *C* in the space after any sentence that is already correct.

1. Peabody Energys commitment to environmental excellence is driven by the companies' mission statement which states that when mining is complete, the company will leave the land in a condition equal or better than it was before mining.

2. In 1998, Blockbuster opened a state of the art distribution center in McKinney, Texas, just North of the company's Dallas Headquarters.

3. Miss Tucci was responsible for developing Terraspring's business plan, establishing the brand, and for launching the company.

4. The principle goals of the new venture will be to offer tailored financial products and meeting the needs of the community.

5. Nestle Waters North America are the number one bottled water company in the US and Canada.

6. The reason egg prices dropped sharply is because of a Post Easter reduction in demand.

7. Joining bank officials during the announcement of the program were U.S. congressman Luis V. Guitierrez, Carlos Manuel Sada Solana, General Consul of Mexico in the Midwest, and "Don Francisco", the leading hispanic entertainment figure in the United States. and Latin America.

8. The summer advertising campaign is the most unique in 7-Eleven's history.

9. Upon introducing it's new Quadruple Fudge flavor, consumers are expected to flock to Baskin-Robbins ice cream parlors.

10. The signing of a Trade Pact between the european union and Chile, is being delayed by european negotiators who insist the deal includes an agreement requiring Chile to stop using the names Cognac, Champagne, and Burgundy.

11. Federal Trade commissioner, Mrs. Sheila F. Anthony called on the dietary supplement industry to institute better self regulation, and called on the media to refuse ads containing claims that are obviously false.

12. Founded in 1971, GSD&M has grown to become a nationally-acclaimed advertising agency with more than 500 employees and having billings of over $1 billion dollars.

13. Although marketing may seem to be the easier place to cut costs during a downturn its actually the last place you should look to make strategic cuts.

14. After closing their plant in Mecosta county, Green Mountain will have less than 200 employees.

15. The purchasing needs of professional's differ from blue collar workers.

Level 3: Document Critique

The following document may contain errors in grammar, capitalization, punctuation, abbreviation, number style, vocabulary, and spelling. You will also find errors relating to topics in this chapter. For example, consider the format, organization, paragraph length, and subject line as you improve this memo. Correct all errors using standard proofreading marks (see Appendix C).

MEMO

TO: George Kimball

FROM: John Mason

SUBJECT: My trip back East

May 31, 2005

Dear George:

I went back to New York for apresentation the 15th of this month and I found it very informative. The sponsor of my visat was Vern Grouper. Vern is the Manager of the data processing-operation at headquarters; that is, their centralized data procesing operation. They've got quite a bit of power out there. And they do encourage us to utilize their capibilities, there services, and experiences to whatever extent will be beneficial to us. However, you could say it would be my observation that although they have a tremendous amount of computing capability that capability is directed toward a business dimension very different than ours and unlike anything we have. However, their are certain services that might be performed in our behalf by headquarters. For example, we could utilize people such as Vern to come and address our data-processing advisory group since I am planning on convening that group on a monthly basis.

By the way, I need to talk to you about the data-processing advicory group when you get a chance. I have 1 or 2 thoughts about some new approaches we can take with it I'd like to run by you if you don't mind. Its not too complicated just some simple ideas.

Let me know what you think of this idea about Vern coming here. If you like it than I will go ahead and set things in motion with Vern.

Sincerely,

John Mason

Supervisor

Spin Cycle: Deciphering Corporate Doublespeak

If there's one product U.S. businesses can manufacture in large amounts, it's doublespeak. Doublespeak is language that only pretends to say something but that in reality hides, evades, or misleads. Like most products, doublespeak comes in many forms, from the popular buzzwords that everyone uses but no one really understands—such as *competitive dynamics* and *empowerment*—to words that try to hide meaning, such as *reengineering, synergy,* and *restructuring.*

With doublespeak, bribes and kickbacks are called *rebates* or *fees for product testing,* used-car-parts dealers have become *auto dismantlers and recyclers,* and travel agents are called *vacation specialists, destination counselors,* or *reservation specialists.* Plus, just about everyone's job title has the word *chief* in it: Chief Nuclear Officer, Chief Learning Officer, Chief Cultural Officer, Chief Ethics Officer, Chief Turnaround Officer, and Chief Creative Officer. After all the "operations improvement" that corporations have undergone, you have to wonder who all those "chiefs" are leading. Never before have so many led so few.

With doublespeak, banks don't have *bad loans* or *bad debts*; they have *nonperforming credits* that are *rolled over* or *rescheduled.* And corporations never lose money; they just experience *negative cash flow, deficit enhancement,* or *negative contributions to profits.*

Of course, no one gets fired these days. People high enough in the corporate pecking order *resign for personal reasons.* Those below the lofty heights of corporate power are *involuntarily terminated* as the result of *downsizing, workforce adjustments,* and *headcount reductions.* Some companies even *implement a skills mix adjustment* or *eliminate redundancies in the human resources area.* One automobile company that closed an entire assembly plant and eliminated over 8,000 jobs called the action *a volume-related production schedule adjustment.*

But don't worry, if you're *dehired, deselected, surplused,* or *uninstalled,* corporations will offer you a *career change opportunity* or *vocational relocation.* In fact, hardly anyone is laid off these days. "We don't characterize it as a layoff," said one corporate doublespeaker (sometimes called a spin doctor). "We're managing our staff resources. Sometimes you manage them up, and sometimes you manage them down."

The goal of good writing is to communicate, not to confuse; to be understood, not to hide behind words. Look at this confusing excerpt from an investment document:

> The applicability of the general information and administrative procedures set forth below accordingly will vary depending on the investor and the record-keeping system established for a shareholder's investment in the Fund. Participants in 401(k) and other plans should first consult with the appropriate persons at their employer or refer to the plan materials before following any of the procedures below.

As discussed in Chapter 4, *plain English* is a way of writing and arranging technical materials so that your audience can understand your meaning. Restating our excerpt in plain English reveals one simple thought: "If you are investing through a large retirement plan or other special program, follow the instructions in your program material."

Some companies are concerned that writing documents in plain English will increase their liability, but many companies are finding just the opposite. "In many ways," notes one Bell Atlantic employee, "we reduced our liability because we have created a document that is much clearer and less ambiguous." Similarly, when Citibank introduced promissory notes written in plain English, the number of collection lawsuits fell dramatically. The clearer writing simply made it easier for borrowers to understand their obligations.

Some lawyers may purposely choose obscure language to control vital information, to take advantage of those who don't know what they're signing, or to profit from people who hire them to interpret the difficult language. But many legal professionals strongly endorse the plain-English movement. The plain-English movement has generated great momentum; perhaps confusing language will become obsolete.

Applications for Success

For more on the subject of doublespeak, read the article "Life Under the Chief Doublespeak Officer" at www.dt.org/html/Doublespeak.html.

Answer the following questions:

1. What do you think? Isn't corporate doublespeak just another way to emphasize the positive in business situa-

tions? Or is it unethical to use business buzzwords and corporate doublespeak to ease negative impressions? Explain your position in a one-page memo or an e-mail message to your instructor.

2. If it's unethical to use doublespeak, would you classify it as an ethical dilemma or an ethical lapse? Explain your position in a one-page memo or e-mail message to your instructor.

3. Do the people in your field appear to value the jargon and buzzwords of their industry? If you use plain English, do you risk your reputation as a professional in your field? Please explain in a one-page memo or e-mail message to your instructor.

4. The president of one company just learned that some of his employees have been playing a popular game called "buzzword bingo," in which participants ridicule doublespeak by tracking the jargon their bosses use during staff meetings on bingo-like cards. Some managers are complaining that it's getting out of control. In fact, as one meeting dragged on, employees tried to steer the conversation to use all the buzzwords on their cards. What can managers do to avoid these silly games?

5. Visit one of the following buzzword bingo websites and print out a card or two:

www.executivespeak.com/buzzword_bingo.html
http://isd.usc.edu/~karl/Bingo/
www.lurkertech.com/chris/bingo

Read the current business section of your favorite newspaper. How many buzzwords did you find?

7

Writing Routine Messages

"Effective communication creates a positive impression—and a positive impression will get more positive responses to your requests. So help your readers by telling them why you're making the request—it gives them an incentive to act. I explain what needs to be done, why it needs to be done, and how the request affects the audience."

—Becky Bumgardner
Senior Corporate Writer
Corporate Relations Department
UnumProvident

Even for routine situations, you need to plan, write, and complete your messages.

Learning Objectives

After studying this chapter, you will be able to

1 Apply the three-step writing process to routine positive messages

2 Illustrate the strategy for writing routine requests

3 Discuss the differences among four types of routine requests

4 Illustrate the strategy for writing routine replies and positive messages

5 Explain the main differences among messages granting a claim when the company, the customer, or a third party is at fault

6 Clarify the importance of goodwill messages, and describe how to make them effective

UnumProvident is the nation's largest disability insurer, aiming to protect individuals' paychecks, assets, and lifestyles from the effects of long-term disability or terminal illness. To succeed, the company must communicate effectively not only externally with brokers, benefit managers, and insured employees but also internally with its own people. Becky Bumgardner is responsible for writing and sending internal messages to more than 10,000 UnumProvident employees in nearly 60 offices across the United States and Canada. She also composes feature articles for the company's monthly newsletter and prepares daily updates for its intranet. Whether she's requesting routine information for the newsletter or reminding employees about an upcoming deadline, Bumgardner is always careful to compose messages that are both concise and clear.[1]

Using the Three-Step Writing Process for Routine Messages

Like Becky Bumgardner, you'll probably compose a lot of routine, good-news, and good-will messages: orders, company policies, claims, credit, information about employees, products, operations, and so on. To produce the best messages possible, apply the three-step writing process (see Figure 7.1 on page 172):

- **Step 1: Planning routine messages.** For routine messages, you may need only a few moments to analyze your purpose and audience, investigate audience needs, and adapt your message to your readers.

- **Step 2: Writing routine messages.** Organizing and composing routine messages can be direct and quick; however, be sure to verify the customs of your intercultural audiences before deciding to use the direct approach.
- **Step 3: Completing routine messages.** No matter how short or straightforward your message, make it professional by allowing plenty of time to revise, produce, and proofread it.

Making Routine Requests

Whenever you ask for something—information, action, products, adjustments, references—you are making a request. A request is routine if it's part of the normal course of business and you anticipate that your audience will want to comply. Don't make unnecessary requests. If you can find information yourself, don't risk your credibility and burden others by asking them to find it for you.

Strategy for Routine Requests

Use the direct approach. Open with your main idea (a clear statement of your request). Use the body to give details and justify your request. Then close by requesting specific action and concluding cordially.

Organize your routine messages according to the direct approach.

State Your Request Up Front

To begin, ask yourself what you want readers to do or to understand as a result of reading your message. Place your request first; however, be careful not to be abrupt or tactless. Follow these guidelines:

Keep your direct approach from being harsh or discourteous.

- **Pay attention to tone.** Even though you expect a favorable response, instead of demanding action ("Send me your catalog no. 33A"), soften your request with words such as *please.*
- **Assume your audience will comply.** Assume that once the reason is clearly understood, your audience will comply with your request. An impatient demand is unnecessary.
- **Avoid beginning with personal introductions.** Don't start with, "I am the senior corporate writer at UnumProvident, and I'm looking for information on . . ." Such a beginning buries the main idea so that the actual request may be lost.
- **Punctuate questions and polite requests differently.** A polite request in question form requires no question mark ("Would you please help us determine whether Kate Kingsley is a suitable applicant for this position"). A direct question does require a question mark ("Did Kate Kingsley demonstrate an ability to work smoothly with clients?").
- **Be specific.** State precisely what you want. For example, if you request the latest census figures from a government agency, be sure to say whether you want a page or two of summary figures or a detailed report running several thousand pages.

Explain and Justify Your Request

Use the body of your message to explain your request. Try to make the explanation grow smoothly and logically from your opening remarks. When Becky Bumgardner requests information from managers, she also tells them why she needs the information and explains how they might benefit from granting the request.

You can use the body of your routine request to list a series of questions. You might ask about the technical specifications, exact dimensions, and precise use of a complex piece of machinery. When listing a series of questions, just keep a few basics in mind:

- **Ask the most important questions first.** Number your questions, and list them logically in descending order of importance. If cost is your main concern, begin by asking, "What does the C-704 cost?" Then you can ask related but more specific questions,

FIGURE 7.1   Applying the Three-Step Writing Process to Routine Messages

Planning

Analyze
- Make your purpose specific.
- Be sure it's worth pursuing at this time.
- Know if readers will react positively.
- Learn more about them if necessary.

Investigate
- Find out what readers need to know.
- Have all the relevant information.
- Gather more information if needed.

Adapt
- Verify effectiveness of written channel.
- If written, choose the best medium.
- Use the "you" attitude.
- Keep your language positive and polite.

Writing

Organize
- Define main idea fairly well before beginning.
- Stick to it by limiting the scope.
- Group relevant points logically.
- Adopt the direct approach.
  - º Open by clearly stating main idea.
  - º Put all necessary details in body.
  - º Close cordially.

Compose
- Adapt style and tone to readers' culture.
- Use conversational tone for U.S. readers.
- Use plain English for U.S. readers.

Completing

Revise
- Evaluate overall effect of the message.
- Be sure you've said what you want to.
- Put content in the order you want.
- Make the message easy to read.
- Make the message concise and clear.

Produce
- Design document to suit your readers.
- Use effective design elements.
- Use appropriate delivery methods.

Proofread
- Check for typos.
- Check for spelling and mechanical errors.
- Look for alignment problems.
- Make sure print quality is acceptable.

1   **2**   **3**

perhaps about the availability of a product ("How many C-704s do you usually have in stock?") or its warranty ("What warranty do you provide with the C-704?").

- **Ask only relevant questions.** Don't waste your reader's time; ask only those questions central to your request. If your questions need simple yes-or-no answers, provide boxes to check; otherwise, use open-ended questions to elicit the information you want: Ask "How fast can you ship the unit?" or "When will you ship the unit?" rather than "Can you ship the unit?"
- **Deal with only one topic per question.** Break down multiple requests. If you have an unusual or complex request, list the request and then provide supporting details in a separate, short paragraph. You may even use paragraph headings to make your reader's job easier.

Request Specific Action in a Courteous Close

Even routine messages require special attention to the close.

Close your message with three important elements:

- **A specific request for action.** Restate your request and ask that readers respond by a specific time ("Please send the figures by April 5 so that I can return first quarter results to you before the May 20 conference").
- **Contact information.** Help your reader respond easily by including your phone number, office hours, and other contact information.
- **An expression of appreciation or goodwill.** Sincerely express your goodwill and appreciation; however, don't thank readers "in advance" for cooperating. If a reader's response warrants a thank you, send it after you've received the reply.

Types of Routine Requests

The types of routine requests are numerous, from asking favors to requesting credit. Many of the routine messages that you'll be writing will likely fall into major categories.

The following sections discuss four of these categories: placing orders, requesting information and action, making claims and requesting adjustments, and requesting recommendations and references.

Placing Orders

Today, many companies make paperless orders by using computer-generated order forms. These forms provide a list of products with a description of each item and information such as the catalog number, name or trade name, color, size, and unit price. Your job is to fill in the quantity, compute the total amount due, and provide the shipping address.

If you do need to draft an order letter, follow the same format as you would on an order blank.

- **Opening.** Start with the general request.
- **Body.** Include specific information about the items you want. Put this information in columns, double-space between the items, and total the price at the end.
- **Close.** Specify the delivery address, which may differ from the billing address. Also indicate how the merchandise is to be shipped. Finally, in any letter including a payment, mention the amount enclosed and explain how the amount was calculated.

When placing orders, be thorough and clear.

Here's an example of an effective order:

Please send the following items to the above address. I am ordering from your current spring–summer catalog:

    ⟵ ——— States general request first

COUNT	STOCK I.D.	DESCRIPTION	ITEM PRICE	TOTAL PRICE
3	139-24	Daily appointment books (black)	$ 8.95	$ 26.85
50	289-90	Mechanical pencils (0.5 mm/black)	1.69	84.50
5	905-18	Wrist pads (gray)	6.99	34.95
10	472-67	CD-R disks (50/box)	17.99	179.90
		TOTAL SALES		$326.20
		SHIPPING		FREE
		AMOUNT DUE		$326.20

Provides all necessary details in a format similar to an order form

Calculates the total amount due (from information on tax and shipping that was provided in catalog)

My check #1738 for $326.20 is enclosed. Please ship these supplies UPS ground to the address in the letterhead.

Includes additional important information in the close

Requesting Information and Action

Basically, a simple request says, "This is what I want to know or what I want you to do, why I'm making the request, and why it may be in your interest to help me." In more complex situations, readers might be unwilling to respond unless they understand how the request benefits them, so be sure to include this information in your explanation. Follow the direct approach:

When requesting information or action, as with any business message, keep your purpose clearly in mind.

- **Opening.** Start with a clear statement of your reason for writing.
- **Body.** Provide whatever explanation is needed to justify your request.
- **Close.** Provide a specific account of what you expect, and include a deadline if appropriate.

Internal requests to fellow employees are often oral and rather casual, but sending a clear, thoughtful memo, e-mail, or instant message can save time and questions by helping readers understand precisely what you want (see Figure 7.2). Requests to outsiders are often made by letter, although some are sent via e-mail or even via instant messaging. These messages are usually short and simple (see Figure 7.3 on page 175).

Follow the same strategy for both internal and external requests.

Making Claims and Requesting Adjustments

When you're dissatisfied with a company's product or service, you make a **claim** (a formal complaint) or request an **adjustment** (a claim settlement). Although a visit, phone call, or

Planning

Analyze
Purpose is to request feedback from fellow employees.

Investigate
Gather accurate, complete information on program benefits and local gym.

Adapt
Office memo or e-mail is appropriate medium. Use "you" attitude, and make responding easy.

1

Writing

Organize
Main idea is saving money while staying healthy. Save time and meet audience expectations using the direct approach.

Compose
Keep style informal but business-like. Using a "we" attitude includes readers in the decision-making process.

2

Completing

Revise
Keep it brief—weed out overly long words and phrases. Avoid unnecessary details.

Produce
No need for fancy design elements in this memo. Include a response form.

Proofread
Review carefully for both content and typographical errors.

3

FIGURE 7.2   Effective Memo Requesting Action from Company Insiders

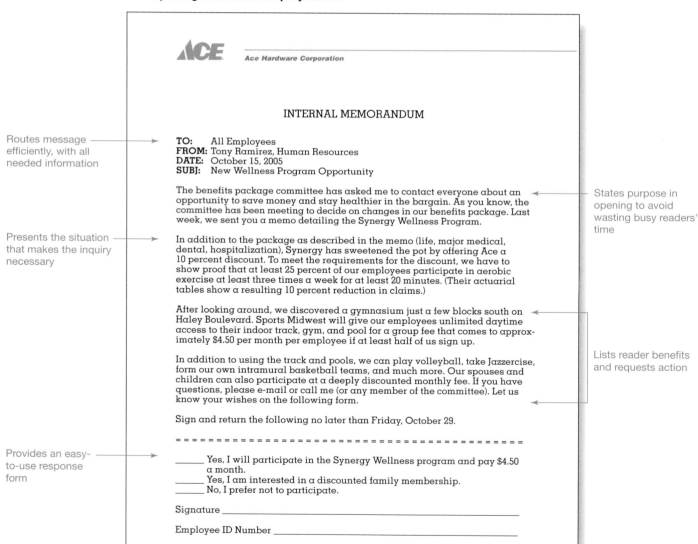

Routes message efficiently, with all needed information

States purpose in opening to avoid wasting busy readers' time

Presents the situation that makes the inquiry necessary

Lists reader benefits and requests action

Provides an easy-to-use response form

ACE
Ace Hardware Corporation

INTERNAL MEMORANDUM

TO: All Employees
FROM: Tony Ramirez, Human Resources
DATE: October 15, 2005
SUBJ: New Wellness Program Opportunity

The benefits package committee has asked me to contact everyone about an opportunity to save money and stay healthier in the bargain. As you know, the committee has been meeting to decide on changes in our benefits package. Last week, we sent you a memo detailing the Synergy Wellness Program.

In addition to the package as described in the memo (life, major medical, dental, hospitalization), Synergy has sweetened the pot by offering Ace a 10 percent discount. To meet the requirements for the discount, we have to show proof that at least 25 percent of our employees participate in aerobic exercise at least three times a week for at least 20 minutes. (Their actuarial tables show a resulting 10 percent reduction in claims.)

After looking around, we discovered a gymnasium just a few blocks south on Haley Boulevard. Sports Midwest will give our employees unlimited daytime access to their indoor track, gym, and pool for a group fee that comes to approx-imately $4.50 per month per employee if at least half of us sign up.

In addition to using the track and pools, we can play volleyball, take Jazzercise, form our own intramural basketball teams, and much more. Our spouses and children can also participate at a deeply discounted monthly fee. If you have questions, please e-mail or call me (or any member of the committee). Let us know your wishes on the following form.

Sign and return the following no later than Friday, October 29.

= =

_____ Yes, I will participate in the Synergy Wellness program and pay $4.50 a month.
_____ Yes, I am interested in a discounted family membership.
_____ No, I prefer not to participate.

Signature _____

Employee ID Number _____

FIGURE 7.3   Effective Letter Requesting Information from a Company Outsider

Pralle Realty

823 Viewpoint Avenue
College Station, TX 77840
979-663-3018   fax: 979-663-3020

September 24, 2005

Mr. Harold Westerman
Agri-Lawn Services
1796 West Commercial Ave.
College Station, TX 77841

Dear Mr. Westerman:

Makes overall request in polite question form (no question mark)

Would you please send us information about the lawn services you provide. Pralle Realty owns approximately 27 pieces of rental property in College Station, and we're looking for a lawn service to handle all of them. We are making a commitment to provide quality housing in this college town, and we are looking for an outstanding firm to work with us.

Keeps reader's interest by hinting at possibility of future business

Avoids making an overly broad request by using a series of specific questions

In addition to brochures or other literature, please respond to the following:

1. **Lawn care.** What is your annual charge for each location for lawn maintenance, including mowing, fertilizing, and weed control?

Itemizes questions in a logical sequence

Avoids useless yes-or-no answers by including open-ended questions

2. **Shrubbery.** What is your annual charge for each location for the care of deciduous and evergreen bushes, including pruning, fertilizing, and replacing as necessary?

3. **Contract.** How does Agri-Lawn Services structure such large contracts? What additional information do you need from us?

Please let us hear from you by February 15. We must have a lawn-care firm in place by March 15.

Specifies a time limit in the courteous close

Sincerely

Kathleen Moriarity

Kathleen Moriarity
Senior Partner

al

Pointers for Making a Routine Request

Direct Statement of the Request

- Be direct since your readers will respond favorably.
- Open by stating the main idea clearly and simply.
- Write in a polite, undemanding, personal tone.
- Before complex requests, include a brief explanation.

Justification, Explanation, and Details

- Justify the request, or explain its importance.
- Explain the benefit of responding.
- State desired actions in a positive, supportive manner.
- Itemize a complex request in a logical, numbered list.
- Limit any question to one topic.

Courteous Close with Request for Specific Action

- Courteously request a specific action.
- Make it easy to comply by including contact information.
- Indicate your gratitude.
- Clearly state any important deadline or time frame.

even instant message may solve the problem, a written claim letter documents your dissatisfaction. Moreover, if you're angry or frustrated, writing the letter will help you cool off and adopt a more objective tone. After all, a courteous, clear, concise explanation will make a far more favorable impression than an abusive, angry letter.

In most cases, and especially in your first letter, assume that a fair adjustment will be made, and follow the plan for direct requests:

- **Opening.** Begin with a straightforward statement of the problem.
- **Body.** Give a complete, specific explanation of the details, providing any information an adjuster would need to verify your claim.
- **Close.** Politely request specific action or convey a sincere desire to find a solution. And don't forget to suggest that the business relationship will continue if the problem is solved satisfactorily.

Companies usually accept the customer's explanation of what's wrong, so ethically it's important to be entirely honest when filing claims. Also, be prepared to back up your claim with invoices, sales receipts, canceled checks, dated correspondence, catalog descriptions, and any other relevant documents. Send copies and keep the originals for your files. Be sure to supply your contact information and the best time to call so that the company can discuss the situation with you if necessary. For more insights into writing these kinds of messages, compare the poor and improved versions of the claim letter in Figure 7.4.

Requesting Recommendations and References

When awarding credit, contracts, jobs, promotions, scholarships, and so on, some companies ask applicants to supply references. If you're an employer considering whether to hire an applicant, you may want to write directly to the person the applicant named as a reference. If you're applying for a job and your potential employer asks for references, you may want to ask a close personal or professional associate to write a letter of recommendation that vouches for your ability, skills, integrity, character, and fitness for the job.

Before you volunteer someone's name as a reference, ask that person's permission. Some people won't let you use their names, perhaps because they don't know enough about you to feel comfortable writing a letter or perhaps because they have a policy of not providing recommendations. You are likely to receive the best recommendation from persons who agree to write about you, so check first.

Because requests for recommendations and references are routine, assume your reader will honor your request, and organize your inquiry using the direct approach.

- **Opening.** Clearly state that you're applying for a position and that you would like your reader to write a letter of recommendation. If you haven't had contact with the person for some time, use the opening to recall the nature of the relationship you had, the dates of your association, and any special events that might bring to mind a clear, favorable picture of you.
- **Body.** Include any information about yourself that the reader might use to support a recommendation—such as a description of the recent related jobs you've held. When you're applying for a job or a scholarship, include a copy of your résumé and refer to it in this middle section. This information will give readers an idea of the direction your life has taken so that they will know what qualities to emphasize to best support your application.
- **Close.** Express your appreciation and include the full name and address of the person to whom the recommendation letter should be sent. When asking for an immediate recommendation, you should also mention the deadline.

You'll make a response more likely if you enclose a stamped, preaddressed envelope. The letter in Figure 7.5 on page 178 covers all these points, and the writer adds important information about some qualifications that might be of special interest to her potential employer.

FIGURE 7.4 Letter Making a Claim

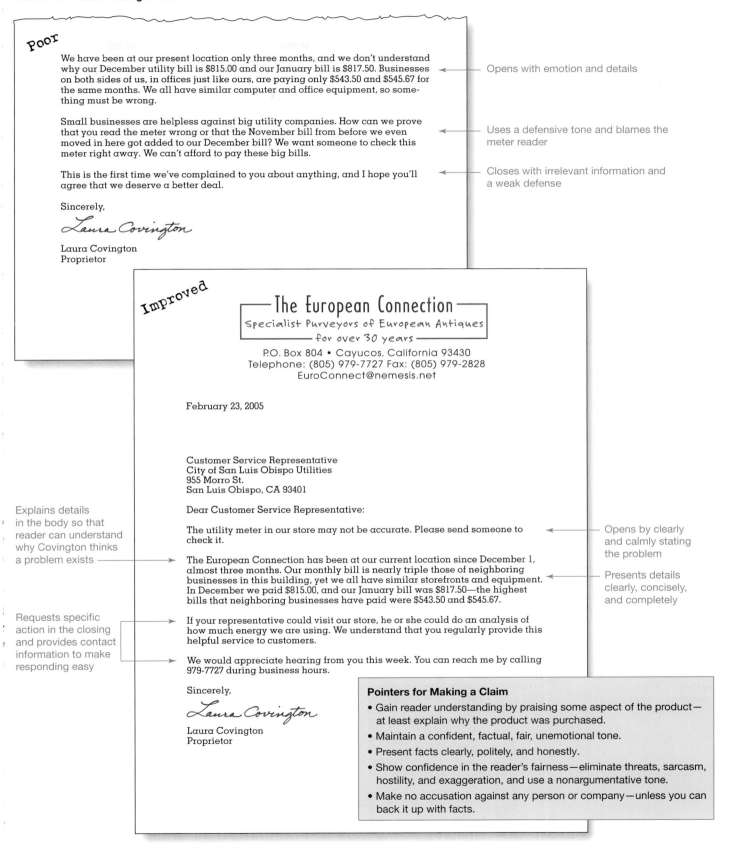

Poor

We have been at our present location only three months, and we don't understand why our December utility bill is $815.00 and our January bill is $817.50. Businesses on both sides of us, in offices just like ours, are paying only $543.50 and $545.67 for the same months. We all have similar computer and office equipment, so something must be wrong.

→ Opens with emotion and details

Small businesses are helpless against big utility companies. How can we prove that you read the meter wrong or that the November bill from before we even moved in here got added to our December bill? We want someone to check this meter right away. We can't afford to pay these big bills.

→ Uses a defensive tone and blames the meter reader

This is the first time we've complained to you about anything, and I hope you'll agree that we deserve a better deal.

→ Closes with irrelevant information and a weak defense

Sincerely,

Laura Covington

Laura Covington
Proprietor

Improved

┌─ The European Connection ─┐
Specialist Purveyors of European Antiques
─ for over 30 years ─
P.O. Box 804 • Cayucos, California 93430
Telephone: (805) 979-7727 Fax: (805) 979-2828
EuroConnect@nemesis.net

February 23, 2005

Customer Service Representative
City of San Luis Obispo Utilities
955 Morro St.
San Luis Obispo, CA 93401

Dear Customer Service Representative:

The utility meter in our store may not be accurate. Please send someone to check it.

→ Opens by clearly and calmly stating the problem

Explains details in the body so that reader can understand why Covington thinks a problem exists →

The European Connection has been at our current location since December 1, almost three months. Our monthly bill is nearly triple those of neighboring businesses in this building, yet we all have similar storefronts and equipment. In December we paid $815.00, and our January bill was $817.50—the highest bills that neighboring businesses have paid were $543.50 and $545.67.

→ Presents details clearly, concisely, and completely

Requests specific action in the closing and provides contact information to make responding easy →

If your representative could visit our store, he or she could do an analysis of how much energy we are using. We understand that you regularly provide this helpful service to customers.

We would appreciate hearing from you this week. You can reach me by calling 979-7727 during business hours.

Sincerely,

Laura Covington

Laura Covington
Proprietor

Pointers for Making a Claim
- Gain reader understanding by praising some aspect of the product— at least explain why the product was purchased.
- Maintain a confident, factual, fair, unemotional tone.
- Present facts clearly, politely, and honestly.
- Show confidence in the reader's fairness—eliminate threats, sarcasm, hostility, and exaggeration, and use a nonargumentative tone.
- Make no accusation against any person or company—unless you can back it up with facts.

Planning

Analyze
Purpose is to request a recommendation letter from your college professor.

Investigate
Gather information to help the reader recall you and to clarify the position you want.

Adapt
A letter format will give your message the formality you need. Be polite.

1

Writing

Organize
Main idea is to convince your professor to send a glowing recommendation to a potential employer. Use the direct approach.

Compose
Make message friendly but businesslike and slightly more formal than usual. Use plain English and an active voice.

2

Completing

Revise
Be concise but thorough. Make sure that concrete detail flows logically.

Produce
Use simple typeface with ample margins and spacing between text. Enclose SASE and perhaps your résumé.

Proofread
Review letter and enclosures for errors.

3

FIGURE 7.5   Effective Letter Requesting a Recommendation

1181 Ashport Drive
Tate Springs, TN 38101
March 14, 2005

Professor Lyndon Kenton
School of Business
University of Tennessee, Knoxville
Knoxville, TN 37916

Dear Professor Kenton:

May I have a letter of recommendation from you? I recently interviewed with Strategic Investments and have been called for a second interview for their Analyst Training Program (ATP). They have requested at least one recommendation from a professor, and I immediately thought of you.

Opens with the request, assumes the reader will honor the request, and names the potential employer

As you may recall, I took BUS 485, Financial Analysis, from you in the fall of 2003. I enjoyed the class and finished the term with an "A." Professor Kenton, your comments on assertiveness and cold-calling impressed me beyond the scope of the actual course material. In fact, taking your course helped me decide on a future as a financial analyst.

Includes information in the opening to refresh reader's memory about this former student

My enclosed résumé includes all my relevant work experience and volunteer activities. But I'd also like to add that I've handled the financial planning for our family since my father passed away several years ago. Although initially, I learned by trial and error, I have increasingly applied my business training in deciding what stocks or bonds to trade. This, I believe, has given me a practical edge over others who may be applying for the same job.

Refers to résumé in the body and mentions experience that could set applicant apart from other candidates

If possible, Ms. Blackmon in Human Resources needs to receive your letter by March 30. For your convenience, I've enclosed a preaddressed, stamped envelope.

Gives a deadline for response in the closing and includes information about the person expecting the recommendation

I appreciate your time and effort in writing this letter of recommendation for me. It will be great to put my education to work, and I'll keep you informed of my progress.

Sincerely,

Joanne Tucker

Joanne Tucker

Enclosure

Sending Routine Replies and Positive Messages

When responding positively to a request, giving good-news, or sending a goodwill message, you have several goals: (1) to communicate the information or good news, (2) to answer all questions, (3) to provide all required details, and (4) to leave your reader with a good impression of you and your firm. Routine positive messages can be quite brief and to the point, but remember to be courteous, stay upbeat, and maintain a you-oriented tone.

Your routine replies and positive messages have four specific goals.

Strategy for Routine Replies and Positive Messages

Like requests, routine replies and positive messages will generally be of interest to your readers, so you'll usually use the direct approach. Open with your main idea (the positive reply or the good news). Use the body to explain all the relevant details. Then close cordially, perhaps highlighting a benefit to your reader.

Start with the Main Idea

Begin your positive message with the main idea or good news and prepare your audience for the detail that follows. Try to make your opening clear and concise. Look at the following introductory statements. They make the same point, but one is so cluttered with unnecessary information that it buries the purpose; the other is brief, to the point, and clear:

Before you begin, have a clear idea of what you want to say.

Instead of This	Write This
I am pleased to inform you that after deliberating the matter carefully, our human resources committee has recommended you for appointment as a staff accountant.	Congratulations. You've been selected to join our firm as a staff accountant, beginning March 20.

Provide Necessary Detail and Explanation

In the body, explain your point completely so that the audience will experience no confusion or lingering doubt. In addition to providing details in the body, maintain the supportive tone you already established in the opening. This tone is easy to continue when your message is purely good news, as in this example:

> Your educational background and internship have impressed us, and we believe you would be a valuable addition to Green Valley Properties. As discussed during your interview, your salary will be $3,300 per month, plus benefits. In that regard, you will meet with our benefits manager, Paula Sanchez, on Monday, March 20, at 8:00 a.m. She will assist you with all the paperwork necessary to tailor our benefit package to your family situation. She will also arrange various orientation activities to help you adapt to our company.

However, if your routine message is mixed and must convey mildly disappointing information, put the negative portion of your message into as favorable a context as possible:

Embed any slightly negative information in a positive context.

Instead of This	Write This
No, we no longer carry the Sportsgirl line of sweaters.	The new Olympic line has replaced the Sportsgirl sweaters that you asked about. Olympic features a wider range of colors and sizes and more contemporary styling.

The more complete description is less negative and emphasizes how the audience can benefit from the change. However, be careful using even only slightly negative information in this type of message: Use it *only* if you're reasonably sure the audience will respond positively. Otherwise, use the indirect approach (discussed in Chapter 8).

Document Makeover

Improve This E-Mail

To practice correcting drafts of actual documents, visit www.prenhall.com/onekey on the web. Click "Document Makeovers," then click Chapter 7. You will find an e-mail message that contains problems and errors relating to what you've learned in this chapter about writing routine, good-news, and goodwill messages. Use the Final Draft decision tool to create an improved version of this e-mail. Check the message for skilled presentation of the main idea, clarity of detail, proper handling of negative information, a positive attitude, and a courteous close.

End with a Courteous Close

Make sure the audience understands what to do next and how that action will benefit them.

Your message is most likely to succeed if your readers are left feeling that you have their personal welfare in mind. Accomplish this task either by highlighting a benefit to the audience or by expressing appreciation or goodwill. If follow-up action is required, clearly state who will do what next.

Types of Routine Replies and Positive Messages

Innumerable types of routine replies and positive messages are used in business every day. Many of these messages fall into four main categories: granting requests for information and action, granting claims and requests for adjustments, providing recommendations and references, and sending goodwill messages.

Granting Requests for Information and Action

If your answer to a request is yes or is straightforward information, use the direct plan: Open with the main idea (or good news), use the body for explanation and detail, and close courteously. Your prompt, gracious, and thorough response will positively influence how people think about your company, its products, your department, and you. For a good example of this type of message, see Herman Miller Inc.'s response to Julian Zamakis's request for information about employment opportunities (see Figure 7.6).

Many companies use form responses to reply to similar requests.

Many of the requests you get will be routine and can get a standardized response. For example, a human resources department gets numerous routine inquiries about job openings. To handle repetitive queries like these, companies usually develop form responses. Although such messages are often criticized as being cold and impersonal, you can put a great deal of thought into wording them, and you can use computers to personalize and mix paragraphs. Thus, a computerized form letter prepared with care may actually be more personal and sincere than a quickly dictated, hastily typed "personal" reply.

Granting Claims and Requests for Adjustment

The claims you receive are your chance to build strong relationships with customers and clients.

Satisfied customers bring additional business to a firm; angry, dissatisfied customers do not. Plus, they complain to anyone who'll listen, creating poor public relations. Therefore, even though claims and adjustments may seem unpleasant, progressive businesspeople treat them as golden opportunities for building customer loyalty.[2]

Finding out who is at fault helps you know how to respond to a claim.

Few people go to the trouble of requesting an adjustment unless they actually have a problem. Thus the most sensible reaction to a routine claim is to assume that the claimant's account of the transaction is an honest statement of what happened—unless the same customer repeatedly submits dubious claims or the dollar amount is very large. When you receive a complaint, investigate the problem first to determine what went wrong and why. In addition, determine whether your company, your customer, or a third party is at fault.

FIGURE 7.6   Effective E-Mail Replying to Request for Information

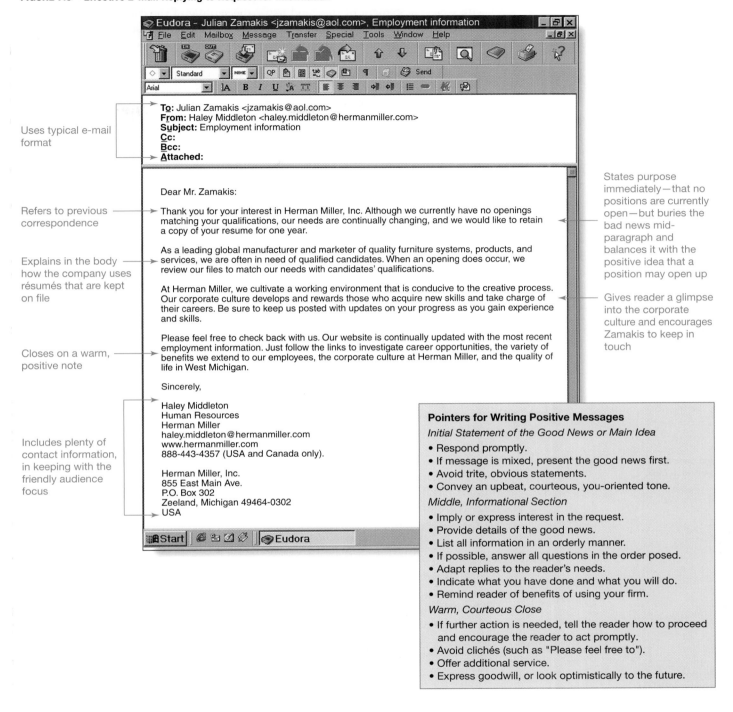

Uses typical e-mail format

Refers to previous correspondence

Explains in the body how the company uses résumés that are kept on file

Closes on a warm, positive note

Includes plenty of contact information, in keeping with the friendly audience focus

States purpose immediately—that no positions are currently open—but buries the bad news mid-paragraph and balances it with the positive idea that a position may open up

Gives reader a glimpse into the corporate culture and encourages Zamakis to keep in touch

To: Julian Zamakis <jzamakis@aol.com>
From: Haley Middleton <haley.middleton@hermanmiller.com>
Subject: Employment information
Cc:
Bcc:
Attached:

Dear Mr. Zamakis:

Thank you for your interest in Herman Miller, Inc. Although we currently have no openings matching your qualifications, our needs are continually changing, and we would like to retain a copy of your resume for one year.

As a leading global manufacturer and marketer of quality furniture systems, products, and services, we are often in need of qualified candidates. When an opening does occur, we review our files to match our needs with candidates' qualifications.

At Herman Miller, we cultivate a working environment that is conducive to the creative process. Our corporate culture develops and rewards those who acquire new skills and take charge of their careers. Be sure to keep us posted with updates on your progress as you gain experience and skills.

Please feel free to check back with us. Our website is continually updated with the most recent employment information. Just follow the links to investigate career opportunities, the variety of benefits we extend to our employees, the corporate culture at Herman Miller, and the quality of life in West Michigan.

Sincerely,

Haley Middleton
Human Resources
Herman Miller
haley.middleton@hermanmiller.com
www.hermanmiller.com
888-443-4357 (USA and Canada only).

Herman Miller, Inc.
855 East Main Ave.
P.O. Box 302
Zeeland, Michigan 49464-0302
USA

Pointers for Writing Positive Messages

Initial Statement of the Good News or Main Idea

- Respond promptly.
- If message is mixed, present the good news first.
- Avoid trite, obvious statements.
- Convey an upbeat, courteous, you-oriented tone.

Middle, Informational Section

- Imply or express interest in the request.
- Provide details of the good news.
- List all information in an orderly manner.
- If possible, answer all questions in the order posed.
- Adapt replies to the reader's needs.
- Indicate what you have done and what you will do.
- Remind reader of benefits of using your firm.

Warm, Courteous Close

- If further action is needed, tell the reader how to proceed and encourage the reader to act promptly.
- Avoid clichés (such as "Please feel free to").
- Offer additional service.
- Express goodwill, or look optimistically to the future.

When Your Company Is at Fault   Refer to company errors carefully. Explain your company's efforts to do a good job, and imply that the error was an unusual incident. Here are some tips on what *not* to do:

When a complaint is the result of company error, word your response carefully.

- Don't blame an individual or a specific department.
- Don't use lame excuses such as "Nobody's perfect" or "Mistakes will happen."
- Don't promise that problems will never happen again (such guarantees are unrealistic and often beyond your control).

Many response letters are written as a personal answer to a unique claim. Such letters start with a clear statement of the good news: the settling of the claim according to the customer's request. For example, when a customer complained about a defective product, Klondike Gear (a large mail-order company) responded with the personal answer in Figure 7.7.

Companies also receive many claims that are quite similar. Klondike Gear has numerous customers who claim they haven't received exactly what was ordered. In response, the company created a form letter (see Figure 7.7) that can be customized through word processing and then individually signed.

When Your Customer Is at Fault   When your customer is at fault (perhaps washing a dry-clean-only sweater in hot water), either you refuse the claim and attempt to justify your refusal or you simply do what the customer asks. Remember, if you refuse the claim, you may lose your customer—as well as many of the customer's friends, who will hear only one side of the dispute. You must weigh the cost of making the adjustment against the cost of losing future business from one or more customers.

If you choose to grant the claim, open with the good news: You're replacing the merchandise or refunding the purchase price. However, the message body needs special attention. After all, if the customer fails to realize what went wrong, you'll be committing your firm to an endless procession of returned merchandise. Your job is to help the customer understand that the merchandise was mistreated, but you must do so without being condescending ("Perhaps you failed to read the instructions carefully") or preachy ("You should know that wool shrinks in hot water"). If you insult the customer, your cash refund will be wasted because you'll lose that customer anyway. Without being offensive, the letter in Figure 7.8 on page 184 educates a customer about how to treat his in-line skates.

> When complying with an unjustified claim, let the customer know that the merchandise was mistreated, but maintain a respectful and positive tone.

When a Third Party Is at Fault   Sometimes neither you nor the claimant is at fault. Perhaps the carrier damaged merchandise in transit. Or perhaps the original manufacturer is responsible for some product defect. When a third party is at fault, you have three options:

> You have three options when a third party is at fault.

- **Simply honor the claim.** This option is the most attractive. You satisfy your customer with a standard good-news letter and no extra explanation. You maintain your reputation for fair dealing but bear no cost (since the carrier, manufacturer, or other third party reimburses you).

- **Honor the claim but explain you're not at fault.** This option corrects any impression that the damage was caused by your negligence. You can still write the standard good-news letter, but stress the explanation.

- **Refer the reader to the third party.** This option is usually a bad choice because you fail to satisfy the reader's needs. However, use this option when you're trying to dissociate yourself from any legal responsibility for the damaged merchandise, especially if it has caused a personal injury, in which case, you would send a bad-news message (see Chapter 8).

Providing Recommendations and References

When writing a letter of recommendation, you want to convince readers that the person being recommended has the characteristics necessary for the job or benefit being sought. Your letter must contain all the relevant details:

> Be thorough when preparing a recommendation.

- Candidate's full name
- Job or benefit being sought
- Nature of your relationship with the candidate
- Whether you're answering a request or taking the initiative
- Facts relevant to the position or benefit sought
- Your overall evaluation of the candidate's suitability for the job or benefit

You want your audience to believe your praise for a candidate's talents and accomplishments. Therefore, illustrate your general points with a specific example or two that

FIGURE 7.7   Personalized and Form Letters Responding to Complaints

Puts customer at
ease with "you"
attitude

Includes resale and
sales promotion in
the body

Personalized
Letter

Klondike Gear
71 Blackfoot Road
Borah, Idaho 83706
(208) 977-3297   fax: (208) 977-3301
www.klondikegear.com

February 7, 2005

Ms. Ellen Seargento
7843 W. Douglas Ave.
Atlanta, GA 30305

Dear Ms. Seargento:

Here is your heather-blue wool-and-mohair sweater (size large) to replace the one returned to Klondike Gear with a defect in the knitting on the left sleeve. Thanks for giving us the opportunity to correct this situation. Customers' needs have come first at Klondike for 27 years. Our sweaters are handmade by the finest knitters in this area.

Our newest catalog is enclosed. Browse through it, and you'll see what wonderful new colors and patterns we have for you. Whether you are skiing or driving a snowmobile, Klondike Gear offers you the best protection available from wind, snow, and cold. Your input helps us serve you better. Please let us know how we may continue to serve you and your sporting needs.

Sincerely,

John Steele
John Steele
Customer Representative

Starts with a "good news" statement: that the correct merchandise has arrived

Thanks customer for writing about the defect

Closes with statement of company's concern for the customer

Form Letter

[Date]

[Name]
[Address]
[City, State, ZIP]

Dear [Name]:

Your letter concerning your recent Klondike order has arrived and has been forwarded to our director of order fulfillment. Your complete satisfaction is our goal; when you are satisfied, we are satisfied. Our customer service representative will contact you soon to assist with the issues raised in your letter.

Whether you're skiing or driving a snowmobile, Klondike Gear offers you the best protection from wind, snow, and cold—and Klondike has been taking care of customers' outdoor needs for over 27 years! Because you're a loyal customer, enclosed is a $5 gift certificate. You may wish to consider our new line of quality snow goggles.

Thank you for taking the time to write to us. Your input helps us better serve you and all our customers.

Puts customer at
ease with "you"
attitude

Includes resale and
sales promotion in
the body

Starts with a "good attitude" statement (not the usual good-news statement since it's going to people with various complaints)

Never suggests that customer was wrong to write to Klondike

Closes with statement of company's concern for all its customers

Analyze

Purpose is to grant a customer's claim, gently educate him, and encourage further business.

Investigate

Gather information on product care, warranties, and resale information.

Adapt

Use letter format to reinforce businesslike tone. Give customer relationship utmost attention.

1

Organize

Main idea is that you're replacing the wheel assembly—even though you are not required to do so.

Compose

Use an upbeat, conversational style, but remain businesslike. Choose words carefully, especially when educating the customer. Include resale information to reinforce future business.

2

Revise

Revise for tone, focusing on conciseness, clarity, and the "you" attitude.

Produce

Avoid confusing your positive message with fussy design elements. Keep it simple.

Proofread

Review for the usual errors, and include all promised enclosures.

3

FIGURE 7.8   Effective Letter Responding to a Claim When the Buyer Is at Fault

---

Skates Alive!

20901 El Dorado Hills
Laguna Niguel, CA 92677
(714) 332-7474 • Fax: (714) 336-5297
skates@speed.net

February 7, 2005

Mr. Steven Cox
1172 Amber Court
Jacksonville, FL 32073

Dear Mr. Cox

Thank you for contacting Skates Alive! about your in-line skates. Even though your six-month warranty has expired, we are mailing you a complete wheel assembly replacement free of charge. The enclosed instructions make removing the damaged wheel line and installing the new one relatively easy. ◄

Acknowledges reader communication, keeps opening positive by avoiding words such as "problem," and conveys the good news right away

The "Fastrax" (model NL 562) you purchased is our best-selling and most reliable skate. However, wheel jams may occur when fine particles of sand block ◄ the smooth rotating action of the wheels. These skates perform best when used on roadways and tracks that are relatively free of sand. We suggest that you remove and clean the wheel assemblies (see enclosed directions) once a month and have them checked by your dealer about every six months.

Explains the problem without blaming the customer by avoiding the pronoun "you" and by suggesting ways to avoid future problems

Includes sales promotion in the body, encouraging the customer to "trade up" ➤

Because of your Florida location, you may want to consider our more advanced "Glisto" (model NL 988) when you decide to purchase new skates. Although more expensive than the Fastrax, the Glisto design helps shed sand and dirt quite efficiently and should provide years of carefree skating.

Enjoy the enclosed copy of "Rock & Roll," with our compliments. Inside, you'll ◄ read about new products, hear from other skaters, and have an opportunity to respond to our customer questionnaire.

Adds value by enclosing a newsletter that invites future response from customer

Closes positively, ending on a "feel good" note that conveys an attitude of excellent customer service ➤

We love hearing from our skaters, so keep in touch. All of us at Skates Alive! wish you good times and miles of healthy skating.

Sincerely

Candace Parker

Candace Parker
Customer Service Representative

Enclosure

Pointers for Granting a Claim

- In the opening, state the good news: you're honoring the claim.
- Thank the reader for writing.
- In the body, explain how you'll grant the claim.
- Don't argue with reader's version of events.
- Keep your explanation objective, nonvindictive, and impersonal.
- Apologize only when appropriate; then do so crisply, with no overly dramatic tone.
- Keep your tone supportive.
- In the closing, remind the reader how you are honoring the claim.
- Encourage reader to look favorably on your company or product.
- Clarify any actions the reader must take.

highlight the person's abilities. Also remember that you have an obligation to mention any shortcomings that are serious and related to job performance.

The danger in writing a critical letter is that you might engage in libel (making a false and malicious written statement that injures the candidate's reputation). On the other hand, if that negative information is truthful and relevant, omitting it from your recommendation may be unethical and illegal. If you must refer to a shortcoming, stick to the facts, avoid value judgments, and place your criticism in the context of a generally favorable recommendation. In Figure 7.9, the writer supports all statements with facts and steers clear of vague, critical judgments.

Recommendation letters are usually confidential. That is, they're sent directly to the person or committee who requested them and are not shown to the candidate. However, recent litigation has made it advisable in some situations to prepare a carefully worded letter that satisfies both parties.

Sending Goodwill Messages

You can enhance your relationships with customers, colleagues, and other businesspeople by sending friendly, unexpected notes with no direct business purpose. Effective goodwill messages must be sincere and honest. Otherwise, the writer appears interested in personal gain. To come across as sincere, avoid exaggeration. To be honest, back up any compliments with specific points. Remember, readers often regard more restrained praise as being more sincere:

Make sure your compliments are grounded in reality.

Instead of This	Write This
Words cannot express my appreciation for the great job you did. Thanks. No one could have done it better. You're terrific! You've made the whole firm sit up and take notice, and we are ecstatic to have you working here.	Thanks again for taking charge of the meeting in my absence. You did an excellent job. With just an hour's notice, you managed to pull the legal and public relations departments together so that we could present a united front in the negotiations. Your dedication and communication abilities have been noted and are truly appreciated.

Congratulations Reasons for sending congratulations include the highlights in people's personal lives—weddings, births, graduations, success in nonbusiness competitions. A prime opportunity for sending goodwill messages is to congratulate someone for a significant business achievement—perhaps for being promoted or for attaining an important civic position. The improved congratulatory note in Figure 7.10 on page 187 moves swiftly to the good news.

Taking note of significant events in someone's personal life helps cement the business relationship.

You may congratulate business acquaintances on their own achievements or on the accomplishments of a spouse or child. You may also take note of personal events, even if you don't know the reader well. Of course, if you're already friendly with the reader, you can get away with a more personal tone.

Appreciation An important business quality is the ability to recognize the contributions of employees, colleagues, suppliers, and other associates. Your praise does more than just make the person feel good; it encourages further excellence. Moreover, a message of appreciation may become an important part of someone's personnel file. Therefore, when you write a message of appreciation, specifically mention the person or people you want to praise. The brief e-mail message that follows expresses gratitude and reveals the happy result:

A message of appreciation documents a person's contributions.

Thank you for sending the air-conditioning components via overnight delivery. You allowed us to satisfy the needs of two customers who were getting very impatient with the heat.

FIGURE 7.9   Effective Recommendation Letter

Discovery

DISCOVERY
COMMUNICATIONS
INCORPORATED

7700 Wisconsin Avenue
Bethesda, Maryland 20814-3579
301-986-1999

November 15, 2005

Ms. Clarice Gailey
Director of Operations
McNally and Associates, Inc.
8688 Southgate Ave.
Augusta, GA 30906

Dear Ms. Gailey:

I am pleased to recommend Talvin Biswas for the marketing position at
McNally and Associates. Talvin has worked with Discovery Communications
as an intern for the past two summers, while working toward his degree in
marketing and advertising.

Clearly states candidate's full name and main point in the opening

As his supervisor, in addition to knowing his work here, I also know that
Talvin has served as secretary for the International Business Association at
the University of Michigan. He tutored other international students in the
university's writing center. His fluency in three languages and thorough knowledge of other cultures will make him an immediate contributor to your international operation.

Specifies duration and nature of relationship in the body to give weight to the evaluation

Although a quiet, introspective young man, Talvin will not hesitate to contribute ideas when invited to do so. In addition, because Talvin learns quickly,
he will learn your company's routine with ease.

Talvin will make an excellent addition to your staff at McNally and Associates.
If you would like to further discuss Talvin's qualifications, please call or fax
me at the numbers above. If you prefer to communicate by e-mail, my address
is Rasmey@discovery.com.

Closes by inviting reader to discuss the candidate further

Begins the close by summarizing the supportive evaluation

Sincerely,

Lim Sok Rasmey

Lim Sok Rasmey
Vice President, Strategy and Development

Pointers for Writing Recommendation Letters

- Take the greatest care to avoid a lawsuit (either for including too much negative information or for omitting too much negative information).
- Consider verifying only the dates of employment and the titles of positions held.
- Release information only to people who have written authorization from former employees.
- Consider writing the letter with the former employee so that the contents satisfy you both.
- Consider asking the former employee to list you as a personal reference, which removes your company from any responsibility for statements you make (however, you can still be held personally responsible).
- Comment only on your own experience working with a former employee.
- Limit your remarks to provable facts (don't exaggerate).
- Always discuss the letter with your human resources department before releasing it.

Analyze
Purpose is to create goodwill with industry business associates.

Investigate
Gather information on specific accomplishments of the reader's firm.

Adapt
Letter format lets reader use your message (perhaps even reproduce it) as an industry testimonial.

Organize
Main idea is to congratulate the reader. The direct approach is perfect for this welcome news.

Compose
A conversational tone complements the slightly formal style, since this is your first contact with the reader. Avoid generalized praise by mentioning specific, concrete accomplishments.

Revise
Review for consistency in tone, word choice, and sentence structure.

Produce
A simple design avoids distracting your reader from the message.

Proofread
Create a positive first impression by being especially careful to send an error-free message.

1 **2** **3**

FIGURE 7.10   Letter Congratulating a Business Acquaintance

Poor

We are so pleased when companies that we admire do well. When we attended our convention in Atlanta last month, we heard about your firm's recent selection to design and print media advertisements for the National Association of Business Suppliers (ABS).

We have long believed that the success of individual franchises is directly linked to the healthy growth of the industry at large. Lambert, Cutchen & Browt is the only firm for the job.

We wish you the best of luck with your new ad campaign. Congratulations on a job well done!

Sincerely,

Janice McCarthy

Janice McCarthy
Director, Media Relations

◄ Sounds condescending and self-centered— expressing the reason but failing to actually congratulate the reader

◄ Seems insincere because of the lack of supporting reasons and the exaggeration ("only you can do the job")

◄ Congratulating the reader in the close seems like an afterthought

Improved

Office DEPOT, Inc.
2200 Old Germantown Road, Delray Beach, FL 33445   407/278-4800

March 3, 2005

Mr. Ralph Lambert, President
Lambert, Cutchen & Browt, Inc.
14355 Pasadena Parkway
Pasadena, TX 74229

Dear Mr. Lambert:

Opens by immediately expressing the reason for congratulating the reader

Congratulations on your firm's recent selection to design and print media advertisements for the National Association of Business Suppliers (ABS). Your appointment was announced at the national convention in Atlanta last month, and here at Office Depot, we can think of no better firm to help our industry achieve wide recognition.

Uses body to make compliment more efective by showing knowledge of the reader's work— without exaggeration

Your success has been admirable in promoting associations of other industries, such as soft drinks, snack foods, and recycling. Your "Dream Vision 2004" ads for the bottling industry were both inspirational and effective in raising consumer awareness. The campaign you design for ABS is sure to yield similar positive responses.

Closes by expressing interest in following the future success of the firm

You can be sure we will follow your media campaign with great interest.

Sincerely,

Janice McCarthy

Janice McCarthy
Director, Media Relations

tw

Special thanks to Susan Brown, who took our initial call and never said, "It can't be done." Her initiative on our behalf is greatly appreciated.

Condolences   In times of serious trouble and deep sadness, written expressions of sympathy leave their mark. Granted, this type of message is difficult to write, but don't let such difficulty keep you from responding promptly. Those who have experienced a health problem, the death of a loved one, or a business misfortune appreciate knowing that they're not alone.

> In condolence messages, try to find a middle path between being superficial and causing additional distress.

Condolences are seldom written on letterhead. Use a plain note card with matching envelope. Open with a brief statement of sympathy, such as "I was deeply sorry to hear of your loss." In the body, mention the good qualities or the positive contributions made by the deceased. State what the person or business meant to you. In the close, you can offer your condolences and your best wishes. One considerate way to end this type of message is to say something that will give the reader a little lift, such as a reference to a brighter future. Here are a few general suggestions for writing condolence messages:

- **Keep reminiscences brief.** Recount a memory or an anecdote (even a humorous one), but don't dwell on the details of the loss, lest you add to the reader's anguish.
- **Write in your own words.** Write as if you were speaking privately to the person. Don't quote "poetic" passages or use stilted or formal phrases. If the loss is a death, refer to it as such rather than as "passing away" or "departing."
- **Be tactful.** Mention your shock and dismay, but remember that bereaved and distressed loved ones take little comfort in lines such as "Richard was too young to die" or "Starting all over again will be so difficult." Try to strike a balance between superficial expressions of sympathy and heartrending references to a happier past or the likelihood of a bleak future.
- **Take special care.** Be sure to spell names correctly and to be accurate in your review of facts. Try to be prompt.
- **Write about special qualities of the deceased.** You may have to rely on reputation to do this, but let the grieving person know you valued his or her loved one.
- **Write about special qualities of the bereaved person.** A pat on the back helps a bereaved family member feel more confident about handling things during such a traumatic time.[3]

For an example of an effective condolence note, see Figure 7.11. George Bigalow sent the message to his administrative assistant, Glenna Case, after learning of the death of Glenna's husband.

FIGURE 7.11   **Effective Note of Condolence**

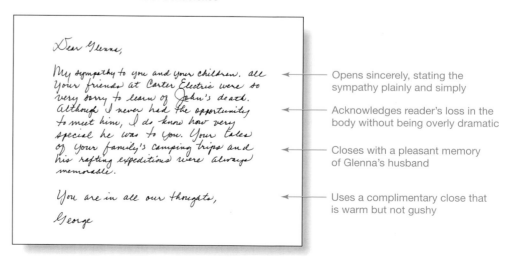

Dear Glenna,

My sympathy to you and your children. All your friends at Carter Electric were so very sorry to learn of John's death. Although I never had the opportunity to meet him, I do know how very special he was to you. Your tales of your family's camping trips and his rafting expeditions were always memorable.

You are in all our thoughts,

George

— Opens sincerely, stating the sympathy plainly and simply

— Acknowledges reader's loss in the body without being overly dramatic

— Closes with a pleasant memory of Glenna's husband

— Uses a complimentary close that is warm but not gushy

Reviewing Key Points

This chapter introduces strategies for routine, good-news, and goodwill messages. Some specific types of routine messages are discussed. The chapter explains how to apply the three-step writing process to routine messages.

In this chapter, you learn how to make routine requests by stating the request up front, explaining and justifying your request, and requesting specific action in a courteous close. You study techniques for placing orders, requesting information and action, making claims, and requesting recommendations. You learn how to prepare positive replies to requests and prepare other types of routine messages. You learn to open with the main idea, provide details and explanations in the body, and close courteously. This chapter explains techniques to use when granting requests for information and action, granting claims, providing recommendations, and sending goodwill messages.

The next chapter focuses on bad-news messages. You'll learn how to apply the three-step writing process to negative messages. The chapter explains the strategies for writing these bad-news messages and discusses various types of negative messages.

Test Your Knowledge

1. When is a request routine?

2. What are three guidelines for asking a series of questions in a routine request?

3. What information should be included in an order request?

4. Should you use the direct or indirect approach for most routine messages? Why?

5. Where in a routine message should you state your actual request?

6. How does a claim differ from an adjustment?

7. How does the question of fault affect what you say in a message granting a claim?

8. What six pieces of information must be included in a letter of recommendation?

9. How can you avoid sounding insincere when writing a goodwill message?

10. What are six guidelines for writing condolence messages?

Apply Your Knowledge

1. When organizing request messages, why is it important to know whether any cultural differences exist between you and your audience? Explain.

2. Your company's error cost an important business customer a new client; you know it and your customer knows it. Do you apologize, or do you refer to the incident in a positive light without admitting any responsibility? Briefly explain.

3. You've been asked to write a letter of recommendation for an employee who is disabled and uses a wheelchair. The disability has no effect on the employee's ability to do the job, and you feel confident about writing the best recommendation possible. Nevertheless, you know the prospective company and its facilities aren't well suited to wheelchair access. Do you mention the employee's disability in your letter? Explain.

4. Every time you send a direct-request memo to Ted Jackson, he delays or refuses to comply. You're beginning to get impatient. Should you send Jackson a memo to ask what's wrong? Complain to your supervisor about Jackson's uncooperative attitude? Arrange a face-to-face meeting with Jackson? Bring up the problem at the next staff meeting? Explain.

5. Ethical Choices   You have a complaint against one of your suppliers, but you have no documentation to back it up. Should you request an adjustment anyway? Why or why not?

Practice Your Knowledge

Exercises for Perfecting Your Writing

Revising Messages: Direct Approach   Revise the following short e-mail messages so that they are more direct and concise; develop a subject line for each revised message.

1. I'm contacting you about your recent order for a High Country backpack. You didn't tell us which backpack you wanted, and you know we make a lot of different ones. We have the canvas models with the plastic frames and vinyl trim and we have the canvas models with leather trim, and we have the ones that have more pockets than the other ones. Plus they come in lots of different colors. Also they make the ones that are large for a big-boned person and the smaller versions for little women or kids.

Subject line: _____

2. Thank you for contacting us about the difficulty you had collecting your luggage at the Denver airport. We are very sorry for the inconvenience this has caused you. As you know, traveling can create problems of this sort regardless of how careful the airline personnel might be. To receive compensation, please send us a detailed list of the items that you lost and complete the following questionnaire. You can e-mail it back to us.

Subject line: _____

Revising Messages: Direct Approach   Rewrite the following sentences so that they are direct and concise.

3. We wanted to invite you to our special 40% off by-invitation-only sale. The sale is taking place on November 9.

4. We wanted to let you know that we are giving a tote bag and a free Phish CD with every $50 donation you make to our radio station.

5. The director planned to go to the meeting that will be held on Monday at a little before 11:00 A.M.

6. In today's meeting, we were happy to have the opportunity to welcome Paul Eccelson. He reviewed some of the newest types of order forms. If you have any questions about these new forms, feel free to call him at his office.

Teamwork   With another student, conduct an audience analysis of the following message topic: A notice to all employees about the placement of recycling bins by the elevator doors

7. What is the purpose of this message?

8. What is the most appropriate format for communicating this written message?

9. How is the audience likely to respond to this message?

10. Based on this audience analysis, would you use the direct or the indirect approach for this message? Explain your reasoning.

Revising Messages: Closing Paragraphs   How would you rewrite each of the following closing paragraphs to be concise, courteous, and specific?

11. I need your response sometime soon so I can order the parts in time for your service appointment. Otherwise your air-conditioning system may not be in tip-top condition for the start of the summer season.

12. Thank you in advance for sending me as much information as you can about your products. I look forward to receiving your package in the very near future.

13. To schedule an appointment with one of our knowledgeable mortgage specialists in your area, you can always call our hotline at 1-800-555-8765. This is also the number to call if you have more questions about mortgage rates, closing procedures, or any other aspect of the mortgage process. Remember, we're here to make the home-buying experience as painless as possible.

Activities

For live links to all websites discussed in this chapter, visit this text's website at www. prenhall.com/bovee. Just log on, select Chapter 7, and click on "Featured Websites." Locate the page or the URL related to the material in the text.

1. **Analyze This Document**   Read the following document, then (1) analyze the strengths and weaknesses of each sentence, and (2) revise the document so that it follows this chapter's guidelines.

Our college is closing its dining hall for financial reasons, so we want to do something to help the students prepare their own food in their dorm rooms if they so choose. Your colorful ad in *Collegiate Magazine* caught our eye. We need the following information before we make our decision.

1. Would you be able to ship the microwaves by August 15th? I realize this is short notice, but our board of trustees just made the decision to close the dining hall last week and we're scrambling around trying to figure out what to do.
2. Do they have any kind of a warranty? College students can be pretty hard on things, as you know, so we will need a good warranty.
3. How much does it cost? Do you give a discount for a big order?
4. Do we have to provide a special outlet?
5. Will students know how to use them, or will we need to provide instructions?

As I said before, we're on a tight time frame and need good information from you as soon as possible to help us make our decision about ordering. You never know what the board might come up with next. I'm looking at several other companies, also, so please let us know ASAP.

2. **Analyze This Document**   Read the following document, then (1) analyze the strengths and weaknesses of each sentence, and (2) revise the document so that it follows this chapter's guidelines.

At a local business-supply store, I recently purchased your "Negotiator Pro" for my computer. I bought the CD because I saw your ad for it in *MacWorld* magazine, and it looked as if it might be an effective tool for use in my corporate seminar on negotiation.

Unfortunately, when I inserted it in my office computer, it wouldn't work. I returned it to the store, but since I had already opened it, they refused to exchange it for a CD that would work or give me a refund. They told me to contact you and that you might be able to send me a version that would work with my computer.

You can send the information to me at the letterhead address. If you cannot send me the correct disk, please refund my $79.95. Thanks in advance for any help you can give me in this matter.

3. **Analyze This Document**   Read the following document, then (1) analyze the strengths and weaknesses of each sentence, and (2) revise the document so that it follows this chapter's guidelines.

We read your letter requesting your deposit refund. We couldn't figure out why you hadn't received it, so we talked to our maintenance engineer as you suggested. He said you had left one of the doors off the hinges in your apartment in order to get a large sofa through the door. He also confirmed that you had paid him $5.00 to replace the door since you had to turn in the U-Haul trailer and were in a big hurry.

This entire situation really was caused by a lack of communication between our housekeeping inspector and the maintenance engineer. All we knew was that the door was off the hinges when it was inspected by Sally Tarnley. You know that our policy states that if anything is wrong with the apartment, we keep the deposit. We had no way of knowing that George just hadn't gotten around to replacing the door.

But we have good news. We approved the deposit refund, which will be mailed to you from our home office in Teaneck, New Jersey. I'm not sure how long that will take, however. If you don't receive the check by the end of next month, give me a call.

Next time, it's really a good idea to stay with your apartment until it's inspected as stipulated in your lease agreement. That way, you'll be sure to receive your refund when you expect it. Hope you have a good summer.

4. Analyze This Document   Read the following document, then (1) analyze the strengths and weaknesses of each sentence, and (2) revise the document so that it follows this chapter's guidelines.

Your letter to Tanaka Asata, President of SONY, was forwarded to me because I am the human resources director. In my job as head of HR, I have access to performance reviews for all of the SONY employees in the United States. This means, of course, that I would be the person best qualified to answer your request for information on Nick Oshinski.

In your letter of the 15th, you asked about Nick Oshinski's employment record with us because he has applied to work for your company. Mr. Oshinski was employed with us from January 5, 1998, until March 1, 2004. During that time, Mr. Oshinski received ratings ranging from 2.5 up to 9.6, with 10 being the top score. As you can see, he must have done better reporting to some managers than to others. In addition, he took all vacation days, which is a bit unusual. Although I did not know Mr. Oshinski personally, I know that our best workers seldom use all the vacation time they earn. I do not know if that applies in this case.

In summary, Nick Oshinski performed his tasks well depending on who managed him.

5. Internet   Visit the business section of the E-Cards site at www.4greeting-cards.com/At_Work/Appreciation/Business_Appreciation, and analyze one of the electronic greeting cards bearing a goodwill message of appreciation for good performance. Under what circumstances would you send this electronic message? How could you personalize it for the recipient and the occasion? What would be an appropriate close for this message?

6. Ethical Choices   Your small supermarket chain has received dozens of complaints about the watery consistency of the ketchup sold under the chain's brand name. You don't want your customers to stop buying other store-brand foods, which are made and packaged for your chain by various suppliers, but you do want to address their concerns about the ketchup. In responding to these complaints, should you explain that the ketchup is actually manufactured by a local supplier and then name the supplier, who has already started bottling a thicker ketchup?

7. Planning a Letter: Air Rage Fiasco   Letter requesting refund from British Airways. You've been administrative assistant to Samantha Alberts, vice president of sales for Richter Office Solutions, for two years. You handle all her travel arrangements and you've never seen her so upset. The "air rage" incident happened on Friday and now it's Monday, but she's still pale and shaky.

"There we were, cruising over the Atlantic, and the guy just erupted! I couldn't believe it!" she says for the third time.

She was flying back from a conference in London to make a presentation at your New York branch. Then she was to catch a plane home to San Francisco on Saturday. With airline security so tight these days, she expected a calm flight and lots of time to prepare her presentation notes as she crossed the ocean. As it turned out, she spent most of that time fearing for her life.

"What made the guy angry?" you ask.

"Apparently some passengers complained about 'offensive images' he was viewing on his laptop. When the steward politely asked him to stop, the guy went nuts and started hitting people, swearing all the while. At first I thought he was a hijacker and I was going to die on that plane! Thank goodness several crew members and passengers were able to subdue him and handcuff him into a back row seat. But we still had hours over the Atlantic before the pilot could land, so we had to listen to him screaming profanity. Finally, a passenger who was a pediatrician injected him with a sedative."

"Did they arrest him?" you want to know.

"As soon as we got on the ground. Police cars were everywhere. He just kept muttering, 'I thought they were going to kill me.'" She shudders. "But the flight attendants and airline officials were wonderful. They told us to write to the airline, explain the details, and ask for a refund."

"Of course, I was late and unprepared for my presentation. When they heard what happened, the folks in our New York office just handed me a cup of herb tea, sat me on a couch with a blanket, and told me to forget about making any presentations that day."

Your task: Samantha leaves you her ticket stubs and other documents. She's expecting you to write the refund request to British Airways Ticket Refunds USA, 75-20 Astoria Blvd., Jackson Heights, NY 11370. Before you begin, consider these questions:[4]

  a. For the purpose of this exercise, what details will you need to make up to write the request?
  b. Will you use a direct or indirect approach? Why?
  c. What tone should you adopt? What should you avoid?
  d. How will you support the claim?
  e. What would be an effective closing for this request?

8. **Planning a Letter: Intercultural Condolences**   Letter conveying sympathy at IBM. You've been working two years as administrative assistant to J. T. "Ted" Childs, Jr., vice president of global workforce diversity at IBM's Learning Center in Armonk, New York. After listening to so many of his speeches on maintaining multicultural sensitivity in the workplace, you know you're facing a sensitive situation right now. You need to stop and think before you act.

   Your co-worker Chana Panichpapiboon's husband was killed in a bus accident yesterday, along with 19 others. The bus skidded on icy pavement into a deep ravine, tipping over and crushing the occupants before rescue workers could get to them.

   You met her husband, Surin, last year at a company banquet. You can still picture his warm smile and the easy way he joked with you and others over chicken Florentine, even though you were complete strangers to him. He was only 32 years old, and he left Chana with two children, a 12-year-old boy, Arsa, and 10-year-old girl, Veera. His death is a terrible tragedy.

   Normally, you'd write a condolence letter immediately. But Chana Panichpapiboon is a native of Thailand, and so was Surin. You know you'd better do a little research first. Is Chana Buddhist or Catholic? Is there anything about the typical Western practice of expressing sympathy that might be inappropriate? Offensive?

   After making some discreet inquiries among Chana's closest friends at work, you learn that she is Theravada Buddhist, as are most people in Thailand. In a reference book your boss lends you about doing business around the world, you read that in Thailand, "the person takes precedence over rule or law" and "people gain their social position as a result of karma, not personal achievement," which means Chana may believe in reincarnation. But the book also says that Theravada Buddhists are free to choose which precepts of their religion, if any, they will follow. So Chana's beliefs are still a mystery.

   You do know that her husband was very important to her and much loved by all their family. That, at least, is universal. And you're considering using a poetic line you remember, "The hand of time lightly lays, softly soothing sorrow's wound." Is it appropriate?

   You've decided to handwrite the condolence note on a blank greeting card you've found that bears a peaceful, "Eastern-flavor" image. You know you're risking a cultural gaffe, but you don't want to commit the offense of not writing at all. Use the following questions to help you think through your choices before you begin writing:[5]

  a. If you had to choose among these sentences, which one would make the best opening?
     1. I was so sorry to hear the news about your husband.
     2. What a terrible tragedy you have suffered.
     3. If there's anything I can do for you, Chana, please let me know.
     4. You and your children must be so upset, and who could blame you?

  b. In the body of the letter, you want to express something meaningful, but you're concerned about Chana's beliefs and you're not sure what's safe. Choose the best idea from the following:
     1. You could quote the poem about "the hand of time" mentioned in the case.
     2. You might say something about the bus driver's terrible carelessness on slippery pavement.

3. You could express your sorrow for Chana's children.
4. You could mention something nice about Surin you learned during your brief meeting.

c. For your closing paragraph, which of these ideas is best?
1. Take a moment to express your thoughts about death and the hereafter.
2. Say something positive and encouraging about Chana.
3. Explain that you don't understand her religious beliefs and aren't sure what's appropriate to say at this time.
4. All of the above.

d. In the following list, circle all of the words you should avoid as you write:
1. Death
2. Departure
3. Karma
4. Unbearable

Now write the condolence letter in your own words. Remember that sincerity is the most important tool in overcoming differences of custom or tradition.

9. **Revising a Letter: Vacation Planning**   Letter requesting routine information about Florida resorts. The following letter requesting information about resorts in Florida contains numerous errors, based on what you've learned in this chapter. Read the letter carefully and analyze its flaws. Then use the steps below to outline and write a better version of the request.

5493 Beechwood Drive
Trenton, NJ 08608
April 12, 2005
Florida Resort Bureau
1555 Palm Beach Lakes Boulevard
West Palm Beach, FL 33401

Dear Sir:

My wife and I are planning a late September vacation with our two teenage children. We need this information in the next two weeks so I can schedule my time off from work in the fall.

I enjoy the beach and the golf course, but we also want to be near night entertainment suitable for the whole family. I am particularly interested in resort areas that have public transportation available; some family members may want to participate in activities away from the resort.

In addition to the brochures your advertisement promises, will you please also tell me which resorts are near large cities, which are reached by public transportation and have attractions for teenagers and do the off-season rates include all the amenities? Can you tell me additionally about the weather during September in Florida, and who we should call for concert schedules during our vacation?

Your advertisement about Florida resorts in the April 2005 issue of *Smithsonian* magazine caught my eye.

FRANK C. ATLAS

a. Describe the flaws you discovered in this letter requesting information.
b. Develop a plan for rewriting the letter. Use the following steps to organize your efforts before you begin writing:
1. Create a clear statement of your request
2. Decide what explanation is needed to justify your request
3. Determine whether you can use lists effectively in your letter
4. Ask for specific action
5. Mention a deadline and reason to respond, if appropriate

c. Now rewrite the letter. Don't forget to leave ample time for revision of your own work before you turn it in.

10. Revising a Letter Betting the company—A team-written letter from Boeing replying to questions about new aircraft plans. You're part of a team in the communication department at Boeing and you've been handed the following form letter, which was written by a temporary worker assisting the corporate chairman. Clearly the letter needs improvement. Your group has been asked to undertake the project, since this letter replying to routine requests for information will be going out to customers, suppliers, the media, and anyone else who inquires about Boeing's plans for developing the new Sonic Cruiser aircraft.

Your task: Working with your classmates as a team, read and discuss the problems you find in the letter, based on what you've learned in this chapter. Then outline a new plan for the letter and choose one person to put your team's ideas in letter form, which you'll all review and discuss before turning in your new, improved version.

Name
Address
City, State, ZIP or postal code
Country

Dear [name]:

We have been inundated with requests for information about Boeing's plans to produce the new Sonic Cruiser high-speed jet since our announcement of this revolutionary design, which resulted from hundreds of hours of research into the future of commercial air travel. So please forgive us for responding to you with a form letter, as we cannot respond effectively to each and every individual who has written to us with an inquiry.

The new jets will take off and land safely on shorter runways, fit comfortably with smaller terminals and taxiways, fly longer ranges. For every 3,000 miles flown, they will shave one hour of traditional flying time because they travel at Mach .95 (twenty percent faster than a 747). The new jets will cost airlines less to operate because of reduced flying time, and the new jets will offer consumers faster transport to their destination, featuring a sleek, delta-wing style, and they will be available in 2008.

For the first time, Boeing's manufacturing division will use outside suppliers for basic parts, so that our engineers can focus their expertise on the sophisticated systems required by the Sonic Cruiser. We're excited about this new efficiency. We expect to reap many benefits from it as Boeing continues to meet the future needs of air travelers, carriers, and the communities we serve.

Boeing envisions that municipalities will be building many more smaller, suburban airports to overcome the traffic congestion now clogging major airport hubs, both in the air and on the ground. To aid in this positive development, we have designed our new Sonic Cruiser.

Sincerely,

Phil Condit

Chairman

Expand Your Knowledge

Exploring the Best of the Web

Recommended Advice for Recommendation Letters
Whether you're continuing on to graduate school or entering the workforce with your undergraduate degree, recommendation letters could play an important role in the next few steps of your career. From selecting the people to ask for recommendation letters to knowing what makes an effective letter, About.com extends the advice offered in this chapter with real-life examples and suggestions. Visit www.about.com, search for "recommendation letters," read the advice you find, then answer the following questions:

Exercises

1. What's a good process for identifying the best people to ask for recommendation letters?

2. What information should you provide to letter writers to help them produce a credible and compelling letter on your behalf?

3. What are the most common mistakes you need to avoid with recommendation letters?

Exploring the Web on Your Own

Learn how to write effective thank-you notes by reviewing the steps at www.brownielocks.com/notes.html.

Need to write a press release but don't have time to become an expert? Learn from any expert at www.stetson.edu/~rhansen/prguide.html.

Get advice on writing sensitive condolence letters at www.ABusinessResource.com (search for "condolence letter").

Learn Interactively

Interactive Study Guide

Go to the Companion Website at www.prenhall.com/bovee. For Chapter 7, take advantage of the interactive "Study Guide" to test your knowledge of the chapter. Get instant feedback on whether you need additional studying. Also, visit this site's "Study Hall," where you'll find an abundance of valuable resources that will help you succeed in this course.

Peak Performance Grammar and Mechanics

To improve your skill with sentences, visit www.prenhall.com/onekey, click "Peak Performance Grammar and Mechanics" and then click "Sentences." Take the Pretest to determine whether you have any weak areas. Then review those areas in the Refresher Course. Take the Follow-Up Test to check your grasp of sentences. For an extra challenge or advanced practice, take the Advanced Test. Finally, for additional reinforcement in sentences, go to the "Improve Your Grammar, Mechanics, and Usage" section that follows, and complete the "Level 1: Self-Assessment" exercises.

Apply each step in Figure 7.1 on page 172 to the following cases, as assigned by your instructor:

1. Unhappy customer: Claim letter from you requesting an adjustment

As a consumer, you've probably bought something that didn't work right, or paid for a service that did not turn out the way you expected. Maybe it was a pair of jeans with a rip in a seam that you didn't find until you got home, or a watch that broke a week after you bought it. Or maybe your family hired a lawn service to do some yard work—and no one from the company showed up on the day promised. When a man finally appeared, he did not do what he'd been hired for, but did other things that wound up damaging valuable plants.

In either case, you'd be wise to write a claim letter asking for a refund, repair, replacement, or other adjustment. You'll need to include all the details of the transaction, plus your contact address and phone number.

Your task: To practice writing claim letters, choose an experience like this from your own background or make up details for these imaginary situations. If your experience is real, you might want to mail the letter. The reply you receive will provide a good test of your claim-writing skills!

2. Step on it: Letter to Floorgraphics requesting information about underfoot advertising

You work for Mary Utanpitak, owner of Better Bike and Ski Shop. You're always unpacking promotional displays and posters from manufacturers, and Mary has you store the extras in the back room or even take some home, since you love ski posters. But now a manufacturer wants to lease a piece of the store's floor!

The Schwinn sales representative, Ruth Beeker, met with Mary yesterday, urging her to sign a contract with Floorgraphics. That company leases floor space from retail stores, and then creates and sells floor ads to manufacturers like Schwinn. Floorgraphics will pay Mary a fee for leasing the floor space, as well as a percentage for every ad it sells. Mary was definitely interested, and turned to you after Beeker left.

"Ruth says that advertising decals on the floor in front of the product reach consumers right where they're standing when making a decision," explained Mary. "She says the ads increase sales from 25 to 75 percent."

You both look down at the dusty floor, and Mary laughs. "It seems funny that manufacturers will pay hard cash to put their names where customers are going to track dirt all over

them! But if Ruth's telling the truth, we could profit three ways: from the leasing fee, the increased sales, and the share in ad revenues. That's not so funny."

Your task: Mary Utanpitak wants you to write to CEO Richard Rebh at Floorgraphics, Inc. (5 Vaughn Drive, Princeton, NJ 08540), asking for financial details and practical information about the ads. For example, how will you clean your floors? Who installs and removes the ads? Can you terminate the lease if you don't like them? She'll sign the letter, but since you've been studying business communication, she thinks you'll do a better job writing the request.[6]

▌E-MAIL ▌WEB SKILLS ▌SKILLS 3. A juicy position: E-mail requesting information about careers at Jamba Juice

You did not expect to find a job while working out at 24-Hour Fitness, but you're willing to explore an opportunity when it appears. As you were buying a smoothie at the Jamba Juice bar inside the gym, you overheard the manager there talking about the company's incentives for employees, especially those interested in becoming managers. You ask her about it and she suggests you log on to the company's website (www.jambajuice.com) for more information.

You're still in business school, and you need a part-time job. Finding one at a company that offers a good future after graduation would be even better than simply earning some money to keep you going now. You check the Jamba Juice website.

You discover that the juice-bar chain has created a good reputation in the health, fitness, and nutrition industry. Also, you can submit your résumé for an entry-level job online. That sounds promising. If you could start now while finishing your degree, you'd be in a prime spot for promotion once you graduate.

But when you look at the careers page (www.jambacareers.com) you find the information a little confusing. The "General Manager J.U.I.C.E. Plan" seems to be about profit-sharing, but the details are not fully explained. You'd like to know more.

Your task: You're going to write an e-mail message requesting additional information about careers and advancement at Jamba Juice. First, visit www.jambajuice.com and www.jambacareers.com to learn all that you can. Then compose your message. Ask for clarification on any points you don't understand, or ask for further instructions on submitting your application. You might want to mention that you're still in school, studying business.[7]

4. Too many hours: Letter requesting letter of recommendation for dot-com dropout

When you took the job as office assistant at Yourtravel.com, you were excited about working for a brand new dot-com company in the travel services industry. You wanted to be on the leading edge of technology and to learn how things are done at a start-up company.

You had no idea how many hours per week you would be expected to work. Executives work at least 70 hours a week, and if they go home before 7 P.M. or fail to show up on Saturday or Sunday, they're considered a poor investment and soon disappear. Office assistants like you are expected to work at least 50 hours per week and at least two weekends per month.

You just can't do it anymore. You've worked here for six months now, and you're exhausted. The pay is good, the atmosphere is exciting, the boss loves your work, but you need time off! You need a reasonable job, 40 hours per week, with weekends off to regain your mental and physical strength. You've looked around and found several openings at more traditional travel companies (whose customers walk in the door rather than surf the Net). You'd love to learn more about Internet technology, but you just don't have the stamina to match the pace at Yourtravel.com.

When you submit your resignation to your boss, creative services director Glenna Evans, she's shocked and disappointed.

"Your work is so good—I wish you'd stay," she says, but you insist you must go.

Your task: You left the company in such a hurry, you forgot to ask for a recommendation. Write to Glenna Evans, Creative Services Director, Yourtravel.com, 145 S. Magnolia Avenue, Atlanta, GA 30333, and ask her to provide a formal letter of recommendation for you.[8]

■E-MAIL ■WEB SKILLS SKILLS 5. Lighten up: E-mail reply to a website designer at Organizers Unlimited

When Kendra Williams, owner of Organizers Unlimited, wanted to create a website to sell her Superclean Organizer, she asked you, her assistant, to find a designer. You researched it and found three promising individuals. Williams chose Pete Womack, whose résumé impressed both of you. Now he's e-mailed his first design proposal and Williams is not happy.

"I detest cluttered websites!" she explodes. "This home-page has too many graphics and animations, too much 'dancing baloney.' He must have included at least 500 kilo-bytes of bouncing cotton balls and jogging soap bars! Clever,

maybe, but we don't want it! If the homepage takes too long to load, our customers won't wait for it and we'll lose sales."

Williams's dislike of clutter is what inspired her to invent the Superclean Organizer in the first place, a neat device for organizing bathroom items.

Your task: "You found him," says Williams, "now you can answer and tell him what's wrong with this design." Before you write the reply to Womack explaining the need for a simpler homepage, read some of the articles offering tips at www.websitetips.com. Use these ideas to support your message.[9]

6. Satellite farming: Letter granting credit from Deere & Company

Your favorite task as a credit assistant at Deere & Company in Moline, Illinois, is writing to farmers like Arlen Ruestman and telling them that yes, the company will grant them credit to purchase new equipment.

Ruestman's farm is in Toluca, Illinois, and he wants to buy your company's new GreenStar satellite system for farmers. The Defense Department developed this technology, naming it the Global Positioning System (GPS). By using a series of satellites orbiting Earth, the system can pinpoint (to the meter) exactly where a farmer is positioned at any given moment as he drives his GreenStar-equipped combine over a field. For farmers like Reustman, GPS means that even 10,000 acres of corn or soybeans can be managed down to the last square foot.

For example, using the GreenStar system, farmers can map and analyze characteristics such as acidity, soil type, or crop yields from a given area. Using this information, they know exactly how much herbicide or fertilizer to spread over precisely which spot, thereby eliminating waste and achieving better results. Farmers can analyze why crops are performing well in some areas and not so well in others. They can even program farm equipment to treat only problem areas. For instance, Ruestman might discover and spray an insect infestation only two meters wide, without having to spray the entire field if it's not infested.

Some farms have already saved as much as $10 an acre on fertilizers alone. For 10,000 acres, that's $100,000 a year. Once Ruestman installs your GreenStar precision package on his old combine, he should have no problem saving enough to pay off the $7,350 credit account you're about to grant him.

Your task: Write a letter to Mr. Ruestman (P.O. Box 4067, Toluca, IL 61369), informing him of the good news.[10]

■TEAM ■WEB SKILLS SKILLS 7. Dot-com trainee: Letter of recommendation for LifeSketch.com intern

Mike Smith is founder, president, and CEO of LifeSketch.com (http://dc.internet.com/news/article.php/451871), an online service offering photo archiving to members. As

Smith's assistant, you've seen a lot of people come and go—but no one you'd rather see stay than your summer intern, Rolanda Winter. When you overheard her ask Smith for a letter of recommendation, you sat up and took notice. Is she leaving already?

"Don't worry, " Smith assures you. "She'll be here until fall term starts. But she wants to be prepared with a recommendation letter because she's already lining up serious job interviews. I wish we could hire her full-time."

"Maybe you'll find a place for her before September," you suggest hopefully.

Winter has been such a patient learner, and a true help to you, that you hate to lose her. Interns usually move on, but in this case, you'd love it if Smith hired her.

For one thing, she learned your filing system overnight, whereas other interns left things in a hopeless mess. She asked lots of intelligent questions about the business. You've been teaching her website design principles, and she's picked them up rapidly, helping you redesign several pages on the LifeSketch site. Most impressive was the fact that she was always on time, neatly dressed, polite, and eager to assist. Also, she didn't mind doing mundane tasks.

On the down side, Winter is a popular student. Early on, you often found her busy on the phone planning her many scheduled activities when you needed her help. After you had a little talk with her, this problem vanished.

"Since you know Rolanda's work better than anyone," says Smith, "I'd like you to draft the letter for me."

Your task: Working with a team of your classmates, discuss what should and should not be in the letter, which will be given to Rolanda Winter for general use. Then outline your ideas on paper. Finally, write the letter for Smith's signature.[11]

8. Midnight mission: Thank-you letter at the Blue Marble bookstore

Tina Moore, owner of the Blue Marble bookstore in Fort Thomas, Kentucky, likes to please her customers. You are her lead salesperson and, with your co-workers, you've been working hard to prepare for the biggest book sales party your store has ever hosted. Tonight's the night.

No one can argue with the popularity of author J. K. Rowling's *Harry Potter* books (and now the movies) about a boy who discovers he's a wizard-in-training and attends a special school for wizards only. Rowling's U.S. publisher, Scholastic, calls the books a "phenomenon" in publishing history, "beyond anything we imagined." It's become a bookstore tradition to host a release party when the newest edition in the series becomes available.

By agreement with the publishers, stores in the United States and Britain are not allowed to sell the new Harry Potter books they receive until a specific, "strict on-sale" date. Many stores open with a big party at midnight on that day. Parents and their children flock to the stores in pajamas, and often buy all the copies on hand before morning.

Like other adults, you've enjoyed the clever stories of Harry and his friends at Hogwarts school of wizardry. When Moore brought up the subject of a Harry Potter party, you quickly volunteered to coordinate the preparations.

Tonight, when the clock chimes midnight, customers will be ushered in by you and your co-workers in costume. An animal trainer with an owl that looks like Harry's "Hedwig" will be there. You'll serve oatmeal and Harry's favorite "butter beer" (apple juice and ginger ale over dry ice) from big black cauldrons the staff's been building all week. The kids will get free lightning-bolt stickers (to create forehead scars like Harry's), and black, round-rimmed imitation "Harry Potter spectacles." It's going to be great fun.

Your task: You've all been donating your free time sewing costumes, making hats, and inventing butter-beer recipes. Moore has asked you, as coordinator, to write a thank-you letter to the entire staff, and she wants you to co-sign it with her. She's going to include a $25 gift certificate in each envelope and give them out tonight before the party begins.[12]

9. Come back to us: Letter from EDS to dot-com deserters

"Now's our chance to get them back," announces director Tom Templeton at a human resources staff meeting. You're his assistant, and for a moment you're confused.

"Get who back?"

"Everyone who left to join dot-com start-ups. You know how many people we lost when the Internet's promise of overnight fortunes lured away some of our best employees. But now it's our turn."

"You mean invite back the 550 employees we lost to dot-coms in recent years?" you ask.

"Exactly. I read that 12,000 dot-com jobs were cut in a nine-month period last year. That number is probably higher now."

You see his point and smile. He'll save EDS considerable money and trouble if some of these individuals return. Finding and keeping good employees is one of the greatest costs of operating any business.

"As dot-coms fail, some of our best people may be out there looking for jobs," Templeton adds. "Are we going to let our competitors have them?"

Your task: After the meeting, Templeton asks you to create a form letter he can send to ex-employees, telling them that EDS will welcome them back if their dot-com jobs haven't worked out as expected.[13]

10. Ranch country: Letter offering a regional sales position with Golight

Nebraska rancher Jerry Gohl hired you when his invention, the Golight, first started to sell. Now Golight, Inc., earns

201

more than $2 million annually, but you're still Gohl's right-hand assistant.

Gohl invented the portable light to fit on his truck so he wouldn't have to get out in the freezing winters to check on his livestock. Then fishing enthusiasts, hunters, and boaters around the world discovered Golight, and sales representatives were soon working in every state and overseas—all except Nebraska. Gohl refused to give up his personal territory until he found the right person.

He's finally decided on Robert Victor, who also grew up on a Nebraska ranch. Victor knows the territory, and best of all, he's been doing well selling agricultural equipment in Montana for two years. Gohl liked him the moment they shook hands.

"He's got the job if he wants it," Gohl says. "Better send him an offer before someone else grabs him. He can start as soon as he's settled."

Your task: Compose the letter offering Victor salary plus commission "as discussed," with full benefits (paid vacation, and health and dental insurance) after six months of employment. Victor's address is 2732A S. Hanson Road, Glendive, MT 59330.[14]

INSTANT MESSAGES   11. Trans-global exchange: Instant message request for information from Chinese manufacturer

Thank goodness your company, Diagonal Imports, chose the enterprise instant messaging software produced by IBM Lotus, called Sametime. Other products might allow you to carry on real-time exchanges with colleagues on the other side of the planet, but Sametime supports bidirectional machine translation, and you're going to need it.

The problem is that production on a popular line of decorative lighting appliances produced at your Chinese manufacturing plant inexplicably came to a halt last month. As Product Manager in the United States, you have many resources you could call on to help, such as new sources for faulty parts. But you can't do anything if you don't know the details. You've tried telephoning top managers in China, but they're evasive, telling you only what they think you want to hear.

Finally, your friend Kuei-chen Tsao has returned from a business trip. You met her during your trip to China last year. She doesn't speak English, but she's the line engineer responsible for this particular product: a fiber-optic lighting display, featuring a plastic base with a rotating color-wheel. As the wheel turns, light emitted from the spray of fiber-optic threads changes color in soothing patterns. Product #3347XM is one of Diagonal's most popular items and you've got orders from novelty stores around the United States waiting to be filled. Kuei-chen should be able to explain the problem, determine whether you can help, and tell you how long before regular shipping resumes.

Your task: Write the first of what you hope will be a productive instant message exchange with Kuei-Chen. Remember your words will be machine-translated.[15]

Improve Your Grammar, Mechanics, and Usage

Level 1: Self-Assessment—Periods, Question Marks, and Exclamation Points

Review Sections 2.1, 2.2, and 2.3 in the Handbook of Grammar, Mechanics, and Usage, and then look at the following 15 items.

In items 1–15, add periods, question marks, and exclamation points wherever they are appropriate.

1. Dr Eleanor H Hutton has requested information on TaskMasters, Inc

2. That qualifies us as a rapidly growing new company, don't you think

3. Our president, Daniel Gruber, is a CPA On your behalf, I asked him why he started the company

4. In the past three years, we have experienced phenomenal growth of 800 percent

5. Contact me at 1358 N Parsons Avenue, Tulsa, OK 74204

6. Jack asked, "Why does he want to know Maybe he plans to become a competitor"

7. The debt load fluctuates with the movement of the US prime rate

8. I can't believe we could have missed such a promising opportunity

9. Is consumer loyalty extinct Yes and No.

10. Johnson and Kane, Inc, has gone out of business What a surprise

11. Will you please send us a check today so that we can settle your account

12. Mr James R Capp will be our new CEO, beginning January 20, 2003

13. The rag doll originally sold for $1098, but we have lowered the price to a mere $599

14. Will you be able to make the presentation at the conference, or should we find someone else

15. So I ask you, "When will we admit defeat" Never

Level 2: Workplace Applications

The following items contain numerous errors in grammar, capitalization, punctuation, abbreviation, number style, word division, and vocabulary. Rewrite each sentence in the space provided, correcting all errors. Write C in the space after any sentence that is already correct.

1. Attached to both the Train Station and the Marriott hotel, one doesnt even need to step outside the convention center to go from train to meeting room.

2. According to Federal statistics, 61 percent of the nations employers have less than 5 workers.

3. "The problem", said Business Owner Mike Millorn, "Was getting vendor's of raw materials to take my endeavor serious."

4. After pouring over trade journals, quizzing industry experts, and talks with other snack makers, the Harpers' decided to go in the pita chip business.

5. A Mac with half as much RAM and a slower processor is as fast or faster than a PC.

6. The couple has done relatively little advertising, instead they give away samples in person at trade shows, cooking demonstrations, and in grocery stores.

7. CME Information Services started by videotaping doctor's conventions, and selling the recorded presentations to nonattending physicians that wanted to keep track of the latest developments.

8. For many companies, the two biggest challenges to using intranets are: getting people to use it and content freshness.

9. Company meetings including 'lunch and learn' sessions are held online often.

10. Most Children's Orchard franchisees, are women between the ages of 30–50; first time business owners lacking even basic computer skills.

11. Joining the company in 1993, she had watched it expand and grow from a single small office to a entire floor of a skyscraper.

12. One issue that effected practically everyone was that they needed to train interns.

13. The website includes information on subjects as mundane as the filling out of a federal express form, and as complex as researching a policy issue.

14. "Some management theories are good, but how many people actually implement them the right way?", says Jack Hartnett President of D. L. Rogers Corp..

15. Taking orders through car windows, customers are served by roller-skating carhops at Sonic restaurants.

Level 3: Document Critique

The following document may contain errors in grammar, punctuation, capitalization, abbreviation, number style, vocabulary, and spelling. You will also find errors relating to topics in this chapter. For example, consider the organization and relevance of material as you improve this routine request for information. Correct all errors using standard proof-reading marks (see Appendix C).

Risa Zenaili

883 Middleton Aven.

Bartlesville OK 74005

918-555-9983

rzenaili@ppri.com

March 13 2002

Tharita Jones Owner

Subway Restaurant

120 W Greenfield Str.

Tulsa, Oklahoma, 74133

Dear Ms. Jones,

I am investigatting careers in vareous fast-food enviroments, since I expect to complete my

degreee in business administration within the next 3 years and that should leave me enough time to grow into a management position. Subway gave me your name when I asked for a franchise owner who might be willing to answer some questions about managment careers with the company. You may be able to provide the kind of informaton I'll never get from coporate brochures.

For example I'd like to know how long I can expect to work at an entry level before promotions are considered. How many levels must I rise before reaching assistant manager. And how many before I would be considered as manager, assuming I've performed well. Sometimes a person is promoted because they are qualified and sometimes it just because they willing to work long hours, so I want to know this before I commit myself!

I'm looking for a company that will offer me the best future in the most promising environment and since there are so many to choose from I am trying to be very careful in making this choice. I'd be really gratefull if you could take a moment to share any advice or encouragment you might have for me because as you know this kind of decision is one we all must make one day and it will effect us for a long, long time to come

I also like to know: How many hour a week can I expect to work to be on management career track? Once I reach management level: will those hours increase?
What qualifications do you look for in your managers and assitant managers? Plus: Benefits the company offers, special training—availibility and qualifications; how to improve my chances for promation if I choose Subway?

Please let me hear from you before the end of the month.

If you prefer to call than write; you reach me at 918 555-9983 day or evening. My cell phone number is (918) 555-8838. Or you can send a reply to me at the address above or to my e-mail address rzeinali@earthlink.net.

Sincerely:

Risa Zeinali

How Direct Is Too Direct?

Is it possible to be too direct, even if you're simply requesting information? At an event in Mexico, the president of the United States spoke bluntly of political realities, but the president of France spoke more abstractly—his style more grand, his words more beautiful. One man addressed the issues directly; the other was less direct. Which one had greater impact?

Neither speech changed global relationships, but the U.S. president was seen as a product of his outspoken culture, whereas the French president was seen as at least making his listeners feel better for a while. Countries such as France, Mexico, Japan, Saudi Arabia, Italy, and the Philippines all tend toward high-context cultures (see discussion in Chapter 1). That is, people in those countries depend on shared knowledge and inferred messages to communicate; they gather meaning more from context and less from direct statement.

Although people in the United States believe that being direct is civil, considerate, and honest, people in high-context cultures view that same directness as abrupt, rude, and intrusive—even dishonest and offensive. You might think you're doing a good thing by offering a little honest and constructive criticism to your Italian assistant, but doing so may actually hurt your assistant's dignity and could even be devastating. In fact, in high-context cultures, don't say outright, "You are wrong." People know when they've made a mistake, but if you put it into words in high-context cultures, you cause them to lose face.

To determine whether your international audience will appreciate a direct or an implied message, consider your audience's attitudes toward four factors: destiny, time, authority, and logic.

- **Destiny.** Do people in this culture believe they can control events themselves? Or are events seen as predetermined and uncontrollable? If you're supervising employees who believe that a construction deadline is controlled by fate, they may not understand your crisp e-mail message requesting them to stay on schedule; they may even find it insulting.
- **Time.** Do people in this culture believe that time is exact, precise, and not to be wasted? Or do they view time as relative, relaxed, and necessary for developing interpersonal relationships? If you believe that time is money and you try to get straight to business in your memo to your Japanese manager, your message may be overlooked in the confusion over your lack of relationship skills and your disregard for social propriety.
- **Authority.** Do the people in this culture conduct business more autocratically or more democratically? In Mexico, rank and status are highly valued, so when communicating with people who have less authority than you do, you may need to be even more direct than you're used to being in the United States. And when communicating with people who have more authority than you do, you may need to be much less direct in Mexico than you're used to being in the United States.
- **Logic.** Do the people in this culture pursue logic in a straight line from point A to point B? Or do they communicate in circular or spiral patterns of logic? If you organize a message in a straightforward and direct manner, your message may be considered illogical, unclear, and disorganized.

You may need to ask not only how direct to be in written messages but also whether to write at all; perhaps a phone call or a visit would be more appropriate. By finding out how much or how little a culture tends toward high-context communication, you can decide whether to be direct or to rely on nuance when communicating with people in that culture.

Applications for Success

For more information on the subject of intercultural communication, go to www.executiveplanet.com.

Answer the following questions:

1. Research a high-context culture such as Japan, Korea, or China, and write a one- or two-paragraph summary of how someone in that culture would go about requesting information.
2. When you are writing in American English to someone in a high-context culture, would it be better to (a) make the request directly in the interest of clarity or (b) try to match your audience's unfamiliar logic and make your request indirectly? Explain your answer.
3. Germany is a low-context culture; by comparison, France and England are more high-context. These three translations of the same message were posted on a lawn in Switzerland:
   a. **German:** "Walking on the grass is forbidden."
   b. **English:** "Please do not walk on the grass."
   c. **French:** "Those who respect their environment will avoid walking on the grass."

   How does the language of each sign reflect the way information is conveyed in the cultural context of each nation? Write a brief (two- to three-paragraph) explanation.

Writing Bad-News Messages

Learning Objectives

After studying this chapter, you will be able to

1 Apply the three-step writing process to bad-news messages

2 Show how to achieve an audience-centered tone and explain why it helps readers

3 Describe the differences between the direct and indirect approaches to bad-news messages, and indicate when it's appropriate to use each one

4 Discuss the three techniques for saying no as clearly and kindly as possible

5 Define *defamation* and explain how to avoid it in bad-news messages

6 List three guidelines for delivering bad news to job applicants

7 Explain five guidelines for accomplishing the main purpose in performance reviews

Bad news in the business world comes in all shapes and sizes. But even though bad news may be commonplace, Jeffrey Caponigro observes that most businesspeople don't know how to communicate this type of news effectively. Working in public relations for over 20 years, Caponigro has helped dozens of companies communicate bad news on such topics as plant closings, product-related lawsuits, criminal investigations, and other unfavorable situations. "The worst mistake is the tendency to clam up and pull back from communicating, rather than recognizing the need to communicate with even greater efficiency and effectiveness," he explains. Of course, communicating bad news isn't always easy, but the proper tone and approach can help people accept and understand your message. As Caponigro advises clients: "Most people will forgive just about anything if you admit to it, take responsibility for it, explain how it happened, and tell what you're doing to ensure it won't occur again."[1]

Using the Three-Step Writing Process for Bad-News Messages

Saying no is difficult.

Nobody likes bad news—as Jeffrey Caponigro can attest. People don't like to get it, and they don't like to give it. Saying no can put knots in your stomach and cost you hours of sleep. The word *no* is terse and abrupt, so negative that a lot of people have trouble saying it. And for most, it's the toughest word to hear or understand. But the most damaging "no" is usually the one you don't explain.[2] The three-step writing process can help you write bad-news messages that are more effective and less damaging (see Figure 8.1 on page 210).

Step 1: Planning Your Bad-News Messages

To be effective, bad-news messages require extremely careful analysis. Studying negative messages closely helps you word your purpose in the best possible way. It helps you make certain that the message should indeed be sent and in writing. Plus, analysis helps you know how your readers will receive your message and whether they prefer receiving it directly or indirectly. Any investigation or research must yield reliable, unmistakable facts that will support your negative decision and provide you with all the facts your audience will need. Finally, maintaining a good relationship with your audience is particularly important, in order to avoid alienating readers, so be sure to adapt your medium and tone to your audience.

Step 2: Writing Your Bad-News Messages

Because your main idea is a refusal, a rejection, or a negative announcement, be careful to define it and cover relevant points thoroughly and logically. Choosing between the direct and indirect approaches takes on added importance in bad-news messages. You need to decide whether to open with the bad news or to prepare your readers with a cogent explanation before giving them the negative bits. Also, pay special attention to word choice so that you can create sentences and paragraphs that are tactful and diplomatic.

Step 3: Completing Your Bad-News Messages

Careful revision ensures that your bad-news message is organized properly, says what you want it to say, and does so concisely and clearly. It gives you a chance to make sure that your design is appropriate for the bad news and contributes to your efforts to be sensitive. And as always, proofreading your message guarantees that misunderstandings won't arise from typos, errors in spelling, or problems with mechanics.

Strategies for Bad-News Messages

Whatever the details of your particular message, when you have bad news, you want your readers to feel that they have been taken seriously, and you want them to agree that your news is fair and reasonable. When delivering bad news, you have five main goals:

- To convey the bad news
- To gain acceptance for it
- To maintain as much goodwill as possible with your audience
- To maintain a good image for your organization
- To reduce or eliminate the need for future correspondence on the matter

Accomplishing so many goals in a single message is not easy. But you can convey negative news more effectively by following these guidelines: First, adopt an audience-centered tone. Second, organize your message to meet your audience's needs and expectations by using either the direct approach, which presents the main idea before the supporting data (fully described in Chapter 7), or the indirect approach, which presents the supporting data before the main idea.

Creating an Audience-Centered Tone

Your tone helps your readers accept that your bad news represents a firm decision. Your audience-centered focus helps readers understand that, under the circumstances, your decision was fair and reasonable. Your tone helps your audience remain well disposed toward your business. And not least, your audience-centered tone helps readers preserve their pride.

FIGURE 8.1   **Applying the Three-Step Writing Process to Bad-News Messages**

Planning →

Analyze
- Verify specific purpose is worth pursuing.
- Know how readers react to bad news.
- Know what readers want: bad news or reasons first.

Investigate
- Ensure information is reliable and accurate.
- Ensure facts support negative news.
- Gather all relevant facts readers need.

Adapt
- Verify effectiveness of written channel.
- Adapt medium and tone to audience.
- Pay particular attention to readers' feelings.

1

Writing →

Organize
- Carefully define negative main idea.
- Cover relevant points thoroughly.
- Group relevant points logically.
- Choose the direct or indirect approach with special care.

Compose
- Adapt style and tone to readers' culture.
- Pay special attention to word choice.
- Create sentences and paragraphs carefully.

2

Completing →

Revise
- Verify message is organized properly.
- Be sure it says what you want it to.
- Ensure message gives bad news concisely and clearly.

Produce
- Ensure design doesn't detract from bad news.
- Ensure design doesn't detract from your efforts to be sensitive.

Proofread
- Ensure there are no misunderstandings.
- Correct spelling and mechanical errors.
- Correct any alignment problems.
- Make sure the print quality is acceptable.

3

Experts suggest that conveying bad news in person requires listening to your audience before talking—building trust by letting people say what they feel. Bad news involves emotions, and you must acknowledge these emotions in your communication.[3] However, if you're delivering bad news in writing, you're unable to "listen" to your audience first. Nevertheless, you can certainly do your research up front and learn as much as you can about your audience. Only then are you able to demonstrate in writing that you're aware of your reader's needs, concerns, and feelings. To adopt an audience-centered tone, pay close attention to several techniques:

> Several techniques will help you establish an audience-centered tone.

- **Use the "you" attitude.** The "you" attitude is crucial to every message you write, but it's especially important in bad-news messages. Point out how your decision might actually further your audience's goals. Convey concern by looking for the best in your audience. And assume that your audience is interested in being fair, even when they are at fault.

- **Choose positive words.** The words you choose can make a letter either offensive or acceptable. You can ease disappointment by using positive words rather than negative, counterproductive ones (see Table 8.1). Just be sure not to hide the bad news.[4] Remember, you want to convey the bad news, not cover it up.

- **Use respectful language.** Protect your audience's pride by using language that conveys respect and avoids an accusing tone. For instance, when your audience is at fault, observe the "you" attitude by avoiding the word *you*. Use impersonal language to explain audience mistakes in an inoffensive way. Say, "The appliance won't work after being immersed in water" instead of "The appliance doesn't work because you immersed it in water."

Using the Direct Approach

> Use the direct approach when your negative answer or information will have little personal impact.

If you know that your audience prefers the bad news first, or if the situation is minor and the news will cause your audience little disappointment, use the direct approach:

- **Opening.** Start with a clear statement of the bad news.

- **Body.** Proceed to the reasons for the decision (perhaps offering alternatives).

- **Close.** End with a positive statement aimed at maintaining a good relationship with the audience.

Table 8.1	Choosing Positive Words
Avoid a Negative Tone	**Use a Positive Tone**
I *cannot understand* what you mean.	Please clarify your request.
There will be a *delay* in your order.	We will ship your order as soon as possible.
Your account is in *error*.	Corrections have been made to your account.
The breakage was not our *fault*.	The merchandise was broken during shipping.
Sorry for your inconvenience.	The enclosed coupon will save you $5 next time.
I was *shocked* to learn that you're unhappy.	Your letter reached me yesterday.
The enclosed statement is *wrong*.	Please recheck the enclosed statement.

Stating the bad news first has two advantages: (1) It makes a shorter message possible, and (2) the audience needs less time to reach the main idea of the message, the bad news itself.

Some bad-news situations are more appropriate for directness than others. You'll sometimes know from experience that your audience simply prefers reading the bad news first in any message. Internal messages are often organized so that the bad news comes before the reasons. Some managers expect all internal correspondence to be brief and direct, regardless of whether the message is positive or negative. Routine external messages often follow the direct approach, especially if they relay decisions that have little or no personal impact. The direct approach is usually used for readers who see bad news frequently (such as candidates searching for employment).[5] The direct approach is also appropriate when you want to present an image of firmness and strength.

Using the Indirect Approach

Beginning a bad news message with a blunt "no" could prevent some people from reading or listening to your reasons. Some people prefer an explanation first, and for them you would use the indirect approach, easing them into your message by explaining your reasons before delivering the bad news:

Use the indirect approach when some preparation will help your audience accept your bad news.

- **Opening.** Start with a buffer.
- **Body.** Continue with a logical, neutral explanation of the reasons for the bad news; then follow with a clear but diplomatic statement of the bad news (emphasizing any good news and de-emphasizing the bad).
- **Close.** End with a positive, forward-looking statement that is helpful and friendly.

Presenting your reasons first increases your chances of gaining audience acceptance by gradually preparing readers for the negative news to come. The indirect approach follows a four-part sequence: buffer, reasons, bad news, positive close.

Begin with a Buffer

A **buffer** is a neutral, noncontroversial statement that is closely related to the point of the message. Some critics believe that using a buffer is manipulative and dishonest, and thus unethical. But buffers are unethical only if they're insincere. Breaking bad news with kindness and courtesy is the humane way. Considering the feelings of others is never dishonest, and that consideration helps your audience accept your message. An effective buffer is tricky to write. A good buffer expresses your appreciation for being thought of, assures the reader of your attention to the request, compliments the reader,

A buffer is a neutral lead-in to bad news.

To write an effective buffer, make it sincere, relevant, neutral, respectful, succinct, assertive, brief, and not misleading.

or indicates your understanding of the reader's needs. To write effective buffers, try to make them

- **Sincere.** Never insult your audience with insincere flattery or self-promoting blather. An effective buffer never makes readers feel they are being set up or "snowed." Imagine writing a memo to tell another supervisor that you can't spare anyone from your staff for a temporary assignment to the order fulfillment department. You might begin with a sentence like this:

  > Our department shares your goal of processing orders quickly and efficiently.

- **Relevant.** Don't use an unrelated buffer. You will seem to be avoiding the issue. You'll appear manipulative and unethical, and you'll lose your audience's respect. In fact, try to base your buffer on statements made by the reader. Doing so shows that you have listened well.

- **Not misleading.** Avoid implying that good news will follow. Building up your audience's expectations at the beginning only makes the actual bad news even more surprising. Imagine your reaction to the following openings:

  > Your résumé indicates that you would be well suited for a management trainee position with our company.

  > Your résumé shows very clearly why you are interested in becoming a management trainee with our company.

  The second opening emphasizes the applicant's interpretation of her qualifications rather than the company's evaluation, so it's less misleading but still positive.

- **Neutral.** Avoid saying no. An audience encountering the blunt refusal right at the beginning usually reacts negatively to the rest of the message, no matter how reasonable and well phrased it is.

- **Respectful.** Avoid using a know-it-all tone. When you use phrases such as "you should be aware that," readers expect your lecture to lead to a negative response, so they resist the rest of your message.

- **Succinct.** Avoid wordy and irrelevant phrases and sentences. Sentences such as "We have received your letter," "This letter is in reply to your request," and "We are writing in response to your request" are irrelevant. Make better use of the space by referring directly to the subject of the letter.

- **Assertive.** Avoid apologizing. Unless warranted by extreme circumstances, an apology only weakens the following explanation of your unfavorable news.

- **Brief.** Avoid writing a buffer that is too long. Identify something that both you and your audience are interested in and agree on before proceeding in a businesslike way.

Table 8.2 shows several types of buffers you could use to open a bad-news message tactfully. After you've composed a buffer, evaluate it by asking yourself four questions: Is it pleasant? Is it relevant? Is it neutral, saying neither yes nor no? Does it provide for a smooth transition to the reasons that follow? If you can answer yes to every question, you can proceed confidently to the next section of your message.

Follow with Reasons

Giving reasons shows that your decision is reasonable and fair.

If you've done a good job of composing the buffer, the reasons will follow naturally. Cover the more positive points first; then move to the less positive ones. Provide enough detail for the audience to understand your reasons, but be concise; a long, roundabout explanation may make your audience impatient. Your goal is to explain *why* you have reached your decision before you explain *what* that decision is. If you present your reasons effectively, they should convince your audience that your decision is justified, fair, and logical.

Table 8.2	Types of Buffers	
Buffer	**Strategy**	**Example**
Agreement	Find a point on which you and the reader share similar views.	We both know how hard it is to make a profit in this industry.
Appreciation	Express sincere thanks for receiving something.	Your check for $127.17 arrived yesterday. Thank you.
Cooperation	Convey your willingness to help in any way you realistically can.	Employee Services is here to smooth the way for all of you who work to achieve company goals.
Fairness	Assure the reader that you've closely examined and carefully considered the problem, or mention an appropriate action that has already been taken.	For the past week, we have carefully monitored those using the photocopying machine to see whether we can detect any pattern of use that might explain its frequent breakdowns.
Good news	Start with the part of your message that is favorable.	A replacement knob for your range is on its way, shipped February 10 via UPS.
Praise	Find an attribute or an achievement to compliment.	Your résumé shows an admirable breadth of experience, which should serve you well as you progress in your career.
Resale	Favorably discuss the product or company related to the subject of the letter.	With their heavy-duty, full-suspension hardware and fine veneers, the desks and file cabinets in our Montclair line have become a hit with value-conscious professionals.
Understanding	Demonstrate that you understand the reader's goals and needs.	So that you can more easily find the printer with the features you need, we are enclosing a brochure that describes all the Panasonic printers currently available.

One way to be tactful when giving your reasons is to highlight how your negative decision benefits your readers (rather than focusing on why the decision is good for you or your company). For example, when denying a request for credit, you can show how your decision will keep the person from becoming overextended financially. Facts and figures are often helpful when convincing readers that you're acting in their best interests.

> Be tactful by focusing on reader benefits, not hiding behind company policy, and not apologizing.

Avoid hiding behind company policy to cushion the bad news. If you say, "Company policy forbids our hiring anyone who does not have two years' management experience," you seem to imply that you haven't considered the person on her or his own merits. Skilled and sympathetic communicators explain company policy (without referring to it as "policy") so that the audience can try to meet the requirements at a later time.

Similarly, avoid apologizing when giving your reasons. Apologies are appropriate only when someone in your company has made a severe mistake or has done something terribly wrong. If no one in the company is at fault, an apology gives the wrong impression. For example, suppose that you're refusing the application of a management trainee. A tactfully worded letter might give these reasons for the decision not to hire:

> Because these management trainee positions are quite challenging, our human relations department has researched the qualifications needed to succeed in them. The findings show that the two most important qualifications are a bachelor's degree in business administration and two years' supervisory experience.

The paragraph does a good job of stating the reasons for the refusal:

> Well-written reasons are
> ■ Detailed
> ■ Tactful
> ■ Individualized
> ■ Unapologetic
> ■ Positive

■ It provides enough detail to make the reason for the refusal logically acceptable.
■ It implies that the applicant is better off avoiding a program in which he or she would probably fail, given the background of potential co-workers.
■ It explains the company's policy as logical rather than rigid.
■ It offers no apology for the decision.
■ It avoids negative personal expressions ("You do not meet our requirements").

Sometimes detailed reasons should not be provided.

Jeffrey Caponigro has learned that even though specific reasons help audiences accept bad news, reasons cannot always be given. Don't include reasons when they involve confidential, excessively complicated, or purely negative information or when they benefit only you or your firm (by enhancing the company's profits, for example). Instead, move directly to the next section.

State the Bad News

When the bad news is a logical outcome of the reasons that come before it, the audience is psychologically prepared to receive it. However, the audience may still reject your message if the bad news is handled carelessly. Three techniques are especially useful for saying no as clearly and as kindly as possible. First, de-emphasize the bad news:

- Minimize the space or time devoted to the bad news.
- Subordinate bad news in a complex or compound sentence ("My department is already shorthanded, so I'll need all my staff for at least the next two months"). This construction pushes the bad news into the middle of the sentence, the point of least emphasis.
- Embed bad news in the middle of a paragraph or use parenthetical expressions ("Our profits, which are down, are only part of the picture").

To handle bad news carefully, use three techniques:
- De-emphasize the bad news visually and grammatically.
- Use a conditional statement.
- Tell what you did do, not what you didn't do.

Second, use a conditional (*if* or *when*) statement to imply that the audience could have received, or might someday receive, a favorable answer ("When you have more managerial experience, you are welcome to reapply"). Such a statement could motivate applicants to improve their qualifications.

Third, tell the audience what you did do, can do, or will do rather than what you did not do, cannot do, or will not do. Say "We sell exclusively through retailers, and the one nearest you that carries our merchandise is . . . " rather than "We are unable to serve you, so please call your nearest dealer." By implying the bad news, you may not need to actually state it ("The five positions currently open have been staffed with people whose qualifications match those uncovered in our research"). By focusing on the positive and implying the bad news, you soften the blow.

Don't let the bad news get lost by overemphasizing the positive.

When implying bad news, be sure your audience understands the entire message—including the bad news. It would be unethical to overemphasize the positive. So if an implied message might leave doubt, state your decision in direct terms. Just be sure to avoid overly blunt statements that are likely to cause pain and anger:

Instead of This	Use This
I *must refuse* your request.	I will be out of town on the day you need me.
We *must deny* your application.	The position has been filled.
I *am unable to* grant your request.	Contact us again when you have established . . .
We *cannot afford to* continue the program.	The program will conclude on May 1.
Much as I would like to attend . . .	Our budget meeting ends too late for me to attend.
We *must reject* your proposal.	We've accepted the proposal from AAA Builders.
We *must turn down* your extension request.	Please send in your payment by June 14.

End with a Positive Close

Make your close positive, final, optimistic, sincere, and confident.

After giving your audience the bad news, your job is to end your message on an upbeat note. You might propose an attainable solution to the audience's problem ("The human resources department has offered to bring in temporary workers when I need them, and they would probably consider doing the same for you"). In a message to a customer or

Document Makeover

Improve This Memo

To practice correcting drafts of actual documents, visit www.prenhall.com/onekey on the web. Click "Document Makeovers," then click Chapter 8. You will find a memo that contains problems and errors relating to what you've learned in this chapter about writing negative business messages. Use the Final Draft decision tool to create an improved version of this memo. Check the message for the use of buffers, apologies, explanations, subordination, embedding, positive action, conditional phrases, and upbeat perspectives.

potential customer, an off-the-subject ending can include **resale information** (favorable comments about a product or service that the customer has already purchased) or **sales promotion** (favorable comments that encourage interest in goods or services the reader has not yet committed to purchase). If you've asked readers to decide between alternatives or to take some action, make sure that they know what to do, when to do it, and how to do it with ease. Whatever type of close you choose, follow these guidelines:

- **Keep it positive.** Don't refer to, repeat, or apologize for the bad news, and refrain from expressing any doubt that your reasons will be accepted (avoid statements such as "I trust our decision is satisfactory").
- **Limit future correspondence.** Encourage additional communication *only* if you're willing to discuss your decision further (avoid wording such as "If you have further questions, please write").
- **Be optimistic about the future.** Don't anticipate problems (avoid statements such as "Should you have further problems, please let us know").
- **Be sincere.** Steer clear of clichés that are insincere in view of the bad news (avoid saying, "If we can be of any help, please contact us").
- **Be confident.** Don't show any doubt about keeping the person as a customer (avoid phrases such as "We hope you will continue to do business with us").

If you are the one who has to reject the applicant for the management trainee position, you can observe these guidelines by writing a close like this:

Many companies seek other qualifications in management trainees, so I urge you to continue your job search. You'll certainly find an opening in which your skills and aspirations match the job requirements exactly.

Keep in mind that the close is the last thing the audience has to remember you by. Try to make the memory a positive one.

Types of Bad-News Messages

In the course of your business career, you will write various types of bad-news messages, from refusing credit to giving negative performance reviews. Many of the messages that you'll be writing will fall into three major categories: negative answers to routine requests, negative organizational news, and negative employment messages.

Sending Negative Answers to Routine Requests

As a businessperson, you can't say yes to everyone. Occasionally, your response to routine requests must simply be "no." It's a mark of your skill as a communicator to be able to say no clearly and yet not cut yourself off from future dealings with the people you refuse.

Refusing Requests for Information

Use either the direct or the indirect approach to tell someone you cannot provide what has been requested.

When people ask you for information and you can't honor the request, you may answer with either the direct approach or the indirect approach. However, using the direct approach may offend readers who are outside the company and may be emotionally involved in the response. Compare the poorly written draft with the improved, revised letter in Figure 8.2.

FIGURE 8.2   Letter Refusing a Request for Information

Poor

Dear Mr. Phuoc:

Our company policy prohibits us from participating in research projects in which disclosure of discretionary information might be necessary. Therefore, we decline your invitation to our sales staff to fill out questionnaires for your study.

Thank you for trying to include Quality Information Services in your research. If we can be of further assistance, please let us know.

Sincerely,

The writer hides behind the blanket "company policy," a policy that the reader may find questionable

Tone is unnecessarily negative and abrupt

The offer to help is an unpleasant irony, given the writer's unwillingness to help in this instance

Improved

Quality
Information Services

1692 Pelham Avenue, New Rochelle, NY 10803
Voice: (914) 927-8219   Fax: (914) 927-8220

April 19, 2005

Mr. Tran Phuoc
774 Claremont Dr.
Wicker Park, Il 60622

Dear Mr. Phuoc:

Buffer is supportive and appreciative →

We at Quality Information Services appreciate and benefit from the research of companies such as yours. Your study sounds interesting, and the questionaire is well developed.

Bad news is implied, not stated explicitly →

Body fully explains reason for decision without falling back on a blanket reference to company policy →

Our board requires strict confidentiality of all sales information until quarterly reports are mailed to stockholders. We release press reports at the same time the quarterly reports go out, and we'll be sure to include you in all our future mailings.

We are more than willing to share information that is part of the public record. I've enclosed several of our past earnings reports for your inspection. We look forward to seeing the results of your study. Please let us know if there is any additional way we can help.

Close is friendly, positive, and helpful →

Sincerely,

Francis Newburgh

Francis Newburgh
Director, Human Resources

Pointers for Writing Bad-News Messages

- Maintain a supportive, audience-centered tone by being sincere, using the "you" attitude, choosing positive words, and using respectful language.
- State the bad news as positively as possible, using tactful wording.
- De-emphasize bad news by minimizing the space devoted to it, subordinating it, or embedding it.
- Emphasize what the firm did do or is doing rather than what it can't or won't do.
- Remind the reader of how his or her needs are being met.
- Eliminate any reference to the bad news, apologies, and uncertainty.
- Suggest actions the reader might take.
- Keep a positive outlook on the future.
- Be confident about keeping the person as a customer.

The improved letter conveys the same negative message but without sounding offensive. As you think about the different effects of these two letters, you can see why good business writers take the time and the trouble to give negative messages the attention they deserve, even when they are only requesting information.

Refusing Invitations and Requests for Favors

When you must say no to an invitation or a requested favor, your use of the direct or the indirect approach depends on your relationship with the reader. For example, suppose the president of the local community college asks your company to host graduation on your corporate grounds, but your sales meetings will be taking place at the same time. If you don't know the president well, you'll probably use the indirect approach. See Figure 8.3, in which May Yee Kwan delivers this bad news in a helpful and supportive way. If you are friends with the president and work frequently on projects for the college, you might use the direct approach:

> Sandra, thanks for asking us to host your graduation. You know we've always supported the college and would love to do this for you. However, our company sales meetings will be going on during the same time. We'll have so many folks tied up with logistics, we won't have the personnel to adequately take care of the graduation.
>
> Have you called Jerry Kane over at the Botanical Gardens? I can't think of a prettier site for graduation. Roberta in my office volunteers over there and knows Jerry. She can fill you in on the details, if you'd like to talk to her first.
>
> Thanks again for considering us. Let's have lunch in mid-June to plan our involvement with the college for the next school year. You can think of all kinds of ways to make me sorry I had to say no! I'll look forward to seeing you and catching up on family news.

This letter gets right to the point but still uses some blow-softening techniques: It compliments the person and organization making the request, suggests an alternative, and looks toward future opportunities for cooperation.

Handling Bad News About Orders

For several reasons, businesses must sometimes convey bad news concerning orders. Also, when delivering bad news to existing or would-be customers, you have an additional challenge—resale. To make readers feel good about continuing to do business with your firm, you want to

- Work toward an eventual sale along the lines of the original order
- Keep instructions or additional information as clear as possible
- Maintain an optimistic, confident tone so that your reader won't lose interest

Reinforcing the customer's confidence in your service or product is an effective way to meet the resale challenge. Just don't overdo it.

When you must back-order for a customer, you have one of two types of bad news to convey: (1) You're able to send only part of the order, or (2) you're able to send none of the order. When sending only part of the order, you actually have both good news and bad news. In such situations, the indirect approach works very well. The buffer contains the good news (that part of the order is en route) along with a resale reminder of the product's attractiveness. After the buffer come the reasons for the delay of the remainder of the shipment. A strong close encourages a favorable attitude toward the entire transaction. For a customer whose order for a recliner and ottoman will be only partially filled, your e-mail message might read like the one in Figure 8.4 on page 219.

When you're unable to send the customer any portion of an order, you still use the indirect approach. However, because you have no good news to give, your buffer only

When turning down an invitation or a request for a favor, base your choice of approach on your relationship with the reader.

The basic goal of a bad-news letter about orders is to protect or make a sale.

Use the indirect approach for both types of bad news about orders.

Planning	Writing	Completing
Analyze Gauge audience's reaction to refusal; gear level of formality to reader familiarity. **Investigate** Collect information on possible alternatives. **Adapt** For a more formal response, letterhead is best. Maintain the relationship with the "you" attitude, and focus on the reader's problem.	**Organize** Main idea is to refuse a request. Respect your reader by showing that the request received serious consideration. Use an indirect approach. **Compose** Make your style conversational but keep it businesslike. Keep the letter brief, clear, and helpful.	**Revise** Maintain a friendly tone by eliminating overly formal words and phrases. Ensure your tone is positive. **Produce** Use letterhead with a straight-forward format. **Proofread** Be careful to review for accuracy, spelling, and mechanics.

| **1** | **2** | **3** |

FIGURE 8.3 **Effective Letter Declining a Favor**

InfoTech

927 Dawson Valley Road, Tulsa, Oklahoma 74151
Voice: (918) 669-4428   Fax: (918) 669-4429
www.infotech.com

March 5, 2005

Dr. Sandra Wofford, President
Whittier Community College
333 Whittier Ave.
Tulsa, OK 74150

Dear Dr. Wofford:

Infotech has been happy to support Whittier Community College in many ways over the years, and we appreciate the opportunities you and your organization provide to so many deserving students. Thank you for considering our grounds for your graduation ceremony.
→ Buffers bad news by demonstrating respect and recapping request

Our company-wide sales meetings will be held during the weeks of May 31 and June 7. We will host over 200 sales representatives and their families, and activities will take place at both our corporate campus and the Ramada Renaissance. As a result, our support staff will be devoting all of their time and effort to these events.
→ States reason for the bad news explicitly and in detail

My assistant, Roberta Seagers, suggests you contact the Municipal Botanical Gardens as a possible graduation site. She recommends calling Jerry Kane, director of public relations. If we can help in any other way with graduation, please let us know.
→ Suggests an alternative—showing that Kwan cares about the college and has given the matter some thought

We remain firm in our commitment to you, President Wofford, and to the fine students you represent. We will continue to be a corporate partner to Whittier College and will support your efforts as you move forward.
→ Closes by renewing the corporation's future support

Sincerely,

May Yee Kwan

May Yee Kwan
Public Relations Director

lc

Pointers for Writing Buffers and Giving Reasons

Buffer

- Express appreciation, cooperation, fairness, good news, praise, resale, or understanding.
- Introduce a relevant topic.
- Avoid apologies and negative-sounding words *(won't, can't, unable to)*.
- Be brief and to the point.

Reasons

- Smooth the transition from the favorable buffer to the reasons.
- Show how the decision benefits your audience.
- Avoid apologies and expressions of sorrow or regret.
- Offer enough detail to show the logic of your position.
- Include only factual information and only business reasons, not personal ones.
- Carefully word the reasons so that readers can anticipate the bad news.

FIGURE 8.4 Effective E-Mail Message Advising of a Back Order

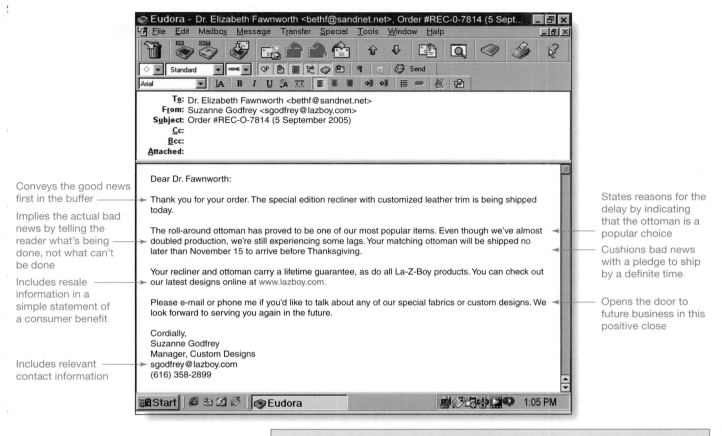

Conveys the good news first in the buffer

Implies the actual bad news by telling the reader what's being done, not what can't be done

Includes resale information in a simple statement of a consumer benefit

Includes relevant contact information

States reasons for the delay by indicating that the ottoman is a popular choice

Cushions bad news with a pledge to ship by a definite time

Opens the door to future business in this positive close

Pointers for Informing Customers about Back Orders

Buffer

- Include all details to identify the order.
- Extend a welcome to a new customer.
- Use resale information to build the customer's confidence in the original choice.
- For partial shipments, include the good news about the fulfilled part.

Reasons

- State the facts without laying blame.
- Specify shipping dates.
- Explain why the item is out of stock (such as exceptional demand, which may stimulate the customer's desire for the item).
- Reinforce the customer's confidence (for consumers, emphasize personal attention, credit, repair services, free delivery, special discounts, telephone shopping, and other services; for dealers, emphasize free counter and window displays, advertising materials, sales manuals, factory guarantees, and nearby warehousing).

The Bad News

- Stress how the reader benefits from the decision to buy.
- Offer a substitute product, if available.

Positive, Friendly, Helpful Close

- Adopt a tone that shows you remain in control of the situation and will continue to give customers' orders personal attention.
- Use resale information to clinch the sale.

confirms the sale, and the explanation section states your reasons for not filling the order promptly.

Refusing Claims and Requests for Adjustment

Use the indirect approach in most cases of refusing a claim.

Almost every customer who makes a claim is emotionally involved; therefore, the indirect approach is usually the best approach for a refusal. Your job as a writer is to avoid accepting responsibility for the unfortunate situation and yet avoid blaming or accusing the customer. To steer clear of these pitfalls, pay special attention to the tone of your letter. Keep in mind that a tactful and courteous letter can build goodwill even while denying the claim. For example, Village Electronics recently received a letter from Daniel Lindmeier, who believes that his warranty covers one year, when it actually covers only three months. For the reply to his letter, see Figure 8.5.

When refusing a claim, avoid language that might have a negative effect on the reader. Instead, demonstrate that you understand and have considered the complaint. Then, even if the claim is unreasonable, rationally explain why you are refusing the request. Remember, don't apologize and don't rely on company policy. End the letter on a respectful note, and try to suggest some alternative action.

When refusing a claim
■ Demonstrate your understanding of the complaint
■ Explain your refusal
■ Suggest alternative action

Avoid defamation by not responding emotionally.

You may be tempted to respond to something particularly outrageous by calling the person responsible a crook, a swindler, or an incompetent. Resist! Otherwise you could be sued for **defamation,** a false statement that tends to damage someone's character or reputation. (Written defamation is called *libel;* spoken defamation is called *slander*). To avoid being accused of defamation, follow these guidelines:

■ Avoid using any kind of abusive language or terms that could be considered defamatory.
■ If you wish to express your own personal opinions about a sensitive matter, use your own stationery (not company letterhead), and don't include your job title or position. Take responsibility for your own actions without involving your company.
■ Provide accurate information and stick to the facts.
■ Never let anger or malice motivate your messages.
■ Consult your company's legal department or an attorney whenever you think a message might have legal consequences.
■ Communicate honestly, and make sure that what you're saying is what you believe to be true.

Sending Negative Organizational News

Refusing a request isn't the only type of bad news. At times, you may have bad news about your company's products or about its operations. Whether you're reporting to a supervisor or announcing your news to the media, the particular situation dictates whether you will use the direct or the indirect approach.

Bad News About Products

Say that you must provide bad news about a product. If you were writing to tell your company's bookkeeping department about increasing product prices, you'd use the direct approach. Although your audience would have to make some arithmetical adjustments, readers would probably be unemotional about the matter. On the other hand, if you were writing to convey the same information to customers or even to your own sales department, you would probably use the indirect approach. Customers never like to pay more, and your sales reps would see the change as weakening your products' competitive edge, threatening their incomes, and possibly threatening their jobs.

Bad News About Company Operations

Use either the direct or the indirect approach when providing bad news about a product.

At least three situations require bad-news letters about company operations or performance: (1) a change in company policy or future plans that will have a negative effect on the reader, (2) problems with company performance, and (3) controversial or unpopular company operations. In trying situations, apologies may be in order. If an apology is appropriate, good writers usually make it brief and bury it somewhere in the middle of

Planning	Writing	Completing

Analyze
Purpose is to explain that the warranty has expired and to offer repairs that the reader can pay for.

Investigate
Briefly gather information on product warranties, terms for repair, and resale information.

Adapt
Use letter format and focus on customer relationship.

1

Organize
Main idea is that you're offering repairs, even though the warranty has expired. Use the indirect approach to help reader accept your message.

Compose
Make the style conversational. Choose your words carefully, and enclose a catalog to encourage future business.

2

Revise
Review for logical order and tone. Be clear but friendly.

Produce
Use a clean letter format on letterhead.

Proofread
Review for accuracy and correctness. Be sure to include promised enclosures.

3

FIGURE 8.5   Effective Letter Refusing a Claim

NUMBER ONE IN ENTERTAINMENT
Village Electronics
68 Lake Itasca Boulevard • Hannover, MN 55341
Voice: (612) 878-1312 • Fax: (612) 878-1316

May 3, 2005

Mr. Daniel Lindmeier
849 Cedar Street
Lake Elmo, MN 55042

Dear Mr. Lindmeier:

Buffers the bad news by emphasizing a point that reader and writer both agree on

Thank you for your letter about the battery release switch on your JVC digital camera. Village Electronics believes, as you do, that electronic equipment should be built to last. That's why we stand behind our products with a 90-day warranty.

States bad news indirectly, tactfully leaving the repair decision to the customer

Even though your JVC camera is a year old and therefore out of warranty, we can still help. Please package your camera carefully and ship it to our store in Hannover. Include your complete name, address, phone number, and a brief description of the malfunction, along with a check for $35. After examining the unit, we will give you a written estimate of the needed parts and labor. Then just let us know whether you want us to make the repairs—either by phone or by filling out the prepaid card we'll send you with the estimate.

Puts company's policy in a favorable light

If you choose to repair the unit, the $35 will be applied toward your bill, the balance of which is payable by check or credit card. If you decide not to repair the unit, the $35 will pay for the technician's time examining the unit. JVC also has service centers available in your area. If you would prefer to take the unit to one of them, please see the enclosed list.

Helps soothe the reader with a positive alternative action

Closes by blending sales promotion with an acknowledgment of customer's interests

Thanks again for inquiring about our service. I've enclosed a catalog of our latest cameras and accessories. In June JVC is offering a "Trade-Up Special," at which time you can receive trade-in credit for your digital camera when you purchase a newer model. Come and visit Village Electronics soon.

Sincerely,

Walter Brodie

Walter Brodie
President

mk

Enclosures: List of service centers
                    Catalog

Pointers for Refusing Claims
- In the buffer, indicate your full understanding of the nature of the complaint.
- Avoid all areas of disagreement and any hint of your final decision.
- In the body, provide an accurate, factual account of the transaction.
- Avoid using a know-it-all tone, and use impersonal, passive language.
- Make the refusal clear, using tactful language (avoid words such as reject and claim).
- Avoid any hint that your decision is less than final.
- Offer a counterproposal, a compromise, or a partial adjustment (if desirable).
- Include resale information for the company or product.
- Emphasize your desire for a good relationship in the future.
- Offer to replace the product or to provide a replacement part at the regular price.
- In the close, make no reference to your refusal.
- Refer to enclosed sales material.
- Make any suggested action easy for readers to comply with.

the letter. Moreover, they try to leave readers with a favorable impression by closing on a positive note.

Companies that produce unpopular products or have controversial operations can find themselves caught in a political crossfire. In such cases, the best strategy might be to explain the reasons the company is manufacturing the controversial item or providing the unpopular service. The idea is to show that reason and need are behind the operation (not villainy, carelessness, or greed).

> **When conveying bad news about your company, focus on the reasons and on possible benefits.**

When a change in company policy will have a negative effect on your audience, state the reasons for the change clearly and carefully. The explanation section of the message convinces readers that the change was necessary and, if possible, explains how the change will benefit them. For example, if your company decided to drop orthodontic coverage from its employee dental plan, you could explain the decision this way:

> By eliminating this infrequently used benefit, we will not have to increase the monthly amount withheld from your paycheck for insurance coverage.

If your company is having serious performance problems, your customers and shareholders want to learn of the difficulty from you, not from newspaper accounts or from rumors. Even if the news leaks out before you announce it, counter with your own explanation as soon as possible. Business is based on mutual trust; if your customers and shareholders can't trust you to inform them of your problems, they may choose to work with someone they can trust. When you do inform stakeholders, use your common sense and present the bad news in as favorable a light as possible.

If your company loses a major business customer or if an important deal falls through, you could present the bad news as an opportunity to focus on smaller, growing businesses or on new products, as the e-mail in Figure 8.6 does. In this example, rather

FIGURE 8.6   Effective E-Mail Message Providing Bad News About Company Operations

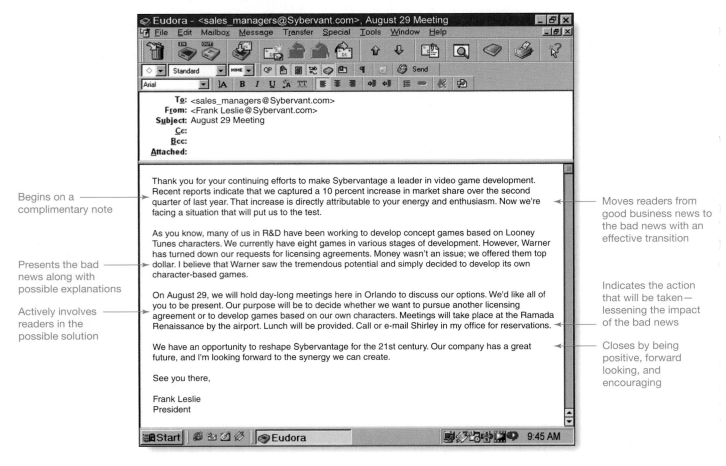

Begins on a complimentary note

Presents the bad news along with possible explanations

Actively involves readers in the possible solution

Moves readers from good business news to the bad news with an effective transition

Indicates the action that will be taken—lessening the impact of the bad news

Closes by being positive, forward looking, and encouraging

then dwell on the bad news, the company focuses on possible options for the future. The upbeat close diminishes the effect of the bad news.

Sending Negative Employment Messages

Most managers must convey bad news to people from time to time. You can use the direct approach when communicating with other companies, sending a negative reference to a prospective employer, or writing to job applicants. But it's best to use the indirect approach when giving negative performance reviews to employees, because they will most certainly be emotionally involved. In addition, choose the media you use for these messages with care.

Refusing Requests for Recommendations and References

Even though many states have passed laws to protect employers who provide open and honest job references for former employees, legal hazards persist.[6] That's why many former employers still refuse to write recommendation letters—especially for people whose job performance has been unsatisfactory. When sending refusals to prospective employers, your message may be brief and direct:

> We received your request for a recommendation for Yolanda Johnson. According to guidelines from our human resources department, we are authorized to confirm only that Ms. Johnson worked for Tandy, Inc., for three years, from June 2003 to July 2005. Best of luck as you interview the administrative applicants.

This message does not say, "We cannot comply with your request." It simply gets down to the business of giving readers the information that is allowable.

Letters to applicants themselves are another matter. Any refusal to cooperate may seem a personal slight and a threat to the applicant's future. Diplomacy and preparation help readers accept your refusal:

> Thank you for letting me know about your job opportunity with Coca-Cola. Your internship there and the MBA you've worked so hard to earn should place you in an excellent position to land the marketing job.
>
> Although we send out no formal recommendations here at PepsiCo, I can certainly send Coke a confirmation of your employment dates. For more in-depth recommendations, be sure to ask the people you worked with during your internship to write evaluations of your work performance, and don't forget to ask several of your professors to write evaluations of your marketing skills. Best of luck to you in your career.

This letter deftly and tactfully avoids hurting the reader's feelings because it makes positive comments about the reader's recent activities, implies the refusal, suggests an alternative, and uses a polite close.

Rejecting Job Applications

It's difficult to tactfully tell job applicants that you won't be offering them employment. But don't let the difficulty stop you from communicating the bad news. Rejecting an applicant with silence is unacceptable. At the same time, poorly written rejection letters do have negative consequences, ranging from the loss of qualified candidates for future openings to the loss of potential customers (not only the rejected applicants but also their friends and family).[7] When delivering bad news to job applicants, follow three guidelines:[8]

■ **Open with the direct approach.** Businesses fare better when they reject applicants up front.[9] Job applicants know that good news will most likely come by phone and that bad news will most likely come by letter. If you try to buffer the bad news that your reader is expecting, you will seem manipulative and insincere.

■ **Clearly state why the applicant was not selected.** Make your rejection less personal by stating that you hired someone with more experience or whose qualifications match the position requirements more closely.

- **Close by suggesting alternatives.** If you believe the applicant is qualified, mention other openings within your company. You might suggest professional organizations that could help the applicant find employment. Or you might simply mention that the applicant's résumé will be considered for future openings. Any of these positive suggestions may help the applicant be less disappointed and view your company more positively.

A rejection letter need not be long. Remember, sending a well-written form letter that follows these three guidelines is better than no letter at all. After all, the applicant wants to know only one thing: Did I land the job? Your brief message conveys the information clearly and with tactful consideration for the applicant's feelings. The e-mail in Figure 8.7 was drafted by Marvin Fichter to communicate the bad news to Carol DeCicco. After reviewing the ineffective first draft, Fitcher made several changes to help DeCicco understand that (1) she would have been hired if she'd had more tax experience, and (2) she shouldn't be discouraged.

Giving Negative Performance Reviews

A performance review is a supervisor's formal or informal evaluation of an employee. Few other communication tasks require such a broad range of skills and strategy as that needed for performance reviews, whether positive or negative. The main purpose of these reviews is to improve employee performance by (1) emphasizing and clarifying job requirements, (2) giving employees feedback on their efforts toward fulfilling those requirements, and (3) guiding continued efforts by developing a plan of action, along with its rewards and opportunities. In addition to improving employee performance, performance reviews help companies set organizational standards and communicate organizational values.[10]

Positive and negative performance reviews share several characteristics: The tone is objective and unbiased, the language is nonjudgmental, and the focus is on resolving any problems.[11] Also, to increase objectivity, more organizations are giving their employees feedback from multiple sources. In these "360-degree reviews," employees get feedback from all directions in the organization: above, below, and horizontally.[12]

Employee performance reviews can play an important role in lawsuits. It's difficult to criticize employees face-to-face, and it's just as hard to include criticism in written performance evaluations. Nevertheless, if you fire an employee for incompetence and the performance evaluations are all positive, the employee can sue your company, maintaining you had no cause to terminate employment.[13] Also, your company could be sued for negligence if an injury is caused by an employee who received a negative evaluation but received no corrective action (such as retraining).[14] So as difficult as it may be, make sure your performance evaluations are well balanced and honest:[15]

- **Confront the problem right away.** Avoiding performance problems only makes them worse. The one acceptable reason to wait is to allow you time to calm down and regain your objectivity.

- **Plan your message.** Be clear about your concerns, and include examples of the employee's specific actions. Think about any possible biases you may have, and get feedback from others. Collect and verify all relevant facts (both strengths and weaknesses).

- **Deliver the message in private.** Whether in writing or in person, address the performance problem privately. Don't send performance reviews by instant message, e-mail, or fax. Conduct a face-to-face review in a meeting that has been arranged expressly for that purpose. Consider holding that meeting in a conference room, the employee's office, or some other neutral area.

- **Focus on the problem.** Discuss the problems caused by the employee's behavior (without attacking the employee). Compare employee performance with what's expected, with company goals, or with job requirements (not with the performance of other employees). Identify the consequences of continuing poor performance, and show that you're committed to helping solve the problem.

FIGURE 8.7 Effective E-Mail Message Rejecting a Job Application

Poor

Dear Ms. DeCicco:

We were so impressed with your résumé and credentials. Your academic record and previous accounting experience are just what we were hoping to see. We just didn't expect to see such sterling qualifications in so many candidates. As you can imagine, with 30 applicants for this position, the selection process was quite difficult.

After much consideration, we were able to narrow down the choices to three, one of which was you. However, I'm sorry to say that you were not chosen to fill the tax accountant position.

If you wouldn't mind, we would like to keep your information on file for six months, on the off chance that another position might open up before you find another position.

Thank you for thinking of us.

Opens using the indirect approach—leading the candidate on and building her expectations before disappointing her

Begins to hint at the bad news rather than just coming out with it

Gives no reasons for why someone else was chosen, leaving the candidate to ponder whatever personal characteristics she might regard as her shortcomings

Finally states the bad news, but does so bluntly, with an apology that makes the reader feel worse than necessary

Closes positively, but asking to keep reader's records on file sounds insincere after handling the rejection so badly

Improved

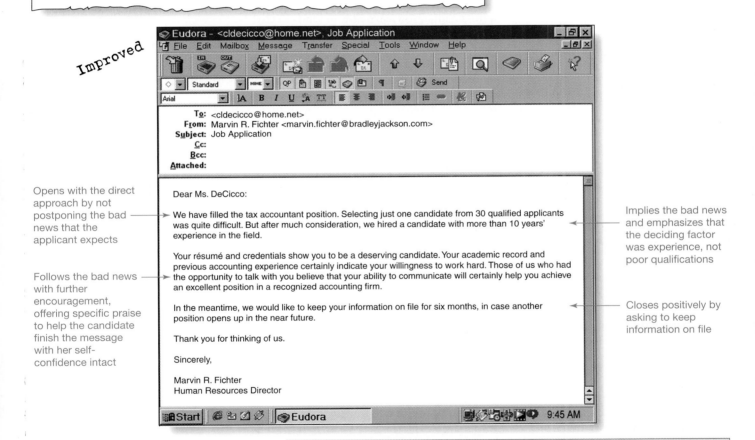

Opens with the direct approach by not postponing the bad news that the applicant expects

Follows the bad news with further encouragement, offering specific praise to help the candidate finish the message with her self-confidence intact

Implies the bad news and emphasizes that the deciding factor was experience, not poor qualifications

Closes positively by asking to keep information on file

Eudora - <cldecicco@home.net>, Job Application

File Edit Mailbox Message Transfer Special Tools Window Help

Standard   MIME   QP   Send

Arial   IA   B   I   U

To: <cldecicco@home.net>
From: Marvin R. Fichter <marvin.fichter@bradleyjackson.com>
Subject: Job Application
Cc:
Bcc:
Attached:

Dear Ms. DeCicco:

We have filled the tax accountant position. Selecting just one candidate from 30 qualified applicants was quite difficult. But after much consideration, we hired a candidate with more than 10 years' experience in the field.

Your résumé and credentials show you to be a deserving candidate. Your academic record and previous accounting experience certainly indicate your willingness to work hard. Those of us who had the opportunity to talk with you believe that your ability to communicate will certainly help you achieve an excellent position in a recognized accounting firm.

In the meantime, we would like to keep your information on file for six months, in case another position opens up in the near future.

Thank you for thinking of us.

Sincerely,

Marvin R. Fichter
Human Resources Director

Start   Eudora   9:45 AM

Pointers for Rejecting Job Applications

- Express the reasons for writing—clearly, completely, and objectively.
- Avoid insincere expressions of regret and impersonal business clichés.
- Whenever possible, embed negative comments in favorable or semifavorable passages.
- Emphasize the positive qualities of the person hired rather than the shortcomings of the rejected applicant.
- Imply negative decisions whenever possible.
- Avoid statements that might involve the company in legal action.
- If candidate is desirable, mention possibilities for future openings.

■ **Ask for a commitment from the employee.** Help the employee understand that planning for and making improvements are the employee's responsibility. However, finalize decisions jointly so that you can be sure any action to be taken is achievable. Set a schedule for improvement and for following up with evaluations of that improvement.

In performance reviews, say what's right as well as what's wrong, and explain how the employee can improve performance.

Even if your employee's performance has been disappointing, you would do well to mention some good points in your performance review. Then, you must clearly and tactfully state how the employee can better meet the responsibilities of the job. If the performance review is to be effective, be sure to suggest ways that the employee can improve.[16] For example, instead of only telling an employee that he damaged some expensive machinery, suggest that he take a refresher course in the correct operation of that machinery. The goal is to help the employee succeed.

Reviewing Key Points

This chapter introduces strategies for bad-news messages and discusses some specific types. The chapter explains how to apply the three-step writing process to bad-news messages.

In this chapter, you learn how to send effective bad-news messages by creating an audience-centered tone and choosing between the direct and indirect approaches. You study techniques for beginning indirect messages with a buffer, following with reasons, stating the bad news, and ending with a positive close. You learn how to prepare negative answers to routine requests, including refusing requests for information, refusing invitations and requests for favors, handling bad news about orders, and refusing claims. This chapter shows you how to send negative news about products and about company operations. It also introduces techniques for sending negative employment messages such as refusing requests for recommendations, rejecting job applicants, and sending negative performance reviews.

The next chapter focuses on persuasive messages. You will learn how to apply the three-step writing process to persuasive messages. The chapter will also explain the strategies for writing persuasive messages and present techniques for preparing persuasive requests and sales messages.

Test Your Knowledge

1. What are the five main goals in delivering bad news?

2. Why is it particularly important to adapt your medium and tone to your audience's needs and preferences when writing a bad-news message?

3. What are the advantages of using the direct approach to deliver the bad news at the beginning of a message?

4. What is the sequence of elements in a bad-news message organized using the indirect approach?

5. What is a buffer, and why do some critics consider it unethical?

6. When using an indirect approach to announce a negative decision, what is the purpose of presenting your reasons before explaining the decision itself?

7. What are three techniques for de-emphasizing bad news?

8. What is defamation, and how does libel differ from slander?

9. What are three guidelines for writing rejection letters to job applicants?

10. When giving a negative review to an employee, what five steps should you follow?

Apply Your Knowledge

1. Why is it important to end your bad-news message on a positive note? Explain.

2. If company policy changes, should you explain those changes to employees and customers at about the same time, or should you explain them to employees first? Why?

3. If the purpose of your letter is to convey bad news, should you take the time to suggest alternatives to your reader? Why or why not?

4. When a company suffers a setback, should you soften the impact by letting out the bad news a little at a time? Why or why not?

5. **Ethical Choices** Is intentionally de-emphasizing bad news the same as distorting graphs and charts to de-emphasize unfavorable data? Why or why not?

Practice Your Knowledge

Exercises for Perfecting Your Writing

Teamwork Working alone, revise the following statements to de-emphasize the bad news. (*Hint:* Minimize the space devoted to the bad news, subordinate it, embed it, or use the passive voice.) Then team up with a classmate and read each other's revisions. Did you both use the same approach in every case? Which approach seems to be most effective for each of the revised statements?

1. The airline can't refund your money. The "Conditions" segment on the back of your ticket states that there are no refunds for missed flights. Sometimes the airline makes exceptions, but only when life and death are involved. Of course, your ticket is still valid and can be used on a flight to the same destination.

2. I'm sorry to tell you, we can't supply the custom decorations you requested. We called every supplier and none of them can do what you want on such short notice. You can, however, get a standard decorative package on the same theme in time. I found a supplier that stocks these. Of course, it won't have quite the flair you originally requested.

3. We can't refund your money for the malfunctioning lamp. You shouldn't have placed a 250-watt bulb in the fixture socket; it's guaranteed for a maximum of 75 watts.

Indirect Approach: Buffers Answer the following questions pertaining to buffers:

4. You have to tell a local restaurant owner that your plans have changed and you have to cancel the 90-person banquet scheduled for next month. Do you need to use a buffer? Why or why not?

5. Write a buffer for a letter declining an invitation to speak at the association's annual fund-raising event. Show your appreciation for being asked.

6. Write a buffer for a letter rejecting a job applicant who speaks three foreign languages fluently. Include praise for the applicant's accomplishments.

Indirect or Direct Approach Select which approach you would use (direct or indirect) for the following bad-news messages:

7. A memo to your boss informing her that one of your key clients is taking its business to a different accounting firm

8. An e-mail message to a customer informing her that one of the books she ordered over the Internet is temporarily out of stock

9. A letter to a customer explaining that the tape backup unit he ordered for his new custom computer is on back order and that, as a consequence, the shipping of the entire order will be delayed

Activities

For live links to all websites discussed in this chapter, visit this text's website at www. prenhall.com/bovee. Just log on, select Chapter 8, and click on "Featured Websites." Locate the page or the URL related to the material in the text.

1. **Analyze This Document** Read the following document, then (1) analyze the strengths and weaknesses of each sentence, and (2) revise each document so that it follows this chapter's guidelines.

Your spring fraternity party sounds like fun. We're glad you've again chosen us as your caterer. Unfortunately, we have changed a few of our policies, and I wanted you to know about these changes in advance so that we won't have any misunderstandings on the day of the party.

We will arrange the delivery of tables and chairs as usual the evening before the party. However, if you want us to set up, there is now a $100 charge for that service. Of course, you might want to get some of the brothers and pledges to do it, which would save you money. We've also added a small charge for cleanup. This is only $3 per person (you can estimate because I know a lot of people come and go later in the evening).

Other than that, all the arrangements will be the same. We'll provide the skirt for the band stage, tablecloths, bar setup, and of course, the barbecue. Will you have the tubs of ice with soft drinks again? We can do that for you as well, but there will be a fee.

Please let me know if you have any problems with these changes and we'll try to work them out. I know it's going to be a great party.

2. **Analyze This Document**   Read the following document, then (1) analyze the strengths and weaknesses of each sentence, and (2) revise each document so that it follows this chapter's guidelines.

I am responding to your letter of about six weeks ago asking for an adjustment on your fax/modem, model FM39Z. We test all our products before they leave the factory; therefore, it could not have been our fault that your fax/modem didn't work.

If you or someone in your office dropped the unit, it might have caused the damage. Or the damage could have been caused by the shipper if he dropped it. If so, you should file a claim with the shipper. At any rate, it wasn't our fault. The parts are already covered by warranty. However, we will provide labor for the repairs for $50, which is less than our cost, since you are a valued customer.

We will have a booth at the upcoming trade fair there and hope to see you or someone from your office. We have many new models of office machines that we're sure you'll want to see. I've enclosed our latest catalog. Hope to see you there.

3. **Ethical Choices**   The insurance company where you work is planning to raise all premiums for health-care coverage. Your boss has asked you to read a draft of her letter to customers announcing the new, higher rates. The first two paragraphs discuss some exciting medical advances and the expanded coverage offered by your company. Only in the final paragraph do customers learn that they will have to pay more for coverage starting next year. What are the ethical implications of this draft? What changes would you suggest?

4. **Planning a Memo: Bad News About Polyester at Coca-Cola**   Polyester went out of style in the 1980s, when no fashionable person would consider the synthetic material. Now polyester is making a comeback in both fashion and food, and the product development department at Coca-Cola wants to use it in the company's plastic drink containers.

To support this proposal, they've presented stacks of material from the chemical companies that produce polyester, such as Amoco, Dow, and Shell. These experts insist that mixing some of their new-generation polyester (polyethylene naphthalate or PEN) into the current plastic used for drink containers (polyethylene terephthalate or PET) will create a harder plastic that will eliminate carbonation loss and solve heat-sensitivity problems. They also say that the resulting material will appeal to consumers because it's clear, lightweight, resealable, and recyclable.

But as a marketing assistant, you've now helped conduct research among a major market segment for soft drinks: young adults. Of all the container materials proposed in the market survey of 1,000 young adults, aluminum ranked highest, with 84 percent of them preferring it. They said they like the feel of the aluminum cans (plastic feels slippery and is harder to hold) and believe that aluminum keeps drinks colder. They also believe that aluminum keeps the carbonation longer, creating a "mouth buzz," whereas plastic lets the fizz out. And finally, they think that aluminum cans look "cool" and that plastic containers look "dorky." They're not likely to buy your drinks in the proposed new containers.

Your research team came up with some suggestions for improving plastic's image among young adults. One approach would be an ad campaign showing "cool young people" drinking from plastic bottles. Another would be ads showing that new technology is helping the plastic containers to hold in the "fizz."

Meanwhile, Shell Chemical's director of polyester research and development, David Richardson, is pushing your company to use the new polyester. "In a few years," he says, "I'll be able to fix you a nice meal, and everything in it will come out of a polyester container." Richard Marion, an executive at Amoco Corporation's Amoco Chemical Company, suggests that "plastic is less deadly than glass when you throw it at a soccer match," so Coca-Cola would be doing the world a good turn, as well.

Your task: You need to report the market research findings to your boss, Tom Ruffenbach, director of marketing at Coca-Cola, in a form he can pass along to other departments during meetings on the proposed conversion to polyester containers. Before you start writing, answer the following questions to help you organize your thinking.

   a. The best format for conveying the information will be
      1. Notes you've made from the study results, organized in neat outline form
      2. An informal e-mail that alerts your boss to the problem uncovered by the study
      3. A formal letter using subheadings to detail the bad news, point by point
      4. A memo that summarizes the bad news from the market study and includes suggestions for overcoming this consumer resistance

   b. Using the direct approach, a good opening sentence for your message would be
      1. "Tom, we've got a problem."
      2. "We can't use plastic containers for our soft drinks."
      3. "While the proposals for the new polyester are convincing and based on scientific data, our market research has uncovered a potential problem with youthful consumers."
      4. "I think you should consider the results of our market study before you proceed."

   c. Explain why you chose your answer for question number b. Then explain why you did not choose each of the other selections.
   d. In the body of your message, you'll want to
      1. Explain the scope of the market study
      2. Summarize the study results, possibly using lists
      3. Suggest positive steps to counteract the bad news
      4. All of the above

   e. What's a good way to close this memo to your boss?
      1. With a restatement of the problem/bad news
      2. On a positive note
      3. With your recommendation for action
      4. With your contact information for further communication

Now that you've thought through these elements, write the bad-news memo in your own words.[17]

5. Revising an E-Mail Message: Budgetary Cutbacks at Black & Decker   The following bad-news e-mail about travel budget cutbacks contains numerous blunders. Using what you've learned in the chapter, read the message carefully and analyze its faults. Then use the questions below to outline and write an improved message.

Date: Wed, 28 May 2005 4:20:15 -0800
From: M. Juhasz, Travel & Meeting Services <mjuhasz@blackanddecker.com>
To: [mailing list]
CC:
BCC:
Attached:
Subject: Travel Budget Cuts Effective Immediately

Dear Traveling Executives:

We need you to start using some of the budget suggestions we are going to issue as a separate memorandum. These include using videoconference equipment instead of traveling to meetings, staying in cheaper hotels, arranging flights for cheaper times, and flying from less convenient but also less-expensive suburban airports.

The company needs to cut travel expenses by fifty percent, just as we've cut costs in all departments of Black & Decker. This means you'll no longer be able to stay in fancy hotels and make last-minute, costly changes to your travel plans.

You'll also be expected to avoid hotel phone surcharges. Compose your e-mail offline when you're in the hotel. And never return a rental car with an empty tank! That causes the rental agency to charge us a premium price for the gas they sell when they fill it up upon your return.

You'll be expected to make these changes in your travel habits immediately.

Sincerely,

M. Juhasz

Travel & Meeting Services

a. Describe the flaws you discovered in this bad-news e-mail about company operations.

b. Develop a plan for rewriting the e-mail, using the direct approach for company insiders. The following steps will help you organize your efforts before you begin writing:
  1. Create an opening statement of the bad news, using the "you" attitude.
  2. Decide what explanation is needed to justify the news.
  3. Determine whether you can use lists effectively.
  4. Choose some positive suggestions you can include to soften the news.
  5. Develop an upbeat closing.

c. Now rewrite the e-mail. Don't forget to leave ample time for revision of your own work before you turn it in.

6. Teamwork: Revising a Letter—Refusal from Home Depot to New Faucet Manufacturer   The following letter rejecting a faucet manufacturer's product presentation contains many errors in judgment. Working with your classmates in a team effort, you should be able to improve its effectiveness as a bad-news message. First, analyze and discuss the letter's flaws. How can it be improved? Use the questions below to help guide your discussion and development of an improved version.

July 15, 2005
Pamela Wilson, Operations Manager
Sterling Manufacturing
133 Industrial Avenue
Gary, IN 46403

Dear Ms. Wilson:

We regret to inform you that your presentation at Home Depot's recent product review sessions in St. Petersburg did not meet our expert panelists' expectations. We require new products that will satisfy our customers' high standards. Yours did not match this goal.

Our primary concern is to continue our commitment to product excellence, customer knowledge, and price competitiveness, which has helped make Home Depot a Fortune 500 company with more than a thousand stores nationwide. The panel found flaws in your design and materials. Also, your cost per unit was too high.

The product review sessions occur annually. You are allowed to try again; just apply as you did this year. Again, I'm sorry things didn't work out for you this time.

Sincerely,

Hilary Buchman
Assistant to the Vice President, Sales

HB:kl

a. Describe the problems you found with this letter rejecting a product presentation.

b. Develop a plan for rewriting the letter, using the indirect approach. First, organize your thinking before you begin writing:
  1. Select a buffer for the opening, using the "you" attitude.
  2. Choose the reasons you'll use to explain the rejection.

3. Develop a way to soften or embed the bad news.
4. Create a conditional (if/then) statement to encourage the recipient to try again.
5. Find a way to close on a positive, encouraging note.

c. Now rewrite the letter. Don't forget to leave ample time for revision of your own work before you turn it in.

Expand Your Knowledge

Exploring the Best of the Web

Protect Yourself When Sending Negative Employment Messages A visit to CCH's Business Owner's Toolkit, www.toolkit.cch.com, can help you reduce your legal liability, whether you are laying off an employee, firing an employee, or contemplating a company-wide reduction in your workforce. Find out the safest way to fire someone from a legal standpoint before it's too late. Learn why it's important to document disciplinary actions. Discover why some bad news should be given face-to-face and never by a letter or over the phone. Read CCH's advice, then answer these questions.

Exercises

1. What should a manager communicate to an employee during a termination meeting?
2. Why is it important to document employee disciplinary actions?

3. What steps should you take before firing an employee for misconduct or poor work?

Exploring the Web on Your Own

Review these chapter-related websites on your own to learn more about the negative issues human resources departments are facing today.

1. Workforce magazine online, www.workforce.com, has the basics and the latest on human resource issues such as recruiting, laws, managing the workforce, incentives, strategies, and more. Read the current edition online.
2. HR.com, www4.hr.com, is the place to go to read about workplace trends, legislation affecting employers, recruiting, compensation, benefits, staffing, and more. Log on and learn.
3. BusinessTown.com, www.businesstown.com, offers information on a wide range of business topics, including advice on conducting successful employee performance reviews.

Learn Interactively

Interactive Study Guide

Go to the Companion Website at www.prenhall.com/bovee. For Chapter 8, take advantage of the interactive "Study Guide" to test your knowledge of the chapter. Get instant feedback on whether you need additional studying. Also, visit this site's "Study Hall," where you'll find an abundance of valuable resources that will help you succeed in this course.

Peak Performance Grammar and Mechanics

To improve your skill with commas, semicolons, and colons, visit www.prenhall.com/onekey, click "Peak Performance

Grammar and Mechanics," click "Punctuation," and then click "Punctuation I." Take the Pretest to determine whether you have any weak areas. Then review those areas in the Refresher Course. Take the Follow-Up Test to check your grasp of commas, semicolons, and colons. For an extra challenge or advanced practice, take the Advanced Test. Finally, for additional reinforcement in commas, go to the "Improve Your Grammar, Mechanics, and Usage" section that follows, and complete the "Level 1: Self-Assessment" exercises.

CASES

Apply each step in Figure 8.1 on page 210 to the following cases, as assigned by your instructor.

▌E-MAIL ▌WEB 1. Too anomalous: SKILLS SKILLS Letter declining an invitation from the Disclosure Project

You work part-time for the president of Mid-State Flying Club, an organization that offers discounts on flying lessons and small plane rentals. In exchange, you get free flying lessons from the president, John Zuniga.

Like most pilots-to-be, you're interested in anomalous aerial phenomena (UFOs), so you paid close attention when Zuniga was asked if the club would sponsor a free public event in Phoenix, a "Campaign for Disclosure." The request came from two Mid-State members, both retired military pilots who are well respected around the airport. You've overheard some of their stories about their UFO encounters during airborne military maneuvers. You also heard them say that they were threatened by superiors to "forget what they'd seen."

These two members met with Zuniga in his office, presenting him with a book and videotape from a nonprofit research organization called the Disclosure Project. It was founded by Dr. Steven Greer, an emergency-room physician who gave up his doctor's salary to document the testimony of more than 400 witnesses to UFO and extraterrestrial events. These witnesses are from the United States, Britain, Russia, and other countries, and from the armed services, the CIA, NASA, and other agencies.

When Zuniga emerges from the meeting, his face is grim, determined. "We can't do it," he tells you when you ask about the sponsorship.

"It's my job to encourage pilots to join this flying club," he explains. "No matter what I believe personally, this isn't an event we should sponsor. I can't have folks referring to us as 'those kooks over in Hangar 5,' much as I'd love to hear Dr. Greer speak. He's got a powerful agenda and I'd love to support him—but officially, I just can't do it."

Your task: Zuniga wants you to write a letter to Dr. Steven Greer (The Disclosure Project, P.O. Box 2365, Charlottesville, VA 22902), declining the sponsorship invitation. "First take a look at the Disclosure website, www. disclosureproject.org, and you'll know why we can't sponsor this. Then write a polite refusal. Use what you've learned to let the doctor know we've given this event our serious consideration. Be encouraging, if you can, and let me sign the letter."[18]

▌E-MAIL ▌WEB 2. Disappearing baby bibs: SKILLS SKILLS E-mail from Home Shopping Network's Craftopia

At Craftopia online, part of the Home Shopping Network (HSN) website, the $12.99 Stamped Cross-Stitch Baby-Bib sewing kit is always popular. Now an on-air TV promotion has totally depleted your stock of the do-it-yourself kits. New kits won't be ready to ship for six weeks.

Your task: As customer service supervisor, notify customers of the delay in receiving their stitchery kits. Soften this news with some resale. First, go online to find resale information you can include in the form message that you must write and send by e-mail. Log on to the HSN homepage at www.HSN.com/cs, then follow the link to Craftopia. Customers who don't want to wait six weeks can call 1-800-373-0343 to request a refund.[19]

3. Cyber-surveillance: Letter refusing claim from Silent Watch victim

You work in human resources for a company called Advertising Inflatables, which designs and builds the huge balloon replicas used for advertising atop retail stores, tire outlets, used-car lots, fast-food outlets, fitness clubs, etc. Since you started, you've seen balloon re-creations of everything from a 50-foot King Kong to a "small" 10-foot pizza.

Not long ago, company management installed the "cyber-surveillance" software, Silent Watch, to track and record employees' computer usage. At the time, you sent out a memo informing all employees that they should limit their computer use and e-mail to work projects only. You also informed them that their work would be monitored. At your boss's request, you did not mention that Silent Watch would record every keystroke of their work or that they could be monitored from a screen in their manager's office.

As expected, Silent Watch caught two of the sales staff spending between 50 and 70 percent of their time surfing Internet sites unrelated to their jobs. The company docked (withheld) their pay accordingly, without warning. Management sent them a memo notifying them that they were not fired but were on probation. You considered this wise, because when they work, both employees are very good at what they do, and talent is hard to find.

But now salesman Jarod Harkington has sent you a letter demanding reinstatement of his pay and claiming he was "spied on illegally." On the contrary, company attorneys have assured management that the courts almost always side with employers on this issue, particularly after employees receive a warning such as the one you wrote. The computer equipment belongs to Advertising Inflatables, and employees are paid a fair price for their time.

Your task: Write a letter refusing Mr. Harkington's claim.[20] His address is 267 Hale Avenue, Anaheim, CA 92801.

4. Not this time: Letter to Union Bank of California customer denying ATM debit adjustments

You work in operations in the ATM Error Resolution Department at Union Bank of California. Your department often adjusts customer accounts for multiple ATM debit errors. Mistakes are usually honest ones—such as a merchant swiping a customer's check debit card two or three times, thinking the first few times didn't "take" when they actually did.

Whenever customers call the bank about problems on their statements, they're instructed to write a claim letter to your department describing the situation and to enclose copies of receipts. Customers are notified of the outcome within 10 to 20 business days.

You usually credit their account. But this time, your supervisor is suspicious about a letter you've received from Margaret Caldwell, who maintains several hefty joint accounts with her husband at Union Bank of California.

Three debits to her checking account were processed on the same day, credited to the same market, Wilson's Gourmet. The debits carry the same transaction reference number, 1440022-22839837109, which is what caught Mrs. Caldwell's attention. But you know that that number changes daily, not hourly, so multiple purchases made on the same day often carry the same number. Also, the debits are for different amounts ($23.02, $110.95, and $47.50), so these transactions weren't a result of repeated card swipes. No receipts are enclosed.

Mrs. Caldwell writes that the store was trying to steal from her, but your supervisor doubts that and asks you to contact Wilson's Gourmet. Manager Ronson Tibbits tells you that he's had no problems with his equipment and mentions that food shoppers commonly return at different times during the day to make additional purchases, particularly for beverages or to pick up merchandise they forgot the first time.

Your supervisor decides this was neither a bank error nor an error on the part of Wilson's Gourmet. It doesn't matter whether Mrs. Caldwell is merely confused or trying to commit an intentional fraud. Bank rules are clear for this situation: You must politely deny her request.

Your task: Write to Margaret Caldwell, 2789 Aviara Parkway, Carlsbad, CA 92008, explaining your refusal of her claim number 7899. Remember, you don't want to lose this wealthy customer's business.[21]

5. Product recall: Letter from Perrigo Company to retailers about children's painkiller

You work at Perrigo Company in customer service, where the atmosphere has been tense lately. Your company discovered that one batch of its cherry-flavored children's painkiller contains too much acetaminophen, and it must immediately inform retailers and the public of this dangerous error. Full and prompt disclosure is especially crucial when consumer health is involved.

Perrigo manufactures more than 900 store-brand, over-the-counter (OTC) pharmaceuticals and nutritional products. Store brands are packaged under store names, such as Sav-On or Kroger. They're priced lower than brand-name products such as Tylenol, Motrin, and NyQuil, but they offer "comparable quality and effectiveness."

Your marketing department calculates that 6,500 four-ounce bottles of the "children's nonaspirin elixir" (a Tylenol look-alike) are already in the hands of consumers. That leaves 1,288 bottles on store shelves. The lab says the acetaminophen contained in the painkilling liquid is up to 29 percent more than labels state, enough to cause an overdose in young children, which can cause liver failure. Fortunately, only lot number 1AD0228 is affected.

The painkiller is sold under the Kroger, Hy-Vee, and Good Sense labels at stores throughout the United States. Consumers must be told not to give the product to children. They must check the lot number, and if the bottle is from the affected batch, they must return it to the store they bought it from for a refund.

Your task: Company news releases have already notified the media about the product recall, but for legal purposes, you've been asked to write a formal letter to retailers. Explain the recall, and instruct stores to remove the product from their shelves for return to your company. Perrigo will reimburse them for refunds to customers. Include a phone number they can call with questions and pass on to customers: 1-800-321-0105.[22]

■TEAM ■SKILLS 6. Safe selling: Memo from The Sports Authority headquarters about dangerous scooters

You're not surprised that the Consumer Product Safety Commission (CPSC) has issued a consumer advisory on the dangers of motorized scooters. As a merchandising assistant at The Sports Authority, you've tried them and you've got the scars to prove it. Like too many riders, you skipped the elbow pads and learned to regret it.

The popular electric or gas-powered scooters, which feature two wheels similar to in-line skates, travel 9 to 14 miles per hour. As sales have grown, so have the reports of broken arms and legs, scraped faces, and bumped heads. The problem is that, unlike a motorcycle or bicycle, a scooter can be mastered by first-timers almost immediately. Both children and adults are hopping on and riding off—without helmets or other safety gear.

Over a six-month period, the CPSC says 2,250 motorized scooter injuries and three deaths were reported by emergency rooms around the country. The riders who were killed, ages 6, 11, and 46, might all have lived if they'd been wearing helmets. As a result, some states have already enacted laws restricting scooter operations.

Your stores sell a wide selection of both the foot-powered ($25 to $150) and motorized scooters ($350 to $1,000). The merchandising experts you work for are as concerned about the rise in injuries as they are about the CPSC advisory's potential negative effect on sales and legality. You've been assigned to a team that will brainstorm ideas for improving the situation.

For example, one team member has suggested developing a safety brochure to give to customers; another wants to train salespeople to discuss safety issues with customers before they buy. "We'd like to see increased sales of reflective gear ($6 to $15), helmets ($24), and elbow and knee pads ($19)," a store executive tells your team, "not to improve on The Sports Authority's $1.5 billion annual revenue, but to save lives."

Your task: Working as a team with classmates, discuss how The Sports Authority can use positive actions, including those mentioned in the case, to soften the effect of the CPSC advisory. Choose the best ideas and decide how to use them in a bad-news memo notifying the chain's 198 store managers about the consumer advisory. Then write the memo your team has outlined.[23]

7. The check's in the mail—almost: Letter from Sun Microsystems explaining late payments

Like everyone else working for Sun Microsystems, you were amazed that the installation of the computer company's new management information system did not go smoothly. When the new computer program was installed, errors were made that caused information to be lost. This embarrassment wasn't discovered until Sun's suppliers started clamoring for payments they never received.

Terence Lenaghan (the corporate controller and your boss) has to tell 6,000 vendors why Sun Microsystems has failed to pay its bills on time—and why it might be late with payments again.

"Until we get these errors corrected," Lenaghan confesses to you, "we're going to have to finish some of the accounting work by hand. That means that some of our payments to vendors will probably be late next month too. I need you to write to our suppliers and let them know that there's nothing wrong with the company's financial status. The last thing we want is for our vendors to think our business is going under."

Your task: Write a form letter to Sun Microsystems' 6,000 vendors explaining that problems with your new manage-

ment information system are responsible for the delays in payment.[24]

E-MAIL
SKILLS **8. Cell phone violations: E-mail message to associates at Wilkes Artis law firm**

"Company policy states that personnel are not to conduct business using cell phones while driving," David Finch reminds you. He's a partner at the law firm of Wilkes Artis in Washington, D.C., where you work as his administrative assistant.

You nod, waiting for him to explain. He already issued a memo about this rule last year, after that 15-year-old girl was hit and killed by an attorney from another firm. Driving back from a client meeting, the attorney was distracted while talking on her cell phone. The girl's family sued the firm and won $30 million, but that's not the point. The point is that cell phones can cause people to be hurt, even killed.

Finch explains, "Yesterday one of our associates called his secretary while driving his car. We can't allow this. According to the National Highway Transportation Safety Administration, 20 to 30 percent of all driving accidents are related to cell phone usage. From now on, any violation of our cell phone policy will result in suspension without pay, unless the call is a genuine health or traffic emergency."

Your task: Finch asks you to write an e-mail message to all employees, announcing the new penalty for violating company policy.[25]

9. Survive this: Recommendation refusal at Bank of America

As a trainee in a Bank of America branch office, you hated working beside Rogan Halliwell. He was highly intelligent, quick, handsome, accurate, and one of the most conceited individuals you've ever met.

This week you're helping your manager, Sandy McCallum, catch up on correspondence, and she's confided that she felt the same way about Halliwell. But since he quit last week, she now faces a communication dilemma.

"I was charmed at first, like everyone else," she explains.

You nod knowingly. Customers loved Halliwell for the same reason.

"But in the eight months he worked here," continues Ms. McCallum, "I had to constantly remind him of new harassment laws prohibiting any behavior that distracts or irritates others. You know, he insisted that at 60 years old, head teller Vera Kopanski should be flattered to be called 'Babe'! And all of you complained about his nonstop chatter, his overbearing ego, and his jokes about customers behind their backs." She sighs. "But he was an excellent teller. His cash drawer almost always balanced, he was fast, and he learned quickly. Some of our older customers even complimented me for hiring that 'nice young man.'"

"Now I have this letter from him. He writes, 'I've moved to Hollywood and I'm about to be hired by one of those *Survivor*-type reality TV shows. I need a character reference from you.' In good conscience, I can't recommend him. Yet his skills as a teller make it risky for me to refuse."

Your task: You boldly volunteer to draft a recommendation refusal for McCallum, using techniques you've learned in this chapter to avoid exposing her or Bank of America to legal repercussions. Address the letter to Rogan Halliwell, 2388 Pitt Avenue, Apt. 4, Hollywood, CA 90028.[26]

INSTANT MESSAGES 10. Midair let-down: Instant message about flight cancellations at United Airlines

It used to be that airline passengers didn't learn about cancelled connecting flights until after they'd landed. Sometimes a captain would announce cancellations just before touching down at a major hub, but how were passengers to notify waiting relatives or business associates on the ground?

As a customer service supervisor for United Airlines, you've just received information that all United flights from Chicago's O'Hare International Airport to Boston's Logan International have been cancelled until further notice. A late winter storm has already blanketed Boston with snow and they're expecting freezing rain overnight. The way the weather report looks, United will probably be lodging Boston-bound connecting passengers in Chicago-area hotels tonight. Meanwhile, you'll be using some of United's newest communication tools to notify travelers of the bad news.

United Airlines now partners with Verizon Airfone® to provide JetConnect[SM] information services, giving travelers access to instant messaging and other resources while they're airborne. For a small fee, they can plug their laptop computers into the Airfone jack, activating their own instant messaging software to send and receive messages. If they've signed up for United's EasyUpdate flight status notification service, they'll also receive instant message alerts for flight cancellations, delays, seating upgrades, and so on.

Your task: Write the cancellation alert, staying within the 65-word limit of many instant-messaging programs. You might want to mention the airline's policy of providing overnight lodging for passengers who planned to use the Boston route as a connecting flight to complete journeys in progress.[27]

11. Quick answer: Instant message turning down employee request at Hewlett-Packard

If she'd asked you a week ago, Lewinda Johnson might be granted her request to attend a conference on the use of "blogging" for business, which is being held in New York City next month. (Blogs are online documents written as a kind of journal posting; some businesses are testing them as a form of low-key promotion.) Instead, Johnson waited until you were stuck in this meeting, and she needs your response within the hour. She'll have to take no for an answer.

For one thing, you'd need budget approval from your group's vice president in order to green-light attendance at any conference longer than a day or further than Denver, a short drive from your Colorado Springs office. The conference in question is not only being held in an expensive New York City hotel, it's going to last four full days. Furthermore, Johnson hasn't given you sufficient justification for her attendance. You'd need a written document from her explaining how the use of business blogs relates to her job as marketing administrator.

Since she waited until precisely one hour before the application deadline, none of these issues can be addressed and you can't possibly say yes.

Your task: Write a 60–75 word instant message to Lewinda Johnson, declining her request. Decide whether the direct or indirect approach is appropriate.[28]

Improve Your Grammar, Mechanics, and Usage

Level 1: Self-Assessment—Semicolons and Colons

Review Sections 2.4 and 2.5 in the Handbook of Grammar, Mechanics, and Usage, and then look at the following 15 items.

In items 1–15, insert all required semicolons, colons, and commas:

1. This letter looks good that one doesn't.

2. I want to make one thing perfectly clear neither of you will be promoted if sales figures don't improve.

3. The Zurich airport has been snowed in therefore I won't be able to meet with you before January 4.

4. His motivation was obvious to get Meg fired.

5. Only two firms have responded to our survey J. J. Perkins and Tucker & Tucker.

6. Send a copy to Mary Kent Marketing Director Robert Bache Comptroller and Dennis Mann Sales Director.

7. Please be sure to inverview these employees next week Henry Gold, Doris Hatch, and George Iosupovich.

8. We have observed your hard work because of it we are promoting you to manager of your department.

9. You shipped three items on June 7 however we received only one of them.

10. The convention kit includes the following response cards, giveaways, brochures, and a display rack.

11. The workers wanted an immediate wage increase they had not had a raise in nearly two years.

12. This, then, is our goal for 2005 to increase sales 35 percent.

13. His writing skills are excellent however he still needs to polish his management style.

14. We would like to address three issues efficiency, profitability, and market penetration.

15. Remember this rule When in doubt, leave it out.

Level 2: Workplace Applications

The following items contain numerous errors in grammar, capitalization, punctuation, abbreviation, number style, word division, and vocabulary. Rewrite each sentence in the space provided, correcting all errors. Write *C* in the space after any sentence that is already correct.

1. Hector's, Julie's, and Tim's report was well-received by the Committee.

2. Everyone who are interested in signing up for the training seminar must do so by 3:00 o'clock PM on friday.

3. David Stern is a management and training expert that has spent a major part of his career coaching, counseling, and giving advise both to managers and workers.

4. Be aware and comply with local "zoning ordnances" and building codes.

5. Garrett didn't seem phased when her supervisor didn't except her excuse for being late, she forgot to set her alarm.

6. Copyright laws on the Internet is not always clearly defined, be sure your research doesn't extend to "borrowing" a competitors' keywords or copy.

7. Sauder Woodworking, in Archibald, Ohio sell a line of ready to assemble computer carts, desks, file cabinets, and furniture that is modular that can be mixed and matched to meet each business owners' personal taste.

8. Spamming is the most certain way to loose you're e-mail account, Web site, and you're reputation.

9. Us programmers have always tried to help others learn the tricks of the trade, especially Roger and myself.

10. The person whom was handling Miss Martinez' account told her that an error had been made by the bank in her favor.

11. "The trouble with focus groups" says Marketing Expert Frances Knight, "Is that consumers rarely act in real life they way they do in a "laboratory" setting."

12. In a industry in which design firms tend to come and go Skyline has licensed seventy products and grown to 8 employees.

13. If youv'e ever wondered why fast food restaurants are on the left and gift shops are on the right as you walk toward the gate into a newly-constructed airport you should read Malcolm Gladwells article, 'The Science of Shopping,' in the *New Yorker*.

14. Anyone whose starting a business should consider using their life story, as a way to generate customer's interest.

15. Having been in business since 1993, over 1000s of sales calls has been made by Mr. Jurzang, on prospects for his minority owned company.

Level 3: Document Critique

The following document may contain errors in grammar, capitalization, punctuation, abbreviation, number style, vocabulary, and spelling. You may also discover problems with wordiness, usage, and appropriateness of tone for bad-news messages. Correct all errors using standard proofreading marks (see Appendix C).

MEMORANDUM

To: all employees

Subject: Health insurance—Changes

Date: Octbr. 22, 2005

From: Lucinda Goodman, Benefits Mangr., Human resources

Unlike many companies, Bright Manufacturing has always paid a hundred % of medical car insurance for it's employees, absorbing the recent 10-20 percent annual cost increases in order to provide this important benefit. This year; Blue Cross gave us some terrible news: the cost increase for our employee's medical coverage would be a staggering fourty percent per month next year

To mange the increase and continue to offer you and your family highquality medical coverage we have negotiated several changes with Blue Cross; a new cost saving alternative is also being offered by us:

1. Under the Blue Cross Plus plan, copay amounts for office visits will be ten dollars next year/ $50 for emergency room visits.

2. 80 % of employees' insurance coverage (including 10 percent of the cost increase) will be paid by Bright next year and 100 % of the prescription drug costs (including a 23 percent cost increase). The remaining twenty percent of medical coverage will be deducted by us monthly from your salary, if you choose to remain on a Blue Cross Plus plan. We realize this is alot, but its still less than many companies charge their employees.

3. A fully paid alternative health plan, Blue Cross HMO, will now be provided by Bright at no cost to employees. But be warned that there is a deadline. If you want to switch to this new plan you must do so during our open enrollment period, Nov. 20 to December 1 2005, and we will not consder applications for the change after that time so don't get your forms in late.

There are forms available in the Human Resources office for changing your coverage. They must be returned between November 20 and December 1, 2005. If you wish to remain on a Blue Cross Plus policy, you do not need to notify us; payroll deductions for company employees on the plan will occur automatic beginning January first, 2005.

If you have questions, please call our new Medical Benefits Information line at ext. 3392. Our Intranet sight will also provide you easy with information about health care coverage online if you click the "Medical Benefits" icon. Since our founding in 1946, we have provided our company employees with the best medical coverage available. We all hate rising costs and although things are looking bleak for the future but we're doing all we can do to hold on to this helpful benefit for you.

Should Employers Use E-Mail to Deliver Negative Employment Messages?

Most people are more comfortable delivering bad news via e-mail than in person or on the phone. But is it appropriate to avoid the dreaded task of explaining layoffs and spending cuts in person by using e-mail to break such bad news? Some think it is.

Few executives advise using e-mail in extremely personal situations such as firing an employee, but some think it's perfectly fine to use e-mail for other uncomfortable scenarios such as job cuts, travel restrictions, hiring freezes, and other significant spending changes. Consider these examples:

- Amazon.com called an in-person meeting to announce job cuts, but telecommuters who couldn't attend the meeting were informed via e-mail. "I want you to know that this was a very difficult decision for the company to make . . . we know this must be very painful to hear," the e-mail read.
- Discovery Communications used e-mail to alert Discover.com workers that staffing changes would take place before announcing layoffs of some of its dot-com full-time employees.
- Motorola sent e-mail to employees in its semiconductor sector explaining layoffs and other cost-cutting steps. Workers being let go were told in person, but word of what was happening went out electronically.
- Ameritrade online brokerage notified more than 2,000 call-center workers of layoffs via e-mail.

Employers who use e-mail to deliver bad news claim that it's a quick and effective way to get information to all employees—especially those in remote locations or home offices. With face-to-face or even voice-to-voice communication, people have a tendency to tune out the worst and sugarcoat the bad news. But delivering bad news via e-mail lets people be more honest. E-mail facilitates straight talk because senders don't see the discomfort of their recipients.

However, critics cry foul when companies break job-related bad news via e-mail. As they see it, e-mail is too impersonal. "The only advantage is that it gives management an opportunity to duck and dodge angry employees," says one communications expert. If you want to maintain good relationships with your employees, "these kinds of things should be done in person."

Applications for Success

For more information about e-mail and employer/employee communication, go to www.vault.com/surveys/email_behavior/email_behavior.jsp.

Do the following:

1. Do you think employers should deliver negative employment messages via e-mail? Explain your answer.
2. Why does e-mail facilitate straight talk?
3. If you are sending bad news in an e-mail message, how can you use an indirect approach and still include an informative subject line? Won't the subject line give away your message before you have the chance to explain your reasons? Briefly explain in a one- to two-paragraph memo or e-mail to your instructor.

9

Writing Persuasive Messages

From the Real World

"You want to make your persuasive messages interesting, and you really do want to keep it simple. Even if the first paragraph is interesting, your reader may think, 'Gee, there's too much detail here. I'll just read this later when I have more time,' and unfortunately, it gets put on that pile—that 'To Do' pile that never gets done!"

—Jeanne Anderson
Sales Director
AT&T Language Line Services

Learning Objectives

After studying this chapter, you will be able to

1 Discuss the planning tasks that need extra attention when preparing persuasive messages

2 Distinguish between emotional and logical appeals, and discuss how to balance them

3 Describe the AIDA plan for persuasive messages

4 List six strategies for sending sales messages

5 Explain how to adapt the AIDA plan to sales messages

6 Compare sales messages with fundraising messages

Jeanne Anderson collects true-life stories—like this one: A frantic husband dialed 911 because his wife was giving birth, and he didn't know what to do. He spoke no English, and the operator couldn't understand what the emergency was. The operator dialed an 800 number for AT&T's Language Line Services, and in minutes a Spanish interpreter was able to help talk the worried husband through the delivery of his first child.

Such stories dramatize the benefits that help Anderson persuade readers about the value of her company's services—connecting dialers with an interpreter in any of 140 languages, 24 hours a day. In her persuasive messages, Anderson targets the needs of audience members—not to manipulate them but to help them make an intelligent, informed decision about her message.[1]

Using the Three-Step Writing Process for Persuasive Messages

Persuasion is the attempt to change someone's attitudes, beliefs, or actions.

Jeanne Anderson and other savvy businesspeople often accomplish communication goals by using techniques of **persuasion**—the attempt to change an audience's attitudes, beliefs, or actions.[2] Effective persuasion is "the ability to present a message in a way that will lead others to support it," says Jay Conger, author of *Winning 'Em Over*. "It makes audiences feel they have a choice, and they choose to agree."[3] In today's competitive marketplace, successful businesspeople must be able to put together a persuasive argument. Applying the three-step writing process to your persuasive messages will help you make them as effective as possible (see Figure 9.1 on page 246).

Step 1: Planning Persuasive Messages

Unlike routine positive messages (discussed in Chapter 7), persuasive messages aim to influence audiences who are inclined to resist. Therefore, persuasive messages are generally longer, are usually more detailed, and often depend heavily on careful planning. Persuasive messages require that you pay particular attention to analyzing your purpose, analyzing your audience, establishing your credibility, and striving for high ethical standards.

For a persuasive message, some planning tasks require more effort.

Analyze Your Purpose

When writing a persuasive message, your purpose is to persuade people to do something different or to try something new. But people are busy, so they're reluctant to act, especially if the action takes time and offers no guarantee of any reward in return. Moreover, people receive competing requests from everywhere. When writing persuasive requests, you must be absolutely sure that your purpose is clear, necessary, and appropriate for written media.

Persuasive requests encounter two problems:
- Audiences are busy.
- Audiences receive many competing requests.

Analyze Your Audience

Chapter 3 discusses the basics of audience analysis, but the process can become much more involved for persuasive messages. Learning about your audience's needs or concerns can take weeks—even months. Everyone's needs differ, so everyone responds differently to any given message.

Gauging Audience Needs   The best persuasive messages are closely connected to your audience's existing desires and interests.[4] Ask yourself these important questions: Who is my audience? What are their needs? What do I want them to do? How might they resist? Are there alternative positions I need to examine? What does the decision maker consider the most important issue? How might the organization's culture influence my strategy?

The questions you ask before writing a persuasive message go beyond those you would ask for other types of messages.

To assess various individual needs, you can refer to specific information. **Demographics** is information about the age, gender, occupation, income, education, and other quantifiable characteristics of your audience. **Psychographics** is information about the personality, attitudes, lifestyle, and other psychological characteristics of an individual. Both types of information are strongly influenced by culture.

Considering Cultural Differences   Persuasion is different in different cultures. To satisfy the needs of audience members and gain their respect, you must understand and respect their cultural differences. For example, in France, using an aggressive, hard-sell technique would probably antagonize your audience. In Germany, where people tend to focus on technical matters, plan on verifying any figures you use for support, and make sure they are exact. In Sweden, audiences tend to focus on theoretical questions and strategic implications, whereas U.S. audiences are usually concerned with more practical matters.[5] By taking into account the cultural expectations and practices of the people in your audience, you will be able to use the appropriate appeal and organize your message in a way that seems familiar and comfortable to them.

Cultural differences influence your persuasion attempts.

Like individuals, organizations also have a culture that heavily influences message effectiveness. All previous messages in an organization establish a tradition that defines persuasive writing in that organization. When you accept and use these traditions, you increase your chances of communicating effectively with co-workers and others in your organization.

Every message written for an organization adds to the organization's tradition.

Establish Your Credibility

To persuade a skeptical or hostile audience, you must convince people that you know what you're talking about and that you're not trying to mislead them. Your *credibility* is your capability of being believed because you're reliable and worthy of confidence.

Your credibility is defined by how reliable, believable, and trustworthy you are.

FIGURE 9.1   Applying the Three-Step Writing Process to Persuasive Messages

Planning

Analyze
- Verify specific purpose is worth pursuing.
- Gauge audience needs, perhaps using specific information from demographics and psychographics.
- Adapt persuasive argument to cultural differences.

Investigate
- Ensure info is reliable and accurate.
- Ensure facts support your persuasive argument.
- Gather all relevant facts readers need.

Adapt
- Verify effectiveness of written channel.
- Establish your credibility.

Writing

Organize
- Define your main idea, limit message scope, and group points meaningfully.
- Choose the indirect approach when appropriate.
- Use the direct approach when:
  - Readers prefer the "bottom line" first.
  - Your firm encourages directness.
  - Your message is long or complex.
  - Your authority warrants doing so.

Compose
- Adapt style and tone to readers.
- Choose words and create sentences and paragraphs carefully.

Completing

Revise
- Judge your argument objectively.
- Appraise your credibility seriously.
- Carefully match purpose and organization to audience needs.

Produce
- Ensure design complements your argument.
- Ensure delivery methods fit your purpose and audience expectations.

Proofread
- Strengthen your persuasive message by correcting spelling and mechanical errors.
- Correct any alignment problems.
- Make sure the print quality is acceptable.

1   2   3

Without such credibility, your efforts to persuade will seem manipulative. Some of the best ways to gain credibility are to

You can do a lot to establish your credibility.

- **Support your message with facts.** Testimonials, documents, guarantees, statistics, and research results all provide seemingly objective evidence for what you have to say, which adds to your credibility. The more specific and relevant your proof, the better.

- **Name your sources.** Telling your audience where your information comes from and who agrees with you always improves your credibility, especially if your sources are already respected by your audience.

- **Be an expert.** Your knowledge of your message's subject area (or even of some other area) helps you give your audience the quality information necessary to make a decision.

- **Establish common ground.** Those beliefs, attitudes, and background experiences that you have in common with members of your audience will help them identify with you.

- **Be enthusiastic.** Your excitement about your subject can infect your audience.

- **Be objective.** Your ability to understand and acknowledge all sides of an issue helps you present fair and logical arguments in your persuasive message.

- **Be sincere.** Your concern, genuineness, good faith, and truthfulness help you focus on your audience's needs.

- **Be trustworthy.** Your honesty and dependability help you earn your audience's respect.

- **Have good intentions.** Your willingness to keep your audience's best interests at heart helps you create persuasive messages that are ethical.

Strive for High Ethical Standards

Some people view the word *persuasion* as negative. They associate persuasion with dishonest and unethical practices, such as coaxing, urging, and even tricking people into accepting an idea, buying a product, or taking an unwanted or unneeded action. However, successful businesspeople make persuasion positive. They influence audience members by providing information and aiding understanding, which allows audiences the freedom to choose.[6]

Positive persuasion leaves your audience free to choose.

To maintain the highest ethics, try to persuade without manipulating.

When trying to influence people's actions, knowing the law is crucial. However, merely avoiding what is illegal may not always be enough. To maintain the highest standards of business ethics, make every attempt to persuade without manipulating. Choose words that won't be misinterpreted, and be sure you don't distort the truth. Focus on the members of your audience by showing honest concern for their needs and interests. Ethical businesspeople inform audiences of the benefits of an idea, a group, a product, or an action so that these audiences can recognize just how well that idea, group, product, or action will satisfy a need they truly have.

Step 2: Writing Persuasive Messages

When writing persuasive messages, you will define your main idea, limit the scope of your message, and group your points in a meaningful way. But you must focus even more effort on choosing the direct or indirect approach. Most persuasive messages use the indirect approach, explaining reasons and building interest before revealing their purpose. Even so, many situations do call for the direct approach.

If audience members are objective, or if you know they prefer the "bottom line" first (perhaps because it saves them time), the direct approach might be the better choice. You'll also want to use the direct approach when your corporate culture encourages directness. In addition, when a message is long or complex, your readers may become impatient if the main idea is buried seven pages in, so you may want to choose the direct approach for these messages as well.

Bette McGiboney is administrative assistant to the athletic director of Auburn University. Each year, after season tickets have been mailed, the cost of the athletic department's toll-free phone number skyrockets as fans call with questions about their seats, complaints about receiving the wrong number of tickets, or orders for last-minute tickets. McGiboney came up with an idea that could solve the problem, so she composed an e-mail message that uses the direct approach (see Figure 9.2). McGiboney supports her idea with benefits, not only for the athletic department but also for the fans who buy season tickets. Plus, her reasons are so logical that the message sounds both confident and convincing.

If you use the direct approach, keep in mind that even though your audience prefers the main point up front, you'll still want to include a justification or explanation, just as Bette McGiboney did. Don't expect your reader to accept your idea on blind faith. For example, consider the following two openers:

> Use the indirect approach when your audience will react unfavorably to your message. Use the direct approach when your message is long or complex, or when your reader prefers directness.

Poor	Improved
I recommend building our new retail outlet on the West Main Street site.	After comparing the four possible sites for our new retail outlet, I recommend West Main Street as the only site that fulfills our criteria for visibility, proximity to mass transportation, and square footage.

Your choice between a direct and an indirect approach is also influenced by the extent of your authority, expertise, or power in an organization. As a first-line manager writing a persuasive message to top management, you may try to be diplomatic and use an indirect approach. However, your choice could backfire if some managers perceive your indirectness as manipulative and time wasting. On the other hand, you may try to save your supervisors time by using a direct approach, which might be perceived as brash and presumptuous. Similarly, when writing a persuasive message to employees, you may use the indirect approach to ease into a major change, but your audience might see your message as weak, even wishy-washy. You need to think carefully about your corporate culture and what your audience expects before selecting your approach.

> Choice of approach is also influenced by your position (or authority within the organization) relative to your audience's.

Step 3: Completing Persuasive Messages

The length and complexity of persuasive messages make applying Step 3 even more crucial to your success. When you evaluate your content, try to judge your argument

> As with other business messages, Step 3 of the writing process helps guarantee the success of your persuasive messages.

FIGURE 9.2   Effective E-Mail Message Presenting an Idea to a Boss

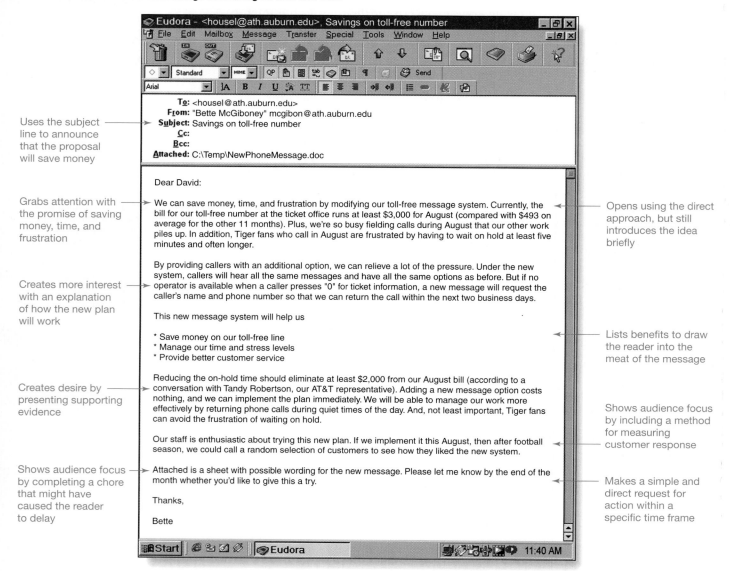

Uses the subject line to announce that the proposal will save money

Grabs attention with the promise of saving money, time, and frustration

Creates more interest with an explanation of how the new plan will work

Creates desire by presenting supporting evidence

Shows audience focus by completing a chore that might have caused the reader to delay

Opens using the direct approach, but still introduces the idea briefly

Lists benefits to draw the reader into the meat of the message

Shows audience focus by including a method for measuring customer response

Makes a simple and direct request for action within a specific time frame

objectively and seriously appraise your credibility. When revising for clarity and conciseness, carefully match the purpose and organization to audience needs.

Your design elements must complement (not detract from) your argument. In addition, make sure your delivery methods fit your audience's expectations as well as your purpose. Finally, meticulous proofreading will identify any mechanical or spelling errors that would weaken your persuasive message.

Sending Persuasive Messages

Your success as a businessperson is closely tied to your ability to convince others to accept or act on your recommendations. You may have been persuading people informally for years, but being able to persuade others in a written letter or memo is vital in today's competitive workplace. In the following section, we discuss some formal strategies you can use to strengthen your persuasive skills.

Strategies for Persuasive Messages

Whether you use a direct or an indirect approach, you must convince your reader that your request or idea is reasonable. You need to make sure that you strike a balance between emotional and logical appeals. Plus, you need to master the AIDA (Attention, Interest, Desire, Action) organizational approach.

Balancing Emotional and Logical Appeals

One way to persuade people is to appeal to their hearts and minds. Most persuasive messages include both emotional and logical appeals. However, finding the right balance between these two types of appeals depends on four factors: (1) the actions you wish to motivate, (2) your reader's expectations, (3) the degree of resistance you must overcome, and (4) how far you feel empowered to go in selling your point of view.[7]

When you're persuading someone to accept a complex idea, take a serious step, or make a large and important decision, try to lean toward logic and make your emotional appeal subtle. However, when you're persuading someone to purchase a product, join a cause, or make a donation, try to rely a bit more on emotion.

Emotional Appeals An **emotional appeal** calls on human feelings, basing the argument on audience needs or sympathies; however, such an appeal must be subtle.[8] For instance, you can make use of the emotion surrounding certain words. The word *freedom* evokes strong feelings, as do words such as *success, prestige, credit record, savings, free, value,* and *comfort.* Such words put your audience in a certain frame of mind and help them accept your message. However, emotional appeals aren't necessarily effective by themselves. Emotion works with logic in a unique way: People need to find rational support for an attitude they've already embraced emotionally.

Logical Appeals A **logical appeal** calls on human reason. In any argument you might use to persuade an audience, you make a claim and then support your claim with reasons or evidence. When appealing to your audience's logic, you might use three types of reasoning:

- **Analogy.** With analogy, you reason from specific evidence to specific evidence. For instance, to persuade employees to attend a planning session, you might use a town meeting analogy, comparing your company to a small community and your employees to valued members of that community.
- **Induction.** With induction, you reason from specific evidence to a general conclusion. To convince potential customers that your product is best, you might report the results of test marketing in which individuals preferred your product over others. After all, if some individuals prefer it, so will others.
- **Deduction.** With deduction, you might reason from a generalization to a specific conclusion. To persuade your boss to hire additional employees, you might point to industrywide projections and explain that industry activity (and thus your company's business) will be increasing rapidly over the next three months, so you'll need more employees to handle increased business.

Using the AIDA Plan

Most persuasive messages follow an organizational plan that goes beyond the indirect approach used for negative messages. The opening does more than serve as a buffer; it grabs your audience's attention. The explanation section does more than present reasons; moreover, it's expanded to two sections. The first incites your audience's interest, and the second changes your audience's attitude. Finally, your close does more than end on a positive note with a statement of what action is needed; it emphasizes reader benefits and motivates readers to take specific action. More intense than the indirect approach of bad-news messages, this persuasive approach is called the **AIDA plan**. In his memo in Figure 9.3, Randy Thumwolt uses the AIDA plan in a persuasive message about his program to reduce

Both emotional and logical appeals are needed to write successful persuasive messages.

Emotional appeals are best if subtle.

Logical appeals can use
- Analogy
- Induction
- Deduction

Organize persuasive messages using the AIDA plan:
- Attention
- Interest
- Desire
- Action

FIGURE 9.3 **Effective Persuasive Memo Using the AIDA Plan**

HOST MARRIOTT SERVICES

INTERNAL MEMORANDUM

TO: Eleanor Tran, Comptroller
FROM: Randy Thumwolt, Purchasing Director
DATE: May 7, 2005
SUBJECT: Cost Cutting in Plastics

In spite of our recent switch to purchasing plastic product containers in bulk, our costs for these containers are exorbitant. In my January 5 memo, I included all the figures showing that

- We purchase five tons of plastic product containers each year
- The price of the polyethylene terephthalate (PET) tends to rise and fall as petroleum costs fluctuate

In January I suggested that we purchase plastic containers in bulk during winter months, when petroleum prices tend to be lower. Because you approved that suggestion, we should realize a 10 percent saving this year. However, our costs are still out of line, around $2 million a year.

In addition to the cost in dollars of these plastic containers is the cost in image. We have recently been receiving an increasing number of consumer letters complaining about our lack of a recycling program for PET plastic containers, both on the airplanes and in the airport restaurants.

After conducting some preliminary research, I have come up with the following ideas:

- Provide recycling containers at all Host Marriott airport restaurants
- Offer financial incentives for the airlines to collect and separate PET containers
- Set up a specially designated dumpster at each airport for recycling plastics
- Contract with A-Batt Waste Management for collection

I've attached a detailed report of the costs involved. As you can see, our net savings the first year should run about $500,000. I've spoken to Ted Macy in marketing. If we adopt the recycling plan, he wants to build a PR campaign around it.

The PET recycling plan will help build our public image while improving our bottom line. If you agree, let's meet with Ted next week to get things started.

Grabs attention by clearly stating an ongoing problem and briefly providing background information that includes specific numbers

Reminds reader of important facts that have already been established by breaking them out into a list

Builds interest by introducing an additional problem with the plastic product containers

Makes suggestions in an easy-to-read list, providing detailed support in an attachment

Creates desire by providing another reader benefit

Urges action within a specific time frame

Pointers for Developing Persuasive Messages
- Balance emotional and logical appeals to help the audience accept your message.
- Open with a reader benefit, a stimulating question, a problem, or an unexpected statement.
- Discuss something your readers can agree with, and show you understand their concerns.
- Elaborate on the main benefit, and explain the relevance of your message to your audience.
- Make audience members want to act by explaining how the action will benefit them.
- Back up your claims with relevant evidence.
- Confidently ask for the audience's cooperation, and stress the positive results of the action.
- Include the due date (if any) for a response, and tie it in with audience benefits.
- Include one last reminder of the audience benefit, and make the desired action easy.

Host Marriott's annual plastics costs while curtailing consumer complaints about the company's recycling record. In persuasive messages, use the AIDA plan to intensify audience reactions in each of four phases:

■ **Attention.** Make your audience want to hear about your problem or idea. Write a brief and engaging opening sentence, with no extravagant claims or irrelevant points. And be sure to find some common ground on which to build your case. Thumwolt's memo gains attention by explaining the specifics of the problem he's trying to solve (see Figure 9.3).

- **Interest.** Explain the relevance of your message to your audience. Continuing the theme you started with, paint a more detailed picture with words. Get your audience thinking. Thumwolt's interest section introduces an additional, unforeseen problem with plastic product containers (see Figure 9.3). Moreover, Thumwolt emphasizes his suggestions with an easy-to-read list.

- **Desire.** Make readers want to change by explaining how the change will benefit them. Reduce resistance by thinking up and answering in advance any questions readers might have. Explain how you would implement complex ideas. Back up your claims to increase reader willingness to take the suggested action. Just be sure that all evidence is relevant to your point. Thumwolt emphasizes a monetary benefit and a possible public relations benefit.

- **Action.** Urge readers to take the action you suggest. Make it more than a statement such as "Please institute this program soon" or "Send me a refund." Remind readers of the benefits of taking action, and make the action easy. You might ask your audience to use an enclosed order form or call a toll-free number. Thumwolt's letter suggests a meeting for further discussion. Include a deadline when applicable.

The AIDA plan is tailor-made for using the indirect approach, allowing you to save your main idea for the action phase. However, it can also be used for the direct approach, in which case you use your main idea as an attention-getter, build interest with your argument, create desire with your evidence, and emphasize your main idea in the action phase with the specific action you want your audience to take.

When your AIDA message uses an indirect approach and is delivered by memo, e-mail, or instant message, keep in mind that your subject line usually catches your readers' eye first. Your challenge is to make it interesting and relevant enough to capture reader attention without revealing your main idea. If you put your request in the subject line, you're likely to get a quick "no" before you've had a chance to present your arguments.

> Using AIDA with the indirect approach allows you to save your idea for the action phase; using it with the direct approach allows you to use your main idea as your attention-getter.

Instead of This	Try This
Proposal to Install New Phone Message System	Savings on Toll-Free Number

Another thing to keep in mind when using the AIDA plan is to narrow your objectives. Focus on your primary goal when presenting your case. For example, if your main idea is to convince your company to install a new phone-messaging system, leave discussions about switching long-distance carriers until another day—unless it's relevant to your argument.

Types of Persuasive Requests

People write innumerable persuasive requests inside and outside an organization. When preparing a persuasive request, be sure to keep it within bounds. Nothing is as distressing

> Make only reasonable requests.

Document Makeover

Improve This E-Mail

To practice correcting drafts of actual documents, visit www.prenhall.com/onekey on the web. Click "Document Makeovers," then click Chapter 9. You will find an e-mail message that contains problems and errors relating to what you've learned in this chapter about writing persuasive business messages. Use the Final Draft decision tool to create an improved version of this e-mail. Check the message for its effectiveness at gaining attention, building interest, stimulating desire, motivating action, focusing on the primary goal, and dealing with resistance.

Highlight the direct and indirect benefits of complying with your request.

as a request so general, so all encompassing, or so inconsiderate that it seems impossible to grant, no matter how worthy the cause. When making a persuasive request, take special care to highlight both the direct and the indirect benefits of fulfilling it.

For example, if you want to persuade your supervisor to institute flextime, a direct benefit for that person might be the reduced workload or the enhanced prestige. An indirect benefit might be better employee morale once flextime is instituted. As examples of persuasive requests, let's look at two specific types: persuasive requests for action and persuasive claims and requests for adjustments.

Persuasive Requests for Action

When making a persuasive request for action, be sure to use the AIDA plan to frame your argument.

Whether you're requesting a favor or a budget increase, use the AIDA plan to frame your message.

- **Attention.** Begin with an attention-getting device. Show readers that you know something about their concerns and that you have some reason for making such a request. In this type of persuasive message, more than in most others, a flattering comment about your reader is acceptable, as long as it's sincere.

- **Interest and Desire.** Cover what you know about the situation you're requesting action on: the facts and figures, the benefits of helping, and any history or experience that will enhance your appeal. Your goals are (1) to gain credibility for you and your request and (2) to convince readers that helping you will indeed help solve a significant problem.

- **Action.** Close with a request for some specific action. Be aware that a persuasive memo to a colleague is more subdued than a persuasive letter to an outsider would be.

Be careful not to doom your request to failure by asking your reader to do all your work for you. For example, don't ask your readers to provide information that you were too lazy to seek, take action that will save you from embarrassment or inconvenience, or provide total financial support for a cause that nobody else is supporting.

Leslie Jorgensen wrote the memo in Figure 9.4. She's excited about the new Airbus A380 and believes that purchasing this plane for appropriate markets could help Qantas Airlines meet its growth needs while lowering its operating costs. She needs her boss's approval for a study of the plane's market potential.

When requesting a favor that is routine (such as asking someone to attend a meeting in your absence), use the direct approach and the format for routine messages (see Chapter 7). However, when asking for a special favor (such as asking someone to chair an event or to serve as the team leader because you can no longer fill that role), use persuasive techniques to convince your reader of the value of the project. Include all necessary information about the project and any facts and figures that will convince your reader that his or her contribution will be enjoyable, easy, important, and of personal benefit.

Persuasive Claims and Requests for Adjustments

The goal of a persuasive claim or request for adjustment is to convince someone to make an adjustment in your favor.

Although persuasive claims and adjustment requests are sometimes referred to as complaint letters, your goal is to persuade someone to make an adjustment in your favor; you're not merely to complain. You accomplish your goal by demonstrating the difference between what you expected and what you actually got.

Most claim letters are routine messages and use the direct approach discussed in Chapter 7. However, suppose you purchase something and, after the warranty expires, you discover that the item was defective. You write the company a routine request asking for a replacement, but your request is denied. You're not satisfied, and you still believe you have a strong case. Perhaps you just didn't communicate it well enough the first time. Persuasion is necessary in such cases.

You can't threaten to withhold payment (the item has already been paid for), so try to convey the essentially negative information in a way that will get positive results. Fortunately, most people in business are open to settling your claim fairly. It's to their advantage to maintain your goodwill and to resolve your problem quickly.

Two key ingredients of a good persuasive claim are (1) a complete and specific review of the facts and (2) a confident and positive tone. Assume that the reader is not trying to

Make your persuasive claims

- Complete and specific when reviewing the facts
- Confident and positive in tone

FIGURE 9.4   Effective Persuasive Memo Requesting Action

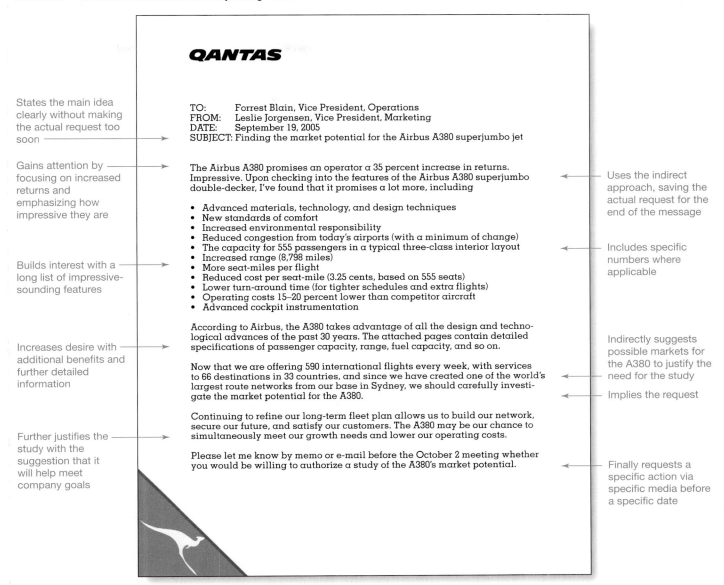

States the main idea clearly without making the actual request too soon

Gains attention by focusing on increased returns and emphasizing how impressive they are

Builds interest with a long list of impressive-sounding features

Increases desire with additional benefits and further detailed information

Further justifies the study with the suggestion that it will help meet company goals

QANTAS

TO: Forrest Blain, Vice President, Operations
FROM: Leslie Jorgensen, Vice President, Marketing
DATE: September 19, 2005
SUBJECT: Finding the market potential for the Airbus A380 superjumbo jet

The Airbus A380 promises an operator a 35 percent increase in returns. Impressive. Upon checking into the features of the Airbus A380 superjumbo double-decker, I've found that it promises a lot more, including

- Advanced materials, technology, and design techniques
- New standards of comfort
- Increased environmental responsibility
- Reduced congestion from today's airports (with a minimum of change)
- The capacity for 555 passengers in a typical three-class interior layout
- Increased range (8,798 miles)
- More seat-miles per flight
- Reduced cost per seat-mile (3.25 cents, based on 555 seats)
- Lower turn-around time (for tighter schedules and extra flights)
- Operating costs 15–20 percent lower than competitor aircraft
- Advanced cockpit instrumentation

According to Airbus, the A380 takes advantage of all the design and technological advances of the past 30 years. The attached pages contain detailed specifications of passenger capacity, range, fuel capacity, and so on.

Now that we are offering 590 international flights every week, with services to 66 destinations in 33 countries, and since we have created one of the world's largest route networks from our base in Sydney, we should carefully investigate the market potential for the A380.

Continuing to refine our long-term fleet plan allows us to build our network, secure our future, and satisfy our customers. The A380 may be our chance to simultaneously meet our growth needs and lower our operating costs.

Please let me know by memo or e-mail before the October 2 meeting whether you would be willing to authorize a study of the A380's market potential.

Uses the indirect approach, saving the actual request for the end of the message

Includes specific numbers where applicable

Indirectly suggests possible markets for the A380 to justify the need for the study

Implies the request

Finally requests a specific action via specific media before a specific date

cheat you but that you have the right to be satisfied with the transaction. Talk only about the complaint at hand, not about other issues involving similar products or other complaints about the company. Your goal is to solve a particular problem, and your audience is most likely to help if you focus on the audience benefits of doing so (rather than focusing on the disadvantages of neglecting your complaint).

- **Attention.** Begin by stating the basic problem (or with a sincere compliment, rhetorical question, agreeable assertion, or brief review of what's been done about the problem). Include a statement that both you and your audience can agree with or that clarifies what you wish to convince your audience about. Be as specific as possible about what you want to happen.

- **Interest and Desire.** Give your reader a good reason for granting your claim. Show how your audience is responsible for the problem, and appeal to your reader's sense of fair play, goodwill, or moral responsibility. Explain how you feel about the problem, but don't get carried away, don't complain too much, and don't make threats. Make sure your request is calm and reasonable.

■ **Action.** State your request specifically and confidently. Make sure your request proceeds logically from the problem and the facts you've explained. Remember to specify a deadline for action (when necessary or desirable). And don't forget to remind your audience of the main benefit of granting your claim.

As Figure 9.5 illustrates, the best approach to resolving problems is to engage in a reasonable exchange rather than an adversarial struggle.

FIGURE 9.5   Effective Letter Making a Persuasive Claim

WORKING WORDS
EDITORIAL AND WRITING SERVICES
761 Sunset Cliffs, Carlsbad, CA 91908   (760) 788-9231 Fax: (760) 788-9241

July 15, 2005

Ms. Ella Carver, Customer Service Representative
Del Mar Home Fashions
8740 Glenmary Dr.
Forrest Hill, TN 38031

Dear Ms. Carver

Working Words purchased five Del Mar cellular window shades through Cellini's Paint and Wall Covering. We bought four shades in June 1999, which were installed in four west-facing double-hung windows. Then in August 1999, we bought an additional shade, which was installed in a much larger north-facing garden window.

A couple of years ago, the individual cells in three of the west-facing shades began coming unglued. Cellini's helped us replace all three shades, in accordance with your company's lifetime guarantee for original owners who have kept the shades in their original windows and who have the original receipts.

Now another of our DelMar shades has come unglued, and we would like you to replace it. This shade was purchased in August 1999, and the sticker under the endcap carries the following information:

No.	Product	Color	Width	Height
C1116	Enchante (7/16) Petite cellular shade	Indigo Seas	42 1/4"	69"

Cellini's has informed us that it no longer deals with Del Mar products. Although we have the receipts for the four shades purchased in June (see enclosed photocopies), we simply cannot locate the receipt for the single shade purchased in August.

Please help us replace this shade. Knowing your exceptional reputation for quality, fairness, and service, we would be happy to deal with you directly or to visit a retailer in our area who handles your products. It's crucial to replace this shade as soon as possible, since August and September are our warmest and brightest months.

Sincerely

Katherine Graham

Katherine Graham
President

**Annotations (left):**

Gains attention with the fact that a number of products have already been purchased from Del Mar

Creates desire to grant the coming request by relating the ease of past replacements and citing Del Mar's guarantee

Refers to attached receipts in the hope they will prove original ownership of the fifth shade

Closes by restating the adjustment requested, by exhibiting a cooperative attitude, and by quietly assuming that the claim will be granted

Implies a deadline

**Annotations (right):**

Increases interest by demonstrating full understanding of product guarantee provisions

Makes the request in positive language that follows logically from the problem and the facts described, including all necessary information

Explains extenuating circumstances after the request

Provides reader with a reason to grant the adjustment (Del Mar's reputation)

Pointers for Persuasive Claims and Adjustments Requests
- Begin by stating something you and your audience can agree on.
- Provide a description that shows readers that their firm is responsible for the problem.
- Make your request factual, logical, and reasonable.
- Appeal to the reader's sense of fair play, desire for customer goodwill, need for a good reputation, or sense of legal or moral responsibility.
- Tell the audience how you feel, without being overly emotional.
- Make the action request a logical conclusion based on the problem and the stated facts.
- Specify a due date for action (when desirable).
- State the main audience benefit as a reminder of benefits in earlier statements.

Sending Sales and Fundraising Messages

Two distinctive types of persuasive messages are sales and fundraising messages. These messages are often sent in special direct-mail packages that can include brochures, reply forms, or other special inserts. Both types of messages are often written by specialized and highly skilled professionals, such as Jeanne Anderson of AT&T's Language Line Services.

> Sales and fundraising letters are distinctive types of persuasive messages that often come in special direct-mail packages.

How do sales messages differ from fundraising messages? Sales messages are usually sent by for-profit organizations persuading readers to spend money on products for themselves. However, fundraising messages are usually sent by nonprofit organizations persuading readers to donate money or time to help others. Aside from these differences, sales and fundraising messages are quite similar. Both require a few more steps than other types of persuasive messages, and both generally use the AIDA sequence.

Strategies for Sales Messages

Since your purpose in writing a sales message is to sell a product, one of the first things to do is gain a thorough understanding of that product. What does it look like? How does it work? How is it priced? Are there any discounts? How is it packaged? How is it delivered?

> When planning a sales message, know your product.

You'll also need to think about the type of sales campaign you'll conduct. Will you send a letter only, or will you include brochures, samples, response cards, and the like? If you send a brochure, how many pages will it run? Will you conduct a multistage campaign, with several mailings and some sort of telephone or in-person follow-up? Or will you rely on a single hard-hitting mailing? Expensive items and hard-to-accept propositions call for a more elaborate campaign than low-cost products and simple actions.

All these decisions depend on the audience you're trying to reach—their characteristics and their likely acceptance of or resistance to your message. You must analyze your audience and focus on their needs, interests, and emotional concerns—just as you would for any persuasive message. But in addition to the usual questions, also ask yourself: What might audience members want to know about this product? How can this product help them? Are they driven by bottom-line pricing, or is quality more important to them?

Determining Selling Points and Benefits

Sales letters require you to know your product's selling points and how each point benefits your particular audience. You'll need to highlight these points when you compose your persuasive message. For example, Jeanne Anderson emphasizes the ease and low cost of dialing up AT&T's Language Line Services.

As Table 9.1 shows, **selling points** are the most attractive features of an idea or product; **benefits** are the particular advantages that readers will realize from those features. Selling points focus on the product. Benefits focus on the user. For example, if you say

> Selling points focus on the product; benefits focus on the user.

Table 9.1	Features Versus Benefits
Product Feature (Selling Point)	**Consumer Benefit**
No money down, no interest payments for 24 months.	You can buy what you want right now at no additional costs.
This printer prints 17 pages a minute.	This printer can turn out one of your 100-page proposals in six minutes.
Our shelter provides 100 adult beds and 50 children's beds for the needy.	Your donation will provide temporary housing for 100 women who don't want to return to abusive husbands.
Your corporate sponsorship of the seminar will pay for the keynote speaker's travel and lodging.	Your corporate sponsorship of the seminar will allow your site manager a five-minute introduction at the beginning of the program to summarize your services.

that your shovel has "an ergonomically designed handle," you've described a good feature. But to persuade someone to buy that shovel, say "the ergonomically designed handle will reduce your risk of back injury." That's a benefit. For your letter and your overall sales efforts to be successful, your product's distinguishing benefit must correspond to your readers' primary needs or emotional concerns.

For example, the sales letter in Figure 9.6 uses the AIDA plan to persuade students to buy a SecureAbel dorm-room alarm system. The features of the system are that it can be installed with a screwdriver, it has an activator that hooks to your key chain or belt loop, and it has a blinking red light to warn intruders to stay away. The benefits are ease of installation, ease of activation, and a feeling of safety and security—all obtainable without investing in a full-blown permanently installed alarm system.

When composing sales messages, be sure to focus on relatively few product benefits. Ultimately, you'll single out one benefit, which will become the hallmark of your campaign. Safety seems to be the key benefit emphasized by SecureAbel Alarms.

Staying Within the Law

As with other persuasive messages, following the letter of the law isn't always enough. Whether you're selling a good, a service, or your company's image, write sales letters of the highest ethical character by focusing on solving your readers' problem rather than on selling your product. When you're genuinely concerned about your audience's needs and interests, you'll find it easier to avoid legal or ethical pitfalls. Even so, to avoid serious legal problems, you need to know the law. For example, consider the following legal issues:

> You can avoid both legal and ethical pitfalls by being genuinely concerned about your audience's needs, but you must also know the law.

- **Letters as contracts.** In many states, sales letters are considered binding contracts. You must be able to do what you say you can do. So avoid even implying offers or promises that you cannot deliver.
- **Facts about fraud.** Misrepresenting the price, quality, or performance of a product in a sales letter is fraud. You can also be committing fraud if you use a testimonial by someone misrepresented as being an expert and if you make a false statement in a sales letter.
- **Invasion of privacy.** Using a person's name, photograph, or other identity in a sales letter without permission usually constitutes invasion of privacy. In addition, legal problems can result from publicizing a person's private life without consent, such as by publishing someone else's prison record, past-due debts, medical records, or X rays.

Using Action Terms

> To give force to a message
> - Use action terms
> - Use colorful verbs and adjectives

Action words give strength to any business message, but they are especially important in sales letters. Compare the following:

Instead of This	Write This
The NuForm desk chair is designed to support your lower back and relieve pressure on your legs.	The NuForm desk chair supports your lower back and relieves pressure on your legs.

The second version says the same thing in fewer words and emphasizes the chair's benefit to the user ("supports") rather than the design team's intentions ("is designed to support").

Use colorful verbs and adjectives that convey a dynamic image. Be careful, however, not to overdo it: "Your factory floors will sparkle like diamonds" is hard to believe and may prevent your audience from believing the rest of your message.

Talking About Price

The price that people are willing to pay for a product depends on several factors, including the prices of similar products, the general state of the economy, and the psychology of the buyer. Price is a complicated issue and often a sensitive one. So you need to be careful whenever you talk about price in your sales messages.

> You can prepare readers for your product's price by subtle choice and arrangement of words.

Whether you highlight or downplay the price of your product, prepare your readers for it. Words such as *luxurious* and *economical* provide unmistakable clues about how your price

Planning	Writing	Completing
Analyze The purpose is to persuade readers to buy the portable alarm system. The audience will be neutral—or even resistant. **Investigate** Gather data on product's features and benefits, as well as on audience needs. **Adapt** Use a typical sales letter format.	**Organize** Make safety the central selling point. Follow the indirect AIDA approach. Get the reader's attention right away. **Compose** Use both logical and emotional appeals. Use a friendly, conversational tone. Include a response card to make reader action easy.	**Revise** Don't emphasize emotional appeals. The point is to help readers, not threaten them. Edit for focus and clarity. **Produce** Use a simple design for the letter and any brochures (in line with reasonable pricing). **Proofread** Be accurate. Remove all typographical distractions.
1	**2**	**3**

FIGURE 9.6   Effective Letter Selling a Product

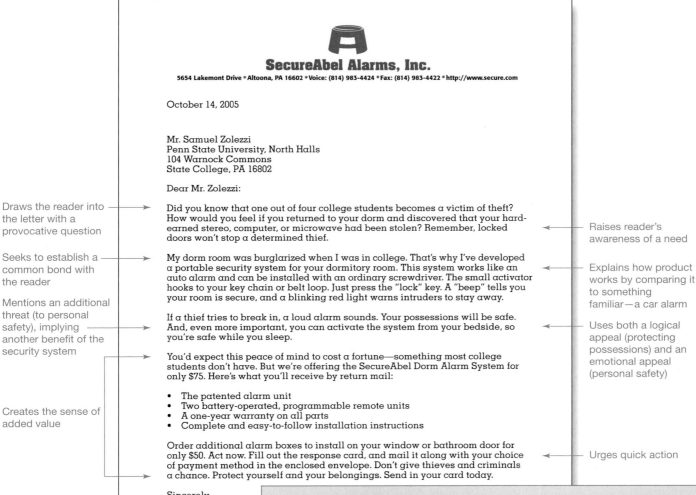

SecureAbel Alarms, Inc.

5654 Lakemont Drive • Altoona, PA 16602 • Voice: (814) 983-4424 • Fax: (814) 983-4422 • http://www.secure.com

October 14, 2005

Mr. Samuel Zolezzi
Penn State University, North Halls
104 Warnock Commons
State College, PA 16802

Dear Mr. Zolezzi:

Draws the reader into the letter with a provocative question

Did you know that one out of four college students becomes a victim of theft? How would you feel if you returned to your dorm and discovered that your hard-earned stereo, computer, or microwave had been stolen? Remember, locked doors won't stop a determined thief.

Raises reader's awareness of a need

Seeks to establish a common bond with the reader

My dorm room was burglarized when I was in college. That's why I've developed a portable security system for your dormitory room. This system works like an auto alarm and can be installed with an ordinary screwdriver. The small activator hooks to your key chain or belt loop. Just press the "lock" key. A "beep" tells you your room is secure, and a blinking red light warns intruders to stay away.

Explains how product works by comparing it to something familiar—a car alarm

Mentions an additional threat (to personal safety), implying another benefit of the security system

If a thief tries to break in, a loud alarm sounds. Your possessions will be safe. And, even more important, you can activate the system from your bedside, so you're safe while you sleep.

Uses both a logical appeal (protecting possessions) and an emotional appeal (personal safety)

You'd expect this peace of mind to cost a fortune—something most college students don't have. But we're offering the SecureAbel Dorm Alarm System for only $75. Here's what you'll receive by return mail:

Creates the sense of added value

- The patented alarm unit
- Two battery-operated, programmable remote units
- A one-year warranty on all parts
- Complete and easy-to-follow installation instructions

Order additional alarm boxes to install on your window or bathroom door for only $50. Act now. Fill out the response card, and mail it along with your choice of payment method in the enclosed envelope. Don't give thieves and criminals a chance. Protect yourself and your belongings. Send in your card today.

Urges quick action

Sincerely,

Dan Abel

Dan Abel, President

Enclosures

Pointers for Composing Sales Letters
- Get attention with a question, a fact, a solution, an offer/gift, a testimonial, and so on.
- Promise a benefit to the reader.
- Develop the central selling point, vividly relating details to the reader's concerns.
- Describe objective details of the product (size, shape, color, scent, sound, texture, etc.).
- Anticipate and answer reader questions, and use an appropriate form of evidence or proof.
- Offer a free trial or a guarantee, and refer to samples if they are included.
- Note any enclosures in conjunction with a selling point or a reader benefit.
- Clearly state the action you desire, along with specifics on how to order the product.
- Ease action with reply cards, preaddressed envelopes, phone numbers, and so on.
- Supply a final reader benefit and offer a special inducement to act now.
- In a postscript, convey important donation information or an important sales point (if desired).

compares with that of competitors. Such words help your readers accept your price when you finally state it. Here's an example from a sales letter offering a product at a bargain price:

All the Features of Name-Brand Pantyhose at Half the Price!
Why pay for fancy packaging or for that little tag with a famous name on it when you can enjoy cotton lining, reinforced toes, and matchless durability for only $1.99?

In this excerpt the price falls right at the end of the paragraph, where it stands out. In addition, the price issue is featured in a bold headline. This technique may even be used as the opening of a letter, if (1) the price is the most important feature, and (2) the audience for the letter is value conscious.

If price is not a major selling point, you can handle it in several ways. You could leave the price out altogether or mention it only in an accompanying brochure. You could de-emphasize the price by putting the actual figures in the middle of a paragraph that comes close to the end of your sales letter, well after you've presented the benefits and selling points.

> *Emphasizes the rarity of the edition to signal value and thus prepare the reader for the big-ticket price that follows*

Only 100 prints of this exclusive, limited-edition lithograph will be created. On June 15, they will be made available to the general public, but you can reserve one now for only $350, the special advance reservation price. Simply rush the enclosed reservation card back today so that your order is in before the June 15 publication date.

> *Buries the actual price in the middle of a sentence and ties it in with another reminder of the exclusivity of the offer*

The pros also use two other techniques for minimizing price. One technique is to break a quantity price into units. Instead of saying that a case of wine costs $144, you might say that each bottle costs $12. The other technique is to compare your product's price with the cost of some other product or activity: "The cost of owning your own exercise equipment is less than you'd pay for a health-club membership." Your aim is to make the cost seem as small and affordable as possible, thereby eliminating price as a possible objection.

Supporting Your Claims

You can't assume that people will believe what you say about your product just because you've said it in writing. You'll have to prove your claims. Support is especially important if your product is complicated, costs a lot, or represents some unusual approach.

Support for your claims may take several forms. Samples and brochures, often with photographs, are enclosed in a sales package and are referred to in the letter. The letter also describes or typographically highlights examples of how the product has benefited others. It includes testimonials (quotations from satisfied customers) or cites statistics from scientific studies of the product's performance. Guarantees of exchange or return privileges may be woven into the letter or set off in a special way, indicating that you have faith in your product and are willing to back it up.

It's almost impossible to provide too much support. Try to anticipate every question your audience may want to ask. Put yourself in your audience's place so that you can discover, and solve, all the "what if" scenarios.[9]

Adapting the AIDA Plan to Sales Messages

Most sales letters are prepared according to the AIDA plan. You begin with an attention-getting device, generate interest by describing some of the product's unique features, increase the desire for your product by highlighting the benefits that are most appealing to your audience, and close by suggesting the action you want the audience to take.

Getting Attention   The emphasis of the attention phase in sales letters is slightly different than in other persuasive messages. Sales letters use some common techniques to attract their audience's attention. You can grab your audience's attention by starting with

- **A provocative question.** "How would you like to get straight A's this semester?"
- **A piece of genuine news.** "In the past 60 days, mortgage rates have fallen to a 30-year low."
- **A personal appeal to the reader's emotions and values.** "The only thing worse than paying taxes is paying taxes when you don't have to."

Margin notes:

To de-emphasize price
- Bury actual figures in the middle of a paragraph near the end
- Mention benefits and favorable money matters before the actual price
- Break a quantity price into units
- Compare the price with the cost of some other product or activity

Types of support for product claims:
- Samples
- Brochures
- Examples
- Testimonials
- Statistics
- Guarantees

Certain tried-and-true attention-getting devices are used in sales letters for a wide variety of products.

- **Your product's most attractive feature along with the associated benefit.** "New control device ends problems with employee pilferage!"
- **An intriguing number.** "Here are three great secrets of the world's most-loved entertainers."
- **A sample of the product.** "Here's your free sample of the new Romalite packing sheet."
- **A concrete illustration with story appeal.** "In 1985, Earl Colbert set out to find a better way to process credit applications. After 10 years of trial and error, he finally developed a procedure so simple and yet thorough that he was cited for service to the industry by the American Creditors Association."
- **A specific trait shared by the audience.** "Busy executives need another complicated 'time-saving' device like they need a hole in the head!"
- **A challenge.** "Don't waste another day wondering how you're going to become the success you've always wanted to be!"
- **A solution to a problem.** "Tired of arctic air rushing through the cracks around your windows? Stay warm and save energy with StormSeal Weather-stripping."

Look at your own mail to see how many sales messages use these few techniques. Such attention-getting devices will give your sales letters added impact.

Textual openings aren't the only way to get attention. In ads and catalogs, companies capture attention and heighten emotional desire by using a variety of formatting devices. You can grab your audience by using special sizes or styles of type, underlining, bullets, color, indentions, and so on. Even so, not all attention-getting devices are equally effective, and using too many can have the reverse effect. In short, the best attention-getter is the one that makes your audience read the rest of your message.

Building Interest   In the interest section of your message, highlight your product's key selling point. Say that your company's alarm device is relatively inexpensive, durable, and tamperproof. Although these are all attractive features, you want to focus on only one. Ask what the competition has to offer, what most distinguishes your product, and what most concerns potential buyers. The answers to these questions will help you select the **central selling point**, the single point around which to build your sales message. Build your audience's interest by highlighting this point, and make it stand out through typography, design, or high-impact writing.[10]

Determining the central selling point will also help you define the benefits to potential buyers. Perhaps your company built its new alarm to overcome competing products' susceptibility to tampering. Being tamperproof is the feature you choose as your central selling point, and its benefit to readers is that burglars won't be able to break in so easily.

To determine your product's central selling point, ask

- What does the competition offer?
- What is special about my product?
- What are potential buyers really looking for?

Increasing Desire   In the desire section, mention your main benefit repeatedly, expanding and explaining as you go. Use both words and pictures, if possible. This main benefit is what will entice recipients to read on and take further action.

As you continue to stress your main benefit, weave in references to other benefits. ("You can get this worry-free protection for much less than you might think," and "The same technology that makes it difficult for burglars to crack your alarm system makes the device durable, even when it must be exposed to the elements.") Remember, sales letters reflect the "you" attitude through references to benefits, so always phrase the selling points in terms of what your product's features can do for potential customers.

To increase desire, expand your main benefit while adding others.

Keep in mind that you don't need to provide every last detail as you explain product benefits. The best letters are short (preferably one but no more than two pages). They include enough detail to spur the reader's interest, but they don't try to be the sole source of information. Also, remember to use bullet points to highlight details whenever possible. You have to assume that your readers are pressed for time and are interested only in what matters most to them.[11]

Motivating Action   In the last section of your letter, you explain clearly how to take the next step. After all, the overriding purpose of a sales letter is to get your reader to do something. Many consumer products sold through the mail simply ask for a check—in other words, an immediate decision to buy. On the other hand, companies selling expensive and more complex items frequently ask for just a small step toward the final buying decision, such as sending for more information or authorizing a call by a sales representative.

Whatever you ask readers to do, try to persuade them to do it right away. Convince them that they must act now, perhaps to guarantee a specific delivery date. If there's no particular reason to act quickly, many sales letters offer discounts for orders placed by a certain date or prizes or special offers to, say, the first 500 people to respond. Others suggest that purchases be charged to a credit card or be paid off over time. Still others offer a free trial, an unconditional guarantee, or a no-strings request card for information—all in an effort to overcome readers' natural inertia.

Of course, adding a postscript (P.S.) is one of the most effective ways to boost audience response. This is the place to make your final impression, so be sure the information is noteworthy. Use the P.S. to reiterate your primary benefit, make an additional offer, or compel the reader to act quickly by emphasizing a deadline.[12]

Finally, use good judgment when distributing your messages to would-be customers. Do not send electronic junk mail (spam). Doing so only irritates consumers, and it can be illegal, depending on the state in which you reside. Laws against spam on the federal level are pending.

Strategies for Fundraising Messages

Most of the techniques used to write sales letters can also be used to write fundraising letters, as long as your techniques match your audience, your goals, and the cause or organization you're representing. Motivating action is a challenge for the best sales letters. Even more of a challenge is motivating action when you're trying to raise funds. Be careful to establish value in the minds of your donors. Above all, don't forget to include the "what's in it for me?" information—for example, telling your readers how good they'll feel by making a donation.[13]

Before you begin writing, read the mail you receive from donors. Learn as much as you can about your audience by noting the tone of these letters, the language used, and the concerns raised. This exercise will help you write letters that donors will both understand and relate to.

Also keep a file of competing fundraising letters. Study these samples to find out what other fundraisers are doing and what new approaches they're taking. Most important, find out what works and what doesn't. Then you can continue with other research efforts, such as conducting interviews, holding focus groups, and reading trade journals to find out what people are concerned about, what they're interested in, and what gets their attention.

Be sure you know whose benefits to emphasize. Make a two-column list; on one side list what your organization does, and on the other side list what your donors want. You'll discover that the two columns are quite different. Make sure that the benefits you emphasize are related to what your donors want, not to what your organization does. Then you can work on stating those donor benefits in specific detail. For example: "Your donation of $100 will provide 15 people with a Christmas dinner."

Because fundraising letters depend so heavily on emotional appeals, keep your message personal. A natural, real-life lead-in is usually the best. People seem to respond best to slice-of-life stories. Storytelling is perfect when your narrative is unforced and goes straight to the heart of the matter.[14] A busy company executive may not be able to identify with the homeless man she passes on the street every day. But every human being understands pain; we've all felt it. So do your best to portray that homeless man's pain using words that the busy executive can understand.[15]

To reach the humanity and compassion of your readers, focus on specific reader benefits, detail the unique need, emphasize the urgency of the situation, and spell out the exact help needed. As director of PETsMART Charities, Rita Gomez has the task of raising millions of dollars to help save the lives of and find families for thousands upon thousands of homeless pets. Her letter in Figure 9.7 makes a compelling case for donations.

FIGURE 9.7 Effective Letter to Raise Funds

Where pets are family™

19601 North 27th Avenue • Phoenix, Arizona 85027 • 623•580•6100

June 17, 2005

Mr. William Hanover, President
Hanover, Jude, and Larson
12785 Sunnyslope Dr.
Phoenix, AZ 85020

Ernie needs your help!

Dear Mr. Hanover:

Ernie deserves a loving home. When Sheila Jenkins found him in the alley behind her apartment, the poor little guy was weak from hunger, infested with fleas, and dragging a broken leg. Under skillful care at the local animal shelter, Ernie recovered fully and won the hearts of all with his indomitable spirit, his quick intelligence, and his perky devotion.

Ernie has been waiting patiently for a family to love, but sometimes homes are hard to find. More than 7 million pets are euthanized every year, simply because they have no family or home to call their own. So in 1992 PETsMART decided not to sell cats and dogs. Instead, the company created PETsMART Charities' Adoption Centers—in-store space that is donated to help local animal welfare organizations make homeless pets available for adoption.

Over the past decade, PETsMART Charities has donated $15 million to animal welfare programs, and through our in-store adoption programs, we've helped save the lives of more than 1 million pets, one by one. These accomplishments are the result of devotion, hard work, and contributions from our own associates and from companies like yours. That's right, we haven't done all this alone. And to continue saving lives, we need your help more than ever.

Mr. Hanover, you and your associates have proved that you care about your community. You know business is about more than merely selling a product or service. Now, with a one-time donation of $100, your company can save the lives of many faithful pet companions. With a yearly or a scheduled monthly donation, you can do even more to rescue these loving family members. Your gift saves lives, makes you feel great, and strengthens your firm's reputation as a caring and responsible company.

Please help Ernie find a good home. Just fill out the enclosed reply form and send it along with your donation in the envelope provided. Ernie can't make it without you, and neither can we.

Sincerely,

Rita E. Gomez

Rita E. Gomez
Director

Enclosure

Annotations (left margin):

Gains attention by personalizing the message with a real-life story

Increases interest by providing hard (even painful) numbers and details of just what PETsMART Charities does

Creates a desire to be involved by sharing specific successes of the program

Makes the request by stating the benefits of the reader's donation to others as well as to the reader

Closes by echoing the real-life story that opened the message and repeating the request for specific action

Annotations (right margin):

Includes a photo to further personalize the message and strengthen the emotional appeal

Avoids sounding like a business communication while getting right to the point

Uses a carefully constructed transition to move reader from what PETsMART has done to what the reader can do

Takes special pains to focus on the reader and his company

Reply form is complete and thorough

TO HELP PETsMART CHARITIES SAVE LIVES

_____ (company)

_____ (address)

WISHES TO DONATE

☐ $100
☐ $ ____ each year
☐ $ ____ a month (for 12 mos.)

☐ By check (enclosed)
☐ By credit card:

____ Visa   ____ Mastercard   ____ Discover

Card no.: _____

Signature: _____

Position: _____

Reviewing Key Points

This chapter highlights how to use the three-step writing process for persuasive messages. It encourages you to pay special attention to planning activities such as analyzing your purpose, analyzing your audience, establishing your credibility, and striving for high ethical standards. The chapter discusses strategies for persuasive messages. It helps you learn about balancing emotional and logical appeals, and using the AIDA plan to develop your messages. You investigated two types of persuasive requests: action requests and claims.

This chapter also describes six strategies for sending sales messages: determining selling points, staying within the law, using action terms, talking about price, supporting your claims, and using the AIDA plan in a special way. It briefly discusses some general strategies for fundraising messages and describes the differences between sales and fundraising messages.

The next chapter will discuss business reports and proposals. You'll learn about the six common purposes of reports, and you'll see how to apply the three-step writing process to business reports and proposals. The coming chapter will also explain the special analysis and investigation tasks that you'll need to complete when planning business reports and proposals.

Test Your Knowledge

1. What are some questions to ask when gauging the audience's needs during the planning of a persuasive message?

2. What role do demographics and psychographics play in audience analysis during the planning of a persuasive message?

3. What are four of the ways you can build credibility with an audience when planning a persuasive message?

4. How do emotional appeals differ from logical appeals?

5. What three types of reasoning can you use in logical appeals?

6. What is the AIDA plan, and how does it apply to persuasive messages?

7. What are the similarities and differences between sales messages and fundraising messages?

8. What are six strategies to use when preparing sales messages?

9. How do benefits differ from features?

10. What four strategies will help your fundraising letters succeed?

Apply Your Knowledge

1. When writing persuasive messages, why is it so important to give special attention to the analysis of your purpose and audience?

2. How are persuasive messages different from routine messages?

3. When is it appropriate to use the direct organizational approach in persuasive messages?

4. As an employee, count how many of your daily tasks require persuasion. List as many as you can think of. Who are your audiences, and how do their needs and characteristics affect the way you develop your persuasive messages at work?

5. Ethical Choices   Are emotional appeals ethical? Why or why not?

Practice Your Knowledge

Exercises for Perfecting Your Writing

Analyzing Persuasive Messages: Teamwork   With another student, analyze the persuasive memo at Host Marriott (Figure 9.3 on page 250) by answering the following questions:

1. What techniques are used to capture the reader's attention?

2. Does the writer use the direct or the indirect organizational approach? Why?

3. Is the subject line effective? Why or why not?

4. Does the writer use an emotional or a logical appeal? Why?

5. What reader benefits are included?

6. How does the writer establish credibility?

7. What tools does the writer use to reinforce his position?

Persuasive Messages: Subject Lines   Compose effective subject lines for the following persuasive memos:

8. A request to your supervisor to purchase a new high-speed laser printer for your office. You've been outsourcing quite a bit of your printing to AlphaGraphics, and you're certain this printer will pay for itself in six months.

9. A direct mailing to area residents soliciting customers for your new business, "Meals à la Car," a carryout dining service that delivers from most local-area restaurants. All local restaurant menus are on the Internet. Mom and Dad can dine on egg rolls and chow mein while the kids munch on pepperoni pizza.

10. A special request to the company president to allow managers to carry over their unused vacation days to the following year. Apparently, many managers canceled their fourth-quarter vacation plans to work on the installation of a new company computer system. Under their current contract, vacation days not used by December 31 aren't accruable.

Sales Letters: Features and Benefits   Determine whether the following sentences focus on features or benefits; rewrite as necessary to focus all the sentences on benefits.

11. All-Cook skillets are coated with a durable, patented nonstick surface.

12. You can call anyone and talk as long you like on Saturdays and Sundays with this new wireless telephone service.

13. We need to raise $25 to provide each needy child with a backpack filled with school supplies.

Activities

For live links to all websites discussed in this chapter, visit this text's website at www.prenhall.com/bovee. Just log on, select Chapter 9, and click on "Featured Websites." Locate the page or the URL related to the material in the text.

1. Analyze This Document Read the following document, then (1) analyze the strengths and weaknesses of each sentence, and (2) revise each document so that it follows this chapter's guidelines:

At Tolson Auto Repair, we have been in business for over 25 years. We stay in business by always taking into account what the customer wants. That's why we are writing. We want to know your opinions to be able to better conduct our business.

Take a moment right now and fill out the enclosed questionnaire. We know everyone is busy, but this is just one way we have of making sure our people do their job correctly. Use the enclosed envelope to return the questionnaire.

And again, we're happy you chose Tolson Auto Repair. We want to take care of all your auto needs.

2. Analyze This Document Read the following document, then (1) analyze the strengths and weaknesses of each sentence, and (2) revise each document so that it follows this chapter's guidelines:

Dear Gateway:

I'm writing to you because of my disappointment with my new TelePath x2 Faxmodem. The modem works all right, but the volume is set wide open and the volume knob doesn't turn it down. It's driving us crazy. The volume knob doesn't seem to be connected to anything but simply spins around. I can't believe you would put out a product like this without testing it first.

I depend on the modem to run my small business and want to know what you are going to do about it. This reminds me of every time I buy electronic equipment from what seems like any company. Something is always wrong. I thought quality was supposed to be important, but I guess not.

Anyway, I need this fixed right away. Please tell me what you want me to do.

3. Analyze This Document Read the following document, then (1) analyze the strengths and weaknesses of each sentence, and (2) revise each document so that it follows this chapter's guidelines:

We know how awful dining hall food can be, and that's why we've developed the "Mealaweek Club." Once a week, we'll deliver food to your dormitory or apartment. Our meals taste great. We have pizza, buffalo wings, hamburgers and curly fries, veggie roll-ups, and more!

When you sign up for just six months, we will ask what day you want your delivery. We'll ask you to fill out your selection of meals. And the rest is up to us. At "Mealaweek," we deliver! And payment is easy. We accept MasterCard and Visa or a personal check. It will save money, especially when compared with eating out.

Just fill out the enclosed card and indicate your method of payment. As soon as we approve your credit or check, we'll begin delivery. Tell all your friends about Mealaweek. We're the best idea since sliced bread!

4. **Ethical Choices**   Your boss has asked you to draft a memo requesting that everyone in your department donate money to the company's favorite charity, an organization that operates a special summer camp for physically challenged children. You wind up writing a three-page memo packed with facts and heartwarming anecdotes about the camp and the children's experiences. When you must work that hard to persuade your audience to take an action such as donating money to a charity, aren't you being manipulative and unethical? Explain.

5. **Internet**   Visit the Federal Trade Commission website and read the "Catch the Bandit in Your Mailbox" consumer warning at www.ftc.gov/bcp/conline/pubs/ tmarkg/bandit.htm. Select one or two sales or fundraising letters you've recently received and see whether they contain any of the suspicious content mentioned in the FTC warning. What does the FTC suggest you do with any materials that don't sound legitimate?

6. **Revising a Letter: Request for a Rent Refund from Kuykendahl Joint, Inc.**   The following persuasive request for adjustment contains many flaws. Using what you've learned in the chapter, read the message carefully and analyze its faults. Then use the questions below to outline and write an improved message.

CMSI
CONTRACT
MANAGEMENT
SERVICES
INCORPORATED

3638 University Boulevard, Suite 302, Houston, Texas 77005-3396
(832) 768-3899   fax: (832) 768-3803   www.cmsi.com

March 22, 2005

Mr. Robert Bechtold, Manager

Kukyendahl Joint, Inc.

88 North Park Road

Houston, TX 77005

Re: Last Warning

Dear Mr. Bechtold:

Enclosed is a summary of recent ETS-related court cases in which landlords and owners were held responsible for providing toxin-free air for their tenants. In most of these cases, owners were also required to reimburse rents and pay damages for the harm done before the environmental tobacco smoke problem was remedied.

We've been plagued with this since we moved in on January 2, 2005. You haven't acted on our complaints, or responded to our explanations that secondhand smoke is making us sick, filtering in from nearby offices. You must act now or you will be hearing from our lawyers. We've told you that we were forced to hire contractors to apply weather stripping and seal openings. This cost us $3,000 (bills attached) and we expect reimbursement. But the smoke is still coming in. We also want a refund for the $9,000 we've paid you in rent since January. Call us immediately at (832) 768-3899, or our attorneys will be calling you.

Cigarette smoke from tenants on either side of us, and perhaps above and below as well, has been infiltrating our space and you have done nothing, despite our pleas, to stop it. This is unacceptable. This is a known human carcinogen. Ask the Environmental Protection Agency which classified it as this Group A toxin. It causes lung, breast, cervical, and endocrine cancer in nonsmokers. You wouldn't want to breathe it, either.

One employee already quit who suffered from asthma. Another is threatening because he's a high risk for heart attack. Migraines, bronchitis, respiratory infections—all caused by the

4,600 chemicals in ETS, including poisons such as cyanide, arsenic, formaldehyde, carbon monoxide, and ammonia. We've had them all—the illnesses, that is.

Secondhand smoke is even more dangerous than what smokers inhale, since the inhalation process burns off some of the toxins. Sick time has already cost CMSI valuable business and lowered productivity. Plus many of us are considering finding other jobs unless our office air becomes safe to breathe again. But as the court cases prove, the responsibility for fixing this problem is yours. We expect you to live up to that responsibility immediately. Frankly, we're fed up with your lack of response.

Kathleen Thomas

Manager

    a. Describe the flaws you discovered in this persuasive request for adjustment.

    b. Develop a plan for rewriting the letter. The following steps will help you organize your thoughts before you begin writing:

        1. Should you use a direct or an indirect approach?

        2. How can you use the "you" attitude to gain attention in the opening?

        3. What can you do to establish your credibility?

        4. How can you improve the order of material presented in the body of the letter?

        5. Create an appropriate closing.

    c. Now rewrite the letter. Don't forget to leave ample time for revision of your own work before you turn it in.

7. Revising a Sales Letter: From ScrubaDub About Its Car Care Club   The following sales letter falls short of its objectives. Use what you know about sales letters to analyze its flaws. Then follow the steps below to produce a better version.

11 locations in Massachusetts and Rhode Island
Bob and Dan Paisner, Owners

Dear Customers:

We are pleased to announce that ScrubaDub has added a new service, the Car Care Club.

It costs $5.95 for a lifetime membership (your car's lifetime) and features our computer automation. You'll be given a bar-coded sticker for your windshield so our computers can identify you as a club member when you pull in. If you sign up within the next 30 days, we will grant you a SuperWash for free.

The new club offers the standard ScrubaDub Touch-less systems to protect your finishes, our private formula Superglo detergent to clean your car safely and thoroughly, wheel sensors to prescribe the right treatment for whitewalls, wire, or chrome, soft, heated well water to eliminate spots, soft-cloth drying for final gloss. We also recycle our water and grant you a free wash on your birthday.

In addition, club members only will have access to a 48-hour guarantee (free rewashes) or 4 days if you purchased the premium Super Wash, Luxury Wash, Special or Works Wash. After ten washes, our computer will award you a free wash. Also available only to club members are $5 rebates for foam waxes (Turtle Wax, Simonize, or Blue Coral). Some additional specials will be granted by us to car club members, on an unplanned basis.

We can handle special requests if you inquire of our Satisfaction Supervisors. We honor our customers with refunds if they remain unsatisfied after a rewash. This is our Bumper-to-Bumper Guarantee.

Sincerely,

Bob and Dan Paisner

a. Describe the mistakes made by the writers of this sales letter.
b. Develop a plan for improving the letter. The following questions will help you organize your thinking:
   1. How can you improve the letterhead, salutation, or subject line (missing here)?
   2. What can you assume about the audience, which is made up of regular customers?
   3. How can you use this information to develop a better opening?
   4. Since customers already know ScrubaDub, what can you do to improve the body of the letter? Can you identify selling points versus benefits? What about the use of language and/or tone of the letter? Formatting?
   5. What can you use as a P.S. to boost sales potential? Could you also make up a special offer to include?

c. Now rewrite the sales letter. Don't forget to leave ample time for revision of your work before you turn it in.

8. **Revising a Persuasive Memo: E-cruiting at Boulder Construction**   This "persuasive" memo probably won't work effectively. Can you identify the mistakes the writer has made? Follow the steps below to analyze and improve on this persuasive request for action.

To: Sheila Young, Human Resources Director
From: Shelby Howard, Vice President
Subject: Recruiting tactics
Date: February 15, 2005

Dear Sheila: I think we should try e-Cruiting. I want you to use the huge data banks of résumés now listed on the Internet. They provide the software for your searches through these thousands of résumés they receive, so it shouldn't be too difficult. But you will have to define the qualifications you want first. Then they'll supply the résumés that fit.

Eventually, you can develop a website for our company that will post job listings. Then you'll get replies from the kinds of people who might not otherwise post their résumés online. Some of them may be good employees we've been looking for.

Costs breakdowns are: About $1300 apiece per candidate for traditional (newspaper ad) hiring. Plus your time for pre-screening. For e-cruiting, approximately $183 per candidate, with prescreening supplied by jobsearch databases such as monster.com, hotjobs.com, or careermosaic.com. They will, however, charge us about $100-300 per month to list our jobs, rather than the $1,000 the local paper charges us for a Sunday ad. Online job posting word length: unlimited.

You might have to wade through the 30,000 to 100,000 Internet sites now devoted to recruiting. Better stick with the names I've already mentioned. You'll be accessing about 150 million Internet users in the United States, 74 percent of them over the age of 18 looking for jobs.

Right now, our competitors aren't using this method and I can't figure out why. I'm thinking it could be a way to reach talent we might otherwise miss. Maybe they just haven't figured this out yet. You know the ones I mean—the talented individuals we compete for with other construction companies, even though we offer good jobs and benefits.

I read that Bank of Montreal relied on e-cruiting this year. They say they saved $1 million, but we'll have to see how accurate that is with our own trial. Only two percent of building industry employers use e-cruiting. Sixty percent of computer companies use it, probably because surfing the Internet is no hassle for them. They insist hiring time per candidate is reduced from six weeks to one hour, but I'll have to see that to believe it! Something about not having to wait for snail mail résumés. But then they also don't get to screen candidates by sight first, so maybe it's a toss-up. On the other hand, they can e-mail questions back and forth.

Well, why don't we give it a go anyway?

a. Describe the flaws in approach and execution of this persuasive request for action.
b. Develop a plan for improving the memo. The following questions should help to stimulate your ideas:
   1. Starting with the subject line, how can you focus on your audience's needs?

2. What would be a better opening? Why?

3. How can you reorganize the body of the memo to improve the reader's interest and receptivity to the new idea?

4. How can you handle facts, statistics, benefits, and appeals more skillfully?

5. What should be included in the conclusion to the memo?

    c. Now rewrite this persuasive request for action. Don't forget to leave ample time for checking your work.

10. **Analyzing a Sales Package: Learning from the Direct-Mail Pros**   The daily mail often brings a selection of sales messages to your front door. Find a direct-mail package from your mailbox that includes a sales letter. Then answer the following questions to help you analyze and learn from the approach used by the communication professionals who prepare these glossy sales messages. Your instructor might also ask you to share the package and your observations in a class discussion.

    a. Who is the intended audience?

    b. What are the demographic and psychographic characteristics of the intended audience?

    c. What is the purpose of the direct-mail package? Has it been designed to solicit a phone-call response, make a mail-order sale, obtain a charitable contribution, or do something else?

    d. What, if any, technique was used to encourage you to open the envelope?

    e. What kind of letter is included? Is it fully printed, printed with a computer fill-in of certain specific information, or fully computer-typed? Is the letter personalized with your name or your family's name? If so, how many times?

    f. Did the letter writer follow the AIDA plan? If not, explain the letter's organization.

    g. What needs does it appeal to?

    h. What emotional appeals and logical arguments does the letter use?

    i. What selling points and consumer benefits does the letter offer?

    j. How many and what kinds of enclosures (such as brochures and order cards) were included for support?

    k. Does the letter or package have an unusual format? Does it use eye-catching graphics?

    l. Is the message in the letter and on the supporting pieces believable? Would the package sell the product or service to you? Why or why not?

Expand Your Knowledge

Exploring the Best of the Web

Influence an Official and Promote Your Cause   At the Thomas site compiled by the Library of Congress, thomas.loc.gov, you'll discover voluminous information about federal legislation, congressional members, and committee reports. You can also access committee homepages and numerous links to government agencies, current issues, and historical documents. You'll find all kinds of regulatory information, including laws and relevant issues that might affect you in the business world. Visit the site and stay informed. Maybe you'll want to convince a government official to support a business-related issue that affects you. Explore the data at the Thomas site, and find an issue you can use to practice your skills at writing a persuasive message.

Exercises

1. What key ideas would you include in an e-mail message to persuade your congressional representative to support an issue important to you?

2. In a letter to a senator or member of Congress, what information would you include to convince the reader to vote for an issue supporting small business?

3. When sending a message to someone who daily receives hundreds of written appeals, what attention-getting techniques can you use? How can you get support for a cause that concerns you as a businessperson?

Exploring the Web on Your Own

Review these chapter-related websites on your own to learn more about writing persuasive messages.

1. Visit the Federal Trade Commission website, www.ftc.gov, to find out how consumers can cut down on the number of unsolicited mailings, calls, and e-mails they receive.

2. Explore some classic examples of persuasive messages at the National Archives' Powers of Persuasion online exhibit, www.archives.gov (enter the Exhibit Hall and find the Power of Persuasion exhibit).

3. See how professional advertising copywriters employ persuasion in their work; take the free tutorial at www.adcopywriting.com/Tutorials_List.htm.

Learn Interactively

Interactive Study Guide

Go to the Companion Website at www.prenhall.com/bovee. For Chapter 9, take advantage of the interactive "Study Guide" to test your knowledge of the chapter. Get instant feedback on whether you need additional studying. Also, visit this site's "Study Hall," where you'll find an abundance of valuable resources that will help you succeed in this course.

Peak Performance Grammar and Mechanics

In Chapter 8 you were referred to the Peak Performance Grammar and Mechanics activities on the web at www.prenhall.com/onekey to improve your skill with commas, semicolons, and colons. For additional reinforcement in semicolons and colons, go to the "Improve Your Grammar, Mechanics, and Usage" section that follows, and complete the "Level 1: Self-Assessment" exercises.

CASES

Apply each step in Figure 9.1 on page 246 to the following cases, as assigned by your instructor.

▌WEB ▌SKILLS 1. No more driving: Persuasive memo about telecommuting to Bachman, Trinity, and Smith

Sitting in your Dallas office at the accounting firm of Bachman, Trinity, and Smith, clacking away on your calculator, you wonder whether you could be doing this work from your home. You've haven't spoken to any co-workers in more than two hours. If you completed your work on time, would your location matter?

As an entry-level accountant, you've participated in location audits at major companies for nearly a year now. If your bosses trust you to work while staying at a hotel, why not let you work from home, where you already have an office with computer, phone, and fax machine? You'd love to regain those two hours you lose commuting to and from work every day.

Your task: To support this idea, visit the website of the International Telework Association and Council website at **www.telecommute.org.** You'll find statistics and other support for a memo persuading your boss, senior partner Marjorie Bachman, to grant you a six-month trial as a telecommuter.[16]

▌E-MAIL ▌SKILLS 2. A laughing matter: Persuasive e-mail to Kinko's manager about making work more fun

You've found that working at Kinko's can be tense. By design, the round-the-clock copy and business service center attracts people who are facing deadlines. They bring a lot of stress in the door with their urgent projects. You and your co-workers pick up their tension, and by the end of the day, your shoulders are aching and your head hurts.

When the economy slows, it's worse. Customers pour in with their résumés and everyone is under pressure. Your co-workers call in sick, your manager gets frustrated, mistakes increase, and morale sinks.

You've read that laughter in the workplace can improve morale and productivity by reducing tension. With a little research, you find support for this idea:

- Dr. Tracy Gaudet, a women's physician and consultant to Oprah Winfrey, says that laughter helps the immune system, lowers blood pressure, decreases heart strain,

and lowers blood levels of the stress hormone cortisol. It also releases endorphins, which are the body's pain relievers. A good belly laugh gives the lungs and heart an aerobic workout, she says, and reduces stress by relaxing muscles.
- Other companies have introduced "fun" activities in the workplace (ice cream socials, pet-matching contests) and found they increased enthusiasm, released creativity, and reduced absenteeism.

Having fun on the job doesn't mean workers are lazy. But it may save them from stress-related illnesses or injuries. At Kinko's, it might also improve customer relations!

Your task: Send a persuasive e-mail to your manager, Brad Attlebury, convincing him to try "laugh therapy" at Kinko's.[17]

3. Ouch, that hurts! Persuasive memo at Technology One requesting equipment upgrade

Working in human resources at Technology One, you've seen three complaints about repetitive stress injuries (RSIs) already this month. With 50 computer programmers on the payroll, this could develop into a serious problem for the software development company.

The three programmers, along with four from last month, are planning to file worker's compensation claims. They're suffering sharp wrist pains, numbness, and decreased range of motion. Company medical consultants have suggested exercises and wrist splints, but if these don't work, your technical experts could be facing surgery or even permanent disability.

Your boss is Philippe Bonsall, director of human resources. He noticed that these complaints began shortly after the company bought a truckload of new computer equipment at a local merchant's going-out-of-business sale, and he has hired an outside consultant to check the used equipment. Mary Li, owner of Li and Associates Ergonomic Consulting, reports back that desk and chair heights are fine, but the old-style keyboards and mousing devices are causing the problem. She suggests replacing the keyboards with divided "ergonomic" keyboards, which allow the wrists to stay straight and relieve pressure on the forearm. She also recommends supplying trackballs, an advanced form of computer mouse that also reduces hand movement by eliminating the need to pick up and roll the pointing device.

Replacing equipment will be expensive, but not nearly as expensive as costs that will arise if more technical workers come in with RSI complaints.

Your task: Bonsall asks you to draft a memo that he can use to persuade company controller Katherine Wilson to replace the equipment. You must convince her of the urgent need to make the upgrades recommended by Li and Associates Ergonomic Consulting.[18]

TEAM SKILLS **4. Always urgent: Letter pleading case for hosting a Red Cross blood drive**

This morning before heading off to your job in the food services department at the Pechanga Casino Entertainment Center in Temecula, California, you heard on the news that the Red Cross has put out a call for blood. National supplies have fallen dangerously low. Donated blood lasts only 72 hours, and the Red Cross is responsible for more than half the nation's supply of emergency and routine blood and blood products for victims of accidents and diseases. Thousands depend on the Red Cross for daily transfusions.

You're one of only five percent of eligible donors who think of giving blood. However, today, you're going to do more than just roll up your own sleeve. You want Pechanga Casino to host the local Red Cross chapter's bloodmobile for a community blood drive. As soon as you get to work, you quickly convince other members of the food services staff to help you out. Working together, you'll have all the skills necessary to organize the event.

Not only is it the right thing to do, but the event will improve

- The casino's community image by demonstrating its interest in the public's welfare
- Pechanga employees' sense of self-esteem, by helping others
- Pechanga customers' personal satisfaction, by having a convenient way to do a good deed
- The Red Cross's blood supply, since Pechanga's hundreds of employees and customers are all potential donors

You also remind your co-workers that the local Red Cross chapter is part of an international humanitarian organization. As part of its mission to "prevent and alleviate human suffering wherever it may be found," all assistance is given free of charge, made possible by people who donate their time, money, and skills.

Your task: With your team of co-workers (classmates), brainstorm additional support for the event. Then work together to write a persuasive letter to the Pechanga Board of Directors, 145 Ocean View Way, Temecula, CA 92590, convincing readers to host the bloodmobile. Research (or make up) details, such as your team's qualifications to organize the event, anecdotes to add emotional appeal, and so on. To donate blood, call 1-800-GIVE-LIFE.[19]

5. Identity theft: Persuasive request to eliminate Social Security numbers from Crossland Data ID cards

As your employer insists, you've always carried your Crossland Data ID card in your wallet. You need the card to get into security doors at work and for other identification purposes outside the office. The problem is that the card prominently features your Social Security number. So when your wallet was stolen recently, you feared that your identity might also be stolen.

According to the Federal Trade Commission, identity theft is the fastest-rising crime in the United States, with as many as 1.1 million victims already. This new type of crime involves using a person's unique, identifying information to tap into bank and credit accounts to steal money. With a few key pieces of information, thieves can set up new accounts, apply for credit, make large purchases, even apply for a new driver's license in your name.

Meanwhile, you might not discover the theft until a suspicious merchant calls your home. Or you might find huge debts on your credit record. Even after the crooks are arrested, some victims have spent hundreds of dollars and hours of phone calls trying to clean up their credit records. To avoid this financial nightmare, law enforcement experts now warn against carrying Social Security numbers in your wallet.

Your task: Write a persuasive letter to Crossland Data's human resources department, requesting that they eliminate Social Security numbers from employee ID cards.[20]

6. No choking matter: Persuasive letter from the Consumer Product Safety Commission about fast-food giveaways

You work in the Office of Compliance at the Consumer Product Safety Commission, under chairperson Ann W. Brown. Right now, she's concerned about increased incidents involving young children and fast-food giveaway toys.

In 1999 two babies died after suffocating on plastic Pokémon balls that their parents got from Burger King. Then three children choked on "Scooter Bugs" that they were given at McDonald's. They weren't seriously injured, but McDonald's undertook a costly recall of 234,000 giveaway toys.

Burger King gives away nearly 100 million toys annually; McDonald's distributes 1.5 billion worldwide. The entire industry accounts for one-third of all toys distributed in the United States, and millions of them have been recalled after children were hurt.

Brown worries that toddlers are being given toys meant for older children. Manufacturing defects also pose a problem. The toys are produced cheaply overseas, and often small parts break off to become serious choking hazards.

Burger King now uses safety tests before, during, and after manufacture to catch hazards in advance. McDonald's developed a testing doll with artificial lungs to check suffocation risks. They've loaned "McBaby" to your department so that other restaurants can copy the design. These industry leaders recognize that protecting child safety is to their advantage. Brown wants other fast-food companies to follow their lead and start checking toys before distribution.

Your task: Develop a letter to fast-food vendors in the United States, urging them to pretest giveaway toys. Use facts, anecdotes, and benefits to support your position.[21]

█WEB
█SKILLS **7. Let's not swim with the sharks: Memo persuading MBC Mortgage Company to relocate its annual sales event**

As assistant to Lucas Waldo, director of meeting planning at MBC Mortgage Company, you help make travel plans for the annual sales-incentive weekend. That's when the company sends its top salespeople to a destination resort somewhere in the United States as a reward for work well done. This year, the "Weekend Adventure in Paradise" is scheduled for West Palm Beach, Florida. But Waldo is concerned about shark attacks and hurricanes.

Florida leads the world in shark attacks, which usually aren't fatal but which grew more vicious last month as sharks were spotted prowling shallow beach waters. A young boy lost an arm, a woman lost her foot and her companion was killed, and another young boy died from massive blood loss after attacks in shallow water. Relatively minor "bites" were recorded up and down Florida's east coast, and many beaches were closed.

Meanwhile, recent climate changes are making hurricanes appear out of season. High winds, heavy rains, and flooding have sent vacationers scurrying for cover.

Waldo thinks management should move the weekend to California, where shark attacks are rare and hurricanes don't exist. "I've heard that the Hotel Del Coronado in San Diego has a classy reputation. Check it out for me," he instructs you, "and then you can help me convince them."

Your task: Explore the websites of San Diego's Hotel Del Coronado at **www.hoteldel.com** and the Shark Attack files at **www.flmnh.ufl.edu/fish/Sharks/Statistics/statsus. htm**. Then use facts, statistics, and anecdotes to write a memo to MBC management, persuading them to relocate the incentive weekend.[22]

8. Not too late for others: Letter to the U.S. Food Safety and Inspection Service requesting recall of Hillshire Farm meat products

As administrative assistant to Veronica Sutfin, marketing manager at TriTech, Inc., you often purchase food for her lunch meetings. You've never had a problem before.

On the afternoon of January 22, you bought lunch meats from Bob and Jill's Market in Baltimore and refrigerated them. Yesterday, January 23, eight people attended Sutfin's lunch meeting, ate the cold cuts you bought, and by 8 P.M., were all at Baltimore City Hospital's emergency room, undergoing treatment for food poisoning.

According to Dr. Samuel Jenkins, the culprit was salmonellosis, which can be fatal. He suggested that the Hillshire Farms cooked, sliced beef or ham might have been contaminated at the factory and should be investigated and recalled to protect others. He gave Suftin the address of the agency to contact.

Your task: Sutfin asks you to write the letter urging a recall of these lunch meats. Address the letter to Elijah Walker, Deputy Administrator, Office of Public Health and Science, Food Safety and Inspection Service, U.S. Department of Agriculture, Washington, DC 20250. Send a copy to Hillshire Farms.[23]

█E-MAIL
█SKILLS **9. Tangled web: Persuasive e-mail to PurelySoftware regarding an online order duplication**

Last week you ordered new design software for your boss, Martin Soderburgh, at ArtAlive, the small art-consulting business where you work. As he requested, you used his Visa card to order Adobe InDesign, Version 1.5, and Adobe Photoshop, Version 6.0, from an Internet vendor, PurelySoftware.com.

When you didn't receive the usual e-mail order confirmation, you called the company's toll-free number. The operator said the company's website was having problems, and he took a second order over the phone: $649 for Adobe InDesign, $564 for Adobe Photoshop, including tax and shipping. Four days later, ArtAlive received two shipments of the software, and your boss's credit card was debited twice for a total of $2,246.

Your task: Technically, you authorized both orders. But you understood during the phone call that the first order was canceled, although you have no written proof. Send a persuasive e-mail to customerservice@purelysoftware.com, requesting (1) an immediate credit to your boss's Visa account and (2) a postage-paid return label for the duplicate order.[24]

10. Cow-spotty text: Letter to Gateway requesting warranty extension

Words Unlimited is a "microbusiness"—just two owners and you, the all-round office assistant. From a small office with two computers, you three provide editorial services to businesses.

When your employers, Tom and Miranda Goodman, decided to add a third computer, they ordered a Professional S1300 business system from Gateway, with a "flat screen" monitor that was supposed to offer superior visual display. They didn't realize that the monitor, recommended by salesman Chris Swanson, uses liquid crystal display (LCD) technology. That's great for graphics, but text is produced as disconnected dots that are hard on the eyes. What they really need is an old-fashioned CRT monitor that displays text as a solid line.

They returned to the store and found one with a fast refresh rate, costing only $20 more, under Gateway's 30-day exchange program. But when they got to the register, they discovered that their 30-day exchange period ran out 5 days ago. Gateway wouldn't take back the LCD monitor, and the Goodmans would have to pay full price for the CRT.

"How did the time run out?" you ask when they return.

"Remember how Swanson forgot to include a modem in our original order and we had to wait for it to be delivered from the factory?" Tom says. "Then UPS delivered the package to the wrong address. When we finally retrieved it, the installation technician was out sick and we had to wait for his return."

Miranda adds, "And then it took Tom forever to set up the new system, between phone calls and other jobs. By the time we saw the flat screen in action, our 30 days had already elapsed."

"At least Swanson apologized," Tom adds. "He thinks his manager will extend our 30-day exchange period if we write her a letter."

Your task: Since your bosses are busy, they've asked you to draft the persuasive letter to Ann Cameron, Manager, Gateway Country Store, 2900 Pine Lake Road, Lincoln, NE 68516. So far Gateway employees have been courteous, quick, and eager to help, despite the mix-ups. You all have high hopes.[25]

11. Broadband blues: Persuasive claim letter to ZippieNet about cable modem failures

When your cable company offered ZippieNet—high-speed, cable modem Internet access—you signed up. You figured $49.95 a month was a bargain for Internet speed.

Your career as a freelance journalist requires you to compete with staff writers at the various publications that buy your work. You need to deliver stories fast to meet short deadlines. Having access to Internet sources "five times faster" than your old dial-up modem should have made your work easier.

At first you were pleased. When the system worked, it worked beautifully. Then the problems began. Three days a week for four weeks, the system failed and you were stuck offline. When you called ZippieNet's support lines, you were put on hold for 30 minutes, and when someone finally answered, they seemed poorly trained and overworked. All you got were vague promises that the system was being repaired.

That was three months ago. Since then, you've experienced total shutdowns at least twice a month. During periods of high usage, the "zippy" speeds that ZippieNet promised slow down to a trickle—not much better than your old dial-up connection.

And now the unthinkable has happened. Last week you were working on an article that you had contracted to sell to *Arete* magazine for $1,000, and the system went down for more than 24 hours. You couldn't access critical information, your story was late, and you lost the sale. Moreover, the editor who'd hired you was so angry, he said he'll never work with you again.

Your task: Write a letter to ZippieNet, 1203 West Barber Avenue, Nashville, TN 37214, demanding a refund for your four months of service, plus $1,000 for lost income on the lost article sale (include a copy of your contract), and $3,000 toward the loss of future sales to the same publication. If ZippieNet pays the $1,000, you'll be satisfied, but don't tell them that. Instead, suggest that you will remain a customer if they can deliver improved service within three weeks. When it works, you love broadband.[26]

12. Selling your goods: Sales letter promoting a product of your own invention

You never intended to become an inventor, but you saw a way to make something work more easily, so you set to work. You developed a model, found a way to mass produce it, and set up a small manufacturing studio in your home. You know that other people are going to benefit from your invention. Now all you need is to reach that market.

Your task: Imagine a useful product that you have invented—perhaps something related to a hobby. For example, one musician wanted to add bass accompaniment to his guitar strumming, so he invented the "Porchboard (Floor) Bass"—a wooden panel you tap with your foot to produce an electronic bass sound. A woman wanted a way to exercise in her short pool, and she invented stretchable "tethers" so that she could keep swimming without hitting the pool's edge.

Now list the benefits and features of your imaginary product (or use one of the examples above). Then write a sales letter for it, using what you've learned in this chapter and making up details as you need them.

INSTANT MESSAGES 13. Instant promotion: Text message from Hilton Hotels to frequent guests

Hilton Hotels now uses an SMS (short messaging service) to send instant text promotions to customers who've signed up as "HHonors" members. But you work in marketing, and that means you're often struggling to condense elaborate travel packages into 65 enticing words (system maximum).

For example, today's promotion offers "A Golfer's Dream Come True: 'I just played a round of golf by the pyramids!'" For $575 (US) per person per day (double room), valid through January 15, 2006, travelers can stay in the Hilton Pyramids Golf Resort in Cairo, Egypt, for 7 nights/8 days, including breakfast, service charge, and tax. They'll be met at the airport, given transportation to the resort, plus two rounds of golf per person at Dreamland Golf course and two rounds of golf per person at Soleimaneia Pyramids Golf & Country Club course. That's 88 words so far.

But you also need to convey that the Dreamland course wraps like a serpent around the Hilton resort. Its lush greens and lakes, designed by Karl Litten, contrast sharply with the golden desert, culminating in a stunning view of the great Pyramids of Giza, one of the seven wonders of the world. The Soleimaneia course features the "biggest floodlit driving course in Egypt." The travel package provides free transportation to this nearby course.

Rates, of course, are subject to availability and other restrictions may apply. But interested travelers should mention code G7 Pyramids Golf Special when they call Hilton Reservations Worldwide. They can also e-mail rm_pyramids_golf@hilton.com or call the Cairo hotel directly at 20 2 8402402. That is, if you can entice them in 65 words.

Your task: Write the persuasive instant message.[27]

14. Helping children: Instant message holiday fund drive at IBM

At IBM, you're one of the coordinators for the annual Employee Charitable Contributions Campaign. Since 1978, the company has helped employees contribute to more than 2,000 health and human service agencies. These groups may offer child care, treat substance abuse, provide health services, or fight illiteracy, homelessness, and hunger. Some offer disaster relief, or care for the elderly. All deserve support. They're carefully screened by IBM, one of the largest corporate contributors of cash, equipment, and people to nonprofit organizations and educational institutions, both in the United States and around the world. As your literature states, the program "has engaged our employees more fully in the important mission of corporate citizenship."

During the winter holidays, you target agencies that cater to the needs of displaced families, women, and children. It's not difficult to raise enthusiasm. The prospect of helping children enjoy the holidays—children who otherwise might have nothing—usually awakens the spirit of your most distracted workers. But some of them wait until the last minute and then forget.

They have until Friday, December 16, to come forth with cash contributions. To make it in time for holiday deliveries, they can also bring in toys, food, and blankets through Tuesday, December 20. They shouldn't have any trouble finding the collection bins; they're everywhere, marked with bright red banners. But some will want to call you with questions or (hopefully) to make credit card contributions: 800-658-3899, ext. 3342.

Your task: It's December 14. Write a 75- to 100-word instant message encouraging last-minute gifts.[28]

Improve Your Grammar, Mechanics, and Usage

Level 1: Self-Assessment—Commas

Review Section 2.6 in the Handbook of Grammar, Mechanics, and Usage, and then look at the following 15 items.

In items 1–15, insert required commas:

1. Please send us four cases of filters two cases of wing nuts and a bale of rags.

2. Your analysis however does not account for returns.

3. As a matter of fact she has seen the figures.

4. Before May 7 1999 they wouldn't have minded either.

5. After Martha has gone talk to me about promoting her.

6. Stoneridge Inc. will go public on September 9 2005.

7. We want the new copier not the old model.

8. "Talk to me" Sandra said "before you change a thing."

9. Because of a previous engagement Dr. Stoeve will not be able to attend.

10. The company started attracting attention during the long hard recession of the mid-1970s.

11. You can reach me at this address: 717 Darby Place Scottsdale Arizona 85251.

12. Transfer the documents from Fargo North Dakota to Boise Idaho.

13. Sam O'Neill the designated representative is gone today.

14. With your help we will soon begin.

15. She may hire two new representatives or she may postpone filling those territories until spring.

Level 2: Workplace Applications

The following items contain numerous errors in grammar, capitalization, punctuation, abbreviation, number style, word division, and vocabulary. Rewrite each sentence in the space provided, correcting all errors. Write C in the space after any sentence that is already correct.

1. A pitfall of internal promotions is, that a person may be given a job beyond their competence.

2. What makes this development possible is the technological advances in todays workplace.

3. We have up to date physical safeguards, such as secure areas in buildings, electronic safeguards, such as passwords and encryption, and we have procedural safeguards, such as customer authentication procedures.

4. When asked why BASF need to bring in a consultant after so many years, process development quality assurance manager Merritt Sink says that experience is extremely important on these type of projects.

5. Looking at just one growth indicator imports to the United States from China "ballooned" to $102 billion in 2005; compared with 15 billion in 1994.

6. Levi Strauss was the first major manufacturer to develop and do publicity about a formal Code of Conduct for it's contract manufacturers.

7. In foreign countries, while the local labor laws may be comparable or even more stringent than in the United States, law enforcement mechanisms are weak or nonexistent often.

8. Hyundai Motor Co., South Koreas' largest-automotive producer are building a $1 billion assembly and manufacturing plant in Montgomery, Alabama.

9. The long term success of some Internet products rest heavily on broadbands wide acceptance.

10. Being creative, flexibility, and dynamic planning are the critical elements of any successful, manufacturing process.

11. "Starbucks expanded the Frappucciono family to satisfy customers by offering a broader array of blended beverages," said Howard Behar, Starbucks president, North American Operations.

12. Internationally-renowned interior designer, Jacques Garcia will be designing the hotel's interiors; the gardens will also be designed by him.

13. Anyone who thinks they know what a CEO does is probably wrong, according to Eric Kriss; a professional Chief Executive.

14. Doctor Ichak Adizes, who founded the Adizes institute, headquartered in Santa Barbara, Calif. has spent decade's studying the life cycle of businesses.

15. The best job-description in the world wont provide you with a trusted executive, finely-honed interviewing skills only will help one do that.

Level 3: Document Critique

The following document may contain errors in grammar, capitalization, punctuation, abbreviation, number style, vocabulary, and spelling. You may also discover problems with wordiness, usage, organization, and tone for a sales message. Correct all errors using standard proofreading marks (see Appendix C).

Date: Monday, 23 June 2005

From: Sasha Morgenstern <smorgenstern@quotesmith.com>

To: <Promotional Customer List2>

Subject: Insurence Service

Dear potential buyers:

You will be able to compare prices from more than three hundredinsurance companies'. Or

find the lower rates for any insurance, such as Term life Automobile; Medical. dental. "No-

exam" whole life, workers' compensation, Medicare supplements; Fixed annuities

$500 Dollar Guaranttes

We'll find you the lowest U.S. rates for term life insurance, or we'll deliver $500 to you overnight. Plus, every quote will carry a $five hundred dollar guarrantee of uptotheday accurracy.

"Quotesmith.com provides rock-bottom quotes."—Forbes

All quotes are free and accurrate;

We offer Lightning-Fast ServicE

What their saying about us can be found at www.quotesmith.com. Our speedy service is being talked about by everyone, which has received high ratings and postive reviews from every major business publication "Nation's Business" "Kiplinger's Personal Finance" Good Housekeeping, The Los Angeles Times,"Money" "U.S. News & World Report"

EXPERT ADVISE WILL BE PROVIDED WITH NO SALES PITCH:

You will not be dealing with insurance agents to save you time and money. But if you want advise our saleried insurance experts are available at our toll-free customer service number. We hope you will take a moment to peruse our webstie, www.quotesmith.com today if possible.

Very truly yours,

Sasha Morgenstern

What You May Legally Say in a Sales Letter

As you prepare to write your sales letter, think carefully about your choice of words. False or misleading statements could land you in court, so make sure your language complies with legal and ethical standards. To keep your sales letters within the limits of the law, review the legal considerations of these typical sales phrases:

■ **"Our product is the best on the market."** This statement is acceptable for a sales letter because the law permits you to express an opinion about your product. In the process of merchandising a product, statements of opinion are known as "puffery," which is perfectly legal as long as you make no deceptive or fraudulent claims.

■ **"Our product will serve you well for many years to come."** This statement from a sales brochure triggered a lawsuit by a disgruntled customer who claimed the manufacturer's product lasted only a few years. The courts ruled that the statement was an acceptable form of puffery because the manufacturer did not promise that the product would last for a specific number of years.

■ **"We're so confident you'll enjoy our products that we've enclosed a sample of our most popular line. This sample can be yours for only $5.00! Please send your payment in the enclosed, prepaid envelope."** If you include a product sample with your sales letter, your readers may keep the merchandise without paying for it. Under the law, consumers may consider unordered goods as gifts. They are not obligated to return the items to you or submit payments for unsolicited merchandise.

■ **"Thousands of high school students—just like you—are already enjoying this fantastic CD collection! Order before March 1 and save!"** If your sales letter appeals to minors, you are legally obligated to honor their contracts. At the same time, however, the law permits minors to cancel their contracts and return the merchandise to you. Sellers are legally obligated to accept contracts voided by minors and any goods returned by them. Legal adult status is defined differently from state to state, ranging from age 18 to age 21.

■ **"You'll find hundreds of bargains at our annual 'scratch and dent' sale! All sales are final on merchandise marked 'as is.'"** When you use the term *as is* in your sales letter, you are not misleading customers about the quality of your products. By warning consumers that the condition of sales items is less than perfect, you are not legally obligated to issue refunds to customers who complain about defects later on.

Applications for Success

You probably receive sales letters through the mail all the time. Review two of these sales letters for content.
Do the following:

1. List the "puffery" statements in each letter.
2. Note any statements in these sales letters that appear questionable to you. Rewrite one of the statements, carefully choosing words that won't be misleading to consumers.
3. What do you think? Are these sales letters convincing? How have they persuaded you? If you don't believe they are convincing, explain how they have failed to persuade you.

Longer Business Messages

Unit 4

10 Understanding and Planning Business Reports and Proposals

Learning Objectives

After studying this chapter, you will be able to

1 Describe four types of informational reports and two types of analytical reports

2 Specify the function of a request for proposals (RFP)

3 Identify seven elements often included in a formal work plan

4 Distinguish between primary and secondary information

5 List the resources you might consult when looking for information in a library

6 Explain how to avoid plagiarism when researching information for reports

7 Define what a conclusion is, and list four things that make a conclusion sound

8 Relate how recommendations differ from conclusions

Since Michael Dell founded Dell Computer Corporation in 1984, the company has become the largest computer manufacturer in the United States and the fastest-growing computer-systems company in the world. But to maintain its leading edge, the company must collect and analyze reams of information. Because information in its raw form doesn't present itself in neat, tidy packages, Michael Dell and his employees rely on well-planned reports to summarize carefully researched data, define problems, discuss pertinent issues, and analyze information.[1]

Working with Business Reports and Proposals

Business reports help companies make decisions and solve business problems.

Like Michael Dell, most managers make decisions and solve problems based on the information and analyses they receive in **reports,** written factual accounts that objectively communicate information about some aspect of business. Reports come in all shapes and sizes, from fleeting images on a computer screen and preprinted forms to memos, letters, and formal three-volume bound manuscripts. Regardless of length or formality, most reports are used for one of six general purposes:

1. To oversee and manage company operations
2. To carry out company rules and ways of doing things
3. To obey government and legal requirements
4. To inform others of what's been done on a project

5. To guide decisions on particular issues
6. To get products, plans, or projects accepted by others

Being familiar with these purposes will help you plan your own reports more effectively.

Informational Reports

Informational reports present data and facts without analyses or recommendations. Common types of informational reports include monitor/control reports, policy/procedure reports, compliance reports, and progress reports.

The purpose of informational reports is to explain.

Reports for Monitoring and Controlling Operations

Managers rely on reports to learn what's happening to the operations under their control. Monitor/control reports focus on data, so they require special attention to accuracy, thoroughness, and honesty. These reports uncover problems to get them out in the open before it is too late, so they avoid covering up bad news and emphasizing only accomplishments.

Monitor/control reports expose any problems that exist.

Some monitor/control reports, such as strategic plans and annual budgets, establish guidelines for future action. Others, such as monthly sales reports, corporate annual reports, and scouting reports, provide detailed information about operations (see Figure 10.1. Finally, some monitor/control reports describe what occurred during some personal activity, such as a conference, convention, or trip.

Reports for Implementing Policies and Procedures

Managers provide policy and procedure reports to be read by anyone who wants a question answered. These reports present information in a straightforward manner. The rules of an organization make up lasting guidelines (such as the process for standardizing quality-control procedures or directions for how to reserve the conference room for special meetings). Less permanent issues are treated as they arise in nonrecurring reports (such as a position paper on the need for extra security precautions after a rash of burglaries in the area).

Policy/procedure reports help managers communicate the company's standards.

Reports for Complying with Government Regulations

All compliance reports are written in response to regulations of one sort or another, most of them imposed by government agencies. The regulatory agency issues instructions on how to write the necessary reports. The important thing in such reports is to be honest, thorough, and accurate. Annual compliance reports include income tax returns and annual shareholder reports. Interim compliance reports include reports from licensed institutions such as nursing homes and child-care facilities.

Compliance reports explain what a company is doing to conform to government regulations.

Reports for Documenting Progress

Whether you're writing a progress report for a client or for your boss, you need to anticipate your reader's needs and provide the required information clearly and tactfully. Interim progress reports give an idea of the work that has been accomplished to date (see Figure 10.2 on page 287). In many cases these interim reports are followed by a final report at the conclusion of the contract or project. Final reports are generally more elaborate than interim reports and serve as a permanent record of what was accomplished. They focus on final results rather than on progress along the way.

Reports documenting progress on a client's contract or an internal project provide all the information readers need.

Analytical Reports

To make informed decisions, managers rely on the supporting information, analyses, and recommendations presented in analytical reports. Typically, an analytical report presents a decision (or solution to a problem), often with recommendations for a number of

The purpose of analytical reports is to convince the audience that the conclusions and recommendations developed in the text are valid.

FIGURE 10.1   Effective Monitor/Control Report—Informational

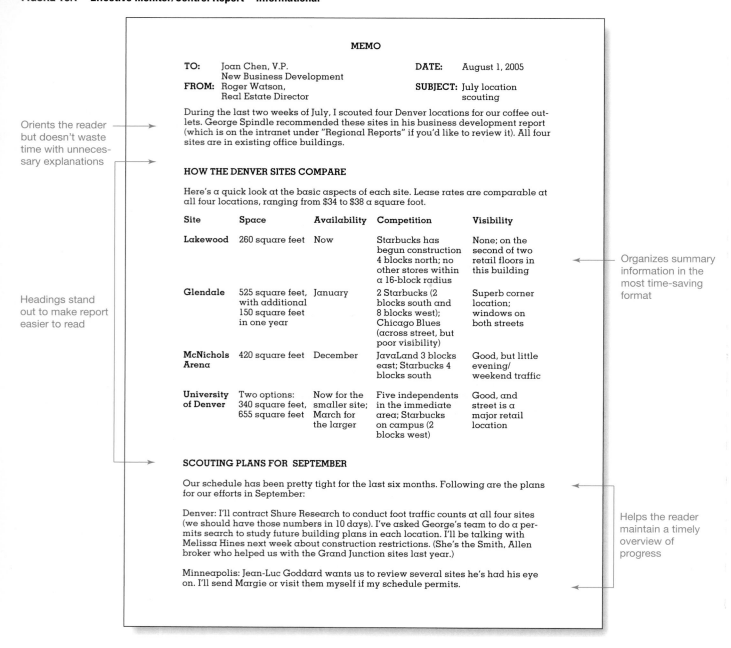

Orients the reader but doesn't waste time with unnecessary explanations

Headings stand out to make report easier to read

> ### MEMO
>
> **TO:**   Joan Chen, V.P.   **DATE:**   August 1, 2005
>   New Business Development
> **FROM:** Roger Watson,   **SUBJECT:** July location
>   Real Estate Director   scouting
>
> During the last two weeks of July, I scouted four Denver locations for our coffee out-
> lets. George Spindle recommended these sites in his business development report
> (which is on the intranet under "Regional Reports" if you'd like to review it). All four
> sites are in existing office buildings.
>
> **HOW THE DENVER SITES COMPARE**
>
> Here's a quick look at the basic aspects of each site. Lease rates are comparable at
> all four locations, ranging from $34 to $38 a square foot.
>
> | Site | Space | Availability | Competition | Visibility |
> |---|---|---|---|---|
> | Lakewood | 260 square feet | Now | Starbucks has begun construction 4 blocks north; no other stores within a 16-block radius | None; on the second of two retail floors in this building |
> | Glendale | 525 square feet, with additional 150 square feet in one year | January | 2 Starbucks (2 blocks south and 8 blocks west); Chicago Blues (across street, but poor visibility) | Superb corner location; windows on both streets |
> | McNichols Arena | 420 square feet | December | JavaLand 3 blocks east; Starbucks 4 blocks south | Good, but little evening/ weekend traffic |
> | University of Denver | Two options: 340 square feet, 655 square feet | Now for the smaller site; March for the larger | Five independents in the immediate area; Starbucks on campus (2 blocks west) | Good, and street is a major retail location |
>
> **SCOUTING PLANS FOR SEPTEMBER**
>
> Our schedule has been pretty tight for the last six months. Following are the plans
> for our efforts in September:
>
> Denver: I'll contract Shure Research to conduct foot traffic counts at all four sites
> (we should have those numbers in 10 days). I've asked George's team to do a per-
> mits search to study future building plans in each location. I'll be talking with
> Melissa Hines next week about construction restrictions. (She's the Smith, Allen
> broker who helped us with the Grand Junction sites last year.)
>
> Minneapolis: Jean-Luc Goddard wants us to review several sites he's had his eye
> on. I'll send Margie or visit them myself if my schedule permits.

Organizes summary information in the most time-saving format

Helps the reader maintain a timely overview of progress

actions. The body of the report presents all the facts (both good and bad) and persuades readers to accept the decision, solution, or recommendations that are detailed throughout the report. To persuade the reader, the writer carefully analyzes the facts and presents a compelling argument. Two of the more common examples of analytical reports are problem-solving reports and proposals.

Reports for Solving Problems

Troubleshooting reports analyze problems and propose solutions.

When solving problems, managers need both basic information and detailed analysis. Problem-solving reports typically require secondary or primary research. They are used when a problem exists and someone must investigate and propose a solution. These troubleshooting reports usually start with some background information on the problem, then analyze alternative solutions, and finally recommend the best approach.

FIGURE 10.2 Effective Progress Report—Informational (Excerpt)

Uses letter format, common for most external interim progress reports (final reports would usually be longer and would often be in manuscript form)

Emphasizes what has been accomplished during the reporting period (if it were a final report, it would focus on results rather than on progress)

Eases reader's understanding by making headings correspond to the tasks performed

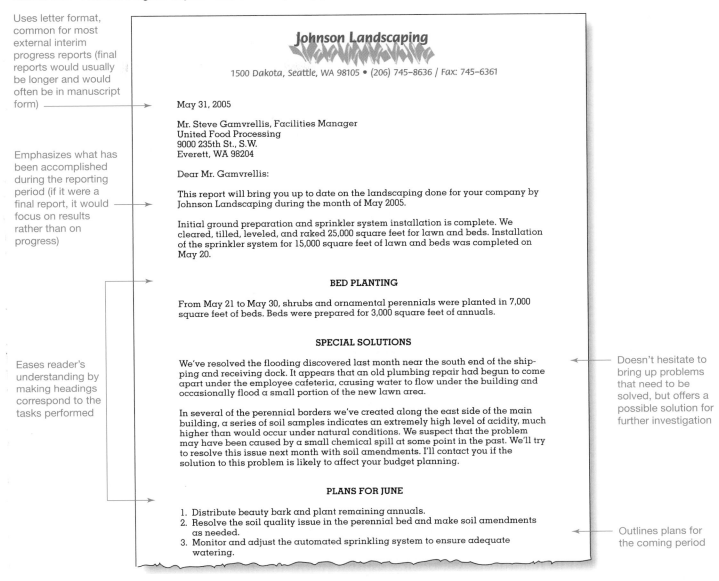

Johnson Landscaping

1500 Dakota, Seattle, WA 98105 • (206) 745–8636 / Fax: 745–6361

May 31, 2005

Mr. Steve Gamvrellis, Facilities Manager
United Food Processing
9000 235th St., S.W.
Everett, WA 98204

Dear Mr. Gamvrellis:

This report will bring you up to date on the landscaping done for your company by Johnson Landscaping during the month of May 2005.

Initial ground preparation and sprinkler system installation is complete. We cleared, tilled, leveled, and raked 25,000 square feet for lawn and beds. Installation of the sprinkler system for 15,000 square feet of lawn and beds was completed on May 20.

BED PLANTING

From May 21 to May 30, shrubs and ornamental perennials were planted in 7,000 square feet of beds. Beds were prepared for 3,000 square feet of annuals.

SPECIAL SOLUTIONS

We've resolved the flooding discovered last month near the south end of the shipping and receiving dock. It appears that an old plumbing repair had begun to come apart under the employee cafeteria, causing water to flow under the building and occasionally flood a small portion of the new lawn area.

In several of the perennial borders we've created along the east side of the main building, a series of soil samples indicates an extremely high level of acidity, much higher than would occur under natural conditions. We suspect that the problem may have been caused by a small chemical spill at some point in the past. We'll try to resolve this issue next month with soil amendments. I'll contact you if the solution to this problem is likely to affect your budget planning.

PLANS FOR JUNE

1. Distribute beauty bark and plant remaining annuals.
2. Resolve the soil quality issue in the perennial bed and make soil amendments as needed.
3. Monitor and adjust the automated sprinkling system to ensure adequate watering.

Doesn't hesitate to bring up problems that need to be solved, but offers a possible solution for further investigation

Outlines plans for the coming period

From time to time, employees and managers write problem-solving reports to evaluate the practicality and advisability of pursuing a course of action (such as buying equipment, changing a procedure, or hiring a consultant). These feasibility reports study proposed options to assess whether any or all of them are sound (see Figure 10.3). Justification reports are written after a course of action has been taken to justify what was done.

Feasibility and justification reports study and qualify courses of action—feasibility reports are prepared before the action is taken, and justification reports are prepared after.

Proposals

A **proposal** is a special type of analytical report designed to get products, plans, or projects accepted by others. Proposals can be one or two pages, or they can be hundreds of pages if they involve large, complex jobs. Regardless of the size and scope, these special types of reports analyze an audience's problem, present a solution, and persuade the audience that the solution presented is the best approach. Proposals are usually read by people in positions of authority.

Solicited proposals are generally prepared at the request of external parties who need something done; however, they may also be requested by such internal sources as

Proposals present ideas and persuade audiences to accept them.

Effective solicited proposals address each item listed in the RFP.

FIGURE 10.3   Effective Problem-Solving Report—Analytical

MEMO

TO: Board of Directors, Executive Committee members
FROM: Alycia Jenn, Business Development Manager
DATE: July 6, 2005
SUBJECT: World Wide Web retailing site

In response to your request, my staff and I investigated the potential for establishing a retailing site on the World Wide Web. After analyzing the behavior of our customers and major competitors and studying the overall development of electronic retailing, we have three recommendations:

1. Yes, we should establish an online presence within the next six months.
2. We should engage a firm that specializes in online retailing to design and develop the website.
3. We must take care to integrate online retailing with our store-based and mail-order operations.

WE SHOULD SET UP A WEBSITE

First, does a website make financial sense today? Studies suggest that our competitors are not currently generating significant revenue from their websites. Stallini's is the leader so far, but its sales haven't broken the $1 million mark. Moreover, at least half of our competitors' online sales are from current customers who would have purchased the same items in-store or by mail order. The cost of setting up a retailing site is around $120,000, so it isn't possible to justify a site solely on the basis of current financial return.

Second, do we need to establish a presence now in order to remain competitive in the future? The online situation is too fluid and unpredictable to answer this question in a quantitative profit-and-loss way, but a qualitative view of strategy indicates that we should set up a site:

- As younger consumers (more comfortable with online shopping) reach their peak earning years (ages 35–54), they'll be more likely to buy online than today's peak spenders.
- The web is erasing geographical shopping limits, presenting both a threat and an opportunity. Even though our customers can now shop websites anywhere in the world (so that we have thousands of competitors instead of a dozen), we can now target customers anywhere in the world.
- If the growth in online retailing continues, this will eventually be a viable market. Establishing a site now and working out any problems will prepare us for high-volume online business in the years ahead.

WE SHOULD ENGAGE A CONSULTANT TO IMPLEMENT THE SITE

Implementing a competitive retailing site can take anywhere from 1,000 to 1,500 hours of design and programming time. We have some of the expertise needed in-house, but the marketing and information systems departments have only 300 person-hours in the next six months. I recommend that we engage a web design consultant to help us with the design and to do all the programming.

Clarifies the purpose and origin of the report in the introduction

Clarifies what's needed by wording recommendations simply and to the point

Presents logical and clear reasons for recommending that the firm establish a website

Includes not only the recommendation to establish a website but also one to hire a consultant to implement the website and integrate it with existing systems

(continued)

---

management or the board of directors. Some external parties prepare an invitation to bid on their contract. Called a **request for proposals (RFP)**, such an invitation includes instructions that specify the exact type of work to be performed, along with guidelines on how and when the company wants the work completed.

Unsolicited proposals are usually written to obtain business or funding without a specific invitation from management or a potential client. In other words, with an unsolicited proposal, the writer makes the first move. Since readers may not know about the problem, the writer must convince them that a problem exists and that he or she can solve it. Thus, unsolicited proposals generally spend considerable time explaining why readers should take action and convincing them of the benefits of buying (or funding) something.

An unsolicited proposal must first establish that a problem exists.

FIGURE 10.3 Continued

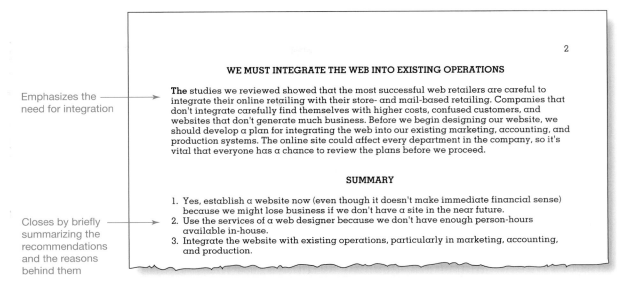

Emphasizes the need for integration

Closes by briefly summarizing the recommendations and the reasons behind them

2

WE MUST INTEGRATE THE WEB INTO EXISTING OPERATIONS

The studies we reviewed showed that the most successful web retailers are careful to integrate their online retailing with their store- and mail-based retailing. Companies that don't integrate carefully find themselves with higher costs, confused customers, and websites that don't generate much business. Before we begin designing our website, we should develop a plan for integrating the web into our existing marketing, accounting, and production systems. The online site could affect every department in the company, so it's vital that everyone has a chance to review the plans before we proceed.

SUMMARY

1. Yes, establish a website now (even though it doesn't make immediate financial sense) because we might lose business if we don't have a site in the near future.
2. Use the services of a web designer because we don't have enough person-hours available in-house.
3. Integrate the website with existing operations, particularly in marketing, accounting, and production.

Internal Proposals **Internal proposals** are submitted to decision makers in one's own organization. They have two primary purposes: (1) to seek approval for a course of action (such as changing recruiting procedures, revising the company's training programs, or reorganizing a department) or (2) to request additional resources (such as new equipment, more employees, or extra operating funds).

Because most internal proposals advocate change, you must take extra care to understand whether your audience will feel threatened by your plan. A good internal proposal is completely unbiased and explains why a project or course of action is needed, what it will involve, how much it will cost, and how the company will benefit (see Figure 10.4).

> Effective internal proposals are unbiased and thoroughly explain the need, application, cost and benefits of the proposed action.

External Proposals **External proposals** are submitted outside an organization to current or potential clients and government agencies. Like internal proposals, they solicit approval for projects or funds, but they differ in several ways. First, because they're directed to outsiders, external proposals are more formal. Second, external proposals are legally binding. Once approved, they form the basis of a contract, so they are prepared with extreme care, spelling out precisely what your company will provide under specific terms and conditions.

> If accepted, external proposals become legally binding documents.

Third, audience members may not know your company, so your proposal must convince them that your organization is the best source of a product or service. You can do so by devoting considerable space to explaining your experience, qualifications, facilities, and equipment. Also, show that you clearly understand your audience's problem or need (see Figure 10.5 on pages 292–293)[2].

Applying the Three-Step Writing Process to Business Reports and Proposals

As with other business messages, your reports and proposals benefit when you follow the three-step writing process: (1) planning, (2) writing, and (3) completing business messages. When preparing these longer messages, you may need to add some tasks to the familiar categories, or you may need to pay special attention to tasks you're already

> The three-step writing process applies to reports as well as to other business messages.

FIGURE 10.4   Effective Internal Proposal—Analytical (Unsolicited)

MEMO

TO: Jamie Engle
FROM: Shandel Cohen
DATE: July 8, 2005
SUBJECT: Proposed automatic mail-response system

THE PROBLEM:
SLOW RESPONSE TO CUSTOMER REQUESTS FOR INFORMATION

Our new produce line has been very well received, and orders have surpassed our projections. This very success, however, has created a shortage of printed catalogs and data sheets, as well as considerable overtime for people in the customer response center. As we introduce upgrades and new options, our printed materials quickly become outdated. If we continue to rely on printed materials for customer information, we have two choices: Distribute existing materials (even though they are incomplete or inaccurate) or discard existing materials and print new ones.

THE SOLUTION:
AUTOMATED MAIL-RESPONSE SYSTEM

With minor modifications to our current computer system and very little additional software, we can set up an automated system to respond to customer requests for information. This system can save us time and money and can keep our distributed information current.

Automated mail-response systems have been tested and proven effective. Many companies already use this method to respond to customer information requests, so we won't have to worry about relying on untested technology. Both customer and company responses have been positive.

Ever-Current Information

Rather than discard and print new materials, we would need to update only the electronic files. We could be able to provide customers and our field sales organization with up-to-date, correct information as soon as the upgrades or options are available.

Instantaneous Delivery

Within a very short time of requesting information, customers would have that information in hand. Electronic delivery would be especially advantageous for our international customers. Regular mail to remote locations sometimes takes weeks to arrive, by which time the information may already be out of date. Both customers and field salespeople will appreciate the automatic mail-response system.

Minimized Waste

With our current method of sending printed information, we discard virtually tons of obsolete catalogs, data sheets, and other materials.

Annotations (left margin):

Describes the problem carefully in a positive light (in terms of the company's success) and shows why a new system is needed

Uses headings to highlight the benefits of the solution

Annotations (right margin):

Hooks reader on solution by highlighting such economic and operational benefits as ease of implementation, affordability, cost and time savings, currency, and proven results

(continued)

---

familiar with (see Figure 10.6 on page 294). Since much of the three-step process is covered in Chapters 3, 4, and 5, the following sections discuss only those tasks that differ for reports and proposals. The rest of this chapter focuses on Step 1, planning business reports and proposals. Chapter 11 focuses on Steps 2 and 3, writing and completing formal business reports and proposals.

Step 1: Planning Business Reports and Proposals

When planning reports and proposals, you focus on the same three tasks as for other business documents: analysis, investigation, and adaptation. Adapting your report to your audience and purpose is no different from adapting other business documents. You choose the best channel and medium, and you establish a good relationship with your

FIGURE 10.4 Continued

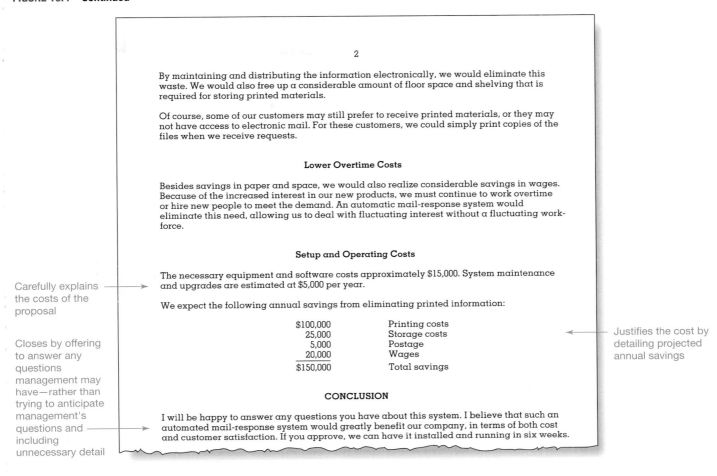

2

By maintaining and distributing the information electronically, we would eliminate this waste. We would also free up a considerable amount of floor space and shelving that is required for storing printed materials.

Of course, some of our customers may still prefer to receive printed materials, or they may not have access to electronic mail. For these customers, we could simply print copies of the files when we receive requests.

Lower Overtime Costs

Besides savings in paper and space, we would also realize considerable savings in wages. Because of the increased interest in our new products, we must continue to work overtime or hire new people to meet the demand. An automatic mail-response system would eliminate this need, allowing us to deal with fluctuating interest without a fluctuating work-force.

Setup and Operating Costs

Carefully explains the costs of the proposal

The necessary equipment and software costs approximately $15,000. System maintenance and upgrades are estimated at $5,000 per year.

We expect the following annual savings from eliminating printed information:

$100,000	Printing costs
25,000	Storage costs
5,000	Postage
20,000	Wages
$150,000	Total savings

Justifies the cost by detailing projected annual savings

CONCLUSION

Closes by offering to answer any questions management may have—rather than trying to anticipate management's questions and including unnecessary detail

I will be happy to answer any questions you have about this system. I believe that such an automated mail-response system would greatly benefit our company, in terms of both cost and customer satisfaction. If you approve, we can have it installed and running in six weeks.

audience. However, you have a few special considerations when analyzing and investigating business reports and proposals.

Analysis for Reports and Proposals

When planning reports and proposals, you will of course need to analyze your audience and purpose. But even before that, you need to analyze your particular situation to see whether it merits writing a report in the first place. Once you decide that you indeed need to write the report, you must determine whether it should be informational or analytical. For informational reports, you define your specific purpose, compose a preliminary outline, and develop a work plan. For analytical reports, you follow the same steps, except that you need to define the problem first.

> When writing reports, pay special attention to analysis tasks such as defining the problem, writing the statement of purpose, developing a preliminary outline, and preparing the work plan.

Define the Problem

Sometimes the person authorizing your report will define the problem you address. Other times, you will have to define the problem to be resolved. Be careful not to confuse a simple topic (campus parking) with a problem (the lack of enough campus parking). To help define the problem that your analytical report will address, ask yourself, What needs to be determined? Why is this issue important? Who is involved in the situation? Where is the trouble located? How did the situation originate? When did it start? Not all these questions apply in every situation, but asking them helps you define the problem and limit the scope of your discussion.

> The problem you need to resolve may be defined by your superior.

FIGURE 10.5   Effective External Proposal—Analytical (Solicited)

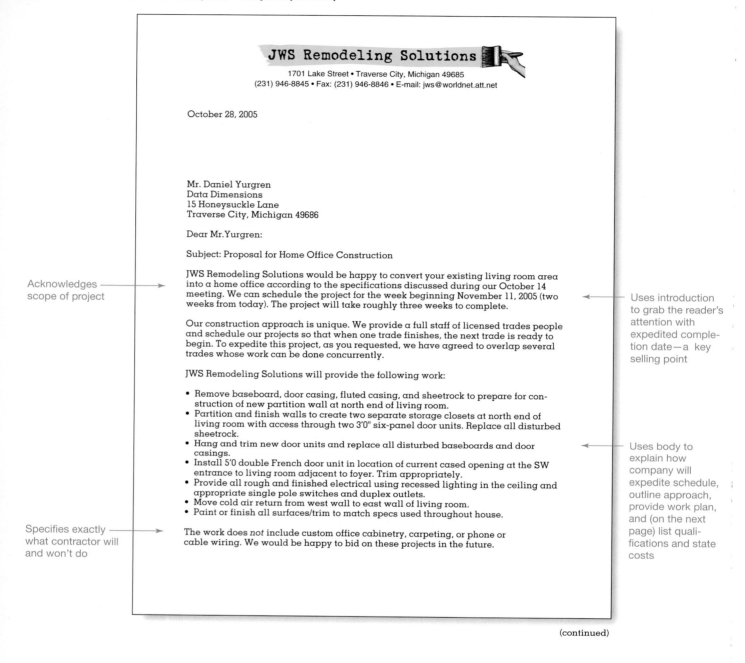

Acknowledges scope of project

Specifies exactly what contractor will and won't do

Uses introduction to grab the reader's attention with expedited completion date—a key selling point

Uses body to explain how company will expedite schedule, outline approach, provide work plan, and (on the next page) list qualifications and state costs

(continued)

Write the Statement of Purpose

The statement of purpose defines the objective of your report.

Writing a statement of purpose will help you keep your report writing on task. Whereas defining the problem helps you know *what* you are going to investigate, the **statement of purpose** defines *why* you are preparing the report. The most useful way to word your purpose statement is to begin with an infinitive phrase (*to* plus a verb). Doing so encourages you to take control and decide where you're going before you begin. For instance, in an informational report, your statement of purpose can be as simple as these:

> To update clients on the progress of the research project (progress report)
>
> To develop goals and objectives for the coming year (monitor/control report)
>
> To explain the building access procedures (policy/procedure report)
>
> To submit required information to the SEC (compliance report)

FIGURE 10.5 Continued

Mr. Daniel Yurgren   October 28, 2005   Page 2

JWS Remodeling Solutions has been in business in the Michigan area for over 17 years. We have a strong reputation for being a quality builder. We take great pride in our work and we treat all projects with the same high-level attention, regardless of their size or scope. Our trades people are all licensed, insured professionals with years of experience in their respective crafts. Enclosed is a copy of our company brochure discussing our qualifications in greater detail, along with a current client list. Please contact any of the names on this list for references.

Increases desire by highlighting qualifications

The total cost for this project is $6,800, broken down as follows:

Materials and supplies	$3,300
Labor	2,700
Overhead	800
Total	$6,800

Justifies cost by providing detail

An initial payment of $3,800 is due upon acceptance of this proposal. The remaining $3,000 is due upon completion of the work.

If you would like to have JWS Remodeling Solutions complete this work, please sign this letter and return it to us with your deposit in the enclosed envelope. We currently anticipate no construction delays, since the materials needed for your job are in stock and our staff of qualified workers is available during the period mentioned. If you have any questions regarding the terms of this proposal, please call me.

Uses brief closing to emphasize fast turnaround and immediate call for action

Sincerely,

Jordan W. Spurrier
President

Enclosures

Accepted by:

_____   _____
Daniel Yurgren   Date

Makes letter a binding contract, if signed

Pointers for Preparing External Proposals

- Review requirements stated in RFP.
- Define scope of work.
- Determine methods and procedures to be used.
- Estimate requirements for time, personnel, and costs.
- Write proposal exactly as RFP specifies—following exact format required and responding meticulously to every point raised.
- Begin by stating the purpose of the proposal, defining the scope of work, presenting background information, and explaining any restrictions that might apply to the contract.
- In the body, give details and specify anticipated results—include methods, schedule, facilities, equipment, personnel, and costs.
- Close by summarizing key points and asking for audience decision.

FIGURE 10.6   The Three-Step Writing Process for Reports

Planning → Writing → Completing

Analyze
Study the situation and define the problem. Write the statement of purpose, compose a preliminary outline, and develop a work plan.

Investigate
Gather primary and secondary information.

Adapt
Establish a good audience relationship and choose the right channel.

1

Organize
Decide on format, length, order, and structure.

Compose
Prepare final outline and draft introduction, body, and closing. Control your style through level of formality and tone. Establish a time perspective and provide supporting detail. Help readers find their way.

2

Revise
Evaluate content and review readability; edit and rewrite for conciseness and clarity.

Produce
Use effective design elements. Include prefatory and supplemental parts.

Proofread
Review text and visuals for errors in layout, spelling, and mechanics.

3

Statements of purpose for analytical reports are often more complex than those for informational reports.

For analytical reports, the statement of purpose is often more comprehensive. Linda Moreno is the cost accounting manager for Electrovision, a high-tech company based in Los Gatos, California. She was recently asked to find ways of reducing employee travel-and-entertainment costs (her complete report appears in Chapter 11). Because Moreno was supposed to suggest specific ways of reducing travel and entertainment costs, she phrased her statement of purpose accordingly:

> . . . to analyze the T&E [travel and entertainment] budget, evaluate the impact of recent changes in airfares and hotel costs, and suggest ways to tighten management's control over T&E expenses.

If Moreno had been assigned an informational report instead, she might have stated her purpose differently:

> To summarize Electrovision's spending on travel and entertainment.

Once you prepare a written statement of your purpose, review it with the person who authorized the study.

You can see from these two examples how much influence the purpose statement has on the scope of your report. Remember, the more specific your purpose statement, the more useful it will be as a guide to planning your report. Also, remember to double-check your statement of purpose with the person who authorized the report. The authorizer may decide that the report needs to go in a different direction. Once your statement is confirmed, you can use it as the basis for your preliminary outline.

Develop a Preliminary Outline

Your preliminary outline establishes the framework for your report and differs from the final outline.

A preliminary outline gives you a visual diagram of your report—its important points, the order in which they will be discussed, and the detail to be included (see Figure. 10.7). Your preliminary outline will guide your research efforts and help you organize and compose your report. Think of your preliminary outline as a working draft that you'll revise and modify as you go along. It will look quite different from the final outline you develop to write your report. Remember, when wording outlines, choose between descriptive (topical) and informative (talking) headings. Although outlines with informative headings take a little longer to write, they're generally more useful in guiding your work and easier for others to review.

Prepare the Work Plan

Writing a report can be a lengthy task with several phrases. In addition to organizing and writing, you'll often need to conduct primary and secondary research and prepare visuals. Developing a work plan is one way to coordinate and monitor your efforts so that you will produce quality reports quickly and efficiently.

FIGURE 10.7   Effective Preliminary Outline of a Research Report Focusing on Conclusions

States the conclusion first: The outsourcing was successful because it met most of the goals established for the program

Emphasizes concrete evidence of improvement in quality

Does not ignore the lack of improvement in employee confidence in three areas

MEASURING QUALITY IMPROVEMENTS

I.   Introduction

II.   Conclusion: Outsourcing employee training has reduced costs and improved quality

III. Cost reductions

   A. Set cost reduction goal at 15 percent over the first year

   B. Achieved actual reduction of 22 percent

   C. Reassigned the three staffers who used to work on training full time

   D. Reduced the management time needed to oversee training

   E. Sold the computers that used to be reserved for training

IV.   Quality improvements

   A. Employees say they are more confident in 7 out of 10 key skill areas

   B. Measurable mistakes have dropped by 12 percent

V.   Areas needing improvement

   A. Two trainers received approval ratings below 80 percent

   B. The outside trainers aren't always up to speed on internal company issues

   C. We've lost some flexibility for scheduling courses

VI.   Summary

Explores the two categories of goals: cost reductions and quality improvements

Discusses some areas of concern

If you are preparing the work plan for yourself, it can be relatively informal: a simple list of the steps you plan to take and an estimate of their sequence and timing. If you're conducting a lengthy, formal study, however, you'll want to develop a detailed work plan that can guide the performance of many tasks over a span of time. A formal work plan might include the following elements (especially the first two):

- **Statement of the problem.** The problem statement clarifies the challenge you face, helps you (and anyone working with you) stay focused on the goal, and helps everyone avoid the distractions that are likely to arise during report preparation.

- **Statement of the purpose and scope of your investigation.** The purpose statement describes what you plan to accomplish and the boundaries of your work. Stating which issues you will and will not cover is especially important with complex, lengthy investigations.

- **List of tasks to be accomplished.** For simple reports, the list of things to do will be short and probably obvious. However, longer, complex investigations require an exhaustive list so that you can plan the time needed for each task. Be sure to indicate your sources of information, the research necessary, and any constraints (on time, money, personnel, or data).

- **Description of any products that will result from your investigation.** Often, the only product of your efforts will be the report itself. In other cases, you'll need to produce something beyond a report, perhaps a new marketing plan or even a new product to sell. Make these expectations clear at the outset, and be sure to schedule enough time and resources to get the job done.

- **Review of project assignments, schedules, and resource requirements.** Indicate who will be responsible for what, when tasks will be completed, and how much the investigation will cost. If more than one person will be involved, include a brief section on coordinating report writing and production.

> Whether you prepare an informal work plan for yourself or a detailed work plan for your team, be sure it identifies all the tasks that must be performed.

FIGURE 10.8   Effective Work Plan for a Formal Study

States the problem clearly enough for anyone to understand without background research

STATEMENT OF THE PROBLEM

The rapid growth of our company over the past five years has reduced the sense of community among our staff. People no longer feel like part of an intimate organization where they matter as individuals.

Lays out the tasks to be accomplished and does so in clear, simple terms

PURPOSE AND SCOPE OF WORK

The purpose of this study is to determine whether a company newsletter would help rebuild employee identification with the organization. The study will evaluate the impact of newsletters in other companies and will attempt to identify features that might be desirable in our own newsletter. Such variables as length, frequency of distribution, types of articles, and graphic design will be considered. Costs will be estimated for several approaches. In addition, the study will analyze the personnel and the procedures required to produce a newsletter.

Delineates exactly what will be covered in the report

SOURCES AND METHODS OF DATA COLLECTION

Sample newsletters will be collected from 50 companies similar to ours in size, growth rate, and types of employees. The editors will be asked to comment on the impact of their publications on employee morale. Our own employees will be surveyed to determine their interest in a newsletter and their preferences for specific features. Production procedures and costs will be analyzed through conversations with newsletter editors and printers.

Presents preliminary outline for guidance, even though no description of the end product is included

PRELIMINARY OUTLINE

The preliminary outline for this study is as follows:

I. Do newsletters affect morale?
   A. Do people read them?
   B. How do employees benefit?
   C. How does the company benefit?
II. What are the features of good newsletters?
   A. How long are they?
   B. What do they contain?
   C. How often are they published?
   D. How are they designed?
III. How should a newsletter be produced?
   A. Should it be written, edited, and printed internally?
   B. Should it be written internally and printed outside?
   C. Should it be totally produced outside?
IV. What would a newsletter cost?
   A. What would the personnel cost be?
   B. What would the materials costs be?
   C. What would outside services cost?
V. Should we publish a company newsletter?
VI. If so, what approach should we take?

Includes no plans for following up

States the assignments and the schedules for completing them

WORK PLAN

Each phase of this study will be completed by the following dates:

Collect/analyze newsletters	September 3 to September 14, 2005
Interview editors by phone	September 16 to September 20, 2005
Survey employees	September 23 to September 27, 2005
Develop sample	September 30 to October 11, 2005
Develop cost estimates	October 8 to October 11, 2005
Prepare report	October 14 to October 25, 2005
Submit final report	October 28, 2005

■ **Plans for following up after delivering the report.** Follow-up can be as simple as making sure people received the information they need or as complex as conducting additional research to evaluate the results of report recommendations. Even informal follow-up can help you improve future reports and show that you care about your work's effectiveness and its impact on the organization.

■ **Working outline.** Some work plans, such as the plan in Figure 10.8, include a tentative outline of the report. This plan was developed for a report on whether to launch a company newsletter.

Investigation for Reports and Proposals

Begin your research by gathering secondary information.

In most cases you'll begin your research by looking for sources of secondary information—information on your subject that already exists and has already been collected, usually in the form of books, periodicals, newspapers, and websites. If secondary information doesn't exist or isn't helpful, then you'll need to collect firsthand, primary information for your specific needs.

Gather Secondary Information

Many sources of secondary information are easily accessible in print and online.[3]

Finding Information in the Library   Libraries are where you'll find business books, electronic databases, newspapers, periodicals, directories, almanacs, and government publications. In additon, you'll find your most important resource: librarians. Reference librarians are trained in research techniques and can show you how to use the library's many resources:

Reference librarians are there to assist you with your research efforts.

- **Business books.** Although less timely than journal articles, business books provide in-depth coverage of a variety of business topics. You may have better luck finding specialized information at company libraries or at a college library.
- **Electronic databases.** These computer-searchable collections of information are often categorized by subject areas (business, law, science, technology, and education). When using an electronic database, try to get a list of the periodicals or publications it includes, as well as the time period it covers so that you can plan to fill in any gaps for items not in the database.
- **Newspapers.** Libraries subscribe to only a select number of newspapers and store a limited number of back issues in print. However, they frequently subscribe to databases containing newspaper articles in full text (available online, on CD-ROM, or on microfilm). Also, most newspapers today offer full-text or limited editions of their papers on the Internet.
- **Periodicals.** Most periodicals fall into four categories: (1) popular magazines (not intended for business, professional, or academic use), (2) trade journals (providing news and other facts about particular professions, industries, and occupations), (3) business magazines (covering all major industries and professions), and (4) academic journals (publishing data from professional researchers and educators).
- **Directories.** Covering everything from accountants to zoos, business directories provide entries for companies, products, and individuals, and they include the names of key contacts.
- **Almanacs.** Almanacs are handy guides to factual and statistical information about countries, politics, the labor force, and so on.
- **Government publications.** For information on a law, a court decision, or current population patterns and business trends, consult government documents. A librarian can direct you to the information you want.

Finding Business Information on the Internet   Today's most popular source of company and industry information is the Internet, offering current news, industry trends, and company-related data on financial performance, products, goals, and employment. Remember that anyone (including you) can post anything on a website. Thus, information on the web may be biased, inaccurate, or exaggerated. Before seriously searching the web for business information, wait until you've had a chance to learn a bit about your topic from journals, books, and commercial databases. Then you'll be able to detect unreliable information and be more selective about which websites and documents you use.

When doing research on the Internet, you need to be selective because anyone can publish anything.

A good place to start on the web is the Internet Public Library at www.ipl.org. Modeled after a real library, this site will provide you with carefully selected links to high-quality business resources. You can find company profiles, trade data, business news, corporate tax and legal advice, small-business information, prepared forms and documents, biographies of executives, financial reports, job postings, online publications, and so on.

To find specific company information, check the company's website (if it maintains one). Company sites generally include detailed information about the firm's products,

You can find all kinds of information about a company on its website.

services, history, mission, strategy, financial performance, and employment needs. Many sites provide links to related company information, such as SEC filings, news releases, and more.

You can obtain news releases and general company news from news release sites such as PRNewswire (www.prnewswire.com) and Business Wire (www.businesswire.com). These sites offer free databases of news releases from companies subscribing to their services. News release sites are also good places to look for announcements of new products, management changes, earnings, dividends, mergers, acquisitions, and other company information.

The web doesn't have everything. You may find nothing about small organizations, or perhaps just their address and phone number. And even if the information exists on the web, you may not be able to find it. The Internet holds hundreds of millions of webpages, with hundreds of pages being added every day, and even the best Internet search engines manage to index only about one-third of the pages on the web.[4]

Understanding Search Engines   Search engines identify and screen web resources. They will often turn up what you're looking for, most likely along with a mountain of stuff you don't need. Not all search engines operate the same way. For instance, some engines index all the pages they find; others index only the most popular pages. Sites such as Yahoo!, Lycos, and Google offer well-known, commercially backed search engines.

Conducting Effective Database Searches   Whether you are using a library database or an Internet search engine, follow these tips to improve your search results:[5]

> *By following a few guidelines, you can improve your database search results.*

- **Use multiple search engines.** Don't limit yourself to a single search engine, especially if you are looking for less popular topics. Try your search on several engines by using **metacrawlers,** special engines that search several search engines at once.

- **Translate concepts into keywords and phrases.** If you're researching the "effect of TQM on company profits," select the keywords *TQM, total quality management, profits, sales, companies,* and *corporations.* Use synonyms or word equivalents whenever possible.

- **Use capitals and lowercase characters correctly.** When a search engine is case sensitive, it will return different documents for the keywords *Chair* and *chair.* If the search engine is not case sensitive, then it will return all documents containing the word *chair,* whether capitalized or not.

- **Use variations of your terms.** Use abbreviations (*CEO, CPA*), synonyms (*man, male*), related terms (*child, adolescent, youth*), different spellings (*dialog, dialogue*), singular and plural forms (*woman, women*), nouns and adjectives (*manager, management, managerial*), and open and compound forms (*online, on line, on-line*).

- **Specify phrases or individual keywords with quotation marks.** To look for an entire phrase (*total quality management*), most search engines allow you to use quotation marks around the phrase. Otherwise, the search engine will look for instances where the separate words (*total, quality,* and *management*) appear somewhere on the webpage.

- **Evaluate the precision and quality of your results to refine your search if necessary.** You'll need to refine your search if you end up with more than 60 to 100 links to sort through or if your first page of results doesn't offer something of interest. Also pay attention to whether you are searching in the title, subject, or document field of the database. Each will return different results.

Collect Primary Information

> *Conduct primary research by collecting basic information yourself.*

Sometimes what you need is not available from sources of secondary information, or you need something beyond what is covered in secondary information. In that case, you go out into the real world to gather data yourself. The main methods of collecting primary information are examining documents, making observations, conducting experiments, surveying people, and conducting interviews.

Documents, Observation, and Experiments   Often the most useful method of collecting primary information is examining internal documents, such as company sales reports, memos, balance sheets, and income statements. You can find a great deal of information in company databases and files. A single document may be a source of both secondary and primary information. For example, when citing summaries of financial and operations data from an annual report, you're using the report as secondary information. However, the same annual report would be considered a primary source if you were analyzing its design features, comparing it with annual reports from other years, or comparing it with reports from other companies.

Documentary evidence and historical records are sources of primary data.

Another common method of collecting primary business information is making formal observations. For instance, you can observe people performing their jobs or customers interacting with a product. Observation is a useful technique when you're studying objects, physical activities, processes, the environment, or human behavior. However, it can be expensive and time-consuming, and the value of the observation depends on the reliability of the observer.

Observation applies your five senses and your judgment to the investigation.

Conducting experiments is another method of collecting primary information, but this method is far more common in technical fields than in general business. An experiment requires extensive, accurate, and measurable manipulation of the factors involved—not only tweaking those variables being tested but also controlling those variables that aren't being tested. This sort of primary information is usually very expensive.

Experiments can be effective, but they are expensive.

Surveys   One of the best methods of collecting primary information is to ask people with relevant experience and opinions. Surveys include everything from a one-time, one-on-one interview to the distribution of thousands of questionnaires. When prepared and conducted properly, surveys can tell you what a cross section of people think about a given topic. Surveys are useful only when they're reliable and valid. A survey is *reliable* if it produces identical results when repeated. A survey is *valid* if it measures what it's intended to measure. For effective surveys, follow these tips:

- **Provide clear instructions.** Respondents need to know exactly how to fill out your questionnaire.

Developing an effective survey questionnaire requires care and skill.

- **Keep the questionnaire short and easy to answer.** Ask only questions that are relevant to your research. Remember that people are most likely to respond if they can complete your questionnaire within 10 to 15 minutes.

- **Develop questions that provide easy-to-analyze answers.** Numbers and facts are easier to summarize than opinions.

- **Avoid leading questions.** Questions that lead to a particular answer bias your survey. If you ask, "Do you prefer that we stay open in the evenings for customer convenience?" you'll get a yes answer. Instead, ask, "What time of day do you normally do your shopping?"

- **Ask only one thing at a time.** A compound question such as "Do you read books and magazines regularly?" doesn't allow for the respondent who reads one but not the other.

- **Pretest the questionnaire.** Have a sample group identify questions that are subject to misinterpretation.

If you're mailing your questionnaire rather than administering it in person, include a return postage-paid envelope along with a persuasive cover letter that explains why you're conducting the research. Your letter must convince your readers that responding is important. Remember that even under the best of circumstances, you may get no more than a 10 to 20 percent response.

Effective interviewers develop a communication plan.

Interviews   Getting information straight from an expert can be another effective method for collecting primary information. **Interviews** are planned conversations with a predetermined purpose that involve asking and answering questions. Before you decide to do one, ask yourself whether an interview is really the best way to get the information you need. Although they are relatively easy to conduct, interviews require careful planning and a lot of time.

- **Plan the interview.** Decide in advance what kind of information you want and how you will use it. Analyze your purpose, learn about the other person, and formulate your main idea. Then decide on the length, style, and organization of the interview.
- **Prepare interview questions.** The answers you receive are influenced by the types of questions you ask, the way you ask them, and your subject's cultural and language background.
- **Prioritize interview questions.** Rate your questions and highlight the ones you really need answers to. If you start to run out of time during the interview, you may have to skip less important questions.
- **Limit the number of questions.** Don't try to cover more questions than you have time for. You can probably handle about 20 questions in a half-hour.
- **Edit your questions.** Try to make your questions as neutral and as easy to understand as possible. Then practice them several times to make sure you're ready for the interview.
- **Process interview information.** After the interview, take a few moments to write down your thoughts, go over your notes, and organize your material. Fill in any blanks while the interview is fresh in your mind.

Document Sources and Give Credit

Always give proper credit when you use someone else's material or ideas.

Whenever you quote or paraphrase, you are using someone else's words or ideas. Doing so without proper credit is **plagiarism**. You can avoid plagiarism by documenting the original source (using one of the systems explained in Appendix B, "Documentation of Report Sources"). Documenting your sources is necessary for books, articles, tables, charts, diagrams, song lyrics, scripted dialogue, letters, speeches—anything that you take from someone else. Even if you paraphrase the material, it's best to give credit to the person you obtained the original information from.

However, you do not have to cite a source for general knowledge or for specialized knowledge that's generally known among your readers. For example, everyone knows that Franklin Roosevelt was elected to the presidency of the United States four times. You can say so on your own authority, even if you've read an article in which the author says the same thing.

Document Makeover

Improve This Report

To practice correcting drafts of actual documents, visit **www.prenhall.com/onekey** on the web. Click "Document Makeovers," then click Chapter 10. You will find a personal activity report that contains problems and errors relating to what you've learned in this chapter about planning business reports and proposals. Use the Final Draft decision tool to create an improved version of this report. Check the message for parallel construction, appropriate headings, suitable content, positive and bias-free language, and use of the "you" attitude.

Interpret Your Findings

By themselves, the data you collect won't offer much meaning or insight. You'll need to search for relationships among the facts and the bits of evidence you've compiled. This analysis allows you to interpret your findings and thus answer the questions or solve the problem that required the report in the first place. Depending on your writing project, you may be summarizing your results, drawing conclusions based on your results, or making recommendations.

Analyze your results before drawing conclusions or developing a set of recommendations.

Summarizing Your Research

If your boss has asked you to summarize the competitive strengths and weaknesses of another company or the recent trends in a particular market, your goal is to provide an unbiased summary that is free of your own opinions, conclusions, or recommendations. If you do uncover something that sparks an idea or raises a concern, by all means communicate this revelation but do so separately; don't include such information in your summary report.

Summaries must be impartial statements of fact.

Summarizing is not always a simple task. Identify the main idea and the key support points, and separate these from details, examples, and other supporting evidence (see Table 10.1). Focus your efforts on your audience, highlighting the information that is most important to the person who assigned the project or to those who will be reading the report.

However, don't mistake audience focus to mean that you're supposed to convey only the information your audience wants to hear. A good summary might contain nothing but bad news or information that runs counter to majority assumptions in the organization. Even if the summary isn't pleasant, effective managers always appreciate and respect honest, complete, and perceptive information from their employees.

Drawing Conclusions

A **conclusion** is a logical interpretation of the facts in your report. Reaching good conclusions based on the evidence at hand is one of the most important skills you can develop in your business career. Make sure your conclusions are sound: First, your conclusion should fulfill the original statement of purpose. After all, drawing a conclusion is why you took on the project in the first place. Second, base your conclusion strictly on the information included in the rest of the report—all the information. Don't ignore anything, even if it

Conclusions are interpretations of the facts.

Table 10.1	Summarizing Effectively	
Original Material (110 Words)	**45-Word Summary**	**22-Word Summary**
Our facilities costs spiraled out of control last year. The 23 percent jump was far ahead of every other cost category in the company and many times higher than the 4 percent average rise for commercial real estate in the Portland metropolitan area. The rise can be attributed to many factors, but the major factors include repairs (mostly electrical and structural problems at the downtown office), energy (most of our offices are heated by electricity, the price of which has been increasing much faster than for oil or gas), and last but not least, the loss of two sublease tenants whose rent payments made a substantial dent in our cost profile for the past five years.	Our facilities costs jumped 23 percent last year, far ahead of every other cost category in the company and many times higher than the 4 percent local average. The major factors contributing to the increase are repairs, energy, and the loss of two sublease tenants.	Our facilities costs jumped 23 percent last year, due mainly to rising repair and energy costs and the loss of sublease income.

Main idea

Major support points

Details

doesn't support your conclusion. Third, don't introduce any new information in your conclusion. (After all, if something is that important, it should be in the body of your report.) And, fourth, make sure your conclusion is logical. A logical conclusion is one that follows accepted patterns of reasoning.

Your conclusions are influenced by your personal values and your organization's values; just be sure that you're aware of how these biases affect your judgment. Also, don't expect all team members to examine the evidence and arrive at the same conclusion. One of the reasons for bringing additional people into a decision is to gain their unique perspectives and experiences.

> **Check the logic that underlies your conclusions.**

Developing Recommendations

> **Recommendations are suggestions for action.**

Whereas a conclusion interprets the facts, a **recommendation** suggests what to do about the facts. The difference between a conclusion and a recommendation can be seen in the following example:

Conclusion	Recommendation
On the basis of its track record and current price, I conclude that this company is an attractive buy.	I recommend that we write a letter to the president offering to buy the company at a 10 percent premium over the market value of its stock.

> **Good recommendations are**
> - Practical
> - Acceptable to readers
> - Explained in enough detail for readers to take action

Be sure to clarify the relationship between your conclusions and your recommendations. Remember, recommendations are inappropriate in a report when you're not expected to supply them. But when you do provide recommendations in a report, try to develop them without bias. Don't let your assumptions and personal values influence them. To be credible, recommendations must be based on logical analysis and sound conclusions. They must also be practical and acceptable to your readers, the people who have to make the recommendations work. Finally, when making a recommendation, be certain that you have adequately described the steps that come next. Don't leave your readers scratching their heads and saying, "This all sounds good, but what do I do on Monday morning?"

Reviewing Key Points

This chapter highlights various types of informational and analytical reports. It discusses when and how these documents are used and summarizes how to apply the three-step writing process to your reports and proposals.

The bulk of this chapter discusses Step 1 of the writing process for business reports and proposals. It talks about the special analysis tasks involved in planning business reports and proposals. The chapter describes defining the problem for analytical reports, writing the statement of purpose, developing a preliminary outline, and preparing the work plan. It also covers the special investigation tasks involved in planning business reports and proposals, including gathering secondary and primary information, documenting sources, analyzing your findings, summarizing your research, drawing conclusions, and developing recommendations.

The next chapter discusses Steps 2 and 3 of the writing process: writing and completing business reports and proposals. You will learn about special organizational considerations when deciding on format and length and when choosing the direct or indirect approach. You'll study the structure of informational and analytical reports, and you'll learn how to choose visual aids. You will learn about developing the text of reports and proposals, and you'll study the various components that go into formal reports and proposals.

Test Your Knowledge

1. How are reports for monitoring and controlling operations used?

2. What functions do progress reports serve?

3. What are the two primary purposes of internal proposals?

4. How do proposal writers use an RFP?

5. How does primary information differ from secondary information?

6. How can you improve your search when using a search engine or a library database?

7. What makes a survey reliable and valid?

8. Why is it important to prioritize your interview questions?

9. What are the characteristics of a sound conclusion?

10. How does a conclusion differ from a recommendation?

Apply Your Knowledge

1. Why are unsolicited proposals more challenging to write than solicited proposals?

2. If you want to make a specific recommendation in your report, should you include information that might support a different recommendation? Explain your answer.

3. If your report includes only factual information, is it objective? Please explain.

4. After an exhaustive study of an important problem, you have reached a conclusion that you believe your company's management will reject. What will you do? Explain your answer.

5. **Ethical Choices**   If you want to make a specific recommendation following your research, should you include information that might support a different recommendation? Explain your answer.

Practice Your Knowledge

Activities

For live links to all websites discussed in this chapter, visit this text's website at www.prenhall. com/bovee. Just log on, select Chapter 10, and click on "Featured Websites." Locate the page or the URL related to the material in the text.

1. **Analyze This Document**   The Securities and Exchange Commission (SEC) requires all public companies to file a comprehensive annual report (form 10-K) electronically. Many companies post links to these reports on their websites along with links to other company reports. Visit the website of Dell at www.dell.com and view the company's most recent annual reports: 10-K and Year in Review. (To view the reports, fol-

low the links at the homepage to About Dell, Investor Relations, and Annual Reports.) Compare the style and format of the two reports. For which audience(s) is the Year in Review targeted? Who besides the SEC might be interested in the Annual Report 10-K? Which report do you find easier to read? More interesting? More detailed?

2. **Understanding Business Reports and Proposals: How Companies Use Reports** Interview several people working in a career you might like to enter, and ask them about the types of written reports they receive and prepare. How do these reports tie in to the decision-making process? Who reads the reports they prepare? Summarize your findings in writing, give them to your instructor, and be prepared to discuss them with the class.

3. **Internet** Read the step-by-step hints and examples for writing a funding proposal at http://www.learnerassociates.net/proposal. Review the entire sample proposal online. What details did the writer decide to include in the appendixes? Why was this material placed in the appendixes and not the main body of the report? According to the writer's tips, when is the best time to prepare a Project Overview?

4. **Analyzing the Situation: Statement of Purpose** Sales at The Style Shop, a clothing store for men, have declined for the third month in a row. Your boss is not sure whether this decline is due to a weak economy or if it's due to another, unknown reason. She has asked you to investigate the situation and to submit a report to her highlighting some possible reasons for the decline. Develop a statement of purpose for your report.

5. **Teamwork: Planning an Unsolicited Proposal** Break into small groups and identify an operational problem occurring at your campus—perhaps involving registration, university housing, food services, parking, or library services. Then develop a workable solution to that problem. Finally, develop a list of pertinent facts that your team will need to gather to convince the reader that the problem exists and that your solution will work.

6. **Preparing the Work Plan** The lawn surrounding the Town Centre shopping center looks as if it could use better care. You're the assistant to the center's general manager, who must approve any new contracts for lawn service. You want to prepare a formal study of the current state of your lawn's health. Your report will include conclusions and recommendations for your boss's consideration. Draft a work plan, including the problem statement, the statement of purpose and scope, a description of what will result from your investigation, the sources and methods of data collection, and a preliminary outline.

7. **Finding Secondary Information** Businesspeople have to know where to look for secondary information when they conduct research. Prepare a list of the most important magazines and professional journals in the following fields of study:
   a. Marketing/advertising
   b. Insurance
   c. Communications
   d. Accounting

8. **Finding Information: Primary Information** Deciding how to collect primary data is an important part of the research process. Which one or more of the five methods of data collection (examining documents, making observations, surveying people, performing experiments, or conducting interviews) would you use if you were researching these questions?
   a. Has the litter problem on campus been reduced since the cafeteria began offering fewer take-out choices this year?
   b. Has the school attracted more transfer students since it waived the formal application process and allowed students at other colleges simply to send their transcripts and a one-page letter of application?
   c. Have the number of traffic accidents at the school's main entrance been reduced since a traffic light was installed?
   d. Has student satisfaction with the campus bookstore improved now that students can order their books over the Internet and pick them up at several campus locations?

9. **Finding Information: Interviews**   You're conducting an information interview with a manager in another division of your company. Partway through the interview, the manager shows clear signs of impatience. How should you respond? What might you do differently to prevent this from happening in the future? Explain your answers.

10. **Processing Information: Documenting Sources**   Select five business articles from sources such as journals, books, newspapers, or websites. Develop a resource list using Appendix B as a guideline.

Expand Your Knowledge

Exploring the Best of the Web

Better Ideas for Better Business Plans   What's involved in a business plan? BizPlanIt.Com (at www.bizplanit.com) offers tips and advice, consulting services, a free e-mail newsletter, and a sample virtual business plan. You'll find suggestions on what details and how much information to include in each section of a business plan. You can explore the site's numerous links to business plan books and software; online magazines; educational programs; government resources; women and minority resources; and even answers to your business plan questions. Review the articles on the site and answer the following questions:

Exercises

1. Why is the executive summary such an important section of a business plan? What kind of information is contained in the executive summary?

2. What is the product/services section? What information should it contain? List some of the common errors to avoid when planning this part.

3. What type of business planning should you describe in the exit strategy section? Why?

Exploring the Web on Your Own

Review these chapter-related websites on your own to learn more about planning and using reports in the workplace.

1. If you need financial information on public companies, just ask Edgar, the Securities and Exchange Commission's online reporting warehouse at www.sec.gov/edgar.

2. Compare annual report styles and formats from hundreds of publicly traded U.S. companies at the Report Gallery, www.reportgallery.com.

3. Researching Companies Online, www.learnwebskills.com, has some good advice for finding company and industry information on the web. Take the tutorial.

Learn Interactively

Interactive Study Guide

Go to the Companion Website at www.prenhall.com/bovee. For Chapter 10, take advantage of the interactive "Study Guide" to test your knowledge of the chapter. Get instant feedback on whether you need additional studying. Also, visit this site's "Study Hall," where you'll find an abundance of valuable resources that will help you succeed in this course.

Peak Performance Grammar and Mechanics

To improve your skill with other types of punctuation, visit www.prenhall.com/onekey, click "Peak Performance Grammar and Mechanics," click "Punctuation," and then click "Punctuation II." Take the Pretest to determine whether you have any weak areas. Then review those areas in the Refresher Course. Take the Follow-Up Test to check your grasp of other types of punctuation. For an extra challenge or advanced practice, take the Advanced Test. Finally, for additional reinforcement in periods, question marks, and exclamation points, go to the "Improve Your Grammar, Mechanics, and Usage" section that follows, and complete the "Level 1: Self-Assessment" exercises.

Informal Informational Reports

1. Your progress to date: Interim progress report on your academic career

As you know, the requirements involved in getting a degree or certificate can be nearly as challenging as any course you could take.

Your task: Plan an interim progress report detailing the steps you've taken toward completing your graduation or certification requirements. After examining the requirements listed in your catalog, indicate a realistic schedule for completing those requirements you have yet to complete. In addition to course requirements, include steps such as completing the residency requirement, filing necessary papers, and paying necessary fees. Plan on using a memo format for your report, and addressing it to anyone who is helping or encouraging you through school.

2. Gavel to gavel: Personal activity report of a meeting

Meetings and conferences can be one-on-one or large gatherings, and you have probably attended your share.

Your task: Plan a personal activity report on a meeting or conference that you recently attended. Plan to use memo format, and direct the report to other students in your class who did not attend.

3. Check that price tag: Informational report on trends in college costs

Are tuition costs going up, going down, or remaining the same? Your school's administration has asked you to compare your tuition costs with those of a nearby school and determine which has risen more quickly. Check your school's annual tuition costs for the last four years. Then check the four-year tuition trends for a neighboring school. For both schools, calculate the percentage change in tuition costs from year to year and between the first and fourth year.

Your task: Plan an informal report (using the letter format) presenting your findings and conclusions to the president of your school. Plan to include graphics that explain and support your conclusions.

4. Get a move on it: Lasting guidelines for moving in with a roommate

Moving in with a roommate is one experience you weren't quite prepared for—lugging your earthly belongings up four flights of stairs in 90-degree heat, channeling electrical cords to the one outlet in the corner of the room, and negotiating with your roommate over who gets the bigger closet. Now that you're a pro, you've offered to write some lasting guidelines for other new roommates so that they know what is expected of them on moving day.

Your task: Plan an informational report for anyone moving in with a roommate, outlining the rules and procedures to follow. Lay out the rules such as establishing a starting time, handling trash and empty boxes, sorting items permitted and not permitted in apartments or dorm rooms, remembering common courtesies, and so on. Be sure to mention any policies for pets, cooking, and overloading electrical circuits. Of course, any recommendations on how to handle disputes with roommates would be helpful. Direct your memo report to fellow students.

Informal Analytical Reports

5. My next career move: Feasibility report organized around recommendations

If you've ever given yourself a really good lecture, you'll be quite comfortable with this project.

Your task: Plan how to write a memo report directed to yourself and signed with a fictitious name. Indicate a possible job that your education will qualify you for, mention the advantages of the position in terms of your long-range goals, and then outline the actions you must take to get the job.

6. Staying the course: Unsolicited proposal

Think of a course you would love to see added to the core curriculum at your school. Or, if you would like to see a course offered as an elective rather than being required, write your e-mail report accordingly.

Your task: Plan a short e-mail proposal. Plan on submitting it to the academic dean. Be sure to include all the reasons supporting your idea.

7. Planning my program: Problem-solving report

Assume that you will have time for only one course next term.

Your task: Plan a report that lists the pros and cons of four or five courses that interest you, and settle on the course that is best for you to take at this time. Plan to make your report a memo addressed to your counselor or academic adviser.

8. "Would you carry it?" Unsolicited proposal recommending a product to a retail outlet

Select a product you are familiar with, and imagine that you work for the manufacturer and that you're trying to get a local retail outlet to carry it. Use the Internet and other resources to gather any information you need about the product.

Your task: Plan an unsolicited proposal to be sent in letter format to the owner (or manager) of the store. You want to propose that the store stock your product. Use the information you gathered to describe some of the product's features and benefits to the store. Then make up some reasonable figures, highlighting what the item costs, what it can be sold for, and what services your company provides (return of unsold items, free replacement of unsatisfactory items, necessary repairs, and so on).

9. Restaurant review: Troubleshooting report on a restaurant's food and operations

Visit any restaurant, possibly your school cafeteria. The workers and fellow customers will assume that you are an ordinary customer, but you are really a spy for the owner.

Your task: After your visit, plan a short memo to the owner, explaining (a) what you did and what you observed, (b) any violations of policy that you observed, and (c) your recommendations for improvement. The first part of your report (what you did and what you observed) will be the longest. Plan to include a description of the premises, inside and out. You'll want to tell how long it took for each step of ordering and receiving your meal. Figure out how you'll describe the service and food thoroughly. You are interested in both the good and bad aspects of the establishment's decor, service, and food. For the second section (violations of policy), use some common sense. If all the servers but one have their hair covered, you may assume that policy requires hair to be covered; a dirty window or restroom obviously violates policy. The last section (recommendations for improvement) involves professional judgment. What management actions will improve the restaurant?

10. On the books: Troubleshooting report on improving the campus bookstore

Imagine that you are a consultant hired to improve the profits of your campus bookstore.

Your task: Visit the bookstore and look critically at its operations. Then plan a memo offering recommendations to the bookstore manager that would make the store more profitable, perhaps suggesting products it should carry, hours that it should remain open, or added services that it should make available to students. Be sure that you plan how to support your recommendations.

11. Press one for efficiency: Unsolicited proposal on a telephone interviewing system

How can a firm be thorough yet efficient when considering dozens of applicants for each position? One tool that may help is IntelliView, a 10-minute question-and-answer session conducted by Touch-Tone telephone. The company recruiter dials up the IntelliView computer and then leaves the room. The candidate punches in answers to roughly 100 questions about work attitudes and other issues. In a few minutes, the recruiter can call Pinkerton (the company offering the service) and find out the results. On the basis of what the IntelliView interview revealed, the recruiter can delve more deeply into certain areas and, ultimately, have more information on which to base the hiring decision.

Your task: As assistant recruiter for Curtis Box and Crate, you think that IntelliView might help your firm. Plan a brief memo to Wallace Jefferson, director of human resources, in which you will suggest a test of the IntelliView system. Your memo should tell your boss why you believe your firm should test the system before making a long-term commitment.[6]

12. Day and night: Problem-solving report on stocking a 24-hour convenience store

When a store is open all day, every day, when's the best time to restock the shelves? That's the challenge at Store 24, a retail chain that never closes. As the assistant manager of a Store 24 branch that just opened near your campus, you want to set up a restocking schedule that won't conflict with prime shopping hours. Think about the number of customers you're likely to serve in the morning, afternoon, evening, and overnight hours. Consider, too, how many employees you might have during these four periods.

Your task: Plan a problem-solving report to be in letter form. You'll be sending your report to the store manager (Isabel Chu) and the regional manager (Eric Angstrom), who must agree on a solution to this problem. Plan on discussing the pros and cons of each of the four periods, and include your recommendations for restocking the shelves.

Improve Your Grammar, Mechanics, and Usage

Level 1: Self-Assessment—Dashes and Hyphens

Review Sections 2.7 and 2.8 in the Handbook of Grammar, Mechanics, and Usage, and then look at the following 15 items.

In items 1–15, insert the required dashes (—) and hyphens (-):

1. Three qualities speed, accuracy, and reliability are desirable in any applicant to the data entry department.

2. A highly placed source explained the top secret negotiations.

3. The file on Marian Gephardt yes, we finally found it reveals a history of late payments.

4. They're selling a well designed machine.

5. A bottle green sports jacket is hard to find.

6. Argentina, Brazil, Mexico these are the countries we hope to concentrate on.

7. Only two sites maybe three offer the things we need.

8. How many owner operators are in the industry?

9. Your ever faithful assistant deserves without a doubt a substantial raise.

10. Myrna Talefiero is this organization's president elect.

11. Stealth, secrecy, and surprise those are the elements that will give us a competitive edge.

12. The charts are well placed on each page unlike the running heads and footers.

13. We got our small business loan an enormous advantage.

14. Ron Franklin do you remember him? will be in town Monday.

15. Your devil may care attitude affects everyone involved in the decision making process.

Level 2: Workplace Applications

The following items contain numerous errors in grammar, capitalization, punctuation, abbreviation, number style, word division, and vocabulary. Rewrite each sentence in the space provided, correcting all errors. Write *C* in the space after any sentence that is already correct.

1. Commerce One helps its customer's to more efficiently lower administrative costs, improve order times, and to manage contract negotiations.

2. The intermodal bus vehicle seats up to 35 passengers, but is equipped with a 20 feet standardized container in the rear. The same container one sees on ships, trains and on planes.

3. "The American Dream of innovation, persistence, and a refusal to except the status quo has just created, in our opinion, Americas newest and most exciting company to watch," said James Gaspard President of Neoplan USA.

4. This new, transportation paradigm may have a global affect and the barriers to entry will be extremely costly too overcome.

5. Autobytel also owns and operates Carsmart.com and Autosite.com as well as AIC [Automotive Information Center] a provider of automotive marketing data and technology.

6. Mymarket.com offers a low cost high reward, entry into e-commerce not only for buyers but also suppliers.

7. Eclipse Aviation's main competitor are another start-up Safire Aircraft of west Palm Beach, Fl.

8. After identifying the factors that improve a industrial process, additional refining experiments must be conducted to confirm the results.

9. The fair labor standards Act regulates minimum wages, establishes overtime compensation, and it outlaws labor for children.

10. The Chinese government are supporting use of the Internet as a business tool because it is seen by it as necessary to enhance competitiveness.

11. At a certain point in a company's growth, the entrepreneur, who wants to control everything, can no longer keep up so they look mistakenly for a better manager and call that person a CEO.

12. City Fresh foods is paid by City health agencies to provide Ethnic food to the homebound "elderly" in the Boston Area.

13. Being in business since 1993, Miss Rosen has boiled down her life story into a 2-minute sound bight for sales prospects.

14. Anyone that wants to gain a new perspective on their product or service must cast aside one's own biases.

15. If I was Bill Gates, I'd handle the Federal government's antitrust lawsuit much different.

Level 3: Document Critique

The following document may contain errors in grammar, capitalization, punctuation, abbreviation, number style, vocabulary, and spelling. You may also find problems with organization, format, and word use. Correct all errors using standard proofreading marks (see Appendix C).

MEMO

SUBJECT: Recruiting and hiring Seminar

To Jeff Black and HR staff

DATE March 14 2005

FROM: Carrie andrews

As you all know the process of recruiting screening and hiring new employees might be a legal minefield. Because we don't have an inhouse lawyer to help us make every decision, its important for all of us to be aware of what actions are legally acceptible and what isn't. Last week I attended a American management Association seminar on this subject. I given enough useful information to warrant updating our online personnel handbook and perhaps developing a quick training session for all interviewing teams. First, heres a quick look at the things I learned.

Avoiding Legal Mistakes

- How to write recruiting ads that accurately portray job openings and not discriminate.
- Complying with the Americans with Disabilities Act
- How to use an employment agency effectively and safe (without risk of legal entanglements)

How to Screen and Interview More Effectively

- How to sort through résumés more efficient (including looking for telltale signs of false information)
- We can avoid interview questions that could get us into legal trouble
- When and how to check criminal records

measuring applicants

- Which type of preemployment tests have been proven most effective?
- Which drug-testing issues and recommendations effect us

as you can see the seminar addresed alot of important information. We covering the basic guidelines for much of this already; but a number of specific recommendations and legal concepts should be emphisized and underline.

It will take me a couple of weeks to get the personel handbook updated: but we don't have any immediate hiring plans anyway so that shouldn't be too much of a problem unless you think I should ocmplete it sooner and then we can talk about that.

I'll keep the seminar handouts and my notes on my desk in case you want to peruse them.

After the handbook is updated by me, we can get together and decide whether we need to train the interviewing team members.

Although we have a lot of new information, what people need to be aware of can be highlighted and the new sections can be read as schedules allow, although they might be reluctant to do this and we can also talk about that later, at a time of your conveinence that you can select later.

If you have any questions in the mean-time; don't hesitate to e-mail me or drop by for a chat.

Communicating Through the Internet

Understanding the Internet

The *Internet* is the world's largest computer network. Started in 1969 by the U.S. Department of Defense, it is a voluntary, cooperative undertaking; no one individual, organization, or government owns it. The Internet is accessible to individuals, companies, colleges, government agencies, and other institutions all over the world.

Accessing the Net

To use the Internet, you need a computer (with a modem) and an *Internet service provider (ISP)*—a company that connects you to the Internet. For a fee, you can dial into one of the ISP's host computers, which will link you to one of the Internet's networked computers. Although many people use a standard phone line, others pay a bit more for the speed and convenience of a cable connection or a *digital subscriber line (DSL)*, a high-speed phone line that carries both voice and data. You can also connect "on the go," using either a handheld computer or a cell phone that is set up for wireless access.

The most widely used part of the Internet is the World Wide Web. Developed in 1990, the web enables users to search for, display, and save multimedia resources such as graphics, text, audio, and video files. This information is stored on a *website*—a series of *webpages* that contain related files of multimedia data. To read webpages, you need a web *browser*—software such as Netscape Navigator or Microsoft's Internet Explorer.

Navigating the Net

The *homepage* of a website is the primary screen that users first access when visiting a site. Each page in a website is identified by a unique address known as a *uniform resource locator (URL)*. An example is http://www.yahoo.com. The address begins with *http* (the abbreviation for *hypertext transfer protocol*, the protocol that allows you to navigate the web). The address continues with *www*, indicating that the site is located on the World Wide Web. The next part of the address is the registered *domain name* (in this case yahoo.com), a name unique to that site. The abbreviation following the period is the *top-level domain (TLD)*. The TLDs now available include com (company), biz (business), info (general information), pro (professional), museum (museum), aero (aviation), name (individual), coop (coop-erative), edu (educational), gov (government), int (international), mil (military), net (network resources), org (non-profit organizations), and numerous country codes such as fr (France) or jp (Japan).

A convenient way to navigate the web is through hyper-links or *hot links*. To automatically jump to another webpage or website, just use your mouse to click on words in *hypertext markup language (HTML)*—colored, underlined, or high-lighted words. Once you get to your new destination, you can *bookmark* the site by using a browser feature that places the site's URL in a file on your computer for future use. You can also navigate your trail backward or forward at any time by using the Back and Forward buttons or menus on your browser.

How Businesses Are Using the Internet

The Internet helps businesses make closer connections with other organizations and customers all over the planet. They use the Internet to

- Share text, photos, slides, videos, and other data within the organization
- Permit employees to *telecommute*, or work away from a conventional office, whether at home, on the road, or across the country
- Recruit employees cost-effectively
- Locate information from external sources
- Find new business partners and attract new customers
- Locate and buy parts and materials from domestic and international suppliers
- Promote and sell goods and services to customers in any location
- Provide customers with service, technical support, and product information
- Collaborate with local, national, and international business partners
- Inform investors, industry analysts, and government regulators about business developments

In addition, companies can set up special employee-only websites using an *intranet*, a private internal corporate network. Intranets use the same technology as the Internet but restrict the information and access to members of the organization (regardless of a member's actual location). Once a company has an intranet, it can add an *extranet* that allows people to communicate and exchange data within a secure network of qualified people outside the organization—such as suppliers, contractors, and customers who use a password to access the system.

Online Reporting

Thanks to the Internet, more and more companies are using online reports to keep employees, managers, investors, and other stakeholders informed. For example, computerized cash registers in Mrs. Fields cookie outlets are the heart of a sophisticated reporting system that monitors and controls operations. Store managers enter data into the computer system by following report formats on their screen. Then they electronically transmit these reports to corporate headquarters in Park City, Utah, where corporate managers immediately receive all the information necessary to track sales trends, productivity figures, and potential problems at more than 700 outlets around the world.

Mrs. Paul's computerized reporting system allows production managers to continuously monitor and control the yield from the company's fish-processing operation. If the reports show that the actual production yield drops below the expected yield, managers can immediately adjust the equipment to improve it. They can find and fix problems much more quickly than if they had to wait for printed reports.

Well-known package-shipper FedEx lets customers access electronic reports to monitor the status of their shipments at any time. This reporting system not only helps FedEx serve its customers better but also puts valuable information in the hands of customers. And like many companies, FedEx posts its annual report and other corporate informational reports on its website for interested customers and investors.

Applications for Success

You can learn more about the Internet by taking the tour at www.learnthenet.com or www.netforbeginners.about.com. Answer the following questions:

1. **Ethical choice:** Do you think companies should monitor their employees' use of the Internet and e-mail? Explain your answer.
2. What kinds of electronic reports might a company want to post on its website?
3. What advantages and disadvantages do you see in asking store managers at Mrs. Fields to go beyond their informational operations reports and start filing electronic problem-solving reports on the company's intranet?

11 Writing and Completing Business Reports and Proposals

Learning Objectives

After studying this chapter, you will be able to

1 Discuss what things you must decide on when organizing a business report or proposal

2 Describe the structure of informational reports

3 Describe the structure of analytical reports

4 List several popular types of visuals and discuss when to use them

5 Name five characteristics of effective report content

6 Explain three tools that writers can use in long reports to help readers stay on track

7 Identify the nine prefatory parts of a formal report

8 Differentiate between a synopsis and an executive summary

9 Name the three supplemental parts of a formal report

Founded by Mark Landiak, Chicago-based Corporate Dynamics provides clients with innovative training and consulting in sales, customer service, and management applications. Landiak's team meets with senior managers from the client company and discusses the challenges the firm is facing, as well as the company's goals and specific needs. Landiak's team further researches these issues, including details on the client's market, competitors, and so on. After weeks—even months—of analysis, Corporate Dynamics sums up its findings in a formal report or proposal that details the client's current position, describes any situations requiring change, states future objectives, points out barriers to success, and recommends strategies for productive organizational change. All the information is useful; however, Landiak knows that to convince clients to use his company's services, he must provide a compelling argument—the key to a successful report.[1]

Step 2: Writing Business Reports and Proposals

Once you've planned out your document (see Chapters 3 and 10), you're ready to begin Step 2, writing business reports and proposals. Since so much of Step 2 is discussed in Chapter 4, the following sections cover only those aspects of writing that differ for reports and proposals. Think carefully about all the relevant tasks as you organize and compose your reports and proposals.

Organizing Reports and Proposals

Before you can compose a business report or proposal, you must organize the material you've collected, arranging it in a logical order that meets your audience's needs. You must carefully choose the format, length, order, and structure for your document before drafting even the first word.

Deciding on Format and Length

At times, the decision about format and length will be made for you by the person who requests the report. When you must select the format for your report, you have four options:

You may present a report in one of four formats: preprinted form, letter, memo, or manuscript.

- **Preprinted form.** Used for fill-in-the-blank reports. Most are relatively short (five or fewer pages) and deal with routine information, often mainly numerical. Use this format when it's requested by the person authorizing the report.
- **Letter.** Commonly used for reports of five or fewer pages that are directed to outsiders. These reports include all the normal parts of a letter, and they may also have headings, footnotes, tables, and figures.
- **Memo.** Commonly used for short (fewer than 10 pages), informal reports distributed within an organization. Like longer reports, they often have internal headings and sometimes include visual aids.
- **Manuscript.** Commonly used for reports that require a formal approach, whether a few pages or several hundred. As length increases, formal reports require more elements before the text (prefatory parts) and after (supplementary parts). The second half of this chapter explains these elements in more detail.

The length of your report often depends on your subject, your purpose, and your relationship with your audience. When your readers are relative strangers, skeptical, or hostile, or if your material is nonroutine or controversial, you usually have to explain your points in greater detail, which results in a longer document. However, you can afford to be brief if you're on familiar terms with your readers, if they are likely to agree with you, and if the information is routine or uncomplicated. Tell your readers what they need to know in a format that is easy for them to use.

Length depends on
- Your subject
- Your purpose
- Your relationship with your audience

Choosing the Direct or Indirect Approach

The direct approach is by far the most popular and convenient order for business reports, saving time and making the report easier to follow. It also produces a more forceful report because stating your conclusions confidently in the beginning makes you sound sure of yourself. However, if your readers have even slight reservations about either you or your material, making strong statements at the beginning may intensify reader resistance. Also, confidence may sometimes be misconstrued as arrogance—especially if you're a junior member of a status-conscious organization. So choose the direct approach for reports only when your credibility is high—when your readers trust you and are willing to accept your conclusions.

The direct approach saves time and makes the report easier to understand by giving readers the main idea first.

If your audience is skeptical or hostile, you may want to use the indirect approach, introducing your complete findings and discussing all supporting details before presenting your conclusions and recommendations. The indirect approach gives you a chance to prove your points and gradually overcome your audience's reservations. Even so, some readers will immediately flip back to the recommendations, thus defeating your purpose. The longer the message, the less effective an indirect approach is likely to be. Also, an

The indirect approach helps overcome resistance by withholding the main idea until later in the report.

FIGURE 11.1   Direct Approach Versus Indirect Approach in an Introduction

THE DIRECT APPROACH

Since the company's founding 25 years ago, we have provided regular repair service for all our electric appliances. This service has been an important selling point as well as a source of pride for our employees. However, we are paying a high price for our image. Last year, we lost $500,000 on our repair business.

Because of your concern over these losses, you have asked me to study the pros and cons of discontinuing our repair service. With the help of John Hudson and Susan Lefkowitz, I have studied the issue for the past two weeks and have come to the conclusion that we have been embracing an expensive, impractical tradition.

By withdrawing from the electric appliance repair business, we can substantially improve our financial performance without damaging our reputation with customers. This conclusion is based on three basic points that are covered in the following pages:
- It is highly unlikely that we will ever be able to make a profit in the repair business.
- Sevice is no longer an important selling point with customers.
- Closing down the service operation will create few internal problems.

THE INDIRECT APPROACH

Since the company's founding 25 years ago, we have provided repair service for all our electric appliances. This service has been an important selling point as well as a source of pride for our employees. However, the repair business itself has consistently lost money.

Because of your concern over these losses, you have asked me to study the pros and cons of discontinuing our repair service. With the help of John Hudson and Susan Lefkowitz, I have studied the issue for the past two weeks. The following pages present my findings for your review. Three basic questions are addressed:
- What is the extent of our losses, and what can we do to turn the business around?
- Would withdrawal hurt our sales of electrical appliances?
- What would be the internal repercussions of closing down the repair business?

indirect argument is harder to follow than a direct one. Therefore, carefully consider report length before deciding on the direct or indirect approach.

Businesspeople often combine the direct and indirect approaches.

Both direct and indirect approaches have merit, so businesspeople often combine them, revealing their conclusions and recommendations as they go along, rather than treating them first or last. Figure 11.1 presents the introductions from two reports with the same general outline. In the direct version, a series of statements summarize the conclusion reached about each main topic on the outline. In the indirect version, the same topics are introduced in the same order but without drawing any conclusions about them. Instead, the conclusions appear in the report body.

Regardless of the format, length, or order you use, you must still decide how your ideas will actually be developed. You must choose the most logical structure—the one that suits your topic and goals and that makes the most sense to your audience.

Structuring Informational Reports

Informational reports provide nothing more than facts. Most readers will respond unemotionally, so you can use the direct approach. However, you need to present the facts logically and accurately so that readers will understand exactly what you mean and be able to use your information easily. For example, when describing a machine, make report headings correspond to each component. Or when describing an event, discuss it chronologically. Let the nature of your subject dictate the structure of your informational reports. Use a **topical organization**, arranging material according to one of the following:

Topical organization is arranging material in order of importance, sequence, chronology, spatial relationships, location, or categories.

- **Importance.** If you're reviewing five product lines, you might organize your report according to product sales, from highest to lowest.
- **Sequence.** If you're studying a process, discuss it step by step—1, 2, 3, and so on.
- **Chronology.** When investigating a chain of events, organize the study according to what happened in January, what happened in February, and so on.

- **Spatial orientation.** If you're explaining how a physical object works, describe it left to right (or right to left in some cultures), top to bottom, outside to inside.
- **Geography.** If location is important, organize your study according to geography, perhaps by region of the United States or by area of a city.
- **Category.** If you're asked to review several distinct aspects of a subject, discuss one category at a time, such as cost, profit, sales, or investment.

Some informational reports (especially compliance reports and internal reports) are prepared on preprinted forms, so they are organized according to the instructions supplied by the person requesting the information.

Structuring Analytical Reports

For analytical reports, your choice of structure depends on the reaction you anticipate. When you expect your audience to agree with you, choose a structure that focuses attention on conclusions and recommendations. When you expect your audience to disagree with you or to be hostile, choose a structure that focuses attention on the reasons behind your conclusions and recommendations. Thus, the three most common approaches to structuring analytical reports are as follows:

The structure of analytical reports depends on audience reaction and whether you focus on

- *Conclusions*
- *Recommendations*
- *Logical arguments*

- **Focusing on conclusions.** When people are likely to accept your conclusions, structure your report around conclusions, using a direct approach. Readers interested mainly in your conclusions can grasp them quickly, and those wanting more detail can examine your analysis and data.
- **Focusing on recommendations.** When asked to solve a problem, structure your report around recommendations, using a direct approach: (1) establish a need for action in the introduction (briefly describing the problem or opportunity), (2) introduce the benefit that can result (without providing any details), (3) list the steps (recommendations) required to achieve the benefit (using action verbs for emphasis), (4) explain each step more fully (giving details of procedures, costs, and benefits), and (5) summarize your recommendations.
- **Focusing on logical arguments.** When encouraging readers to weigh all the facts before presenting your conclusions or recommendations, use the indirect approach and arrange your ideas around the reasoning behind your report's conclusions and recommendations. Organize your material to reflect the thinking process that will lead readers to your conclusions.

Structuring Business Proposals

Just as with reports, choosing a structural approach for proposals depends on whether you expect your audience to be receptive. In general, your audience may be more receptive with solicited proposals, since the problem and the solution have already been identified. The writer structures the proposal as specified in the RFP (request for proposals) using a direct approach and focusing on recommendations.

Solicited proposals are best organized by using the client's criteria as the main points.

The indirect approach may be a better choice for unsolicited proposals. You must first convince your audience that a problem exists and establish your credibility if you are unknown to the reader. Unfold your solution to the problem by focusing on your logical argument. As you unfold your solution, (1) try to persuade readers to accept your idea and award you a contract, and (2) spell out the terms of your proposal in the report's content.

Organizing Visual Aids

When preparing reports, you'll often include graphics, or visual aids, to convey important points. Carefully prepared visuals can help your audience understand your message and make your report more interesting. Even so, don't overdo the number of graphics. Use

Use visual aids to simplify, clarify, and emphasize important information.

visuals selectively to support your primary message—to supplement your words, not to replace them.

Some information is clearest in words; other information is clearest as a graphic. For instance, detailed facts and figures may be confusing and tedious in paragraph form, but tables and charts organize and display such detail concisely and conveniently. Information that requires detailed description of physical relationships or procedures is clearest in a flowchart. Or you can simply draw attention to a particular fact or detail by reinforcing that information visually.

Be sure to maintain a balance between your visuals and your words. The ideal blend depends on the nature of your subject. But illustrating every point dilutes the effectiveness of visuals. Plus, readers usually assume that the amount of space allocated to a topic indicates its relative importance. So by using visuals to illustrate a minor point, you may be sending a misleading message about its significance.

Choosing the Right Visual for the Job

Once you decide which points to illustrate visually, select the type of graphic that will present your data most clearly and effectively to your audience. Some types of visuals depict certain kinds of data better than others.

Use tables to help your audience understand detailed information.

Tables To present detailed, specific information, choose a **table**, a systematic arrangement of data in columns and rows, with useful headings along the top and side (see Table 11.1). If a table has too many columns to fit comfortably between the margins of the page, turn the paper horizontally and insert it in the report with the top toward the binding. When preparing tables, be sure to

- Use common, understandable units, and clearly identify them: dollars, percentages, price per ton, and so on
- Express all items in a column in the same unit, and round off for simplicity
- Label column headings clearly, and use a subhead if necessary
- Separate columns or rows with lines or extra space to make the table easy to follow
- Document the source of data using the same format as a text footnote (see Appendix B)

Use line charts

- **To indicate changes over time**
- **To plot the relationship of two variables**

Line and Surface Charts A **line chart** illustrates trends over time or plots the relationship of two variables. In line charts showing trends, the vertical, or y, axis shows the amount, and the horizontal, or x, axis shows the time or the quantity being measured. Ordinarily, both scales begin at zero and proceed in equal increments; however, in Figure 11.2 the vertical axis is broken to show that some of the increments have been left out. A broken axis is appropriate when the data are plotted far above zero, but be sure to clearly indicate the omission of data points.

Table 11.1	Parts of a Table			
	Multicolumn Head[*]			
Stub Head	**Subhead**	**Subhead**	**Single-column head**	**Single-column head**
Row head	XXX	XXX	XX	XX
Row head				
Subhead	XX	XXX	XX	X
Subhead	XX	XXX	XX	XX
Total	XXX	XXX	XX	XX

Source: (In the same format as a text footnote; see Appendix A.)
[*]Footnote (for explanation of elements in the table; a superscript number or small letter may be used instead of an asterisk or other symbol.)

FIGURE 11.2   Line Chart with Broken Axis

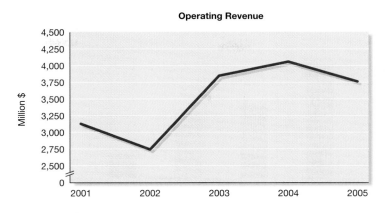

FIGURE 11.3   Line Chart with Multiple Lines

FIGURE 11.4   Surface Chart

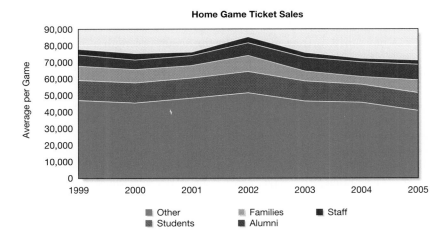

A simple line chart may be arranged in many ways. One of the most common is to plot several lines on the same chart for comparative purposes, as shown in Figure 11.3. Try to use no more than three lines on any given chart, particularly if the lines cross.

A **surface chart**, also called an **area chart**, is a form of line chart with a cumulative effect; all the lines add up to the top line, which represents the total (see Figure 11.4). This form of chart helps you illustrate changes in the composition of something over time.

A surface chart is a kind of line chart showing a cumulative effect.

FIGURE 11.5   The Versatile Bar Chart

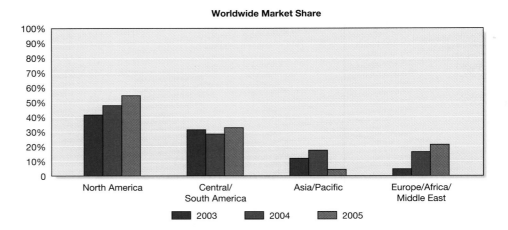

When preparing a surface chart, put the most important segment against the baseline, and restrict the number of strata to four or five.

Bar Charts   A **bar chart** portrays numbers by the height or length of its rectangular bars, making a series of numbers easy to read or understand. Bar charts are particularly valuable when you want to

- Compare the size of several items at one time
- Show changes in one item over time
- Indicate the composition of several items over time
- Show the relative size of components of a whole

As Figure 11.5 shows, bar charts can be singular ("CommuniCo Staff Computer Skills") or grouped ("CommuniCo Worldwide Market Share"), comparing more than one set of data by using a different color or pattern for each set. Segmented bar charts ("CommuniCo Preferred Communication Media") show how individual components contribute to a total number—using a different color or pattern for each component. Combination bar and line charts ("CommuniCo Employee Training Costs") compare quantities that require different intervals.

You can be creative with bar charts in many ways. You can align the bars either vertically or horizontally ("Conference Attendance by Gender"). But be careful to keep all the bars in the chart the same width; otherwise, you seem to mislead viewers by implying a relative importance for various bars. Also space the bars evenly and place them in a logical order such as chronological or alphabetical.

> Bar charts, in which numbers are visually portrayed by rectangular bars, can take a variety of forms.

FIGURE 11.5   Continued

CommuniCo Preferred Communication Media

Legend: IM, E-Mail, Telephone, Text Messaging, Face-to-Face

CommuniCo Employee Training Costs

Legend: Headcount, Training Costs

Conference Attendance by Gender

Women in Attendance	Men in Attendance	
750	600	San Diego Conference
590	800	Las Vegas Conference
950	450	Miami Conference

Pie Charts   Like segmented bar charts and area charts, **pie charts** show how parts of a whole are distributed. Each segment represents a slice of a complete circle, or *pie*. As you can see in Figure 11.6, pie charts are an effective way to show percentages or to compare one segment with another. You can combine pie charts with tables to expand the usefulness of such visuals.

When composing pie charts, restrict the number of slices in the pie. Otherwise, the chart looks cluttered and is difficult to label. If necessary, lump the smallest pieces together in a "miscellaneous" category. Ideally, the largest or most important slice of the pie is placed at the twelve o'clock position; the rest are arranged clockwise either in order of size or in some other logical progression. Use different colors or patterns to distinguish the various pieces. To emphasize one piece, you can explode it or pull it away from the rest of the pie. Label all segments, and indicate their value either in percentages or in units of measure. Remember, the segments must add up to 100 percent if percentages are used or to the total number if numbers are used.

Flowcharts   If you need to show physical or conceptual relationships rather than numerical ones, you might want to use a **flowchart**, illustrating a sequence of events from start to finish. Flowcharts are indispensable when illustrating processes, procedures, and

Use pie charts to show the relative sizes of the parts of a whole.

Use flowcharts
- To show a series of steps from beginning to end
- To show sequential relationships

FIGURE 11.6   Pie Chart Combined with a Table

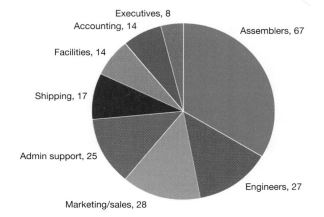

Year-End Head Count by Function

Function	Head Count
Assemblers	67
Engineers	27
Marketing/sales	28
Admin support	25
Shipping	17
Facilities	14
Accounting	14
Executives	8

sequential relationships. The various elements in the process you want to portray may be represented by pictorial symbols or geometric shapes, as shown in Figure 11.7.

Use organization charts to depict the interrelationships among the parts of an organization.

Organization Charts   As the name implies, an **organization chart** illustrates the positions, units, or functions of an organization and the way they interrelate. An organization's normal communication channels are almost impossible to describe without the benefit of a chart like the one in Figure 11.8.

FIGURE 11.7   Flowchart

FIGURE 11.8   Organization Chart

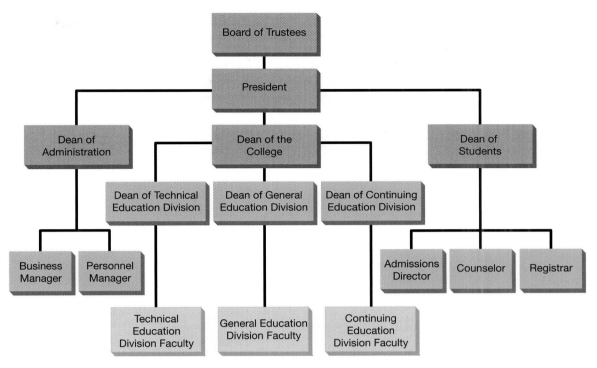

Administration and Faculty of Atlantic College

Creating Visuals with Computers

Professional-looking graphics used to be extremely expensive and time-consuming to produce, but personal computer technology has changed all that. Instead of relying on graphic designers, businesspeople are turning out their own professional-looking visual aids with **computer graphics**: visuals created and produced using a computer program. You can create freehand drawings, manipulate existing images, and display numbers in graphic form using software programs such as CorelDraw!, PowerPoint, Photoshop, Painter, Excel, Lotus 1-2-3, and Visio—to name just a few.

Using computer graphics gives you several advantages, including speed, accuracy, and ease of use. You also gain the ability to save the results and use the visuals over and over again in various reports. But before using any computer-graphics tools, think about the kind of image you want to project. The style of your visuals communicates a subtle message about your relationship with your audience. The image you want to project should determine the visual you use, whether it's a simple, hand-drawn diagram for a working meeting or full-color visuals for a formal presentation or report.

> Computer-graphics systems cut the time and cost involved in producing visuals.

Composing Reports and Proposals

Effective writers begin composing their first draft by preparing a final outline. In addition to guiding your writing effort, a final outline forces you to reevaluate the information and visuals you've selected and the order in which you present them. Preparing a final outline also gives you a chance to rephrase your outline points to set the tone of your report.

As you compose your report or proposal, use the writing process discussed in Chapter 5: Control your style and tone, select the best words, and create effective sentences and paragraphs. When writing reports, additional tasks include developing the text, drafting the content for your reports and proposals, using a proper degree of formality, sticking with a consistent time perspective, and providing clues to help readers navigate your document.

> A final outline is a work in progress.

Developing the Text

As with other written business communications, the text of a report or proposal has three major sections: an introduction, a body, and a close. The content and length of each section varies with the type and purpose of the document, the document's organizational structure, the length and depth of the material, the degree of document formality, and the writer's relationship with the audience.

The quality of your report's content will likely influence your professional success. After all, the content shows how well you think, gather and analyze data, draw conclusions, and develop and support your recommendations. You'll create more successful reports if your content is

- **Accurate.** In addition to checking for typos, double-check your facts and references.
- **Complete.** Include all the necessary information—no more, no less.
- **Balanced.** Present all sides of the issue fairly and equitably.
- **Structured clearly and logically.** Write uncluttered sentences and paragraphs that organize your ideas and proceed logically with clear, helpful transitions.[2]
- **Documented properly.** Properly give credit to your sources, as explained in Appendix B.

Proposals are a special kind of report whose general purpose is to persuade readers to do something (purchase goods or services, fund a project, implement a program). Thus, writing a proposal is similar to writing persuasive sales messages (see Chapter 9). Use the AIDA plan to gain attention, build interest, create desire, and motive action. In addition, be sure to do the following:[3]

- **Demonstrate your knowledge.** Show readers that you have the knowledge and experience to solve the problem. Remember to disclose enough information to win the job without giving away your ideas so that your services aren't needed.
- **Provide concrete examples.** Avoid vague, unsupported generalizations such as "we are losing money on this program." Instead, provide quantifiable details such as the amount of money being lost, how, why, and so on. Explain how much money your proposed solution will save. Spell out your plan, and give details on how the job will be done.
- **Research the competition.** Use trade publications and the Internet to become familiar with your competitors' product lines, services, and prices. This strategy is especially important if you are competing against others for a job.
- **Prove that your proposal is workable.** Your proposal must be feasible for the audience. For instance, it would be foolish to recommend a solution that doubles the budget or requires three times the number of current employees.
- **Adopt a "you" attitude.** Relate your product, service, or personnel to the reader's exact needs, either as stated in the RFP for a solicited proposal or as discovered through your own investigation for an unsolicited proposal.
- **Package your proposal attractively.** Make sure your proposal is letter-perfect, inviting, and readable. Readers will judge the type of work you perform by your submitted proposal. If it contains errors, omissions, or inconsistencies, they will likely withhold approval.

Drafting the Introduction   In the *introduction*, prepare your readers for the information that follows. Invite them to continue reading by telling them what the report is about, why the audience should be concerned, and how the report is organized. Your introduction should accomplish four tasks:

- Tie the report or proposal to a problem or an assignment.
- Introduce the report's subject (purpose) and indicate why that subject is important.
- Preview the main ideas and the order in which they'll be covered.
- Establish the tone of the document and your relationship with the audience.

In proposals, use the introduction to present the problem you want to solve and to summarize your solution. Orient readers to the remainder of the text. In a solicited proposal, refer to the RFP in your introduction; in an unsolicited one, use the introduction to mention any factors that led you to submit your proposal.

Drafting the Body   In the *body* of your reports and proposals, include the major divisions or chapters that present, analyze, and interpret the information you gathered during your investigation. Give complete details of your proposed solution and specify what results you anticipate. The body contains the "proof," the detailed information necessary to support your conclusions and recommendations.

The body contains the substance of your report or proposal.

Drafting the Close   The *close* is the final section of the text in your report or proposal. Leave a strong and lasting impression. This is your last chance to make sure that your report says what you intended.[4] In proposals, the close is your last opportunity to persuade readers to accept your suggestions. In both formal and informal proposals, be brief, assertive, and confident. Your close should accomplish four goals:

The close reemphasizes your main ideas.

- Emphasize the main points of the message.
- Summarize reader benefits (if some change or other course of action is suggested).
- Refer back to all the pieces and remind readers how those pieces fit together.
- Bring all the action items together in one place and give details about who should do what, when, where, and how.

For examples of some of the topics you might include in the introduction, body, and close of reports and proposals, see Table 11.2.

Choosing the Proper Degree of Formality

If you know your readers reasonably well and if your report is likely to meet with their approval, you can generally adopt a fairly informal tone. You can speak to readers in the first person, referring to yourself as *I* and to your readers as *you*. This personal approach is often used in brief memo or letter reports, although there are many exceptions.

For informal reports, adopt a personal style, using the pronouns I and you.

Use a more formal tone for longer reports, especially those dealing with controversial or complex information, and for reports that will be sent to other parts of the organization or to customers or suppliers. Also, communicating with people in other cultures often calls for more formality. Use an impersonal style, and eliminate all references to *you* and *I* (including *we, us,* and *our*). However, make sure that avoiding personal pronouns doesn't lead to overuse of phrases such as *there is* and *it is*, which are both dull and wordy. Also, be careful not to slip into passive voice more than necessary.

Being formal means putting your readers at a distance and establishing an objective, businesslike relationship.

You can often tell what tone is appropriate for your readers by looking at other reports of a similar type in your company. If all the other reports on file are impersonal, you should probably adopt a formal tone yourself, unless you're confident that your readers prefer a more personal style.

Establishing a Consistent Time Perspective

By switching from tense to tense throughout your report, you only confuse your readers. They wonder whether the shift is significant or whether you are just being sloppy. Eliminate such confusion by using tense consistently.

Be consistent in the verb tense you use, and follow a proper chronological sequence.

Also be careful to observe the chronological sequence of events in your report. If you're describing the history or development of something, start at the beginning and cover each event in the order of its occurrence. If you're explaining the steps in a process, take each step in proper sequence.

Helping Readers Find Their Way

Readers have no concept of how the various pieces of your report relate to one another. Although you can see how each page fits into the overall structure, readers see your report one page at a time. So give them a preview or road map of your report's structure, and

Readers can lose their way unless you give them directions about where they are and where they're going.

Table 11.2	Report and Proposal Contents

Report Contents

Introduction

- **Authorization.** Review who authorized the report (when, how), who wrote it, when it was submitted.

- **Problem/purpose.** Explain the reason for the report's existence and what the report will achieve.

- **Scope.** Describe what will and won't be covered in the report—indicating size and complexity.

- **Background.** Review historical conditions or factors that led up to the report.

- **Sources and methods.** Discuss the primary and secondary sources consulted and methods used.

- **Definitions.** List terms and their definitions—including any terms that might be misinterpreted. Terms may also be defined in the body, explanatory notes, or glossary.

- **Limitations.** Discuss factors beyond your control that affect report quality—not an excuse for a poor study or bad report.

- **Report organization.** Tell what topics are covered in what order.

Body

- **Explanations.** Give complete details of the problem, project, or idea.

- **Facts, statistical evidence, and trends.** Lay out the results of studies or investigations.

- **Analysis of action.** Discuss potential courses of action.

- **Pros and cons.** Explain advantages, disadvantages, costs, and benefits of a particular course of action.

- **Procedures.** Outline steps for a process.

- **Methods and approaches.** Discuss how you've studied a problem (or gathered evidence) and arrived at your solution (or collected your data).

- **Criteria.** Describe the benchmarks for evaluating options and alternatives.

- **Conclusions and recommendations.** Discuss what you believe the evidence reveals and what you propose should be done about it.

- **Support.** Give the reasons behind your conclusions or recommendations.

Close

- **For direct order.** Summarize key points (except in short memos), listing them in the order they appear in the body. Briefly restate your conclusions or recommendations, if appropriate.

- **For indirect order.** You may use the close to present your conclusions or recommendations for the first time—just be sure not to present any new facts.

- **For motivating action.** Spell out exactly what should happen next and provide a schedule with specific task assignments.

Proposal Contents

Introduction

- **Background or statement of the problem.** Briefly review the reader's situation, establish a need for action, and explain how things could be better. In unsolicited proposals, convince readers that a problem or opportunity exists.

- **Solution.** Briefly describe the change you propose, highlighting your key selling points and their benefits to show how your proposal will solve the reader's problem.

- **Scope.** State the boundaries of the proposal—what you will and will not do.

- **Report organization.** Orient the reader to the remainder of the proposal and call attention to the major divisions of thought.

Body

- **Facts and evidence to support your conclusions.** Give complete details of the proposed solution and the anticipated results.

- **Proposed approach.** Describe your concept, product, or service. Stress reader benefits and emphasize any advantages you have over your competitors.

- **Work plan.** Describe how you'll accomplish what must be done (unless you're providing a standard, off-the-shelf item). Explain the steps you'll take, their timing, the methods or resources you'll use, and the person(s) responsible. State when work will begin, how it will be divided into stages, when you'll finish, and whether follow-up will be needed.

- **Statement of qualifications.** Describe your organization's experience, personnel, and facilities—relating it all to readers' needs. Include a list of client references.

- **Costs.** Prove that your costs are realistic—break them down so that readers can see the cost of labor, materials, transportation, travel, training, and other categories.

Close

- **Review of argument.** Briefly summarize the key points.

- **Review of reader benefits.** Briefly summarize how your proposal will help the reader.

- **Review of the merits of your approach.** Briefly summarize why your approach will be more effective than that of competitors.

- **Restatement of qualifications.** Briefly reemphasize why you and your firm should do the work

- **Request.** Ask for a decision from the reader.

FIGURE 11.9 Heading Format for Reports

TITLE

The title is centered at the top of the page in all capital letters, usually, bold-faced (or underlined if typewritten), often in a large font (type size), and often using a sans serif typeface. When the title runs to more than one line, the lines are usually double-spaced and arranged as an inverted pyramid (longer line on the top).

FIRST-LEVEL HEADING

A first-level heading indicates what the following section is about, perhaps by describing the subdivisions. All first-level headings are grammatically parallel, with the possible exception of such headings as "Introduction," "Conclusions," and "Recommendations." Some text appears between every two headings, regardless of their levels. Still boldfaced and sans serif, the font may be smaller than that used in the title but still larger than the typeface used in the text and still in all capital letters.

Second-Level Heading

Like first-level headings, second-level headings indicate what the followed material is about. All second-level headings within a section are grammatically parallel. Still boldfaced and sans serif, the font may either remain the same or shrink to the size used in the text, and the style is now initial capitals followed with lowercase. Never use only one second-level heading under a first-level heading. (The same is true for every other level of heading.)

Third-Level Heading

A third-level heading is worded to reflect the content of the material that follows. All third-level headings beneath a second-level heading should be grammatically parallel.

Fourth-Level Heading. Like all the other levels of heading, fourth-level headings reflect the subject that will be developed. All fourth-level headings within a subsection are parallel.

Fifth-level headings are generally the lowest level of heading used. However, you can indicate further breakdowns in your ideas by using a list:

1. *The first item in a list.* You may indent the entire item in block format to set it off visually. Numbers are optional.
2. *The second item in a list.* All lists have at least two items. An introductory phrase or sentence may be italicized for emphasis, as shown here.

clarify how the various parts are related. Give them a sense of the overall structure of your document by using three tools:

- **Headings.** These brief titles cue readers about the content of a section. They improve readability (see Chapter 6) and clarify a report's framework. *Subheadings* (lower-level headings) help show which ideas are more important. Many companies specify a format for headings; if yours does, use it. Otherwise, use the scheme shown in Figure 11.9.
- **Transitions.** These words or phrases tie ideas together and show how one thought is related to another. Whether words, sentences, or complete paragraphs, use transitions to help readers move from one section of a report to the next. When writing transitions, be sure to list coming topics in the order they are discussed.
- **Previews and reviews.** *Preview sections* introduce an important topic, helping readers get ready for new information. *Review sections* come after a body of material and summarize the information for readers, helping them absorb details while keeping track of the big picture.

Document Makeover

Improve This Report

To practice correcting drafts of actual documents, visit **www.prenhall.com/onekey** on the web. Click "Document Makeovers," then click Chapter 11. You will find a policy report that contains problems and errors relating to what you've learned in this chapter about composing business reports and proposals. Use the Final Draft decision tool to create an improved version of this report. Check the message for an effective opening, consistent levels of formality or informality, consistent time perspective, and the use of headings, transitions, previews and reviews to help orient readers.

Step 3: Completing Business Reports and Proposals

Producing documents requires some special considerations when working with reports.

The process of writing a report or proposal doesn't end with a first draft. As Chapter 5 points out, once you have finished your first draft, you perform three tasks to complete your document: revise, produce, and proofread. Revising and proofreading reports and proposals is basically the same as for any business message, although these tasks may take longer for lengthy documents. However, you have a few special considerations when producing business reports and proposals.

As personal computers have become commonplace in the business office, more and more employees are expected to handle most or even all the formatting and production of their own reports. Make sure you've scheduled enough time for production. Corrupted disk files, printing problems, and other glitches can consume hours. If you're preparing a long, formal report, you'll need extra time to prepare and assemble all the various components.

Components of a Formal Report

The three basic divisions of a formal report:
- *Prefatory parts*
- *Text*
- *Supplementary parts*

The parts included in a report depend on the type of report you are writing, the requirements of your audience, the organization you're working for, and the length of your report. The components listed in Figure 11.10 fall into three categories, according to their location in a report: prefatory parts, text, and supplementary parts.

Most prefatory parts (such as the table of contents) should be placed on their own pages. However, the various parts in the report text are often run together and seldom stand alone. If your introduction is only a paragraph long, don't bother with a page break before moving into the body of your report. If the introduction runs longer than a page, however, a page break can signal the reader that a major shift is about to occur in the flow of the report.

For an illustration of how the various parts fit together in an actual report, see Figure 11.11 beginning on page 332. This 14-page report was prepared by Linda Moreno, manager of the cost accounting department at Electrovision, a high-tech company based in Los Gatos, California. Electrovision's main product is optical character recognition equipment, which is used by the U.S. Postal Service for sorting mail. Moreno's job is to help analyze the company's costs. Moreno used direct order and organized her report based on conclusions and recommendations.

Prefatory Parts

Prefatory parts come before the text but may be written after the text has been completed.

Prefatory parts are front-end materials that provide preliminary information so that readers can decide whether to and how to read the report.[5] Many of these parts—such as the table of contents, list of illustrations, and executive summary—are easier to prepare

FIGURE 11.10   Parts of a Formal Report

PREFATORY PARTS	TEXT PARTS	SUPPLEMENTARY PARTS
Synopsis or executive summary	Notes	Index
List of illustrations	Recommendations	Bibliography
Table of contents	Conclusions	Appendixes
Letter of transmittal	Summary	
Letter of authorization	Body	
Title page	Introduction	
Title fly		
Cover		

after the text has been completed, because they directly reflect the contents. Other parts can be prepared at almost any time.

- **Cover.** Many companies have standard covers for reports. If your company doesn't provide them, you can find something suitable in a good stationery store. Report titles are either printed on these covers or attached with gummed labels. Think carefully about the title you put on the cover. Give readers all the information they need (the who, what, when, where, why, and how of the subject), but try to be reasonably concise.

- **Title fly.** Formal reports begin with a plain sheet of paper that has only the title of the report on it. You don't really need a title fly, but it adds a touch of formality.

- **Title page.** The title page includes four blocks of information (see Moreno's Electrovision report): (1) the title of the report; (2) the name, title, and address of the person, group, or organization that authorized the report (usually the intended audience); (3) the name, title, and address of the person, group, or organization that prepared the report; and (4) the date on which the report was submitted.

- **Letter of authorization.** If you received written authorization to prepare the report, you may want to include that letter or memo in your report.

- **Letter of transmittal.** This routine document (which can also be a memo) begins with the main idea ("Here is the report you asked me to prepare on . . ."). The opening discusses scope, methods, and limitations. The middle can highlight important sections of the report, suggest follow-up studies, offer details to help readers use the report, and acknowledge help from others. The close can include a note of thanks for the assignment, an expression of willingness to discuss the report, and an offer to assist with future projects, (see Figure 11.11 on page 333).

- **Table of contents.** The contents page lists report parts and text headings to indicate the location and relative importance of the information in the report. You may show only the top two or three levels of headings or only first-level headings. Word headings exactly as they are in the report text. List all prefatory parts (except those that come before the contents page) and all supplementary parts. If you have fewer than four visual aids, you may wish to list them in the table of contents (see Figure 11.11 on page 334).

(continued on page 345)

FIGURE 11.11   **Linda Moreno's Effective Formal Report**

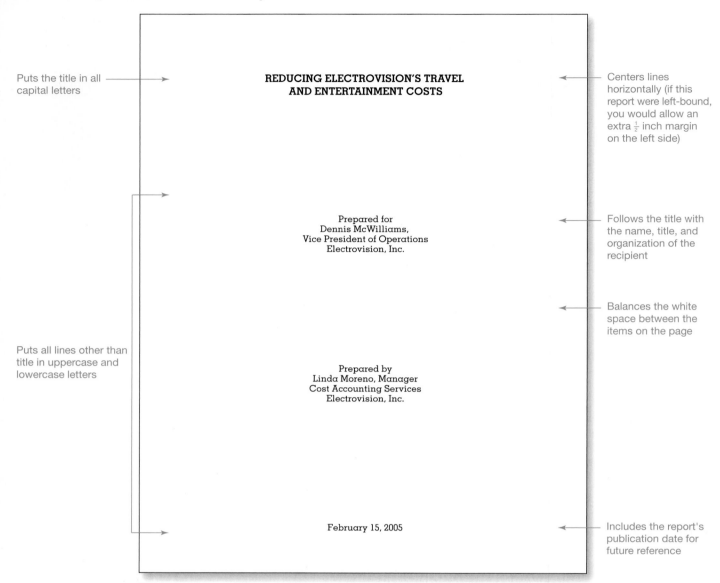

Puts the title in all capital letters

Puts all lines other than title in uppercase and lowercase letters

REDUCING ELECTROVISION'S TRAVEL
AND ENTERTAINMENT COSTS

Prepared for
Dennis McWilliams,
Vice President of Operations
Electrovision, Inc.

Prepared by
Linda Moreno, Manager
Cost Accounting Services
Electrovision, Inc.

February 15, 2005

Centers lines horizontally (if this report were left-bound, you would allow an extra $\frac{1}{2}$ inch margin on the left side)

Follows the title with the name, title, and organization of the recipient

Balances the white space between the items on the page

Includes the report's publication date for future reference

The "how to" tone of Moreno's title is appropriate for an action-oriented report that emphasizes recommendations. A more neutral title, such as "An Analysis of Electrovision's Travel and Entertainment Costs," would be more suitable for an informational report.

FIGURE 11.11 Continued

Uses memo format for transmitting this internal report; otherwise, letter format would be used for transmitting external reports

Presents the main conclusion right away (because Moreno expects a positive response)

Uses an informal, conversational style

Acknowledges help that has been received

Closes with thanks and an offer to discuss results (when appropriate, you could also include an offer to help with future projects)

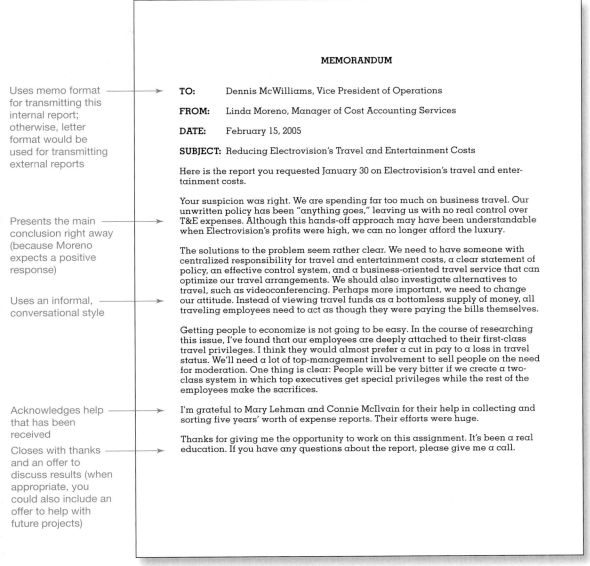

MEMORANDUM

TO: Dennis McWilliams, Vice President of Operations

FROM: Linda Moreno, Manager of Cost Accounting Services

DATE: February 15, 2005

SUBJECT: Reducing Electrovision's Travel and Entertainment Costs

Here is the report you requested January 30 on Electrovision's travel and entertainment costs.

Your suspicion was right. We are spending far too much on business travel. Our unwritten policy has been "anything goes," leaving us with no real control over T&E expenses. Although this hands-off approach may have been understandable when Electrovision's profits were high, we can no longer afford the luxury.

The solutions to the problem seem rather clear. We need to have someone with centralized responsibility for travel and entertainment costs, a clear statement of policy, an effective control system, and a business-oriented travel service that can optimize our travel arrangements. We should also investigate alternatives to travel, such as videoconferencing. Perhaps more important, we need to change our attitude. Instead of viewing travel funds as a bottomless supply of money, all traveling employees need to act as though they were paying the bills themselves.

Getting people to economize is not going to be easy. In the course of researching this issue, I've found that our employees are deeply attached to their first-class travel privileges. I think they would almost prefer a cut in pay to a loss in travel status. We'll need a lot of top-management involvement to sell people on the need for moderation. One thing is clear: People will be very bitter if we create a two-class system in which top executives get special privileges while the rest of the employees make the sacrifices.

I'm grateful to Mary Lehman and Connie McIlvain for their help in collecting and sorting five years' worth of expense reports. Their efforts were huge.

Thanks for giving me the opportunity to work on this assignment. It's been a real education. If you have any questions about the report, please give me a call.

In this report, Moreno decided to write a brief memo of transmittal and include a separate executive summary. Short reports (fewer than 10 pages) often combine the synopsis or executive summary with the memo or letter of transmittal.

FIGURE 11.11   Continued

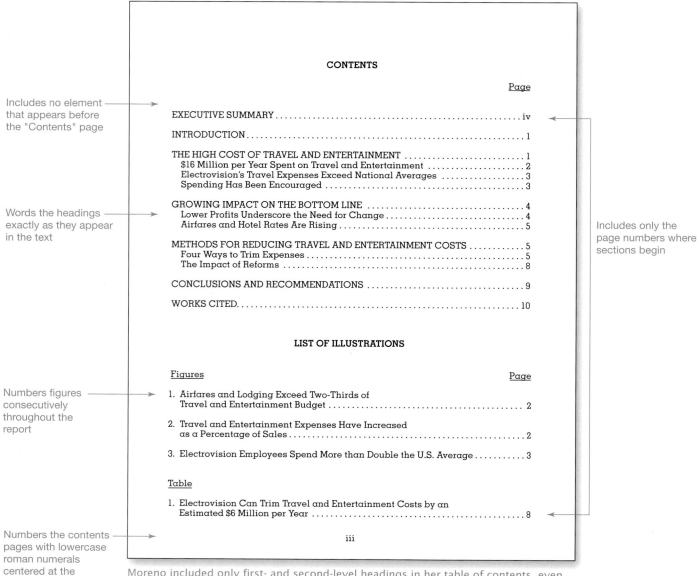

Includes no element that appears before the "Contents" page

Words the headings exactly as they appear in the text

Numbers figures consecutively throughout the report

Numbers the contents pages with lowercase roman numerals centered at the bottom margin

Includes only the page numbers where sections begin

CONTENTS

LIST OF ILLUSTRATIONS

iii

Moreno included only first- and second-level headings in her table of contents, even though the report contains third-level headings. She prefers a shorter table of contents that focuses attention on the main divisions of thought. She used informative titles, which are appropriate for a report to a receptive audience.

FIGURE 11.11   Continued

Begins by stating the purpose of the report

EXECUTIVE SUMMARY

This report analyzes Electrovision's travel and entertainment (T&E) costs and presents recommendations for reducing those costs.

Uses subheadings that summarize the content of the main sections of the report without repeating what appears in the text

Travel and Entertainment Costs Are Too High

Travel and entertainment is a large and growing expense category for Electrovision. The company spends over $16 million per year on business travel, a cost that is increasing 12 percent annually. Employees make some 3,500 trips a year, each trip averaging $4,720. Airfares are the largest expense, followed by hotels and meals.

The nature of Electrovision's business requires extensive travel, but the company's costs seem excessive. Electrovision employees spend more than double what the average business traveler spends. Although the location of company facilities may partly explain this discrepancy, the firm's philosophy and managerial style invite employees to go first class and pay relatively little attention to travel costs.

Presents the points in the executive summary in the same order as they appear in the report

Cuts Are Essential

Electrovision management now recognizes the need to gain more control over this element of costs. The company is entering a period of declining profits, prompting management to look for every opportunity to reduce spending. Also, rising airfares and hotel rates are making T&E expenses more important to the bottom line.

Targets a receptive audience with a hard-hitting tone in the executive summary (a more neutral approach would be better for hostile or skeptical readers)

Electrovision Can Save $6 Million per Year

Fortunately, Electrovision should be able to save up to $6 million per year, based on the experience of other companies. A sensible travel-management program can save firms up to 35 percent a year (Gilligan 39–40). Since we purchase more first-class tickets than the average, we should be able to achieve even greater savings.

The first priority should be hiring a director for T&E spending. This director should develop a written T&E policy, establish a cost-control system, retain a national travel agency, and investigate electronic alternatives to travel. Electrovision should make employees aware of the need to reduce T&E spending by forgoing unnecessary travel and by economizing on tickets, hotels, meals, and rental cars.

Appears in the same typeface and type style as the text of the report. Uses single-spacing because the report is single-spaced, and follows the text's format for margins, paragraph indentions, and headings

Continues numbering the executive summary pages with lowercase roman numerals centered about 1 inch from the bottom of the page

We should also negotiate preferential rates with travel providers. These changes are likely to hurt short-term morale. Management will need to explain the rationale for reduced spending and set an example by economizing on their own travel arrangements. On the plus side, cutting travel will reduce the burden on employees and help them balance their business and personal lives.

iv

Moreno included an executive summary because her audience was mixed—some readers would be interested in the details of her report and some would prefer to focus on the big picture.

Moreno's impersonal style adds to the formality of her report. She chose an impersonal style for several reasons: (1) several members of her audience were considerably higher up in the organization and she did not want to sound too familiar, (2) she wanted the executive summary to be compatible with the text, and (3) her company prefers the impersonal style for formal reports.

Some writers prefer a more personal approach. Generally, you should gear your choice of style to your relationship with the readers.

FIGURE 11.11   Continued

Centers the title of the report on the first page of the text, 2 inches from the top of the page (2½ inches if top-bound)

REDUCING ELECTROVISION'S
TRAVEL AND ENTERTAINMENT COSTS

INTRODUCTION

Electrovision has always encouraged a significant amount of business travel. To compensate employees for the inconvenience and stress of frequent trips, management has authorized generous travel and entertainment (T&E) allowances. This philosophy has been good for morale, but last year Electrovision spent $16 million on T&E—$7 million more than it spent on research and development.

Begins the introduction by establishing the need for action

This year's T&E costs will affect profits even more, due to changes in airfares and hotel rates. Also, the company anticipates that profits will be relatively weak for a variety of other reasons. Therefore, Dennis McWilliams, Vice President of Operations, asked the accounting department to look into the T&E budget.

The purpose of this report is to analyze the T&E budget, evaluate the effect of changes in airfares and hotel costs, and suggest ways to tighten management's control over T&E expenses. The report outlines several steps to reduce our expenses, but the precise financial impact of these measures is difficult to project. Estimates are a "best guess" view of what Electrovision can expect to save.

For this report, the accounting department analyzed internal expense reports for the past five years to determine how much Electrovision spends on T&E. These figures were compared with average statistics compiled by Dow Jones (publisher of *The Wall Street Journal*) and presented as the Dow Jones Travel Index. We also analyzed trends and suggestions published in a variety of business journal articles to see how other companies are coping with the high cost of business travel.

This report reviews the size and composition of Electrovision's T&E expenses, analyzes trends in travel costs, and recommends ways to reduce the T&E budget.

THE HIGH COST OF TRAVEL AND ENTERTAINMENT

Many companies view T&E as an "incidental" cost of business, but the dollars add up. Electrovision's bill for airfares, hotels, rental cars, meals, and entertainment totaled $16 million last year and has increased by 12 percent per year for the past five years. Compared with the average U.S. business, Electrovision's expenditures are high, largely because of management's generous policy on travel benefits.

Mentions sources and methods to increase credibility and to give readers a complete picture of the study's background

Uses the arabic numeral 1 for the first page, centering the number about 1 inch from the bottom of the page

1

In her brief introduction, Moreno omitted the subheadings within the introduction and relied on topic sentences and on transitional words and phrases to indicate that she is discussing the purpose, scope, and limitations of the study. To conserve space, Moreno used single-spacing and 1-inch side margins.

FIGURE 11.11   Continued

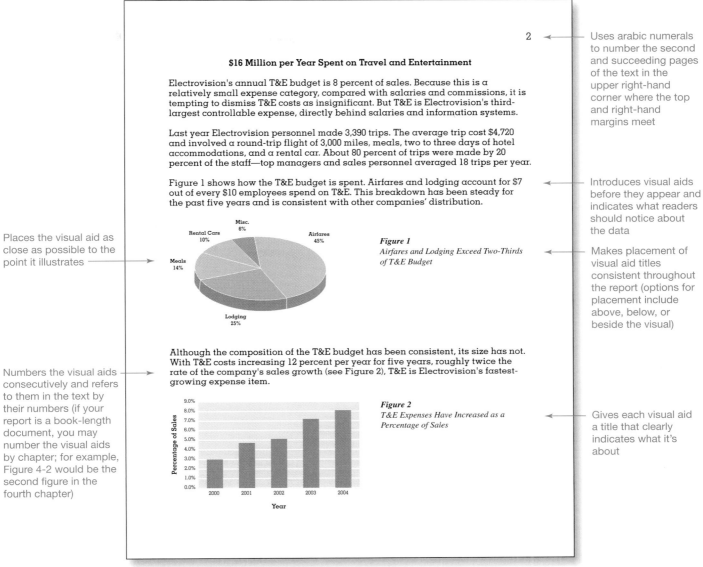

2

Uses arabic numerals to number the second and succeeding pages of the text in the upper right-hand corner where the top and right-hand margins meet

$16 Million per Year Spent on Travel and Entertainment

Electrovision's annual T&E budget is 8 percent of sales. Because this is a relatively small expense category, compared with salaries and commissions, it is tempting to dismiss T&E costs as insignificant. But T&E is Electrovision's third-largest controllable expense, directly behind salaries and information systems.

Last year Electrovision personnel made 3,390 trips. The average trip cost $4,720 and involved a round-trip flight of 3,000 miles, meals, two to three days of hotel accommodations, and a rental car. About 80 percent of trips were made by 20 percent of the staff—top managers and sales personnel averaged 18 trips per year.

Figure 1 shows how the T&E budget is spent. Airfares and lodging account for $7 out of every $10 employees spend on T&E. This breakdown has been steady for the past five years and is consistent with other companies' distribution.

Introduces visual aids before they appear and indicates what readers should notice about the data

Places the visual aid as close as possible to the point it illustrates

Misc. 6%
Rental Cars 10%
Airfares 45%
Meals 14%
Lodging 25%

Figure 1
Airfares and Lodging Exceed Two-Thirds of T&E Budget

Makes placement of visual aid titles consistent throughout the report (options for placement include above, below, or beside the visual)

Although the composition of the T&E budget has been consistent, its size has not. With T&E costs increasing 12 percent per year for five years, roughly twice the rate of the company's sales growth (see Figure 2), T&E is Electrovision's fastest-growing expense item.

Numbers the visual aids consecutively and refers to them in the text by their numbers (if your report is a book-length document, you may number the visual aids by chapter; for example, Figure 4-2 would be the second figure in the fourth chapter)

Figure 2
T&E Expenses Have Increased as a Percentage of Sales

9.0%
8.0%
7.0%
6.0%
5.0%
4.0%
3.0%
2.0%
1.0%
0.0%

Percentage of Sales

2000 2001 2002 2003 2004
Year

Gives each visual aid a title that clearly indicates what it's about

Moreno opened the first main section of the body with a topic sentence that introduces an important fact about the subject of the section. Then she oriented the reader to the three major points developed in the section.

Moreno decided to use a bar chart in Figure 2 to express the main idea in terms of percentage and make the main idea easy to grasp.

FIGURE 11.11   Continued

3

Electrovision's Travel Expenses Exceed National Averages

Much of our travel budget is justified. Two major contributing factors are

- Our headquarters are on the West Coast and our major customer is on the East Coast, so we naturally spend a lot on cross-country flights.

- Corporate managers and division personnel make frequent trips between our headquarters here on the West Coast and the manufacturing operations in Detroit, Boston, and Dallas to coordinate these disparate operations.

However, even with such justifiable expenses, Electrovision spends considerably more on T&E than the average business traveler spends (see Figure 3).

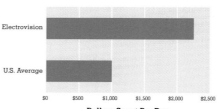

Figure 3
Electrovision Employees Spend More than Double the U.S. Average

Source: *Wall Street Journal and company records*

The Dow Jones Travel Index calculates the average cost per day of business travel in the United States, based on average rates for airfare, hotel, and rental car. This average fluctuates weekly as travel companies change their rates, but it has been running about $1,000 per day for the last year or so. In contrast, Electrovision's average daily expense over the past year has been $2,250—125 percent higher than average. This figure is based on the average trip cost of $4,720 and an average trip length of 2.1 days.

Spending Has Been Encouraged

Although a variety of factors may contribute to this differential, Electrovision's relatively high T&E costs are at least partially due to the company's philosophy and management style. Since many employees do not enjoy business travel, management has tried to make the trips more pleasant by authorizing first-class airfare, luxury hotel accommodations, and full-size rental cars. The sales staff is encouraged to entertain clients at top restaurants and to invite them to cultural and sporting events.

Leaves a bit more white space above a heading than below to help readers associate that heading with the text it describes

The chart in Figure 3 is very simple, but it creates an effective visual comparison. Moreno included just enough data to make her point. She was as careful about the appearance of her report as she was about its content.

FIGURE 11.11 Continued

4

The cost of these privileges is easy to overlook, given the weakness of Electrovision's system for keeping track of T&E expenses:

Uses bulleted list to make it easy for readers to identify and distinguish related points

- Monthly financial reports have no separate T&E category; this information is buried in Cost of Goods Sold and in Selling and General Expenses.

- Department heads can approve expense reports, no matter how large.

- Receipts are not required for expenditures of less than $100.

- Individuals are allowed to make their own travel arrangements.

- No one has responsibility for controlling the company's total T&E spending.

GROWING IMPACT ON THE BOTTOM LINE

Uses informative headings to focus reader attention on the main points (such headings are appropriate when a report is in direct order and intended for a receptive audience; however, descriptive headings are more effective when a report is in indirect order and readers are less receptive)

During the past three years, the company's healthy profits have disguised the need for tighter controls over all aspects of the business. However, as we all know, the projection is for flat to declining profits over the next two years, which has prompted all of us to search for ways to cut costs. Also, rising airfares and hotel rates have increased the impact of T&E expenses on the company's finances.

Lower Profits Underscore the Need for Change

The next two years promise to be difficult for Electrovision. After several years of steady spending increases, the Postal Service is tightening procurement policies for automated mail-handling equipment. Funding for our A-12 optical character reader has been canceled. As a result, our marketing people expect sales to drop 15 percent. Even though Electrovision is negotiating several R&D contracts with nongovernment clients, the marketing department foresees no major procurements for two to three years.

At the same time, Electrovision is facing cost increases on several fronts. As we have known for several months, the new production facility now under construction in Salt Lake City, Utah, is behind schedule and over budget. Labor contracts in Boston and Dallas will expire within the next six months, and plant managers there anticipate that significant salary and benefits concessions may be necessary to avoid strikes.

Moreover, marketing and advertising costs are expected to increase as we attempt to strengthen these activities to better cope with competitive pressures. Given the expected decline in revenues and increase in costs, the Executive Committee's prediction that profits will fall by 12 percent in the coming fiscal year does not seem overly pessimistic.

Moreno designed her report to include plenty of white space so that pages having no graphics would appear inviting and easy to read.

FIGURE 11.11   Continued

5

Airfares and Hotel Rates Are Rising

Business travelers got used to frequent fare wars and discounting in the travel industry. Excess capacity and aggressive price competition made travel a relative bargain. However, that situation has changed as weaker competitors have been forced out and the remaining players have grown stronger and smarter. Airlines and hotels are better at managing inventory and keeping occupancy rates high, which translates into higher prices since suppliers have less reason to compete on price. Last year we saw some of the steepest rate hikes in years. Business airfares jumped 40 percent in many markets. The trend is expected to continue, with rates increasing another 5 to 10 percent overall (Phillips 331; Dahl B6).

Since air and hotel costs account for 70 percent of Electrovision's T&E budget, the trend toward higher prices in these two categories will have serious effects on the company's expenses, unless management takes action to control these costs.

METHODS FOR REDUCING T&E COSTS

By implementing a number of reforms, management can expect to reduce Electrovision's T&E budget by as much as 40 percent. This estimate is based on the general assessment made by American Express (Gilligan 39–40) and our chance to reduce or eliminate first-class travel. However, these measures are likely to be unpopular with employees. To gain acceptance for such changes, management will need to sell employees on the need for moderation in T&E allowances.

Four Ways to Trim Expenses

By researching what other companies are doing to curb T&E expenses, the accounting department has identified four prominent opportunities that should enable Electrovision to save about $6 million annually in travel-related costs.

Institute Tighter Spending Controls

One person should be appointed director of travel and entertainment to lead the T&E budget-control effort. More than a third of all U.S. companies now employ travel managers to keep costs in line ("Businesses Use Savvy Managers" 4). Reporting to the vice president of operations, the director should be familiar with the travel industry and well versed in both accounting and information technology. The director should establish a written T&E policy and implement a system for controlling T&E costs. Electrovision currently has no written policy on travel and entertainment, a step widely recommended by air travel experts (Smith D4). Creating a policy would clarify management's position and serve as a vehicle for

---

Documents the facts to add weight to Moreno's argument

Gives recommendations an objective flavor by pointing out both the benefits and the risks of taking action

---

Because airfares represent Electrovision's biggest T&E expense, Moreno included a subsection that deals with the possible impact of trends in the airline industry. Airfares are rising, so it is especially important to gain more control over employees' air travel arrangements.

Moreno created a forceful tone by using action verbs in the third-level subheadings of this section. This approach is appropriate to the nature of the study and the attitude of the audience. However, in a status-conscious organization, the imperative verbs might sound a bit too presumptuous coming from a junior member of the staff.

FIGURE 11.11   Continued

6

communicating the need for moderation. At a minimum, the policy should include provisions such as the following:

- Limiting all T&E to business purposes and getting approval in advance

- Ensuring that all employees travel by coach and stay in mid-range business hotels (with rare exceptions to be approved on a case-by-case basis)

- Applying policy equally to employees at all levels

To implement the new policy, Electrovision must create a system for controlling T&E expenses. Each department should prepare an annual T&E budget. These budgets should be presented in detail so that management can evaluate how T&E dollars will be spent and can recommend appropriate cuts. To help management monitor performance relative to these budgets, the T&E director should prepare monthly financial statements showing actual T&E expenditures by department.

The director of travel should also be responsible for retaining a business-oriented travel service that will schedule all employee business trips and look for the best travel deals, especially in airfares. In addition to centralizing Electrovision's reservation and ticketing activities, the agency will negotiate reduced group rates with hotels and rental car agencies. The agency should have offices nationwide so that all Electrovision facilities can channel their reservations through the same company. This step is particularly important in light of the differing airfares available from city to city. It's common to find dozens of fares along commonly traveled routes (Rowe 30). Plus, the director can help coordinate travel across the company to secure group discounts when possible (Barker 31; Miller B6).

Reduce Unnecessary Travel and Entertainment

One of the easiest ways to reduce expenses is to reduce the amount of traveling and entertaining that occurs. An analysis of last year's expenditures suggests that as much as 30 percent of Electrovision's T&E is discretionary. The professional staff spent $2.8 million attending seminars and conferences last year. Some of these gatherings are undoubtedly beneficial, but the company could save money by sending fewer people and eliminating the less valuable functions.

Electrovision could also economize on trips between headquarters and divisions by reducing these visits and sending fewer people each time. Although face-to-face meetings are often necessary, management could try to resolve more internal issues through telephone, electronic, and written communication.

Electrovision can urge employees to economize by flying tourist instead of first class or by taking advantage of discount fares. Instead of taking clients to dinner, Electrovision personnel can hold breakfast meetings, which tend to be less costly.

Breaks up text with bulleted lists, which not only call attention to important points but also add visual interest (you can also use visual aids, headings, and direct quotations to break up large, solid blocks of print)

Specifies the steps required to implement recommendations

Moreno decided to single-space her report to create a formal, finished look; however, double-spacing can make the text of a long report somewhat easier to read and provide more space for readers to write comments.

FIGURE 11.11   Continued

Rather than ordering a $50 bottle of wine, employees can select a less expensive bottle or dispense with alcohol entirely. People can book rooms at moderately priced hotels and drive smaller rental cars.

Obtain Lowest Rates from Travel Providers

Apart from urging individual employees to economize, Electrovision can also save money by searching for the lowest available rates for airfares, hotels, and rental cars. Few Electrovision employees have the time or specialized knowledge to seek out travel bargains, making the most convenient and comfortable arrangements. However, by contracting with a professional travel service, the company will have access to professionals who can more efficiently obtain lower rates.

Judging by the experience of other companies, Electrovision may be able to trim 30 to 40 percent from the travel budget by looking for bargains in airfares and negotiating group rates with hotels and rental car companies. The company should be able to achieve these economies by analyzing travel patterns, identifying frequently visited locations, and selecting a few hotels that are willing to reduce rates in exchange for guaranteed business. Also, the company should be able to save up to 40 percent on rental car charges by negotiating a corporate rate.

The possibilities for economizing are promising; however, making the best arrangements is a complicated undertaking, requiring trade-offs such as the following:

- The best fares may not always be the lowest (e.g., indirect flights often cost less than direct ones, but they take longer, costing more in lost work time).

- The cheapest tickets may need to be booked far in advance, often impossible.

- Nonrefundable discount tickets are a drawback if the trip must be canceled.

Replace Travel with Technological Alternatives

We might be able to replace a major portion of our interdivisional travel with electronic meetings, such as videoconferencing or real-time on-screen document sharing. Many companies use these tools to cut costs and reduce employee stress.

Rather than make specific recommendations in this report, I suggest that the new T&E director conduct an in-depth study of the company's travel patterns. An analysis of why employees travel and what they accomplish will highlight any opportunities for replacing face-to-face meetings. Part of this study should include limited testing of various electronic systems as a way of measuring their effect on both workplace effectiveness and overall costs.

Points out possible difficulties to show that all angles have been considered and to build reader confidence in the writer's judgment

Note how Moreno made the transition from section to section. The first sentence under the first heading on this page refers to the subject of the previous paragraph and signals a shift in thought.

FIGURE 11.11   Continued

8

The Impact of Reforms

By implementing tighter controls, reducing unnecessary expenses, negotiating more favorable rates, and exploring "electronic travel," Electrovision should be able to reduce its travel and entertainment budget significantly. As Table 1 illustrates, the combined savings should be in the neighborhood of $6 million, although precise figures are somewhat difficult to project.

Table 1

Electrovision Can Trim Travel and Entertainment Costs by an Estimated $6 Million per Year

Source of Savings	Amount Saved
Switching from first-class to coach airfare	$2,300,000
Negotiating preferred hotel rates	940,000
Negotiating preferred rental car rates	460,000
Systematically searching for lower airfares	375,000
Reducing interdivisional travel	675,000
Reducing seminar and conference attendance	1,250,000
TOTAL POTENTIAL SAVINGS	**$6,000,000**

To achieve the economies outlined in the table, Electrovision will incur expenses for hiring a director of travel and for implementing a T&E cost-control system. These costs are projected at $95,000: $85,000 per year in salary and benefits for the new employee and a one-time expense of $10,000 for the cost-control system. The cost of retaining a full-service travel agency is negligible because agencies receive a commission from travel providers rather than a fee from clients.

The measures required to achieve these savings are likely to be unpopular with employees. Electrovision personnel are accustomed to generous travel and entertainment allowances, and they are likely to resent having these privileges curtailed. To alleviate their disappointment

- Management should make a determined effort to explain why the changes are necessary.

- The director of corporate communication should develop a multifaceted campaign to communicate the importance of curtailing T&E costs.

- Management should set an example by adhering strictly to the new policies.

- The limitations should apply equally to employees at all levels in the organization.

Uses informative title in the table, which is consistent with the way headings are handled and is appropriate for a report to a receptive audience

Table title is worded to help readers focus immediately on the point of the illustrations

Includes dollar figures to help management envision the impact of the suggestions, even though estimated savings are difficult to project

Note how Moreno calls attention in the first paragraph to items in the following table, without repeating the information in the table.

The table puts Moreno's recommendations in perspective. She calls attention to the most important sources of savings and also spells out the costs required to achieve those results.

FIGURE 11.11   Continued

Uses a descriptive heading for the last section of the text (in informational reports, this section is often called "Summary"; in analytical reports, it is called "Conclusions" or "Conclusions and Recommendations")

Emphasizes the recommendations by presenting them in list format

9

CONCLUSIONS AND RECOMMENDATIONS

Electrovision is currently spending $16 million per year on travel and entertainment. Although much of this spending is justified, the company's costs are high relative to competitors', mainly because Electrovision has been generous with its travel benefits.

Electrovision's liberal approach to T&E expenses made sense during years of high profitability; however, the company is facing the prospect of declining profits for the next several years. Thus management is motivated to cut costs in all areas of the business. Reducing T&E spending is particularly important because the impact of these costs will increase as airfares and hotel accommodations increase.

Electrovision should be able to reduce T&E costs by as much as 40 percent by taking four important steps:

1. *Institute tighter spending controls.* Management should hire a T&E director to assume overall responsibility for relevant activities. Within the next six months, this director should develop a written travel policy, institute a T&E budget and a cost-control system, and retain a professional, business-oriented travel agency.

2. *Reduce unnecessary travel and entertainment.* Electrovision should encourage employees to economize on T&E spending. Management can authorize fewer trips and urge employees to be more conservative in their spending.

3. *Obtain lowest rates from travel providers.* Electrovision should focus on obtaining the best rates on airline tickets, hotel rooms, and rental cars. By channeling all arrangements through a professional travel agency, the company can optimize its choices and gain clout in negotiating preferred rates.

4. *Replace travel with technological alternatives.* With the number of computers already installed in our facilities, it seems likely that we could take advantage of desktop videoconferencing and other distance-meeting tools. This won't be quite as feasible with customer sites, since these systems require compatible equipment at both ends of a connection, but it is certainly a possibility for communication with Electrovision's own sites.

Because these measures may be unpopular with employees, management should make a concerted effort to explain the importance of reducing travel costs. The director of corporate communication should be given responsibility for developing a plan to communicate the need for employee cooperation.

Summarizes conclusions in the first two paragraphs —a good approach because Moreno organized her report around conclusions and recommendations, so readers have already been introduced to them

Uses a simple list to remind readers of the four main recommendations

Moreno introduces no new facts in this entire section. In a longer report, she might have divided this section into subsections, labeled "Conclusions" and "Recommendations," to distinguish between the two.

FIGURE 11.11   Continued

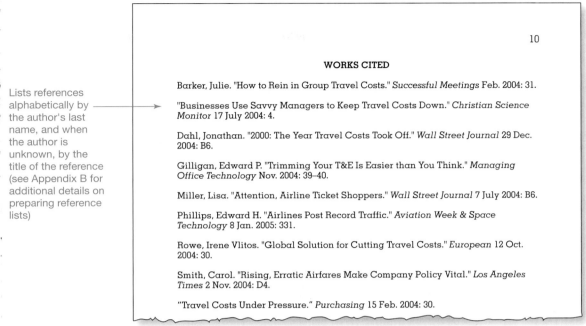

Lists references alphabetically by the author's last name, and when the author is unknown, by the title of the reference (see Appendix B for additional details on preparing reference lists)

10

WORKS CITED

Barker, Julie. "How to Rein in Group Travel Costs." *Successful Meetings* Feb. 2004: 31.

"Businesses Use Savvy Managers to Keep Travel Costs Down." *Christian Science Monitor* 17 July 2004: 4.

Dahl, Jonathan. "2000: The Year Travel Costs Took Off." *Wall Street Journal* 29 Dec. 2004: B6.

Gilligan, Edward P. "Trimming Your T&E Is Easier than You Think." *Managing Office Technology* Nov. 2004: 39–40.

Miller, Lisa. "Attention, Airline Ticket Shoppers." *Wall Street Journal* 7 July 2004: B6.

Phillips, Edward H. "Airlines Post Record Traffic." *Aviation Week & Space Technology* 8 Jan. 2005: 331.

Rowe, Irene Vlitos. "Global Solution for Cutting Travel Costs." *European* 12 Oct. 2004: 30.

Smith, Carol. "Rising, Erratic Airfares Make Company Policy Vital." *Los Angeles Times* 2 Nov. 2004: D4.

"Travel Costs Under Pressure." *Purchasing* 15 Feb. 2004: 30.

Moreno's list of references follows the style recommended in *The MLA Style Manual*.

■ **List of illustrations.** The list of illustrations gives the titles and page numbers of visual aids. If you have enough space on a single page, include the list of illustrations directly beneath the table of contents. Otherwise, put the list on the page after the contents page. When tables and figures are numbered separately, they should also be listed separately. The two lists can appear on the same page if they fit; otherwise, start each list on a separate page.

■ **Synopsis.** A **synopsis** is a brief overview (one page or less) of a report's most important points—it can also be called an **abstract**. The phrasing of a synopsis can be either informative (presenting the main points in the order they appear in the text) or descriptive (simply telling what the report is about), depending on whether the report is in direct or indirect order.

■ **Executive summary.** Instead of a synopsis or abstract, many report writers prefer an **executive summary**—a fully developed "mini" version of the report itself, which may contain headings, transitions, and even visual aids. Executive summaries are for readers who lack the time or motivation to study the complete text. Keep the length of an executive summary proportionate to the length of the report. Linda Moreno's Electrovision report provides one example of an executive summary.

Many reports require neither a synopsis nor an executive summary. Length is usually the determining factor. Most reports of fewer than 10 pages either omit such a preview or combine it with the letter of transmittal. However, if your report is over 30 pages long, you'll probably include either a synopsis or an executive summary as a convenience for readers. Which one you'll provide depends on the traditions of your organization.

Text of the Report

Although reports may contain a variety of components, the heart of a report is always the text, with its introduction, body, and conclusion. If your report has a synopsis or an executive summary, avoid redundancy by balancing your introduction with the material in your summary as Moreno does in her report (Figure 11.11 on page 335). Moreno's executive

Three main text parts of a report are
■ Introduction
■ Body
■ Closing

summary is fairly detailed, so she makes her introduction relatively brief (see Figure 11.1 on page 336). If you believe that your introduction must repeat information that has already been covered in one of the prefatory parts, simply use different wording.

Linda Moreno's Electrovision report gives you a good idea of the types of supporting detail commonly included in the text body. Pay close attention to her effective use of visuals. Most inexperienced writers have a tendency to include too much data in their reports or to place too much data in paragraph format instead of using tables and charts. Include only the essential supporting data in the body, use relevant visuals, and place any additional information in an appendix.

In a long report, the closing section may be labeled "Summary" or "Conclusions and Recommendations." Since Moreno organized her report in a direct pattern, her closing is relatively brief. When using the indirect approach, you may use the close to present your recommendations and conclusions for the very first time, in which case, this section could be relatively extensive.

Supplementary Parts

Supplementary parts present additional details and come after the text.

Supplementary parts follow the text of the report and provide information for readers who seek more detailed discussion. Supplements are more common in long reports than in short ones. They typically include appendixes, bibliography, and index.

- **Appendixes.** An appendix contains additional information for those readers who want it—information related to the report but not included in the text because it is too lengthy, is too bulky, or lacks direct relevance. Appendixes contain sample questionnaires and cover letters, sample forms, computer printouts, spreadsheets, and so on. Include each type of material in a separate appendix, mention all appendixes in the text, and list them in the table of contents.
- **Bibliography.** The bibliography lists the secondary sources you consulted. In Moreno's report, she labeled her bibliography "Works Cited" because she listed only the works that were mentioned in the report. Moreno's Electrovision report uses the author-date system. An alternative is to use numbered footnotes (bottom of the page) or endnotes (end of the report). For more on citing sources, see Appendix B, "Documentation of Report Sources."
- **Index.** An index is an alphabetical list of names, places, and subjects mentioned in the report, along with the pages on which they occur (see the index for this book). An index is rarely included in unpublished reports.

Components of a Formal Proposal

Formal proposals contain many of the same components as other formal reports (see Figure 11.12). The difference lies mostly in the text, although a few of the prefatory parts are also different. With the exception of an occasional appendix, most proposals have few supplementary parts.

Prefatory Parts

Formal proposals contain most of the same prefatory parts as other formal reports.

The cover, title fly, title page, table of contents, and list of illustrations are handled the same as in other formal reports. However, other prefatory parts are handled quite differently, such as the copy of the RFP, the synopsis or executive summary, and the letter of transmittal.

- **Copy of the RFP.** Instead of having a letter of authorization, a formal proposal may have a copy of the request for proposals (RFP), which is a letter or memo soliciting a proposal or a bid for a particular project. If the RFP includes detailed specifications, it may be too long to bind into the proposal; in that case, you may want to include only the introductory portion of the RFP. Another option is to omit the RFP and simply refer to it in your letter of transmittal.
- **Synopsis or executive summary.** Although you may include a synopsis or an executive summary, these components are often less useful in a formal proposal than in a report.

FIGURE 11.12   Parts of a Formal Proposal

PREFATORY PARTS	TEXT PARTS	SUPPLEMENTARY PARTS
Synopsis or executive summary	Summary	Appendixes
List of illustrations	Body	
Table of contents	Introduction	
Letter of transmittal		
Request for proposal		
Title page		
Title fly		
Cover		

In an unsolicited proposal, your transmittal letter will already have caught the reader's interest. In a solicited proposal, the introduction would provide an adequate preview of the contents. Plus, the reader would already be committed to studying your proposal to find out how you intend to satisfy the terms of a contract.

■ **Letter of transmittal.** If the proposal is solicited, the transmittal letter follows the pattern for good-news messages, highlighting those aspects of your proposal that may give you a competitive advantage. If the proposal is unsolicited, the transmittal letter follows the pattern for persuasive messages (see Chapter 9). The letter must persuade the reader that you have something worthwhile to offer that justifies reading the entire proposal. Because the transmittal letter may be all that the client reads, it must be especially convincing.

Text of the Proposal

Just as with reports, the text of a proposal is composed of an introduction, body, and close. The introduction presents and summarizes the problem you intend to solve and your solution. It includes any benefits the reader will receive from the solution. The body explains the complete details of the solution: how the job will be done, how it will be broken into tasks, what method will be used to do it (including the required equipment, material, and personnel), when the work will begin and end, how much the entire job will cost (including a detailed breakdown), and why your company is qualified. The close emphasizes the benefits readers will realize from your solution, and it urges readers to act.

> Just like other business reports, proposals have three divisions of text: introduction, body, and close.

Figure 11.13 on pages 348–357 is an informal proposal submitted by Dixon O'Donnell, vice president of O'Donnell & Associates, a geotechnical engineering firm that conducts a variety of environmental testing services. The company is bidding on the mass grading and utility work specified by AGI Builders. As you review this document, pay close attention to the specific items addressed in the proposal's introduction, body, and closing.

Reviewing Key Points

This chapter discusses Step 2 of the three-step process: writing business reports and proposals. In this chapter, you have learned that in addition to the organizational tasks presented in earlier chapters for short business messages, you need to attend to special report

(continued on page 352)

FIGURE 11.13   Dixon O'Donnell's Effective Informal Solicited Proposal

O'Donnell
&
Associates, Inc.

1793 East Westerfield Road, Arlington Heights, Illinois 60005
(847) 398-1148 Fax: (847) 398-1149 E-mail: dod@ix.netcom.com

July 28, 2005

Ms. Joyce Colton, P.E.
AGI Builders, Inc.
1280 Spring Lake Drive
Belvidere, Illinois, 61008

Dear Ms. Colton:

Subject: Proposal No. F-0087 for AGI Builders, Elgin Manufacturing Campus

Uses opening paragraph in place of an introduction →

O'Donnell & Associates is pleased to submit the following proposal to provide construction testing services for the mass grading operations and utility work at the Elgin Manufacturing Campus, 126th St., Elgin, Illinois. Our company has been providing construction-testing services in the Chicago area since 1972 and has performed over 100 geotechnical investigations at airports within the State of Illinois—including O'Hare International Airport, Midway Airport, and Meig's Field.

← *Grabs reader's attention by highlighting company qualifications*

Background

It is our understanding that the work consists of two projects: (1) the mass grading operations will require approximately six months, and (2) the utility work will require approximately three months. The two operations are scheduled as follows:

← *Acknowledges the two projects and their required time lines*

Mass Grading Operation	September 2005–February 2006
Utility Work	March 2006–May 2006

Uses headings to divide proposal into logical segments for easy reading →

Proposed Approach and Work Plan

Describes scope of project and outlines specific tests the company will perform →

O'Donnell & Associates will perform observation and testing services during both the mass grading operations and the excavation and backfilling of the underground utilities. Specifically, we will perform field density tests on the compacted material as required by the job specifications using a nuclear moisture/density gauge. We will also conduct appropriate laboratory tests such as ASTM D-1557 Modified Proctors. We will prepare detailed reports summarizing the results of our field and laboratory testing. Fill materials to be placed at the site may consist of natural granular materials (sand), processed materials (crushed stone, crushed concrete, slag) or clay soils.

(continued)

FIGURE 11.13   Continued

O'Donnell & Associates, Inc.   July 28, 2005   Page 2

Explains who will be responsible for the various tasks

O'Donnell & Associates will provide qualified personnel to perform the necessary testing. Mr. Kevin Patel will be the lead field technician responsible for the project. A copy of Mr. Patel's résumé is included with this proposal for your review. Kevin will coordinate field activities with your job site superintendent and make sure that appropriate personnel are assigned to the job site. Overall project management will be the responsibility of Mr. Joseph Proesel. Project engineering services will be performed under the direction of Mr. Dixon O'Donnell, P.E. All field personnel assigned to the site will be familiar with and abide by the Project Site Health and Safety Plan prepared by Carlson Environmental, Inc., dated April 2005.

Encloses résumé rather than listing qualifications in the document

Qualifications

O'Donnell & Associates has been providing quality professional services since 1972 in the areas of

- Geotechnical engineering
- Materials testing and inspection
- Pavement evaluation
- Environmental services
- Engineering and technical support (CADD) services

Grabs attention by mentioning distinguishing qualifications

The company provides Phase I and Phase II environmental site assessments, preparation of LUST site closure reports, installation of groundwater monitoring wells, and testing of soil/groundwater samples of environmental contaminants. Geotechnical services include all phases of soil mechanics and foundation engineering, including foundation and lateral load analysis, slope stability analysis, site preparation recommendations, seepage analysis, pavement design, and settlement analysis.

O'Donnell & Associates' materials testing laboratory is certified by AASHTO Accreditation Program for the testing of Soils, Aggregate, Hot Mix Asphalt and Portland Cement Concrete. A copy of our laboratory certification is included with this proposal. In addition to in-house training, field and laboratory technicians participate in a variety of certification programs, including those sponsored by American Concrete Institute (ACI) and Illinois Department of Transportation (IDOT).

Gains credibility by describing certifications

Costs

On the basis of our understanding of the scope of the work, we estimate the total cost of the two projects to be $100,260.00, as follows:

(continued)

FIGURE 11.13   Continued

O'Donnell & Associates, Inc.   July 28, 2005   Page 3

Table of Cost Estimates

Builds interest by describing all services provided by the company →

Cost Estimate: Mass Grading	Units	Rate ($)	Total Cost ($)
Field Inspection			
Labor	1,320 hours	$38.50	$ 50,820.00
Nuclear Moisture Density Meter	132 days	35.00	4,620.00
Vehicle Expense	132 days	45.00	5,940.00
Laboratory Testing			
Proctor Density Tests (ASTM D-1557)	4 tests	130.00	520.00
Engineering/Project Management			
Principal Engineer	16 hours	110.00	1,760.00
Project Manager	20 hours	80.00	1,600.00
Administrative Assistant	12 hours	50.00	600.00
Subtotal			**$ 65,860.00**

Itemizes costs by project and gives supporting detail →

Cost Estimate: Utility Work	Units	Rate ($)	Total Cost ($)
Field Inspection			
Labor	660 hours	$ 38.50	$ 25,410.00
Nuclear Moisture Density Meter	66 days	5.00	2,310.00
Vehicle Expense	66 days	45.00	2,970.00
Laboratory Testing			
Proctor Density Tests (ASTM D-1557)	2 tests	130.00	260.00
Engineering/Project Management			
Principal Engineer	10 hours	110.00	1,100.00
Project Manager	20 hours	80.00	1,600.00
Administrative Assistant	15 hours	50.00	750.00
Subtotal			**$ 34,400.00**

Total Project Costs			**$100,260.00**

This estimate assumes full-time inspection services. However, our services may also be performed on an as-requested basis, and actual charges will reflect time associated with the project. We have attached our standard fee schedule for your review. Overtime rates are for hours in excess of 8.0 hours per day, before 7:00 a.m., after 5:00 p.m., and on holidays and weekends.

← Provides alternative option in case full-time service costs exceed client's budget

(continued)

FIGURE 11.13   Continued

Uses brief closing
to emphasize
qualifications and
ask for client
decision

O'Donnell & Associates, Inc.   July 28, 2005   Page 4

Authorization

With a staff of over 30 personnel, including registered professional engineers,
resident engineers, geologists, construction inspectors, laboratory technicians,
and drillers, we are convinced that O'Donnell & Associates is capable of
providing the services required for a project of this magnitude.

If you would like our firm to provide the services as outlined in this proposal,
please sign this letter and return it to us along with a certified check in the
amount of $10,000 (our retainer) by August 15, 2005. Please call me if you have
any questions regarding the terms of this proposal or our approach.

Provides deadline
and makes
response easy

Sincerely,

Dixon O'Donnell

Dixon O'Donnell
Vice President

Enclosures

Accepted for AGI BUILDERS, INC.

Makes letter a
binding contract,
if signed

By_____   Date _____

requirements when deciding on format and length and when choosing the direct or indirect approach. The chapter discusses structuring informational reports according to topic and structuring analytical reports according to whether you focus on conclusions, recommendations, or logical argument.

The chapter talks about how to choose the right visuals. It also summarizes composition tasks, such as developing the text, choosing the proper degree of formality, establishing a consistent time perspective, and helping readers find their way. The chapter also discusses Step 3 of the three-step process: completing business reports and proposals. It talks about all the various components of formal reports and proposals, including prefatory parts, text, and supplementary parts.

The next chapter discusses giving oral business presentations. You will learn how to plan, write, and complete business speeches and presentations. You will learn about the various types of presentation visuals, and you will find out how to master the art of delivery, including practicing, overcoming anxiety, and handling questions.

Test Your Knowledge

1. What are your options for selecting a report format?

2. What are your options for structuring an informational report?

3. What are your options for structuring an analytical report?

4. What tools can you use to help readers follow the structure and flow of information in a long report?

5. What chart type would you use to compare one part with a whole?

6. What chart type would you use to present detailed, exact values?

7. How does a flowchart differ from an organization chart?

8. What information is included on the title page of a report?

9. What is a letter of transmittal, and where is it positioned within a report?

10. What is the equivalent of a letter of authorization for a proposal?

Apply Your Knowledge

1. Should a report always explain the writer's method of gathering evidence or solving a problem? Why or why not?

2. Would you use the direct or indirect approach to document inventory shortages at your manufacturing plant? To propose an employee stock-option plan? Why?

3. What similarities do you see between visuals and nonverbal communication? Explain your answer.

4. You're writing a report to the director of human resources on implementing teams throughout your company. You want to emphasize that since the new approach was implemented six months ago, absenteeism and turnovers have been sharply reduced in all but two departments. How do you visually present your data in the most favorable light? Explain.

5. Ethical Choices   How would you report on a confidential survey in which employees rated their managers' capabilities? Both employees and managers expect to see the results. Would you give the same report to employees and managers? What components would you include or exclude for each audience? Explain your choices.

Practice Your Knowledge

Activities

For live links to all websites discussed in this chapter, visit this text's website at www.prenhall.com/bovee. Just log on, select Chapter 11, and click on "Featured Websites." Locate the page or the URL related to the material in the text.

1. **Organizing Reports: Deciding on Format**   Go to the library or visit the Internet site www.annualreportservice.com and review the annual reports recently released by two corporations in the same industry. Analyze each report and be prepared to discuss the following questions in class:
   a. What organizational differences, if any, do you see in the way each corporation discusses its annual performance? Are the data presented clearly so that shareholders can draw conclusions about how well the company performed?
   b. What goals, challenges, and plans do top managers emphasize in their discussion of results?
   c. How do the format and organization of each report enhance or detract from the information being presented?

2. **Organizing Reports: Choosing the Direct or Indirect Approach**   Of the organizational approaches introduced in the chapter, which is best suited for writing a report that answers the following questions? Briefly explain why. (Note, you will write one report for each question item.)
   a. In which market segment—root beer, cola, or lemon-lime—should Fizz Drinks, Inc., introduce a new soft drink to take advantage of its enlarged research and development budget?
   b. Should Major Manufacturing, Inc., close down operations of its antiquated Bellville, Arkansas, plant despite the adverse economic impact on the town that has grown up around the plant?
   c. Should you and your partner adopt a new accounting method to make your financial statements look better to potential investors?
   d. Should Grand Canyon Chemicals buy disposable test tubes to reduce labor costs associated with cleaning and sterilizing reusable test tubes?
   e. What are some reasons for the recent data loss at the college computer center, and how can we avoid similar problems in the future?

3. **Teamwork: Report Structure**   You and a classmate are helping Linda Moreno prepare her report on Electrovision's travel and entertainment costs (see Figure 11.11 on

pages 332–345). This time, however, the report is to be informational rather than analytical, so it will not include recommendations. Review the existing report and determine what changes would be needed to make it an informational report. Be as specific as possible. For example, if your team decides the report needs a new title, what title would you use? Now draft a transmittal memo for Moreno to use in conveying this informational report to Dennis McWilliams, Electrovision's vice president of operations.

4. **Organizing Reports: Structuring Informational Reports** Assume that your college president has received many student complaints about campus parking problems. You are appointed to chair a student committee organized to investigate the problems and recommend solutions. The president gives you the file labeled "Parking: Complaints from Students," and you jot down the essence of the complaints as you inspect the contents. Your notes look like this:

- Inadequate student spaces at critical hours
- Poor night lighting near the computer center
- Inadequate attempts to keep resident neighbors from occupying spaces
- Dim marking lines
- Motorcycles taking up full spaces
- Discourteous security officers
- Spaces (usually empty) reserved for college officials
- Relatively high parking fees
- Full fees charged to night students even though they use the lots only during low-demand periods
- Vandalism to cars and a sense of personal danger
- Inadequate total space
- Resident harassment of students parking on the street in front of neighboring houses

Now prepare an outline for an informational report to be submitted to committee members. Use a topical organization for your report that categorizes this information.

5. **Choosing the Right Visual** You're preparing the annual report for FretCo Guitar Corporation. For each of the following types of information, select the right chart or visual to illustrate the text. Explain your choices.
   a. Data on annual sales for the past 20 years
   b. Comparison of FretCo sales, product by product (electric guitars, bass guitars, amplifiers, acoustic guitars), for this year and last year
   c. Explanation of how a FretCo acoustic guitar is manufactured
   d. Explanation of how the FretCo Guitar Corporation markets its guitars
   e. Data on sales of FretCo products in each of 12 countries
   f. Comparison of FretCo sales figures with sales figures for three competing guitar makers over the past 10 years

6. **Internet** One of the best places to see how data can be presented visually is in government statistical publications, which are often available on the Internet. For example, the International Trade Administration (ITA), a branch of the U.S. Department of Commerce, publishes monthly reports about U.S. trade with other countries. Visit the report page of its website at http://www.ita.doc.gov/td/industry/otea/ustrade.html, and follow the link to the latest monthly trade update. Using what you learned in this chapter, evaluate the charts in the report. Do they present the data clearly? Are they missing any elements? What would you do to improve the charts? Print out a copy of the report to turn in with your answers, and indicate which charts you are evaluating.

7. **Composing Reports: Navigational Clues** Review a long business article in a journal or newspaper. Highlight examples of how the article uses headings, transitions, and previews and reviews to help the readers find their way.

8. **Ethical Choices** Your boss has asked you to prepare a feasibility report to determine whether the company should advertise its custom-crafted cabinetry in the weekly neighborhood newspaper. Based on your primary research, you think they should. As you draft the introduction to your report, however, you discover that the survey

administered to the neighborhood newspaper subscribers was flawed. Several of the questions were poorly written and misleading. You used the survey results, among other findings, to justify your recommendation. The report is due in three days. What actions might you want to take, if any, before you complete your report?

9. **Producing Reports: Letter of Transmittal** You are president of the Friends of the Library, a nonprofit group that raises funds and provides volunteers to support your local library. Every February, you send a report of the previous year's activities and accomplishments to the County Arts Council, which provides an annual grant of $1,000 toward your group's summer reading festival. Now it's February 6, and you've completed your formal report. Here are the highlights:

- Back-to-school book sale raised $2,000.
- Holiday craft fair raised $1,100.
- Promotion and prizes for summer reading festival cost $1,450.
- Materials for children's program featuring local author cost $125.
- New reference databases for library's career center cost $850.
- Bookmarks promoting library's website cost $200.

Write a letter of transmittal to Erica Maki, the council's director. Because she is expecting this report, you can use the direct approach. Be sure to express gratitude for the council's ongoing financial support.

10. **Analyze This Document** Visit the U.S. Department of Justice reports page at http://uscis.gov/graphics/aboutus/repsstudies/addition.html. Read the brief description of the department's Triennial Comprehensive Report on Immigration and follow the link to the executive summary. Using the information in this chapter, analyze the executive summary and offer specific suggestions for revising it.

11. **Internet** Government reports vary in purpose and structure. Read through the Department of Education's report on how population growth is affecting school enrollment, posted online at www.ed.gov/pubs/bbecho00/index.html. What is the purpose of this document? Does the title communicate this purpose? What type of report is this, and what is the report's structure? Which prefatory and supplementary parts are included? Now analyze the visuals. What types are included in this report? Are they all necessary? Are the titles and legends sufficiently informative?

Expand Your Knowledge

Exploring the Best of the Web

Preview Before You Produce A good way to get ideas for the best style, organization, and format of a report is by looking at copies of professional business reports. To find samples of various types of reports, you can use a metasearch engine such as Ixquick Metasearch, at www.ixquick.com. Enter the phrase *business reports*, then choose a report and review it. Answer the following questions:

Exercises

1. What is the purpose of the report you read? Who is its target audience? Explain why the structure and style of the report make it easy or difficult to follow the main idea.

2. What type of report did you read? Briefly describe the main message. Is the information well organized? If you answer "yes," explain how you can use the report as a guide for a report you might write. If you answer "no," explain why the report is not helpful.

3. Drawing on what you know about the qualities of a good business report, review a report and describe what features contribute to its readability.

Exploring the Web on Your Own

Review these chapter-related websites to learn more about writing reports and proposals.

1. Plan your way to profit by learning how to write effective business plans. Refer to the Business Planning sec-

tion on the Small Business Administration website, www.sba.gov (look under "Starting Your Business").

2. Improve the quality of your reports by following an effective proofreading strategy. Visit Purdue University's Online Writing Lab, owl.english.purdue.edu, and search for "Editing and Proofreading Strategies."

3. Resolve any grammar question you come across in your proofreading by consulting the online grammar directory at www.clearenglish.net.

Learn Interactively

Interactive Study Guide

Go to the Companion Website at www.prenhall.com/bovee. For Chapter 11, take advantage of the interactive "Study Guide" to test your knowledge of the chapter. Get instant feedback on whether you need additional studying. Also, visit this site's "Study Hall," where you'll find an abundance of valuable resources that will help you succeed in this course.

Peak Performance Grammar and Mechanics

In Chapter 10 you were referred to the Peak Performance Grammar and Mechanics activities on the web at www.prenhall.com/onekey to improve your skill with other types of punctuation. For additional reinforcement in quotation marks, parentheses, and ellipses, go to the "Improve Your Grammar, Mechanics, and Usage" section that follows, and complete the "Level 1: Self-Assessment" exercises.

CASES

The "Cases" section of Chapter 10 asked you to complete planning tasks for 12 informal cases (both informational and analytical). Your instructor may ask you to go back and choose some of those cases to prepare and write as fully developed reports. Following are some formal reports your instructor may assign.

Short Formal Reports

1. Climbing the ladder: Short report summarizing data about corporate opportunities for women (no additional research required)

As assistant to the director of human resources for a large advertising firm, you hear the concerns of many employees. Lately, increasing numbers of women have been complaining about being passed up for promotions and management positions. They feel that men receive preferential treatment, even though many women are more highly qualified.

Your team has already conducted some research into the problem. Table 11.3 shows several key statistics about the men and women working for your company. Table 11.4 depicts how executives in Fortune 1000 companies see the barriers to the advancement of women, and Table 11.5 shows why female executives believe that women should have more opportunities in the corporate world. These data may help shed light on the possibility of sex discrimination at your company. Because your company believes in fair and equal treatment for all employees,

Table 11.3	Statistics for Male and Female Managers	
Employee Statistics	**Female Managers**	**Male Managers**
Average number of years with the company	12.3	9.5
Average number of years of management experience	7.2	6.9
Percentage who have an MBA or other advanced degree	74%	63%
Average annual salary	$76,000	$84,000
Average number of times promoted	4.2	4.4

Table 11.4	Why Female Executives Don't Advance into Corporate Leadership Positions	
Reason Cited	**According to Female Executives**	**According to Male CEOs**
Male stereotyping preconceptions	52%	25%
Exclusion from informal networks	49	15
Lack of general management/line experience	47	82
Inhospitable corporate culture	35	18
Women not in pipeline long enough	29	64

Table 11.5	Why Female Executives Think Companies Should Increase the Number of Female Senior Managers	
Reason	**Agree**	**Strongly Agree**
Women are large part of management talent pool	29%	69%
Women contribute unique perspective	32	61
Women are large part of consumer base	45	36
Companies have social responsibility	41	10
Shareholders want more executive women	41	7
Customers want more executive women	34	7
Lawsuits are increasing	40	5

regardless of gender, you know your boss will be interested in this information.

Your task: Write a short report to the director of human resources, interpreting and summarizing the information in these tables. Suggest a possible course of action to remedy the situation at your company.[6]

WEB SKILLS 2. Picking the better path: Short research report assisting a client in a career choice (additional research required)

You are employed by Open Options, a career-counseling firm, where your main function is to help clients make career choices. Today a client with the same name as yours (what a coincidence!) came to your office and asked for help deciding between two careers—careers that you yourself had been interested in (an even greater coincidence!).

Your task: Research the two careers, and prepare a short report that your client can study. Your report should compare at least five major areas, such as salary, working conditions, and educational requirements. Interview the client to understand her or his personal preferences regarding each of the five areas. For example, what is the minimum salary the client will accept? By comparing the client's preferences with the research material you collect, you will have a basis for concluding which of the two careers is best. The report should end with a career recommendation. (Note: One good place for career-related information is the *Occupational Outlook Handbook*, published by the U.S. Bureau of Labor Statistics, available in print at the library and online at **http://stats.bls.gov/oco/ocoiab.htm**.)

Long Formal Reports Requiring Additional Research

3. Is there any justice? Report critiquing legislation

Plenty of people complain about their state legislators, but few are specific about their complaints. Here's your chance.

Your task: Write a formal report about a law that you believe should have been, or should not have been, enacted. Be objective. Write the report using specific facts to support your beliefs. Reach conclusions and offer your recommendation at the end of the report. As a final step, you might send a copy of your report to an appropriate state official or legislator.

4. Travel opportunities: Report comparing two destinations

You are planning to take a two-week trip abroad sometime within the next year. Because a couple of destinations appeal to you, you are going to have to do some research before you can make a decision.

Your task: Prepare a lengthy report comparing two countries that you would like to visit. Begin by making a list of important questions you will need to answer. Do you want a relaxing vacation or an educational experience? What types of services will you require? What will your transportation needs be? Where will you have the least difficulty with the language? Using resources in your library, on the Internet, and perhaps from travel agencies, analyze the two destinations to see which one meets your own travel criteria. At the end of the report, recommend the better country for you to visit this year.

5. Secondary sources: Report based on library research

Perhaps one of the following questions has been on your mind:

 a. Which is the best college at which to pursue an undergraduate degree in business?
 b. How can you organize a student group to make your campus safer at night?
 c. Which of three companies that you would like to work for has the most responsible environmental policies?
 d. What market factors led to the development of a product that you use frequently, and how are those factors different today?
 e. Which three U.S. companies have had the best stock price performance over the past 30 years and why?
 f. What are the best small-business opportunities available today?

Your task: Answer one of those questions, using secondary sources for information. Be sure to document your sources in the correct form (see Appendix B). Give conclusions and recommendations in your report.

6. Doing business abroad: Report summarizing the social and business customs of a foreign country

Your company would like to sell its products overseas. But first, management must have a clear understanding of the social and business customs of the foreign countries where they intend to do business.

Your task: Choose a non-English-speaking country, and write a long formal report summarizing the country's social and business customs. Review appropriate sections of

Chapter 1 as a guide for the types of information you could include in your report.

7. Brewing up sales: Formal proposal to supply coffee to Peter's Doughnuts

You are assistant to the president of Lighthouse Roasters, a small but growing coffee-roasting company. Lighthouse has made a name for itself by offering fresh, dark-roasted gourmet coffees; however, Lighthouse Roasters does not operate its own stores (unlike Starbucks and other competitors). Instead, Lighthouse sells roasted gourmet coffee beans to retailers such as restaurants, bakeries, and latte carts. These retailers use the Lighthouse beans to make the coffee beverages they sell.

Lighthouse's total cost to produce a pound of roasted gourmet beans is $2.75. The company wholesales a pound of roasted gourmet beans for an average price of $4.50. Competitors who sell regular coffee beans typically charge about $3.00 per pound. However, the average price of a gourmet coffee beverage is $1.50, about $.50 more than beverages made with regular coffee (including both brewed coffee and espresso drinks). Each pound of coffee yields about 40 beverages.

With 76 doughnut shops across 13 states, Peter's Doughnuts has seen its sales decline in recent months, after Starbucks began opening stores close by Peter's shops. Starbucks not only sells gourmet coffee but also carries a selection of delicious pastries that compete with doughnuts. Peter's management figures that by offering gourmet coffee, it will win back customers who like doughnuts but who also want darker-roasted gourmet coffees. Therefore, Peter's has invited you to submit a proposal to be its exclusive supplier of coffee. Peter's anticipates that it will need 400 pounds of coffee a month during the colder months (October–March) and 300 pounds during the warmer months (April–September). The company has said it wants to pay no more than $3.75 per pound for Lighthouse coffee.

Your task: Using your imagination to supply the details, write a proposal describing your plan to supply coffee to Peter's Doughnuts. Considering your costs, will you meet Peter's pricing demands, or will you attempt to gain a higher price?

Improve Your Grammar, Mechanics, and Usage

Level 1: Self-Assessment—Quotation Marks, Parentheses, Ellipses, Underscores, and Italics

Review Sections 2.10, 2.11, 2.12, and 2.13 in the Handbook of Grammar, Mechanics, and Usage, and then look at the following 15 items.

In items 1–15, insert quotations marks, parentheses, ellipses, and underscores (for italics) wherever necessary:

1. Be sure to read How to Sell by Listening in this month's issue of Fortune.

2. Her response see the attached memo is disturbing.

3. Contact is an overused word.

4. We will operate with a skeleton staff during the holiday break December 21 through January.

5. The SBP's next conference, the bulletin noted, will be held in Minneapolis.

6. Sara O'Rourke a reporter from The Wall Street Journal will be here on Thursday.

7. I don't care why you didn't fill my order; I want to know when you'll fill it.

8. The term up in the air means undecided.

9. Her assistant the one who just had the baby won't be back for four weeks.

10. Ask not what your country can do for you is the beginning of a famous quotation from John F. Kennedy.

11. Whom do you think Time magazine will select as its Man of the year?

12. Do you remember who said And away we go?

13. Refinements in robotics may prove profitable. More detail about this technology appears in Appendix A.

14. The resignation letter begins Since I'll never regain your respect and goes on to explain why that's true.

15. You must help her distinguish between i.e. which means that is and e.g. which means for example.

Level 2: Workplace Applications

The following items contain numerous errors in grammar, capitalization, punctuation, abbreviation, number style, word division, and vocabulary. Rewrite each sentence in the space provided, correcting all errors. Write *C* in the space after any sentence that is already correct.

1. For the lst time, thank's to largely deals with the big chains like Stop & Shop, Sheila's Snak Treetz are showing a profit.

2. The premise for broadband, sometimes called the 'next generation of Internet', is that consumers need a more fast pipeline for getting digital information in our homes.

3. After moving into they're own factory, the Anderson's found theirselves in the market for an oven with airflow controls.

4. Cash-strapped entrepreneurs have learned penny-pinching, cost-cutting, credit-stretching techniques.

5. Designs in the Rough send out some 7 million catalogs a year yet until recently the company did'nt need a warehouse and they hadn't hardly any carrying costs.

6. Blockbuster estimates that 70 percent of the US population live within a 10 minute drive of a Blockbuster store.

7. Nestle Waters North America are the exclusive importer of globally-recognized brands such as: Perrier and Vittel from France and, S. Pelligrino from Italy,

8. The U.S. hispanic community; the largest Minority Group in the country; commands a impressive total purchasing power estimated at $499 billion dollars.

9. We conducted a six-month pilot in Chicago, to insure the affectiveness of the program.

10. A series of 7-Eleven television spots help make the term brain freeze part of every day American language.

11. The ad agencies accounts include the following consumer-brands; Wal-Mart, Southwest airlines, Kinko's, Land Rover, and Krispy Kreme.

12. PETsMART allows pets and their humans to together stroll the aisles of its stores; the number one Specialty Retailer of pet supplies.

13. Signature Fruit Co. has confirmed its closing it's Gridley, CA peach plant this Fall.

14. To unite the company's 91 franchisees around a common corporate identity WingsToGo have setup a corporate intranet.

15. It would be well for you to contract with an Internet service provider—a ISP - to both run and to maintain your website.

Level 3: Document Critique

The following document may contain errors in grammar, capitalization, punctuation, abbreviation, number style, vocabulary, and spelling. You may also find problems with organization, format, and word use. Correct all errors using standard proofreading marks (see Appendix C).

MEMORANDUM

From: Kris Beiersdorf

Date: 18 April 2005

RE PROJECT: Contract no. 79371 DuPage county

To: Ken Estes, Northern Illinois concrete

Memco Construction is pleased to submit a road construction proposal for the above project. Our company has been providing quality materials and subcontracting services for highway reconstruction projects for over twenty-three years. Our most recent jobs in Illinois have included Illinois State Route 60 resurfacing, and reconstructing Illinois tollway 294.

Should you have any questions about this proposal please contact me at the company 847-672-0344, direct extension #30) or by e-mail at kbeirsdorf@memcocon.com.

Based on the scope of the work outlined: the total cost of this job is projected by us to run ninety-nine thousand, two hundred eighty-three dollars. Because material quantities can vary once a project gets underway a separate page will be attached by us to this memorandum detailing our per-unit fees. Final charges will be based on the exact quantity of materials used for the job, and anything that accedes this estimate will be added of course.

Our proposal assumes that the following items will be furnished by other contractors (at no cost to Memco). All forms, earthwork and clearing; All prep work; Water at project site; Traffic control setup, devices, and maintenance—Location for staging, stockpiling, and storing material and equipment at job sight.

If we win this bid, we are already to begin when the apropriate contracts have been signed by us and by you.

Top Tips for Writing Reports That Tell the Truth

Put nothing in writing that you're unwilling to say in public, and write nothing that may embarrass or jeopardize your employer. Does this mean you should cover up problems? Of course not. However, when you're dealing with sensitive information, be discreet. Present the information in such a way that it will help readers solve a problem. Avoid personal gripes, criticisms, alibis, attempts to blame other people, sugarcoated data, and unsolicited opinions.

To be useful, the information must be accurate, complete, and honest. But remember, being honest is not always a simple matter. Everyone sees reality a little differently, and individuals describe what they see in their own way. To restrict the distortions introduced by differences in perception, follow these guidelines:

- **Describe facts or events in concrete terms.** Indicate quantities whenever you can. Say that "Sales have increased 17 percent," or that "Sales have increased from $40,000 to $43,000 in the past two months." Don't say, "Sales have skyrocketed."

- **Report all relevant facts.** Regardless of whether these facts support your theories or please your readers, they must be included. Omitting the details that undermine your position may be convenient, but it is misleading and inaccurate.

- **Put the facts in perspective.** Taken out of context, the most concrete facts are misleading. If you say "Stock values have doubled in three weeks," you offer an incomplete picture. Instead, say "Stock values have doubled in three weeks, rising from $2 to $4 per share."

- **Give plenty of evidence for your conclusions.** Statements such as "We have to reorganize the sales force or we'll lose market share" may or may not be true. Readers have no way of knowing unless you provide enough data to support your claim.

- **Present only verifiable conclusions.** Check facts, and use reliable sources. Don't draw conclusions too quickly (one rep may say that customers are unhappy, but that doesn't mean they all are). And don't assume that one event caused another (sales may have dipped right after you switched ad agencies, but that doesn't mean the new agency is at fault—the general state of the economy may be responsible).

- **Keep your personal biases in check.** Even if you feel strongly about your topic, keep those feelings from influencing your choice of words. Don't say, "Locating a plant in Kraymore is a terrible idea because the people there are mostly students who would rather play than work and who don't have the ability to operate our machines." Such language not only offends but also obscures the facts and provokes emotional responses.

Applications for Success

You may already have written some business reports, or you may have written papers for class. Consider the top tips just discussed when completing these three activities.

Do the following:

1. When would you use vague language instead of concrete detail in a business report? Would this action be unethical or merely one form of emphasizing the positive?
2. Recent budget cuts have endangered the day-care program at your local branch of a national company. You're writing a report for headquarters about the grave impact on employees. Describe the situation in a single sentence that reveals nothing about your personal feelings but that clearly shows your position.
3. When writing an unsolicited proposal to a potential client, you need to persuade your audience to consider hiring your firm or purchasing your product. How can you be persuasive and completely truthful at the same time?

12 Preparing and Giving Oral Business Presentations

Learning Objectives

After studying this chapter, you will be able to

1 Explain how planning an oral presentation differs from planning a written document

2 Describe the five tasks that go into organizing oral presentations

3 List three challenges you must keep in mind while composing your presentation

4 Discuss four elements involved in creating effective slides

5 List 10 ways to overcome your anxiety and feel more confident

6 Discuss two factors in presenting visuals effectively

7 Discuss six guidelines for handling questions effectively

Leanne Anderson helps businesspeople become better public speakers by training them to focus on their audience's needs. She believes that knowing your audience is the most important element of a successful speech. She also advocates being a ruthless editor, because a good way to make your presentation stand out from others is to write a well-organized speech that is clear, concise, and focused. "Economy of language is the real key to good communication," she says. "That means choosing the best way of saying something to get the desired result."[1]

The Three-Step Oral Presentation Process

Like Leanne Anderson, chances are you'll have an opportunity to deliver a number of oral presentations throughout your career. You may not speak before large audiences of employees or the media, but you'll certainly be expected to present ideas to your colleagues, make sales presentations to potential customers, or engage in other kinds of spoken communication. For instance, if you're in the human resources department, you may give orientation briefings to new employees or explain company policies, procedures, and benefits at assemblies. If you're familiar with your department's procedures, you may conduct training programs. Regardless of your job or the purpose of your presentation, you will be more effective if you adopt an oral presentation process that follows three familiar steps (see Figure 12.1 on page 368):

The process for preparing oral presentations has three familiar steps.

1. Plan your presentation.
2. Write your presentation.
3. Complete your presentation.

Step 1: Planning Speeches and Presentations

Planning oral presentations is similar to planning any other business message: It requires analyzing your purpose and your audience, investigating necessary information, and adapting your message to the occasion and your audience so that you can establish a good relationship. However, because presentations are delivered orally under relatively public circumstances, they require a few special communication techniques. For one thing, a presentation is a one-time event; your audience cannot leaf back through printed pages to review something you said earlier. So you must make sure that audience members will hear what you say and remember it. You must capture their attention immediately and keep them interested. Therefore, begin by defining your purpose clearly while thinking of ways to engage your audience.

Preparing oral presentations requires some special communication techniques to ensure your audience hears what you say.

Clarify Your Purpose

The four basic reasons for giving a presentation are to inform, to persuade, to motivate, and to entertain. The purpose of your oral presentation will govern the content you include and the style in which you present the content. Most of your presentations or speeches will be informative, requiring a straightforward statement of the facts. If you're involved in marketing or sales, however, you'll probably be writing and delivering persuasive presentations and speeches using the organizational and writing techniques discussed in Chapter 9. Motivational speeches tend to be more specialized, so many companies bring in outside professional speakers to handle this type of presentation. Entertainment speeches are perhaps the rarest in the business world; they are usually limited to after-dinner speeches and to speeches at conventions or retreats.

The content and style of speeches and presentations vary, depending on your purpose.

Analyze Your Audience

Whatever your purpose, your speech will be more effective if you keep your audience interested in your message. To do so, you must understand who your audience members are and what they need. If you're involved in selecting the audience or if you're speaking to a group of peers at work, you'll certainly have information about listener characteristics. But in many cases, you'll be speaking to a group of people you know very little about. You'll want to investigate their needs and characteristics before showing up to speak. You can also ask your host or some other contact person for help with audience analysis, and you can supplement that information with some educated estimates of your own. For a reminder of how to analyze an audience, review Chapter 3's "Develop an Audience Profile" and see Figure 12.2. For even more insight into audience evaluation (including emotional and cultural issues), consult a good public-speaking textbook.

What you know about your audience affects your main idea, scope, approach, outline, and style.

Step 2: Writing Speeches and Presentations

You may never actually write out a presentation word for word. But that doesn't mean that developing its content will be any easier or quicker than preparing a written document. Speaking intelligently about a topic may actually involve more work and more time than preparing a written document about the same topic.

Organize Your Speech or Presentation

Organize an oral message just as you would organize a written message, by focusing on your audience as you define your main idea, limit your scope, choose your approach, prepare your outline, and decide on the most effective style for your presentation.

FIGURE 12.1   The Three-Step Oral Presentation Process

Planning ➤   **Writing** ➤   **Completing** ➤

Analyze
Study your purpose, lay out your schedule, and profile your audience.

Investigate
Gather needed information through formal or informal research methods.

Adapt
Adapt your presentation to occasion and audience; then establish a good relationship with your audience.

Organize
Define your main idea, limit the scope, choose your approach, prepare your outline, and decide on style.

Compose
Compose your presentation, ensuring that the introduction, body, close, and question-and-answer period all accomplish the necessary tasks for an oral medium.

Revise
Edit presentation for content, conciseness, and clarity.

Produce
Review everything for typos, improper grammar, and mechanical errors.

Proofread
Practice your presentation, check the location, overcome your anxiety, and field questions responsibly.

1   **2**   **3**

The tasks you perform when organizing oral messages are similar to those you perform for written messages.

- **Define the main idea.** What is the one message you want audience members to walk away with? The "you" attitude helps keep your audience's attention and convinces people that your points are relevant.

- **Limit your scope.** Tailor the material to the time allowed, which is often strictly regulated. Speakers can deliver about one paragraph (125 to 150 words) a minute (or between 20 and 25 double-spaced, typed pages per hour). To make three basic points in a 10-minute presentation, allow about 2 minutes (about two paragraphs) to explain each point, devote a minute each to the introduction and the conclusion, and leave 2 minutes for questions.

- **Choose your approach.** If you have 10 minutes or less to deliver your message, organize your presentation like a letter or a brief memo. Organize longer presentations like reports. Regardless of length, use direct order if the audience is receptive and indirect if

FIGURE 12.2   Analyzing the Audience for Oral Presentations

AUDIENCE ANALYSIS CHECKLIST

Determine Audience Size and Composition
✓ Estimate how many people will attend.
✓ Consider whether they have some political, religious, professional, or other affiliation in common.
✓ Analyze the mix of men and women, ages, socioeconomic and ethnic groups, occupations, and geographic regions represented.

Predict the Audience's Probable Reaction
✓ Analyze why audience members are attending the presentation.
✓ Determine the audience's general attitude toward the topic: interested, moderately interested, open-minded, unconcerned, or hostile.
✓ Analyze the mood that people will be in when you speak to them.
✓ Find out what kind of backup information will most impress the audience: technical data, historical information, financial data, demonstrations, samples, and so on.
✓ Consider whether the audience has any biases that might work against you.
✓ Anticipate possible objections or questions.

Gauge the Audience's Level of Understanding
✓ Analyze whether everybody has the same background and experience.
✓ Determine what the audience already knows about the subject.
✓ Decide what background information the audience will need to better understand the subject.
✓ Consider whether the audience is familiar with your vocabulary.
✓ Analyze what the audience expects from you.
✓ Think about the mix of general concepts and specific details you will need to present.

FIGURE 12.3   Effective Outline for a 30-Minute Presentation

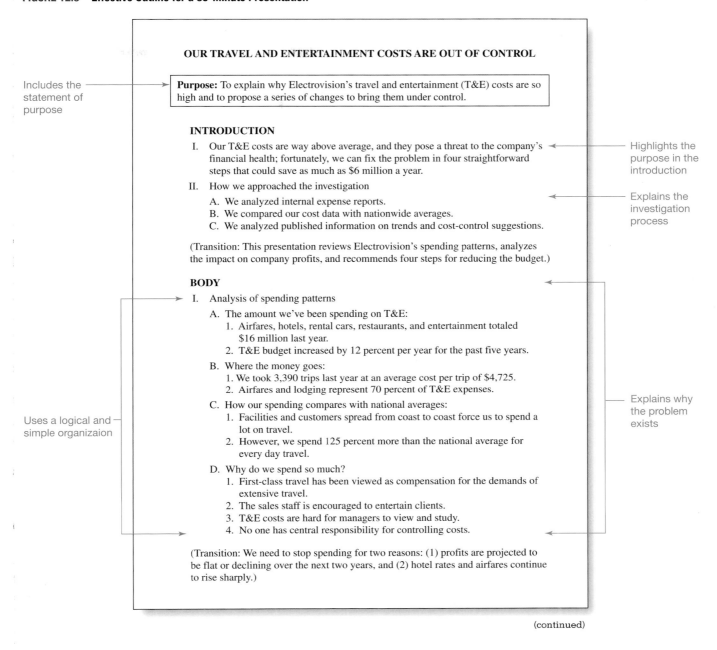

Includes the statement of purpose

Highlights the purpose in the introduction

Explains the investigation process

Uses a logical and simple organizaion

Explains why the problem exists

(continued)

you expect resistance. Simplicity of organization is especially valuable in oral presentations, since listeners can't review a paragraph or flip pages back and forth, as they can when reading.

■ **Prepare your outline.** Your outline helps you keep your presentation both audience centered and within the allotted time. Figure 12.3 is the outline for a 30-minute analytical presentation based on Linda Moreno's Electrovision report (see Chapter 11). It is organized around conclusions and presented in direct order. If you plan to give your presentation from notes rather than from written text, your outline can also become your final "script."

■ **Decide on an appropriate style.** Choose your style to fit the occasion, audience size, subject, purpose, budget, location, and preparation time. When speaking to a small group in a conference room, encourage participation with a casual style. For

FIGURE 12.3   Continued

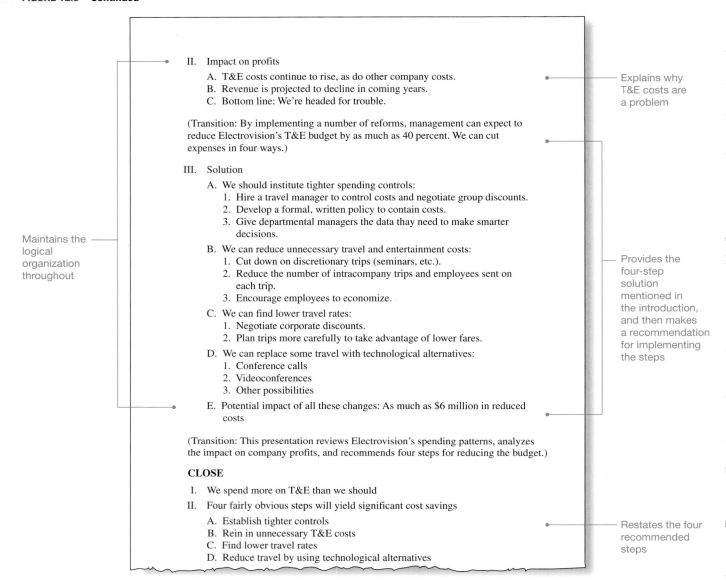

II. Impact on profits
    A. T&E costs continue to rise, as do other company costs.
    B. Revenue is projected to decline in coming years.
    C. Bottom line: We're headed for trouble.

Explains why T&E costs are a problem

(Transition: By implementing a number of reforms, management can expect to reduce Electrovision's T&E budget by as much as 40 percent. We can cut expenses in four ways.)

III. Solution
    A. We should institute tighter spending controls:
      1. Hire a travel manager to control costs and negotiate group discounts.
      2. Develop a formal, written policy to contain costs.
      3. Give departmental managers the data thay need to make smarter decisions.
    B. We can reduce unnecessary travel and entertainment costs:
      1. Cut down on discretionary trips (seminars, etc.).
      2. Reduce the number of intracompany trips and employees sent on each trip.
      3. Encourage employees to economize.
    C. We can find lower travel rates:
      1. Negotiate corporate discounts.
      2. Plan trips more carefully to take advantage of lower fares.
    D. We can replace some travel with technological alternatives:
      1. Conference calls
      2. Videoconferences
      3. Other possibilities
    E. Potential impact of all these changes: As much as $6 million in reduced costs

Maintains the logical organization throughout

Provides the four-step solution mentioned in the introduction, and then makes a recommendation for implementing the steps

(Transition: This presentation reviews Electrovision's spending patterns, analyzes the impact on company profits, and recommends four steps for reducing the budget.)

CLOSE

I. We spend more on T&E than we should

II. Four fairly obvious steps will yield significant cost savings

    A. Establish tighter controls
    B. Rein in unnecessary T&E costs
    C. Find lower travel rates
    D. Reduce travel by using technological alternatives

Restates the four recommended steps

a large audience at an important event, establish a more formal atmosphere: perhaps speaking from a stage or platform, standing behind a lectern, and using a microphone.

Compose Your Speech or Presentation

Formal presentations offer opportunities that written reports do not.

Developing a major presentation is much like writing a formal report, except that you need to adjust your technique to an oral channel. Speaking before a group offers certain opportunities:

■ **Immediate audience feedback.** You can transmit information, but you can also receive audience feedback without delay.

■ **Immediate modification to suit audience needs.** You can adjust both the content and the delivery of your message as you go along, in order to clarify or to be more compelling. Instead of simply expressing your ideas, you can draw ideas from your audience and then reach a mutually acceptable conclusion.

Table 12.1	Five Ways to Get Attention and Keep It
Use humor	Even though the subject of most business presentations is serious, including a light comment now and then can perk up the audience. Just be sure the humor is relevant to the presentation and not offensive to the audience.
Tell a story	Slice-of-life stories are naturally interesting and can be compelling. Be sure your story illustrates an important point.
Pass around a sample	Psychologists say that you can get people to remember your points by appealing to their senses. The best way to do so is to pass around a sample. If your company is in the textile business, let the audience handle some of your fabrics. If you sell chocolates, give everybody a taste.
Ask a question	Asking questions will get the audience actively involved in your presentation and, at the same time, will give you information about them and their needs.
State a startling statistic	People love details. If you can interject an interesting statistic, you can often wake up your audience.

- **Nonverbal reinforcement.** You also have the opportunity to use nonverbal cues to express your meaning and emphasize what's important.

Using an oral communication channel presents you with challenges you need not face in written reports. As you compose each part of your presentation, think about how you will face each challenge:

> Oral presentations offer challenges that written reports do not.

- **Maintaining control.** The more you expect to interact with your audience, the less control you'll have of the situation.
- **Helping your audience follow what you're saying.** Since listeners cannot refer back and forth to what has been or will be said, you must work harder to clarify where you're going and help them stay on track.
- **Shifting topics smoothly.** Halfway through your presentation, a comment from someone in the audience might force you to shift topics. If you anticipate such shifts, you can prepare for them as you compose your presentation.

As you develop your speech, think carefully about how to handle each part: introduction, body, and, close.

Introduction

A good introduction arouses the audience's interest in your topic, establishes your credibility, and prepares the audience for what will follow. That's a lot to pack into the first few minutes of your presentation. So, of the total time you allocate to writing your oral presentation, plan on spending a disproportionate amount on developing your introduction. In the introduction, you want to

> The introduction must capture attention, inspire confidence, and preview the contents.

- **Arouse audience interest.** Get a good start by capturing the audience's attention (several methods are listed in Table 12.1). If you are presenting to a small group, you can involve the audience by encouraging comments from listeners. However, when speaking to a large group, responding to comments can interrupt the flow of information, weaken your argument, and reduce your control of the situation. In that case, it's often best to ask people to hold questions until you're finished—be sure to allow ample time after your remarks.
- **Build your credibility.** Establish your credentials quickly—people will decide about you within a few minutes.[2] Building credibility is easy for a familiar, open-minded

audience. For strangers (especially skeptical ones), try letting someone else introduce you. If introducing yourself, keep your comments simple, and don't be afraid to mention your accomplishments:

> I'm Karen Whitney. I've worked in the telemarketing department for the past five years, specializing in small-business markets. Vice President John Barre asked me to talk to you about our telemarketing methods so that you'll have a better idea of how to get started.

■ **Preview your presentation.** Help your audience understand the structure and contents of your message. Give them cues to figure out how the main points of the message fit together. Summarize the main idea, identify the supporting points, and indicate the order in which you'll develop them. Establish the framework so that your audience will understand how the facts and figures are related to your main idea as you move into the body of your presentation.

Body

Simplify the body by covering no more than three or four main points.

The bulk of your speech or presentation is devoted to a discussion of the three or four main points in your outline. Use the same organizational patterns you would use in a letter, memo, or report, but keep things simple—limit the body to three or four main points. Make sure that your organization is clear and that your presentation holds the audience's attention.

Connecting Your Ideas　To show how ideas are related, a written report uses typographical and formatting clues: headings, paragraph indentions, white space, and lists. However, an oral presentation must rely on words to link various parts and ideas.

Help your audience follow your presentation by using clear transitions between sentences and paragraphs, as well as between major sections.

For the small links between sentences and paragraphs, use one or two transitional words: *therefore, because, in addition, in contrast, moreover, for example, consequently, nevertheless,* or *finally.* To link major sections of a presentation, use complete sentences or paragraphs, such as "Now that we've reviewed the problem, let's take a look at some solutions." Every time you shift topics, be sure to stress the connection between ideas. Summarize what's been said, then preview what's to come.

Emphasize your transitions by repeating key ideas, using gestures, changing your tone of voice, or introducing a visual aid.

The longer your presentation, the more important your transitions become. If you will be presenting many ideas, audience members may have trouble absorbing them and seeing the relationships among them. Your listeners need clear transitions to guide them to the most important points. Furthermore, they need transitions to pick up any ideas they may have missed. So by repeating key ideas in your transitions, you can compensate for lapses in your audience's attention. When you actually give your presentation, you might also want to call attention to the transitions by using gestures, changing your tone of voice, or introducing a visual aid (discussed later in this chapter).

Make a special effort to capture wandering attention.

Holding Your Audience's Attention　To communicate your points effectively, you must do more than connect your ideas with clear transitions. You also have to hold your audience's attention. Here are a few helpful tips for engaging an audience:

■ **Relate your subject to your audience's needs.** People are interested in things that affect them personally. Present every point in light of your audience's needs and values.

■ **Anticipate your audience's questions.** Try to anticipate as many questions as you can, and address these questions in the body of your presentation. You'll also want to prepare and reserve additional material to use during the question-and-answer period should the audience ask for greater detail.

■ **Use clear, vivid language.** People become bored when they don't understand the speaker. If your presentation will involve abstract ideas, plan to show how those abstractions connect with everyday life. Use familiar words, short sentences, and concrete examples.

■ **Explain the relationship between your subject and familiar ideas.** Show how your subject is related to ideas that audience members already understand, so that you give people a way to categorize and remember your points.[3]

- **Ask opinions or pause occasionally for questions or comments.** Getting audience feedback helps you determine whether your listeners have understood a key point. Feedback also gives your audience a change from listening to participating. Plan your pauses, even noting them in your outline so that you won't forget to pause once you're on stage.

Close

The close of a speech or presentation is almost as important as the beginning because audience attention peaks at this point. Plan to devote about 10 percent of your writing time to the ending. When developing your conclusion, begin by telling listeners that you're about to finish, so that they'll make one final effort to listen intently. Don't be afraid to sound obvious. Consider saying something such as "in conclusion" or "to sum it all up." You want people to know that this is the home stretch.

- **Restating your main points.** Repeat your main idea in the close. Emphasize what you want your audience to do or think, state the key motivating factor, and restate the three or four main supporting points. A few sentences are enough to refresh people's memories. One speaker ended a presentation by repeating his four specific recommendations and concluding with a memorable statement to motivate his audience:

  > We can all be proud of the way our company has grown. If we want to continue that growth, however, we will have to adjust our executive compensation program to reflect competitive practices. If we don't, our best people will look for opportunities elsewhere.
  >
  > In summary, our survey has shown that we need to do four things to improve executive compensation:
  >
  > - Increase the overall level of compensation
  > - Install a cash bonus program
  > - Offer a variety of stock-based incentives
  > - Improve our health insurance and pension benefits
  >
  > By making these improvements, we can help our company cross the threshold of growth into the major leagues.

- **Describing the next steps.** If listeners agree on an issue, say so in a sentence or two. If they don't agree, you might say, "We seem to have some disagreement on this issue," and be ready to suggest ways to resolve differences. If you expect listeners to take action, explain who is responsible for doing what. (You might present a slide listing each item with a completion date and the name of persons responsible.) Alert people to potential difficulties or pitfalls.
- **Ending on a strong note.** Make your final remarks encouraging and memorable. Conclude with a quote, a call to action, or some encouraging words. You might stress the benefits of action, express confidence in the listeners' ability to accomplish the work ahead, or end with a question or statement that leaves people thinking. Your final words give the audience a satisfied feeling of completeness. Don't introduce new ideas or alter the mood of the speech.

The close should leave a strong and lasting impression.

Step 3: Completing Speeches and Presentations

To complete your oral presentation, evaluate the content of your message and edit your remarks for clarity and conciseness—as you would for any business message. Develop any visual aids for your presentation, and coordinate them with your delivery. Finally, master the art of delivery through practice and preparation, by building your confidence, and by polishing the way you present visuals and handle questions.

Using Visual Aids in Your Speech or Presentation

Visual aids can improve the quality and impact of your oral presentation by creating interest, illustrating points that are difficult to explain in words alone, adding variety, and increasing the audience's ability to absorb and remember information. Visual aids help your audience; they are estimated to improve learning by 400 percent, because humans can process visuals 60,000 times faster than text.[4] Visual aids also help you as speaker; they help you remember the details of your message (no small feat in a lengthy presentation), and they improve your professional image (speakers who use visuals generally appear better prepared and more knowledgeable than other speakers).

Selecting the Right Type of Visual

To enhance oral presentations, you can choose from a variety of visual aids. Among the most popular types are overhead transparencies, electronic presentations, chalkboards and whiteboards, flip charts, and 35-millimeter slides:

- **Overhead transparency.** This piece of clear plastic contains text or a graphic. You show a transparency by placing it on the lit window of an overhead projector, which casts the image onto a large screen. You can create transparencies by hand, but you're more likely to use word-processing, page-layout, or presentation software. We sometimes refer to transparencies as slides because their content and design elements are so similar to electronic slides.

- **Electronic presentation.** This slide show is a series of electronic slides created and stored on computer. Using software such as Microsoft PowerPoint, Lotus Freelance Graphics, or Corel Draw!, you can incorporate text, photos, sound, video, graphics, and animation into your slides. You show these slides on a personal computer monitor, a special projector that puts the image of a computer monitor onto a large screen, or a liquid crystal display (LCD) projector.[5]

- **Chalkboard or whiteboard.** These writing surfaces are effective tools for recording points made during small-group brainstorming sessions. Because these visual aids are produced on the spot, they offer flexibility; however, they're too informal for some situations.

- **Flip chart.** These large sheets of paper are attached at the top like a tablet and can be propped on an easel so that you can flip the pages as you speak. With felt-tip markers, you can also record ideas generated during a discussion.

- **35-millimeter slide.** The content of a 35-millimeter slide may be text, graphics, or pictures. Slide presentations can create a polished, professional atmosphere, particularly if you're addressing a crowd and don't mind speaking in a darkened room. You will need to coordinate your slides with your speech and perhaps appoint someone to operate the projector.

- **Other visual aids.** Product or material samples help your audience experience your subject directly. Scale models represent objects conveniently. Audiotapes supplement a slide show or present a precisely worded message. Filmstrips and movies grab attention with color and movement. Television and videotapes show demonstrations, interviews, and other events. Also, filmstrips, movies, TV, and videos can stand alone (without a speaker) to communicate with dispersed audiences at various times.

The two most popular visual aids are overhead transparencies and electronic presentations. Even though these two visual aids differ in some features and delivery, both are a collection of slides that must be well written and well designed to be effective. Once the slides are created, they are either printed on clear plastic sheets (for overhead transparencies) or stored electronically and further embellished with multimedia effects (for electronic presentations). Both overhead transparencies and electronic slides have advantages and disadvantages, as Table 12.2 points out.

Table 12.2	Advantages and Disadvantages of Overhead Transparencies and Electronic Slides

Overhead Transparencies	Electronic Slides
Advantages	**Advantages**
• Slides are inexpensive and easy to create. You can prepare high-quality overheads using a computer and a high-resolution color inkjet or laser printer.	• Slides are easy to change in real time. You can change a graphic, add a bulleted phrase, even alter slide sequence with a simple click of the mouse.
• Slides are simple to use. They require little extra equipment to show: Most conference rooms or classrooms have overhead projectors.	• Slides make dazzling professional presentations. You can add animation, video clips, sound, hypertext, and other multimedia effects, as well as preprogram and automate the release of text and graphic elements.
• Slides can be projected in full daylight. Speakers can maintain eye contact with their listeners.	• Slides are easy to store, transport, and customize for different audiences.
• Slides can be altered during presentation. Speakers can use special markers to write on transparencies as they present information.	
Disadvantages	**Disadvantages**
• Slides must be replaced if content changes.	• Display equipment is expensive, can be complicated to use, and may not be available in all situations.
• Slides must be manually renumbered to add or remove a slide from the sequence.	• Most people spend too much time focusing on the technical components of a presentation, paying more attention to the animation and special effects than to the contents of each slide.
• Slides are fragile. They easily chip, flake, scratch, and tear. Protective frames of cardboard or plastic and transparent sleeves are costly and bulky to store and transport.	• Inexperienced presenters tend to use too many special effects, creating a visual feast of pictures and graphics that dazzle the audience but blur the key message.
• Overhead projectors can be noisy and difficult to talk over.	
• Slides must be aligned carefully (one at a time) on the overhead projector, limiting the speaker's ability to move freely about the room.	

Limiting the Number of Visuals

Even if you produce an outstanding set of slides, they'll do you no good if you can't complete your presentation in the allotted time. Having too many visuals can detract from your message. It forces you either to rush through a presentation or to skip visuals—some of which may be critical to your message.

Covering less information in a relaxed style is much better than covering too much information in a hurried and disorganized manner. Build enough time into your presentation for a smile, an anecdote, or further illustration of a point. Remember that audiences won't be angry if you let them out early, but they might be upset if you keep them late.

Gauging the correct number of visuals depends on the length of your presentation and the complexity of the subject matter. If you are using electronic slides, try to average one slide for every 90 seconds you speak. For a 30-minute presentation, you would create about 20 slides.[6] Of course, you may spend more time discussing some slides than others, so the best way to find the "right" number is to time your presentation as you practice.

Limit the number of slides to a few good ones.

Creating Effective Slides

Once you've planned out what a slide is going to say, organize the content as you would for any written message. Then compose and polish the written content before focusing on the slide's design elements.

Simplicity is the key to effective design. Since people cannot read and listen at the same time, your slides must be simple enough for the audience to understand in a moment or two. Therefore, keep content and graphics simple and readable, select design

Slides are most effective when they are simple.

Table 12.3	Color and Emotion	
Color	**Emotional Associations**	**Best Use**
	Peaceful, soothing, tranquil, cool, trusting	Background for electronic business presentations (usually dark blue): safe and conservative
	Neutral, Innocent, pure,	Font color of choice for most electronic business presentations with a dark background
	Warm, bright, cheerful, enthusiastic	Text bullets and subheadings with a dark background
	Losses in business, passion, danger, action, pain	Promote action or stimulate audience; seldom used as a background
	Money, growth, assertiveness, prosperity, envy, relaxation	Highlight and accent color

elements that enhance your message without overshadowing it, be consistent in your design selections, and use special effects selectively.

Color can increase the appeal and impact of your slides.

Choosing Color   Color is a critical design element. It grabs the viewer's attention, emphasizes important ideas, creates contrast, and isolates slide elements. Color can make your slides more attractive, lively, and professional (see Table 12.3). Indeed, color visuals can account for 60 percent of an audience's acceptance or rejection of an idea.[7] When choosing color, remember these important guidelines:

- **Use color to stimulate the right emotions.** If you wish to excite your audience, add some warm colors such as red and orange to your slides. If you wish to achieve a more relaxed and receptive environment, stick to blue.[8]
- **Be sensitive to cultural differences.** When creating slides for international audiences, remember that color may have a different meaning from culture to culture.
- **Limit color selections to a few complementary ones.** Avoid using too many colors in your slides. Also, remember that some colors work together better than others.
- **Use contrasting colors to increase readability.** For backgrounds, titles, and text, avoid choosing colors that are close in hue: yellow text on a white background, brown on green, blue on black, blue on purple, and so on.[9]
- **Adjust color choices to room light.** Since most electronic presentations are shown in a dark room, use dark colors such as blue for the background, a midrange of brightness for illustrations, and light colors for text. If you are showing overhead transparencies in well-lit rooms, reverse the colors: Use light colors for the background and dark colors for text.
- **Order colors from dark to light.** Dark colors appear heavier than light colors. So when assigning color to graphic elements, ordering them from dark to light makes it easier on viewers' eyes.[10]

Choosing Background Designs   A slide's background can silently persuade viewers to pay attention or encourage them to look the other way. Many companies hire professional graphic artists to develop a custom background design to be used in all company slides. These custom designs generally include a company logo and company colors.

Select a background design that fits with your message and your audience.

    If you're not using a company design, you have several options. Popular software programs such as Microsoft's PowerPoint come with a collection of professionally developed background designs. Some designs are effective for business presentations; others are too busy or too colorful to be used in business settings. You can also purchase collections of slide backgrounds over the Internet, obtain them from other software packages, or create your own.

FIGURE 12.4   PowerPoint's Predefined Layouts

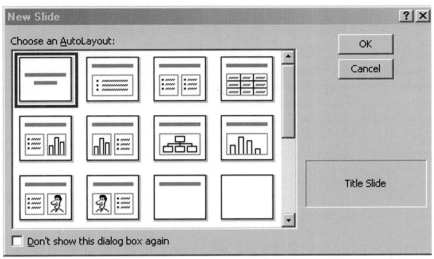

When designing a new slide for a presentation, beginning with one of PowerPoint's preformatted layouts can save you time and improve the consistency of your presentation.

Regardless of your source, be careful when choosing slide backgrounds. Avoid backgrounds whose heavy color, busy patterns, or strong graphics compete with your text. Choose a design that is simple, is appropriate for the presentation subject, and will appeal to the audience. Make sure that graphic elements such as borders and company logos repeat on every visual. Such consistency not only makes your slides easier to read but gives your presentation a clean, professional look. Another way to achieve design consistency is to use the layout templates that are included with most presentation software packages. As Figure 12.4 shows, each layout contains placeholders for specific slide elements such as a title, graphic art, or bulleted text.

Layout templates are easy to use.

Choosing Fonts and Type Styles   Most software programs offer an immense selection of fonts. However, even though decorative fonts appear attractive, few of them project well on screen. When selecting fonts and type styles for slides, follow these guidelines:

- Avoid script or decorative fonts.
- Limit your fonts to one or two per slide (if two fonts are used, reserve one for headings and the other for bulleted items).
- Use boldface type for electronic slides so that letters won't look washed out.
- Avoid italicized type because it is difficult to read when projected.
- Use both uppercase and lowercase letters, with extra white space between lines of text.

Bigger is not always better when it comes to type size. Large type can force text from one line to two and diminish the slide's white space. Use between 24- and 36-point type for electronic presentations, reserving the larger size for titles and the smaller size for bullet items. Headings of the same level of importance should use the same font, type size, and color. Once you've selected your fonts and type styles, test them for readability by viewing sample slides from a distance.

Test your font and typeface selections by viewing slides from the back of a room.

Adding Animation and Special Effects   Unlike transparencies, electronic slide shows can include a number of special effects, such as sound, animation, and video. You can even automate your program to move from one slide to the next without the speaker's intervention. The biggest challenge to overcome is the tendency to use too many of these features, which can include

Don't overdo special effects.

- **Transitions.** The way that one electronic slide replaces another on screen is called a *transition.* Effective transitions can make your presentation flow smoothly from slide to slide so that you keep your audience's attention. Most electronic software packages include a number of effective transition effects, such as blind, box, checkerboard, dissolve, wipe, fade, paintbrush, and split. Use the same transitions throughout your presentation.

- **Builds.** The way that text and graphics are released for viewing is called a *build*. You can make your bullet points appear one at a time, line by line, to draw audience attention to the point being discussed. The most basic build effects are flys (making an element appear to fly in) and dissolves (altering the intensity of an element's color as you discuss it while fading the other colors into the background). Use the same builds throughout your presentation.

- **Hyperlinks.** By coding text, graphics, or pictures with hypertext markup language, you can build interactivity into electronic slides. When you click on a slide's hyperlink with a mouse, you are taken to a different slide in your presentation, to other files on your computer, or even to a webpage on the Internet. Hyperlinks are a great tool for illustrating fine details without having to incorporate each detail into a slide.

Electronic presentation software can help you plan, write, and revise your slides. As Figure 12.5 shows, the *slide sorter view* lets you see a file's entire batch of slides at once,

FIGURE 12.5 Slide Sorter View

Examining thumbnails of slides on one screen is the best way to check the overall design of your final product. Note how each slide in this group looks uncluttered (not overburdened with text) and uses consistent colors and design elements.

making it relatively easy to add and delete slides, reposition slides, and check slides for design consistency. You can also use this view to preview animation and transition effects and experiment with design elements.

Slide sorter view makes it easier to check your slides for consistency and logical organization.

Creating Effective Handouts

Handouts are a terrific way to offer your audience additional material without over-loading your slides with information. Candidates for good handout material include the following:[11]

- **Complex charts and diagrams.** Charts and tables that are too unwieldy for the screen or that demand thorough analysis make good handouts. One common approach is to create a stripped-down version of a chart or graphic for the presentation slide and include a more detailed version in your handout.
- **Company reports.** In most cases lengthy research reports promise information over-load and are inappropriate for handouts. But photocopies of specific pages that high-light or underline relevant text are welcome material.
- **Magazine articles.** Magazine articles make good handout materials. They are easy to photocopy and they are already formatted in an easy-to-read layout. However, be sure to create quality copies. Nothing is more frustrating than an illegible handout.
- **Websites.** Lists of websites related to your topic are useful. In addition to providing the URL address, annotate each item with a one-or-two sentence summary of each site's content.
- **Copies of presentation slides.** In many cases, audiences like to have small print ver-sions of the slides used by the speaker (about three to a page) along with accompany-ing comments and blank lines for note-taking.

Good handouts keep the audience informed without overwhelming them with information.

Other good handout materials include brochures, pictures, outlines, and a copy of the presentation agenda.

Timing the distribution of handouts is a difficult decision. You must base that deci-sion on the content of your handouts, the nature of your presentation, and your personal preference. Some speakers distribute handout materials before the presentation begins. The downside of doing so is that it allows your audience to read ahead instead of listening to you. Other speakers simply advise the audience of the types of information they are including in handouts but delay distributing anything until they have finished speaking.

Handouts can be both useful and distracting.

To help you decide when to distribute handouts, how many visuals to include, or how to coordinate your slides with what you have to say, you'll need to practice delivering your speech.

Mastering the Art of Delivery

Giving a speech is quite different from preparing one. Once you've planned and written your presentation and developed your visuals, you're ready to begin practicing your deliv-ery. You have a variety of delivery methods to choose from, some of which are easier to handle than others:

- **Memorizing.** Unless you're a trained actor, avoid memorizing your speech, especially a long one. You're likely to forget your lines, and your speech will sound stilted. Besides, you'll often need to address audience questions during your speech, so you must be flexible enough to adjust your speech as you go. However, memorizing a quotation, an opening paragraph, or a few concluding remarks can bolster your confidence and strengthen your delivery.
- **Reading.** If you're delivering a technical or complex presentation, you may want to read it. Policy statements by government officials are sometimes read because the wording may be critical. If you choose to read your speech, practice enough so that you can still maintain eye contact with your audience. Triple-spaced copy, wide margins,

and large type will help. You might even want to include stage cues, such as *pause, raise hands, lower voice*.

■ **Speaking from notes.** Making a presentation with the help of an outline, note cards, or visual aids is probably the most effective and easiest delivery mode. This approach gives you something to refer to and still allows for eye contact and interaction with the audience. If your listeners look puzzled, you can expand on a point or rephrase it. (Generally, note cards are preferable to sheets of paper, because nervousness is easier to see in shaking sheets of paper.)

■ **Impromptu speaking.** You might have to give an impromptu, or unrehearsed, speech if you're called on to speak unexpectedly or if you've agreed to speak but neglected to prepare your remarks. Avoid speaking unprepared unless you've spoken countless times on the same topic or are an extremely good public speaker. When you're asked to speak "off the cuff," take a moment to think through what you'll say. Then avoid the temptation to ramble.

Prepare to Speak

Regardless of which delivery mode you use, be sure that you're thoroughly familiar with your subject. Knowing what you're talking about is the best way to build your self-confidence. Also, practicing helps keep you on track, helps you maintain a conversational tone with your audience, and boosts your confidence and composure. Practicing in front of a mirror is always a good idea. Try to visualize the room filled with listeners. Put your talk on tape to check the sound of your voice, as well as your timing, phrasing, and emphasis. If possible, rehearse on videotape to see yourself as your audience will. If you're concerned about the content of your presentation and the effectiveness of your slides, nothing beats practicing in front of people who are willing to stop you when they don't understand your message or when they need you to clarify a point on your slide.

In addition to knowing your material and practicing your delivery, check the location of your presentation in advance. Make sure the room is ready and that you will have everything you need. Check the seating arrangements to ensure they're appropriate for your needs. If you want audience members to sit at tables, be sure tables are available. Check for any outlets you'll need for projection equipment or a microphone. Locate light switches and dimmers. If you need a flip-chart easel or a chalkboard, be sure it's on hand. Check for chalk, an eraser, a pointer, extension cords, and any other small but crucial items you might need.

Also, make sure you're prepared to address audiences from other cultures. You may need to adapt the content of your presentation. Be sure to consider any cultural differences in appearance, mannerisms, and other speaking customs. Find out whether any changes are necessary for a specific audience or a particular occasion.

Overcome Anxiety and Stage Fright

If you're nervous about facing an audience and experience stage fright, you're not alone. Even speakers with years of experience feel some anxiety about getting up in front of an audience. Although you might not be able to make your nervous feelings disappear, you can learn to cope with your anxiety.

Feeling More Confident   Nervousness shows that you care about your audience, your topic, and the occasion. If your palms get wet or your mouth goes dry, don't think of nerves, think of excitement. Such stimulation can give you the extra energy you need to make your presentation sparkle. Here are some ways to become a more confident speaker:[12]

■ **Prepare more material than necessary.** Combined with a genuine interest in your topic, extra knowledge will reduce your anxiety.

■ **Rehearse.** The more familiar you are with your material, the less panic you'll feel.

■ **Think positively.** See yourself as polished and professional, and your audience will too.

- **Visualize your success.** Use the few minutes before you actually begin speaking to tell yourself you're on and you're ready.
- **Take a few deep breaths.** Before you begin to speak, remember that your audience is silently wishing you success.
- **Be ready.** Have your first sentence memorized and on the tip of your tongue.
- **Be comfortable.** If your throat is dry, drink some water.
- **Don't panic.** If you feel that you're losing your audience during your speech, try to pull them back by involving them in the action; ask for their opinions or pause for questions.
- **Keep going.** Things usually get better as you go.
- **Focus on your message and audience.** Perhaps the best way to feel more confident is to focus outside yourself. If you're busy thinking about your subject and observing your audience's response, you'll tend to forget your fears.

Appearing More Confident   As you practice delivering your presentation, try to be aware of the nonverbal signals you're transmitting. Regardless of how you feel inside, your effectiveness greatly depends on how you look and sound.

Well-delivered presentations start with your first minute at the podium, so don't rush. As you approach the speaker's lectern, walk slowly, breathe deeply, and stand up straight. Face your audience, adjust the microphone, count to three slowly, and then survey the room. When you find a friendly face, make eye contact and smile. Count to three again and begin your presentation.[13] If you are nervous, this slow, controlled beginning will help you establish rapport and appear more confident.

Don't rush the opening.

Be particularly careful to practice maintaining eye contact with your audience. You'll pick out several people positioned around the room, and shift your gaze from one to another. Looking directly at your listeners will make you appear sincere, confident, and trustworthy. It also helps you get an idea of the impression you're creating.

Use eye contact, posture, gestures, and voice to convey an aura of mastery and to keep your audience's attention.

Your posture is also important in projecting more confidence. Stand tall, with your weight on both feet and your shoulders back. Avoid gripping the lectern. In fact, practice stepping out from behind the lectern to help your audience feel more comfortable with you and to express your own comfort and confidence in what you're saying. Use your hands to emphasize your remarks with appropriate gestures. Meanwhile, vary your facial expressions to make the message more dynamic.

Finally, think about the sound of your voice. Studies indicate that people who speak with lower vocal tones at a slightly faster than average rate are perceived as being more credible.[14] Practice speaking in a normal, conversational tone but with enough volume for everyone to hear you. Try to sound poised and confident, varying your pitch and speaking rate to add emphasis. Don't ramble. Use silence instead of meaningless filler words such as *um, you know, okay,* and *like.* Silence adds dramatic punch and gives the audience time to think about the message. Remember, speak clearly and crisply, articulating all the syllables, and sound enthusiastic about what you're saying.

Present Visuals Effectively

When practicing your presentation, run through it about five times using your visuals. Your credibility is dramatically enhanced when you move seamlessly through your presentation.

Speaking Without Reading   The most common mistake people make when delivering a presentation is reading their slides. When you read to audience members, you lose contact with them. As your voice loses its inflection, listeners lose interest and eventually stop paying attention. Plus, listeners expect you to add valuable information not included on the slides. You must know enough about the subject of your presentation to elaborate on your visuals, so do your research.

Don't read your slides to the audience.

As you practice, try not to be so dependent on your slides that you're unable to function without them. Some people can deliver a perfect presentation without notes. But for those who require notes, electronic software gives you an added advantage. Speaker's notes

Use speaker's notes to jog your memory.

FIGURE 12.6   Speaker's Notes

Figure 12.6a Speaker's notes

Figure 12.6b Corresponding slide

Speaker's notes, such as the ones displayed in Figure 12.6a, are an added benefit of using electronic presentations. The notes are displayed only on the presenter's screen while the corresponding slide, Figure 12.6b, is presented to the audience.

(as shown in Figure 12.6a) are a helpful tool included with most popular electronic presentation software packages. You can display these notes along with a scaled-down version of your slide (as shown in Figure 12.6b) on a computer screen so that only you can see the notes. As with visuals, don't read your speaker's notes aloud word for word. Instead, use them to list important facts or to remind yourself of comments you should make as you present the slide. For instance, you might include a note such as "Explain the impact of last year's bad weather on sales."

Introducing Visuals   All visual aids must be properly introduced. Too many speakers show a visual first and then introduce it. Introduce the next visual aid before you show it. State your transition out loud:

> "We can get started with this new program by introducing these policies . . . "

> "The next segment of my presentation discusses . . ."

> "The three most significant issues facing our company are . . ."

Also avoid referring to a slide in your transitional comments. For instance, don't say "The next slide illustrates . . ." Instead, match your words to the slide and let the audience make the proper connection.

If you're using overhead transparencies, the best approach is to introduce the next overhead as you remove the old one and position the new one on the projector. Immediately cover all but the first bulleted phrase with a sheet of paper to prevent the audience from reading ahead. Then step aside to give the audience about five seconds to look it over before you start discussing it. As you advance through your discussion, you can move the paper down the transparency to uncover the next bullet, waiting a few seconds for the audience to find your point of reference. When you are finished using the transparency, it's often a good idea to cover it until you're ready to introduce a new slide. Keep in mind that placing overhead transparencies on a projector takes a bit more time than clicking a mouse to advance electronic slides, so you may be introducing a new topic while the old one is still displayed. Don't be concerned. The audience will probably have little interest in reading the old transparency once your comments move forward.[15]

If you are using electronic slides, the best approach is to introduce the slide before you show it and then give the audience a few seconds to view the title and design elements. With electronic slides, you have more control over the release of information. For instance, you can release bulleted points or sections of a graph as you discuss them. This

Introduce your slides before you show them.

Practice placing overhead transparencies on a projector so it becomes second nature.

With electronic slides, you are not tied to the projector or front of the room.

control gives you more flexibility to move about the room. Take advantage of this benefit. Moving around can increase audience involvement and enhance your impact. You may even want to invest in a mouse with an extended cord or a battery-operated remote mouse to maximize your freedom to walk around.

If you're using a pointer, keep in mind that it's a tool meant to guide the audience to a specific part of a visual. It is not a riding crop, conductor's baton, leg scratcher, or walking stick. Use the pointer only at the time you need it, then fold it and remove it from sight. If you are using a laser pointer that puts a focused dot of light on the desired part of your visual, don't overdo it. A laser pointer is an excellent tool if used judiciously, but in the hands of the overzealous presenter, it can become a distraction.[16]

Handle Questions Responsively

The question-and-answer period is one of the most important parts of an oral presentation. Questions give you a chance to obtain important information and feedback, to emphasize points you made earlier, to work in material that didn't fit into the formal presentation, and to overcome audience resistance by building enthusiasm for your point of view. Without questions, you might just as well write a report.

Many speakers do well delivering their oral presentation, only to falter during the question-and-answer period. But if you spend time anticipating these questions, you'll be ready with answers. Some experts recommend that you hold back some dramatic statistics as ammunition for the question-and-answer session.[17] If your message is unpopular, you should also be prepared for hostile questions. Treat them as legitimate requests for information. Maintaining your professionalism will improve your credibility. Follow these guidelines to ensure an effective question-and-answer period:

- **Focus on the questioner.** Pay attention to body language and facial expression to determine what the question really means. Nod your head in acknowledgment, and repeat the question aloud to confirm your understanding and ensure that everyone has heard it. If a question is vague, ask for clarification before giving a simple, direct answer. If asked to choose between two alternatives, don't feel you must. Offer your own choice if it makes more sense.[18]

- **Respond appropriately.** Answer the question you're asked. Don't sidestep it, ignore it, or laugh it off. If an adequate answer would take too long, say, "I'm sorry, we don't have time to explore that issue right now, but if you'll see me after the presentation, I'll be happy to discuss it with you." If you don't know the answer, don't pretend to. Say, "I don't have those figures. I'll get them for you as quickly as possible."

- **Maintain control of the situation.** Prevent anyone from monopolizing this period. State a time or question limit per person. Asking people to identify themselves before they speak helps them behave themselves.[19] Avoid lengthy debate. You might respond with a brief answer before moving on to the next questioner. Or you might admit that you and the questioner have different opinions and offer to get back to the questioner once you've done more research.[20]

- **Maintain self-control.** If a question flusters or angers you, answer honestly but stay cool. Maintain eye contact, answer the question as well as you can, and try not to show your feelings. Don't get into an argument. Defuse hostility by paraphrasing the question and asking the questioner to confirm that you've understood it correctly. Break long, complicated questions into parts. Respond accurately and unemotionally; then move on.

- **Motivate questions.** If listeners are too timid or hostile to ask questions, consider planting your own. If a friend or the event organizer starts off, others will join in. Or ask a question yourself: "Would you like to know more about . . ." If someone answers, act as if the question came from that person. When all else fails, say something like "I know from experience that most questions are asked after the question period. So I'll be around afterward to talk."[21]

- **Signal the end of your speech.** When your allotted time is up, halt the question-and-answer session, even if people still want to talk. Say, "Our time is almost up. Let's have one last question." After you reply, summarize the main idea of the presentation and

Be ready with answers so that you can
- Emphasize your most important points
- Refer to material that didn't fit in the formal presentation
- Overcome audience resistance

Answer questions effectively by
- Using body language to show you're listening
- Keeping answers short and to the point
- Stating some ground rules to maintain control
- Responding unemotionally
- Helping listeners ask you questions

Document Makeover

Improve This Speech

To practice correcting drafts of actual documents, visit www.prenhall.com/onekey on the web. Click "Document Makeovers," then click Chapter 12. You will find a speech that contains problems and errors relating to what you've learned in this chapter about preparing effective oral presentations. Use the Final Draft decision tool to create an improved version of this speech. Check the message for effective choices in scope, style, opening, use of transitions, and closing.

thank people for their attention. Conclude the way you began, by looking around the room and making eye contact. Then gather your notes and leave the podium, shoulders straight, head up.

Reviewing Key Points

This chapter discusses giving business speeches and oral presentations. You have learned to plan your speeches and presentations by studying your purpose and profiling your audience. The chapter talks about how to organize and compose your presentation, and how to develop the introduction, body, and close.

The chapter discusses using visual aids in oral presentations and talks about the pros and cons of overhead transparencies and electronic slides. You have learned how to create effective slides by choosing color, background design, fonts, and typestyles. This chapter also talks about mastering the art of delivery. You have learned how to get ready to speak, overcome anxiety, present visuals effectively, and handle questions responsively.

The next chapter discusses searching for employment. You will learn how to seek a job in today's changing workplace. You will also learn how to prepare your résumé, and you'll study how to prepare application letters.

Test Your Knowledge

1. What are the four basic purposes for giving an oral presentation?

2. Why is simplicity of organization important in oral communication?

3. What three goals should you accomplish during the introduction of an oral presentation?

4. How can a speaker get and keep the audience's attention?

5. What three tasks should you accomplish in the close of your presentation?

6. When creating slides for oral presentations, which should you do first: select the background design for your slides or write your bulleted phrases? Explain your answer.

7. What is the advantage of practicing an oral presentation with visual aids before a live audience?

8. As a speaker, what nonverbal signals can you send to appear more confident?

9. When should you introduce slides?

10. What can speakers do to maintain control during the question-and-answer period of a presentation?

Apply Your Knowledge

1. Why is it important to limit the scope of oral presentations?

2. How might the audience's attitude affect the amount of audience interaction during or after a presentation? Explain your answer.

3. If you were giving an oral presentation on the performance of a company product, what three attention-getters might you use to enliven your talk?

4. From the speaker's perspective, what are the advantages and disadvantages of responding to questions from the audience throughout an oral presentation, rather than just afterward? From the listener's perspective, which approach would you prefer? Why?

5. **Ethical Choices**   How can you use design elements and special effects to persuade an audience? Is it ethical to do so?

Practice Your Knowledge

Activities

For live links to all websites discussed in this chapter, visit this text's website at www. prenhall.com/bovee. Just log on, select Chapter 12, and click on "Featured Websites." Locate the page or the URL related to the material in the text.

1. **Analyze This Document**   Pick a speech from *Vital Speeches of the Day,* a publication containing recent speeches on timely and topical subjects. As an alternative, select a speech from an online source such as the speech archives of NASA (www.nasa.gov) or AT&T (go to www.att.com/speeches and enter "speeches" in the search window to find the most recent speeches by AT&T executives.) Examine both the introduction and the close; then analyze how these two sections work together to emphasize the main idea. What action does the speaker want the audience to take? Next, identify the transitional sentences or phrases that clarify the speech's structure for the listener, especially those that help the speaker shift between supporting points. Using these transitions as clues, list the main message and supporting points; then indicate how each transitional phrase links the current supporting point to the succeeding one. Now, prepare a brief (two- to three-minute) oral presentation summarizing your analysis for your class.

2. **Internet**   For many years, Toastmasters has been dedicated to helping its members give speeches. Instruction, good speakers as models, and practice sessions aim to teach members to convey information in lively and informative ways. Visit the

Toastmasters website at www.toastmasters.org, and carefully review the linked pages about listening, speaking, voice, and body. Evaluate the information and outline a three-minute presentation to your class telling why Toastmasters and its website would or would not help you and your classmates write and deliver an effective speech.

3. **Mastering Delivery: Analysis** Attend a presentation at your school or in your town, or watch a speech on television. Categorize the speech as one that motivates or entertains, one that informs or analyzes, or one that persuades or urges collaboration. Then compare the speaker's delivery with the concepts presented in this chapter. Write a two-page report analyzing the speaker's performance and suggesting improvements.

4. **Mastering Delivery: Nonverbal Signals** Observe and analyze the delivery of a speaker in a school, work, or other setting. What type of delivery did the speaker use? Was this delivery appropriate for the occasion? What nonverbal signals did the speaker use to emphasize key points? Were these signals effective? Which nonverbal signals would you suggest to further enhance the delivery of this oral presentation—and why?

5. **Ethical Choices** Think again about the oral presentation you observed and analyzed in Activity 4 above. How could the speaker have used nonverbal signals to unethically manipulate the audience's attitudes or actions?

6. **Teamwork** You've been asked to give an informative 10-minute talk on vacation opportunities in your home state. Draft your introduction, which should last no more than 2 minutes. Then pair off with a classmate and analyze each other's introductions. How well do these two introductions arouse the audience's interest, build credibility, and preview the presentation? Suggest how these introductions might be improved.

7. **Completing Oral Presentations: Self-Assessment** How good are you at planning, writing, and delivering oral presentations? Rate yourself on each of the following elements of the oral presentation process. Then examine your ratings to identify where you are strongest and where you can improve, using the tips in this chapter.

Elements of the Presentation Process	Always	Frequently	Occasionally	Never
1. I start by defining my purpose.	_____	_____	_____	_____
2. I analyze my audience before writing an oral presentation.	_____	_____	_____	_____
3. I match my presentation length to the allotted time.	_____	_____	_____	_____
4. I begin my oral presentations with an attention-getting introduction.	_____	_____	_____	_____
5. I look for ways to build credibility as a speaker.	_____	_____	_____	_____
6. I cover only a few main points in the body of my presentation.	_____	_____	_____	_____
7. I use transitions to help listeners follow my ideas.	_____	_____	_____	_____
8. I review main points and describe next steps in the close.	_____	_____	_____	_____
9. I practice my presentation beforehand.	_____	_____	_____	_____
10. I prepare in advance for questions and objections.	_____	_____	_____	_____
11. I conclude oral presentations by summarizing my main idea.	_____	_____	_____	_____

8. Delivering Oral Presentations: Possible Topics   Perhaps one of the following topics interests you:

    a. What I expect to learn in this course.

    b. Past public speaking experiences: the good, the bad, and the ugly.

    c. I would be good at teaching _____.

    d. I am afraid of _____.

    e. It's easy for me to _____.

    f. I get angry when _____.

    g. I am happiest when I _____.

    h. People would be surprised if they knew that I _____.

    i. My favorite older person.

    j. My favorite charity.

    k. My favorite place.

    l. My favorite sport.

    m. My favorite store.

    n. My favorite television show.

    o. The town you live in suffers from a great deal of juvenile vandalism. Explain to a group of community members why juvenile recreational facilities should be built instead of a juvenile detention complex.

    p. You are speaking to the Humane Society. Support or oppose the use of animals for medical research purposes.

    q. You are talking to civic leaders of your community. Try to convince them to build an art gallery.

    r. You are speaking to a first-grade class at an elementary school. Explain why they should brush their teeth after meals.

    s. You are speaking to a group of traveling salespeople. Convince them that they should wear their seatbelts while driving.

    t. You are speaking to a group of elderly people. Convince them to adopt an exercise program.

    u. Environmental concerns (energy conservation, global warming, pollution, population control, rare species and wildlife extinction, world hunger, etc.).

    v. Financial issues (banking, investing, financial issues in the 1990s, the challenges faced by two-income families, etc.).

    w. Government (domestic policy, foreign policy, social security taxes, welfare, etc.).

    x. Information age and computers (electronic mail, Internet, technophobes, voice mail, etc.).

    y. Politics (Democrats and Republicans, elections, legislative bodies and legislation, the presidency, etc.).

    z. Sports (amateur and professional, baseball, football, golf, hang gliding, hockey, rock climbing, tennis, etc.).

Your task: Choose a topic and prepare a brief presentation (5–10 minutes) to be given before your class.

Expand Your Knowledge

Exploring the Best of the Web

Speak with Flair   The Virtual Presentation Assistant, www. ukans.edu/cwis/units/coms2/vpa/vpa.htm, offers abundant resources with related links to other websites that contain useful articles, reviews, or supplemental materials for planning presentations. You can also connect to popular media and library pages with worldwide research information. You'll find examples of presentation types, suggestions for selecting and focusing your topic, tips on audience analysis, delivery, use of visual aids, and various other guidelines to help you prepare and deliver an effective oral presentation. Check out this site, then answer the following questions:

Exercises

1. Suppose you have been asked to prepare an oral presentation on a business issue currently in the news. How could you use what you've discovered at the VPA site to help you select a topic? How could you use this site to find additional information or supplementary materials related to your topic?

2. According to this website, what factors should you consider when analyzing your audience?

3. What topics or information will entice you to return to this site or its links? (If you don't find the Virtual Presentation Assistant useful, explain why.)

Exploring the Web on Your Own

Review these chapter-related websites on your own to enhance your oral presentation skills and knowledge.

1. Visit Abraham Lincoln Online, showcase.netins.net/web/creative/Lincoln, to retrieve some of President Lincoln's classic speeches. Not only can you see examples of great writing, but you can also see how speechwriting has changed in the past century and a half.

2. Visit the Advanced Public Speaking Institute, at www.public-speaking.org, and learn how to be the best public speaker you can be.

3. Learn to prepare, write, and polish your oral presentations at SpeechTips.com, www.speechtips.com.

Learn Interactively

Interactive Study Guide

Go to the Companion Website at www.prenhall.com/bovee. For Chapter 12, take advantage of the interactive "Study Guide" to test your knowledge of the chapter. Get instant feedback on whether you need additional studying. Also, visit this site's "Study Hall," where you'll find an abundance of valuable resources that will help you succeed in this course.

Peak Performance Grammar and Mechanics

To improve your skill with mechanics, visit www.prenhall.com/onekey, click "Peak Performance Grammar and Mechanics," and then click "Mechanics of Style." Take the Pretest to determine whether you have any weak areas. Then review those areas in the Refresher Course. Take the Follow-Up Test to check your grasp of mechanics. For an extra challenge or advanced practice, take the Advanced Test. Finally, for additional reinforcement in capitals, italics, and abbreviations, go to the "Improve Your Grammar, Mechanics, and Usage" section that follows, and complete the "Level 1: Self-Assessment" exercises.

Improve Your Grammar, Mechanics, and Usage

Level 1: Self-Assessment—Capitals and Abbreviations

Review Sections 3.1 and 3.2 in the Handbook of Grammar, Mechanics, and Usage, and then look at the following 15 items.

In items 1–15, indicate proper capitalization by underlining appropriate letters with three underscores. Circle abbreviations that should be spelled out, and insert abbreviations where appropriate.

1. Dr. paul hansen is joining our staff.

2. New caressa skin cream should be in a position to dominate that market.

3. Send this report to mister h. k. danforth, rural route 1, warrensburg, new york 12885.

4. You are responsible for training my new assistant to operate the xerox machine.

5. She received her master of business administration degree from the university of michigan.

6. The building is located on the corner of madison and center streets.

7. Call me at 8 tomorrow morning, pacific standard time, and I'll have the information you need.

8. When jones becomes ceo next month, we'll need your input asap.

9. Address it to art bowers, chief of production.

10. Please rsvp to sony corp. just as soon as you know your schedule.

11. The data-processing department will begin work on feb. 2, just one wk. from today.

12. You are to meet him on friday at the un building in nyc.

13. Whenever you can come, professor, our employees will greatly enjoy your presentation.

14. At 50 per box, our std. contract forms are $9 a box, and our warranty forms are $7.95 a box.

15. We plan to establish a sales office on the west coast.

Level 2: Workplace Applications

The following items contain numerous errors in grammar, capitalization, punctuation, abbreviation, number style, word division, and vocabulary. Rewrite each sentence in the space provided, correcting all errors. Write *C* in the space after any sentence that is already correct.

1. Mc'Donalds and Sears' have partnered with the television program, "Its Showtime At The Apollo." To offer talented kids the opportunity too appear on national television.

2. Tiffany & Co., the internationally-renowned jeweler and specialty retailer plan to open a 5000 square feet store in Walnut Creek, CA next year.

3. If none of the solutions seem satisfying, pick the more easier one.

4. Ken Baker, the west coast bureau chief for Us magazine, will be responsible for overseeing all of magazine reporting in Hollywood, conducting high profile, celebrity interviews, for identifying news stories, and assist in the generation of cover concepts.

5. With experience managing numerous enthusiast brands, including "Kawasaki" and "Skechers," Juxt Interactive are cementing their role as a leader in strategic, integrated campaigns.

6. You're message, tone, and product positioning has to be right on to be excepted and successful.

7. As I begun to put the team together, it became apparent to myself that my idea was ahead of it's time.

8. Many think that the primary market for newspapers are the readers, however advertisers generate the majority of revenues.

9. REIs new website, www.REI-outlet.com, features items that are not available at REI's physical stores, catalog, or main website.

10. The company's C.E.O., who we had saw at the awards dinner wednesday night, was fired the next day.

11. A designer of high priced purses such as Kate Spade or Louis Vitton generally limit distribution to exclusive boutiques or high end retail stores: such as Neiman-Marcus.

12. There is many indications that an economic recovery is underway, and will continue to stabilize and build however modestly.

13. We bought the equipment at a second hand store which turned out to be shoddy and defective.

14. Experts site 2 principle reasons for Webvan's failure; consumer resistance and over expansion.

15. Implementation of the over time hours guidelines will be carried out by the Human Resources Staff members.

Level 3: Document Critique

The following document may contain errors in grammar, punctuation, capitalization, abbreviation, number style, vocabulary, and spelling. You may also find problems with organization, format, and word use. Correct all errors using standard proofreading marks (see Appendix C).

Date: Thu, 25 April, 2005

From: Steve Pendergrass <spender@manchcc.edu>

To: Gregory Hansford <gregory.hansford@manchcc.edu>

CC:

BCC:

Attached:

Subject: Library Hours

Dear Mr. Hansford,

There is a favorite place in which Manchester students study on our campus: the library because of the quiet atmosphere excellent resources, and helpful staff. With a ajustment in library hours there assets could be taken advantage of by more students.

In an informal survey of the students in my English class, a desire for the library to be open more hours on the weekends became evident. Many students find weekends best for researching term papers: because that's when large blocks of time can be found in their schedules.

I'd like to sight several reasons for the change I am about to propose to encourage your interest and desire for my suggestion. Understandable, librarians need a day off. Perhaps students and librarians could both be accomodated if the library closed at five p.m. on Friday night. Friday night is the time most students like to relax and attend sports events or parties. The libary could then be open on Saturdays from ten a.m. until 4:30 p.m. To make this arrangement fair to librarians; perhaps their schedules could be staggered so that nobody would have to work every Saturday or those scheduled to work on Saturdays could be given Mondays or Fridays off.

Consider implementing this new schedule this Fall. Another much-appreciated service for students will be performed if you do this.

Sincerely: Steve Pendergrass, student

Nerves: The Secret Weapon of Polished Presenters

What do Barbra Streisand, Liza Minnelli, and Donny Osmond have in common? These professional performers and many others admit to being nervous about public speaking. If the pros can feel fear, it's no wonder beginners are sometimes scared speechless. Survey after survey has confirmed that public speaking is the number one fear in the United States—so if you're anxious about stepping in front of an audience, you're not alone.

Nervousness might make your hands tremble, your knees knock, your mouth feel dry, or your stomach churn. As bad as these symptoms can be, remember that nerves are a good indicator of your concern for the occasion, your subject, and your audience. If you didn't care, you wouldn't be anxious. A speaker who cares is more likely to seek out every method of communicating with the audience.

Remember also that you'll feel a little less nervous with every oral presentation. Once you see how the audience responds to your first attempt, you'll realize that you did better than you feared you would. People in the audience want you to succeed; they're interested in learning from you or being inspired by your words, not in straining to hear the sound of your knees knocking together.

You can harness your nerves by focusing on what you want to accomplish. In the words of actress Carol Channing, "I don't call it nervousness—I prefer to call it concentration." Like Channing, you can concentrate your efforts on making that all-important connection with your audience. But don't make the mistake of expecting perfection. Put that nervous energy into planning, preparing, and practicing. Turn your negative fears into positive energy, and you'll be better equipped to face your audience the first time and every time.

You might start by listing statements that describe each of your fears: (1) the behavior that will show your fear, (2) the effect this behavior will have, and (3) the action you can take to change the behavior and get rid of the fear. For example, if you're afraid that you won't be as good as you would like to be, you might say, "I'll leave out parts of my speech or act nervous (behavior), so I won't impress the audience or get my message across (effect)." The solution is to make the speech your own before addressing your audience (action). Practice, practice, practice. Tape-record your speech or videotape yourself and look for strengths and weaknesses. Practice out loud until you've mastered the speech and it's yours. If you like your speech, your audience will like it, and you'll get your message across.

Or perhaps you're saying something like "I'll look scared (behavior), and the audience will sense my nervousness and will snicker and make fun of me (effect)." The solution is to act confident—even if you don't feel it (action). Listeners want you to succeed, and they can't see what's happening inside you. Don't apologize for anything. If you make a mistake, don't start over; just keep going. Then enjoy the applause—your moment in the spotlight.

Applications for Success

Learn how to overcome your fear of public speaking by visiting www.businessknowhow.com/manage/fearspeak.htm, www.stresscure.com/jobstress/speak.html, and www.pe2000.com/pho-speaking.htm.

Do the following:

1. Think of any lectures or presentations you've recently attended. Have you ever noticed a speaker's level of anxiety? Did any speakers succeed in overcoming this fear? Describe the ways a particular speaker visibly conquered his or her nervousness. If that speaker failed, what techniques might have helped?
2. As a member of the audience, what can you do to help a speaker overcome his or her nervousness? Briefly explain.
3. Using the "behavior-effect-action" structure, list one of your fears and show how you plan to counter it in your next speech.

Employment Messages

Unit 5

13

Searching for Employment and Preparing Employment Messages

Learning Objectives

After studying this chapter, you will be able to

1 Discuss three results of how today's constantly changing workplace is affecting the employment-search process

2 Explain three things you can do to help you adapt to the changing workplace

3 Summarize six tasks you can do before and during your job search

4 Discuss how to choose the appropriate résumé organization, and list the advantages or disadvantages of the three options

5 List the major elements to include in a traditional résumé

6 Describe what you can do to adapt your résumé to a scannable format

7 Define the purpose of application letters, and explain how to apply the AIDA organizational approach to them

Recreational Equipment Incorporated (REI) is a national outdoor gear and clothing cooperative. The company is listed by *Fortune* magazine as one of the 100 best places to work in the United States, and as employment manager, Doug Halm receives over 400 résumés each month. "Someone who is a leader, who worked after school, and who understands teamwork may do better than someone who got good grades but didn't do these things," says Halm. Of course, even if you have all these attributes, you won't get a call from Halm if your résumé doesn't look professional. But the best résumés can't say all there is to know about a person's qualifications. The application letter gives you the chance to say why you want the job and why you would be good for the job. It fills in the blanks and it answers questions that your résumé might create.[1]

Building Toward a Career

As Doug Halm will tell you, getting the job that's right for you takes more than sending out a few résumés and application letters. Before entering the workplace, you need to learn as much as you can about your capabilities and the job marketplace.

Understanding Today's Changing Workplace

The workplace today is changing constantly.[2] The attitudes and expectations of both employers and employees are being affected not only by globalization, technology, diversity, and teams but also by deregulation, shareholder activism, corporate downsizing, mergers and acquisitions, outsourcing, and entrepreneurialism (people starting their own business or buying a franchise).[3] The results of constant change are threefold:

- **How often people look for work.** Rather than looking for lifelong employees, many employers now hire temporary workers and consultants on a project-by-project basis. Likewise, rather than staying with one employer for their entire career, growing numbers of employees are moving from company to company.

- **Where people find work.** Fewer jobs are being created by large companies. One expert predicts that soon 80 percent of the labor force will be working for firms employing fewer than 200 people. Moreover, self-employment seems to be an increasingly attractive option for many former employees.[4]

- **The type of people who find work.** Employers today are looking for people who are able and willing to adapt to diverse situations and who continue to learn throughout their careers. Companies want team players with strong work records, leaders who are versatile, and employees with diversified skills and varied job experience.[5] Plus, most employers expect employees to be sensitive to intercultural differences.[6]

Numerous forces are changing today's workplace.

Adapting to the Changing Workplace

Before you limit your employment search to a particular industry or job, do some advance preparation. Analyze what you have to offer, what you hope to get from your work, and how you can make yourself more valuable to potential employers. This preliminary analysis will help you identify employers who are likely to want you and vice versa.

Learn What You Have to Offer

When seeking employment, you must tell people about yourself, about who you are. So you need to know what talents and skills you have. You'll need to explain how these skills will benefit potential employers. Follow these guidelines:

To determine what you have to offer, carefully examine your functional skills, your education and experience, and your personality traits.

- **Jot down 10 achievements you're proud of.** Did you learn to ski, take a prize-winning photo, tutor a child, edit your school paper? Think about what skills these achievements demanded (leadership skills, speaking ability, and artistic talent may have helped you coordinate a winning presentation to your school's administration). You'll begin to recognize a pattern of skills, many of which might be valuable to potential employers.

- **Look at your educational preparation, work experience, and extracurricular activities.** What do your knowledge and experience qualify you to do? What have you learned from volunteer work or class projects that could benefit you on the job? Have you held any offices, won any awards or scholarships, mastered a second language?

- **Take stock of your personal characteristics.** Are you aggressive, a born leader? Or would you rather follow? Are you outgoing, articulate, great with people? Or do you prefer working alone? Make a list of what you believe are your four or five most important qualities. Ask a relative or friend to rate your traits as well.

Your college placement office may be able to administer a variety of tests to help you identify interests, aptitudes, and personality traits. These tests won't reveal your "perfect" job, but they'll help you focus on the types of work best suited to your personality.

Decide What You Want to Do

When deciding what you want to do, envision your ideal day at work: your activities, independence, salary, career goals, environment, location, position, and relationships.

Knowing what you *can* do is one thing. Knowing what you *want* to do is another. Don't lose sight of your own values. Discover the things that will bring you satisfaction and happiness on the job.

- **What would you like to do every day?** Talk to people in various occupations about their typical workday. You might consult relatives, local businesses, or former graduates (through your school's alumni relations office). Read about various occupations. Start with your college library or placement office.

- **How would you like to work?** Consider how much independence you want on the job, how much variety you like, and whether you prefer to work with products, machines, people, ideas, figures, or some combination thereof. Do you like physical work, mental work, or a mix? Constant change or a predictable role?

- **What specific compensation do you expect?** What do you hope to earn in your first year? What kind of pay increase do you expect each year? What's your ultimate earnings goal? Would you be comfortable getting paid on commission, or do you prefer a steady paycheck? Are you willing to settle for less money in order to do something you really love?

- **Can you establish some general career goals?** Consider where you'd like to start, where you'd like to go from there, and the ultimate position you'd like to attain. How soon after joining the company would you like to receive your first promotion? Your next one? What additional training or preparation will you need to achieve them?

- **What size of company would you prefer?** Do you like the idea of working for a small, entrepreneurial operation? Or would you prefer a large corporation?

- **What type of operation is appealing to you?** Do you prefer to work for a profit-making company or a nonprofit organization? Are you attracted to service businesses or manufacturing operations? Do you want regular, predictable hours, or do you thrive on flexible, varied hours? Would you enjoy a seasonally varied job such as education (which may give you summers off) or retailing (with its selling cycles)?

- **What location would you like?** Would you like to work in a city, a suburb, a small town, an industrial area, or an uptown setting? Do you favor a particular part of the country? A country abroad? Do you like working indoors or outdoors?

- **What facilities do you envision?** Is it important to you to work in an attractive place, or will simple, functional quarters suffice? Do you need a quiet office to work effectively, or can you concentrate in a noisy, open setting? Is access to public transportation or freeways important?

- **What sort of corporate culture are you most comfortable with?** Would you be happy in a formal hierarchy with clear reporting relationships? Or do you prefer less structure? Are you looking for a paternalistic firm or one that fosters individualism? Do you like a competitive environment? One that rewards teamwork? What qualities do you want in a boss?

Make Yourself More Valuable to Employers

Make yourself more valuable to potential employers by tracking what you've done, broadening your experience, and constantly improving your skills.

Take positive steps toward building your career. Before you graduate from college or while you're seeking employment, you can do a lot. The following suggestions will help potential employers recognize the value of hiring you:

- **Keep an employment portfolio.** Get a three-ring notebook and a package of plastic sleeves that open at the top. Collect anything that shows your ability to perform (classroom or work evaluations, certificates, awards, papers you've written). Your portfolio is a great resource for writing your résumé, and it gives employers tangible evidence of your professionalism.

- **Take interim assignments.** As you search for a permanent job, consider temporary or freelance work. Also gain a competitive edge by participating in an internship program. These temporary assignments not only help you gain valuable experience and relevant contacts but also provide you with important references and with items for your portfolio.[7]

- **Work on polishing and updating your skills.** Whenever possible, join networks of professional colleagues and friends who can help you keep up with your occupation and industry. While waiting for responses to your résumé, take a computer course, or seek out other educational or life experiences that would be hard to get while working full-time.

Even after you've been hired, continue improving your skills. Distinguish yourself from your peers and continue increasing your value to current and potential employers. Becoming a lifelong learner will help you reach your personal goals in the workplace:[8]

- Obtain as much technical knowledge as you can.
- Learn to accept and adapt to change.
- Regularly read publications such as *The Wall Street Journal, Business Week,* and *U.S. News & World Report.*
- View each job as a chance to expand your knowledge, experience, and social skills.
- Take on as much responsibility as you can (listen to and learn from others while actively pursuing new or better skills).
- Stay abreast of what's going on in your organization and industry.
- Share what you know with others.
- Understand the big picture.

> Your career-building efforts don't stop after you are hired.

Seeking Employment in the Changing Workplace

Look at Figure 13.1 for an idea of what an employment search entails. The first two tasks are discussed in this chapter; the rest are discussed in Chapter 14. Gather as much information as you can, narrowing it as you go until you know precisely the companies you want to approach.

> The search for employment is a process.

Begin by finding out where the job opportunities are, which industries are strong, which parts of the country are booming, and which specific job categories offer the best prospects for the future. From there you can investigate individual organizations, doing your best to learn as much about them as possible. To prepare for and successfully complete your search for employment, do the following:

- **Stay abreast of business and financial news.** Subscribe to a major newspaper (print or online) and scan the business pages every day. Watch some television programs that

> To learn all you can about the job opportunities available, consistently pursue six tasks.

FIGURE 13.1 The Employment Search

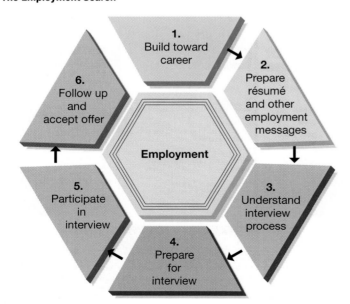

focus on business. Consult the *Dictionary of Occupational Titles* (U.S. Employment Service), employment publications of Science Research Associates, and the *Occupational Outlook Handbook* (U.S. Bureau of Labor Statistics—in print and online at www.bls.gov/oco.

- **Research specific companies.** Compile a list of specific organizations that appeal to you (by consulting directories of employers at the library, at your career center, or on the web). Consult company profiles, press releases, financial information, and information on employment opportunities. Find out about a company's mission, products, annual reports, and employee benefits. Send an e-mail request for annual reports, brochures, or newsletters.

- **Look for job openings.** Check company websites for job openings, or find sites that list openings from multiple companies—many of which allow you to search by region, industry, job title, company, skills, or requirements (see Figure 13.2). And don't forget to look in newspapers, sign up for campus interviews, network, and find career counseling.

- **Respond to job openings.** You can respond directly to job listings by posting tailor-made résumés (that match required qualifications) and by sending e-mail résumés and focused cover letters directly to the people doing the hiring. Since companies receive thousands of electronic résumés a day, also consider a printed letter or a phone call.[9]

- **Network.** Find people in your field by participating in student business organizations (such as the American Marketing Association or the American Management Association). Visit organizations, contact their personnel departments, and talk with key employees. On the web, locate and communicate with potential employers using discus-

FIGURE 13.2   CareerBuilder
CareerBuilder is just one of the many websites that job seekers turn to for career advice, as well as for employer information and company job postings.

sion groups, Usenet newsgroups (that post messages on electronic bulletin boards), and listservs (that e-mail messages to every member). Once you locate a potential contact, send an e-mail requesting information about the company or about job openings.

■ **Find career counseling.** College placement offices offer counseling, credential services, job fairs, on-campus interviews, and job listings. They provide workshops in job-search techniques, résumé preparation, interview techniques, and more.[10] College- and university-run online career centers are excellent. Commercial career centers (online and off) range from award winning to depressing, so find those with advice that is useful and sensible.

Preparing Résumés

While looking for employment, you'll need to send out messages such as résumés and application letters. Whenever you send out such employment messages, you have an opportunity to showcase your communication skills—skills valued highly by the majority of employers. So write these messages carefully by following the three-step writing process (see Figure 13.3).

> As with other business messages, the three-step writing process can help you plan, write, and complete your résumé and other employment messages.

Planning Your Résumé

A **résumé** is a structured, written summary of a person's education, employment back-ground, and job qualifications. Many people have misconceptions about the value and function of résumés—see Table 13.1. As with other business messages, planning a résumé means analyzing your purpose and audience, gathering information, and adapting the document to your purpose and audience.

> Your résumé concisely summarizes your educational and employment background and shows your qualifications for a job.

■ **Analyze your purpose and audience.** Your résumé must be more than a simple list of jobs you've held. It is a form of advertising intended to stimulate an employer's interest in you—in meeting you and learning more about you. With this purpose in mind, put yourself in your audience's position and tailor your résumé to satisfy audience needs.

■ **Investigate pertinent information.** Gather every scrap of pertinent personal history you can and have it at your fingertips: all details of previous jobs (dates, duties, accomplishments), all relevant educational experience (formal degrees, skill certificates, academic or civic awards), all relevant information about personal endeavors (dates of

> To get an interview, analyze your audience's needs, have all the facts at your fingertips, and tailor your résumé to various audiences and situations.

FIGURE 13.3   Three-Step Writing Process for Employment Messages

Planning →

Analyze
Study your purpose and your audience to tailor your message for maximum effect.

Investigate
Gather relevant information about you and about the employer you're targeting.

Adapt
Establish a good relationship by highlighting those skills and qualifications that match each employer.

1

Writing →

Organize
Use the AIDA approach in letters and choose the most appropriate résumé format to highlight your strongest points.

Compose
Make your letters friendly, businesslike, and slightly more formal than usual. For résumés, use action verbs and make your style direct, brief, and crisp.

2

Completing →

Revise
Evaluate content, revising for both clarity and conciseness.

Produce
Ensure a clean, sharp look whether your message is printed, e-mailed, or placed online.

Proofread
Look carefully for errors in spelling and mechanics that can detract from your professionalism.

3

Table 13.1	Fallacies and Facts About Résumés	
Fallacy		**Fact**
⊗ The purpose of a résumé is to list all your skills and abilities.		☑ The purpose of a résumé is to kindle employer interest and generate an interview.
⊗ A good résumé will get you the job you want.		☑ All a résumé can do is get you in the door.
⊗ Your résumé will be read carefully and thoroughly by an interested employer.		☑ Your résumé probably has less than 45 seconds to make an impression.
⊗ The more good information you present about yourself in your résumé, the better.		☑ Too much information on a résumé may actually kill the reader's appetite to know more.
⊗ If you want a really good résumé, have it prepared by a résumé service.		☑ Prepare your own résumé—unless the position is especially high-level or specialized. Even then, you should check carefully before using a service.

membership in an association, offices you held in a club or organization, presentations you made to a community group).

- **Adapt your résumé to your audience.** Your résumé must make an impression quickly. Focus on your audience. Ask yourself what key qualifications this employer will be looking for. Decide which qualifications are your greatest strengths. Choose three or four of your most relevant accomplishments and what resulted from these accomplishments. A good résumé is flexible and can be customized for various situations and employers.

Don't exaggerate, and don't alter the past or claim skills you don't have. However, don't dwell on negatives, either. By knowing yourself and your audience, you'll focus successfully on the strengths needed by potential employers.

Writing Your Résumé

To write a successful résumé, you need to convey seven qualities that employers seek. You want to show that you (1) think in terms of results, (2) know how to get things done, (3) are well rounded, (4) show signs of progress, (5) have personal standards of excellence, (6) are flexible and willing to try new things, and (7) possess strong communication skills. As you organize and compose your résumé, think about how you can convey those seven qualities.

Organize Your Résumé Around Your Strengths

Select an organizational pattern that focuses attention on your strengths.

Although you may want to include a little information in all categories, emphasize the information that has a bearing on your career objective, and minimize or exclude any that is irrelevant or counterproductive. Call attention to your best features and downplay your weaknesses—but be sure you do so without distorting or misrepresenting the facts.[11] To focus attention on your strongest points, adopt the appropriate organizational approach—make your résumé chronological, functional, or a combination of the two. The "right" choice depends on your background and your goals.

The Chronological Résumé   In a **chronological résumé**, the "Work Experience" section dominates and is placed immediately after the name and address and the objective. You list your jobs sequentially in reverse order, beginning with the most recent position and working backward toward earlier jobs. Under each job listing, describe your responsibilities and accomplishments, giving the most space to the most recent positions. If you're just starting your career, you can vary this chronological approach by putting your educational qualifications before your experience, thereby focusing attention on your training and academic credentials.

FIGURE 13.4   Ineffective Chronological Résumé

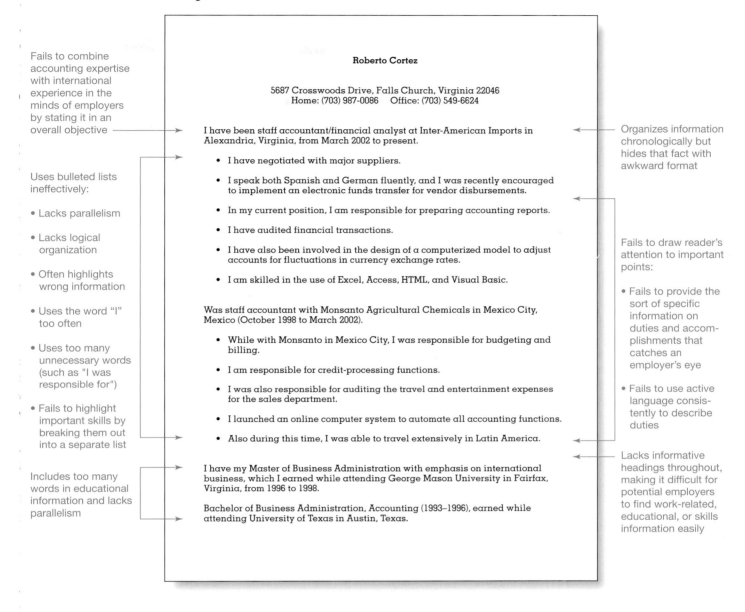

Fails to combine accounting expertise with international experience in the minds of employers by stating it in an overall objective

Uses bulleted lists ineffectively:

• Lacks parallelism

• Lacks logical organization

• Often highlights wrong information

• Uses the word "I" too often

• Uses too many unnecessary words (such as "I was responsible for")

• Fails to highlight important skills by breaking them out into a separate list

Includes too many words in educational information and lacks parallelism

Roberto Cortez

5687 Crosswoods Drive, Falls Church, Virginia 22046
Home: (703) 987-0086   Office: (703) 549-6624

I have been staff accountant/financial analyst at Inter-American Imports in Alexandria, Virginia, from March 2002 to present.

• I have negotiated with major suppliers.

• I speak both Spanish and German fluently, and I was recently encouraged to implement an electronic funds transfer for vendor disbursements.

• In my current position, I am responsible for preparing accounting reports.

• I have audited financial transactions.

• I have also been involved in the design of a computerized model to adjust accounts for fluctuations in currency exchange rates.

• I am skilled in the use of Excel, Access, HTML, and Visual Basic.

Was staff accountant with Monsanto Agricultural Chemicals in Mexico City, Mexico (October 1998 to March 2002).

• While with Monsanto in Mexico City, I was responsible for budgeting and billing.

• I am responsible for credit-processing functions.

• I was also responsible for auditing the travel and entertainment expenses for the sales department.

• I launched an online computer system to automate all accounting functions.

• Also during this time, I was able to travel extensively in Latin America.

I have my Master of Business Administration with emphasis on international business, which I earned while attending George Mason University in Fairfax, Virginia, from 1996 to 1998.

Bachelor of Business Administration, Accounting (1993–1996), earned while attending University of Texas in Austin, Texas.

Organizes information chronologically but hides that fact with awkward format

Fails to draw reader's attention to important points:

• Fails to provide the sort of specific information on duties and accomplishments that catches an employer's eye

• Fails to use active language consistently to describe duties

Lacks informative headings throughout, making it difficult for potential employers to find work-related, educational, or skills information easily

The chronological approach is the most common way to organize a résumé, and many employers prefer it. This approach has three key advantages: (1) employers are familiar with it and can easily find information, (2) it highlights growth and career progression, and (3) it highlights employment continuity and stability.[12] The chronological approach is especially appropriate if you have a strong employment history and are aiming for a job that builds on your current career path. This is the case for Roberto Cortez. Compare the ineffective and effective versions of Cortez's résumé in Figures 13.4 and 13.5.

Most recruiters prefer the chronological plan: a historical summary of your education and work experience.

The Functional Résumé   A **functional résumé** emphasizes a list of skills and accomplishments, identifying employers and academic experience in subordinate sections. This pattern stresses individual areas of competence, so it's useful for people who are just entering the job market, who want to redirect their careers, or who have little continuous career-related experience. The functional approach also has three advantages: (1) without having to read through job descriptions, employers can see what you can do for them, (2) you can emphasize earlier job experience, and (3) you can de-emphasize any lack of career progress or lengthy unemployment.

A functional résumé focuses attention on your areas of competence.

Planning

Analyze
Decide how best to combine accounting expertise with international experience.

Investigate
Gather data from contacts and research.

Adapt
Point out specific achievements to interest potential employers.

1

Writing

Organize
A chronological résumé will best emphasize years of work experience.

Compose
The style is direct, brief, and crisp, using action verbs to focus on employment history, professional achievements, and international abilities.

2

Completing

Revise
Make content clear and concise.

Produce
Give traditional résumé a clean, sharp look with dates set off in margin.

Proofread
Review for spelling and mechanical errors.

3

FIGURE 13.5   Effective Chronological Résumé

Combines accounting expertise with international experience in the minds of employers by stating it in an overall objective

Organizes information chronologically and emphasizes that organization with format

Makes each description concise, easy to read, and informative:

• Avoids the word "I" throughout

• Uses no unnecessary words

Highlights important skills by breaking them out into a list in a separate section

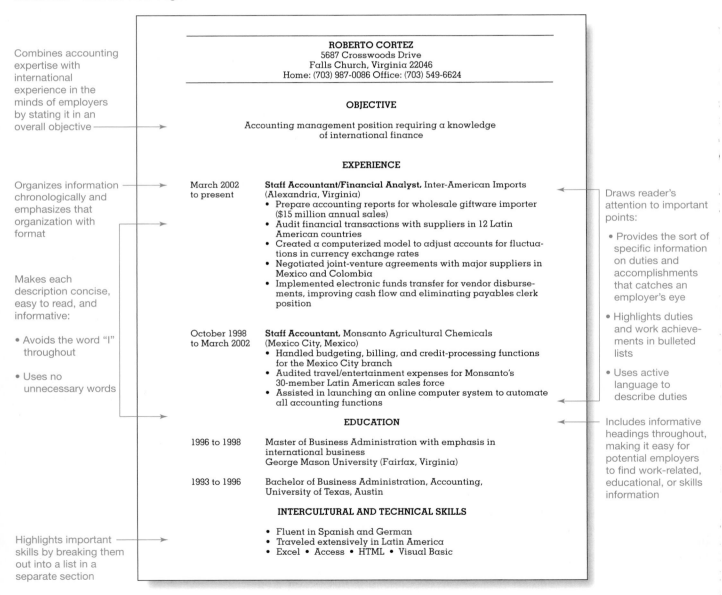

ROBERTO CORTEZ
5687 Crosswoods Drive
Falls Church, Virginia 22046
Home: (703) 987-0086 Office: (703) 549-6624

OBJECTIVE

Accounting management position requiring a knowledge
of international finance

EXPERIENCE

March 2002
to present

Staff Accountant/Financial Analyst, Inter-American Imports
(Alexandria, Virginia)
• Prepare accounting reports for wholesale giftware importer
  ($15 million annual sales)
• Audit financial transactions with suppliers in 12 Latin
  American countries
• Created a computerized model to adjust accounts for fluctua-
  tions in currency exchange rates
• Negotiated joint-venture agreements with major suppliers in
  Mexico and Colombia
• Implemented electronic funds transfer for vendor disburse-
  ments, improving cash flow and eliminating payables clerk
  position

October 1998
to March 2002

Staff Accountant, Monsanto Agricultural Chemicals
(Mexico City, Mexico)
• Handled budgeting, billing, and credit-processing functions
  for the Mexico City branch
• Audited travel/entertainment expenses for Monsanto's
  30-member Latin American sales force
• Assisted in launching an online computer system to automate
  all accounting functions

EDUCATION

1996 to 1998   Master of Business Administration with emphasis in
                international business
                George Mason University (Fairfax, Virginia)

1993 to 1996   Bachelor of Business Administration, Accounting,
                University of Texas, Austin

INTERCULTURAL AND TECHNICAL SKILLS

• Fluent in Spanish and German
• Traveled extensively in Latin America
• Excel • Access • HTML • Visual Basic

Draws reader's attention to important points:

• Provides the sort of specific information on duties and accomplishments that catches an employer's eye

• Highlights duties and work achieve-ments in bulleted lists

• Uses active language to describe duties

Includes informative headings throughout, making it easy for potential employers to find work-related, educational, or skills information

FIGURE 13.6   Effective Functional Résumé

Describes relevant skills first because Johns is a recent graduate

Uses action verbs to enhance résumé effectiveness

Describes but does not emphasize Johns's sketchy work history

Calls attention to leadership abilities and experience by listing her leadership positions in a separate section

---

Figure 13.6 illustrates how Glenda Johns uses the functional approach to showcase her qualifications for a career in retail. Although she has not held any paid, full-time positions in retail sales, Johns has participated in work-experience programs, and she knows a good deal about the profession from research and from talking with people in the industry. She organized her résumé in a way that demonstrates her ability to handle such a position. Bear in mind, however, that many employment professionals assume that candidates who use this organization are trying to hide something.[13]

The Combination Résumé   A **combination résumé** includes the best features of the chronological and functional approaches. Nevertheless, it is not commonly used, and it has two major disadvantages: (1) it tends to be longer, and (2) it can be repetitious if you have to list your accomplishments and skills in both the functional section and the

A combination résumé is a hybrid of the chronological and functional résumés.

FIGURE 13.7 Effective Combination Résumé

Erica Vorkamp

993 Church Street, Barrington, Illinois 60010
(847) 884-2153

OBJECTIVE

To obtain a position as a special event coordinator that will utilize my skills and experience

SKILLS AND CAPABILITIES

- Plan and coordinate large-scale public events
- Develop community support for concerts, festivals, and the arts
- Manage publicity for major events
- Coordinate activities of diverse community groups
- Establish and maintain financial controls for public events
- Negotiate contracts with performers, carpenters, electricians, and suppliers

SPECIAL EVENT EXPERIENCE

- Arranged 2004's week-long Arts and Entertainment Festival for the Barrington Public Library, involving performances by 25 musicians, dancers, actors, magicians, and artists
- Supervised the 2003 PTA Halloween Carnival, an all-day festival with game booths, live bands, contests, and food service that raised $7,600 for the PTA
- Organized the 2002 Midwestern convention for 800 members of the League of Women Voters, which extended over a three-day period and required arrangements for hotels, meals, speakers, and special tours
- Served as chairperson for the 2001 to 2003 Children's Home Society Fashion Show, a luncheon for 400–500 that raised $5,000–$6,700 for orphans and abused children

EDUCATION

- Associate of Applied Science, Administrative Assistant program with specialization in General Business, Lincoln School of Commerce (Lincoln, Nebraska), 1990

EMPLOYMENT HISTORY

- First National Bank of Chicago, 1990 to 1992, operations processor; processed checks with a lost/stolen status, contacted customers by phone, inspected checks to determine risk characteristics, processed payment amounts, verified receipt reports, researched check authenticity, managed orientation program for entry-level trainees
- Lincoln School of Commerce, 1988 to 1990, part-time administrative assistant for admissions (Business Department)

Relates all capabilities and experience to the specific job objective, giving a selective picture of the candidate's abilities

Includes event attendance statistics and fund-raising results to quantify accomplishments

Includes work history (even though it has little bearing on job target) because Vorkamp believes recruiters want to see evidence that she's held a paying position

chronological job descriptions.[14] When Erica Vorkamp developed her résumé, she chose not to use a chronological pattern, which would focus attention on her lack of recent work experience. As Figure 13.7 shows, she used a combination approach to emphasize her abilities, skills, and accomplishments while also including a complete job history.

Compose Your Résumé to Impress

To save your readers time and to state your information as forcefully as possible, write your résumé using a simple and direct style. Use short, crisp phrases instead of whole sentences, and focus on what your reader needs to know. Avoid using the word *I*. Instead, start your phrases with impressive action verbs such as the ones listed in Table 13.2. For instance, you might say, "Coached a Little League team to the regional playoffs" or "Managed a fast-food restaurant and four employees." Here are some additional examples of how to phrase your accomplishments using active statements that show results:

To capture attention quickly, leave out the word I, and begin your phrases with strong, action verbs.

Table 13.2	Action Verbs to Use in Résumés			
accomplished	coordinated	initiated	participated	set up
achieved	created	installed	performed	simplified
administered	demonstrated	introduced	planned	sparked
approved	developed	investigated	presented	streamlined
arranged	directed	joined	proposed	strengthened
assisted	established	launched	raised	succeeded
assumed	explored	maintained	recommended	supervised
budgeted	forecasted	managed	reduced	systematized
chaired	generated	motivated	reorganized	targeted
changed	identified	operated	resolved	trained
compiled	implemented	organized	saved	transformed
completed	improved	oversaw	served	upgraded

Avoid Weak Statements	Use Active Statements That Show Results
Responsible for developing a new filing system	Developed a new filing system that reduced paperwork by 50 percent
I was in charge of customer complaints and all ordering problems	Handled all customer complaints and resolved all product order discrepancies
Won a trip to Europe for opening the most new customer accounts in my department	Generated the highest number of new customer accounts in my department
Member of special campus task force to resolve student problems with existing cafeteria assignments	Assisted in implementing new campus dining program allowing students to eat at any college dorm

Elements to include in your résumé are your name and address, academic credentials, employment history, activities and achievements, and relevant personal data.

Name and Address   The first thing an employer needs to know is who you are and where you can be reached: your name, address, and phone number (as well as your e-mail address or URL, if you have one). If you have contact information at school and at home, you can include both. Similarly, if you have a work phone and a home phone, list both and indicate which is which. Many résumé headings are nothing more than the name and address centered at the top of the page. You don't really need to include the word *résumé*. Just make sure the reader can tell in an instant who you are and how to communicate with you.

The opening section shows at a glance
- Who you are
- How to reach you

Career Objective or Summary of Qualifications   Experts disagree about the need to state a career objective on your résumé. Some argue that your objective is obvious from your qualifications. Some also maintain that such a statement only limits you as a candidate (especially if you want to be considered for a variety of openings) because it labels you as being interested in only one thing. Other experts argue that employers will try to categorize you anyway, so you might as well make sure they attach the right label. Remember, your goal is to generate interest immediately. If you decide to state your objective, make it effective by being as specific as possible about what you want:

Stating your objective or summarizing your qualifications helps the recruiter categorize you.

A software sales position in a growing company requiring international experience

Advertising assistance with print media emphasis requiring strong customer-contact skills

If you have different types of qualifications (such as a certificate in secretarial science and two years' experience in retail sales), prepare separate résumés, each with a different objective. If your immediate objective differs from your ultimate one, combine the two in a single statement:

A marketing position with an opportunity for eventual managerial status

Proposal writer, with the ultimate goal of becoming a contracts administrator

Instead of stating your objective, you might summarize your qualifications in a brief statement that highlights your strongest points, particularly if you have had a good deal of varied experience. Use a short, simple phrase:

Summary of qualifications: Ten years of experience in commission selling with track record of generating new customer leads through creative advertising and community leadership positions

The career objective or summary may be the only section read fully by the employer, so if you include either one, make it strong, concise, and convincing.

Education If you're still in school, education is probably your strongest selling point. Present your educational background in depth, choosing facts that support your objective. Give this section a heading such as "Education," "Professional College Training," or "Academic Preparation." Then, starting with the school you most recently attended, list the name and location of each one, the term of your enrollment (in months and years), your major and minor fields of study, significant skills and abilities you've developed in your course work, and the degrees or certificates you've earned. If you're working on an uncompleted degree, include in parentheses the expected date of completion. Showcase your qualifications by listing courses that have directly equipped you for the job you are seeking, and indicate any scholarships, awards, or academic honors you've received.

> If education is your strongest selling point, discuss it thoroughly and highlight it visually.

The education section also includes off-campus training sponsored by business or government. Include any relevant seminars or workshops you've attended, as well as the certificates or other documents you've received. Mention high school or military training only if the associated achievements are pertinent to your career goals. Whether you list your grades depends on the job you want and the quality of your grades. If you choose to show a grade-point average, be sure to mention the scale, especially if a five-point scale is used instead of a four-point scale.

Education is usually given less emphasis in a résumé after you've worked in your chosen field for a year or more. If work experience is your strongest qualification, save the section on education for later in the résumé and provide less detail.

Work Experience, Skills, and Accomplishments Like the education section, the work-experience section focuses on your overall theme. Tailor your description to highlight the relationship between your previous responsibilities and your target field. Call attention to skills you've developed and your progression from jobs of lesser to greater responsibility.

> The work experience section lists all the related jobs you've had:
> - Name and location of employer
> - What the organization does (if not clear from its name)
> - Your functional title
> - How long you worked there
> - Your duties and responsibilities
> - Your significant achievements or contributions

When describing your work experience, list your jobs in chronological order, with the current or last one first. Include any part-time, summer, or intern positions, even if unrelated to your current career objective. Employers will see that you have the ability to get and hold a job—an important qualification in itself. If you have worked your way through school, say so. Employers interpret this behavior as a sign of character.

Each listing includes the name and location of the employer. If readers are unlikely to recognize the organization, briefly describe what it does. When you want to keep the name of your current employer confidential, identify the firm by industry only ("a large film-processing laboratory") or use the name but request confidentiality in the application letter or in an underlined note ("Résumé submitted in confidence") at the top or bottom of the résumé. If an organization's name or location has since changed, state the current name and location and then "formerly . . ."

Before or after each job listing, state your functional title, such as "clerk typist" or "salesperson." If you were a dishwasher, say so. Don't try to make your role seem more important by glamorizing your job title, functions, or achievements. Employers are checking on candidates' backgrounds more than they used to, so inaccuracies are likely to be exposed sooner or later. Also state how long you worked on each job, from month/year to month/year. Use the phrase "to present" to denote current employment. If a job was part-time, say so.

Devote the most space to the jobs that are related to your target position. If you were personally responsible for something significant, be sure to mention it ("Devised a new collection system that accelerated payment of overdue receivables"). Facts about your skills and accomplishments are the most important information you can give a prospective employer, so quantify them whenever possible:

Quantify your accomplishments whenever possible.

Designed a new ad that increased sales by 9 percent

Raised $2,500 in 15 days for cancer research

You may also include a section describing other aspects of your background that pertain to your career objective. If you were applying for a position with a multinational organization, you would mention your command of another language or your travel experience. Other skills you might mention include the ability to operate a computer, word processor, or other specialized equipment. You might title a special section "Computer Skills" or "Language Skills" and place it near your "Education" or "Work Experience" section.

Include miscellaneous facts that are related to your career objective:
- *Command of other languages*
- *Computer expertise*
- *Date you can start working*

If samples of your work might increase your chances of getting the job, insert a line at the end of your résumé offering to supply them on request. You may put "References available upon request" at the end of your résumé, but doing so is not necessary; the availability of references is usually assumed. Don't include actual names of references. List your references on a separate sheet and take them to your interview.

Activities and Achievements Your résumé should also describe any volunteer activities that demonstrate your abilities. List projects that require leadership, organization, teamwork, and cooperation. Emphasize career-related activities such as "member of the Student Marketing Association." List skills you learned in these activities, and explain how these skills are related to the job you're applying for. Include speaking, writing, or tutoring experience; participation in athletics or creative projects; fund-raising or community-service activities; and offices held in academic or professional organizations. (However, mention of political or religious organizations may be a red flag to someone with differing views, so use your judgment.)

Nonpaid activities may provide evidence of work-related skills.

Note any awards you've received. Again, quantify your achievements whenever possible. Instead of saying that you addressed various student groups, state how many and the approximate audience sizes. If your activities have been extensive, you may want to group them into divisions such as "College Activities," "Community Service," "Professional Associations," "Seminars and Workshops," and "Speaking Activities." An alternative is to divide them into two categories: "Service Activities" and "Achievements, Awards, and Honors."

Personal Data Experts advise you to leave personal interests off your résumé—unless including them enhances the employer's understanding of why you would be the best candidate for the job.[15] For instance, candidates applying for a bodyguard position with Pinkerton's security division may want to list martial arts achievements among their personal interests. Someone applying to REI may want to list outdoor activities. According to REI's Doug Halm, such information helps show how a candidate will fit in with the organization's culture.

Provide only the personal data that will help you get the job.

Some information is best excluded from your résumé. Civil rights laws prohibit employers from discriminating on the basis of gender, marital or family status, age (although only persons aged 40 to 70 are protected), race, religion, national origin, and physical or mental disability. So be sure to exclude any items that could encourage discrimination. Experts also recommend excluding salary information, reasons for leaving jobs, names of previous supervisors, your Social Security number, and other identification codes. Save these items for the interview, and offer them only if the employer specifically requests them.

If military service is relevant to the position, you may list it in this section (or under "Education" or "Work Experience"). List the date of induction, the branch of service, where you served, the highest rank you achieved, any accomplishments related to your career goals, and the date you were discharged.

Avoid Résumé Deception

In an effort to put your best foot forward, you may be tempted to waltz around a few points that could raise questions about your résumé. Although statistics on the prevalence of résumé inflation are difficult to gather, the majority of recruiters agree that distortion is common. Avoid the most frequent forms of deception:

> Do not misrepresent your background or qualifications.

- **Do not claim educational credits you don't have.** Candidates may state (or imply) that they earned a degree when, in fact, they never attended the school or attended but did not complete the regular program. A typical claim might read, "Majored in business administration at Wayne State University."

- **Do not inflate your grade-point average.** Students who feel pressured to impress employers with their academic performance may claim a higher GPA than they actually achieved.

- **Do not stretch dates of employment to cover gaps.** Many candidates try to camouflage gaps in their work history by giving vague dates of employment. For example, a candidate who left a company in January 1992 and joined another in December 1993 might cover up by showing that the first job ended in 1992 and the next began in 1993.

- **Do not claim to be self-employed.** Another common way people cover a period of unemployment is by saying that they were "self-employed" or a "consultant." The candidate claims to have operated an independent business during the period in question.

- **Do not claim to have worked for companies that are out of business.** Candidates who need to fill a gap in their work record sometimes say they worked for a firm that has gone out of business. Checking such claims is difficult because the people who were involved in the disbanded business are hard to track down.

- **Do not omit jobs that might cause embarrassment.** Being fired from one or two jobs is understandable when corporate mergers and downsizing are commonplace. However, a candidate who has lost several jobs in quick succession may seem a poor employee to recruiters. To cover a string of job losses, candidates may decide to leave out a few positions and stretch the dates of employment for the jobs held before and after.

- **Do not exaggerate expertise or experience.** Candidates often inflate their accomplishments by using verbs somewhat loosely. Words such as *supervised, managed, increased, improved,* and *created* imply that the candidate was personally responsible for results that, in reality, were the outcome of a group effort.

Think twice before trying one of these ploys yourself. If you misrepresent your background and your résumé raises suspicion, you will probably get caught, and your reputation will be damaged. A deceptive résumé can seriously affect your ability to get hired and pursue your career.

Experienced recruiters are familiar with the games that candidates play to enhance their image. Many employers fire people who lied on their résumés, and companies today are hiring highly skilled investigators who can access much-improved databases to seek the truth. Sure, it's fine to present your strongest, most impressive qualifications and to minimize your weaknesses. But don't exaggerate, alter the past, or claim to have skills you don't have (see Table 13.3).

Completing Your Résumé

The last step in the three-step writing process for résumés is no less important than the other two. As with any other business message, you need to revise your résumé, produce it in an appropriate form, and proofread it for any errors.

Table 13.3	How Far Can You Go to Make Your Résumé Strong and Positive?

Do	Don't
☑ **Tell the truth.** If you lie, you will almost certainly get caught, and the damage to your career could be significant.	⊗ **Fabricate.** Fake academic degrees and nonexistent jobs are checked first and will cost you the job, before or after you're hired.
☑ **Make your story positive.** Most blemishes on your record can be framed in a positive way.	⊗ **Make blatant omissions.** Failing to disclose a job that didn't work out is almost as bad as making one up.
☑ **Sanitize your record.** Clear up unresolved issues such as tax liens and lawsuits.	⊗ **Exaggerate successes.** Be ready to prove any claim about your accomplishments.
☑ **Think small.** Candidates with criminal histories or other career impediments should focus on smaller companies, which are less likely to conduct background checks.	⊗ **Go overboard.** There's usually no need to disclose career or personal history that's more than 15 years old. If asked directly, answer truthfully—but with a minimum of elaboration.

Revise Your Résumé

The key to writing a successful résumé is to adopt the "you" attitude and focus on your audience. Think about what the prospective employer needs, and then tailor your résumé accordingly. Employers read thousands of résumés every year, and they complain about common problems. Do not submit a résumé that is

- **Too long.** The résumé is not concise, relevant, and to the point.
- **Too short or sketchy.** The résumé does not give enough information for a proper evaluation of the applicant.
- **Hard to read.** A lack of "white space" and of devices such as indentions and boldfacing makes the reader's job more difficult.
- **Wordy.** Descriptions are verbose, with numerous words used for what could be said more simply.
- **Too slick.** The résumé appears to have been written by someone other than the applicant, which raises the question of whether the qualifications have been exaggerated.
- **Amateurish.** The applicant appears to have little understanding of the business world or of a particular industry, as revealed by including the wrong information or presenting it awkwardly.
- **Poorly reproduced.** The print is faint and difficult to read.
- **Misspelled and ungrammatical throughout.** Recruiters conclude that candidates who make spelling and grammar mistakes lack good verbal skills, which are important on the job.
- **Boastful.** The overconfident tone makes the reader wonder whether the applicant's self-evaluation is realistic.
- **Dishonest.** The applicant claims to have expertise or work experience that he or she does not possess.
- **Gimmicky.** The words, structure, decoration, or material used in the résumé depart so far from the usual as to make the résumé ineffective.

Avoid common résumé problems.

Produce Your Résumé

With less than a minute to make a good impression, your résumé needs to look sharp and grab a recruiter's interest in the first few lines. A typical recruiter devotes 45 seconds to each résumé before tossing it into either the "maybe" or the "reject" pile. Most recruiters scan a résumé rather than read it from top to bottom. If yours doesn't stand out—or if it stands out in a negative way—chances are a recruiter won't look at it long enough to judge your qualifications.[16]

Effective résumé designs are simple, clean, and professional—not gaudy, clever, or cute.

Good design is a must, and it's not hard to achieve. As you can see in Figures 13.5, 13.6, and 13.7, good designs feature simplicity, order, plenty of white space, and straightforward typefaces such as Times Roman or Arial (most of the fonts on your computer are not appropriate for a résumé). Make your subheadings easy to read and easy to find, placing them either above each section or in the left margin. Use lists to itemize your most important qualifications, and leave plenty of white space, even if doing so forces you to use two pages rather than one. Color is not necessary by any means, but if you add color, make it subtle and sophisticated, such as adding color to a thin horizontal line under your name and address.

The most common way to get into trouble with résumé design is going overboard. If any part of the design "jumps out at you," get rid of it. You want people to be impressed with the information on your résumé, not with the number of colors in your printer. To see how jarring and unprofessional a poor design looks to an employer, compare Figures 13.5, 13.6, and 13.7 with the "creative" design in Figure 13.8.

FIGURE 13.8   Ineffective Résumé Design

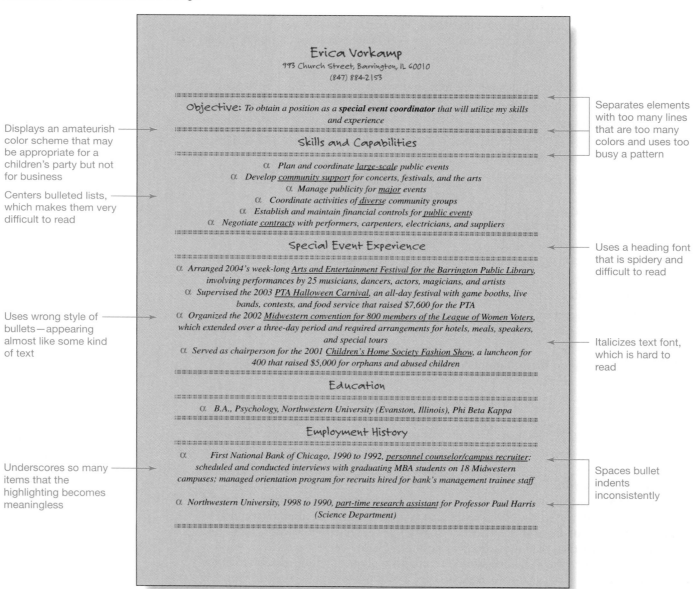

Until just a few years ago, producing résumés was a simple matter: you printed or photocopied as many as you needed and mailed them out. Not any more. Depending on the companies you apply to, you might want to produce your résumé in as many as six forms:

■ **Printed traditional résumé.** Format your traditional résumé simply but elegantly to make the best impression on your employer. Naturally, printed versions must be delivered by hand or through the post.

■ **Printed scannable résumé.** Prepare a printed version of your résumé that is unformatted and thus electronically scannable so that employers can store your information in their database.

■ **Electronic plain-text file.** Create an electronic plain-text file to use when uploading your résumé information into web forms or inserting it into e-mail messages.

■ **Microsoft Word file.** Keep a Microsoft Word file of your traditional résumé so that you can upload it on certain websites

■ **HTML format.** By creating an HTML version, you can post your resume on your own website, on a page provided by your college, or some of the many job board sites now available.

■ **Electronic PDF File.** This is an optional step, but a PDF file of your traditional résumé provides a simple, safe format to attach to e-mail messages. Although creating PDFs requires special software, using it can be helpful when an employer asks you to e-mail your résumé.

Don't panic; most of these versions are easy to do, as you'll see in the following sections.

Printing a Traditional Résumé   Spend a few minutes in the paper aisle at an office supply store, and you'll notice that paper falls into three general categories:

■ Avoid using basic white bond paper used for photocopying and printing; they make your résumé look cheap.

■ Avoid predesigned papers with borders and backgrounds; they make your résumé look gimmicky and unprofessional.

■ Use heavier, higher-quality papers designed specifically for résumés and other important documents; they give your résumé the professional appearance you're looking for.

Choose a white or off-white paper from this third category; these papers are more expensive, but you don't need much, and it's a worthwhile investment.

When you're ready to print your résumé, find a well-maintained, quality printer. Don't tolerate any streaks, stray lines, or poor print quality. You wouldn't walk into an interview looking messy, so make sure your résumé doesn't look that way, either.

Printing a Scannable Résumé   To cope with the flood of unsolicited paper résumés in recent years, many companies now optically scan incoming résumés into a database. When hiring managers want to interview candidates for job openings, they search the database for the most attractive candidates, using keywords appropriate to a specific position. The system then displays a list of possible candidates, each with a percentage score indicating how closely the résumé reflects the employer's requirements.[17] Nearly all large companies now use these systems, as do many mid-sized companies and even some smaller firms.[18]

The use of such scanning systems affects the way you produce your résumé. First, design your résumé as simply as possible, with no formatting. Computers are capable only of matching information to the key words requested; they cannot judge artistic attempts at résumé design. Since a human being may never actually see the résumé as you submitted it, don't worry about it looking depressingly dull.

Second, use a plain font. *Optical character recognition (OCR) software* doesn't actually "read" anything; it merely looks for shapes that match stored profiles of characters. Although printing your name in some gothic font might look grand to you, it will look

Start with a traditional printed résumé, but realize that you may need to create several other versions during your job search.

Strive for a clean, classy look in your printed résumé, using professional-grade paper and a clean, high-quality printer.

Converting your résumé to scannable format is easy to do—and extremely important.

FIGURE 13.9   Effective Scannable Résumé

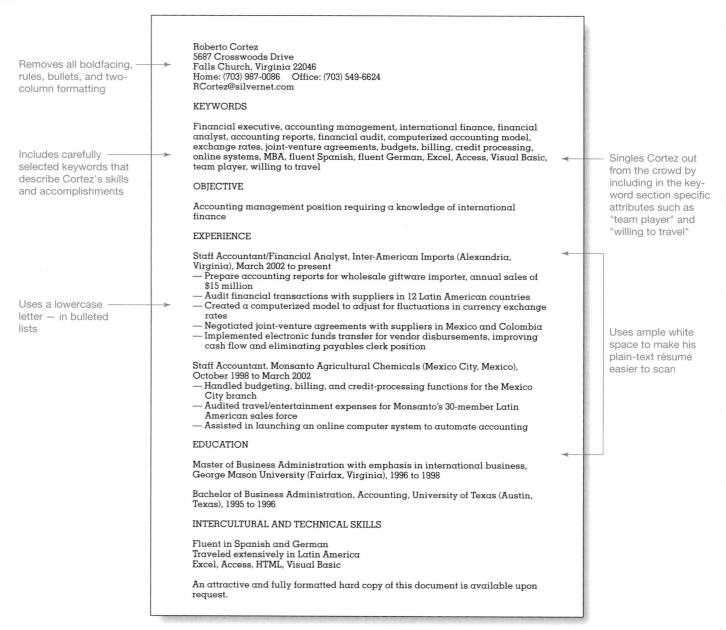

Removes all boldfacing, rules, bullets, and two-column formatting

Includes carefully selected keywords that describe Cortez's skills and accomplishments

Uses a lowercase letter — in bulleted lists

Singles Cortez out from the crowd by including in the key-word section specific attributes such as "team player" and "willing to travel"

Uses ample white space to make his plain-text résumé easier to scan

> Roberto Cortez
> 5687 Crosswoods Drive
> Falls Church, Virginia 22046
> Home: (703) 987-0086   Office: (703) 549-6624
> RCortez@silvernet.com
>
> KEYWORDS
>
> Financial executive, accounting management, international finance, financial analyst, accounting reports, financial audit, computerized accounting model, exchange rates, joint-venture agreements, budgets, billing, credit processing, online systems, MBA, fluent Spanish, fluent German, Excel, Access, Visual Basic, team player, willing to travel
>
> OBJECTIVE
>
> Accounting management position requiring a knowledge of international finance
>
> EXPERIENCE
>
> Staff Accountant/Financial Analyst, Inter-American Imports (Alexandria, Virginia), March 2002 to present
> — Prepare accounting reports for wholesale giftware importer, annual sales of $15 million
> — Audit financial transactions with suppliers in 12 Latin American countries
> — Created a computerized model to adjust for fluctuations in currency exchange rates
> — Negotiated joint-venture agreements with suppliers in Mexico and Colombia
> — Implemented electronic funds transfer for vendor disbursements, improving cash flow and eliminating payables clerk position
>
> Staff Accountant, Monsanto Agricultural Chemicals (Mexico City, Mexico), October 1998 to March 2002
> — Handled budgeting, billing, and credit-processing functions for the Mexico City branch
> — Audited travel/entertainment expenses for Monsanto's 30-member Latin American sales force
> — Assisted in launching an online computer system to automate accounting
>
> EDUCATION
>
> Master of Business Administration with emphasis in international business, George Mason University (Fairfax, Virginia), 1996 to 1998
>
> Bachelor of Business Administration, Accounting, University of Texas (Austin, Texas), 1995 to 1996
>
> INTERCULTURAL AND TECHNICAL SKILLS
>
> Fluent in Spanish and German
> Traveled extensively in Latin America
> Excel, Access, HTML, Visual Basic
>
> An attractive and fully formatted hard copy of this document is available upon request.

like nonsense to the OCR software. If the OCR software can't make sense of your fancy fonts or creative page layout, it will enter gibberish into the database (for instance, your name might go in as "W{$..3r ?00!#" instead of "Walter Jones").

Third, compile your list of keywords carefully. Even the most sophisticated databases cannot conduct a search with the nuance and intuition of an experienced human recruiter. Therefore, choosing the keywords for your résumé is a critical step. A human might know that "data-driven webpage design" means that you know XML, but the database probably won't make that connection.

A scannable résumé contains the same information as your traditional résumé but is formatted to be OCR-friendly (see Figure 13.9):[19]

- Use a clean, common sans serif font such as Optima or Arial, and size it between 10 and 14 points.

- Make sure that characters do not touch one another (whether numbers, letters, or symbols—including the slash [/]).
- Don't use side-by-side columns (the OCR software reads one line all the way across the page).
- Don't use ampersands (&), percent signs (%), foreign-language characters (such as é and ö), or bullet symbols (use a dash—not a lower-case 'o'—in place of a bullet symbol).
- Put each phone number and e-mail address on its own line.
- Print on white, plain paper (speckles and other background coloration can confuse the OCR software).

Your scannable résumé will probably be longer than your traditional résumé because you can't compress text into columns and because you need plenty of white space between headings and sections. If your scannable résumé runs more than one page, make sure your name appears on every subsequent page (in case the pages become separated). Before sending a scannable résumé, check the company's website or call the human resources department to see whether that company has any specific requirements other than those discussed here.

When adding a keyword summary to your résumé, keep your audience in mind. Employers generally search for nouns, so make your keywords nouns as well. Use abbreviations sparingly and only when they are well-known and clear, such as *MBA*. Include in your list between 20 and 30 words and phrases that define your skills, experience, education, professional affiliations, and so on. Place this list right after your name and address. Look back at Figure 13.9 for an example of a keyword summary for an accountant.

> Think carefully about the keywords you include in your scannable résumé; they need to appeal to recruiters and reflect your qualities accurately.

One good way to identify which keywords to include in your summary is to underline all the skills listed in ads for the types of jobs you're interested in. Also, if you stay current by reading periodicals, networking, and so on, you'll develop a good ear for current terminology. Be sure to include only those keywords that correspond with your skills and experience. Don't try to get ahead of the competition by listing skills that you don't have. Doing so would be unethical; moreover, your efforts would be exposed right away when your keywords don't match your job experience or educational background.

Creating a Plain Text File of Your Résumé An increasingly common way to get your information into an employer's database is by entering your résumé into an online form, using a *plain text* version (sometimes referred to as an *ASCII text version*). This approach has the same goal as a scannable résumé, but it's faster, easier, and less prone to errors than the scanning process. If you have the option of mailing a scannable résumé or submitting plain text online, choose the "plain text online" method.

> A plain-text version of your résumé is simply a computer file without any of the formatting that you typically apply using a word processor.

In addition, some employers or networking contacts will ask you to e-mail your résumé in a plain text format right in the body of your e-mail message. Many employers will refuse to open e-mail attachments, thanks to the prevalence of computer viruses these days.

Plain text is just what it sounds like: no font selections, no bullet symbols, no colors, no lines or boxes, and so on. A plain text version is easy to create with your word processor. Start with the file you used to create your traditional printed résumé, use the *save as* choice to save it as "plain text" or whichever similarly labeled option your software has, and then verify the result.

The verification step is crucial because you can never be quite sure what happens to your layout. Open the text file to view the layout, but don't use your word processor; instead, open the file with a basic text editor (such as Notepad on Windows PCs). If necessary, reformat the page manually, moving text and inserting spaces as needed. For simplicity's sake, left-justify all your headings, rather than trying to center them manually. You can put headings in all caps or underline them with a row of dashes to separate them from blocks of text.

> Make sure you verify the plain-text file that you output from your word processor; it might need a few manual adjustments (make these using a text editor such as NotePad, not your word processor).

Creating a Word File of Your Traditional Résumé   In some cases, an employer or job-posting website will let you upload a Microsoft Word file directly. (Although there are certainly other word processors on the market, particularly on Apple and Linux systems, Microsoft Word on the PC is the generally accepted standard in business these days.) This method of transferring information preserves the design and layout of your traditional printed résumé and saves you the trouble of creating a plain text version. However, read the instructions carefully. For instance, you can upload a Word résumé to Monster.com, but the site asks you to follow some specific formatting instructions to make sure that your file isn't garbled.[20] Before you submit a Word file to anyone, make sure your system is free from viruses. Infecting a potential employer's PC won't make the good first impression that you're hoping for.

Creating a Webpage Version of Your Résumé   You can probably find several uses for an HTML version of your résumé. Although employers probably won't try to find you via a search engine, you can send e-mail to a potential employer and include the URL that links back to your site. Providing an HTML version lets you show a fully formatted résumé without the virus risks of e-mailing a Word file. Plus, you can provide links to supporting details and other materials from within your résumé. You can also use the HTML file in your e-portfolio, if you choose to create one. Even if you don't have HTML experience, you can save your résumé as a webpage from within Microsoft Word.

As you design your website résumé, think of important keywords to use as hyperlinks—words that will grab an employer's attention and make the recruiter want to click on that hyperlink to learn more about you. You can link to papers you've written, recommendations you've received, and sound or video clips that directly support your résumé. However, don't distract potential employers from your credentials by providing hyperlinks to other organizations or other websites (unless you designed a website and want to show it to recruiters). Also, in addition to the HTML version of your résumé, include a plain-text version on your webpage so that prospective employers can download it into their company's database.

> You have several options for posting your résumé online, but remember that you could be displaying your personal information for all the world to see, so think carefully about privacy and security.

Proofread Your Résumé

Employers view your résumé as a concrete example of how you will prepare material on the job. Your résumé doesn't need to be good or pretty good; it needs to be perfect. Job seekers have committed every error imaginable, from forgetting to put their own names on their résumés to misspelling "Education."[21] Not only is your résumé one of the most important documents you'll ever write, it's also one of the shortest, so there's every reason to make it perfect. Check all headings and lists for clarity and parallelism, and be sure that your grammar, spelling, and punctuation are correct. Ask at least three or four other people to read it, too. As the creator of the material, you could stare at a mistake for weeks and not see it.

> Your résumé can't be "pretty good" or "almost perfect"—it needs to be *perfect,* so proofread it thoroughly and ask several other people to verify it, too.

You also need to make sure your résumé works in every format you create, so double- and triple-check your scannable and plain-text résumés. Many personal computer users now have low-cost scanners with OCR software, so you can even test the scannability of your résumé. These OCR tools aren't as accurate as commercial systems, but you'll get a rough idea of what your résumé will look like on the other end of the scanning process. And always test your plain-text version. Simply copy it into an e-mail message and send it to yourself and several friends on different e-mail systems. Doing so will let you know whether previously hidden characters are suddenly showing up or whether your formatting fell apart on the receiving end.

Once your résumé is complete, update it continuously. As flexible as employment has become these days, you'll probably want or need to change employers several times in your career. You'll also need a current résumé to apply for membership in professional organizations and to apply for a promotion. Moreover, updating your résumé frequently helps you see how your career is progressing. Some people even create "future résumés" that list skills and experience they'd like to have. By pursuing those attributes, they can become the person they want to be, the one in that résumé.

Document Makeover

Improve This Résumé

To practice correcting drafts of actual documents, visit www.prenhall.com/onekey on the web. Click "Document Makeovers," then click Chapter 13. You will find a résumé that contains problems and errors relating to what you've learned in this chapter about preparing effective résumés. Use the Final Draft decision tool to create an improved version of this résumé. Check the message for spelling and grammatical errors, effective use of verbs and pronouns, inclusion of unnecessary information, or omission of important facts.

Distribute Your Résumé

What you do to distribute your résumé depends on the number of employers you target and their preferences for receiving résumés. Employers usually list their preferences on their websites, so verify this information to make sure that your résumé ends up in the right format and in the right channel. Beyond that, here are some general delivery tips:

- **Mailing your traditional and scannable résumés.** Take some care with the packaging. Spend a few extra cents to mail these documents in a flat 9x12 envelope, or better yet, use Priority Mail, which gives you a sturdy cardboard mailer and faster delivery for just a few dollars. Consider sending both formats to each employer. In your cover letter, explain that for the employer's convenience, you're sending both standard and scannable versions.

- **Faxing your traditional and scannable résumés.** If you know that an employer prefers résumés via fax, be sure to include a standard fax cover sheet, along with your cover letter, followed by your résumé(s). Set the fax machine to "fine" mode to help ensure a high-quality printout on the receiving end.

- **E-mailing your résumé.** Unless someone specifically asks for a Word document as an attachment, don't send it—it probably won't be opened. Instead, insert plain text into the body of the e-mail message or simply include a hyperlink in the e-mail that links back to your webpage résumé (or do both). If you know a reference number or a job ad number, include it in your e-mail subject line.

- **Submitting your résumé online.** The details of submitting résumés online vary from site to site, so be sure to read the instructions thoroughly. Some sites let you grab a file from your hard disk and upload it as is; others instruct you to cut and paste blocks of plain text into specific fields in an online form. Whenever you do this, be sure to cut and paste, rather than re-typing information; you've already proofed this material, and you don't want to create any new mistakes while re-keying it.

- **Posting a résumé on your website.** If you wish to post your résumé on your website, you'll need to find some way of providing potential employers with your URL; most recruiters won't take the time to use search engines to find your site.[22]

- **Posting your résumé with an index service or job site.** Websites such as Monster.com, CareerBuilder.com, and Yahoo Hotjobs have rapidly become a major force in recruiting. Don't forget to check specialty sites as well, such as those maintained by professional societies in your fields of interest. However, before you upload your résumé to any site, learn about its confidentiality protection. Some sites allow you to specify levels of confidentiality, such as letting employers search your qualifications without seeing your personal contact information or preventing your current employer from seeing your résumé. In any case, carefully limit the amount of personal information you provide

The most important advice you can get about distributing your résumé is to pay close attention to the specific wishes of each organization, whether it's an individual company or a job site online; some want printed résumés, some want Microsoft Word files, some want plain text in an online form, and so on.

online. Never put your Social Security number, student ID number, or driver's license number online

Preparing Other Types of Employment Messages

Although your résumé will take the greatest amount of time and effort, you'll also need to prepare other employment messages, including application letters, job-inquiry letters, application forms, and follow-up notes.

Application Letters

Application letters are intended to interest readers enough to read your résumé.

Whenever you submit your résumé, accompany it with a cover, or application, letter to let readers know what you're sending, why you're sending it, and how they can benefit from reading it. Because your application letter is in your own style (rather than the choppy, shorthand style of your résumé), it gives you a chance to show your communication skills and some personality.

Always send your résumé and application letter together, because each has a unique job to perform. The purpose of your résumé is to get employers interested enough to contact you for an interview. The purpose of your application letter is to get employers interested enough to read your résumé.

Before drafting a letter, learn something about the organization you're applying to; then focus on your audience so that you can show you've done your homework. Imagine yourself in the recruiter's situation, and show how your background and talents will solve a particular problem or fill a specific need the company has. The more you can learn about the organization, the better you'll be able to capture the reader's attention and convey your interest in the company.[23] During your research, find out the name, title, and department of the person you're writing to. Reaching and addressing the right person is the most effective way to gain attention. Avoid phrases such as "To Whom It May Concern" and "Dear Sir."

When putting yourself in your reader's shoes, remember that this person's in-box is probably overflowing with résumés and cover letters. So respect your reader's time. Steer clear of gimmicks, which almost never work, and include nothing in your cover letter that already appears in your résumé. Keep your letter straightforward, fact-based, short, upbeat, and professional. Some quick tips for application letters include the following:[24]

- **Be specific.** Avoid general objectives. Be as clear as possible about the kind of opportunity and industry you're looking for.
- **Include salary.** If you've been working in your field, include your current salary, but make sure your reader understands that this information is not a demand but intended to inform and assist.
- **Make e-mail covers even shorter.** When sending a cover letter by e-mail, make it a bit shorter than traditional application letters. Remember, e-mail readers want the gist very quickly.
- **Aim for high quality.** Meticulously check your spelling, mechanics, and grammar. Recruiters are complaining about the declining quality of written communication, including cover letters.

A good application letter should be no longer than three paragraphs. It should maintain a friendly, conversational tone. "The letter is a sales piece," advises Doug Halm. "Look at the job advertisement and highlight the specific points the company is looking for. Show that you know the job."

FIGURE 13.10   Effective Solicited Application Letter

2893 Jack Pine Road
Chapel Hill, NC 27514
February 3, 2005

Ms. Angela Clair
Director of Administration
Cummings and Welbane, Inc.
770 Campus Point Drive
Chapel Hill, NC 27514

Dear Ms. Clair:

In the January 31 issue of the *Chapel Hill Post*, your ad mentioned "proven skills." I believe I have what you are looking for in an administrative assistant. In addition to experience in a variety of office settings, I am familiar with the computer software used in your office.

I recently completed a three-course sequence at Hamilton College on Microsoft Office applications, including Word, Excel, PowerPoint, and Access, and I've created files using all four of these applications. In addition, a workshop on "Designing and Producing Professional Documents with Microsoft Publisher" gave me experience designing, formatting, and printing the wide variety of reports and sales materials used in your office.

These skills have been invaluable to me as assistant to the chief nutritionist at our campus cafeteria (please refer to my résumé). I'm particularly proud of the order-confirmation system I designed, which has sharply reduced the problems of late shipments and depleted inventories.

Because "proven skills" are best explained in person, I would appreciate an interview with you. Please phone me any afternoon between 3 and 5 p.m. at (919) 220-6139 to let me know the day and time most convenient for you.

Sincerely,

Kenneth Sawyer

Kenneth Sawyer

*Annotations (left):*
States the reason for writing and links the writer's experience to stated qualifications

Explains an achievement mentioned in the résumé and refers the reader to the enclosure

*Annotations (right):*
Discusses how specific skills apply to the job sought, showing that Sawyer understands the job's responsibilities

Asks for an interview and facilitates action

If you're sending a **solicited application letter**—in response to an announced job opening—you'll usually know what qualifications the organization is seeking. You'll also have more competition because hundreds of other job seekers will have seen the listing and may be sending applications too. The letter in Figure 13.10 was written in response to a help-wanted ad. Kenneth Sawyer highlights his chief qualifications and mirrors the requirements specified in the ad. He actually grabs attention by focusing on the phrase "proven skills" used in the ad: He elaborates on his own proven skills throughout the letter and even mentions the term in the closing paragraph.

In some respects, an **unsolicited letter**—sent to an organization that has not announced an opening—stands a better chance of being read and receiving individualized attention. In her unsolicited application letter in Figure 13.11, Glenda Johns manages to give a snapshot of her qualifications and skills without repeating what is said in her résumé (which appears in Figure 13.6 on page 405). She gains attention by focusing on the needs of the employer.

Both solicited and unsolicited letters present your qualifications similarly. The main difference is in the opening paragraph. In a solicited letter, you need no special attention-getter

Margin notes:
You write a solicited application letter in response to an announced job opening.

You write an unsolicited application letter to an organization that has not announced a job opening.

FIGURE 13.11   Effective Unsolicited Application Letter

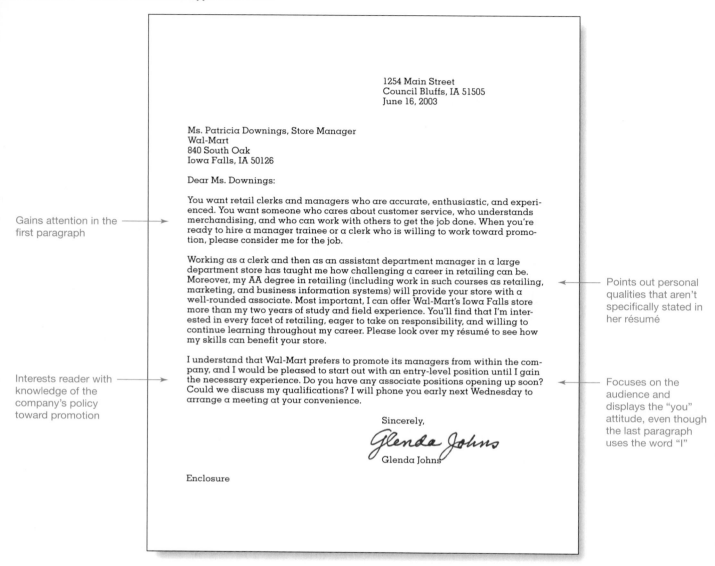

Gains attention in the first paragraph

Interests reader with knowledge of the company's policy toward promotion

Points out personal qualities that aren't specifically stated in her résumé

Focuses on the audience and displays the "you" attitude, even though the last paragraph uses the word "I"

1254 Main Street
Council Bluffs, IA 51505
June 16, 2003

Ms. Patricia Downings, Store Manager
Wal-Mart
840 South Oak
Iowa Falls, IA 50126

Dear Ms. Downings:

You want retail clerks and managers who are accurate, enthusiastic, and experienced. You want someone who cares about customer service, who understands merchandising, and who can work with others to get the job done. When you're ready to hire a manager trainee or a clerk who is willing to work toward promotion, please consider me for the job.

Working as a clerk and then as an assistant department manager in a large department store has taught me how challenging a career in retailing can be. Moreover, my AA degree in retailing (including work in such courses as retailing, marketing, and business information systems) will provide your store with a well-rounded associate. Most important, I can offer Wal-Mart's Iowa Falls store more than my two years of study and field experience. You'll find that I'm interested in every facet of retailing, eager to take on responsibility, and willing to continue learning throughout my career. Please look over my résumé to see how my skills can benefit your store.

I understand that Wal-Mart prefers to promote its managers from within the company, and I would be pleased to start out with an entry-level position until I gain the necessary experience. Do you have any associate positions opening up soon? Could we discuss my qualifications? I will phone you early next Wednesday to arrange a meeting at your convenience.

Sincerely,

Glenda Johns

Glenda Johns

Enclosure

because you have been invited to apply. In an unsolicited letter, you need to start by capturing the reader's attention and interest.

Getting Attention

Follow the AIDA approach when writing your application letter: attention, interest, desire, action.

Like your résumé, your application letter is a form of advertising, so organize it as you would a sales letter: Use the AIDA approach, focus on your audience, and emphasize reader benefits (as discussed in Chapter 9). Make sure your style projects confidence. To sell a potential employer on your merits, you must believe in them and sound as though you do.

The opening of an application letter captures attention, gives the reason you're writing, and states which job you're applying for.

The opening paragraph of your application letter must also state your reason for writing and the position you are applying for. Table 13.4 highlights some important ways to spark interest and grab attention in your opening paragraph. All these openings demonstrate the "you" attitude, and many indicate how the applicant can serve the employer. You can give your reason for writing by saying something like the following examples:

Please consider my application for an entry-level position in technical writing.

Table 13.4	Tips for Getting Attention in Application Letters

Tip	Example
Unsolicited Application Letters	
• Show how your strongest skills will benefit the organization. A 20-year-old in her third year of college might begin like this:	When you need a secretary in your export division who can take shorthand at 125 words a minute and transcribe notes at 70—in English, Spanish, or Portuguese—call me.
• Describe your understanding of the job's requirements and then show how well your qualifications fit them	Your annual report states that Mobil Corporation runs employee-training programs about workforce diversity. The difficulties involved in running such programs can be significant, as I learned while tutoring inner-city high school students last summer. My 12 pupils were enrolled in vocational training programs and came from diverse ethnic and racial backgrounds. The one thing they had in common was a lack of familiarity with the typical employer's expectations. To help them learn the "rules of the game," I developed exercises that cast them in various roles: boss, customer, new recruit, and co-worker. Of the 12 students, 10 subsequently found full-time jobs and have called or written to tell me how much they gained from the workshop.
• Mention the name of a person known to and highly regarded by the reader	When Janice McHugh of your franchise sales division spoke to our business communication class last week, she said you often need promising new marketing graduates at this time of year.
• Refer to publicized company activities, achievements, changes, or new procedures	Today's issue of the *Detroit News* reports that you may need the expertise of computer programmers versed in robotics when your Lansing tire plant automates this spring.
• Use a question to demonstrate your understanding of the organization's needs	Can your fast-growing market research division use an interviewer with 1 1/2 years of field survey experience, a B.A. in public relations, and a real desire to succeed? If so, please consider me for the position.
• Use a catchphrase opening if the job requires ingenuity and imagination	*Haut monde*—whether said in French, Italian, or Arabic, it still means "high society." As an interior designer for your Beverly Hills showroom, not only could I serve and sell to your distinguished clientele, but I could do it in all these languages. I speak, read, and write them fluently.
Solicited Application Letters	
• Identify the publication in which the ad ran; then describe what you have to offer	Your ad in the April issue of *Travel & Leisure* for a cruise-line social director caught my eye. My eight years of experience as a social director in the travel industry would allow me to serve your new Caribbean cruise division well.

Your firm advertised a fleet sales position (on September 23, 2005, in the *Baltimore Sun*).

With my 16 months of new-car sales experience, won't you consider me for that position?

Another way to state your reason for writing is to use a title at the opening of your letter:

Subject: Application for bookkeeper position

Building Interest and Increasing Desire

The middle section of your application letter presents your strongest selling points in terms of their potential benefit to the organization, thereby building interest in you and creating a desire to interview you. If you already mentioned your selling points in the opening, don't repeat them. Simply give supporting evidence. Be careful not to repeat the

The middle section of an application letter

- ■ Summarizes your relevant qualifications
- ■ Emphasizes your accomplishments
- ■ Suggests desirable personal qualities
- ■ Justifies salary requirements
- ■ Refers to your résumé

facts presented in your résumé; simply interpret those facts for the reader. Otherwise, spell out a few of your key qualifications, and back up your assertions with some convincing evidence of your ability to perform:

Poor: I completed three college courses in business communication, earning an A in each course, and have worked for the past year at Imperial Construction.

Improved: Using the skills gained from three semesters of college training in business communication, I developed a collection system for Imperial Construction that reduced its 2004 bad-debt losses by 3.7 percent, or $9,902, over those of 2003. Instead of using timeworn terminology, the new system's collection letters offered discount incentives for speedy payment.

Improved: Experience in customer relations and college courses in public relations have taught me how to handle the problem-solving tasks that arise in a leading retail clothing firm like yours. Such important tasks include identifying and resolving customer complaints, writing letters that build good customer relations, and above all, promoting the organization's positive image.

When writing a solicited letter responding to an advertisement, be sure to discuss each requirement specified in the ad. If you are deficient in any of these requirements, stress other solid selling points to help strengthen your overall presentation.

The middle of your application letter also demonstrates a few significant job-related qualities, such as your diligence or your ability to work hard, learn quickly, handle responsibility, or get along with people:

> While attending college full-time, I trained 3 hours a day with the varsity track team. In addition, I worked part-time during the school year and up to 60 hours a week each summer in order to be totally self-supporting while in college. I can offer your organization the same level of effort and perseverance.

Another matter you might bring up in this section is your salary requirements—but *only* if the organization has asked you to state them. Unless you know approximately what the job pays, suggest a salary range, or indicate that the salary is negotiable or open. You might consult the latest government "Area Wage Survey" at the library to get an idea of the salary range for various job classifications and geographic areas. If you do state a target salary, tie it to the benefits you would bring to the organization (much as you would handle price in a sales letter):

> For the past two years, I have been helping a company similar to yours organize its database. I would therefore like to receive a salary in the same range (the mid-20s) for helping your company set up a more efficient customer database.

Toward the end of this section, refer the reader to your résumé by citing a specific fact or general point covered there:

> You will find my people skills an asset. As you can see in the attached résumé, I've been working part-time with a local publisher since my sophomore year, and during that time, I have successfully resolved more than a few "client crises."

Motivating Action

Close by asking for an interview and making the interview easy to arrange.

The final paragraph of your application letter has two important functions: to ask the reader for a specific action and to make a reply easy. In almost all cases, the action you request is an interview. Don't demand it, however; try to sound natural and appreciative. Offer to come to the employer's office at a convenient time or, if the firm is some distance away, to meet with its nearest representative. Make the request easy to fulfill by stating your phone number and the best time to reach you—or, if you wish to be in control, by mentioning that you will follow up with a phone call in a few days. Refer again to your strongest selling point and, if desired, your date of availability:

> After you have reviewed my qualifications, could we discuss the possibility of putting my marketing skills to work for your company? Because I will be on spring break the week of March 8, I would like to arrange a time to talk then. I will call in late February to schedule a convenient time when we could discuss employment opportunities at your company.

Once you have edited and proofread your application letter, mail it and your résumé promptly, especially if they have been solicited.

Adapting Style and Approach to Culture

The AIDA approach isn't appropriate for job seekers in every culture. If you're applying for a job abroad or want to work with a subsidiary of an organization that is based in another country, you may need to adjust your tone. Blatant self-promotion is considered bad form in some cultures. Other cultures stress group performance over individual contributions. As for format, recruiters in some countries (including France) prefer handwritten letters to printed or typed ones—another good reason to research a company carefully before drafting your application letter. Be yourself, but be businesslike too; avoid sounding cute. Don't use slang or a gimmicky layout.

You may need to vary your approach according to your reader's culture.

Application Forms and Job-Inquiry Letters

Before considering you for a position, some organizations require you to fill out and submit an **application form**, a standardized data sheet that simplifies the comparison of applicants' qualifications. To request such a form, send a job-inquiry letter and include enough information about yourself in the letter to show that you have at least some of the requirements for the position you are seeking:

Use a job-inquiry letter to request an application form, which is a standardized data sheet that simplifies comparison of applicants' credentials.

> Please send me an application form for work as an interior designer in your home furnishings department. For my certificate in design, I took courses in retail merchandising and customer relations. I have also had part-time sales experience at Capwell's department store.

Instead of writing a letter of this kind, you may want to drop in at the office you're applying to. You probably won't be able to talk to anyone other than the receptionist or a human resources assistant, but you can pick up the form, get an impression of the organization, and demonstrate your initiative and energy.

Organizations will use your application form as a convenient one-page source for information about your qualifications. So try to be thorough and accurate when filling it out. Have your résumé with you to remind you of important information, and if you can't remember something and have no record of it, provide the closest estimate possible. If you cannot provide some information because you have no such background (military experience, for example), write "Not applicable." When filling out applications, use a pen (unless specifically requested to use a pencil) and print legibly.

Application forms rarely give you enough space or ask you the right questions to reflect your skills and abilities accurately. Nevertheless, show your cooperation by doing your best to fill out the form completely. If you get an interview, you'll have an opportunity to fill in the gaps. You might also ask whether you might submit a résumé and an application letter along with the application.

Application Follow-Ups

Use a follow-up letter to let the employer know you're still interested in the job.

If your application letter and résumé fail to bring a response within a month or so, follow up with a second letter to keep your file active. This follow-up letter also gives you a chance to update your original application with any recent job-related information:

> Since applying to you on May 3 for an executive secretary position, I have completed a course in office management at South River Community College. I received straight A's in the course. I now am a proficient user of MS Word, including macros and other complex functions.
>
> Please keep my application in your active file, and let me know when you need a skilled executive secretary.

Even if you've received a letter acknowledging your application and saying that it will be kept on file, don't hesitate to send a follow-up letter three months later to show that you are still interested:

> Three months have elapsed since I applied to you for an underwriting position, but I want to let you know that I am still very interested in joining your company.
>
> I recently completed a four-week temporary work assignment at a large local insurance agency. I learned several new verification techniques and gained experience in using the online computer system. This experience could increase my value to your underwriting department.
>
> Please keep my application in your active file, and let me know when a position opens for a capable underwriter.

Unless you state otherwise, the human resources office is likely to assume that you've already found a job and are no longer interested in the organization. Moreover, requirements change. A follow-up letter can demonstrate that you're sincerely interested in working for the organization, that you're persistent in pursuing your goals, and that you're upgrading your skills to make yourself a better employee. And it might just get you an interview.

Reviewing Key Points

This chapter discusses searching for employment and sending employment messages. You have learned how to build toward a career by understanding and adapting to today's changing workplace. You have also learned how to stay abreast of business news, research specific companies, make contacts, and find career counseling.

The chapter discusses how to prepare effective résumés using the three-step writing process. You have learned about the three types of résumé organization: chronological, functional, and combination. And you've learned about the types of sections to include in your résumé. In addition, the chapter explains how to produce six versions of your résumé, depending on what potential employers require. It also explains how to proof and distribute your résumé.

The chapter also discusses preparing employment messages, such as application letters, job-inquiry letters, and application follow-ups. You have learned about how to get attention in your application letters, as well as how to build interest, increase desire, and motivate action.

The next chapter discusses interviewing for employment. You will learn about the sequence and types of interviews, as well as what employers are looking for. You'll learn how to prepare for a job interview by planning ahead for questions and answers. You'll also learn about the various stages of an interview and how to take notes. Finally, you'll learn about following up after the interview with thank-you messages and letters of inquiry.

Test Your Knowledge

1. In what three ways is the employment search affected by the results of today's changing workplace?

2. What three things can you do to make yourself more valuable to an employer?

3. What is a résumé, and why is it important to adopt a "you" attitude when preparing one?

4. How does a chronological résumé differ from a functional résumé, and when is each appropriate?

5. What elements are commonly included in a résumé?

6. What are some of the most common problems with résumés?

7. Why is it important to provide a keyword summary in a scannable or electronic résumé?

8. What advantages do résumés sent by e-mail have over résumés sent by fax or by mail?

9. How does a solicited application letter differ from an unsolicited letter?

10. How does the AIDA approach apply to an application letter?

Apply Your Knowledge

1. According to experts in the job-placement field, the average job seeker relies too heavily on the résumé and not enough on other elements of the job search. Which elements do you think are most important? Please explain.

2. One of the disadvantages of résumé scanning is that some qualified applicants will be missed because the technology isn't perfect. However, more companies are using this approach. Do you think that résumé scanning is a good idea? Please explain.

3. Stating your career objective on a résumé or application might limit your opportunities by labeling you too narrowly. Not stating your objective, however, might lead an employer to categorize you incorrectly. Which outcome is riskier? Do summaries of qualifications overcome such drawbacks? If so, how? Explain briefly.

4. When writing a solicited application letter and describing the skills requested in the employer's ad, how can you avoid using *I* too often? Explain and give examples.

5. **Ethical Choices**   Between your sophomore and junior year, you quit school for a year to earn the money to finish college. You worked as a clerk in a finance company, checking references on loan applications, typing, and filing. Your manager made a lot of the fact that he had never attended college. He seemed to resent you for pursuing your education, but he never criticized your work, so you thought you were doing okay. After you'd been working there for six months, he fired you, saying that you failed to be thorough enough in your credit checks. You were actually glad to leave, and you found another job right away at a bank doing similar duties. Now that you've graduated from college, you're writing your résumé. Will you include the finance company job in your work history? Please explain.

Practice Your Knowledge

Activities

For live links to all websites discussed in this chapter, visit this text's website at www. prenhall.com/bovee. Just log on, select Chapter 13, and click on "Featured Websites." Locate the page or the URL related to the material in the text.

1. **Analyze This Document**   Read the following résumé, then (1) analyze the strengths or weaknesses, and (2) revise the document so that it follows the guidelines presented in this chapter.

Sylvia Manchester
765 Belle Fleur Blvd.
New Orleans, LA 70113
(504) 312-9504
smanchester@rcnmail.com

PERSONAL: Single, excellent health, 5'8", 116 lbs.; hobbies include cooking, dancing, and reading.

JOB OBJECTIVE: To obtain a responsible position in marketing or sales with a good company.

Education: BA degree in biology, University of Louisiana. Graduated with a 3.0 average. Member of the varsity cheerleading squad. President of Panhellenic League. Homecoming queen.

WORK EXPERIENCE

Fisher Scientific Instruments, 2001 to present, field sales representative. Responsible for calling on customers and explaining the features of Fisher's line of laboratory instruments. Also responsible for writing sales letters, attending trade shows, and preparing weekly sales reports.

Fisher Scientific Instruments, 1998-2000, customer service representative. Was responsible for handling incoming phone calls from customers who had questions about delivery, quality, or operation of Fisher's line of laboratory instruments. Also handled miscellaneous correspondence with customers.

Medical Electronics, Inc. 1995-98, administrative assistant to the vice president of marketing. In addition to handling typical secretarial chores for the vice president of marketing, I was in charge of compiling the monthly sales reports, using figures provided by members of the field sales force. I also was given responsibility for doing various market research activities.

<u>New Orleans Convention and Visitors Bureau. 1992-95, summers. tour guide</u>. During the summers of my college years, I led tours of New Orleans for tourists visiting the city. My duties included greeting conventioneers and their spouses at hotels, explaining the history and features of the city during an all-day sight-seeing tour, and answering questions about New Orleans and its attractions. During my fourth summer with the bureau, I was asked to help train the new tour guides. I prepared a handbook that provided interesting facts about the various tourist attractions, as well as answers to the most commonly asked tourist questions. The Bureau was so impressed with the handbook they had it printed up so that it could be given as a gift to visitors.

<u>University of Louisiana. 1992-95. part-time clerk in admissions office</u>. While I was a student in college, I worked 15 hours a week in the admissions office. My duties included filing, processing applications, and handling correspondence with high school students and administrators.

2. **Analyze This Document**   Read the following letter, then (1) analyze its strengths and weaknesses, and (2) revise it so that it follows the guidelines presented in this chapter.

I'm writing to let you know about my availability for the brand manager job you advertised. As you can see from my enclosed résumé, my background is perfect for the position. Even though I don't have any real job experience, my grades have been outstanding considering that I went to a top-ranked business school.

I did many things during my undergraduate years to prepare me for this job:

■ Earned a 3.4 out of a 4.0 with a 3.8 in my business courses

■ Elected representative to the student governing association

■ Selected to receive the Lamar Franklin Award

■ Worked to earn a portion of my tuition

I am sending my résumé to all the top firms, but I like yours better than any of the rest. Your reputation is tops in the industry, and I want to be associated with a business that can pridefully say it's the best.

If you wish for me to come in for an interview, I can come on a Friday afternoon or anytime on weekends when I don't have classes. Again, thanks for considering me for your brand manager position.

3. **Analyze This Document**   Read the following letter, then (1) analyze the strengths or weaknesses, and (2) revise it so that it follows the guidelines presented in this chapter.

Did you receive my résumé? I sent it to you at least two months ago and haven't heard anything. I know you keep résumés on file, but I just want to be sure that you keep me in mind. I heard you are hiring health-care managers and certainly would like to be considered for one of those positions.

Since I last wrote you, I've worked in a variety of positions that have helped prepare me for management. To wit, I've become lunch manager at the restaurant where I work, which involved a raise in pay. I now manage a wait-staff of 12 girls and take the lunch receipts to the bank every day.

Of course, I'd much rather be working at a real job, and that's why I'm writing again. Is there anything else you would like to know about me or my background? I would really like to know more about your company. Is there any literature you could send me? If so, I would really appreciate it.

I think one reason I haven't been hired yet is that I don't want to leave Atlanta. So I hope when you think of me, it's for a position that wouldn't require moving. Thanks again for considering my application.

4. **Work-Related Preferences: Self-Assessment**   What work-related activities and situations do you prefer? Evaluate your preferences in each of the following areas. Use the results as a good start for guiding your job search.

	Strongly Agree	Agree	Disagree	No Preference
1. I want to work independently.	_____	_____	_____	_____
2. I want variety in my work.	_____	_____	_____	_____
3. I want to work with people.	_____	_____	_____	_____
4. I want to work with products or machines.	_____	_____	_____	_____
5. I want physical work.	_____	_____	_____	_____
6. I want mental work.	_____	_____	_____	_____
7. I want to work for a large organization.	_____	_____	_____	_____
8. I want to work for a nonprofit organization.	_____	_____	_____	_____
9. I want to work for a small family business.	_____	_____	_____	_____
10. I want to work for a service business.	_____	_____	_____	_____
11. I want regular, predictable work hours.	_____	_____	_____	_____
12. I want to work in a city location.	_____	_____	_____	_____
13. I want to work in a small town or suburb.	_____	_____	_____	_____
14. I want to work in another country.	_____	_____	_____	_____
15. I want to work outdoors.	_____	_____	_____	_____
16. I want to work in a structured environment.	_____	_____	_____	_____

5. **Teamwork** Working with another student, change the following statements to make them more effective for a traditional résumé by using action verbs.
   a. Have some experience with database design.
   b. Assigned to a project to analyze the cost accounting methods for a large manufacturer.
   c. I was part of a team that developed a new inventory control system.
   d. Am responsible for preparing the quarterly department budget.
   e. Was a manager of a department with seven employees working for me.
   f. Was responsible for developing a spreadsheet to analyze monthly sales by department.
   g. Put in place a new program for ordering supplies.

6. **Résumé Preparation: Work Accomplishments** Using your team's answers to Activity 5 above, make the statements stronger by quantifying them (make up any numbers you need).

7. **Ethical Choices** Assume that you achieved all the tasks shown in Activity 5 above not as an individual employee, but as part of a work team. In your résumé, must you mention other team members? Explain your answer.

8. **Résumé Preparation: Electronic Version** Using your revised version of the résumé in Activity 1 on page 427, prepare a fully formatted print résumé. What formatting changes would Sylvia Manchester need to make if she were sending her résumé electronically? Develop a keyword summary and make all the changes needed to complete this electronic résumé.

Expand Your Knowledge

Exploring the Best of the Web

Post an Online Résumé At CareerBuilder, www.career builder.com, you'll find sample résumés, tips on preparing different types of résumés (including scannable ones), links to additional articles, and expert advice on creating résumés that bring positive results. After you've polished your résumé-writing skills, you can search for jobs online using the site's numerous links to national and international industry-specific websites. You can access the information at CareerBuilder to develop your résumé and then post it with prospective employers—all free of charge. Take advantage of what this site offers, and get ideas for writing or improving a new résumé.

Exercises

1. Before writing a new résumé, make a list of action verbs that describe your skills and experience.
2. Describe the advantages and disadvantages of chronological and functional résumé formats. Do you think a combination résumé would be an appropriate format for your new résumé? Explain why or why not.
3. List some of the tips you learned for preparing an electronic résumé.

Exploring the Web on Your Own

Review these chapter-related websites on your own to learn more about writing résumés and cover letters.

1. To find out what happens when résumés are scanned, log on to Proven Résumés, www.provenresumes.com/reswkshps/electronic/scnres.html.
2. Take measures to ensure that your e-mail résumé arrives intact by following the helpful advice at www.businessweek.com/careers/content/nov2001/ca20011113_7790.
3. Accepted.com, www.accepted.com, can give you advice on getting into graduate school or on writing the perfect résumé.

Learn Interactively

Interactive Study Guide

Go to the Companion Website at www.prenhall.com/bovee. For Chapter 13, take advantage of the interactive "Study Guide" to test your knowledge of the chapter. Get instant feedback on whether you need additional studying. Also, visit this site's "Study Hall," where you'll find an abundance of valuable resources that will help you succeed in this course.

Peak Performance Grammar and Mechanics

In Chapter 12 you were referred to the Peak Performance Grammar and Mechanics activities on the web at www.prenhall.com/onekey to improve your skill with mechanics. For additional reinforcement in numbers, go to the "Improve Your Grammar, Mechanics, and Usage" section that follows, and complete the "Level 1: Self-Assessment" exercises.

Apply each step in Figure 13.3 on page 401 to the following cases, as assigned by your instructor.

Building Toward a Career

1. Taking stock and taking aim: Application package for the right job

Think about yourself. What are some things that come easily to you? What do you enjoy doing? In what part of the country would you like to live? Do you like to work indoors? Outdoors? A combination of the two? How much do you like to travel? Would you like to spend considerable time on the road? Do you like to work closely with others or more independently? What conditions make a job unpleasant? Do you delegate responsibility easily, or do you like to do things yourself? Are you better with words or numbers? Better at speaking or writing? Do you like to work under fixed deadlines? How important is job security to you? Do you want your supervisor to state clearly what is expected of you, or do you like the freedom to make many of your own decisions?

Your task: After answering these questions, gather information about possible jobs that suit your profile by consulting reference materials (from your college library or placement center) and by searching the Internet (using some of the search strategies discussed in Chapter 10). Next, choose a location, a company, and a job that interests you. With guidance from your instructor, decide whether to apply for a job you're qualified for now or one you'll be qualified for with additional education. Then, as directed by your instructor, write one or more of the following: (a) a job-inquiry letter, (b) a résumé, (c) a letter of application, (d) a follow-up letter to your application letter.

■ WEB SKILLS 2. Scanning the possibilities: Résumé for the Internet

In your search for a position, you discover Career Magazine, a website that lists hundreds of companies advertising on the Internet. Your chances of getting an interview with a leading company will be enhanced if you submit your résumé and cover letter electronically. On the web, explore www.careermag.com.

Your task: Prepare a scannable résumé that could be submitted to one of the companies advertising at the Career Magazine website. Print out the résumé for your instructor.

■ WEB SKILLS 3. Online application: Electronic cover letter introducing a résumé

Motley Fool (www.fool.com) is a "Generation X" online magazine accessed via the web. Although its founders and writers are extremely creative and motivated, they lack business experience and need a fellow "X'er" to help them manage the business. Among articles in a recent edition was one titled "The Soul of the Dead," about the influence of the Grateful Dead on more than one generation of concertgoers. Other articles deal with lifestyle issues, pop movies, music, and "trends for an old-young generation."

Your task: Write an e-mail message that will serve as your cover letter and address your message to Louis Corrigan, Managing Editor. Try to limit your message to one screen (about 23 lines). You'll need a creative "hook" and a reassuring approach that identifies you as the right person to help Motley Fool become financially viable.

Writing a Résumé and an Application Letter

4. "Help wanted": Application for a job listed in the classified section

Among the jobs listed in today's *Chicago Tribune* (435 N. Michigan Avenue, Chicago, IL 60641) are the following:

ACCOUNTING ASSISTANT
Established leader in the vacation ownership industry has immediate opening in its Northbrook corp. accounting dept. for an Accounting Assistant. Responsibilities include: bank reconciliation, preparation of deposits, AP, and cash receipt posting. Join our fast-growing company and enjoy our great benefits package. Flex work hours, medical, dental insurance. Fax résumé to Lisa: 847-564-3876.

ADMINISTRATIVE ASSISTANT
Fast-paced Wood Dale office seeks professional with strong computer skills. Proficient in MS Word & Excel, PowerPoint a plus. Must be detail oriented, able to handle multiple tasks, and possess strong communication skills. Excellent benefits, salary, and work environment. Fax résumé to 630-350-8649.

CUSTOMER SERVICE

A nationally known computer software developer has an exciting opportunity in customer service and inside sales support in its fast-paced downtown Chicago office. You'll help resolve customer problems over the phone, provide information, assist in account management, and administer orders. If you're friendly, self-motivated, energetic, and have 2 years of experience, excellent problem-solving skills, organizational, communication, and PC skills, and communicate well over the phone, send résumé to J. Haber, 233 North Lake Shore Drive, Chicago, IL 60641.

SALES-ACCOUNT MANAGER

MidCity Baking Company is seeking an Account Manager to sell and coordinate our programs to major accounts in the Chicago market. The candidate should possess strong analytical and selling skills and demonstrate computer proficiency. Previous sales experience with major account level assignment desired. A degree in business or equivalent experience preferred. For confidential consideration please mail résumé to Steven Crane, Director of Sales, MidCity Baking Company, 133 N. Railroad Avenue, Northlake IL 60614.

Your task: Send a résumé and an application letter to one of these potential employers.

Writing Other Types of Employment Messages

5. Crashing the last frontier: Letter of inquiry about jobs in Alaska

Your friend can't understand why you would want to move to Alaska. So you explain: "What really decided it for me was that I'd never seen the northern lights."

"But what about the bears? The 60-degree-below winters? The permafrost?" asks your friend.

"No problem. Anchorage doesn't get much colder than Buffalo does. It is just windier and wetter. Anyhow, I want to live near Fairbanks, which is near the gold-mining area—and the university is there. Fairbanks has lots of small businesses, like a frontier town in the West about 150 years ago. I think it still has homesteading tracts for people who want to do their own building and are willing to stay for a certain number of years."

"Your plans seem a little hasty," your friend warns. "Maybe you should write for information before you just take off. How do you know you could get a job?"

Your task: Take your friend's advice and write to the Chamber of Commerce, Fairbanks, AK 99701. Ask what types of employment are available to someone with your education and experience, and ask who specifically is hiring year-round employees.

Improve Your Grammar, Mechanics, and Usage

Level 1: Self-Assessment—Numbers

Review Section 3.3 in the Handbook of Grammar, Mechanics, and Usage, and then look at the following 15 items.

For items 1–15, correct number style wherever necessary:

1. We need to hire one office manager, four bookkeepers, and twelve clerk-typists.

2. The market for this product is nearly six million people in our region alone.

3. Make sure that all 1835 pages are on my desk no later than nine o'clock a.m.

4. 2004 was the year that José Guiterez sold more than $50 thousand dollars worth of stock.

5. Our deadline is 4/7, but we won't be ready before 4/11.

6. 95 percent of our customers are men.

7. More than 1/2 the U.S. population is female.

8. Cecile Simmons, thirty-eight, is the first woman in this company to be promoted to management.

9. Last year, I wrote 20 15-page reports, and Michelle wrote 24 three-page reports.

10. Of the 15 applicants, seven are qualified.

11. Our blinds should measure 38 inches wide by 64 and one-half inches long by 7/16 inches deep.

12. Deliver the couch to seven eighty-three Fountain Rd., Suite three, Procter Valley, CA 92074.

13. Here are the corrected figures: 42.7% agree, 23.25% disagree, 34% are undecided, and the error is .05%.

14. You have to agree that 50,000,000 U.S. citizens cannot be wrong.

15. We need a set of shelves 10 feet, eight inches long.

Level 2: Workplace Applications

The following items contain numerous errors in grammar, capitalization, punctuation, abbreviation, number style, word division, and vocabulary. Rewrite each sentence in the space provided, correcting all errors. Write *C* in the space after any sentence that is already correct.

1. Speaking at a recent software conference Alan Nichols; ceo of Tekco Systems; said the companys' goal is to reduce response time to 2 to 4 hrs., using software as an enabler.

2. Selling stocks short are the latest rage on wall street, where lately things have just gone from bad to worst.

3. As Electronic Commerce grows people are trying to find new ways to make money off of it.

4. We give a notification not only to the customer but also our salespeople that the product has been shipped because they will want to follow up.

5. When deciding between these various suppliers, we found that each of them offer both advantages and also disadvantages.

6. I found the book, "Marketing is Easy, Selling is Hard," for three different prices on the Internet: $14, $13.25, and $12.00.

7. United Agra Products, a distributor of fertilizers and seeds, in transmission of customer orders over it's private network faced the possibility of serious bottlenecks.

8. The answers you receive on your questionnaire, are influenced by the types of question you ask, the way they are asked, and your subjects cultural and language background.

9. The creation of hazardous by products, like silver in film processing, require us to collect our used chemicals for disposal at a hazardous-waste-facility.

10. As a source of ingredients for our products, we try to establish relationships with small cooperative or farming communities - often in developing countries – because, we believe that the best way to improve peoples' lives is to give them a chance at self reliance.

11. A entrepreneur really should never be in any organization that get's so big that it looses intimacy.

12. Racecar Driver Eddie Cheever, is founder of Aleanza Marketing Group, a seven-person company that handles $10 million dollars in sponsorship campaigns for Cheevers' team Red Bull Cheever Racing.

13. Over the last six years, Business Cluster Development have started 13 technology related incubators, that they call 'business clusters.'

14. In an interview, Gary Hoover said "When I dreamed up Bookstop, we asked people, "If there was a bookstore that carried a huge selection of books and had them all at discount prices, would you go there"? and we got a lot of yawns".

15. The chief attraction of vending machines are their convenience, they are open 24 hours a day, on the other hand, vending machine prices are no bargain.

Level 3: Document Critique

The following document may contain errors in grammar, capitalization, punctuation, abbreviation, number style, vocabulary, and spelling. You may also find problems with word use and format. Correct all errors using standard proofreading marks (see Appendix C).

THE EXECUTVE SUMMARY

(EXCERPT)

Purpose of the Proposal

This document will acquaint the reader with 3 principle topics by

■ Showing what the San Diego State University (SDSU) *Suntrakker* project is

■ Showing that the team-oriented, inerdepartmental diciplines at SDSU possesses the
tenacity and knowhow to build and race a solar-powered vehical in the World solar
Challenge Race in Austrailia in 1993;

■ Define and articulate how this business team expect to promote and generate the
neccesary support; funds, and materials from the student body, alumni, community and
local businesses to sieze and executive this opportunity;

Project Profile

The *Suntrakker* Solar Car project was conceived in July; 1990, when a small group of San
Diego State university engineering students motivated by the successof of the General
motors "Sunrayce," committed itself to designing and building a superior solar-powered
vehicle to compete in the world Solar Challenge.

From modest Beginnings, the *Suntrakker* project quickly revolved into a cross-disciplinary
educational effort encompassing students from many colleges of San Diego State
University. The project has provides students participants and volunteers with valuable real

life experiences and has brought them together in an effort that benefits not only the students and the university but also the environment.

Sponsors of this project are not only contributing to the successful achievment of the overall *Suntrakker* project but will also enhance their goodwill, advertising, and name promotion by association with the project. In addition, the *Suntrakker* offers a unique opportunity for the companies who can donate parts and accessories to showcase their name and test field their products in public in this highly publicized international contest.

Netting a Job on the Web

Can the web provide the answer to all your employment dreams? Perhaps . . . or perhaps not. As the web grows, the employment information it provides is constantly expanding. And you're fortunate because you don't have to start from scratch like some intrepid adventurer. For helpful hints and useful web addresses, you can turn to books such as *What Color Is Your Parachute?* by Richard Nelson Bolles. Other places to check out online include the following:*

- **4Work** (www.4work.com). One of the few sites that includes listings of internships and volunteer opportunities.
- **America's Career InfoNet** (www.acinet.org). Good place to begin. Offers information on typical wages and employment trends. Gives education, knowledge, and skills requirements for most occupations. Includes links to multiple career resources on the Internet.
- **America's CareerOneStop** (www.careeronestop.org). Comprehensive, government-funded site that includes America's Career InfoNet and America's Job Bank; learn more about the workplace in general as well as specific careers; offers information on typical wages and employment trends and identifies education, knowledge, and skills requirements for most occupations.
- **America's Job Bank** (www.ajb.dni.us). An average of 5,000 new openings posted each day by state agencies. Companies contribute another 3,000.
- **CareerBuilder** (www.careerbuilder.com). Offers a network of career services, job-search information, and tips on how to succeed once you're hired. Includes a database of 20,000 openings.
- **IMDiversity** (www.imdiversity.com). Good resource on diversity in the workplace, with job postings from companies that have made a special commitment to promoting diversity in their workforces.
- **InternshipPrograms.com** (www.internships.wetfeet.com). Posts listings from companies looking for interns in a wide variety of professions.
- **The Monster Board** (www.monster.com). Posts more than 25,000 openings and 300,000 résumés. Heavily mar-

keted, it brings a flood of employers (many with under 500 employees).

- **NationJob Network** (www.nationjob.com). Posts more than 15,000 jobs nationwide, with an emphasis on those in the Midwest.
- **Net-Temps** (www.net-temps.com). Maintained by career consultants; offers several thousand updated listings and real-time seminars. Network forums help you develop new contacts and job leads. Includes chat room for online interviews.
- **MonsterTrak** (www.monstertrak.com). Has formed partnerships with 750 campuses nationwide and serves as a virtual career center for students and alumni. Many entry-level postings.
- **USA Jobs** (www.usajobs.opm.gov). The official job search site for the U.S. government, featuring everything from economists to astronauts to Border patrol agents.
- **Yahoo! HotJobs** (hotjobs.yahoo.com). A member-based site that charges companies a hefty fee to post openings or search through résumés. Job seekers can create a personal page to manage their search and collect statistics on how many companies have retrieved their résumé.

Applications for Success

Looking for employment on the web can be both convenient and confusing. You'll be ahead of the competition if you understand that job sites offer both advantages and drawbacks.

Do the following:

1. Surfing the web can chew up a disproportionate amount of your job-seeking time. Explain how you can limit the amount of time you spend on the web and still make it work for you.
2. When posting your résumé on the web, you're revealing a lot of information about yourself that could be used by people other than employers (salespeople, people competing for similar positions, con artists). What sort of information might you leave off your web résumé that would certainly appear on a traditional résumé?
3. Visit at least two of these online indexes, and check out features such as job searches, career centers, and tips for finding employment. Compare the features of the indexes and choose the one you find the most convenient and helpful. Explain your choice in a one-page e-mail to your instructor.

---

*Direct links to these websites can be accessed at the Riley Guide (www.rileyguide.com).

14 Interviewing for Employment and Following Up

Learning Objectives

After studying this chapter, you will be able to

1 Define *employment interview* and explain its dual purpose

2 Discuss the three stages in a typical sequence of interviews

3 Identify and briefly describe six types of employment interviews

4 List six tasks you need to complete to prepare for a successful job interview

5 Explain the three stages of a successful employment interview

6 Describe four ways you can respond to unethical or illegal questions during an interview

7 Name three common employment messages that follow an interview and state briefly when you would use each one

When evaluating candidates, Microsoft's Jodi DeLeon asks how they set priorities for all the various projects they're currently working on. That's where demonstrating an ability to juggle school with extracurricular activities can help. She also looks at a student's drive and ambition, resourcefulness, and analytical ability. Good grades help, of course, but she's more interested in how well a person listens to and thinks through what she says.[1]

Understanding the Interviewing Process

"Interviewers are not trying to intimidate or scare people," explains Jodi DeLeon. "We just want to find out as much as we can." Employment interviews have a dual purpose:

- **Organization's main objective.** To find the best person available for the job
- **Applicant's main objective.** To find the job best suited to his or her goals and capabilities

An interview helps both the interviewer and the applicant achieve their goals.

While recruiters are trying to decide whether you are right for them, you must decide whether the company is right for you.

An **employment interview** is a formal meeting during which both employer and applicant ask questions and exchange information to see whether the applicant and the organization are a good match. Because interviewing takes time, you'll want to begin

438

seeking jobs well in advance of the date you want to start work. Some students begin their job search as much as nine months before graduation. After all, it takes an average of 10 interviews to get one job offer, so if you hope to have several offers to choose from, expect to go through 20 or 30 interviews during your job search.[2] Also plan on facing a series of interviews, each with a different purpose.

In a typical job search, you can expect to have many interviews before you accept a job offer.

The Typical Sequence of Interviews

Not all organizations interview potential candidates the same way. However, most employers interview an applicant two or three times before deciding to make a job offer.

The Screening Stage

The preliminary *screening stage* is generally held on campus to help employers screen out unqualified applicants. These interviews are fairly structured: Applicants are often asked roughly the same questions so that all the candidates will be measured against the same criteria. In some cases, technology has transformed the initial, get-to-know-you interview, allowing employers to screen candidates by phone, video, or computer.[3]

Your best approach to the screening stage is to follow the interviewer's lead. Keep your responses short and to the point. Time is limited, so talking too much can be a big mistake. However, try to differentiate yourself from other candidates. Without resorting to gimmicks, call attention to one key aspect of your background. Then the recruiter can say, "Oh yes, I remember Jones—the one who sold used Toyotas in Detroit." Just be sure the trait you accentuate is relevant to the job in question. Also be ready to demonstrate a particular skill (perhaps problem solving) if asked to do so. Candidates who meet the company's requirements are invited to visit company offices for further evaluation.

During the screening stage of interviews, try to differentiate yourself from other candidates with a memorable headline.

The Selection Stage

The next stage of interviews helps the organization narrow the field a little further. Typically, if you're invited to visit a company, you'll talk with several people: a member of the human resources department, one or two potential colleagues, and your potential supervisor. You might face a panel of several interviewers who ask you questions during a single session. By noting how you listen, think, and express yourself, they can decide how likely you are to get along with colleagues.

Your best approach during this stage of interviews is to show interest in the job. Relate your skills and experience to the organization's needs. Broaden your sales pitch. Instead of telegraphing the "headline," give the interviewer the whole story. Touch briefly on all your strengths, but explain three or four of your best qualifications in depth. At the same time, probe for information that will help you evaluate the position objectively. As important as it is to get an offer, it's also important to learn whether the job is right for you. Also, be sure to listen attentively, ask insightful questions, and display enthusiasm. If the interviewers agree that you're a good candidate, you may receive a job offer, either on the spot or a few days later by phone or mail.

During the selection stage of interviews, expand on the headline, covering all your strengths and relating them to the organization's needs.

The Final Stage

You may be invited back for a final evaluation by a higher-ranking executive with the authority to make an offer and negotiate terms. This person may already have concluded that your background is right and may be more concerned with sizing up your personality. You both need to see whether there is a good psychological fit, so be honest about your motivations and values. If the interview goes well, your goal is to clinch the deal on the best possible terms. An underlying objective of the *final stage* is often to sell you on the advantages of joining the organization.

During the final stage, emphasize your personality, describing your motivations and values honestly.

Types of Interviews

Organizations use various types of interviews to discover as much as possible about applicants.

Interviews vary from employer to employer.

- **Structured interviews.** Generally used in the screening stage, structured interviews are controlled by the employer, who asks a series of prepared questions in a set order. All answers are noted. Although useful in gathering facts, the structured interview is generally a poor measure of an applicant's personal qualities. Nevertheless, some companies use structured interviews to create uniformity in their hiring process.[4]

- **Open-ended interviews.** Less formal and unstructured, these interviews often have a relaxed format. The interviewer asks broad, open-ended questions, encouraging applicants to talk freely. Such interviews bring out an applicant's personality and test professional judgment. However, some candidates reveal too much, rambling on about personal or family problems, so strike a balance between being friendly and remembering that you're in a business situation.

- **Group interviews.** To judge interpersonal skills, some employers meet with several candidates simultaneously to see how they interact. For example, the Walt Disney Company uses group interviews when hiring people for its theme parks. During a 45-minute session, the Disney recruiter watches how three candidates relate to one another. Do they smile? Are they supportive of one another's comments? Do they try to score points at each other's expense?[5]

- **Stress interviews.** Perhaps the most unnerving, stress interviews are set up to see how well a candidate handles stressful situations (an important qualification for certain jobs). You might be asked pointed questions designed to irk or unsettle you. You might be subjected to long periods of silence, criticisms of your appearance, deliberate interruptions, and abrupt or even hostile reactions by the interviewer.

- **Video interviews.** To cut travel costs, many large companies use videoconferencing systems. You need to prepare a bit differently for a video interview by (1) requesting a preliminary phone conversation to establish rapport with the interviewer, (2) arriving early enough to get used to the equipment and setting, (3) speaking clearly but no more slowly than normal, (4) sitting straight and looking up but not down, and (5) showing some animation (but not too much, since it will appear blurry to the interviewer).[6]

- **Situational interviews.** Many companies claim that interviewing is about the job, not about a candidate's five-year goals, weaknesses or strengths, challenging experiences, or greatest accomplishments. An interviewer describes a situation and asks, "How would you handle this?" So the situational interview is a hands-on, at-work meeting between an employer who needs a job done and a worker who must be fully prepared to do the work.[7]

Regardless of the type of interview you may face, a personal interview is vital because your résumé can't show whether you're lively and outgoing or subdued and low-key, able to take direction or able to take charge. Each job requires a different mix of personality traits. The interviewer's task is to find out whether you will be effective on the job.

Preparing for a Job Interview

Just as written messages need planning, employment interviews need preparation.

It's perfectly normal to feel a little anxious before an interview. But good preparation will help you perform well. Be sure to consider any cultural differences when preparing for interviews, and base your approach on what your audience expects. The advice in this chapter is most appropriate for companies and employers in the United States and Canada. Before the interview, do some follow-up research, think ahead about questions, bolster your confidence, polish your interview style, plan to look good, and be ready when you arrive.

Table 14.1 Finding Out About the Organization and the Job

Where to Look for Information

• Annual report	Summarizes operations; describes products, lists events, names key personnel
• In-house magazine or newspaper	Reveals information about company operations, events, personnel
• Product brochure or publicity release	Gives insight into firm's operations and values (obtain from public relations office)
• Stock research report	Helps assess stability and growth prospects (obtain online or from stockbroker)
• Newspaper's business or financial pages	Contain news items about organizations, current performance figures
• Periodicals indexes	Contain descriptive listings of magazine/newspaper articles about firms (obtain from library)
• Better Business Bureau and Chamber of Commerce	Distribute information about some local organizations
• Former and current employees	Have insight into job and work environment
• College placement office	Collects information on organizations that recruit and on job qualifications and salaries

What to Find Out About the Organization

• Full name	How the firm is officially known (e.g., 3M is Minnesota Mining & Manufacturing Company)
• Location	Where the organization's headquarters, branch offices, and plants are
• Age	How long the organization has been in business
• Products	What goods and services the organization produces and sells
• Industry position	What the organization's current market share, financial position, and profit picture are
• Earnings	What the trends in the firm's stock prices and dividends are (if firm is publicly held)
• Growth	How the firm's earnings/holdings have changed in recent years and prospects for expansion
• Organization	What subsidiaries, divisions, and departments make up the whole

What to Find Out About the Job

• Job title	What you will be called
• Job functions	What the main tasks of the job are
• Job qualifications	What knowledge and skills the job requires
• Career path	What chances for ready advancement exist
• Salary range	What the firm typically offers and what is reasonable in this industry and geographic area
• Travel opportunities	How often, long, and far you'll be allowed (or required) to travel
• Relocation opportunities	Where you might be allowed (or required) to move and how often

Do Some Follow-Up Research

You will already have researched the companies you sent your résumé to. But now that you've been invited for an interview, you'll want to fine-tune your research and brush up on the facts you've collected (see Table 14.1). Learning about the organization and the job enables you to show the interviewer just how you will meet the organization's particular needs.

Be prepared to relate your qualifications to the organization's needs.

Think Ahead About Questions

Planning ahead for the interviewer's questions will help you handle them more confidently and intelligently. Moreover, you will want to prepare intelligent questions of your own.

Table 14.2	Twenty-Five Common Interview Questions

Questions About College

1. What courses in college did you like most? Least? Why?
2. Do you think your extracurricular activities in college were worth the time you spent on them? Why or why not?
3. When did you choose your college major? Did you ever change your major? If so, why?
4. Do you feel you did the best scholastic work you are capable of?
5. Which of your college years was the toughest? Why?

Questions About Employers and Jobs

6. What jobs have you held? Why did you leave?
7. What percentage of your college expenses did you earn? How?
8. Why did you choose your particular field of work?
9. What are the disadvantages of your chosen field?
10. Have you served in the military? What rank did you achieve? What jobs did you perform?
11. What do you think about how this industry operates today?
12. Why do you think you would like this particular type of job?

Questions About Personal Attitudes and Preferences

13. Do you prefer to work in any specific geographic location? If so, why?
14. How much money do you hope to be earning in 5 years? In 10 years?
15. What do you think determines a person's progress in a good organization?
16. What personal characteristics do you feel are necessary for success in your chosen field?
17. Tell me a story.
18. Do you like to travel?
19. Do you think grades should be considered by employers? Why or why not?

Questions About Work Habits

20. Do you prefer working with others or by yourself?
21. What type of boss do you prefer?
22. Have you ever had any difficulty getting along with colleagues or supervisors? With instructors? With other students?
23. Would you prefer to work in a large or a small organization? Why?
24. How do you feel about overtime work?
25. What have you done that shows initiative and willingness to work?

Planning for the Employer's Questions

Employers usually gear their interview questions to specific organizational needs. You can expect to be asked about your skills, achievements, and goals, as well as about your attitude toward work and school, your relationships with others (work supervisors, colleagues, and fellow students), and occasionally your hobbies and interests. For a look at the types of questions often asked, see Table 14.2. Jot down a brief answer to each one. Then read over the answers until you feel comfortable with each of them.

Practice answering interview questions.

Although practicing your answers will help you feel prepared and confident, you don't want to memorize responses or sound over-rehearsed. Try giving a list of interview questions to a friend or relative and have that person ask you various questions at random. Such practice helps you learn to articulate answers and to look at the person as you answer.

Planning Questions of Your Own

The questions you ask in an interview are just as important as the answers you provide. By asking intelligent questions, you demonstrate your understanding of the organization, and you can steer the discussion into those areas that allow you to present your qualifications to best advantage. Before the interview, prepare a list of about a dozen questions you need answered in order to evaluate the organization and the job.

Don't limit your questions to those you think will impress the interviewer, or you won't get the information you'll need to make a wise decision if and when you're offered the job. Here's a list of some things you might want to find out:

- **Are these my kind of people?** Observe the interviewer, and if you can, arrange to talk with other employees.
- **Can I do this work?** Compare your qualifications with the requirements described by the interviewer.
- **Will I enjoy the work?** Know yourself and what's important to you. Will you find the work challenging? Will it give you feelings of accomplishment, of satisfaction, and of making a real contribution?
- **Is the job what I want?** You may never find a job that fulfills all your wants, but the position you accept should satisfy at least your primary ones. Will it make use of your best capabilities? Does it offer a career path to the long-term goals you've set?
- **Does the job pay what I'm worth?** By comparing jobs and salaries before you're interviewed, you'll know what's reasonable for someone with your skills in your industry.
- **What kind of person would I be working for?** If the interviewer is your prospective boss, watch how others interact with that person, tactfully query other employees, or pose a careful question or two during the interview. If your prospective boss is someone else, ask for that person's name, job title, and responsibilities. Try to learn all you can.
- **What sort of future can I expect with this organization?** How healthy is the organization? Can you look forward to advancement? Does the organization offer insurance, pension, vacation, or other benefits?

Rather than bombarding the interviewer with these questions the minute you walk in the room, use a mix of formats to elicit this information. Start with a warm-up question to help break the ice. You might ask, "What departments usually hire new graduates?" After that, you might build rapport by asking an open-ended question that draws out the interviewer's opinion ("How do you think Internet sales will affect the company's continued growth?"). Indirect questions can elicit useful information and show that you've prepared for the interview ("I'd really like to know more about the company's plans for expanding its corporate presence on the web" or "That recent *Business Week* article about the company was very interesting"). Any questions you ask should be in your own words so that you don't sound like every other candidate. For a list of other good questions you might use as a starting point, see Table 14.3.

Take your list of questions to the interview on a notepad. If you need to, jot down brief notes during the meeting, and be sure to record answers in more detail afterward. Having a list of questions should impress the interviewer with your organization and thoroughness. It will also show that you're there to evaluate the organization and the job as well as to sell yourself.

Bolster Your Confidence

Building your confidence helps you make a better impression. The best way to counteract any apprehension is to remove its source. You may feel shy or self-conscious because you think you have some flaw that will prompt others to reject you. But you're much more conscious of your limitations than other people are.

You are responsible for deciding whether the work and the organization are compatible with your goals and values.

Types of questions to ask during an interview:
- Warm-up
- Open-ended
- Indirect

Table 14.3	Fifteen Questions to Ask the Interviewer
Questions About the Job	**Questions About the Organization**
What are the job's major responsibilities?	What are the organization's major strengths? Weaknesses?
What qualities do you want in the person who fills this position?	Who are your organization's major competitors, and what are their strengths and weaknesses?
Do you want to know more about my related training?	What makes your organization different from others in the industry?
What is the first problem that needs the attention of the person you hire?	What are your organization's major markets?
Would relocation be required now or in the future?	Does the organization have any plans for new products? Acquisitions?
Why is this job now vacant?	How would you define your organization's managerial philosophy?
What can you tell me about the person I would report to?	What additional training does your organization provide?
	Do employees have an opportunity to continue their education with help from the organization?

If you feel shy or self-conscious, remember that recruiters are human too.

If some aspect of your appearance or background makes you uneasy, correct it or off-set it by exercising positive traits such as warmth, wit, intelligence, or charm. Instead of dwelling on your weaknesses, focus on your strengths so that you can emphasize them to an interviewer. Make a list of your good points and compare them with what you see as your shortcomings. Remember that you're not alone. All the other candidates for the job are just as nervous as you are. Even the interviewer may be nervous.

Polish Your Interview Style

Staging mock interviews with a friend is a good way to hone your style.

Confidence helps you walk into an interview, but once you're there, you want to give the interviewer an impression of poise, good manners, and good judgment. You can develop an adept style by staging mock interviews with a friend. After each practice session, try to identify opportunities for improvement. Have your friend critique your performance, using the list of interview faults shown in Figure 14.1. You can tape-record or videotape these mock interviews and then evaluate them yourself. The taping process can be intimidating, but it helps you work out any problems before you begin actual job interviews.

Nonverbal behavior has a significant effect on the interviewer's opinion of you.

As you stage your mock interviews, pay particular attention to your nonverbal behavior. In the United States, you are more likely to have a successful interview if you maintain eye contact, smile frequently, sit in an attentive position, and use frequent hand gestures. These nonverbal signals convince the interviewer that you're alert, assertive, dependable, confident, responsible, and energetic.[8] Some companies based in the United States are owned and managed by people from other cultures, so during your research, find out about the company's cultural background and preferences regarding nonverbal behavior.

The sound of your voice can also have a major impact on your success in a job interview.[9] You can work with a tape recorder to overcome voice problems. If you tend to speak too rapidly, practice speaking more slowly. If your voice sounds too loud or too soft, practice adjusting it. Work on eliminating speech mannerisms such as *you know, like,* and *um,* which might make you sound inarticulate.

Plan to Look Good

To look like a winner
- Dress conservatively
- Be well groomed
- Smile when appropriate

Physical appearance is important because clothing and grooming reveal something about a candidate's personality and professionalism. When it comes to clothing, the best policy is to dress conservatively. Wear the best-quality businesslike clothing you can, preferably in a dark, solid color. Avoid flamboyant styles, colors, and prints. Even in companies

FIGURE 14.1   Marks Against Applicants (in General Order of Importance)

> ### WHAT EMPLOYERS DON'T LIKE TO SEE IN CANDIDATES
>
> ☑ Poor personal appearance
> ☑ Overbearing, overaggressive, conceited demeanor; a "superiority complex"; know-it-all attitude
> ☑ Inability to express ideas clearly; poor voice, diction, grammar
> ☑ Lack of knowledge or experience
> ☑ Poor preparation for the interview
> ☑ Lack of interest in the job
> ☑ Lack of planning for career; lack of purpose, goals
> ☑ Lack of enthusiasm; passive and indifferent demeanor
> ☑ Lack of confidence and poise; appearance of being nervous and ill at ease
> ☑ Insufficient evidence of achievement
> ☑ Failure to participate in extracurricular activities
> ☑ Overemphasis on money; interest only in the best dollar offer
> ☑ Poor scholastic record; just got by
> ☑ Unwillingness to start at the bottom; expecting too much too soon
> ☑ Tendency to make excuses
> ☑ Evasive answers; hedges on unfavorable factors in record
> ☑ Lack of tact
> ☑ Lack of maturity
> ☑ Lack of courtesy; ill-mannered
> ☑ Condemnation of past employers
> ☑ Lack of social skills
> ☑ Marked dislike for schoolwork
> ☑ Lack of vitality
> ☑ Failure to look interviewer in the eye
> ☑ Limp, weak handshake

where interviewers may dress casually, it's important to show good judgment by dressing (and acting) in a professional manner. Some candidates are asking interviewers ahead of time what they should wear. One human resources executive tells job seekers to dress business casual, because dressing in a suit, for example, looks awkward at his company.[10]

Good grooming makes any style of clothing look better. Make sure your clothes are clean and unwrinkled, your shoes unscuffed and well shined, your hair neatly styled and combed, your fingernails clean, and your breath fresh. If possible, check your appearance in a mirror before entering the room for the interview. Finally, remember that one of the best ways to look good is to smile at appropriate moments.

Be Ready When You Arrive

Plan to take a small notebook, a pen, a list of the questions you want to ask, two copies of your résumé (protected in a folder), an outline of what you have learned about the organization, and any past correspondence about the position. You may also want to take a small calendar, a transcript of your college grades, a list of references, and a portfolio containing samples of your work, performance reviews, and certificates of achievement. In an era when many people exaggerate their qualifications, visible proof of your abilities carries a lot of weight.[11]

Be sure you know when and where the interview will be held. The worst way to start any interview is to be late. Check the route you will take, even if it means phoning the interviewer's secretary to ask. Find out how much time it takes to get there; then plan to arrive early. Allow a little extra time in case you run into a problem on the way.

Be prepared for the interview by
- Taking proof of your accomplishments
- Arriving on time
- Waiting graciously

Once you arrive, relax. You may have to wait a little while, so bring along something to read or occupy your time (the less frivolous or controversial, the better). If company literature is available, read it while you wait. In any case, be polite to the interviewer's assistant. If the opportunity presents itself, ask a few questions about the organization or express enthusiasm for the job. Refrain from smoking before the interview (nonsmokers can smell smoke on the clothing of interviewees), and avoid chewing gum in the waiting room. Anything you do or say while you wait may well get back to the interviewer, so make sure your best qualities show from the moment you enter the premises. That way you'll be ready for the interview itself once it actually begins.

Interviewing for Success

As discussed earlier, how you handle a particular interview depends on where you stand in the sequence of interviews. Is this your first interview in the screening process? Have you made it to the selection interview or even the final interview? Regardless of where you are in the process, every interview will proceed through three stages: the warm-up, the question-and-answer session, and the close.

The Warm-Up

The first minute of the interview is crucial.

Of the three stages, the warm-up is the most important, even though it may account for only a small fraction of the time you spend in the interview. Psychologists say that 50 percent of an interviewer's decision is made within the first 30 to 60 seconds, and another 25 percent is made within 15 minutes. If you get off to a bad start, it's extremely difficult to turn the interview around.[12]

Body language is important at this point. Because you won't have time to say much in the first minute or two, you must sell yourself nonverbally. Begin by using the interviewer's name if you're sure you can pronounce it correctly. If the interviewer extends a hand, respond with a firm but gentle handshake, and wait until you're asked to be seated. Let the interviewer start the discussion, and listen for cues that tell you what he or she is interested in knowing about you as a potential employee.

The Question-and-Answer Stage

Questions and answers will consume the greatest part of the interview. The interviewer will ask you about your qualifications and discuss many of the points mentioned in your résumé. You'll also be asking questions of your own.

Dealing with Questions

Tailor your answers to emphasize your strengths.

Let the interviewer lead the conversation, and never answer a question before he or she has finished asking it. Surprisingly, the last few words of the question might alter how you respond. As questions are asked, tailor your answers to make a favorable impression. Don't limit yourself to yes-or-no answers. If you're asked a difficult question, be sure you pause to think before responding.

If you periodically ask a question or two from the list you've prepared, you'll not only learn something but also demonstrate your interest. Probe for what the company is looking for in its new employees so that you can show how you meet the firm's needs. Also try to zero in on any reservations the interviewer might have about you so that you can dispel them.

Listening to the Interviewer

Paying attention to both verbal and nonverbal messages can help you turn the question-and-answer stage to your advantage.

Paying attention when the interviewer speaks can be as important as giving good answers or asking good questions. Listening should make up about half the time you spend in an interview. For tips on becoming a better listener, see Chapter 2.

The interviewer's facial expressions, eye movements, gestures, and posture may tell you the real meaning of what is being said. Be especially aware of how your comments are received. Does the interviewer nod in agreement or smile to show approval? If so, you're making progress. If not, you might want to introduce another topic or modify your approach.

Fielding Discriminatory Questions

Employers cannot legally discriminate against a job candidate on the basis of race, color, gender, age (from 40 to 70), marital status, religion, national origin, or disability. In general, the following topics should not be directly or indirectly introduced by an interviewer:[13]

- Your religious affiliation or organizations and lodges you belong to
- Your national origin, age, marital status, or former name
- Your spouse, spouse's employment or salary, dependents, children, or child-care arrangements
- Your height, weight, gender, pregnancy, or any health conditions or disabilities that are not reasonably related to job performance
- Arrests or criminal convictions that are not related to job performance

Some questions should not be asked by interviewers.

Although federal law does not specifically prohibit questions that touch on these areas, the Equal Employment Opportunity Commission (EEOC) considers such questions with "extreme disfavor." Table 14.4 compares specific questions that may and may not be asked during an employment interview.

How to Respond   If your interviewer asks these personal questions, how you respond depends on how badly you want the job, how you feel about revealing the information asked for, what you think the interviewer will do with the information, and whether you want to work for a company that asks such questions. If you don't want the job, you can tell the interviewer that you think a particular question is unethical or simply refuse to answer—responses that will leave an unfavorable impression.[14] If you do want the job, you might (1) ask how the question is related to your qualifications, (2) explain that the information is personal, (3) respond to what you think is the interviewer's real concern, or (4) answer both the question and the concern. If you answer an unethical or unlawful question, you run the risk that your answer may hurt your chances, so think carefully before answering.[15]

Think in advance about how you might respond to unlawful interview questions.

Table 14.4	Interview Questions That May and May Not Be Asked
You may ask this . . .	**But not this**
What is your name?	What was your maiden name?
Are you over 18?	When were you born?
Did you graduate from high school?	When did you graduate from high school?
[No questions about race are allowed.]	What is your race?
Can you perform [specific tasks]?	Do you have physical or mental disabilities?
	Do you have a drug or alcohol problem?
	Are you taking any prescription drugs?
Would you be able to meet the job's requirement to frequently work weekends?	Would working on weekends conflict with your religion?
Do you have the legal right to work in the United States?	What country are you a citizen of?
Have you ever been convicted of a felony?	Have you ever been arrested?
This job requires that you speak Spanish. Do you?	What language did you speak in your home when you were growing up?

Where to File a Complaint   When a business can show that the safety of its employees or customers is at stake, it may be allowed to ask questions that would seem discriminatory in another context. Despite this exception, if you believe an interviewer's questions are unreasonable, unrelated to the job, or an attempt to discriminate, you may complain to the EEOC or to the state agency that regulates fair employment practices. To report discrimination on the basis of age or physical disability, contact the employer's equal opportunity officer or the U.S. Department of Labor. If you file a complaint, be prepared to spend a lot of time and effort—and keep in mind that you may not win.[16]

The Close

Like the opening, the end of the interview is more important than its duration would indicate. In the last few minutes, you need to evaluate how well you've done. You also need to correct any misconceptions the interviewer might have.

Concluding Gracefully

Conclude the interview with courtesy and enthusiasm.

You can generally tell when the interviewer is trying to conclude the session. He or she may ask whether you have any more questions, sum up the discussion, change position, or indicate with a gesture that the interview is over. When you get the signal, respond promptly, but don't rush. Be sure to thank the interviewer for the opportunity and express an interest in the organization. If you can do so comfortably, try to pin down what will happen next, but don't press for an immediate decision.

If this is your second or third visit to the organization, the interview may culminate with an offer of employment. You have two options: Accept it or request time to think it over. The best course is usually to wait. If no job offer is made, the interviewer may not have reached a decision yet, but you may tactfully ask when you can expect to know the decision.

Discussing Salary

Be realistic in your salary expectations and diplomatic in your negotiations.

If you do receive an offer during the interview, you'll naturally want to discuss salary. However, let the interviewer raise the subject. If asked your salary requirements, say that you would expect to receive the standard salary for the job in question. If you have added qualifications, point them out: "With my 18 months of experience in the field, I would expect to start in the middle of the normal salary range." Some applicants find the Internet a terrific resource for salary information.

When to Negotiate   If you don't like the offer, you might try to negotiate, provided you're in a good bargaining position and the organization has the flexibility to accommodate you. You'll be in a fairly strong position if your skills are in short supply and you have several other offers. It also helps if you're the favorite candidate and the organization is booming. However, many organizations are relatively rigid in their salary practices, particularly at the entry level. In the United States and some European countries, it is perfectly acceptable to ask, "Is there any room for negotiation?"

What to Negotiate   Even if you can't bargain for more money, you may be able to win some concessions on benefits and perquisites. The value of negotiating can be significant because benefits often cost the employer 25 to 45 percent of your salary. In other words, if you're offered an annual salary of $20,000, you'll ordinarily get an additional $5,000 to $9,000 in benefits: life, health, and disability insurance; pension and savings plans; vacation time; or even tuition reimbursement.[17]

If you can trade one benefit for another, you may be able to enhance the value of the total package. For example, life insurance may be relatively unimportant to you if you're single, whereas extra vacation time might be very valuable indeed. Don't inquire about benefits, however, until you know you have a job offer.

Interview Notes

Keep a written record of your job interviews.

If yours is a typical job search, you'll have many interviews before you accept an offer. For that reason, keeping a notebook or binder of interview notes can help you refresh your memory of each conversation. As soon as the interview ends, jot down the names and titles of the people you met. Briefly summarize the interviewer's answers to your questions. Then quickly evaluate your performance during the interview, listing what you handled well and what you didn't. Going over these notes can help you improve your performance in the future.[18] In addition to improving your performance during interviews, interview notes will help you keep track of any follow-up messages you'll need to send.

Following Up After the Interview

Touching base with the prospective employer after the interview, either by phone or in writing, shows that you really want the job and are determined to get it. Following up brings your name to the interviewer's attention once again and reminds him or her that you're waiting for the decision.

The two most common forms of follow-up are the thank-you message and the inquiry. These messages are often handled by letter, but an e-mail or a phone call can be just as effective, particularly if the employer seems to favor a casual, personal style. Other types of follow-up messages are sent only in certain cases—such as a letter requesting a time extension. Such messages are best handled in a letter, in order to be able to document your employment-related communications.

Three types of follow-up messages:
- Thank-you message
- Inquiry
- Request for a time extension

Thank-You Message

Express your thanks within two days after the interview, even if you feel you have little chance for the job. Acknowledge the interviewer's time and courtesy, and be sure to restate the specific job you're applying for. Convey your continued interest, then ask politely for a decision.

Keep your thank-you message brief (less than five minutes for a phone call or only one page for a letter), and organize it like a routine message. Demonstrate the "you" attitude, and sound positive without sounding overconfident. The following sample thank-you letter shows how to achieve all this in three brief paragraphs:

A note or phone call thanking the interviewer
- Is organized like a routine message
- Closes with a request for a decision or future consideration

Reminds the interviewer of the reasons for meeting and graciously acknowledges the consideration shown to the applicant

After talking with you yesterday, touring your sets, and watching the television commercials being filmed, I remain very enthusiastic about the possibility of joining your staff as a television/film production assistant. Thanks for taking so much time to show me around.

During our meeting, I said that I would prefer not to relocate, but I've reconsidered the matter. I would be pleased to relocate wherever you need my skills in set decoration and prop design.

Now that you've explained the details of your operation, I feel quite strongly that I can make a contribution to the sorts of productions you're lining up. You can also count on me to be an energetic employee and a positive addition to your crew. Please let me know your decision as soon as possible.

Ends with a request for decision

Indicates the writer's flexibility and commitment to the job if hired

Reminds the recruiter of special qualifications

Closes on a confident, "you"-oriented note

Even if the interviewer has said that you're unqualified for the job, a thank-you message may keep the door open. Miguel Espinosa followed up a recent job interview with a thank-you message sent by e-mail the same day (see Figure 14.2).

Letter of Inquiry

If you're not advised of the interviewer's decision by the promised date or within two weeks, you might make an inquiry. A letter of inquiry is particularly appropriate if you've

An inquiry about a hiring decision follows the plan for a direct request.

FIGURE 14.2   Effective Thank-You by E-Mail

Uses a subject line that tells the reader the purpose of the message

Uses a formal salutation for e-mail to the interviewer

Shows interest in future openings for the position and confirms the writer's commitment to follow the interviewer's advice

Includes contact information in case the interviewer wants to keep it on file

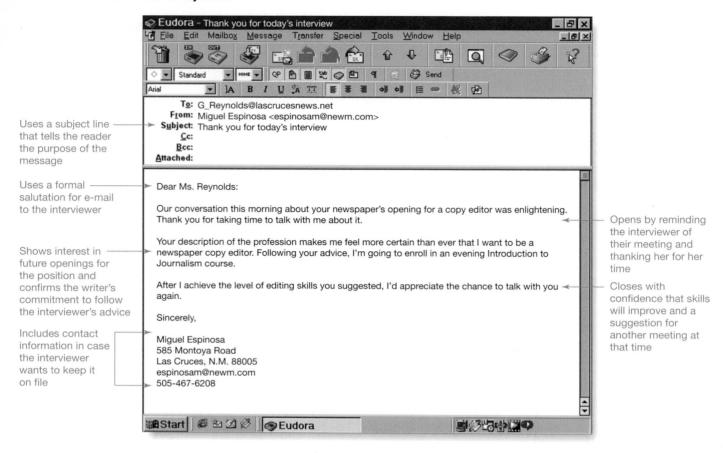

Opens by reminding the interviewer of their meeting and thanking her for her time

Closes with confidence that skills will improve and a suggestion for another meeting at that time

received a job offer from a second firm and don't want to accept it before you have an answer from the first. The following letter illustrates the general plan for a direct request; the writer assumes that a simple oversight, and not outright rejection, is the reason for the delay:

Identifies the position and introduces the main idea

Places the reason for the request second

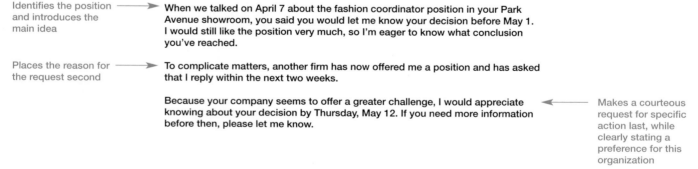

Makes a courteous request for specific action last, while clearly stating a preference for this organization

Request for a Time Extension

If you receive a job offer while other interviews are still pending, you'll probably want more time to decide, so write to the offering organization and ask for a time extension. Employers understand that candidates often interview with several companies. They want you to be sure you're making the right decision, so most are happy to accommodate you with a reasonable extension.

A request for a time extension follows the plan for a direct request but pays extra attention to easing the reader's disappointment.

Preface your request with a friendly opening. Ask for more time, stressing your enthusiasm for the organization. Conclude by allowing for a quick decision if your request for additional time is denied. Ask for a prompt reply confirming the time exten-

FIGURE 14.3   Effective Request for a Time Extension

Begins with a strong statement of interest in the job →

Emphasizes specific reasons for preferring the first job offer to help reassure the reader of sincerity →

1448 Solsbury Avenue
Thunderhawk, SD 57655
January 5, 2005

Mr. Frank Lapuzo, Vice President
Customer Relations
Lone Star Foods
7499 Hackberry Parkway
San Antonio, TX 78210

Dear Mr. Lapuzo:

The customer relations position in your snack foods division seems like an exciting challenge and a great opportunity. I'm very pleased that you offered it to me.

Because of another commitment, I would appreciate your giving me until February 16 to make a decision. Before our interview, I scheduled a follow-up interview with another company. I'm interested in your organization because of its impressive quality-control procedures and friendly, attractive work environment. But I do feel obligated to keep my appointment.

If you need my decision immediately, I'll gladly let you know. However, If you can allow me the added time to fulfill the earlier commitment, I'd be grateful. Please let me know right away by telephoning me at (605) 234-6897.

Sincerely,

Chang Li

Chang Li

← Stresses professional obligations, not the desire to learn what the other company may offer

← Closes with expression of willingness to yield or compromise, conveying continued interest in the position

sion if the organization grants it. This type of letter is, in essence, a direct request. However, because the recipient may be disappointed, be sure to temper your request for an extension with statements indicating your continued interest. The request in Figure 14.3 is a good example.

Reviewing Key Points

This chapter discusses interviewing for employment and following up. You have learned about the typical sequence of interviews: screening, selection, and final. You have also learned about the various types of possible interviews. The chapter covers how to prepare for a job interview by doing some follow-up research, thinking ahead about questions, bolstering your confidence, polishing your interview style, planning to look good, and being ready when you arrive.

This chapter also discusses the three parts of any interview: the important warm-up stage, the question-and-answer stage, and the equally important close. You've learned about following up after an interview with a thank-you message and perhaps with a letter of inquiry or a request for a time extension.

Document Makeover

Improve This Letter

To practice correcting drafts of actual documents, visit www.prenhall.com/onekey on the web. Click "Document Makeovers," then click Chapter 14. You will find a letter that contains problems and errors relating to what you've learned in this chapter about interviewing for employment and following up. Use the Final Draft decision tool to create an improved version of this letter. Check the message for all the elements necessary to reassure the potential employer, ask for the extension, explain the reasons for the request, offer to compromise, and facilitate a quick reply.

You have worked hard to complete this course, and as promised, you have learned how to create effective business messages and you've increased your skills in business communication. No matter what career you pursue, successfully completing this course will help you succeed. Just remember that successful businesspeople never stop learning. As you pursue your career, continue your education and keep polishing the skills you've gained in this course. This text's superb collection of communication examples can jog your memory and serve as a helpful reference throughout your career.

Test Your Knowledge

1. What should your objective be during a selection interview?

2. How does a structured interview differ from an open-ended interview and a situational interview?

3. What typically occurs during a stress interview?

4. Why are the questions you ask during an interview as important as the answers you give to the interviewer's questions?

5. What is the best way to polish your interview style?

6. What are the three stages of every interview, and which is the most important?

7. How should you respond if an interviewer at a company where you want to work asks you a question that seems too personal or unethical?

8. What should you include in your interview notes?

9. What should you say in a thank-you message after an interview?

10. What is the purpose of sending a letter of inquiry after an interview?

Apply Your Knowledge

1. How can you distinguish yourself from other candidates in a screening interview and still keep your responses short and to the point? Explain.

2. What can you do to make a favorable impression when you discover that an open-ended interview has turned into a stress interview? Briefly explain your answer.

3. If you want to switch jobs because you can't work with your supervisor, how can you explain this situation to a prospective employer? Give an example.

4. During a group interview you notice that one of the other candidates is trying to monopolize the conversation. He's always the first to answer, his answer is the longest, and he even interrupts the other candidates while they are talking. The interviewer doesn't seem to be concerned about his behavior, but you are. You would like to have more time to speak so that the interviewer could get to know you better. What should you do?

5. Ethical Choices   Why is it important to distinguish unethical or illegal interview questions from acceptable questions? Explain.

Practice Your Knowledge

Activities

For live links to all websites discussed in this chapter, visit this text's website at www. prenhall.com/bovee. Just log on, select Chapter 14, and click on "Featured Websites." Locate the page or the URL related to the material in the text.

1. Analyze This Document   Read the following document, then (1) analyze its strengths and weaknesses, and (2) revise it so that it follows this chapter's guidelines.

> Thank you for the really marvelous opportunity to meet you and your colleagues at Starret Engine Company. I really enjoyed touring your facilities and talking with all the people there. You have quite a crew! Some of the other companies I have visited have been so rigid and uptight that I can't imagine how I would fit in. It's a relief to run into a group of people who seem to enjoy their work as much as all of you do.
>
> I know that you must be looking at many other candidates for this job, and I know that some of them will probably be more experienced than I am. But I do want to emphasize that my two-year hitch in the Navy involved a good deal of engineering work. I don't think I mentioned all my shipboard responsibilities during the interview.
>
> Please give me a call within the next week to let me know your decision. You can usually find me at my dormitory in the evening after dinner (phone: 877-9080).

2. Analyze This Document   Read the following document, then (1) analyze its strengths and weaknesses, and (2) revise it so that it follows this chapter's guidelines.

> I have recently received a very attractive job offer from the Warrington Company. But before I let them know one way or another, I would like to consider any offer that your firm may extend. I was quite impressed with your company during my recent interview, and I am still very interested in a career there.
>
> I don't mean to pressure you, but Warrington has asked for my decision within ten days. Could you let me know by Tuesday whether you plan to offer me a position? That would give me enough time to compare the two offers.

3. **Analyze This Document** Read the following document, then (1) analyze its strengths and weaknesses, and (2) revise it so that it follows this chapter's guidelines.

> I'm writing to say that I must decline your job offer. Another company has made me a more generous offer, and I have decided to accept. However, if things don't work out for me there, I will let you know. I sincerely appreciate your interest in me.

4. **Teamwork** Divide the class into two groups. Half the class will be recruiters for a large chain of national department stores looking to fill manager trainee positions (there are 15 openings). The other half of the class will be candidates for the job. The company is specifically looking for candidates who demonstrate these three qualities: initiative, dependability, and willingness to assume responsibility.
   a. Have each recruiter select and interview an applicant for 10 minutes.
   b. Have all the recruiters discuss how they assessed the applicant against each of the three desired qualities. What questions did they ask or what did they use as an indicator to determine whether the candidate possessed the quality?
   c. Have all the applicants discuss what they said to convince the recruiters that they possessed each of these qualities.

5. **Internet** Select a large company (one that you can easily find information about) where you might like to work. Use Internet sources to gather some preliminary research on the company.
   a. What did you learn about this organization that would help you during an interview there?
   b. What Internet sources did you use to obtain this information?
   c. Armed with this information, what aspects of your background do you think might appeal to this company's recruiters?
   d. If you choose to apply for a job with this company, what keywords would you include on your résumé, and why?

6. **Interviews: Being Prepared** Prepare written answers to 10 of the questions listed in Table 14.2, "Twenty-Five Common Interview Questions" (see page 442).

7. **Interviews: Understanding Qualifications** Write a short memo to your instructor discussing what you believe are your greatest employment strengths and weaknesses. Next, explain how these strengths and weaknesses would be viewed by interviewers evaluating your qualifications.

Expand Your Knowledge

Exploring the Best of the Web

Planning for a Successful Interview How can you practice for a job interview? What are some questions that you might be asked, and how should you respond? What questions are you not obligated to answer? Job-interview.net, www.job-interview.net, provides mock interviews based on actual job openings. It provides job descriptions, questions and answers for specific careers and jobs, and links to company guides and annual reports. You'll find a step-by-step plan that outlines key job requirements, lists practice interview questions, and helps you put together practice interviews. The site offers tips on the keywords to look for in a job description, which will help you narrow your search and anticipate the questions you might be asked on your first or next job interview. Have a look around, then answer these questions:

Exercises

1. What are some problem questions you might be asked during a job interview? How would you handle these questions?
2. Choose a job title from the list, and read more about it. What did you learn that could help during an actual interview for the job you selected?
3. Developing an "interview game plan" ahead of time helps you make a strong, positive impression during an interview. What are some of the things you can practice to help make everything you do during an interview seem to come naturally?

Exploring the Web on Your Own

Review these chapter-related websites on your own to learn more about interviewing for jobs.

1. Get over 2,000 pages of career advice at Monster.com, www.monster.com, and talk to career experts in your choice of industry or profession.

2. For a humorous but effective take on cover letters, visit www.soyouwanna.com, click on Work, then find the article about cover letters.

3. Among the many helpful pages of advice you'll find at the Online Writing Lab is a section on writing cover letters; check it out at owl.english.purdue. edu/handouts/ pw/p_applettr.html.

Learn Interactively

Interactive Study Guide

Go to the Companion Website at www.prenhall.com/bovee. For Chapter 14, take advantage of the interactive "Study Guide" to test your knowledge of the chapter. Get instant feedback on whether you need additional studying. Also, visit this site's "Study Hall," where you'll find an abundance of valuable resources that will help you succeed in this course.

Peak Performance Grammar and Mechanics

To improve your skill with vocabulary, visit www.prenhall. com/bovee, click "Peak Performance Grammar and Mechanics." First click "Vocabulary" and take the Pretest under Vocabulary I and Vocabulary II. Then click "Misspelled Words" and take the Pretest there. These tests will help you determine whether you have any weak areas. Then review those areas in the Refresher Courses. Take the Follow-Up Tests to check your grasp of frequently confused, misused, and misspelled words. For an extra challenge or advanced practice, take the Advanced Tests. Finally, for additional reinforcement in vocabulary and spelling, go to the "Improve Your Grammar, Mechanics, and Usage" section that follows, and complete the Level 1: Self-Assessment exercises.

Interviewing with Potential Employers

1. Interviewers and interviewees: Classroom exercise in interviewing

Interviewing is clearly an interactive process involving at least two people. The best way to practice for interviews is to work with others.

Your task: You and all other members of your class are to write letters of application for an entry-level or management-trainee position requiring a pleasant personality and intelligence but a minimum of specialized education or experience. Sign your letter with a fictitious name that conceals your identity. Next polish (or prepare) a résumé that accurately identifies you and your educational and professional accomplishments.

Now, three members of the class who volunteer as interviewers divide among themselves all the anonymously written application letters. Then each interviewer selects a candidate who seems the most pleasant and convincing in his or her letter. At this time the selected candidates identify themselves and give the interviewers their résumés.

Each interviewer then interviews his or her chosen candidate in front of the class, seeking to understand how the items on the résumé qualify the candidate for the job. At the end of the interviews, the class may decide who gets the job and discuss why this candidate was successful. Afterward, retrieve your letter, sign it with the right name, and submit it to the instructor for credit.

WEB SKILLS 2. Internet interview: Exercise in interviewing

Using the Web 100 site at www.hotjobs.com/htdocs/tools/index-us.html, locate the homepage of a company you would like to work for. Then identify a position within the company for which you would like to apply. Study the company using any online business resources you choose, and prepare for an interview with that company.

Your task: Working with a classmate, take turns interviewing each other for your chosen positions. Interviewers should take notes during the interview. Once the interview is complete, critique each other's performance (interviewers should critique how well candidates prepared for the interview and answered the questions; interviewees should critique the quality of the questions asked). Write a follow-up letter thanking your interviewer, and submit the letter to your instructor.

Following Up After the Interview

3. A slight error in timing: Letter asking for delay of an employment decision

You botched your timing and applied for your third-choice job before going after what you really wanted. What you want to do is work in retail at Neiman Marcus in Dallas; what you have been offered is a retail job with Longhorn Leather and Lumber, 25 dry and dusty miles away in Commerce, just south of the Oklahoma panhandle.

You review your notes. Your Longhorn interview was three weeks ago with the human resources manager, R. P. Bronson, a congenial person who has just written to offer you the position. The store's address is 27 Sam Rayburn Dr., Commerce, TX 75428. Mr. Bronson notes that he can hold the position open for 10 days. You have an interview scheduled with Neiman Marcus next week, but it is unlikely that you will know the store's decision within this 10-day period.

Your task: Write to R. P. Bronson, requesting a reasonable delay in your consideration of his job offer.

4. Job hunt: Set of employment-related letters to a single company

Where would you like to work? Pick a real or an imagined company, and assume that a month ago you sent your résumé and application letter. Not long afterward, you were invited to come for an interview, which seemed to go very well.

Your task: Use your imagination to write the following: (a) a thank-you letter for the interview, (b) a note of inquiry, and (c) a request for more time to decide.

Improve Your Grammar, Mechanics, and Usage

Level 1: Self-Assessment—Vocabulary

Review Sections 4.1, 4.2, and 4.3 in the Handbook of Grammar, Mechanics, and Usage, and then look at the following 15 items.

In items 1–7, write the correct word in the space provided:

1. Everyone (*accept/except*) _____ Barbara King has registered for the company competition.

2. We need to find a new security (*device/devise*) _____.

3. The Jennings are (*loath/loathe*) _____ to admit that they are wrong.

4. The judge has ruled that this town cannot enforce such a local (*ordinance/ordnance*) _____.

5. To stay on schedule, we must give (*precedence/precedents*) _____ to the Marley project.

6. This month's balance is greater (*than/then*) _____ last month's.

7. That decision lies with the director, (who's/whose) _____ in charge of this department.

In items 8–15, underline errors and write corrections in the space provided:

8. _____ In this department, we see alot of mistakes like that.

9. _____ In my judgement, you'll need to redo the cover.

10. _____ He decided to reveal the information, irregardless of the consequences.

11. _____ Why not go along when it is so easy to accomodate his demands?

12. _____ When you say that, do you mean to infer that I'm being unfair?

13. _____ She says that she finds this sort of ceremony embarassing.

14. _____ All we have to do is try and get along with him for a few more days.

15. _____ A friendly handshake should always preceed negotiations.

Level 2: Workplace Applications

The following items contain numerous errors in grammar, capitalization, punctuation, abbreviation, number style, word division, and vocabulary. Rewrite each sentence in the space provided, correcting all errors. Write *C* in the space after any sentence that is already correct.

1. An entrepreneur and their business, are so closely tied together that a bank will want to see how they handle their personal affairs, before granting a small business line of credit.

2. The companys' annual meeting will be held from 2-4 PM on May 3d in the Santa Fe room at the Marriott hotel..

3. Well over four hundred outstanding students from coast-to-coast, have realized their dreams of a college education thanks to the NASE Scholarship program.

4. If you're home is you're principle place of business you can deduct generally the cost of traveling from you're home, to any business destination.

5. Companies like McLeod USA sprung into being in the 1990's to provide cut rate phone services to small- and medium-size businesses in competition with the established baby bells.

6. Some question whether a 'new economy' exists and if so how it differs from the old economy?

7. When the music industry claimed by stealing intellectual property Napster were committing piracy - Napster argued that it was'nt doing anything illegal or un-ethical.

8. The World Bank plays an important roll in todays fast changing closely-meshed global economy.

9. When it comes to consumer rights the F.D.A., F.T.C., and Agriculture department are concerned not only with safety but also accurate information.

10. Fujitsu, a $50 billion company with 190,000 employees, dominates the Japanese computer industry.

11. The fortune 500 ranks not only corporations by size but also offers brief company descriptions; along with industry statistics, and additional measures of corporate performance.

12. Having bought 55 companies over the past decade, plans to make ten to 15 new acquisitions each year are being made by Cisco Systems.

13. In 1984 Michael Dell decided to sell P.C.'s direct and built to order, now everybody in the industry are trying to imitate Dells' strategy.

14. Resulting in large cost savings for the company, American Express have reduced the number of field office's from 85 to 7 by using virtual teams.

15. In Europe and Asia, people are using mobile phones to send text messages to other users; exchange e-mail; read the morning news; surfing certain websites; and to make purchases such as movie tickets and charge it to they're monthly phone bill.

Level 3: Document Critique

The following document may contain errors in grammar, capitalization, punctuation, abbreviation, number style, vocabulary, and spelling. Based on what you've learned in this chapter, you may also find problems with organization, usage, and word choice. Correct all errors using standard proofreading marks (see Appendix C).

MORGAN MITRAS

2397 Glencrest ridge, Fort Worth, TEX 76119

(817/ 226-1804

February 2 2005:

Norton Acctg. Group

Ms Nancy Remington, Human Resources

3778 Parkway North

Indianapolis, Indiana 46205

Dear Ms. Remington—

With your companys' reputation for quality, customer service, employee empowerment, you'll will want to hire someone who is not only accurrate and efficient but also self motivated and results-oriented—someone who is able to make decisions as well as coperate with team members and clients. The ad you placed in the February 1st issue of *The Wall Street Journal* for someone to fill a financial management position really has me very excited and eager.

During my 3 years at Tandy corporation -see attached résumé- I've conducted internal auditing for accounts valued at $450 million dollars. Some of my many, countless accomplishments include

- ■ Increasing both internal and client support for the auditing process
- ■ I save the company over 2.5 million dollars when I discovered billing errors
- ■ Suggest ways accounts receivable processes could be streamlined

In addition it might be that Norton Accounting may appreciate my ability to complete projects on time as well as keeping them under budget. One of my priorities is a position in which my expereince will be broaden: so any opportunity to travel would be welcomed by me!

I'll be in your area during the weak of February 20; I'll call your office on Feb. 8 to see whether we can arrange to meet. I hope you'll give me a chance, please.

Sincerely,

Morgan Mitras,

Applicant

Interview Strategies: Answering the 16 Toughest Questions

The answers to challenging interview questions can reveal a lot about a candidate. You can expect to face several such questions during every interview. If you're prepared with thoughtful answers that are related to your specific situation, you're bound to make a good impression. Here are 16 tough questions and guidelines for planning answers that put your qualities in the best light.

1. **What was the toughest decision you ever had to make?** Be prepared with a good example, explaining why the decision was difficult and how you decided.
2. **Why do you want to work for this organization?** Show that you've done your homework, and cite some things going on in the company that appeal to you.
3. **Why should we employ you?** Emphasize your academic strengths, job skills, and enthusiasm for the firm. Tie specific skills to the employer's needs, and give examples of how you can learn and become productive quickly. Cite past activities to prove you can work with others as part of a team.
4. **If we hire you, what changes would you make?** No one can know what to change in a position before settling in and learning about the job and company operations. State that you would take a good hard look at everything the company is doing before making recommendations.
5. **Can we offer you a career path?** Reply that you believe so, but you need to know more about the normal progression within the organization.
6. **What are your greatest strengths?** Answer sincerely by summarizing your strong points: "I can see what must be done and then do it" or "I'm willing to make decisions" or "I work well with others."
7. **What are your greatest weaknesses?** Describe a weakness so that it sounds like a virtue—honestly revealing something about yourself while showing how it works to an employer's advantage. If you sometimes drive yourself too hard, explain that it has helped when you've had to meet deadlines.
8. **What didn't you like about previous jobs you've held?** State what you didn't like and discuss what the experience taught you. Avoid making slighting references to former employers.
9. **How do you spend your leisure time?** Rather than focusing on just one, mention a cross section of interests—active and quiet, social and solitary.
10. **Are there any weaknesses in your education or experience?** Take stock of your weaknesses before the interview, and practice discussing them in a positive light. You'll see they're minor when discussed along with the positive qualities you have to offer.
11. **Where do you want to be five years from now?** This question tests (1) whether you're merely using this job as a stopover until something better comes along and (2) whether you've given thought to your long-term goals. Saying that you'd like to be company president is unrealistic, and yet few employers want people who are content to sit still. Your answer should reflect your long-term goals and the organization's advancement opportunities.
12. **What are your salary expectations?** If you're asked this at the outset, say, "Why don't we discuss salary after you decide whether I'm right for the job?" If the interviewer asks this after showing real interest in you, speak up. Do your homework, but if you need a clue about salary levels, say, "Can you discuss the salary range with me?"
13. **What would you do if . . .** This question tests your resourcefulness. For example: "What would you do if your computer broke down during an audit?" Your answer is less important than your approach to the problem—and a calm approach is best.
14. **What type of position are you interested in?** Job titles and responsibilities vary from firm to firm. So state your skills ("I'm good with numbers") and the positions that require those skills ("accounts payable").
15. **Tell me something about yourself.** Answer that you'll be happy to talk about yourself, and ask what the interviewer wants to know. If this point is clarified, respond. If it isn't, explain how your skills can contribute to the job and the organization. This is a great chance to sell yourself.
16. **Do you have any questions about the organization or the job?** Employers like candidates who are interested in the organization. Convey your interest and enthusiasm.

Be sure that your answers are sincere, truthful, and positive. Take a moment to compose your thoughts before responding, so that your answers are to the point.

Applications for Success

Improve your interviewing skills by visiting the "Interview" section at *Hotjobs* (www.hotjobs.com/htdobs/tools/index. html).

Do the following:

1. When an interviewer asks you a question, what makes one answer more effective than another? List some of the ways that answers can vary: specific versus general, assertive versus passive, informal versus formal.
2. Think of four additional questions that pertain specifically to your résumé. Practice your answers.
3. Which of these 16 questions seems the toughest to you? In no more than two paragraphs, write out your answer to the question that you think is the toughest of all. Then submit your work to your instructor.

Format and Layout of Business Documents

The format and layout of business documents vary from country to country; they even vary within regions of the United States. In addition, many organizations develop their own variations of standard styles, adapting documents to the types of messages they send and the kinds of audiences they communicate with. The formats described here are more common than others.

First Impressions

Your documents tell readers a lot about you and about your company's professionalism. So all your documents must look neat, present a professional image, and be easy to read. Your audience's first impression of a document comes from the quality of its paper, the way it is customized, and its general appearance.

Paper

To give a quality impression, businesspeople consider carefully the paper they use. Several aspects of paper contribute to the overall impression:

- **Weight.** Paper quality is judged by the weight of four reams (each a 500-sheet package) of letter-size paper. The weight most commonly used by U.S. business organizations is 20-pound paper, but 16- and 24-pound versions are also used.
- **Cotton content.** Paper quality is also judged by the percentage of cotton in the paper. Cotton doesn't yellow over time the way wood pulp does, plus it's both strong and soft. For letters and outside reports, use paper with a 25 percent cotton content. For memos and other internal documents, you can use a lighter-weight paper with lower cotton content. Airmail-weight paper may save money for international correspondence, but make sure it isn't too flimsy.[1]
- **Size.** In the United States, the standard paper size for business documents is 8½ by 11 inches. Standard legal documents are 8½ by 14 inches. Executives sometimes have heavier 7-by-10-inch paper on hand (with matching envelopes) for personal messages such as congratulations and recommendations.[2] They may also have a box of note cards imprinted with their initials and a box of plain folded notes for condolences or for acknowledging formal invitations.
- **Color.** White is the standard color for business purposes, although neutral colors such as gray and ivory are sometimes used. Memos can be produced on pastel-colored paper to distinguish them from external correspondence. In addition, memos are sometimes produced on various colors of paper for routing to separate departments. Light-colored papers are appropriate, but bright or dark colors make reading difficult and may appear too frivolous.

Customization

For letters to outsiders, U.S. businesses commonly use letterhead stationery, which may be either professionally printed or designed in-house using word-processing templates and graphics. The letterhead includes the company's name and address, usually at the top of the page but sometimes along the left side or even at the bottom. Other information may be included in the letterhead as well: the company's telephone number, fax number, cable address, website address, product lines, date of establishment, officers and directors, slogan, and symbol (logo). Well-designed letterhead gives readers[3]

- Pertinent reference data
- A favorable image of the company
- A good idea of what the company does

For as much as it's meant to accomplish, the letterhead should be as simple as possible. Too much information makes the page look cluttered, occupies space needed for the message, and might become outdated before all the stationery can be used. If you correspond frequently with people abroad, your letterhead must be intelligible to foreigners. It must include the name of your country in addition to your cable, telex, e-mail, or fax information.

In the United States, businesses always use letterhead for the first page of a letter. Successive pages are usually plain sheets of paper that match the letterhead in color and quality. Some companies use a specially printed second-page letterhead that bears only the company's name. Other countries have other conventions.

Many companies also design and print standardized forms for memos and frequently written reports that always require the same sort of information (such as sales reports and expense reports). These forms may be printed in sets for use with carbon paper or in carbonless-copy sets that produce multiple copies automatically. More and more organizations use computers to generate their standardized forms, which can save them both money and time.[4]

Appearance

Produce almost all of your business documents using either a printer (letter-quality, not a dot matrix) or a typewriter. Certain documents, however, should be handwritten (such as a short informal memo or a note of condolence). Be sure to handwrite, print, or type the envelope to match the document. However, even a letter on the best-quality paper with the best-designed letterhead may look unprofessional if it's poorly produced. So pay close attention to all the factors affecting appearance, including the following:

- **Margins.** Companies in the United States make sure that documents (especially external ones) are centered on the page, with margins of at least an inch all around. Using word-processing software, you can achieve this balance simply by defining the format parameters. When using a typewriter, either establish a standard line length (usually about 6 inches) or establish a "picture frame."

- **Line length.** Lines are rarely right-hand justified, because the resulting text looks too much like a form letter and can be hard to read (even with proportional spacing). Varying line length makes the document look more personal and interesting. Pica type (12 points) gives you 60 characters in a line; elite type (10 points) gives you 72 characters in a line.

- **Line spacing.** You can adjust the number of blank lines between elements (such as between the date and the inside address) to ensure that a short document fills the page vertically or that a longer document extends at least two lines of the body onto the last page.

- **Character spacing.** Use proper spacing between characters and after punctuation. For example, U.S. conventions include leaving one space after commas, semicolons, colons, and sentence-ending periods. Each letter in a person's initials is followed by a period and a single space. However, abbreviations such as U.S.A. or MBA may or may not have periods, but they never have internal spaces.

- **Special symbols.** When using a computer, use appropriate symbols to give your document a professional look (see Table A.1 for examples). When using a typewriter, use a hyphen for the en dash, and use two hyphens (with no space before, between, or after) for the em dash. Find other details of this sort in your company's style book or in most secretarial handbooks.

- **Corrections.** Messy corrections are obvious and unacceptable in business documents. Reprint or retype any letter, report, or memo requiring a lot of corrections. Word-processing software and self-correcting typewriters can produce correction-free documents at the push of a button.

Letters

All business letters have certain elements in common. Several of these elements appear in every letter; others appear only when desirable or appropriate. In addition, these letter parts are usually arranged in one of three basic formats.

Table A.1	Special Symbols on Computer	
	Computer symbol	**Typed symbol**
Case fractions	½	1/2
Copyright	©	(c)
Registered trademark	®	(R)
Cents	¢	None
British pound	£	None
Paragraph	¶	None
Bullets	●, ◆, ■, □, ✓, ☑, ⊗	˚, #, 0
Em dash	—	-- (two hyphens)
En dash	–	- (one hyphen)

Standard Letter Parts

The letter in Figure A.1 shows the placement of standard letter parts. The writer of this business letter had no letterhead available but correctly included a heading. All business letters typically include these seven elements.

Heading

Letterhead (the usual heading) shows the organization's name, full address, telephone number (almost always), and e-mail address (often). Executive letterhead also bears the name of an individual within the organization. Computers allow you to design your own letterhead (either one to use for all correspondence or a new one for each piece of correspondence). If letterhead stationery is not available, the heading includes a return address (but no name) and starts 13 lines from the top of the page, which leaves a two-inch top margin.

Date

If you're using letterhead, place the date at least one blank line beneath the lowest part of the letterhead. Without letterhead, place the date immediately below the return address. The standard method of writing the date in the United States uses the full name of the month (no abbreviations), followed by the day (in numerals, without *st, nd, rd,* or *th*), a comma, and then the year: July 14, 2003 (7/14/03). Some organizations follow other conventions (see Table A.2). To maintain the utmost clarity in international correspondence, always spell out the name of the month in dates.[5]

When communicating internationally, you may also experience some confusion over time. Some companies in the United States refer to morning (A.M.) and afternoon (P.M.), dividing a 24-hour day into 12-hour blocks so that they refer to four o'clock in the morning (4:00 A.M.) or four o'clock in the afternoon (4:00 P.M.). The U.S. military and European companies refer to one 24-hour period so that 0400 hours (4:00 A.M.) is always in the morning and 1600 hours (4:00 P.M.) is always in the afternoon.[6] Make sure your references to time are as clear as possible, and be sure you clearly understand your audience's time references.

FIGURE A.1 Standard Letter Parts

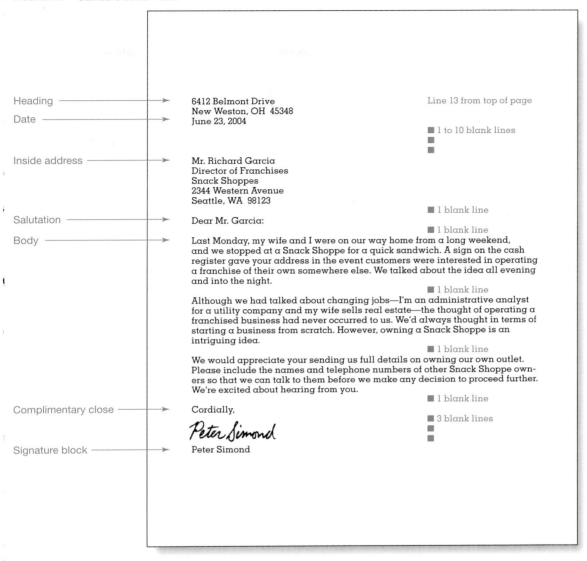

Heading → 6412 Belmont Drive / New Weston, OH 45348

Date → June 23, 2004

Inside address → Mr. Richard Garcia / Director of Franchises / Snack Shoppes / 2344 Western Avenue / Seattle, WA 98123

Salutation → Dear Mr. Garcia:

Body →

Complimentary close → Cordially,

Signature block → Peter Simond

Line 13 from top of page

■ 1 to 10 blank lines

■ 1 blank line

■ 1 blank line

■ 1 blank line

■ 1 blank line

■ 1 blank line

■ 3 blank lines

Inside Address

The inside address identifies the recipient of the letter. For U.S. correspondence, begin the inside address at least one line below the date. Precede the addressee's name with a courtesy title, such as *Dr.*, *Mr.*, or *Ms.* The accepted courtesy title for women in business is *Ms.*, although a woman known to prefer the title *Miss* or *Mrs.* is always accommodated. If you don't know whether a person is a man or a woman (and you have no way of finding out), omit the courtesy title. For example, *Terry Smith* could be either a man or a woman. The first line of the inside address would be just

Table A.2	Common Date Forms		
Convention	**Description**	**Date—Mixed**	**Date—All Numerals**
U.S. standard	Month (spelled out) day, year	July 14, 2003	7/14/03
U.S. government and some U.S. industries	Day (in numerals) month (spelled out) year	14 July 2003	14/7/03
European	Replace U.S. solidus (diagonal line) with periods	14 July 2003	14.7.2003
International standard	Year month day	2003 July 14	2003,7,14

Table A.3	Forms of Address	
Person	**In Address**	**In Salutation**
Personal Titles		
Man	Mr. [first & last name]	Dear Mr. [last name]:
Woman (marital status unknown)	Ms. [first & last name]	Dear Ms. [last name]:
Woman (single)	Ms. or Miss [first & last name]	Dear Ms. or Miss [last name]:
Woman (married)	Ms. or Mrs. [wife's first & last name] or Mrs. [husband's first & last name]	Dear Ms. or Mrs. [last name]:
Woman (widowed)	Ms. or Mrs. [wife's first name & last name]	Dear Ms. or Mrs. [last name]:
Woman (separated or divorced)	Ms. or Mrs. [first & last name]	Dear Ms. or Mrs. [last name]:
Two men (or more)	Mr. [first & last name] and Mr. [first & last name]	Dear Mr. [last name] and Mr. [last name] or Messrs. [last name] and [last name]:
Two women (or more)	Ms. [first & last name] and Ms. [first & last name] or Mrs. [first & last name] and Mrs. [first & last name]	Dear Ms. [last name] and Ms. [last name] or Mses. [last name] and [last name]: Dear Mrs. [last name] and Mrs. [last name]: or Dear Mesdames [last name] and [last name] or Mesdames:
	Miss [first & last name] Mrs. [first & last name]	Dear Miss [last name] and Mrs. [last name]:
One woman and one man	Ms. [first & last name] and Mr. [first & last name]	Dear Ms. [last name] and Mr. [last name]:
Couple (married)	Mr. and Mrs. [husband's first & last name]	Dear Mr. and Mrs. [last name]:
Couple (married with different last names)	[title] [first & last name of husband] [title] [first & last name of wife]	Dear [title] [husband's last name] and [title] [wife's first & last name]:
Couple (married professionals with same title and same last name)	[title in plural form] [husband's first name] and [wife's first & last name]	Dear [title in plural form] [last name]:
Couple (married professionals with different titles and same last name)	[title] [first & last name of husband] and [title] [first & last name of wife]	Dear [title] and [title] [last name]:

(continued)

Terry Smith, and the salutation would be *Dear Terry Smith.* The same is true if you know only a person's initials, as in *S. J. Adams.*

Spell out and capitalize titles that precede a person's name, such as *Professor* or *General* (see Table A.3 for the proper forms of address). The person's organizational title, such as *Director,* may be included on this first line (if it is short) or on the line below; the name of a department may follow. In addresses and signature lines, don't forget to capitalize any professional title that follows a person's name:

Mr. Ray Johnson, Dean

Ms. Patricia T. Higgins
Assistant Vice President

However, professional titles not appearing in an address or signature line are capitalized only when they directly precede the name.

President Kenneth Johanson will deliver the speech.

Maria Morales, president of ABC Enterprises, will deliver the speech.

The Honorable Helen Masters, senator from Arizona, will deliver the speech.

If the name of a specific person is unavailable, you may address the letter to the department or to a specific position within the department. Also, be sure to spell out company

Table A.3	Continued	
Person	**In Address**	**In Salutation**
Professional Titles		
President of a college or university (doctor)	Dr. [first & last name], President	Dear Dr. [last name]:
Dean of a school of college	Dean [first & last name] *or* Dr., Mr., Mrs., *or* Miss [first & last name] Dean of (title)	Dear Dean [last name]: Dear Dr., Mr., Ms., Mrs., *or* Miss [last name]:
Professor	Professor [first & last name]	Dear Professor [last name]:
Physician	[first & last name], M.D.	Dear Dr. [last name]:
Lawyer	Mr., Ms., Mrs., *or* Miss [first & last name]	Dear Mr., Ms., Mrs., *or* Miss [last name]:
Service personnel	[full rank, first & last name, abbreviation of service designation] (add *Retired* if applicable)	Dear [rank] [last name]:
Company or corporation	[name of organization]	Ladies and Gentlemen *or* Gentlemen and Ladies
Governmental Titles		
President of the United States	The President	Dear Mr. *or* Madam President:
Senator of the United States	Honorable [first & last name]	Dear Senator [last name]:
Cabinet member Postmaster General Attorney General	Honorable [first & last name]	Dear Mr. *or* Madam Secretary: Dear Mr. *or* Madam Postmaster General: Dear Mr. *or* Madam Attorney General:
Mayor	Honorable [first & last name] Mayor of [name of city]	Dear Mayor [last name]:
Judge	The Honorable	Dear Judge [last name]:
Religious Titles		
Priest	The Reverend [first & last name], [initials of order, if any]	Reverend Sir: (formal) *or* Dear Father [last name]: (informal)
Rabbi	Rabbi & [first & last name]	Dear Rabbi [last name]:
Minister	The Reverend [first & last name] [title, if any]	Dear Reverend [last name]:

names in full, unless the company itself uses abbreviations in its official name.

Other address information includes the treatment of buildings, house numbers, and compass directions (see Table A.4 on the following page). The following example shows all the information that may be included in the inside address and its proper order for U.S. correspondence:

Ms. Linda Coolidge, Vice President
Corporate Planning Department
Midwest Airlines
Kowalski Building, Suite 21-A
7279 Bristol Avenue
Toledo, OH 43617

Canadian addresses are similar, except that the name of the province is usually spelled out:

Dr. H. C. Armstrong
Research and Development
Commonwealth Mining Consortium
The Chelton Building, Suite 301
585 Second Street SW
Calgary, Alberta T2P 2P5

Table A.4	Inside Address Information	
Description		**Example**
Capitalize building names.		Empire State Building
Capitalize locations within buildings (apartments, suites, rooms).		Suite 1073
Use numerals for all house or building numbers, except the number *one*.		One Trinity Lane 637 Adams Avenue, Apt. 7
Spell out compass directions that fall within a street address		1074 West Connover Street
Abbreviate compass directions that follow the street address		783 Main Street, N.E., Apt. 27

The order and layout of address information vary from country to country. So when addressing correspondence for other countries, carefully follow the format and information that appear in the company's letterhead. However, when you're sending mail from the United States, be sure that the name of the destination country appears on the last line of the address in capital letters. Use the English version of the country name so that your mail is routed from the United States to the right country. Then, to be sure your mail is routed correctly within the destination country, use the foreign spelling of the city name (using the characters and diacritical marks that would be commonly used in the region). For example, the following address uses *Köln* instead of *Cologne*:

H. R. Veith, Director	Addressee
Eisfieren Glaswerk	Company Name
Blaubachstrabe 13	Street address
Postfach 10 80 07	Post office box
D-5000 Köln I	District, city
GERMANY	Country

For additional examples of international addresses, see Table A.5.

Be sure to use organizational titles correctly when addressing international correspondence. Job designations vary around the world. In England, for example, a managing director is often what a U.S. company would call its chief executive officer or president, and a British deputy is the equivalent of a vice president. In France, responsibilities are assigned to individuals without regard to title or organizational structure, and in China the title *project manager* has meaning, but the title *sales manager* may not.

To make matters worse, businesspeople in some countries sign correspondence without their names typed below. In Germany, for example, the belief is that employees represent the company, so it's inappropriate to emphasize personal names.[7] Use the examples in Table A.5 as guidelines when addressing correspondence to countries outside the United States.

Salutation

In the salutation of your letter, follow the style of the first line of the inside address. If the first line is a person's name, the salutation is *Dear Mr.* or *Ms. Name.* The formality of the salutation depends on your relationship with the addressee. If in conversation you would say "Mary," your letter's salutation should be *Dear Mary,* followed by a colon. Otherwise, include the courtesy title and last name, followed by a colon. Presuming to write

Dear Lewis instead of *Dear Professor Chang* demonstrates a disrespectful familiarity that the recipient will probably resent.

If the first line of the inside address is a position title such as *Director of Personnel,* then use *Dear Director.* If the addressee is unknown, use a polite description, such as *Dear Alumnus, Dear SPCA Supporter,* or *Dear Voter.* If the first line is plural (a department or company), then use *Ladies and Gentlemen* (look again at Table A.3). When you do not know whether you're writing to an individual or a group (for example, when writing a reference or a letter of recommendation), use *To whom it may concern.*

In the United States some letter writers use a "salutopening" on the salutation line. A salutopening omits *Dear* but includes the first few words of the opening paragraph along with the recipient's name. After this line, the sentence continues a double space below as part of the body of the letter, as in these examples:

Thank you, Mr. Brown,	Salutopening
for your prompt payment of your bill.	Body
Congratulations, Ms. Lake!	Salutopening
Your promotion is well deserved.	Body

Whether your salutation is informal or formal, be especially careful that names are spelled right. A misspelled name is glaring evidence of carelessness, and it belies the personal interest you're trying to express.

Body

The body of the letter is your message. Almost all letters are single-spaced, with one blank line before and after the salutation or salutopening, between paragraphs, and before the complimentary close. The body may include indented lists, entire paragraphs indented for emphasis, and even subheadings. If it does, all similar elements should be treated in the same way. Your department or company may select a format to use for all letters.

Complimentary Close

The complimentary close begins on the second line below the body of the letter. Alternatives for wording are available, but currently the trend seems to be toward using one-word closes, such as *Sincerely* and *Cordially.* In any case, the complimentary close reflects the relationship between you and the person you're writing to. Avoid cute closes, such as *Yours for bigger profits.* If your audience doesn't know you well, your sense of humor may be misunderstood.

| Table A.5 | International Addresses and Salutations | | |

Country	Postal Address	Address Elements	Salutations
Argentina	Sr. Juan Pérez Editorial Internacional S.A. Av. Sarmiento 1337, 8° P. C. C1035AAB BUENOS AIRES - CF ARGENTINA	S.A. = Sociedad Anónima (corporation) Av. Sarmiento (name of street) 1337 (building number) 8° = 8th. P = Piso (floor) C (room or suite) C1035AAB (postcode + city) CF = Capital Federal (federal capital)	Sr. = Señor (Mr.) Sra. = Señora (Mrs.) Srta. = Señorita (Miss) Don't use given names except with people you know well.
Australia	Mr. Roger Lewis International Publishing Pty.Ltd. 166 Kent Street, Level 9 GPO Box 3542 SYDNEY NSW 2001 AUSTRALIA	Pty.Ltd. = Proprietory Limited (corp.) 166 (building number) Kent Street (name of street) Level (floor) GPO Box (post office box) city + state (abbrev.) + postcode	Mr. and Mrs. used on first contact. Ms. not common (avoid use). Business is informal—use given name freely.
Austria	Herrn Dipl.-Ing. J. Gerdenitsch International Verlag Ges.m.b.H. Glockengasse 159 1010 WIEN AUSTRIA	Herrn = To Mr. (separate line) Dipl.-Ing. (engineering degree) Ges.m.b.H. (a corporation) Glockengasse (street name) 159 (building number) 1010 (postcode + city) WIEN (Vienna)	Herr (Mr.) Frau (Mrs.) Fräulein (Miss) obsolete in business, so do not use. Given names are almost never used in business.
Brazil	Ilmo. Sr. Gilberto Rabello Ribeiro Editores Internacionais S.A. Rua da Ajuda, 228-6° Andar Caixa Postal 2574 20040-000 RIO DE JANEIRO - RJ BRAZIL	Ilmo. = Ilustrissimo (honorific) Ilma. = Ilustrissima (hon. female) S.A. = Sociedade Anônima (corporation) Rua = street, da Ajuda (street name) 228 (building number) 6° = 6th. Andar (floor) Caixa Postal (P.O. box) 20040-000 (postcode + city) - RJ (state abbrev.)	Sr. = Senhor (Mr.) Sra. = Senhora (Mrs.) Srta. = Senhorita (Miss) Family name at end, e.g., Senhor Ribeiro (Rabello is mother's family—as in Portugal) Given names readily used in business.
China	Xia Zhiyi International Publishing Ltd. 14 Jianguolu Chaoyangqu BEIJING 100025 CHINA	Ltd. (limited liability corporation) 14 (building number) Jianguolu (street name), lu (street) Chaoyangqu (district name) (city + postcode)	Family name (single syllable) first. Given name (2 syllables) second, sometimes reversed. Use Mr. or Ms. at all times (Mr. Xia).
France	Monsieur LEFÈVRE Alain Éditions Internationales S.A. Siège Social Immeuble Le Bonaparte 64–68, av. Galliéni B.P. 154 75942 PARIS CEDEX 19 FRANCE	S.A. = Société Anonyme Siège Social (head office) Immeuble (building + name) 64–68 (building occupies 64, 66, 68) av. = avenue (no initial capital) B.P. = Boîte Postale (P.O. box) 75942 (postcode) CEDEX (postcode for P.O. box)	Monsieur (Mr.) Madame (Mrs.) Mademoiselle (Miss) Best not to abbreviate. Family name is sometimes in all caps with given name following.
Germany	Herrn Gerhardt Schneider International Verlag GmbH Schillerstraße 159 44147 DORTMUND GERMANY	Herrn = To Herr (on a separate line) GmbH (inc.—incorporated) -straße (street—'ß' often written 'ss') 159 (building number) 44147 (postcode + city)	Herr (Mr.) Frau (Mrs.) Fräulein (Miss) obsolete in business. Business is formal: (1) do not use given names unless invited, and (2) use academic titles precisely.

(continued)

Table A.5   Continued

Country	Postal Address	Address Elements	Salutations
India	Sr. Shyam Lal Gupta International Publishing (Pvt.) Ltd. 1820 Rehaja Centre 214, Darussalam Road Andheri East BOMBAY - 400049 INDIA	(Pvt.) (privately owned) Ltd. (limited liability corporation) 1820 (possibly office #20 on 18th floor) Rehaja Centre (building name) 214 (building number) Andheri East (suburb name) (city + hyphen + postcode)	Shri (Mr.), Shrimati (Mrs.) but English is common business language, so use Mr., Mrs., Miss. Given names are used only by family and close friends.
Italy	Egr. Sig. Giacomo Mariotti Edizioni Internazionali S.p.A. Via Terenzio, 21 20138 MILANO ITALY	Egr. = Egregio (honorific) Sig. = Signor (not nec. a separate line) S.p.A. = Società per Azioni (corp.) Via (street) 21 (building number) 20138 (postcode + city)	Sig. = Signore (Mr.) Sig.ra = Signora (Mrs.) Sig.a (Ms.) Women in business are addressed as Signora. Use given name only when invited.
Japan	Mr. Taro Tanaka Kokusai Shuppan K.K. 10–23, 5-chome, Minamiazabu Minato-ku TOKYO 106 JAPAN	K.K. = Kabushiki Kaisha (corporation) 10 (lot number) 23 (building number) 5-chome (area #5) Minamiazabu (neighborhood name) Minato-ku (city district) (city + postcode)	Given names not used in business. Use family name + job title. Or use family name + "-san" (Tanaka-san) or more respectfully, add "-sama" or "-dono."
Korea	Mr. Kim Chang-ik International Publishers Ltd. Room 206, Korea Building 33-4 Nonhyon-dong Kangnam-ku SEOUL 135-010 KOREA	English company names common Ltd. (a corporation) 206 (office number inside the building) 33-4 (area 4 of subdivision 33) -dong (city neighborhood name) -ku (subdivision of city) (city + postcode)	Family name is normally first but sometimes placed after given name. A two-part name is the given name. Use Mr. or Mrs. in letters, but use job title in speech.
Mexico	Sr. Francisco Pérez Martínez Editores Internacionales S.A. Independencia No.322 Col. Juárez 06050 MEXICO D.F.	S.A. = Sociedad Anónima (corporation) Independencia (street name) No. = Número (number) 322 (building number) Col. = Colonia (city district) Juárez (locality name) 06050 (postcode + city) D.F. = Distrito Federal (federal capital)	Sr. = Señor (Mr.) Sra. = Señora (Mrs.) Srta. = Señorita (Miss) Family name in middle: e.g., Sr. Pérez (Martínez is mother's family). Given names are used in business.
South Africa	Mr. Mandla Ntuli International Publishing (Pty.) Ltd. Private Bag X2581 JOHANNESBURG 2000 SOUTH AFRICA	Pty. = Proprietory (privately owned) Ltd. (a corporation) Private Bag (P.O. Box) (city + postcode) or (postcode + city)	Mnr = Meneer (Mr.) Mev. = Mevrou (Mrs.) Mejuffrou (Miss) is not used in business. Business is becoming less formal, so the use of given names is possible.
United Kingdom	Mr. N. J. Lancaster International Publishing Ltd. Kingsbury House 12 Kingsbury Road EDGEWARE Middlesex HA8 9XG ENGLAND	N. J. (initials of given names) Ltd. (limited liability corporation) Kingsbury House (building name) 12 (building number) Kingsbury Road (name of street/road) EDGEWARE (city—all caps) Middlesex (county—not all caps) HA8 9XG (postcode)	Mr. and Ms. used mostly. Mrs. and Miss sometimes used in North and by older women. Given names—called Christian names—are used in business after some time. Wait to be invited.

Signature Block

Leave three blank lines for a written signature below the complimentary close, and then include the sender's name (unless it appears in the letterhead). The person's title may appear on the same line as the name or on the line below:

Cordially,

Raymond Dunnigan
Director of Personnel

Your letterhead indicates that you're representing your company. However, if your letter is on plain paper or runs to a second page, you may want to emphasize that you're speaking legally for the company. The accepted way of doing that is to place the company's name in capital letters a double space below the complimentary close and then include the sender's name and title four lines below that:

Sincerely,

WENTWORTH INDUSTRIES

(Mrs.) Helen B. Taylor
President

If your name could be taken for either a man's or a woman's, a courtesy title indicating gender should be included, with or without parentheses. Also, women who prefer a particular courtesy title should include it:

Mrs. Nancy Winters
(Miss) Juana Flores
Ms. Pat Li
(Mr.) Jamie Saunders

Additional Letter Parts

Letters vary greatly in subject matter and thus in the identifying information they need and the format they adopt. The letter in Figure A.2 on page A-10 shows how these additional parts should be arranged. The following elements may be used in any combination, depending on the requirements of the particular letter:

- **Addressee notation.** Letters that have a restricted readership or that must be handled in a special way should include such addressee notations as *Personal, Confidential,* or *Please Forward.* This sort of notation appears a double space above the inside address, in all-capital letters.
- **Attention line.** Although not commonly used today, an attention line can be used if you know only the last name of the person you're writing to. It can also direct a letter to a position title or department. Place the attention line on the first line of the inside address and put the company name on the second.[8] Match the address on the envelope with the style of the inside address. An attention line may take any of the following forms or variants of them:

Attention Dr. McHenry
Attention Director of Marketing
Attention Marketing Department

- **Subject line.** The subject line tells recipients at a glance what the letter is about (and indicates where to file the letter for future reference). It usually appears below the salutation, either against the left margin, indented (as a paragraph in the body), or centered. It can be placed above the salutation or at the very top of the page, and it can be underscored. Some businesses omit the word *Subject,* and some organizations replace it with *Re:* or *In re:* (meaning "concerning" or "in the matter of"). The subject line may take a variety of forms, including the following:

Subject: RainMaster Sprinklers
About your February 2, 2004, order
FALL 2004 SALES MEETING
Reference Order No. 27920

- **Second-page heading.** Use a second-page heading whenever an additional page is required. Some companies have second-page letterhead (with the company name and address on one line and in a smaller typeface). The heading bears the name (person or organization) from the first line of the inside address, the page number, the date, and perhaps a reference number. Leave two blank lines before the body. Make sure that at least two lines of a continued paragraph appear on the first and second pages. Never allow the closing lines to appear alone on a continued page. Precede the complimentary close or signature lines with at least two lines of the body. Also, don't hyphenate the last word on a page. All the following are acceptable forms for second-page headings:

Ms. Melissa Baker
May 10, 2004
Page 2

Ms. Melissa Baker, May 10, 2004, Page 2

Ms. Melissa Baker   -2-   May 10, 2004

- **Company name.** If you include the company's name in the signature block, put it all in capital letters a double space below the complimentary close. You usually include the company's name in the signature block only when the writer is serving as the company's official spokesperson or when letterhead has not been used.
- **Reference initials.** When businesspeople keyboard their own letters, reference initials are unnecessary, so they are becoming rare. When one person dictates a letter and another person produces it, reference initials show who helped prepare it. Place initials at the left margin, a double space below the signature block. When the signature block includes the writer's name, use only the preparer's initials. If the signature block includes only the department, use both sets of initials, usually in one of the following forms: *RSR/sm, RSR:sm,* or *RSR:SM* (writer/

FIGURE A.2 Additional Letter Parts

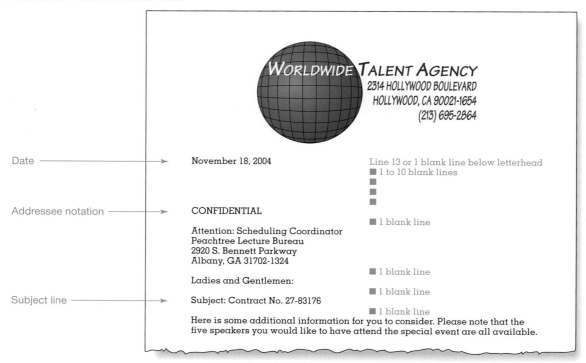

preparer). When the writer and the signer are different people, at least the file copy should bear both their initials as well as the typist's: *JFS/RSR/sm* (signer/writer/preparer).

- **Enclosure notation.** Enclosure notations appear at the bottom of a letter, one or two lines below the reference initials. Some common forms include the following:

  Enclosure

  Enclosures (2)

  Enclosures: Résumé

                 Photograph

                 Attachment

- **Copy notation.** Copy notations may follow reference initials or enclosure notations. They indicate who's receiving a *courtesy copy* (*cc*). Some companies indicate copies made on a photocopier (*pc*), or they simply use *copy* (*c*). Recipients are listed in order of rank or (rank being equal) in alphabetical order. Among the forms used are the following:

  cc: David Wentworth, Vice President

  pc: Dr. Martha Littlefield

  Copy to Hans Vogel

             748 Chesterton Road

             Snowhomish, WA 98290

             c: Joseph Martinez with brochure and technical sheet

When sending copies to readers other than the person receiving the original letter, place *bc, bcc,* or *bpc* ("blind copy," "blind courtesy copy," or "blind photocopy") along with the name and any other information only on the copy, not on the original.

- **Mailing notation.** You may place a mailing notation (such as *Special Delivery* or *Registered Mail*) at the bottom of the letter, after reference initials or enclosure notations (whichever one is last) and before copy notations. Or you may place it at the top of the letter, either above the inside address on the left-hand side or just below the date on the right-hand side. For greater visibility, mailing notations may appear in capital letters.

- **Postscript.** A postscript is an afterthought to the letter, a message that requires emphasis, or a personal note. It is usually the last thing on any letter and may be preceded by *P.S., PS., PS:,* or nothing at all. A second afterthought would be designated *P.P.S.* (post postscript). Since postscripts usually indicate poor planning, generally avoid them. However, they're common in sales letters as a punch line to remind readers of a benefit for taking advantage of the offer.

Letter Formats

A letter format is the way of arranging all the basic letter parts. Sometimes a company adopts a certain format as its policy; sometimes the individual letter writer or preparer is allowed to choose the most appropriate format. In the United States, three major letter formats are commonly used:

- **Block format.** Each letter part begins at the left margin. The main advantage is quick and efficient preparation (see Figure A.3 on page A-12).

FIGURE A.2   Continued

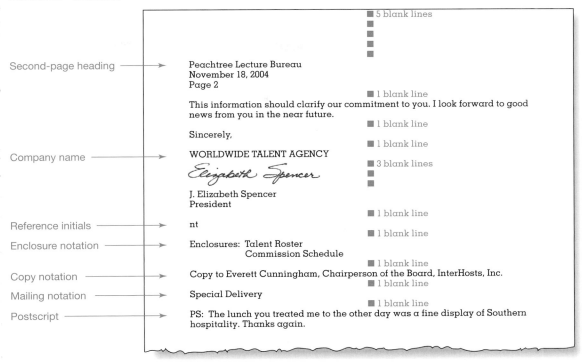

Second-page heading → Peachtree Lecture Bureau / November 18, 2004 / Page 2

Company name → WORLDWIDE TALENT AGENCY / *Elizabeth Spencer* / J. Elizabeth Spencer / President

Reference initials → nt

Enclosure notation → Enclosures: Talent Roster / Commission Schedule

Copy notation → Copy to Everett Cunningham, Chairperson of the Board, InterHosts, Inc.

Mailing notation → Special Delivery

Postscript → PS: The lunch you treated me to the other day was a fine display of Southern hospitality. Thanks again.

(Figure text: 5 blank lines; 1 blank line; This information should clarify our commitment to you. I look forward to good news from you in the near future.; 1 blank line; Sincerely,; 1 blank line; 3 blank lines; 1 blank line; 1 blank line; 1 blank line; 1 blank line)

- **Modified block format.** Same as block format, except that the date, complimentary close, and signature block start near the center of the page (see Figure A.4 on page A-13). The modified block format does permit indentions as an option. This format mixes preparation speed with traditional placement of some letter parts. It also looks more balanced on the page than the block format does.

- **Simplified format.** Instead of using a salutation, this format often weaves the reader's name into the first line or two of the body and often includes a subject line in capital letters (see Figure A.5 on page A-14). With no complimentary close, your signature appears after the body, followed by your printed (or typewritten) name (usually in all capital letters). This format is convenient when you don't know the reader's name; however, some people object to it as mechanical and impersonal (a drawback you can overcome with a warm writing style). Because certain letter parts are eliminated, some line spacing is changed.

These three formats differ in the way paragraphs are indented, in the way letter parts are placed, and in some punctuation. However, the elements are always separated by at least one blank line, and the printed (or typewritten) name is always separated from the line above by at least three blank lines to allow space for a signature. If paragraphs are indented, the indention is normally five spaces. The most common formats for intercultural business letters are the block style and the modified block style.

In addition to these three letter formats, letters may also be classified according to their style of punctuation. *Standard,* or *mixed, punctuation* uses a colon after the salutation (a comma if the letter is social or personal) and a comma after the complimentary close. *Open punctuation* uses no colon or comma after the salutation or the complimentary close. Although the most popular style in business communication is mixed punctuation, either style of punctuation may be used with block or modified block letter formats. Because the simplified letter format has no salutation or complimentary close, the style of punctuation is irrelevant.

Envelopes

For a first impression, the quality of the envelope is just as important as the quality of the stationery. Letterhead and envelopes should be of the same paper stock, have the same color ink, and be imprinted with the same address and logo. Most envelopes used by U.S. businesses are No. 10 envelopes (9½ inches long), which are sized for an 8½-by-11-inch piece of paper folded in thirds. Some occasions call for a smaller, No. 6¾, envelope or for envelopes proportioned to fit special stationery. Figure A.6 on page A-15 shows the two most common sizes.

Addressing the Envelope

No matter what size the envelope, the address is always single-spaced with all lines aligned on the left. The address on the envelope is in the same style as the inside address and presents the same information. The order to follow is from the smallest division to the largest:

1. Name and title of recipient
2. Name of department or subgroup
3. Name of organization
4. Name of building
5. Street address and suite number, or post office box number
6. City, state or province, and ZIP code or postal code
7. Name of country (if the letter is being sent abroad)

FIGURE A.3   Block Letter Format

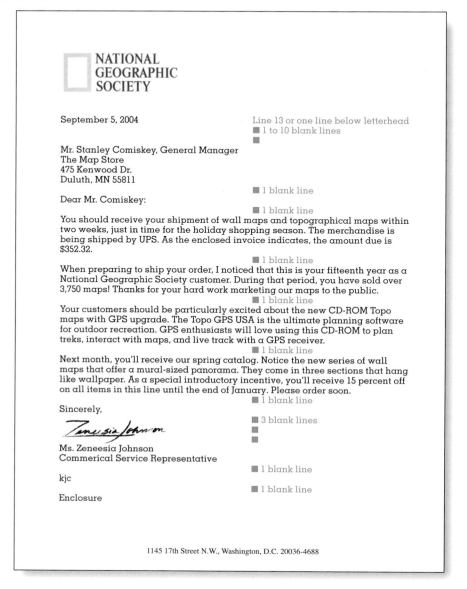

Because the U.S. Postal Service uses optical scanners to sort mail, envelopes for quantity mailings, in particular, should be addressed in the prescribed format. Everything is in capital letters, no punctuation is included, and all mailing instructions of interest to the post office are placed above the address area (see Figure A.6 on page A-15). Canada Post requires a similar format, except that only the city is all in capitals, and the postal code is placed on the line below the name of the city. The post office scanners read addresses from the bottom up, so if a letter is to be sent to a post office box rather than to a street address, the street address should appear on the line above the box number. Figure A.6 also shows the proper spacing for addresses and return addresses.

The U.S. Postal Service and the Canada Post Corporation have published lists of two-letter mailing abbreviations for states, provinces, and territories (see Table A.6 on page A-16). Postal authorities prefer no punctuation with these abbreviations, but some executives prefer to have state and province names spelled out in full and set off from city names by a comma. The issue is unresolved, although the comma is most often included. Quantity mailings follow post office requirements. For other letters, a reasonable compromise is to use traditional punctuation, uppercase and lowercase letters for names and street addresses, but two-letter state or province abbreviations, as shown here:

Mr. Kevin Kennedy

2107 E. Packer Drive

Amarillo, TX 79108

For all out-of-office correspondence, use ZIP and postal codes that have been assigned to speed mail delivery. The U.S. Postal Service has divided the United States and its territories into 10 zones (0 to 9); this digit comes first in the ZIP code. The second and third digits represent smaller geographical areas within a state, and the last two digits identify a "local delivery area." Canadian postal codes are alphanumeric, with a three-character "area code" and a three-character "local code" sepa-

FIGURE A.4   Modified Block Letter Format

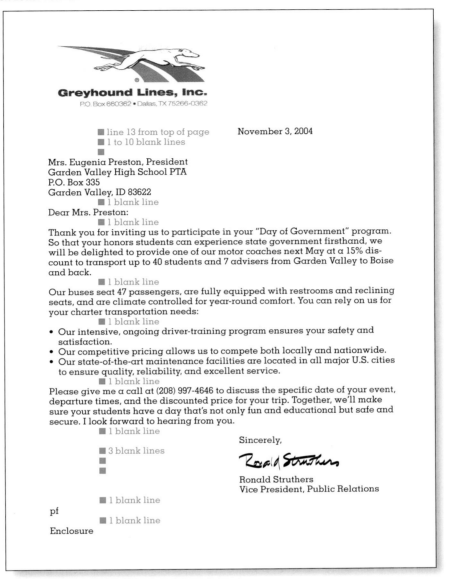

rated by a single space (K2P 5A5). ZIP codes should be separated from state and province names by one space. Canadian postal codes may be treated the same or may be put in the bottom line of the address all by itself.

The U.S. Postal Service has added ZIP + 4 codes, which add a hyphen and four more numbers to the standard ZIP codes. The first two of the new numbers may identify an area as small as a single large building, and the last two digits may identify one floor in a large building or even a specific department of an organization. The ZIP + 4 codes are especially useful for business correspondence. The Canada Post Corporation achieves the same result with special postal codes assigned to buildings and organizations that receive a large volume of mail.

Folding to Fit

The way a letter is folded also contributes to the recipient's overall impression of your organization's professionalism.

When sending a standard-size piece of paper in a No. 10 envelope, fold it in thirds, with the bottom folded up first and the top folded down over it (see Figure A.7 on page A-17); the open end should be at the top of the envelope and facing out. Fit smaller stationery neatly into the appropriate envelope simply by folding it in half or in thirds. When sending a standard-size letterhead in a No. 6¾ envelope, fold it in half from top to bottom and then in thirds from side to side.

International Mail

Postal service differs from country to country. For example, street addresses are uncommon in India, and the mail there is unreliable.[9] It's usually a good idea to send international correspondence by airmail and to ask that responses be sent that way as well. Also, remember to check the postage; rates for sending mail to most other countries differ from the rates for sending mail within your own country.

FIGURE A.5   Simplified Letter Format

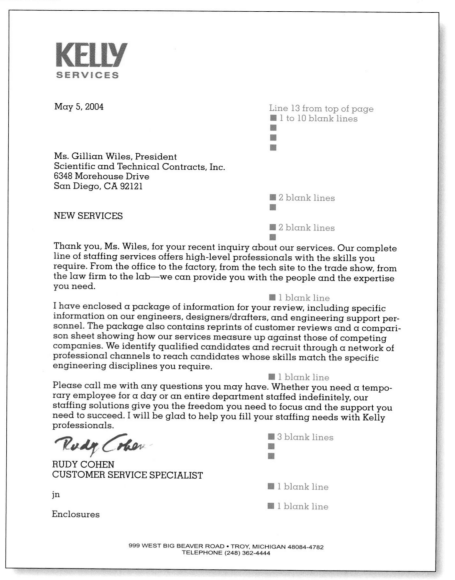

International mail falls into three main categories:

- **LC mail.** An abbreviation of the French *Lettres et Cartes* ("letters and cards"); this category consists of letters, letter packages, aerograms, and postcards.
- **AO mail.** An abbreviation of the French *Autres Objets* ("other articles"); this category includes regular printed matter, books and sheet music, matter for the blind, small packets, and publishers' periodicals (second class).
- **CP mail.** An abbreviation of the French *Colis Postaux* ("parcel post"); this category resembles fourth-class mail, including packages of merchandise or any other articles not required to be mailed at letter rates.

Along with several optional special services, the U.S. Postal Service also offers the following:

- **Express Mail International Service (EMS).** A high-speed mail service to many countries
- **International Priority Airmail (IPA).** An international service that's as fast as or faster than regular airmail service
- **International Surface Air Lift (ISAL).** A service providing quicker delivery and lower cost for all kinds of printed matter
- **Bulk Letter Service to Canada.** An economical airmail service for letters weighing 1 ounce or less
- **VALUEPOST/CANADA.** A reduced postage rate for bulk mailings
- **International Electronic Post (INTELPOST).** A service offering same- or next-day delivery of fax documents
- **International Postal Money Orders.** A service for transferring funds to other countries

FIGURE A.6   Prescribed Envelope Format

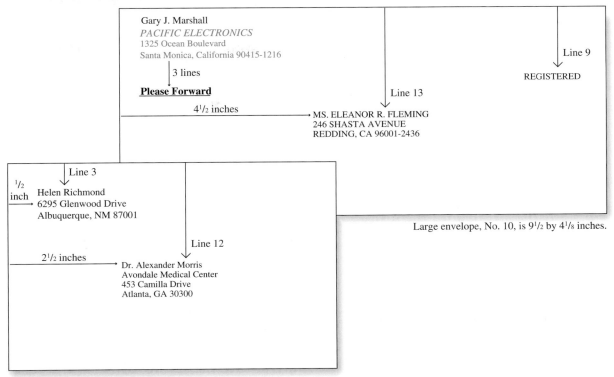

Gary J. Marshall
PACIFIC ELECTRONICS
1325 Ocean Boulevard
Santa Monica, California 90415-1216

3 lines

Please Forward

4½ inches

Line 13

MS. ELEANOR R. FLEMING
246 SHASTA AVENUE
REDDING, CA 96001-2436

Line 9

REGISTERED

Large envelope, No. 10, is 9½ by 4⅛ inches.

Line 3

Helen Richmond
6295 Glenwood Drive
Albuquerque, NM 87001

½ inch

Line 12

2½ inches

Dr. Alexander Morris
Avondale Medical Center
453 Camilla Drive
Atlanta, GA 30300

Small envelope, No. 6¾, is 6½ by 3⅝ inches.

To prepare your mail for international delivery, follow the instructions in the U.S. Postal Service Publication 51, *International Postal Rates and Fees*. Be sure to note instructions for the address, return address, and size limits. Envelopes and wrappers must be clearly marked to show their classification (letter, small packet, printed matter, airmail). All registered letters, letter packages, and parcel post packages must be securely sealed. Printed matter may be sealed only if postage is paid by permit imprint, postage meter, precanceled stamps, or second-class imprint. Otherwise, prepare contents so that they're protected without hindering inspection. Finally, because international mail is subject to customs examination in the country of destination, the contents and value must be declared on special forms.

Memos

Many organizations have memo forms preprinted, with labeled spaces for the recipient's name (or sometimes a checklist of all departments in an organization or all persons in a department), the sender's name, the date, and the subject (see Figure A.8 on page A-17). If such forms don't exist, you can use a memo template (which comes with word-processing software and provides margin settings, headings, and special formats), or you can use plain paper.

On your document, include a title such as *MEMO* or *INTEROFFICE CORRESPONDENCE* (all in capitals) centered at the top of the page or aligned with the left margin. Also at the top, include the words *To, From, Date,* and *Subject*—followed by the appropriate information—with a blank line between, as shown here:

MEMO

TO:

FROM:

DATE:

SUBJECT:

Sometimes the heading is organized like this:

MEMO

TO: DATE:
FROM: SUBJECT:

You can arrange these four pieces of information in almost any order. The date sometimes appears without the heading *Date*. The subject may be presented with the letters *Re:* (in place of *SUBJECT:*) or may even be presented without any heading (but in capital letters so that it stands out clearly). You may want to include a file or reference number, introduced by the word *File*.

The following guidelines will help you effectively format specific memo elements:

■ **Addressees.** When sending a memo to a long list of people, include the notation *See distribution list* or *See below* in the *To* position at the top; then list the names at the end of the memo. Arrange this list alphabetically, except when high-ranking officials deserve more prominent placement. You can also address memos to groups of people—*All Sales Representatives, Production Group, New Product Team.*

| Table A.6 | | Two-Letter Mailing Abbreviations for the United States and Canada | | | |

State/Territory/Province	Abbreviation	State/Territory/Province	Abbreviation	State/Territory/Province	Abbreviation
United States		Massachusetts	MA	Texas	TX
Alabama	AL	Michigan	MI	Utah	UT
Alaska	AK	Minnesota	MN	Vermont	VT
American Samoa	AS	Mississippi	MS	Virginia	VA
Arizona	AZ	Missouri	MO	Virgin Islands	VI
Arkansas	AR	Montana	MT	Washington	WA
California	CA	Nebraska	NE	West Virginia	WV
Canal Zone	CZ	Nevada	NV	Wisconsin	WI
Colorado	CO	New Hampshire	NH	Wyoming	WY
Connecticut	CT	New Jersey	NJ	**Canada**	
Delaware	DE	New Mexico	NM	Alberta	AB
District of Columbia	DC	New York	NY	British Columbia	BC
Florida	FL	North Carolina	NC	Labrador	NL
Georgia	GA	North Dakota	ND	Manitoba	MB
Guam	GU	Northern Mariana	CM	New Brunswick	NB
Hawaii	HI	Ohio	OH	Newfoundland	NL
Idaho	ID	Oklahoma	OK	Northwest Territories	NT
Illinois	IL	Oregon	OR	Nova Scotia	NS
Indiana	IN	Pennsylvania	PA	Ontario	ON
Iowa	IA	Puerto Rico	PR	Prince Edward Island	PE
Kansas	KS	Rhode Island	RI	Quebec	PQ
Kentucky	KY	South Carolina	SC	Saskatchewan	SK
Louisiana	LA	South Dakota	SD	Yukon Territory	YT
Maine	ME	Tennessee	TN		
Maryland	MD	Trust Territories	TT		

- **Courtesy titles.** You need not use courtesy titles anywhere in a memo; first initials and last names, first names, or even initials alone are often sufficient. However, use a courtesy title if you would use one in a face-to-face encounter with the person.

- **Subject line.** The subject line of a memo helps busy colleagues quickly find out what your memo is about. Although the subject "line" may overflow onto a second line, it's most helpful when it's short (but still informative).

- **Body.** Start the body of the memo on the second or third line below the heading. Like the body of a letter, it's usually single-spaced with blank lines between paragraphs. Indenting paragraphs is optional. Handle lists, important passages, and subheadings as you do in letters. If the memo is very short, you may double-space it.

- **Second page.** If the memo carries over to a second page, head the second page just as you head the second page of a letter.

- **Writer's initials.** Unlike a letter, a memo doesn't require a complimentary close or a signature, because your name is already prominent at the top. However, you may initial the memo—either beside the name appearing at the top of the memo or at the bottom of the memo—or you may even sign your name at the bottom, particularly if the memo deals with money or confidential matters.

- **Other elements.** Treat elements such as reference initials, enclosure notations, and copy notations just as you would in a letter.

Memos may be delivered by hand, by the post office (when the recipient works at a different location), or through interoffice mail. Interoffice mail may require the use of special reusable envelopes that have spaces for the recipient's name and department or room number; the name of the previous recipient is simply crossed out. If a regular envelope is used, the words

FIGURE A.7   Folding Standard-Size Letterhead

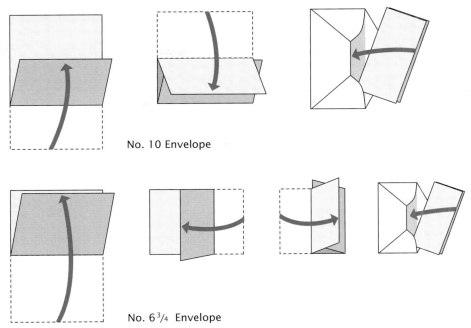

No. 10 Envelope

No. 6 3/4 Envelope

Interoffice Mail appear where the stamp normally goes, so that it won't accidentally be stamped and mailed with the rest of the office correspondence.

Informal, routine, or brief reports for distribution within a company are often presented in memo form (see Chapter 10). Don't include report parts such as a table of contents and appendixes, but write the body of the memo report just as carefully as you'd write a formal report.

E-Mail

Because e-mail messages can act both as memos (carrying information within your company) and as letters (carrying information outside your company and around the world), their format depends on your audience and purpose. You may choose to have your e-mail resemble a formal letter or a detailed report, or you may decide to keep things as simple as an interoffice memo. A modified memo format is appropriate for most e-mail messages.[10] All e-mail programs include two major elements: the header and the body (see Figure A.9 on the following page).

Header

The e-mail header depends on the particular program you use. Some programs even allow you to choose between a shorter and a longer version. However, most headers contain similar information.

- **To:** Contains the audience's e-mail address (see Figure A.10 on page A-19). Most e-mail programs also allow you to send mail to an entire group of people all at once. First, you create a distribution list. Then you type the name of the list in the *To:* line instead of typing the addresses of every person in the group.[11] The most common e-mail addresses are addresses such as

  NMAA.BETSY@C.SI.EDU (Smithsonian Institute's National Museum of American Art)

  webwsj@dowjones.com (*Wall Street Journal*'s home page)

  relpubli@mairie-toulouse.mipnet.fr (Municipal Services, Toulouse, France)

- **From:** Contains your e-mail address.

FIGURE A.8   Preprinted Memo Form

MEMO	
TO: _____	
DEPT: _____	FROM: _____
DATE: _____	TELEPHONE: _____
SUBJECT: _____	*For your* ☐ APPROVAL ☐ INFORMATION ☐ COMMENT

FIGURE A.9   A Typical E-Mail Message

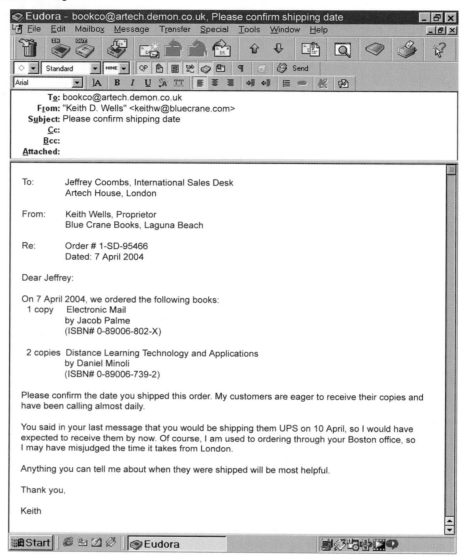

- **Date:** Contains the day of the week, date (day, month, year), time, and time zone.

- **Subject:** Describes the content of the message and presents an opportunity for you to build interest in your message.

- **Cc:** Allows you to send copies of a message to more than one person at a time. It also allows everyone on the list to see who else received the same message.

- **Bcc:** Lets you send copies to people without the other recipients knowing—a practice considered unethical by some.[12]

- **Attachments:** Contains the name(s) of the file(s) you attach to your e-mail message. The file can be a word-processing document, a digital image, an audio or video message, a spreadsheet, or a software program.[13]

Most e-mail programs now allow you the choice of hiding or revealing other lines that contain more detailed information, including

- **Message-Id:** The exact location of this e-mail message on the sender's system

- **X-mailer:** The version of the e-mail program being used

- **Content type:** A description of the text and character set that is contained in the message

- **Received:** Information about each of the systems your e-mail passed through en route to your mailbox.[14]

Body

The rest of the space below the header is for the body of your message. In the *To:* and *From:* lines, some headers actually print out the names of the sender and receiver (in addition to their e-mail addresses). Other headers do not. If your mail program includes only the e-mail addresses, you might consider including your own memo-type header in the body of your message, as in Figure A.9. The writer even included a second, more specific subject line in his memo-type header. Some

FIGURE A.10   Anatomy of an E-Mail Address

recipients may applaud the clarity of such second headers; however, others will criticize the space it takes. Your decision depends on how formal you want to be.

Do include a greeting in your e-mail. As pointed out in Chapter 6, greetings personalize your message. Leave one line space above and below your greeting to set it off from the rest of your message. You may end your greeting with a colon (formal), a comma (conversational), or even two hyphens (informal)—depending on the level of formality you want.

Your message begins one blank line space below your greeting. Just as in memos and letters, skip one line space between paragraphs and include headings, numbered lists, bulleted lists, and embedded lists when appropriate. Limit your line lengths to a maximum of 80 characters by inserting a hard return at the end of each line.

One blank line space below your message, include a simple closing, often just one word. A blank line space below that, include your signature. Whether you type your name or use a signature file, including your signature personalizes your message.

Time-Saving Messages

Telephone and e-mail systems are quick, as are mailgrams, telegrams, faxes, and the like. Organizations have developed special formats to reduce the amount of time spent writing and typing short messages:

- **Fax cover sheets.** When faxing messages, you may use a fax cover sheet, which includes the recipient's name, company, fax number, and city; the sender's name, complete address, fax number, and telephone number; the number of pages being sent; a phone number to call if the faxed transmission isn't successful; and enough space for any brief message.[15] The format for this information varies widely. When a document is self-explanatory, a cover sheet may be unnecessary, so be sure not to waste paper or transmission time.

- **Short-note reply technique.** Popular in many organizations, this technique can be used even without a special form. The recipient of a memo (or sometimes a letter) simply handwrites a response on the original document, makes a copy for the files, and sends the annotated original back to the person who wrote it.

- **Letterhead postcards.** Ideal for short, impersonal messages, letterhead postcards are preprinted with a list of responses so that the "writer" merely checks the appropriate response(s) and slips the postcard into the mail. Organizations such as mail-order companies and government agencies use these time-saving devices to communicate frequently with individuals by mail.

Reports

Enhance your report's effectiveness by paying careful attention to its appearance and layout. Follow whatever guidelines your organization prefers, always being neat and consistent throughout. If it's up to you to decide formatting questions, the following conventions may help you decide how to handle margins, headings, spacing and indention, and page numbers.

Margins

All margins on a report page are at least 1 inch wide. For double-spaced pages, use 1-inch margins; for single-spaced pages, set margins between 1¼ and 1½ inches. The top, left, and right margins are usually the same, but the bottom margins can be 1½ times deeper. Some special pages also have deeper top margins. Set top margins as deep as 2 inches for pages that contain major titles: prefatory parts (such as the table of contents or the executive summary), supplementary parts (such as the reference notes or bibliography), and textual parts (such as the first page of the text or the first page of each chapter).

If you're going to bind your report at the left or at the top, add half an inch to the margin on the bound edge (see Figure A.11).

FIGURE A.11   Margins for Formal Reports

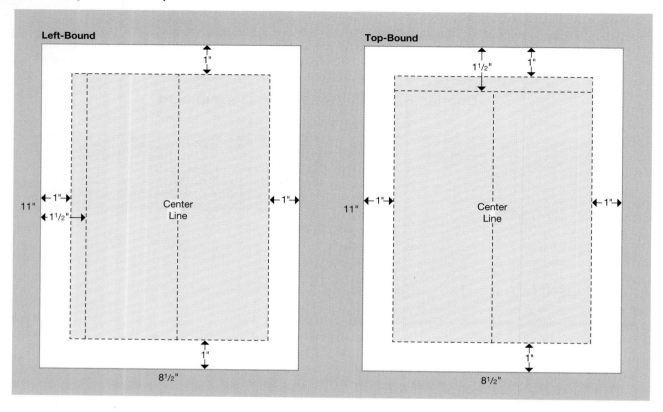

The space taken by the binding on left-bound reports makes the center point of the text a quarter inch to the right of the center of the paper. Be sure to center headings between the margins, not between the edges of the paper. Computers can do this for you automatically. Other guidelines for report formats are in the Chapter 11 sample.

Headings

Headings of various levels provide visual clues to a report's organization. Figure 11.9, on page 329, illustrates one good system for showing these levels, but many variations exist. No matter which system you use, be sure to be consistent.

Spacing and Indentions

If your report is double-spaced (perhaps to ease comprehension of technical material), indent all paragraphs five character spaces (or about ½ inch). In single-spaced reports, block the paragraphs (no indentions) and leave one blank line between them.

Make sure the material on the title page is centered and well balanced, as on the title page of the sample report in Chapter 11. When using a typewriter, proper spacing takes some calculation. To center text in left-bound reports, start a quarter inch to the right of the paper's center. From that point, backspace once for each two letters in the line. The line will appear centered once the report is bound.

To place lines of type vertically on the title page, follow these steps:

1. Count the number of lines in each block of copy, including blank lines.
2. Subtract that total from 66 (the number of lines on an 11-inch page); the result is the number of unused lines.
3. Divide the number of unused lines by the number of blank areas (always one more than the number of blocks of copy). The result is the number of blank lines to allocate above, between, and below the blocks of copy.

A computer with a good word-processing program will do these calculations for you at the click of a mouse.

Page Numbers

Remember that every page in the report is counted; however, not all pages show numbers. The first page of the report, normally the title page, is unnumbered. All other pages in the prefatory section are numbered with a lowercase roman numeral, beginning with *ii* and continuing with *iii, iv, v,* and so on. The unadorned (no dashes, no period) page number is centered at the bottom margin.

Number the first page of the text of the report with the unadorned arabic numeral 1, centered at the bottom margin (double- or triple-spaced below the text). In left-bound reports, number the following pages (including the supplementary parts) consecutively with unadorned arabic numerals (2, 3, and so on), placed at the top right-hand margin (double- or triple-spaced above the text). For top-bound reports and for special pages having 2-inch top margins, center the page numbers at the bottom margin.

Documentation of Report Sources

Documenting a report is too important a task to undertake haphazardly. By providing information about your sources, you improve your own credibility as well as the credibility of the facts and opinions you present. Documentation gives readers the means for checking your findings and pursuing the subject further. Also, documenting your report is the accepted way to give credit to the people whose work you have drawn from.

What style should you use to document your report? Experts recommend various forms, depending on your field or discipline. Moreover, your employer or client may use a form different from those the experts suggest. Don't let this discrepancy confuse you. If your employer specifies a form, use it; the standardized form is easier for colleagues to understand. However, if the choice of form is left to you, adopt one of the styles described here. Whatever style you choose, be consistent within any given report, using the same order, punctuation, and format from one reference citation or bibliography entry to the next.

A wide variety of style manuals provide detailed information on documentation. Here is a brief annotated list:

■ American Psychological Association, *Publication Manual of the American Psychological Association,* 5th ed. (Washington, DC: American Psychological Association, 2001). Details the author-date system, which is preferred in the social sciences and often in the natural sciences as well.

■ *The Chicago Manual of Style,* 15th ed. (Chicago: University of Chicago Press, 1993). Often referred to only as *Chicago* and widely used in the publishing industry; provides detailed treatment of documentation in Chapters 15 and 16.

■ Joseph Gibaldi, *MLA Style Manual and Guide to Scholarly Publishing,* 2d ed. (New York: Modern Language Association, 1998). Serves as the basis for the note and bibliography style used in much academic writing and is recommended in many college textbooks on writing term papers; provides a lot of examples in the humanities.

■ Andrew Harnack and Eugene Kleppinger, *Online! A Reference Guide to Using Internet Sources—2000* (New York: St. Martin's Press, 2000). Offers an approach to style for citing online references.

Although many schemes have been proposed for organizing the information in source notes, all of them break the information into parts: (1) information about the author (name), (2) information about the work (title, edition, volume number), (3) information about the publication (place, publisher), (4) information about the date, and (5) information on relevant page ranges.

In the following sections, we summarize the major conventions for documenting sources in three styles: *The Chicago Manual of Style* (Chicago), the *Publication Manual of the American Psychological Association* (APA), and the *MLA Style Manual* (MLA).

Chicago Humanities Style

The Chicago Manual of Style recommends two types of documentation systems. The *documentary-note,* or *humanities,* style gives bibliographic citations in notes—either footnotes (when printed at the bottom of a page) or endnotes (when printed at the end of the report). The humanities system is often used in literature, history, and the arts. The other system strongly recommended by Chicago is the *author-date* system, which cites the author's last name and the date of publication in the text, usually in parentheses, reserving full documentation for the reference list (or bibliography). For the purpose of comparing styles, we will concentrate on the humanities system, which is described in detail in Chicago.

In-Text Citation—Chicago Humanities Style

To document report sources in text, the humanities system relies on superscripts—arabic numerals placed just above the line of type at the end of the reference:

> Toward the end of his speech, Myers sounded a note of caution, saying that even though the economy is expected to grow, it could easily slow a bit.[10]

The superscript lets the reader know how to look for source information in either a footnote or an endnote (see Figure B.1 on the following page). Some readers prefer footnotes so that they can simply glance at the bottom of the page for information. Others prefer endnotes so that they can read the text without a clutter of notes on the page. Also, endnotes relieve the writer from worrying about how long each note will be and how much space it will take away from the page. Both footnotes

FIGURE B.1   Sample Endnotes—Chicago Humanities Style

NOTES

Journal article with volume and issue numbers

1. James Assira, "Are They Speaking English in Japan?" *Journal of Business Communication* 36, no. 4 (Fall 2004): 72.

Brochure

2. BestTemp Staffing Services, *An Employer's Guide to Staffing Services*, 2d ed. (Denver: BestTemp Information Center, 2002), 31.

Newspaper article, no author

3. "Buying Asian Supplies on the Net," *Los Angeles Times*, 12 February 2002, sec. D, p. 3.

Annual report

4. Eurotec, *2003 Annual Report* (New York: Eurotec, Inc., 2003), 48.

Magazine article

5. Holly Graves, "Prospecting Online," *Business Week*, 17 November 2004, 43–5.

Television broadcast

6. Daniel Han, "Trade Wars Heating Up Around the Globe," *CNN Headline News* (Atlanta: CNN, 5 March 2004).

Internet, World Wide Web

7. "Intel—Company Capsule," Hoover's Online [cited 8 March 2005], 3 screens; available from www.hoovers.com/capsules/13787.html.

Book, component parts

8. Sonja Kuntz, "Moving Beyond Benefits," in *Our Changing Workforce*, ed. Randolf Jacobson (New York: Citadel Press, 2003), 213–27.

Unpublished dissertation or thesis

9. George H. Morales, "The Economic Pressures on Industrialized Nations in a Global Economy" (Ph.D. diss., University of San Diego, 2003), 32–47.

Paper presented at a meeting

10. Charles Myers, "HMOs in Today's Environment" (paper presented at the Conference on Medical Insurance Solution, Chicago, Ill., August 2003), 16–17.

Online magazine article

11. Preston Norwalk, "Training Managers to Help Employees Accept Change," in *Business Line* [online] (San Francisco, 2003 [updated 17 September 2004; cited 3 October 2004]); available from www.busline.com/news.

CD-ROM encyclopedia article, one author

12. Robert Parkings, "George Eastman," *The Concise Columbia Encyclopedia* (New York: Columbia University Press, 2000) [CD-ROM].

Interview

13. Georgia Stainer, general manager, Day Cable and Communications, interview by author, Topeka, Kan., 2 March 2002.

Newspaper article, one author

14. Evelyn Standish, "Global Market Crushes OPEC's Delicate Balance of Interests," *Wall Street Journal*, 19 January 2004, sec. A, p. 1.

Book, two authors

15. Miriam Toller and Jay Fielding, *Global Business for Smaller Companies* (Rocklin, Calif.: Prima Publishing, 2003), 102–3.

Government publication

16. U.S. Department of Defense, *Stretching Research Dollars: Survival Advice for Universities and Government Labs* (Washington, D.C.: GPO, 2004), 126.

and endnotes are handled automatically by today's word-processing software.

For the reader's convenience, you can use footnotes for **content notes** (which may supplement your main text with asides about a particular issue or event, provide a cross-reference to another section of your report, or direct the reader to a related source). Then you can use endnotes for **source notes** (which document direct quotations, paraphrased passages, and visual aids). Consider which type of note is most common in your report, and then choose whether to present these notes all as endnotes or all as footnotes. Regardless of the method you choose for referencing textual information in your report, notes for visual aids (both content notes and source notes) are placed on the same page as the visual.

Bibliography—Chicago Humanities Style

The humanities system may or may not be accompanied by a bibliography (because the notes give all the necessary bibliographic information). However, endnotes are arranged in order of appearance in the text, so an alphabetical bibliography can be valuable to your readers. The bibliography may be titled *Bibliography, Reference List, Sources, Works Cited* (if you include only those sources you actually cited in your report), or *Works Consulted* (if you include uncited sources as well). This list of sources may also serve as a reading list for those who want to pursue the subject of your report further, so you may want to annotate each entry—that is, comment on the subject matter and viewpoint of the source, as well as on its usefulness to readers. Annotations may be written in either complete or incom-

FIGURE B.2   Sample Bibliography—Chicago Humanities Style

BIBLIOGRAPHY

Journal article with volume and issue numbers	Assira, James. "Are They Speaking English in Japan?" *Journal of Business Communication* 36, no. 4 (Fall 2004): 72.
Brochure	BestTemp Staffing Services. *An Employer's Guide to Staffing Services.* 2d ed. Denver: BestTemp Information Center, 2002.
Newspaper article, no author	"Buying Asian Supplies on the Net." *Los Angeles Times,* 12 February 2002, sec. D, p. 3.
Annual report	Eurotec. *2003 Annual Report.* New York: Eurotec, Inc., 2003.
Magazine article	Graves, Holly. "Prospecting Online." *Business Week,* 17 November 2004, 43–5.
Television broadcast	Han, Daniel. "Trade Wars Heating Up Around the Globe." *CNN Headline News.* Atlanta: CNN, 5 March 2004.
Internet, World Wide Web	"Intel—Company Capsule." *Hoover's Online* [cited 8 March 2005]. 3 screens; Available from www.hoovers.com/capsules/13787.html.
Book, component parts	Kuntz, Sonja. "Moving Beyond Benefits." In *Our Changing Workforce*, edited by Randolf Jacobson. New York: Citadel Press, 2003.
Unpublished dissertation or thesis	Morales, George H. "The Economic Pressures on Industrialized Nations in a Global Economy." Ph.D. diss., University of San Diego, 2003.
Paper presented at a meeting	Myers, Charles. "HMOs in Today's Environment." Paper presented at the Conference on Medical Insurance Solutions, Chicago, Ill., August 2003.
Online magazine article	Norwalk, Preston. "Training Managers to Help Employees Accept Change." In *Business Line* [online]. San Francisco, 2003 [updated 17 September 2004; cited 3 October 2004]. Available from www.busline.com/news.
CD-ROM encyclopedia article, one author	Parkings, Robert. "George Eastman." *The Concise Columbia Encyclopedia.* New York: Columbia University Press, 2000. [CD-ROM].
Interview	Stainer, Georgia, general manager, Day Cable and Communications. Interview by author. Topeka, Kan., 2 March 2002.
Newspaper article, one author	Standish, Evelyn. "Global Market Crushes OPEC's Delicate Balance of Interests." *Wall Street Journal,* 19 January 2004, sec. A, p. 1.
Book, two authors	Toller, Miriam, and Jay Fielding. *Global Business for Smaller Companies.* Rocklin, Calif.: Prima Publishing, 2003.
Government publication	U.S. Department of Defense. *Stretching Research Dollars: Survival Advice for Universities and Government Labs.* Washington, D.C.: GPO, 2004.

plete sentences. (See the annotated list of style manuals early in this appendix.) A bibliography may also be more manageable if you subdivide it into categories (a classified bibliography), either by type of reference (such as books, articles, and unpublished material) or by subject matter (such as government regulation, market forces, and so on). Following are the major conventions for developing a bibliography according to Chicago style (see Figure B.2):

■ Exclude any page numbers that may be cited in source notes, except for journals, periodicals, and newspapers.

■ Alphabetize entries by the last name of the lead author (listing last name first). The names of second and succeeding authors are listed in normal order. Entries without an author name are alphabetized by the first important word in the title.

■ Format entries as hanging indents (indent second and succeeding lines three to five spaces).

■ Arrange entries in the following general order: (1) author name, (2) title information, (3) publication information, (4) date, (5) periodical page range.

■ Use quotation marks around the titles of articles from magazines, newspapers, and journals—capitalizing the first and last words, as well as all other important words (except prepositions, articles, and coordinating conjunctions).

■ Use italics to set off the names of books, newspapers, journals, and other complete publications—capitalizing the first and last words, as well as all other important words.

■ For journal articles, include the volume number and the issue number (if necessary). Include the year of publication inside parentheses and follow with a colon and the page range of the article: *Journal of Business Communication* 36, no. 4 (2001): 72. (In this source, the volume is 36, the number is 4, and the page is 72.)

■ Use brackets to identify all electronic references: [Online database] or [CD-ROM].

■ Explain how electronic references can be reached: Available from www.spaceless.com/WWWVL.

■ Give the citation date for online references: Cited 23 August 2002.

■ For additional information about documenting online sources, go to www.lib.ohio-state.edu/guides/chicagogd.html.

APA Style

The American Psychological Association (APA) recommends the author-date system of documentation, which is popular in the physical, natural, and social sciences. When using this system, you simply insert the author's last name and the year of publication within parentheses following the text discussion of the material cited. Include a page number if you use a direct quote. This approach briefly identifies the source so that readers can locate complete information in the alphabetical reference list at the end of the report. The author-date system is both brief and clear, saving readers time and effort.

In-Text Citation—APA Style

To document report sources in text using APA style, insert the author's surname and the date of publication at the end of a statement. Enclose this information in parentheses. If the author's name is referred to in the text itself, then the number can be omitted from parenthetical material.

> Some experts recommend both translation and back-translation when dealing with any non-English-speaking culture (Assira, 2001).

> Toller and Fielding (2000) make a strong case for small companies succeeding in global business.

Personal communications and interviews conducted by the author would not be listed in the reference list at all. Such citations would appear in the text only.

> Increasing the role of cable companies is high on the list of Georgia Stainer, general manager at Day Cable and Communications (personal communication, March 2, 2001).

List of References—APA Style

For APA style, list only those works actually cited in the text (so you would not include works for background or for further reading). Report writers must choose their references judiciously. Following are the major conventions for developing a reference list according to APA style (see Figure B.3):

■ Format entries as hanging indents.

■ List all author names in reversed order (last name first), and use only initials for the first and middle names.

■ Arrange entries in the following general order: (1) author name, (2) date, (3) title information, (4) publication information, (5) periodical page range.

■ Follow the author name with the date of publication in parentheses.

■ List titles of articles from magazines, newspapers, and journals without underlines or quotation marks. Capitalize only the first word of the title, any proper nouns, and the first word to follow an internal colon.

■ Italicize titles of books, capitalizing only the first word, any proper nouns, and the first word to follow a colon.

■ Italicize names of magazines, newspapers, journals, and other complete publications—capitalizing all the important words.

■ For journal articles, include the volume number (in italics) and, if necessary, the issue number (in parentheses). Finally, include the page range of the article: *Journal of Business Communication, 36*(4), 72. (In this example, the volume is 36, the number is 4, and the page number is 72.)

■ Include personal communications (such as letters, memos, e-mail, and conversations) only in text, not in reference lists.

■ Electronic references include author, date of publication, title of article, name of publication (if one), volume, date of retrieval (month, day, year), and the source.

■ For electronic references, indicate the actual year of publication, and the exact date of retrieval.

■ For electronic references, specify the URL, leave periods off the ends of URLs.

■ For additional information about documenting online sources, go to www.apastyle.org/elecref.html.

MLA Style

The style recommended by the Modern Language Association of America is used widely in the humanities, especially in the study of language and literature. Like APA style, MLA style uses brief parenthetical citations in the text. However, instead of including author name and year, MLA citations include author name and page reference.

In-Text Citation—MLA Style

To document report sources in text using MLA style, insert the author's last name and a page reference inside parentheses following the cited material: (Matthews 63). If the author's name is mentioned in the text reference, the name can be omitted from the parenthetical citation: (63). The citation indicates that the reference came from page 63 of a work by Matthews. With the author's name, readers can find complete publication information in the alphabetically arranged list of works cited that comes at the end of the report.

> Some experts recommend both translation and back-translation when dealing with any non-English-speaking culture (Assira 72).

> Toller and Fielding make a strong case for small companies succeeding in global business (102–03).

FIGURE B.3   Sample References—APA Style

<table>
<tr><td>Journal article with volume and issue numbers</td><td>

REFERENCES

Assira, J. (2004). Are they speaking English in Japan? *Journal of Business Communication, 36*(4), 72.</td></tr>
<tr><td>Brochure</td><td>BestTemp Staffing Services. (2002). *An employer's guide to staffing services* (2d ed.) [Brochure]. Denver: BestTemp Information Center.</td></tr>
<tr><td>Newspaper article, no author</td><td>Buying Asian supplies on the net. (2002, February 12). *Los Angeles Times*, p. D3.</td></tr>
<tr><td>Annual report</td><td>Eurotec. (2003). *2003 annual report*. New York: Eurotec.</td></tr>
<tr><td>Magazine article</td><td>Graves, H. (2004, November 17). Prospecting online. *Business Week*, 43–45.</td></tr>
<tr><td>Television broadcast</td><td>Han, D. (2004, March 5). Trade wars heating up around the globe. *CNN Headline News*. [Television broadcast]. Atlanta, GA: CNN.</td></tr>
<tr><td>Internet, World Wide Web</td><td>Hoover's Online. (2005). *Intel—Company Capsule*. Retrieved March 8, 2005, from http://www.hoovers.com/capsules/13787.html</td></tr>
<tr><td>Book, component parts</td><td>Kuntz, S. (2003). Moving beyond benefits. In Randolph Jacobson (Ed.), *Our changing workforce* (pp. 213–227). New York: Citadel Press.</td></tr>
<tr><td>Unpublished dissertation or thesis</td><td>Morales, G. H. (2003). *The economic pressures on industrialized nations in a global economy*. Unpublished doctoral dissertation, University of San Diego.</td></tr>
<tr><td>Paper presented at a meeting</td><td>Myers, C. (2003, August). *HMOs in today's environment*. Paper presented at the Conference on Medical Insurance Solutions, Chicago, IL.</td></tr>
<tr><td>Online magazine article</td><td>Norwalk, P. (2004, July 17). Training managers to help employees accept change. *Business Line*. Retrieved October 3, 2004, from http://www.busline.com/news</td></tr>
<tr><td>CD-ROM encyclopedia article, one author</td><td>Parkings, R. (2000). George Eastman. *The concise Columbia encyclopedia*. [CD-ROM]. New York: Columbia University Press.</td></tr>
<tr><td>Interview</td><td>*Cited in text only, not in the list of references.*</td></tr>
<tr><td>Newspaper article, one author</td><td>Standish, E. (2004, January 19). Global market crushes OPEC's delicate balance of interests. *Wall Street Journal*, p. A1.</td></tr>
<tr><td>Book, two authors</td><td>Toller, M., & Fielding, J. (2003). *Global business for smaller companies*. Rocklin, CA: Prima Publishing.</td></tr>
<tr><td>Government publication</td><td>U.S. Department of Defense. (2004). *Stretching research dollars: Survival advice for universities and government labs*. Washington, DC: U.S. Government Printing Office.</td></tr>
</table>

List of Works Cited—MLA Style

The *MLA Style Manual* recommends preparing the list of works cited first so that you will know what information to give in the parenthetical citation (for example, whether to add a short title if you're citing more than one work by the same author, or whether to give an initial or first name if you're citing two authors who have the same last name). The list of works cited appears at the end of your report, contains all the works that you cite in your text, and lists them in alphabetical order. Following are the major conventions for developing a reference list according to MLA style (see Figure B.4).

- Format entries as hanging indents.
- Arrange entries in the following general order: (1) author name, (2) title information, (3) publication information, (4) date, (5) periodical page range.
- List the lead author's name in reverse order (last name first), using either full first names or initials. List second and succeeding author names in normal order.
- Use quotation marks around the titles of articles from magazines, newspapers, and journals—capitalize all important words.
- Italicize the names of books, newspapers, journals and other complete publications, capitalizing all main words in the title.

FIGURE B.4   Sample Works Cited—MLA Style

WORKS CITED

Journal article with volume and issue numbers	Assira, James. "Are They Speaking English in Japan?" *Journal of Business Communication* 36.4 (2004): 72.
Brochure	BestTemp Staffing Services. *An Employer's Guide to Staffing Services*. 2d ed. Denver: BestTemp Information Center, 2002.
Newspaper article, no author	"Buying Asian Supplies on the Net." *Los Angeles Times* 12 Feb. 2002: D3.
Annual report	Eurotec. *2005 Annual Report*. New York: Eurotec, Inc., 2005.
Magazine article	Graves, Holly. "Prospecting Online." *Business Week* 17 Nov. 2004: 43–45.
Television broadcast	Han, Daniel. "Trade Wars Heating Up Around the Globe." *CNN Headline News*. CNN, Atlanta. 5 Mar. 2004.
Internet, World Wide Web	"Intel—Company Capsule." *Hoover's Online*. 2005. Hoover's Company Information. 8 Mar. 2005 <http://www.hoovers.com/capsules/13787.html>.
Book, component parts	Kuntz, Sonja. "Moving Beyond Benefits." *Our Changing Workforce*. Ed. Randolf Jacobson. New York: Citadel Press, 2003. 213–27.
Unpublished dissertation or thesis	Morales, George H. "The Economic Pressures on Industrialized Nations in a Global Economy." Diss. U of San Diego, 2003.
Paper presented at a meeting	Myers, Charles. "HMOs in Today's Environment." Conference on Medical Insurance Solutions. Chicago. 13 Aug. 2003.
Online magazine article	Norwalk, Preston. "Training Managers to Help Employees Accept Change." *Business Line* 17 July 2003. 3 Oct. 2004 <http://www.busline.com/news/>.
CD-ROM encyclopedia article, one author	Parkings, Robert. "George Eastman." *The Concise Columbia Encyclopedia*. CD-ROM. New York: Columbia UP, 2000.
Interview	Stainer, Georgia, general manager, Day Cable and Communications. Telephone interview. 2 Mar. 2002.
Newspaper article, one author	Standish, Evelyn. "Global Market Crushes OPEC's Delicate Balance of Interests." *Wall Street Journal* 19 Jan. 2004: A1.
Book, two authors	Toller, Miriam, and Jay Fielding. *Global Business for Smaller Companies*. Rocklin, CA: Prima Publishing, 2003.
Government publication	United States. Department of Defense. *Stretching Research Dollars: Survival Advice for Universities and Government Labs*. Washington: GPO, 2004.

- For journal articles, include the volume number and the issue number (if necessary). Include the year of publication inside parentheses and follow with a colon and the page range of the article: *Journal of Business Communication* 36.4 (2001): 72. (In this source, the volume is 36, the number is 4, and the page is 72.)
- Electronic sources are less fixed than print sources, and they may not be readily accessible to readers. So citations for electronic sources must provide more information. Always try to be as comprehensive as possible, citing whatever information is available.
- The date for electronic sources should contain both the date assigned in the source and the date accessed by the researcher.
- The URL for electronic sources must be as accurate and complete as possible, from access-mode identifier (http, ftp, gopher, telnet) to all relevant directory and file names. Be sure to enclose this path inside angle brackets: < http://www.hoovers.com/capsules/13787.html>.
- For additional information about documenting online sources, go to http://owl.english.purdue.edu/handouts/research/r_mla.html#Electronic

Correction Symbols

Instructors often use these short, easy-to-remember correction symbols and abbreviations when evaluating students' writing. You can use them too, to understand your instructor's suggestions and to revise and proofread your own letters, memos, and reports. Refer to the Handbook of Grammar, Mechanics, and Usage (pp. H-1–H-29) for further information.

Content and Style

Acc	Accuracy. Check to be sure information is correct.
ACE	Avoid copying examples.
ACP	Avoid copying problems.
Adp	Adapt. Tailor message to reader.
App	Follow proper organization approach. (Refer to Chapter 4.)
Assign	Assignment. Review instructions for assignment.
AV	Active verb. Substitute active for passive.
Awk	Awkward phrasing. Rewrite.
BC	Be consistent.
BMS	Be more sincere.
Chop	Choppy sentences. Use longer sentences and more transitional phrases.
Con	Condense. Use fewer words.
CT	Conversational tone. Avoid using overly formal language.
Depers	Depersonalize. Avoid attributing credit or blame to any individual or group.
Dev	Develop. Provide greater detail.
Dir	Direct. Use direct approach; get to the point.
Emph	Emphasize. Develop this point more fully.
EW	Explanation weak. Check logic; provide more proof.
Fl	Flattery. Avoid compliments that are insincere.
FS	Figure of speech. Find a more accurate expression.
GNF	Good news first. Use direct order.
GRF	Give reasons first. Use indirect order.

GW	Goodwill. Put more emphasis on expressions of goodwill.
H/E	Honesty/ethics. Revise statement to reflect good business practices.
Imp	Imply. Avoid being direct.
Inc	Incomplete. Develop further.
Jar	Jargon. Use less specialized language.
Log	Logic. Check development of argument.
Neg	Negative. Use more positive approach or expression.
Obv	Obvious. Do not state point in such detail.
OC	Overconfident. Adopt humbler language.
OM	Omission.
Org	Organization. Strengthen outline.
OS	Off the subject. Close with point on main subject.
Par	Parallel. Use same structure.
Pom	Pompous. Rephrase in down-to-earth terms.
PV	Point of view. Make statement from reader's perspective rather than your own.
RB	Reader benefit. Explain what reader stands to gain.
Red	Redundant. Reduce number of times this point is made.
Ref	Reference. Cite source of information.
Rep	Repetitive. Provide different expression.
RS	Resale. Reassure reader that he or she has made a good choice.
SA	Service attitude. Put more emphasis on helping reader.
Sin	Sincerity. Avoid sounding glib or uncaring.
SL	Stereotyped language. Focus on individual's characteristics instead of on false generalizations.
Spec	Specific. Provide more specific statement.
SPM	Sales promotion material. Tell reader about related goods or services.

Stet	Let stand in original form.
Sub	Subordinate. Make this point less important.
SX	Sexist. Avoid language that contributes to gender stereotypes.
Tone	Tone needs improvement.
Trans	Transition. Show connection between points.
UAE	Use action ending. Close by stating what reader should do next.
UAS	Use appropriate salutation.
UAV	Use active voice.
Unc	Unclear. Rewrite to clarify meaning.
UPV	Use passive voice.
USS	Use shorter sentences.
V	Variety. Use different expression or sentence pattern.
W	Wordy. Eliminate unnecessary words.
WC	Word choice. Find a more appropriate word.
YA	"You" attitude. Rewrite to emphasize reader's needs.

Grammar, Mechanics, and Usage

Ab	Abbreviation. Avoid abbreviations in most cases; use correct abbreviation.
Adj	Adjective. Use adjective instead.
Adv	Adverb. Use adverb instead.
Agr	Agreement. Make subject and verb or noun and pronoun agree.
Ap	Appearance. Improve appearance.
Apos	Apostrophe. Check use of apostrophe.
Art	Article. Use correct article.
BC	Be consistent.
Cap	Capitalize.
Case	Use cases correctly.
CoAdj	Coordinate adjective. Insert comma between coordinate adjectives; delete comma between adjective and compound noun.

CS	Comma splice. Use period or semicolon to separate clauses.
DM	Dangling modifier. Rewrite so that modifier clearly relates to subject of sentence.
Exp	Expletive. Avoid expletive beginnings, such as it is, there are, there is, this is, and these are.
F	Format. Improve layout of document.
Frag	Fragment. Rewrite as complete sentence.
Gram	Grammar. Correct grammatical error.
HCA	Hyphenate compound adjective.
lc	Lowercase. Do not use capital letter.
M	Margins. Improve frame around document.
MM	Misplaced modifier. Place modifier close to word it modifies.
NRC	Nonrestrictive clause (or phrase). Separate from rest of sentence with commas.
P	Punctuation. Use correct punctuation.
Par	Parallel. Use same structure.
PH	Place higher. Move document up on page.
PL	Place lower. Move document down on page.
Prep	Preposition. Use correct preposition.
RC	Restrictive clause (or phrase). Remove commas that separate clause from rest of sentence.
RO	Run-on sentence. Separate two sentences with comma and coordinating conjunction or with semicolon.
SC	Series comma. Add comma before *and*.
SI	Split infinitive. Do not separate *to* from rest of verb.
Sp	Spelling error. Consult dictionary.
S-V	Subject-verb pair. Do not separate with comma.
Syl	Syllabification. Divide word between syllables.
WD	Word division. Check dictionary for proper end-of-line hyphenation.
WW	Wrong word. Replace with another word.

Proofreading Marks

Symbol	Meaning	Symbol Used in Context	Corrected Copy
≡	Align horizontally	meaningful result	meaningful result
||	Align vertical	1. Power cable 2. Keyboard	1. Power cable 2. Keyboard
bf	Boldface	Recommendations (bf)	**Recommendations**
≡	Capitalize	Pepsico, Inc.	PepsiCo, Inc.
⊐⊏	Center	Awards Banquet	Awards Banquet
◡	Close up space	self- confidence	self-confidence
e	Delete	harrassment and abuse	harassment
ds	Double-space	text in first line text in second line (ds)	text in first line text in second line
∧	Insert	tirquoise shirts	turquoise and white shirts
∨	Insert apostrophe	our teams goals	our team's goals
∧	Insert comma	a, b and c	a, b, and c
⹀	Insert hyphen	third quarter sales	third-quarter sales
⊙	Insert period	Harrigan et al	Harrigan et al.
∨ ∨	Insert quotation marks	This team isn't cooperating.	This "team" isn't cooperating.
#	Insert space	real estate testcase	real estate test case
ital	Italics	Quarterly Report (ital)	*Quarterly Report*
/	Lowercase	TULSA, South of here	Tulsa, south of here
⌴	Move down	Sincerely,	Sincerely,
⊏	Move left	Attention: Security	Attention: Security
⊐	Move right	February 2, 2003	February 2, 2003
⌐⌐	Move up	THIRD-QUARTER SALES	THIRD-QUARTER SALES
STET	Restore	staff talked openly and frankly STET	staff talked openly
ᔕ	Run lines together	Manager, Distribution	Manager, Distribution
ss	Single space	text in first line (ss) text in second line	text in first line text in second line
◯	Spell out	COD	cash on delivery
sp	Spell out	(sp) Assn. of Biochem. Engrs.	Association of Biochemical Engineers
⌐⌐	Start new line	Marla Fenton, Manager, Distri-bution	Marla Fenton, Manager, Distribution
¶	Start new paragraph	¶ The solution is easy to determine but difficult to implement in a competitive environment like the one we now face.	The solution is easy to determine but difficult to implement in a competitive environment like the one we now face.
∼	Transpose	airy, light, casual tone	light, airy, casual tone

Your instructor may elect to show you one or more of the videos described on the following pages. These programs supplement course concepts with real-life examples of businesspeople meeting important communication challenges. This video guide includes several review and analysis questions as well as exercises for each video. Be sure to review the appropriate page ahead of time so that you'll know what to look for when you watch the video.

Ethical Communication

Learning Objectives

After viewing this video, you will be able to

1. Describe a process for deciding what is ethical or unethical
2. Explain the importance of meeting your personal and professional responsibilities in an ethical manner
3. Discuss the possible consequences of ethical and unethical choices and talk about the impact of these choices on direct and related audiences

Background Information

Communication is ethical when it includes all relevant information, when it's true in every sense, and when it isn't deceptive in any way. In contrast, communication is unethical when it includes false information, fails to include important information, or otherwise misleads an audience. To avoid unethical choices in your communication efforts, you must consider not only legal issues but also the needs of your audience and the expectations of society and your employer. In turn, companies that demonstrate high standards of ethics maintain credibility with employees, customers, and other stakeholders.

The Video

This video identifies two important tools in a communicator's toolbox: honesty and objectivity. These tools help businesspeople resolve ethical dilemmas and avoid ethical lapses, both within the company and during interactions with outside audiences. Poor ethical choices can damage a company's credibility and put employees, customers, and the surrounding community at risk. Unfortunately, some ethical choices are neither clear nor simple, and you may face situations in which the needs of one group or individual must be weighed against the needs of another.

Discussion Questions

1. Would you ever consider compromising your ethics for self-gain? If so, under what circumstances? If not, why?
2. The video mentions the role of misrepresentations in the collapse of Enron. If you were the head of communications at Enron and had some knowledge of the true nature of the company's financial condition, what would you have done?
3. Identify risks involved when you choose to act in an unethical manner.
4. How can you be an effective business communicator without credibility?
5. Is it ethical to call in sick to work, even though you are not ill? What happens to your credibility if someone finds out you were not sick?

Follow-Up Assignment

Many businesses, from small companies to large corporations, formulate codes of ethics that outline ethical standards for employees. Review IBM's guidelines, which are posted on its website at **www.ibm.com/investor/corpgovernance/cgbcg.phtml**. Now answer the following questions:

1. What does IBM want employees to do if they are aware of unethical situations within the organization?
2. How does IBM view misleading statements or innuendos about competitors?
3. What advice does IBM give employees on the subject of receiving gifts from people outside the company?

For Further Research

Advertising communications, particularly advertising aimed at children, can present a variety of ethical concerns. The article provided at **www.mediascope.org/pubs/ibriefs/cha.htm** reports statistics on the advertising of alcohol and tobacco products and discusses the negative effect these advertisements can have on children. To what extent was it ethical for Anheuser Busch to use the Budweiser frog or for Philip Morris to use Joe Camel in its advertisements, given that many children were able to identify with both characters?

Learning to Listen: Second City Communications

Learning Objectives

After viewing this video, you will be able to

1. Understand the functions of interpersonal communication in the workplace
2. Identify the ways to overcome barriers to effective communication
3. Discuss the importance of active listening both socially and professionally

Background Information

Chicago's Second City Improv is more than the world's best-known comedy theater. Second City now brings its famous brand of humor to corporate giants such as Coca-Cola, Motorola, and Microsoft. With over 40 years of experience in corporate services, Second City's teachers help business professionals develop communication skills through lessons in improvisational theater. Business Communications Training is Second City's fastest growing practice, fueled by the demands of more than two hundred Fortune 500 companies. Workshops are tailored to client's needs in such areas as listening and giving presentations, collaborative leadership and team skills, interviewing, breaking down barriers to successful communication, and using humor to convey important messages. The next time you watch improvisational sketch comedy, ask yourself how a lesson in the art of "improv" might give your career a boost.

The Video

In these two video segments, you'll see Second City's training techniques in action. The first segment addresses the need to listen actively, and the second explores techniques for encouraging innovation. The second clip is less focused on communication, but you can see how the techniques for stimulating innovation work equally well for fostering meaningful, two-way conversation that encourages people to open up rather than shut down.

Discussion Questions

1. How do the exercises featured in this video address the contrasting needs of the trial lawyer, the divorce lawyer, and the media buyer?
2. Would ABC's talkative guest Kay Jarman, the 47-year-old award winning salesperson, be a good candidate for Second City's training workshop?
3. What other workshops might Tom Yorton want to offer companies in response to the current economic and political climate?
4. How might the "yes and" rule of improvisation be used to train customer service representatives at an L.L. Bean or a Dell computer call center? Without physical cues, such as facial expression and body language, is the "yes and" rule still effective?

5. As President and Managing Director of Second City Communications, Tom Yorton says the following: "You have to be willing to fail to be able to get the results you want...to connect with an audience." Do you agree that this statement is as true in business as it is in comedy? Support your chosen position.

Follow-Up Assignment

Enjoy Second City Communication's website at www.secondcity.com. If you are a loyal fan, you might want to check out the book titles offered and read more about the group's history. Now explore Second City's Corporate Services: Scan the client roster, read the testimonials, and then select a case study that you find compelling. If you are currently employed, which workshop would be most beneficial to you and to your work team? Explain your choice. If you are not currently employed, how might you and your fellow business students benefit from a Second City workshop? Which workshop would you most like to participate in? Explain how you think it might help you in terms of your social life, your career planning, and your interviewing skills.

For Further Research

The importance of active listening is at the core of *consultative selling*, an approach that emphasizes posing questions to the potential buyer in order to identify needs and expectations—rather than rattling off a prepared sales speech. PublicSpeakingSkills.com (www.publicspeakingskills.com) is one of many companies that offer training in consultative selling. Review the description of the company's Consultative Selling and Negotiating Skills course. Do the principles espoused match the concept of the "you" attitude and the elements of ethical communication that you've learned so far?

Communicating in the Global Workplace

Learning Objectives

After viewing this video, you will be able to

1. Discuss the challenges of communicating in the global workplace
2. Identify barriers to effective communication across borders
3. Explain the critical role of time in global communication efforts

Background Information

Many businesses are crossing national boundaries to engage in international business. However, operating in a global environment presents a variety of challenges related to culture and communication. Understanding and respecting these challenges can mean the difference between success and failure, so executives must make sure that employees are educated on cultural issues before attempting to do business in other countries.

The Video

This video identifies the challenges to effective communication in the global marketplace, including the barriers posed by language, culture, time, and technology. You will see that a significant amount of research needs to be conducted before a company can engage in successful global business ventures. For instance, if communicators are unaware of differences in gestures, expressions, and dialect, they can inadvertently offend or confuse their audiences. In addition, time zone differences require organizations to plan carefully in advance so that they can develop, translate, and deliver information in a timely manner.

Discussion Questions

1. Language can be a barrier to effective communication. What steps can a company take to minimize language barriers across borders?
2. What characteristics of a country's culture need to be researched to ensure business success across borders?
3. How does a company ensure that a message is properly translated into the local language and dialect of the people it conducts business with?
4. What challenges does a company face when trying to hold a conference call or video meeting with affiliates and employees around the world?
5. The video mentions that some companies have trusted contacts in a country they wish to do business with, while other companies rely on a significant amount of research to learn more about culture and other local characteristics. What method do you feel is most effective for gathering useful, accurate, and up-to-date information regarding cultural issues?

Follow-Up Assignment

The Coca-Cola Company has local operations in more than 200 countries throughout the world. Visit www.coca-cola.com to learn more about the company's business activities in a variety of countries. What steps does Coke take to communicate through its website with customers around the world? Does the company strive to develop products that meet local tastes and needs? If so, how and why?

For Further Research

Choose a country other than the United States, and research your selection using both online and library resources to identify important cultural characteristics specific to that country. For example, you may want to gather information about gestures and other nonverbal communication that would be considered offensive, about work habits, or about laws related to conducting business in that country. The characteristics you identify should be useful and accurate.

Based on what you've learned about this country and your personal beliefs, values, and life experiences, is there any risk that you might have a prejudiced or ethnocentric viewpoint regarding people from this country? Why or why not?

Impact of Culture on Business: Spotlight on Latin America

Learning Objectives

After viewing this video, you will be able to

1. List key aspects of Latin American culture and indicate the influences on their development
2. Identify factors that might lead to cultural change in Latin America
3. Explain some of the major cultural contrasts within Latin America and their impact on international business operations

Background Information

To a large degree, culture defines the way all human beings interpret and respond to life's changing circumstances. When you interact with people from your own culture, your shared experiences and expectations usually enhance the communication process by providing a common language and frame of reference. However, when you communicate across cultural boundaries, a lack of awareness of your audience's culture—and the subconscious ways that your own culture shapes your perceptions—can result in partial or even total failure of the communication process. Moreover, culture is rarely static, so impressions you may have gathered at one point in your life may need to be revisited and revised over time.

The Video

This video takes a broad look at Latin America's various countries and cultures and explores the business implications of cultural similarities and differences. You'll learn how cultural groups that may appear identical on the surface can in fact have subtle but profound differences. Although communication is just one of many topics discussed in the video, you will get a sense of just how important—and challenging—communication can be when conducting business across cultural boundaries.

Discussion Questions

1. Explain what the video means when it says that your own culture can "sneak up on you."
2. How is business influencing the economic gulf between urban and rural populations in Latin America?
3. How have imperial conquests and slavery affected the populations and cultures of Latin America?
4. How do many outsiders view the issue of business and government corruption in Latin America?
5. Is business etiquette in most of Latin America considered relatively formal or relatively informal?

Follow-Up Assignment

The World Bank plays an important role in today's fast-changing, closely meshed global economy. Visit the bank's website at www.worldbank.org and explore the initiatives programs underway in the Latin American region. How is the bank using this website to foster better communication between Latin America and the rest of the world?

For Further Research

In today's global marketplace, knowing as much as possible about your international customers' business practices and customs could give you a strategic advantage. To help you successfully conduct business around the globe, navigate the resources at the U.S. Government Export Portal. Start at www.export.gov, then click on "Market Research" and then on "Country Information—Quick Reference (TIC)." Click anywhere on the world map to learn more about each country.

How can resources such as this website help U.S. businesses communicate more successfully with customers, employees, and other groups in Latin America?

Technology and the Tools of Communication

Learning Objectives

After viewing this video, you will be able to

1. Identify technology-related issues to consider when developing communication strategies
2. Identify advantages of using technology as a tool for effective communication
3. Differentiate between "push" and "pull" communication

Background Information

From instant messaging to online meetings, technology has become an integral element of business communication. When used with care, technological tools can help you reach more people in less time with more effective messages. However, when technology is misused or misunderstood, it can cause more problems than it solves. Knowing which technologies to use in every situation—and knowing how to use each one—are vital to your success.

The Video

This video discusses how the Internet, e-mail, voicemail, and other devices have revolutionized the way people communicate. These technological tools increase the speed, frequency, and range of business communication. The video also discusses factors to consider when choosing the most appropriate vehicle for your communication, including the all-important challenge of getting and keeping your audience's attention. The advantages of using technological communication tools are presented throughout the video.

Discussion Questions

1. Identify six questions you need to consider when choosing a technology vehicle for your messages.
2. List the advantages of communicating via e-mail within an organization.
3. What role does technology play in ensuring effective communication within an organization?
4. What are some of the more common challenges that business communicators can encounter when they use technology for communication purposes?
5. Identify the difference between "push" and "pull" communications, and provide an example of each method.

Follow-Up Assignment

VolResource (at www.volresource.org.uk/samples/olcomms. htm) provides practical and informative resources for volunteer organizations that are trying to develop online communication strategies. The VolResource website further details questions that need to be addressed in the process of developing an effective communication strategy for any organization. What issues do you think are the most important to consider? Why?

For Further Exploration

Visit the Yellow Freight website at www.yellowfreight.com and explore the various e-commerce tools this company utilizes to communicate effectively with its customers. Examine these tools and consider their effectiveness. What are some of the advantages of these online communication tools? How do they benefit the client? How do they benefit Yellow Freight?

Grammar and mechanics are nothing more than the way words are combined into sentences. Usage is the way words are used by a network of people—in this case, the community of business-people who use English. You'll find it easier to get along in this community if you know the accepted standards of grammar, mechanics, and usage. This handbook offers you valuable opportunities in three sections:

■ **Diagnostic Test of English Skills.** Testing your current knowledge of grammar, mechanics, and usage helps you find out where your strengths and weaknesses lie. This test offers 60 items taken from the topics included in this Handbook.

■ **Assessment of English Skills.** After completing the diagnostic test, use the assessment form to highlight those areas you most need to review.

■ **Essentials of Grammar, Mechanics, and Usage with Practice Sessions.** This section helps you quickly review the basics. You can study the things you've probably already learned but may have forgotten about grammar, punctuation, capitalization, mechanics (including capitalization, abbreviation, number style, and word division), and vocabulary (including frequently confused words, frequently misused words, frequently misspelled words, and transitional words and phrases). Practice sessions throughout this section help you test yourself and reinforce what you learn. Use this essential review not only to study and improve your English skills but also as a reference for any questions you may have during this course.

Without a firm grasp of the basics of grammar, punctuation, mechanics, and vocabulary, you risk being misunderstood, damaging your company's image, losing money for your company, and possibly even losing your job. However, once you develop strong English skills, you will create clear and concise messages, you will enhance your company's image as well as your own, and you will not only increase your company's profits but expand your own chances of success.

Diagnostic Test of English Skills

Use this test to help you determine whether you need more practice with grammar, punctuation, mechanics, or vocabulary. When you've answered all the questions, ask your instructor for an answer sheet so that you can score the test. On the Assessment of English Skills form (page H-2), record the number of questions you answered correctly in each section.

The following choices apply to items 1–10. In each blank, write the letter of the choice that best describes the problem with each sentence.

A. sentence incomplete
B. too many phrases/clauses strung together
C. modifying elements misplaced (dangling)
D. structure not parallel
E. nothing wrong

_____ **1.** Stop here.
_____ **2.** Your duties are interviewing, hiring, and also to fire employees.
_____ **3.** After their presentation, I was still undecided.
_____ **4.** Speaking freely, the stock was considered a bargain.
_____ **5.** Margaret, pressed for time, turned in unusually sloppy work.
_____ **6.** Typing and filing, routine office chores.
_____ **7.** With care, edit the report.
_____ **8.** When Paul came to work here, he brought some outmoded ideas, now he has accepted our modern methods.
_____ **9.** To plan is better than improvising.
_____ **10.** Hoping to improve performance, practice is advisable.

The following choices apply to items 11–20. In each blank, write the letter of the choice that identifies the underlined word(s) in each sentence.

A. subject
B. predicate (verb)
C. object
D. modifier
E. conjunction/preposition

_____ **11.** Take his <u>memo</u> upstairs.
_____ **12.** Before leaving, he <u>repaired</u> the photocopier.
_____ **13.** <u>Velnor, Inc.</u>, will soon introduce a new product line.
_____ **14.** We must hire only <u>qualified</u>, ambitious graduates.
_____ **15.** They <u>are having</u> trouble with their quality control systems.
_____ **16.** <u>After</u> she wrote the report, Jill waited eagerly for a response.
_____ **17.** The route to the plant isn't paved <u>yet</u>.
_____ **18.** See <u>me</u> after the meeting.
_____ **19.** Your new <u>home</u> is ready and waiting.
_____ **20.** BFL is large <u>but</u> caring.

In the blanks for items 21–30, write the letter of the word that best completes each sentence.

_____ 21. Starbucks (A. is, B. are) opening five new stores in San Diego in the next year.

_____ 22. There (A. is, B. are) 50 applicants for the job opening.

_____ 23. Anyone who wants to be (A. their, B. his or her) own boss should think about owning a franchise.

_____ 24. Neither of us (A. was, B. were) prepared for the meeting.

_____ 25. Another characteristic of a small business is that (A. they tend, B. it tends) to be more innovative than larger firms.

_____ 26. After he had (A. saw, B. seen) the revised budget, Raymond knew he wouldn't be getting a new desk.

_____ 27. The number of women-owned small businesses (A. has, B. have) increased sharply in the past two decades.

_____ 28. If I (A. was, B. were) you, I'd stop sending personal e-mails at work.

_____ 29. Eugene (A. lay, B. laid) the files on the desk.

_____ 30. Either FedEx or UPS (A. has, B. have) been chosen as our preferred shipping service.

The following choices apply to items 31–40. In each blank, write the letter of the choice that best describes each sentence.

A. all punctuation used correctly
B. some punctuation used incorrectly or incorrectly omitted

_____ 31. The president who rarely gave interviews, agreed to write an article for the company newsletter.

_____ 32. Give the assignment to Karen Schiff, the new technical writer.

_____ 33. Could you please send a replacement for Item No. 3-303.

_____ 34. Debbie said that, "technicians must have technical degrees."

_____ 35. We'll have branches in Bakersfield, California, Reno, Nevada, and Medford, Oregon.

_____ 36. Before leaving her secretary finished typing the memo.

_____ 37. How many of you consider yourselves "computer literate?"

_____ 38. This, then, is our goal: to increase market share by 50 percent.

_____ 39. They plan to move soon, however, they still should be invited.

_____ 40. Health, wealth, and happiness—those are my personal goals.

The following choices apply to items 41–50. In each blank, write the letter of the choice that best describes the problem with each sentence.

A. error in punctuation
B. error in use of abbreviations or symbols
C. error in use of numbers
D. error in capitalization
E. no errors

_____ 41. Most of last year's sales came from the midwest.

_____ 42. We can provide the items you are looking for @ $2 each.

_____ 43. Alex noted: "few of our competitors have tried this approach."

_____ 44. Address the letter to professor Elliott Barker, Psychology Department, North Dakota State University.

_____ 45. They've recorded 22 complaints since yesterday, all of them from long-time employees.

_____ 46. Leslie's presentation—"New Markets for the Nineties"—was well organized.

_____ 47. We're having a sale in the childrens' department, beginning Wednesday, August 15.

_____ 48. About 50 of the newly inducted members will be present.

_____ 49. Mister Spencer has asked me to find ten volunteers.

_____ 50. Let's meet in Beth and Larry's office at one o'clock.

In the blanks for items 51–60, write the letter of the word that best completes each sentence.

_____ 51. Will having a degree (A. affect, B. effect) my chances for promotion?

_____ 52. Place the latest drawings (A. beside, B. besides) the others.

_____ 53. Try not to (A. loose, B. lose) this key; we will charge you a fee to replace it.

_____ 54. Let us help you choose the right tie to (A. complement, B. compliment) your look.

_____ 55. The five interviewers should discuss the candidates' qualifications (A. among, B. between) themselves.

_____ 56. New employees spend their time looking for (A. perspective, B. prospective) clients.

_____ 57. Are the goods you received different (A. from, B. than) the goods you ordered?

_____ 58. He took those courses to (A. farther, B. further) his career.

_____ 59. We are (A. anxious, B. eager) to see you next Thursday.

_____ 60. All commissions will be (A. disbursed, B. dispensed, C. dispersed) on the second Friday of every month.

Assessment of English Skills

In the space provided below, record the number of questions you answered correctly.

Questions	Number You Got Correct	Skill Area
1–10	———	Sentence structure
11–20	———	Grammar: Parts of speech
21–30	———	Grammar: Verbs and agreement
31–40	———	Punctuation
41–50	———	Punctuation and mechanics
51–60	———	Vocabulary

If you scored 8 or lower in any of the skills areas, focus on those areas in the appropriate sections of this Handbook.

Essentials of Grammar, Mechanics, and Usage

The sentence below looks innocent, but is it really?

> We sell tuxedos as well as rent.

You might sell rent, but it's highly unlikely. Whatever you're selling, some people will ignore your message because of a blunder like this. The following sentence has a similar problem:

> Vice President Eldon Neale told his chief engineer that he would no longer be with Avix, Inc., as of June 30.

Is Eldon or the engineer leaving? No matter which side the facts are on, the sentence can be read the other way. Now look at this sentence:

> The year before we budgeted more for advertising sales were up.

Confused? Perhaps this is what you meant:

> The year before, we budgeted more for advertising. Sales were up.

Maybe you meant this:

> The year before we budgeted more for advertising, sales were up.

The meaning of language falls into bundles called sentences. A listener or reader can take only so much meaning before filing a sentence away and getting ready for the next one. So, as a business writer, you have to know what a sentence is. You need to know where one ends and the next one begins.

If you want to know what a sentence is, you have to find out what goes into it, what its ingredients are. Luckily, the basic ingredients of an English sentence are simple: The parts of speech combine with punctuation, mechanics, and vocabulary to convey meaning.

1.0 Grammar

Grammar is the study of how words come together to form sentences. Categorized by meaning, form, and function, English words fall into various parts of speech: nouns, pronouns, verbs, adjectives, adverbs, prepositions, conjunctions, articles, and interjections. You will communicate more clearly if you understand how each of these parts of speech operates in a sentence.

1.1 Nouns

A noun names a person, place, or thing. Anything you can see or detect with one of your other senses has a noun to name it. Some things you can't see or sense are also nouns—ions, for example, or space. So are things that exist as ideas, such as accuracy and height. (You can see that something is accurate or that a building is tall, but you can't see the idea of accuracy or the

idea of height.) These names for ideas are known as abstract nouns. The simplest nouns are the names of things you can see or touch: car, building, cloud, brick.

1.1.1 Proper Nouns and Common Nouns

So far, all the examples of nouns have been common nouns, referring to general classes of things. The word *building* refers to a whole class of structures. Common nouns such as *building* are not capitalized.

If you want to talk about one particular building, however, you might refer to the Glazier Building. The name is capitalized, indicating that *Glazier Building* is a proper noun.

Here are three sets of common and proper nouns for comparison:

Common	Proper
city	Kansas City
company	Blaisden Company
store	Books Galore

1.1.2 Nouns as Subject and Object

Nouns may be used in sentences as subjects or objects. That is, the person, place, idea, or thing that is being or doing (subject) is represented by a noun. So is the person, place, idea, or thing that is being acted on (object). In the following sentence, the nouns are underlined.

> The <u>secretary</u> keyboarded the <u>report</u>.

The secretary (subject) is acting in a way that affects the report (object). The following sentence is more complicated:

> The <u>installer</u> delivered the <u>carpeting</u> to the <u>customer</u>.

Installer is the subject. *Carpeting* is the object of the main part of the sentence (acted on by the installer), whereas *customer* is the object of the phrase *to the customer*. Nevertheless, both *carpeting* and *customer* are objects.

1.1.3 Plural Nouns

Nouns can be either singular or plural. The usual way to make a plural noun is to add *s* to the singular form of the word:

Singular	Plural
rock	rocks
picture	pictures
song	songs

Many nouns have other ways of forming the plural. (Letters, numbers, and words used as words are sometimes made plural by adding an apostrophe and an *s*.) Very often, *'s* is used with abbreviations that have periods, lowercase letters that stand alone, and capital letters that might be confused with words when made into plurals:

> Spell out all *St.*'s and *Ave.*'s.
>
> He divided the page with a row of *x*'s.
>
> Sarah will register the *A*'s through the *G*'s at the convention.

In other cases, however, the apostrophe may be left out:

They'll review their ABCs.

The stock market climbed through most of the 1980s.

Circle all *the*s in the paragraph.

In some of these examples, the letters used as letters and words used as words are *italicized* (a mechanics issue that is discussed later).

Other nouns, such as those below, are so-called irregular nouns; they form the plural in some way other than by simply adding *s*:

Singular	Plural
tax	taxes
specialty	specialties
cargo	cargoes
shelf	shelves
child	children
woman	women
tooth	teeth
mouse	mice
parenthesis	parentheses
son-in-law	sons-in-law
editor-in-chief	editors-in-chief

Rather than memorize a lot of rules about forming plurals, use a dictionary. If the dictionary says nothing about the plural of a word, it's formed the usual way: by adding *s*. If the plural is formed in some irregular way, the dictionary often shows the plural spelling.

1.1.4 Possessive Nouns

A noun becomes possessive when it's used to show the ownership of something. Then you add *'s* to the word:

the man's car   the woman's apartment

However, ownership does not need to be legal:

the secretary's desk   the company's assets

Also, ownership may be nothing more than an automatic association:

a day's work   the job's prestige

An exception to the rule about adding *'s* to make a noun possessive occurs when the word is singular and already has two "s" sounds at the end. In cases like the following, an apostrophe is all that's needed:

crisis' dimensions   Mr. Moses' application

When the noun has only one "s" sound at the end, however, retain the *'s*:

Chris's book   Carolyn Nuss's office

With hyphenated nouns (compound nouns), add *'s* to the last word:

Hyphenated Noun	Possessive Noun
mother-in-law	mother-in-law's
mayor-elect	mayor-elect's

To form the possessive of plural nouns, just begin by following the same rule as with singular nouns: add *'s*. However, if the plural noun already ends in an *s* (as most do), drop the one you've added, leaving only the apostrophe:

the clients' complaints   employees' benefits

Practice Session: Nouns

Underline the preferred choice within each set of parentheses in the following sentences.

1. We are moving company headquarters to New York (*City, city*).
2. The historic Bradbury (*Building, building*) is the site of the press conference; the (*Building, building*) is located in downtown Los Angeles.
3. During the conference, our staff will be staying at the Hyatt, Hilton, and Marriott (*Hotels, hotels*).
4. Accuracy requires that you cross your (*ts, t's*) and dot your (*is, i's*).
5. The industry has been on a downward spiral since the early (*1990's, 1990s*).
6. The new (*shelfs, shelves*) will be installed on Friday.
7. Our (*specialtys, specialties*) are unparalleled service and premium brands.
8. As a result of several Internet-related (*cases, case's*), the copyright laws are under scrutiny.
9. Before a job interview, you should learn about the (*company's, companies'*) mission statement.
10. Sending the newsletter to the printer is the (*editor's-in-chief, editor-in-chief's*) responsibility.
11. All the downtown (*business', businesses', businesses's*) signs must be repainted.
12. Because the (*passenger's, passengers'*) luggage had been damaged, they had to file claims with the airline.
13. Dealing with angry customers is all in a (*days, day's, days'*) work for Mr. Jemas.
14. Its large airport is one of (*Dallases, Dallas', Dallas's*) main appeals for industrial firms.
15. We were skeptical of (*Jone's, Jones', Jones's*) plan.

1.2 Pronouns

A pronoun is a word that stands for a noun; it saves repeating the noun:

Drivers have some choice of weeks for vacation, but *they* must notify this office of *their* preference by March 1.

The pronouns *they* and *their* stand in for the noun *drivers*. The noun that a pronoun stands for is called the antecedent of the pronoun; *drivers* is the antecedent of *they* and *their*.

When the antecedent is plural, the pronoun that stands in for it has to be plural; *they* and *their* are plural pronouns because *drivers* is plural. Likewise, when the antecedent is singular, the pronoun has to be singular:

> We thought the *contract* had expired, but we soon learned that *it* had not.

1.2.1 Multiple Antecedents

Sometimes a pronoun has a double (or even a triple) antecedent:

> *Kathryn Boettcher* and *Luis Gutierrez* went beyond *their* sales quotas for January.

If taken alone, *Kathryn Boettcher* is a singular antecedent. So is *Luis Gutierrez*. However, when together they are the plural antecedent of a pronoun, so the pronoun has to be plural. Thus the pronoun is *their* instead of *her* or *his*.

1.2.2 Unclear Antecedents

In some sentences the pronoun's antecedent is unclear:

> Sandy Wright sent Jane Brougham *her* production figures for the previous year. *She* thought they were too low.

To which person does the pronoun *her* refer? Someone who knew Sandy and Jane and knew their business relationship might be able to figure out the antecedent for *her*. Even with such an advantage, however, a reader might receive the wrong meaning. Also, it would be nearly impossible for any reader to know which name is the antecedent of *she*.

The best way to clarify an ambiguous pronoun is usually to rewrite the sentence, repeating nouns when needed for clarity:

> Sandy Wright sent her production figures for the previous year to Jane Brougham. *Jane* thought they were too low.

The noun needs to be repeated only when the antecedent is unclear.

1.2.3 Gender-Neutral Pronouns

The pronouns that stand for males are *he, his,* and *him.* The pronouns that stand for females are *she, hers,* and *her.* However, you'll often be faced with the problem of choosing a pronoun for a noun that refers to both females and males:

> Each manager must make up (his, her, his or her, its, their) own mind about stocking this item and about the quantity that (he, she, he or she, it, they) can sell.

This sentence calls for a pronoun that's neither masculine nor feminine. The issue of gender-neutral pronouns responds to efforts to treat females and males evenhandedly. Here are some possible ways to deal with this issue:

> Each manager must make up *his* . . .
> (Not all managers are men.)

> Each manager must make up *her* . . .
> (Not all managers are women.)

> Each manager must make up *his* or *her* . . .
> (This solution is acceptable but becomes awkward when repeated more than once or twice in a document.)

> Each manager must make up *her* . . . Every manager will receive *his* . . . A manager may send *her* . . .
> (A manager's gender does not alternate like a windshield wiper!)

> Each manager must make up *their* . . .
> (The pronoun can't be plural when the antecedent is singular.)

> Each manager must make up *its* . . .
> (*It* never refers to people.)

The best solution is to make the noun plural or to revise the passage altogether:

> Managers must make up *their* minds . . .
> Each manager must decide whether . . .

Be careful not to change the original meaning.

1.2.4 Case of Pronouns

The case of a pronoun tells whether it's acting or acted upon:

> *She sells* an average of five packages each week.

In this sentence, *she* is doing the selling. Because *she* is acting, *she* is said to be in the nominative case. Now consider what happens when the pronoun is acted upon:

> After six months, Ms. Browning promoted *her*.

In this sentence, the pronoun *her* is acted upon. The pronoun *her* is thus said to be in the objective case.

Contrast the nominative and objective pronouns in this list:

Nominative	Objective
I	me
we	us
he	him
she	her
they	them
who	whom
whoever	whomever

Objective pronouns may be used as either the object of a verb (such as *promoted*) or the object of a preposition (such as *with*):

> Rob worked with *them* until the order was filled.

In this example, *them* is the object of the preposition *with* because Rob acted upon—worked with—them. Here's a sentence with three pronouns, the first one nominative, the second the object of a verb, and the third the object of a preposition:

> *He* paid *us* as soon as the check came from *them.*

He is nominative; *us* is objective because it's the object of the verb *paid; them* is objective because it's the object of the preposition *from.*

Every writer sometimes wonders whether to use *who* or *whom:*

> (Who, Whom) will you hire?

Because this sentence is a question, it's difficult to see that *whom* is the object of the verb *hire*. You can figure out which pronoun to use if you rearrange the question and temporarily try *she* and *her* in place of *who* and *whom:* "Will you hire *she?*" or "Will you hire *her?*" *Her* and *whom* are both objective, so the correct choice is "*Whom* will you hire?" Here's a different example:

> (Who, Whom) logged so much travel time?

Turning the question into a statement, you get:

> *He* logged so much travel time.

Therefore, the correct statement is:

> *Who* logged so much travel time?

1.2.5 Possessive Pronouns

Possessive pronouns work like possessive nouns: They show ownership or automatic association.

her job	their preferences
his account	its equipment

However, possessive pronouns are different from possessive nouns in the way they are written. That is, possessive pronouns never have an apostrophe.

Possessive Noun	**Possessive Pronoun**
the woman's estate	her estate
Roger Franklin's plans	his plans
the shareholders' feelings	their feelings
the vacuum cleaner's attachments	its attachments

The word *its* is the possessive of *it.* Like all other possessive pronouns, its has no apostrophe. Some people confuse *its* with *it's,* the contraction of *it is.* Contractions are discussed later.

Practice Session: Pronouns

Underline the preferred choice within each set of parentheses in the following sentences.

1. Just between you and (*I, me*), I don't think we will make the deadline.
2. The final speaker at the luncheon was (*she, her*).
3. When you are finished, give the report to (*he, him*).
4. (*We, Us*) telemarketers have a tarnished reputation.
5. The company is sending the marketing communications staff—Mary-Ann, Alan, and (*I, me, myself*)—to the conference.
6. The company will issue (*their, its*) annual report next month.
7. Anyone who hasn't yet turned in (*their, his or her*) questionnaire should do so by tomorrow.
8. (*Who, Whom*) shall I say called?
9. To (*who, whom*) should I address the letter?
10. (*Who, Whom*) will they hire?
11. We need more people in our department like (*she, her*).
12. When dealing with an angry customer, try to calm (*him, him or her, them*) down.
13. It was either Sarah or Charlene who left (*her, their*) briefcase on the train.
14. The company needs to update (*its, it's*) website.
15. (*Who, Whom*) do you think will be given the promotion?
16. Be sure to include (*your, you're*) e-mail address on the form.
17. Each brand should have (*its, their*) own trademark.
18. The "dynamic duo"—Bruce and (*I, me*)—are in charge of next week's office party.
19. The supervisor thanked the team members for (*their, they're*) support.
20. The pharmaceutical giant agreed to take (*their, its*) diet drug off the market.

1.3 Verbs

A verb describes an action:

> They all *quit* in disgust.

It may also describe a state of being:

> Working conditions *were* substandard.

The English language is full of action verbs. Here are a few you'll often run across in the business world:

verify	perform	fulfill
hire	succeed	send
leave	improve	receive
accept	develop	pay

You could undoubtedly list many more.

The most common verb describing a state of being instead of an action is *to be* and all its forms:

> I *am, was,* or *will be;* you *are, were,* or *will be*

Other verbs also describe a state of being:

> It *seemed* a good plan at the time.
>
> She *sounds* impressive at a meeting.

These verbs link what comes before them in the sentence with what comes after; no action is involved. (See Section 1.7.5 for a fuller discussion of linking verbs.)

1.3.1 Verb Tenses

English has three simple verb tenses: present, past, and future.

Present: Our branches in Hawaii *stock* other items.

Past: We *stocked* Purquil pens for a short time.

Future: Rotex Tire Stores *will stock* your line of tires when you begin a program of effective national advertising.

With most verbs (the regular ones), the past tense ends in *ed,* and the future tense always has *will* or *shall* in front of it. But the present tense is more complex, depending on the subject:

	First Person	Second Person	Third Person
Singular	I stock	you stock	he/she/it stocks
Plural	we stock	you stock	they stock

The basic form, *stock,* takes an additional *s* when *he, she,* or *it* precedes it. (See Section 1.3.4 for more on subject-verb agreement.)

In addition to the three simple tenses, there are three perfect tenses using forms of the helping verb *have.* The present perfect tense uses the past participle (regularly the past tense) of the main verb, *stocked,* and adds the present-tense *have* or *has* to the front of it:

> (I, we, you, they) *have stocked.*
>
> (He, she, it) *has stocked.*

The past perfect tense uses the past participle of the main verb, *stocked,* and adds the past-tense *had* to the front of it:

> (I, you, he, she, it, we, they) *had stocked.*

The future perfect tense also uses the past participle of the main verb, *stocked,* but adds the future-tense *will have:*

> (I, you, he, she, it, we, they) *will have stocked.*

Keep verbs in the same tense when the actions occur at the same time:

> When the payroll checks *came* in, everyone *showed* up for work.
>
> We *have found* that everyone *has pitched* in to help.

When the actions occur at different times, you may change tense accordingly:

> The shipment *came* last Wednesday, so if another one *comes* in today, please *return* it.
>
> The new employee *had been* ill at ease, but now she *has become* a full-fledged member of the team.

1.3.2 Irregular Verbs

Many verbs don't follow in every detail the patterns already described. The most irregular of these verbs is *to be:*

Tense	Singular	Plural
Present:	I *am*	we *are*
	you *are*	you *are*
	he, she, it *is*	they *are*
Past:	I *was*	we *were*
	you *were*	you *were*
	he, she, it *was*	they *were*

The future tense of *to be* is formed in the same way that the future tense of a regular verb is formed.

The perfect tenses of *to be* are also formed as they would be for a regular verb, except that the past participle is a special form, *been,* instead of just the past tense:

Present perfect:	you have been
Past perfect:	you had been
Future perfect:	you will have been

Here's a sampling of other irregular verbs:

Present	Past	Past Participle
begin	began	begun
shrink	shrank	shrunk
know	knew	known
rise	rose	risen
become	became	become
go	went	gone
do	did	done

Dictionaries list the various forms of other irregular verbs.

1.3.3 Transitive and Intransitive Verbs

Many people are confused by three particular sets of verbs:

> lie/lay   sit/set   rise/raise

Using these verbs correctly is much easier when you learn the difference between transitive and intransitive verbs.

Transitive verbs convey their action to an object; they "transfer" their action to an object. Intransitive verbs do not.

Here are some sample uses of intransitive and transitive verbs:

Intransitive	Transitive
We should include in our new offices a place to *lie* down for a nap.	The workers will be here on Monday to *lay* new carpeting.
Even the way an interviewee *sits* is important.	That crate is full of stemware, so *set* it down carefully.
Salaries at Compu-Link, Inc., *rise* swiftly.	They *raise* their level of production every year.

The workers *lay* carpeting, you *set* down the crate, they *raise* production; each action is transferred to something. In the intransitive sentences, one *lies* down, an interviewee *sits,* and salaries *rise* without (at least grammatically) affecting anything else. Intransitive sentences are complete with only a subject and a verb; transitive sentences are not complete unless they also include an object, or something to transfer the action to.

Tenses are a confusing element of the *lie/lay* problem:

Present	Past	Past Participle
I lie	I lay	I have lain
I lay (something down)	I laid (something down)	I have laid (something down)

The past tense of *lie* and the present tense of *lay* look and sound alike, even though they're different verbs.

1.3.4 Subject-Verb Agreement
Whether regular or irregular, every verb must agree with its subject, both in person (first, second, or third) and in number (single or plural).

	First Person	Second Person	Third Person
Singular	I *am;* I *write*	you *are;* you *write*	he/she/it *is;* he/she/it *writes*
Plural	we *are;* we *write*	you *are;* you *write*	they *are;* they *write*

In a simple sentence, making a verb agree with its subject is a straightforward task:

Hector Ruiz *is* a strong competitor. (third-person singular)

We *write* to you every month. (first-person plural)

Confusion sometimes arises when sentences are a bit more complicated. For example, be sure to avoid agreement problems when words come between the subject and verb. In the following examples, the verb appears in italics, and its subject is underlined:

The <u>analysis</u> of existing documents *takes* a full week.

Even though *documents* is a plural, the verb is in the singular form. That's because the subject of the sentence is *analysis,* a singular noun. The phrase *of existing documents* can be disregarded. Here is another example:

The <u>answers</u> for this exercise *are* in the study guide.

Take away the phrase *for this exercise* and you are left with the plural subject *answers.* Therefore, the verb takes the plural form.

Verb agreement is also complicated when the subject is not a specific noun or pronoun and when the subject may be considered either singular or plural. In such cases, you have to analyze the surrounding sentence to determine which verb form to use.

The <u>staff</u> *is* quartered in the warehouse.

The <u>staff</u> *are* at their desks in the warehouse.

The <u>computers</u> and the <u>staff</u> *are* in the warehouse.

Neither the staff nor the <u>computers</u> *are* in the warehouse.

<u>Every</u> computer *is* in the warehouse.

Many a <u>computer</u> *is* in the warehouse.

Did you notice that words such as *every* use the singular verb form? In addition, when an *either/or* or a *neither/nor* phrase combines singular and plural nouns, the verb takes the form that matches the noun closest to it.

In the business world, some subjects require extra attention. Company names, for example, are considered singular and therefore take a singular verb in most cases—even if they contain plural words:

<u>Stater Brothers</u> *offers* convenient grocery shopping.

In addition, quantities are sometimes considered singular and sometimes plural. If a quantity refers to a total amount, it takes a singular verb; if a quantity refers to individual, countable units, it takes a plural verb:

Three <u>hours</u> *is* a long time.

The eight <u>dollars</u> we collected for the fund *are* tacked on the bulletin board.

Fractions may also be singular or plural, depending on the noun that accompanies them:

One-third of the <u>warehouse</u> *is* devoted to this product line.

One-third of the <u>products</u> *are* defective.

For a related discussion, see Section 1.7.2, "Longer Sentences," later in this Handbook.

1.3.5 Voice of Verbs
Verbs have two voices, active and passive. When the subject comes first, the voice is active. When the object comes first, the voice is passive:

| **Active:** | The buyer paid a large amount. |
| **Passive:** | A large amount was paid by the buyer. |

The passive voice uses a form of the verb *to be,* which adds words to a sentence. In the example, the passive-voice sentence uses eight words, whereas the active-voice sentence uses only six to say the same thing. The words *was* and *by* are unnecessary to convey the meaning of the sentence. In fact, extra words usually clog meaning. So be sure to opt for the active voice when you have a choice.

At times, however, you have no choice:

> Several items *have been taken,* but so far we don't know who took them.

The passive voice becomes necessary when you don't know (or don't want to say) who performed the action; the active voice is bolder and more direct.

1.3.6 Mood of Verbs

You have three moods to choose from, depending on your intentions. Most of the time you use the indicative mood to make a statement or to ask a question:

> The secretary *mailed* a letter to each supplier.
>
> Did the secretary *mail* a letter to each supplier?

When you wish to command or request, use the imperative mood:

> Please *mail* a letter to each supplier.

Sometimes, especially in business, a courteous request is stated like a question; in that case, however, no question mark is required:

> Would you *mail* a letter to each supplier.

The subjunctive mood, most often used in formal writing or in presenting bad news, expresses a possibility or a recommendation. The subjunctive is usually signaled by a word such as *if* or *that.* In these examples, the subjunctive mood uses special verb forms:

> If the secretary *were to mail* a letter to each supplier, we might save some money.
>
> I suggested that the secretary *mail* a letter to each supplier.

Although the subjunctive mood is not used as often as it once was, it's still found in such expressions as *Come what may* and *If I were you.* In general, it is used to convey an idea that is contrary to fact: If iron *were* lighter than air.

Practice Session: Verbs

Underline the preferred choice within each set of parentheses in the following sentences.

1. When Hastings (*come, comes, came*) in, tell him I (*want, wanted*) to see him.
2. Even though Sheila (*knowed, knew*) the right password, she typed it incorrectly.
3. The presentation had not yet (*began, begun*) when Charles arrived.
4. What I always say is, let sleeping dogs (*lay, lie*).
5. The workers (*lay, laid*) the tile in the executive bathroom yesterday.
6. This is where the president of the board (*sits, sets*) during meetings.
7. Just (*sit, set*) the boxes down over there.
8. Do you think management will (*raise, rise*) prices across the board next week?
9. A list of promotions (*was, were*) posted on the company intranet.
10. The supervisor of the assembly-line workers (*is, are*) being replaced.
11. The committee (*is, are*) considering the proposal today.
12. The board and the committee (*is, are*) having a joint meeting on June 25.
13. Neither the board nor the committee (*is, are*) expected to approve the proposal.
14. Every member of the board (*is, are*) going to make a statement.
15. Katten and Associates (*represent, represents*) clients in the entertainment industry.
16. Five hours (*is, are*) all I can give you to get the project done.
17. Half of the vacant lots (*is, are*) already sold.
18. Half of the hall (*is, are*) reserved for the luncheon.
19. Mario suggested that the public relations department (*send, sends*) out a news release about the merger.
20. If I (*was, were*) CEO, I'd fire the whole accounting staff.

1.4 Adjectives

An adjective modifies (tells something about) a noun or pronoun. Each of the following phrases says more about the noun or pronoun than the noun or pronoun would say alone.

an *efficient* staff	a *heavy* price
brisk trade	*poor* you

Adjectives always tell us something that we wouldn't know without them. So you don't need to use adjectives when the noun alone, or a different noun, will give the meaning:

> a *company* employee
>
> (An employee ordinarily works for a company.)
>
> a *crate-type* container
>
> (*Crate* gives the entire meaning.)

Verbs in the *ing* (present participle) form can be used as adjectives:

> A *boring* job can sometimes turn into a *fascinating* career.

So can the past participle of verbs:

> A freshly *painted* house is a *sold* house.

Adjectives modify nouns more often than they modify pronouns. When adjectives do modify pronouns, however, the sentence usually has a linking verb:

They were *attentive.*   It looked *appropriate.*
He seems *interested.*   You are *skillful.*

At times, a series of adjectives precedes a noun:

It was a *long* and *active* workday.

Such strings of adjectives are acceptable as long as they all convey a different part of the phrase's meaning. However, adjectives often pile up in front of a noun, like this:

The *superficial, obvious* answer was the one she gave.
The most valuable animal on the ranch is a *small black* horse.

The question is whether a comma should be used to separate the adjectives. The answer is to use a comma when the two adjectives independently modify the noun; do not use a comma when one of the adjectives is closely identified with the noun. In the first example above, the answer was both superficial and obvious. But in the second example, the black horse is small.

Another way to think about this is to use the word *and* as a replacement for the comma. Study the following example:

We recommend a diet of leafy green vegetables.
We recommend a diet of green, leafy vegetables.

Because some green vegetables are not leafy (cucumbers and zucchini, for example), it is correct to leave out the comma in the first example so that you know which kind of green vegetables are being discussed. But because all leafy vegetables are also green (green and leafy), the comma must be included in the second example.

You might also try switching the adjectives. If the order of the adjectives can be reversed without changing the meaning of the phrase, you should use a comma. If the order cannot be reversed, you should not use a comma. Consider these examples:

Here's our *simplified credit* application.
Here's our *simplified, easy-to-complete* application.
Here's our *easy-to-complete, simplified* application.

A credit application may be simple or complex; however, you cannot talk about a credit, simplified application; therefore, leave the comma out of the first example. The application in the second and third examples is both simplified and easy to complete, no matter how you arrange the words, so include the comma in these examples.

1.4.1 Comparative Degree
Most adjectives can take three forms: simple, comparative, and superlative. The simple form modifies a single noun or pronoun. Use the comparative form when comparing two

items. When comparing three or more items, use the superlative form.

Simple	Comparative	Superlative
hard	harder	hardest
safe	safer	safest
dry	drier	driest

The comparative form adds *er* to the simple form, and the superlative form adds *est.* (The *y* at the end of a word changes to *i* before the *er* or *est* is added.)

A small number of adjectives are irregular, including these:

Simple	Comparative	Superlative
good	better	best
bad	worse	worst
little	less	least

When the simple form of an adjective is two or more syllables, you usually add *more* to form the comparative and *most* to form the superlative:

Simple	Comparative	Superlative
useful	more useful	most useful
exhausting	more exhausting	most exhausting
expensive	more expensive	most expensive

The most common exceptions are two-syllable adjectives that end in *y:*

Simple	Comparative	Superlative
happy	happier	happiest
costly	costlier	costliest

If you choose this option, change the *y* to *i,* and tack *er* or *est* onto the end.

Some adjectives cannot be used to make comparisons because they themselves indicate the extreme. For example, if something is perfect, nothing can be more perfect. If something is unique or ultimate, nothing can be more unique or more ultimate.

1.4.2 Hyphenated Adjectives
Many adjectives used in the business world are actually combinations of words: *up-to-date* report, *last-minute* effort, *fifth-floor* suite, *well-built* engine. As you can see, they are hyphenated when they come before the noun they modify. However, when they come after the noun they modify, they are not hyphenated. In the following example, the adjectives appear in italics and the nouns they modify are underlined:

The <u>report</u> is *up to date* because of our team's *last-minute* <u>efforts</u>.

Hyphens are not used when part of the combination is a word ending in *ly* (because that word is usually not an adjective). Hyphens are also omitted from word combinations that are used frequently.

We live in a *rapidly shrinking* world.

Our *highly motivated* employees will be well paid.

Please consider renewing your *credit card* account.

Send those figures to our *data processing* department.

Our new intern is a *high school* student.

1.5 Adverbs

An adverb modifies a verb, an adjective, or another adverb:

Modifying a verb: Our marketing department works *efficiently*.

Modifying an adjective: She was not dependable, although she was *highly* intelligent.

Modifying another adverb: His territory was *too* broadly diversified, so he moved *extremely* cautiously.

Most of the adverbs mentioned are adjectives turned into adverbs by adding *ly*, which is how many adverbs are formed:

Adjective	Adverb
efficient	efficiently
extreme	extremely
high	highly
official	officially
separate	separately
special	specially

Some adverbs are made by dropping or changing the final letter of the adjective and then adding *ly*:

Adjective	Adverb
due	duly
busy	busily

Other adverbs don't end in *ly* at all. Here are a few examples of this type:

often	fast	too
soon	very	so

Some adverbs are difficult to distinguish from adjectives. For example, in the following sentences, is the underlined word an adverb or an adjective?

They worked <u>well</u>.

The baby is <u>well</u>.

In the first sentence, *well* is an adverb modifying the verb worked. In the second sentence, *well* is an adjective modifying the noun *baby*. To choose correctly between adverbs and adjec-tives, remember that verbs of being link a noun to an adjective describing the noun. In contrast, you would use an adverb to describe an action verb.

Adjective	Adverb
He is a *good* worker. (What kind of worker is he?)	He works *well*. (How does he work?)
It is a *real* computer. (What kind of computer is it?)	It *really* is a computer. (To what extent is it a computer?)
The traffic is *slow*. (What quality does the traffic have?)	The traffic moves *slowly*. (How does the traffic move?)

1.5.1 Negative Adverbs

Negative adverbs (such as *neither, no, not, scarcely,* and *seldom*) are powerful words and therefore do not need any help in conveying a negative thought. In fact, using double negatives gives a strong impression of illiteracy, so avoid sentences like these:

I don't want no mistakes.
(Correct: "I don't want any mistakes," or "I want no mistakes.")

They couldn't hardly read the report.
(Correct: "They could hardly read the report," or "They couldn't read the report.")

They scarcely noticed neither one.
(Correct: "They scarcely noticed either one," or "They noticed neither one.")

1.5.2 Comparative Degree

Like adjectives, adverbs can be used to compare items. Generally, the basic adverb is combined with *more* or *most,* just as long adjectives are. However, some adverbs have one-word comparative forms:

One Item	Two Items	Three Items
quickly	more quickly	most quickly
sincerely	less sincerely	least sincerely
fast	faster	fastest
well	better	best

Practice Session: Adjectives and Adverbs

Underline the preferred choice within each set of parentheses in the following sentences.

1. I always choose the (*less, least*) expensive brand.
2. Which would be (*better, best*), the store brand or the generic brand?
3. This audit couldn't have come at a (*worse, worst*) time.
4. When it comes to data analysis, Claire is (*more competent, competenter*) than Alexander.
5. The ad agency's campaign for our new vitamin supplement is (*unique, very unique, most unique*), to say the least.
6. A corporation can benefit from a (*well written, well-written*) annual report.

7. The chairman's introductory message to the annual report was (*well written, well-written*).
8. Even a (*beautifully written, beautifully-written*) report can be hampered by poor design and production.
9. According to Bank of America, the number of (*credit-card, credit card*) applications has tripled in the past year.
10. Angela wasn't feeling (*good, well*), so she went home early.
11. Harrison and Martinez work (*good, well*) together.
12. We are (*real, really*) excited about next week's product launch.
13. Could this project be moving any more (*slow, slowly*) through the bureaucratic system?
14. We (*could hardly, couldn't hardly*) wait to see how the brochure had turned out.
15. Today TeKTech is (*more heavy, more heavily, most heavily*) involved in nanotechnology, compared to five years ago.

1.6 Other Parts of Speech

Nouns, pronouns, verbs, adjectives, and adverbs carry most of the meaning in a sentence. Four other parts of speech link them together in sentences: prepositions, conjunctions, articles, and interjections.

1.6.1 Prepositions

Prepositions are words like these:

of	to	for	with
at	by	from	about

Some prepositions consist of more than one word—like these:

because of   in addition to   out of   except for

And some prepositions are closely linked with a verb. When using phrases such as *look up* and *wipe out,* keep the phrase intact and do not insert anything between the verb and the preposition.

Prepositions most often begin prepositional phrases, which function like adjectives and adverbs by telling more about a pronoun, noun, or verb:

of a type	*by* Friday
to the point	*with* characteristic flair

To prevent misreading, prepositional phrases should be placed near the element they modify:

Of all our technicians, <u>she</u> is the best trained.

They couldn't see the <u>merit</u> *in my proposal.*

Someone left a <u>folder</u> *on my desk.*

It was once considered totally unacceptable to put a preposition at the end of a sentence. Now you may:

I couldn't tell what they were interested in.

What did she attribute it to?

However, be careful not to place prepositions at the end of sentences when doing so is unnecessary. In fact, avoid using any unnecessary preposition. In the following examples, the prepositions in parentheses should be omitted:

All (of) the staff members were present.

I almost fell off (of) my chair with surprise.

Where was Mr. Steuben going (to)?

They couldn't help (from) wondering.

The opposite problem is failing to include a preposition when you should. Consider the two sentences that follow:

Sales were over $100,000 for Linda and Bill.

Sales were over $100,000 for Linda and for Bill.

The first sentence indicates that Linda and Bill had combined sales over $100,000; the second, that Linda and Bill each had sales over $100,000, for a combined total in excess of $200,000. The preposition *for* is critical here.

Prepositions are also required in sentences like this one:

Which type of personal computer do you prefer?

Certain prepositions are used with certain words. When the same preposition can be used for two or more words in a sentence without affecting the meaning, only the last preposition is required:

We are familiar (*with*) and satisfied *with* your company's products.

But when different prepositions are normally used with the words, all the prepositions must be included:

We are familiar *with* and interested *in* your company's products.

Here is an incomplete list of prepositions that are used in a particular way with particular words:

among/between: *Among* is used to refer to three or more (*Circulate the memo among the staff*); *between* is used to refer to two (*Put the copy machine between Judy and Dan*).

as if/like: *As if* is used before a clause (*It seems as if we should be doing something*); *like* is used before a noun or pronoun (*He seems like a nice guy*).

have/of: *Have* is a verb used in verb phrases (*They should have checked first*); *of* is a preposition and is never used in such cases.

in/into: *In* is used to refer to a static position (*The file is in the cabinet*); *into* is used to refer to movement toward a position (*Put the file into the cabinet*).

And here is an incomplete list of some prepositions that have come to be used with certain words:

according to	different from	prior to
agree to (a proposal)	get from (receive)	reason with
agree with (a person)	get off (dismount)	responsible for
buy from	in accordance with	similar to
capable of	in search of	talk to (without interaction)
comply with	independent of	talk with (with interaction)
conform to	interior to	wait for (person or thing)
differ from (things)	plan to	wait on (like a waiter)
differ with (person)	prefer to	

1.6.2 Conjunctions

Conjunctions connect the parts of a sentence: words, phrases, and clauses. You are probably most familiar with coordinating conjunctions such as the following:

and	for	or	yet
but	nor	so	

Conjunctions may be used to connect clauses (which have both a subject and a predicate) with other clauses, to connect clauses with phrases (which do not have both a subject and a predicate), and to connect words with words:

We sell designer clothing *and* linens.

(Words with words)

Their products are expensive *but* still appeal to value-conscious consumers.

(Clauses with phrases)

I will call her on the phone today, *or* I will visit her office tomorrow.

(Clauses with clauses)

Some conjunctions are used in pairs:

both . . . and	neither . . . nor	whether . . . or
either . . . or	not only . . . but also	

With paired conjunctions, you must be careful to construct each phrase in the same way.

They *not only* <u>are out of</u> racquets *but also* <u>are out of</u> balls.
They are *not only* <u>out of</u> racquets *but also* <u>out of</u> balls.
They <u>are out of</u> *not only* racquets *but also* balls.

In other words, the construction that follows each part of the pair must be parallel, containing the same verbs, prepositions, and so on. The same need for parallelism exists when using conjunctions to join the other parts of speech:

He is listed in *either* <u>your</u> roster *or* <u>my</u> roster.
He is listed *neither* <u>in</u> your roster *nor* <u>on</u> the master list.
They *both* <u>gave</u> *and* <u>received</u> notice.

A certain type of conjunction is used to join clauses that are unequal—that is, to join a main clause to one that is subordinate or dependent. Here is a partial list of conjunctions used to introduce dependent clauses:

although	before	once	unless
as soon as	even though	so that	until
because	if	that	when

Using conjunctions is also discussed in Sections 1.7.3 and 1.7.4.

1.6.3 Articles and Interjections

Only three articles exist in English: *the, a,* and *an.* These words are used, like adjectives, to specify which item you are talking about.

Interjections are words that express no solid information, only emotion:

Wow!	Well, well!
Oh, no!	Good!

Such purely emotional language has its place in private life and advertising copy, but it only weakens the effect of most business writing.

Practice Session: Prepositions, Conjunctions, and Articles
Circle the letter of the preferred choice in each pair of sentences.

1. a. If we want to have the project done next week, we'll need those balance sheets by Wednesday.
   b. If we want to have the project done next week, by Wednesday we'll need those balance sheets.

2. a. From where did that information come?
   b. Where did that information come from?

3. a. Please look up the shipping rates for packages to France.
   b. Please look the shipping rates up for packages to France.

4. a. You need to indicate the type job you're seeking.
   b. You need to indicate the type of job you're seeking.

5. a. Michael got the actuarial data off of the Internet.
   b. Michael got the actuarial data off the Internet.

6. a. When the meeting is over, Michelle will prepare the minutes.
   b. When the meeting is over with, Michelle will prepare the minutes.

7. a. Sharon is familiar and knowledgeable about HTML coding.
   b. Sharon is familiar with and knowledgeable about HTML coding.

8. a. We'll be deciding among the four applicants this afternoon.
   b. We'll be deciding between the four applicants this afternoon.

9. a. Since Marshall isn't here, it looks like the conference call will have to be canceled.
   b. Since Marshall isn't here, it looks as if the conference call will have to be canceled.

10. a. I would have had the memo done sooner, but my computer crashed.
    b. I would of had the memo done sooner, but my computer crashed.

11. **a.** Once we have the survey results, we can put them in the report.
    b. Once we have the survey results, we can put them into the report.

12. **a.** If you agree with the settlement, I can prepare the final papers.
    b. If you agree to the settlement, I can prepare the final papers.

13. **a.** It is important that you provide not only your name but also your address and telephone number.
    b. It is important that you provide not only your name but also address and telephone number.

14. **a.** The conference will be held in either March or July.
    b. The conference will be held either in March or July.

15. **a.** Please prepare an RFP for the construction job.
    b. Please prepare a RFP for the construction job.

1.7 Sentences

Sentences are constructed with the major building blocks, the parts of speech.

> Money talks.

This two-word sentence consists of a noun (*money*) and a verb (*talks*). When used in this way, the noun works as the first requirement for a sentence, the subject, and the verb works as the second requirement, the predicate. Now look at this sentence:

> They merged.

The subject in this case is a pronoun (*they*), and the predicate is a verb (*merged*). This is a sentence because it has a subject and a predicate. Here is yet another kind of sentence:

> The plans are ready.

This sentence has a more complicated subject, the noun *plans* and the article *the;* the complete predicate is a state-of-being verb (*are*) and an adjective (*ready*).

Without a subject (who or what does something) and a predicate (the doing of it), you have merely a collection of words, not a sentence.

1.7.1 Commands

In commands, the subject (always *you*) is only understood, not stated:

> (You) Move your desk to the better office.
> (You) Please try to finish by six o'clock.

1.7.2 Longer Sentences

More complicated sentences have more complicated subjects and predicates, but they still have a simple subject and a predicate verb. In the following examples, the subject is underlined once, the predicate verb twice:

> <u>Marex</u> and <u>Contron</u> <u>enjoy</u> higher earnings each quarter.
>
> (*Marex* [and] *Contron* do something; *enjoy* is what they do.)

> My <u>interview</u>, coming minutes after my freeway accident, <u>did</u> not <u>impress</u> or <u>move</u> anyone.
>
> (*Interview* is what did something. What did it do? It *did* [not] *impress* [or] *move.*)

> In terms of usable space, a steel <u>warehouse</u>, with its extremely long span of roof unsupported by pillars, <u>makes</u> more sense.
>
> (*Warehouse* is what *makes.*)

These three sentences demonstrate several things. First, in all three sentences, the simple subject and predicate verb are the "bare bones" of the sentence, the parts that carry the core idea of the sentence. When trying to find the subject and predicate verb, disregard all prepositional phrases, modifiers, conjunctions, and articles.

Second, in the third sentence the verb is singular (*makes*) because the subject is singular (*warehouse*). Even though the plural noun *pillars* is closer to the verb, *warehouse* is the subject. So *warehouse* determines whether the verb is singular or plural. Subject and predicate must agree.

Third, the subject in the first sentence is compound (*Marex* [and] *Contron*). A compound subject, when connected by *and*, requires a plural verb (*enjoy*). Also in the second sentence, compound predicates are possible (*did* [not] *impress* [or] *move*).

Fourth, the second sentence incorporates a group of words—*coming minutes after my freeway accident*—containing a form of a verb (*coming*) and a noun (*accident*). Yet this group of words is not a complete sentence for two reasons:

- Not all nouns are subjects: *Accident* is not the subject of *coming.*
- Not all verbs are predicates: A verb that ends in *ing* can never be the predicate of a sentence (unless preceded by a form of *to be,* as in *was coming*).

Because they don't contain a subject and a predicate, the words *coming minutes after my freeway accident* (called a phrase) can't be written as a sentence. That is, the phrase cannot stand alone; it cannot begin with a capital letter and end with a period. So a phrase must always be just one part of a sentence.

Sometimes a sentence incorporates two or more groups of words that do contain a subject and a predicate; these word groups are called clauses:

> My *interview,* because it <u>came</u> minutes after my freeway accident, <u>did</u> not <u>impress</u> or <u>move</u> anyone.

The independent clause is the portion of the sentence that could stand alone without revision:

> My <u>interview</u> <u>did</u> not <u>impress</u> or <u>move</u> anyone.

The other part of the sentence could stand alone only by removing *because:*

(because) It <u>came</u> minutes after my freeway accident.

This part of the sentence is known as a dependent clause; although it has a subject and a predicate (just as an independent clause does), it's linked to the main part of the sentence by a word (*because*) showing its dependence.

In summary, the two types of clauses—dependent and independent—both have a subject and a predicate. Dependent clauses, however, do not bear the main meaning of the sentence and are therefore linked to an independent clause. Nor can phrases stand alone, because they lack both a subject and a predicate. Only independent clauses can be written as sentences without revision.

1.7.3 Sentence Fragments

An incomplete sentence (a phrase or a dependent clause) that is written as though it were a complete sentence is called a fragment. Consider the following sentence fragments:

> Marilyn Sanders, having had pilferage problems in her store for the past year. Refuses to accept the results of our investigation.

This serious error can easily be corrected by putting the two fragments together:

> Marilyn Sanders, having had pilferage problems in her store for the past year, refuses to accept the results of our investigation.

Not all fragments can be corrected so easily. Here's more information on Sanders's pilferage problem.

> Employees a part of it. No authority or discipline.

Only the writer knows the intended meaning of those two phrases. Perhaps the employees are taking part in the pilferage. If so, the sentence should read:

> Some employees are part of the pilferage problem.

On the other hand, it's possible that some employees are helping with the investigation. Then the sentence would read:

> Some employees are taking part in our investigation.

It's just as likely, however, that the employees are not only taking part in the pilferage but are also being analyzed:

> Those employees who are part of the pilferage problem will accept no authority or discipline.

Even more meanings could be read into these fragments. Because fragments can mean so many things, they mean nothing. No well-written memo, letter, or report ever demands the reader to be an imaginative genius.

One more type of fragment exists, the kind represented by a dependent clause. Note what *because* does to change what was once a unified sentence:

> Our stock of sprinklers is depleted.
> Because our stock of sprinklers is depleted.

Although the second version contains a subject and a predicate, adding *because* makes it a fragment. Words such as *because* form a special group of words called subordinating conjunctions. Here's a partial list:

after	if	unless
although	since	whenever
even if	though	while

When a word of this type begins a clause, the clause is dependent and cannot stand alone as a sentence. However, if a dependent clause is combined with an independent clause, it can convey a complete meaning. The independent clause may come before or after the dependent clause:

> We are unable to fill your order because our stock of sprinklers is depleted.
> Because our stock of sprinklers is depleted, we are unable to fill your order.

Also, to fix a fragment that is a dependent clause, remove the subordinating conjunction. Doing so leaves a simple but complete sentence:

> Our stock of sprinklers is depleted.

The actual details of a situation will determine the best way for you to remedy a fragment problem.

The ban on fragments has one exception. Some advertising copy contains sentence fragments, written knowingly to convey a certain rhythm. However, advertising is the only area of business in which fragments are acceptable.

1.7.4 Fused Sentences and Comma Splices

Just as there can be too little in a group of words to make it a sentence, there can also be too much:

> All our mail is run through a postage meter every afternoon someone picks it up.

This example contains two sentences, not one, but the two have been blended so that it's hard to tell where one ends and the next begins. Is the mail run through a meter every afternoon? If so, the sentences should read:

> All our mail is run through a postage meter every afternoon. Someone picks it up.

Perhaps the mail is run through a meter at some other time (morning, for example) and is picked up every afternoon:

> All our mail is run through a postage meter. Every afternoon someone picks it up.

The order of words is the same in all three cases; sentence division makes all the difference. Either of the last two cases is grammatically correct. The choice depends on the facts of the situation.

Sometimes these so-called fused sentences have a more obvious point of separation:

> Several large orders arrived within a few days of one another, too many came in for us to process by the end of the month.

Here the comma has been put between two independent clauses in an attempt to link them. When a lowly comma separates two complete sentences, the result is called a comma splice. A comma splice can be remedied in one of three ways:

- Replace the comma with a period and capitalize the next word: ". . . one another. Too many . . ."
- Replace the comma with a semicolon and do not capitalize the next word: ". . . one another; too many . . ." This remedy works only when the two sentences have closely related meanings.
- Change one of the sentences so that it becomes a phrase or a dependent clause. This remedy often produces the best writing, but it takes more work.

The third alternative can be carried out in several ways. One is to begin the blended sentence with a subordinating conjunction:

> Whenever several large orders arrived within a few days of one another, too many came in for us to process by the end of the month.

Another way is to remove part of the subject or the predicate verb from one of the independent clauses, thereby creating a phrase:

> Several large orders arrived within a few days of one another, too many for us to process by the end of the month.

Finally, you can change one of the predicate verbs to its *ing* form:

> Several large orders arrived within a few days of one another, too many coming in for us to process by the end of the month.

At other times a simple coordinating conjunction (such as *or*, *and*, or *but*) can separate fused sentences:

> You can fire them, or you can make better use of their abilities.
>
> Margaret drew up the designs, and Matt carried them out.
>
> We will have three strong months, but after that sales will taper off.

Be careful using coordinating conjunctions: Use them only to join simple sentences that express similar ideas.

Also, because they say relatively little about the relationship between the two clauses they join, avoid using coordinating conjunctions too often: *and* is merely an addition sign; *but* is just a

turn signal; *or* only points to an alternative. Subordinating conjunctions such as *because* and *whenever* tell the reader a lot more.

1.7.5 Sentences with Linking Verbs

Linking verbs were discussed briefly in the section on verbs (Section 1.3). Here you can see more fully the way they function in a sentence. The following is a model of any sentence with a linking verb:

> A (*verb*) B.

Although words such as *seems* and *feels* can also be linking verbs, let's assume that the verb is a form of *to be*:

> A *is* B.

In such a sentence, A and B are always nouns, pronouns, or adjectives. When one is a noun and the other is a pronoun, or when both are nouns, the sentence says that one is the same as the other:

> She is president.
>
> Rachel is president.

When one is an adjective, it modifies or describes the other:

> She is forceful.

Remember that when one is an adjective, it modifies the other as any adjective modifies a noun or pronoun, except that a linking verb stands between the adjective and the word it modifies.

1.7.6 Misplaced Modifiers

The position of a modifier in a sentence is important. The movement of *only* changes the meaning in the following sentences:

> Only we are obliged to supply those items specified in your contract.
>
> We are obliged only to supply those items specified in your contract.
>
> We are obliged to supply only those items specified in your contract.
>
> We are obliged to supply those items specified only in your contract.

In any particular set of circumstances, only one of those sentences would be accurate. The others would very likely cause problems. To prevent misunderstanding, place such modifiers as close as possible to the noun or verb they modify.

For similar reasons, whole phrases that are modifiers must be placed near the right noun or verb. Mistakes in placement create ludicrous meanings.

> Antia Information Systems has bought new computer chairs for the programmers *with more comfortable seats.*

The anatomy of programmers is not normally a concern of business writers. Obviously, the comfort of the chairs was the issue:

Antia Information Systems has bought new computer chairs *with more comfortable seats* for the programmers.

Here is another example:

I asked him to file all the letters in the cabinet that had been answered.

In this ridiculous sentence the cabinet has been answered, even though no cabinet in history is known to have asked a question. *That had been answered* is too far from *letters* and too close to *cabinet*. Here's an improvement:

I asked him to file in the cabinet all the letters that had been answered.

In some cases, instead of moving the modifying phrase closer to the word it modifies, the best solution is to move the word closer to the modifying phrase.

Practice Session: Sentences

Circle the letter of the preferred choice in each group of sentences.

1. **a.** Cyberterrorism—orchestrated attacks on a company's information systems for political or economic purposes—is a very real threat.
   b. Cyberterrorism—orchestrated attacks on a company's information systems for political or economic purposes—are a very real threat.

2. **a.** E-mail, phone calls, and faxes, each one a distraction, interrupts employees when they work.
   b. E-mail, phone calls, and faxes, each one a distraction, interrupt employees when they work.

3. **a.** About 35 percent of major U.S. companies keep tabs on workers. Because they want to protect valuable company information.
   b. About 35 percent of major U.S. companies keep tabs on workers, because they want to protect valuable company information.
   c. About 35 percent of major U.S. companies keep tabs on workers; because they want to protect valuable company information.

4. **a.** Despite its small size and relative isolation in the Arctic Circle. Finland leads the pack in mobile phone technology and its applications.
   b. Despite its small size and relative isolation in the Arctic Circle; Finland leads the pack in mobile phone technology and its applications.
   c. Despite its small size and relative isolation in the Arctic Circle, Finland leads the pack in mobile phone technology and its applications.

5. **a.** Many employees erroneously believe that their e-mail and voice mail messages are private they're surprised when e-mail ends up in places where they did not intend it to go.
   b. Many employees erroneously believe that their e-mail and voice mail messages are private, they're surprised when e-mail ends up in places where they did not intend it to go.
   c. Many employees erroneously believe that their e-mail and voice mail messages are private, so they're surprised when e-mail ends up in places where they did not intend it to go.

6. **a.** Each day people in the United States treat themselves to more than 3 million Krispy Kreme doughnuts, they buy more than 11,000 dozen of those doughnuts every hour.
   b. Each day people in the United States treat themselves to more than 3 million Krispy Kreme doughnuts, buying more than 11,000 dozen of those doughnuts every hour.

7. **a.** The procedure for making Krispy Kreme doughnuts takes about an hour, the manufacturing process begins long before local stores crank up their production lines.
   b. The procedure for making Krispy Kreme doughnuts takes about an hour; the manufacturing process begins long before local stores crank up their production lines.
   c. The procedure for making Krispy Kreme doughnuts takes about an hour. But the manufacturing process begins long before local stores crank up their production lines.

8. **a.** After blending the ingredients, the doughnut mix is stored in Krispy Kreme's warehouse for a week.
   b. After blending the ingredients, Krispy Kreme's warehouse is used to store the doughnut mix for a week.
   c. After the ingredients have been blended, the doughnut mix is stored in Krispy Kreme's warehouse for a week.

9. **a.** All the company's bikes are custom-made by Green Gear Cycling to meet the rider's size and component preferences.
   b. All the company's bikes are custom-made to meet the rider's size and component preferences by Green Gear Cycling.

10. **a.** Catering to its customers, about 2,000 bikes are built annually by Green Gear Cycling.
    b. Catering to its customers, about 2,000 bikes are built by Green Gear Cycling annually.
    c. Catering to its customers, Green Gear Cycling builds about 2,000 bikes annually.

2.0 Punctuation

On the highway, signs tell you when to slow down or stop, where to turn, when to merge. In similar fashion, punctuation helps readers negotiate your prose. The proper use of punctuation keeps readers from losing track of your meaning.

2.1 Periods

Use a period (1) to end any sentence that is not a question, (2) with certain abbreviations, and (3) between dollars and cents in an amount of money.

2.2 Question Marks

Use a question mark after any direct question that requests an answer:

Are you planning to enclose a check, or shall we bill you?

Don't use a question mark with commands phrased as questions for the sake of politeness:

> Will you send us a check today.

2.3 Exclamation Points

Use exclamation points after highly emotional language. Because business writing almost never calls for emotional language, you will seldom use exclamation points.

2.4 Semicolons

Semicolons have three main uses. One is to separate two closely related independent clauses:

> The outline for the report is due within a week; the report itself is due at the end of the month.

A semicolon should also be used instead of a comma when the items in a series have commas within them:

> Our previous meetings were on November 11, 1998; February 20, 1999; and April 28, 2000.

Finally, a semicolon should be used to separate independent clauses when the second one begins with a word such as *however, therefore,* or *nevertheless* or a phrase such as *for example* or *in that case:*

> Our supplier has been out of part D712 for 10 weeks; however, we have found another source that can ship the part right away.
>
> His test scores were quite low; on the other hand, he has a lot of relevant experience.

Section 4.4 has more information on using transitional words and phrases.

2.5 Colons

Use a colon after the salutation in a business letter. You also use a colon at the end of a sentence or phrase introducing a list or (sometimes) a quotation:

> Our study included the three most critical problems: insufficient capital, incompetent management, and inappropriate location.

In some introductory sentences, phrases such as *the following* or *that is* are implied by using a colon.

A colon should not be used when the list, quotation, or idea is a direct object or part of the introductory sentence:

> We are able to supply
> staples
> wood screws
> nails
> toggle bolts

> This shipment includes 9 videotapes, 12 CDs, and 14 cassette tapes.

Another way you can use a colon is to separate the main clause and another sentence element when the second explains, illustrates, or amplifies the first:

> Management was unprepared for the union representatives' demands: this fact alone accounts for their arguing well into the night.

However, in contemporary usage, such clauses are frequently separated by a semicolon.

Practice Session: Punctuation 1
Circle the letter of the preferred choice in the following groups of sentences.

1. **a.** She asked me whether we should increase our insurance coverage?
   b. She asked me whether we should increase our insurance coverage.

2. **a.** Would you please let me know when the copier is free.
   b. Would you please let me know when the copier is free?

3. **a.** You won't want to miss this exciting seminar!
   b. You won't want to miss this exciting seminar.

4. **a.** The officers of the board of directors are John Rogers, president, Robin Doug Donlan, vice president for programming, Bill Pittman, vice president for operations, and Mary Sturhann, secretary.
   b. The officers of the board of directors are John Rogers, president; Robin Doug Donlan, vice president for programming; Bill Pittman, vice president for operations; and Mary Sturhann, secretary.
   c. The officers of the board of directors are John Rogers, president; Robin Doug Donlan, vice president for programming; Bill Pittman, vice president for operations, and Mary Sturhann, secretary.

5. **a.** Edward Jones is the best brokerage house in America; it's got more offices than any other brokerage house.
   b. Edward Jones is the best brokerage house in America, it's got more offices than any other brokerage house.

6. **a.** One of the SEC's top priorities is to crack down on insider trading, however it readily admits that it has not been very successful to date.
   b. One of the SEC's top priorities is to crack down on insider trading; however, it readily admits that it has not been very successful to date.

7. **a.** To keep on top of financial news, you should consult newspapers aimed specifically at investors, such as *Investor's Business Daily* and *Barron's.*
   b. To keep on top of financial news, you should consult newspapers aimed specifically at investors; such as, *Investor's Business Daily* and *Barron's.*
   c. To keep on top of financial news, you should consult newspapers aimed specifically at investors; such as *Investor's Business Daily* and *Barron's.*

8. **a.** Dear Dr. Schatzman,
   b. Dear Dr. Schatzman:

9. **a.** The three basic concepts that guide accountants are: the fundamental accounting equation, double-entry book-keeping, and the matching principle.
   b. The three basic concepts that guide accountants are the fundamental accounting equation, double-entry book-keeping, and the matching principle.
   c. The three basic concepts that guide accountants are the fundamental accounting equation; double-entry book-keeping; and the matching principle.

10. **a.** Accountants are guided by three basic concepts, the fundamental accounting equation, double-entry book-keeping, and the matching principle.
    b. Accountants are guided by three basic concepts: the fundamental accounting equation; double-entry book-keeping; and the matching principle.
    c. Accountants are guided by three basic concepts: the fundamental accounting equation, double-entry book-keeping, and the matching principle.

2.6 Commas

Commas have many uses; the most common is to separate items in a series:

> He took the job, learned it well, worked hard, and succeeded.
>
> Put paper, pencils, and paper clips on the requisition list.

Company style often dictates omitting the final comma in a series. However, if you have a choice, use the final comma; it's often necessary to prevent misunderstanding.

A second place to use a comma is between independent clauses that are joined by a coordinating conjunction (*and, but,* or *or*) unless one or both are very short:

> She spoke to the sales staff, and he spoke to the production staff.
>
> I was advised to proceed and I did.

A third use for the comma is to separate a dependent clause at the beginning of a sentence from an independent clause:

> Because of our lead in the market, we may be able to risk introducing a new product.

However, a dependent clause at the end of a sentence is separated from the independent clause by a comma only when the dependent clause is unnecessary to the main meaning of the sentence:

> We may be able to introduce a new product, although it may involve some risk.

A fourth use for the comma is after an introductory phrase or word:

> Starting with this amount of capital, we can survive in the red for one year.

> Through more careful planning, we may be able to serve more people.
>
> Yes, you may proceed as originally planned.

However, with short introductory prepositional phrases and some one-syllable words (such as *hence* and *thus*), the comma is often omitted:

> Before January 1 we must complete the inventory.
>
> Thus we may not need to hire anyone.
>
> In short the move to Tulsa was a good idea.

Fifth, commas are used to surround nonrestrictive phrases or words (expressions that can be removed from the sentence without changing the meaning):

> The new owners, the Kowacks, are pleased with their purchase.

Sixth, commas are used between adjectives modifying the same noun (coordinate adjectives):

> She left Monday for a long, difficult recruiting trip.

To test the appropriateness of such a comma, try reversing the order of the adjectives: *a difficult, long recruiting trip.* If the order cannot be reversed, leave out the comma (*a good old friend* isn't the same as *an old good friend*). A comma is also not used when one of the adjectives is part of the noun. Compare these two phrases:

> a distinguished, well-known figure
>
> a distinguished public figure

The adjective-noun combination of *public* and *figure* has been used together so often that it has come to be considered a single thing: *public figure.* So no comma is required.

Seventh, commas are used both before and after the year in sentences that include month, day, and year:

> It will be sent by December 15, 1999, from our Cincinnati plant.

Some companies write dates in another form: 15 December 2000. No commas should be used in that case. Nor is a comma needed when only the month and year are present (December 2000).

Eighth, commas are used to set off a variety of parenthetical words and phrases within sentences, including state names, dates, abbreviations, transitional expressions, and contrasted elements:

> They were, in fact, prepared to submit a bid.
>
> Our best programmer is Ken, who joined the company just a month ago.
>
> Habermacher, Inc., went public in 1999.
>
> Our goal was increased profits, not increased market share.
>
> Service, then, is our main concern.
>
> The factory was completed in Chattanooga, Tennessee, just three weeks ago.
>
> Joanne Dubiik, M.D., has applied for a loan from First Savings.

I started work here on March 1, 2001, and soon received my first promotion.

Ninth, a comma is used to separate a quotation from the rest of the sentence:

> Your warranty reads, "These conditions remain in effect for one year from date of purchase."

However, the comma is left out when the quotation as a whole is built into the structure of the sentence:

> He hurried off with an angry "Look where you're going."

Finally, a comma should be used whenever it's needed to avoid confusion or an unintended meaning. Compare the following:

> Ever since they have planned new ventures more carefully.

> Ever since, they have planned new ventures more carefully.

2.7 Dashes

Use a dash to surround a comment that is a sudden turn in thought:

> Membership in the IBSA—it's expensive but worth it—may be obtained by applying to our New York office.

A dash can also be used to emphasize a parenthetical word or phrase:

> Third-quarter profits—in excess of $2 million—are up sharply.

Finally, use dashes to set off a phrase that contains commas:

> All our offices—Milwaukee, New Orleans, and Phoenix—have sent representatives.

Don't confuse a dash with a hyphen. A dash separates and emphasizes words, phrases, and clauses more strongly than a comma or parentheses can; a hyphen ties two words so tightly that they almost become one word.

On computer, use the em dash symbol. When typing a dash in e-mail or on a typewriter, type two hyphens with no space before, between, or after.

2.8 Hyphens

Hyphens are mainly used in three ways. The first is to separate the parts of compound words beginning with such prefixes as *self-, ex-, quasi-,* and *all-*:

self-assured	quasi-official
ex-wife	all-important

However, omit hyphens from and close up those words that have prefixes such as *pro, anti, non, re, pre, un, inter,* and *extra*:

prolabor	nonunion
antifascist	interdepartmental

Exceptions occur when (1) the prefix occurs before a proper noun, or (2) the vowel at the end of the prefix is the same as the first letter of the root word:

pro-Republican	anti-American
anti-inflammatory	extra-atmospheric

When in doubt, consult your dictionary.

Hyphens are also used in some compound adjectives, which are adjectives made up of two or more words. Specifically, you should use hyphens in compound adjectives that come before the noun:

> an interest-bearing account   well-informed executives

However, you need not hyphenate when the adjective follows a linking verb:

> This account is interest bearing.

> Their executives are well informed.

You can shorten sentences that list similar hyphenated words by dropping the common part from all but the last word:

> Check the costs of first-, second-, and third-class postage.

Finally, hyphens may be used to divide words at the end of a typed line. Such hyphenation is best avoided, but when you have to divide words at the end of a line, do so correctly (see Section 3.4). A dictionary will show how words are divided into syllables.

2.9 Apostrophes

Use an apostrophe in the possessive form of a noun (but not in a pronoun):

> On *his* desk was a reply to Bette *Ainsley's* application for the *manager's* position.

Apostrophes are also used in place of the missing letter(s) of a contraction:

Whole Words	Contraction
we will	we'll
do not	don't
they are	they're

2.10 Quotation Marks

Use quotation marks to surround words that are repeated exactly as they were said or written:

> The collection letter ended by saying, "This is your third and final notice."

Remember: (1) When the quoted material is a complete sentence, the first word is capitalized. (2) The final comma or period goes inside the closing quotation marks.

Quotation marks are also used to set off the title of a newspaper story, magazine article, or book chapter:

You should read "Legal Aspects of the Collection Letter" in *Today's Credit*.

The book title is shown here in italics. When typewritten, the title is underlined. The same treatment is proper for newspaper and magazine titles. (Appendix B explains documentation style in more detail.)

Quotation marks may also be used to indicate special treatment for words or phrases, such as terms that you're using in an unusual or ironic way:

Our management "team" spends more time squabbling than working to solve company problems.

When you are defining a word, put the definition in quotation marks:

The abbreviation *etc.* means "and so forth."

When using quotation marks, take care to insert the closing marks as well as the opening ones.

Although periods and commas go inside any quotation marks, colons and semicolons go outside them. A question mark goes inside the quotation marks only if the quotation is a question:

All that day we wondered, "Is he with us?"

If the quotation is not a question but the entire sentence is, the question mark goes outside:

What did she mean by "You will hear from me"?

2.11 Parentheses
Use parentheses to surround comments that are entirely incidental:

Our figures do not match yours, although (if my calculations are correct) they are closer than we thought.

Parentheses are also used in legal documents to surround figures in arabic numerals that follow the same amount in words:

Remittance will be One Thousand Two Hundred Dollars ($1,200).

Be careful to put punctuation (period, comma, and so on) outside the parentheses unless it is part of the statement in parentheses.

2.12 Ellipses
Use ellipsis points, or dots, to indicate that material has been left out of a direct quotation. Use them only in direct quotations and only at the point where material was left out. In the following example, the first sentence is quoted in the second:

The Dow Jones Industrial Average, which skidded 38.17 points in the previous five sessions, gained 4.61 to end at 2213.84.

According to the Honolulu *Star Bulletin*, "The Dow Jones Industrial Average . . . gained 4.61" on June 10.

The number of dots in ellipses is not optional; always use three. Occasionally, the points of ellipsis come at the end of a sentence, where they seem to grow a fourth dot. Don't be fooled: One of the dots is a period.

Practice Session: Punctuation 2
Circle the letter of the preferred choice in each group of sentences.

1. **a.** Capital One uses data mining to predict what customers might buy, and how the company can sell those products to them.
   b. Capital One uses data mining to predict what customers might buy and how the company can sell those products to them.

2. **a.** During the three-year lawsuit, pressure built to settle out of court.
   b. During the three-year lawsuit pressure built to settle out of court.

3. **a.** The music store, which had been in the Harper family for three generations, was finally sold to a conglomerate.
   b. The music store which had been in the Harper family for three generations was finally sold to a conglomerate.

4. **a.** After the fire, Hanson resolved to build a bigger better bottling plant.
   b. After the fire, Hanson resolved to build a bigger, better bottling plant.

5. **a.** Wild Oats, a chain of natural food grocery stores, uses kiosks to deliver nutrition information to customers.
   b. Wild Oats; a chain of natural food grocery stores; uses kiosks to deliver nutrition information to customers.

6. **a.** Management consultant Peter Drucker said "The aim of marketing is to know the customer so well that the product or service sells itself.
   b. Management consultant Peter Drucker said, "The aim of marketing is to know the customer so well that the product or service sells itself."

7. **a.** Companies use a wide variety of techniques - contests, displays, and giveaways, to name a few - to sell you things.
   b. Companies use a wide variety of techniques—contests, displays, and giveaways, to name a few—to sell you things.
   c. Companies use a wide variety of techniques—contests, displays, and giveaways to name a few—to sell you things.

8. **a.** Self-insurance plans are not subject to state regulation or premium taxes.
   b. Self insurance plans are not subject to state regulation or premium taxes.
   c. Selfinsurance plans are not subject to state regulation or premium taxes.

9. **a.** Because ours is a non-profit corporation, we don't pay federal taxes.
    b. Because ours is a nonprofit corporation, we don't pay federal taxes.

10. **a.** The decision-making process depends on a buyer's culture, social class, and self-image.
    b. The decision-making process depends on a buyer's culture, social class, and self image.
    c. The decision making process depends on a buyer's culture, social class, and self-image.

11. **a.** Situation factors also play a role in consumer decision-making.
    b. Situation factors also play a role in consumer decision making.

12. **a.** Joel told me, "I can't stop humming this song in my head, 'There's a Moon Out Tonight."
    b. Joel told me, "I can't stop humming this song in my head, 'There's a Moon Out Tonight'."
    c. Joel told me, "I can't stop humming this song in my head, 'There's a Moon Out Tonight.'"

13. **a.** An insider at Arthur Andersen said that "the fall of the accounting giant stemmed from a series of poor management decisions made over decades."
    b. An insider at Arthur Andersen said that, "The fall of the accounting giant stemmed from a series of poor management decisions made over decades."

14. **a.** Have you read Jason Zein's article "Measuring the Internet?"
    b. Have you read Jason Zein's article "Measuring the Internet"?

15. **a.** According to Jamba Juice founder Kirk Peron, "jamba" is a West African word meaning *to celebrate.*
    b. According to Jamba Juice founder Kirk Peron, *jamba* is a West African word meaning "to celebrate."
    c. According to Jamba Juice founder Kirk Peron, "jamba" is a West African word meaning to celebrate.

3.0 Mechanics

The most obvious and least tolerable mistakes that a business writer makes are probably those related to grammar and punctuation. However, a number of small details, known as writing mechanics, demonstrate the writer's polish and reflect on the company's professionalism.

3.1 Capitals

Capitals are used at the beginning of certain word groups:

■ **Complete sentence:**
Before hanging up, he said, "*We'll* meet here on Wednesday at noon."

■ **Formal statement following a colon:**
She has a favorite motto: Where there's a will, there's a way. (Otherwise, the first word after a colon should not be capitalized—see Section 2.5.)

■ **Phrase used as sentence:**
Absolutely not!

■ **Quoted sentence embedded in another sentence:**
Scot said, "Nobody was here during lunch hour except me."

■ **List of items set off from text:**
Three preliminary steps are involved:
  Design review
  Budgeting
  Scheduling

Capitalize proper adjectives and proper nouns (the names of particular persons, places, and things):

Darrell Greene lived in a Victorian mansion.

We sent Ms. Larson an application form, informing her that not all applicants are interviewed.

Let's consider opening a branch in the West, perhaps at the west end of Tucson, Arizona.

As office buildings go, the Kinney Building is a pleasant setting for TDG Office Equipment.

Ms. Larson's name is capitalized because she is a particular applicant, whereas the general term *applicant* is left uncapitalized. Likewise, *West* is capitalized when it refers to a particular place but not when it means a direction. In the same way, *office* and *building* are not capitalized when they are general terms (common nouns), but they are capitalized when they are part of the title of a particular office or building (proper nouns).

Titles within families, governments, or companies may also be capitalized:

I turned down Uncle David when he offered me a job, since I wouldn't be comfortable working for one of my relatives.

We've never had a president quite like President Sweeney.

People's titles are capitalized when they are used in addressing a person, especially in a formal context. They are not usually capitalized, however, when they are used merely to identify the person:

Address the letter to Chairperson Anna Palmer.

I wish to thank Chairperson Anna Palmer for her assistance.

Please deliver these documents to board chairperson Anna Palmer.

Anna Palmer, chairperson of the board, took the podium.

Also capitalize titles if they are used by themselves in addressing a person:

Thank you, Doctor, for your donation.

Always capitalize the first word of the salutation and complimentary close of a letter:

Dear Mr. Andrews: *Yours* very truly,

The names of organizations are capitalized, of course; so are the official names of their departments and divisions. However, do not use capitals when referring in general terms to a department or division, especially one in another organization:

> Route this memo to Personnel.
>
> Larry Tien was transferred to the Microchip Division.
>
> Will you be enrolled in the Psychology Department?
>
> Someone from the engineering department at EnerTech stopped by the booth.
>
> Our production department has reorganized for efficiency.
>
> Send a copy to their school of business administration.

Capitalization is unnecessary when using a word like *company, corporation,* or *university* alone:

> The corporation plans to issue 50,000 shares of common stock.

Likewise, the names of specific products are capitalized, although the names of general product types are not:

> Compaq computer   Tide laundry detergent

One problem that often arises in writing about places is the treatment of two or more proper nouns of the same type. When the common word comes before the specific names, it is capitalized; when it comes after the specific names, it is not:

> Lakes Ontario and Huron
>
> Allegheny and Monongahela rivers

The names of languages, races, and ethnic groups are capitalized: *Japanese, Caucasian, Hispanic.* But racial terms that denote only skin color are not capitalized: *black, white.*

When referring to the titles of books, articles, magazines, newspapers, reports, movies, and so on, you should capitalize the first and last words and all nouns, pronouns, adjectives, verbs, adverbs, and prepositions and conjunctions with five letters or more. Except for the first and last words, do not capitalize articles:

> *Economics During the Great War*
>
> "An Investigation into the Market for Long-Distance Services"
>
> "What Successes Are Made Of"

When *the* is part of the official name of a newspaper or magazine, it should be treated this way too: *The Wall Street Journal.*

References to specific pages, paragraphs, lines, and the like are not capitalized: *page 73, line 3.* However, in most other numbered or lettered references, the identifying term is capitalized: *Chapter 4, Serial No. 382-2203, Item B-11.*

Finally, the names of academic degrees are capitalized when they follow a person's name but are not capitalized when used in a general sense:

> I received a bachelor of science degree.
>
> Thomas Whitelaw, Doctor of Philosophy, will attend.

Similarly, general courses of study are not capitalized, but the names of specific classes are:

> She studied accounting as an undergraduate.
>
> She is enrolled in Accounting 201.

3.2 Underscores and Italics

Usually a line typed underneath a word or phrase either provides emphasis or indicates the title of a book, magazine, or newspaper. If possible, use italics instead of an underscore. Italics (or underlining) should also be used for defining terms and for discussing words as words:

> In this report *net sales* refers to after-tax sales dollars.
>
> The word *building* is a common noun and should not be capitalized.

3.3 Abbreviations

Abbreviations are used heavily in tables, charts, lists, and forms. They're used sparingly in prose paragraphs, however. Here are some abbreviations often used in business writing:

Abbreviation	Full Term
b/l	bill of lading
ca.	circa (about)
dol., dols.	dollar, dollars
etc.	et cetera (and so on)
FDIC	Federal Deposit Insurance Corporation
Inc.	Incorporated
L.f.	Ledger folio
Ltd.	Limited
mgr.	manager
NSF or N/S	not sufficient funds
P&L or P/L	profit and loss
reg.	regular
whsle.	wholesale

One way to handle an abbreviation that you want to use throughout a document is to spell it out the first time you use it, follow it with the abbreviation in parentheses, and then use the abbreviation in the remainder of the document.

Because *etc.* contains a word meaning "and," never write *and etc.* In fact, try to limit your use of such abbreviations to tables and parenthetical material.

3.4 Numbers

Numbers may be correctly handled many ways in business writing, so follow company style. In the absence of a set style, however, generally spell out all numbers from one to nine and use arabic numerals for the rest.

There are some exceptions to this general rule. For example, never begin a sentence with a numeral:

> *Twenty* of us produced *641* units per week in the first *12* weeks of the year.

Use numerals for the numbers one through ten if they're in the same list as larger numbers:

Our weekly quota rose from *9* to *15* to *27.*

Use numerals for percentages, time of day (except with *o'clock*), dates, and (in general) dollar amounts.

Our division is responsible for *7* percent of total sales.

The meeting is scheduled for *8:30* A.M. on August *2.*

Add *$3* for postage and handling.

Use a comma in numbers expressing thousands (*1,257*), unless your company specifies another style. When dealing with numbers in the millions and billions, combine words and figures: *7.3 million, 2 billion.*

When writing dollar amounts, use a decimal point only if cents are included. In lists of two or more dollar amounts, use the decimal point either for all or for none:

He sent two checks, one for *$67.92* and one for *$90.00.*

When two numbers fall next to each other in a sentence, use figures for the number that is largest, most difficult to spell, or part of a physical measurement; use words for the other:

I have learned to manage a classroom of 30 twelve-year-olds.

She's won a bonus for selling 24 thirty-volume sets.

You'll need twenty 3-inch bolts.

In addresses, all street numbers except *One* are in figures. So are suite and room numbers and ZIP codes. For street names that are numbered, practice varies so widely that you should use the form specified on an organization's letterhead or in a reliable directory. All of the following examples are correct:

One Fifth Avenue   297 Ninth Street
1839 44th Street   11026 West 78 Place

Telephone numbers are always expressed in figures. Parentheses may separate the area code from the rest of the number, but a slash or a dash may be used instead, especially if the entire phone number is enclosed in parentheses:

(602) 382-8329   (602/382-8329)   602-382-8329

Percentages are always expressed in figures. The word *percent* is used in most cases, but *%* may be used in tables, forms, and statistical writing.

Physical measurements such as distance, weight, and volume are also often expressed in figures: *9 kilometers, 5 feet 3 inches, 7 pounds 10 ounces.*

Ages are usually expressed in words—except when a parenthetical reference to age follows someone's name:

Mrs. Margaret Sanderson is seventy-two.

Mrs. Margaret Sanderson, 72, swims daily.

Also, ages expressed in years and months are treated like physical measurements that combine two units of measure: *5 years 6 months.*

Decimal numbers are always written in figures. In most cases, add a zero to the left of the decimal point if the number is less than one and does not already start with a zero:

1.38   .07   0.2

In a series of related decimal numbers with at least one number greater than one, make sure that all numbers smaller than one have a zero to the left of the decimal point: *1.20, 0.21, 0.09.* Also, express all decimal numbers in a series to the same number of places by adding zeroes at the end:

The responses were Yes, 37.2 percent; No, 51.0; Not Sure, 11.8.

Simple fractions are written in words, but more complicated fractions are expressed in figures or, if easier to read, in figures and words:

two-thirds   9/32   2 hundredths

A combination of whole numbers and a fraction should always be written in figures. Note that a hyphen is used to separate the fraction from the whole number when a slash is used for the fraction: *2-11/16.*

3.5 Word Division

In general, avoid dividing words at the ends of lines. When you must do so, follow these rules:

- Don't divide one-syllable words (such as *since, walked,* and *thought*); abbreviations (*mgr.*); contractions (*isn't*); or numbers expressed in numerals (*117,500*).
- Divide words between syllables, as specified in a dictionary or word-division manual.
- Make sure that at least three letters of the divided word are moved to the second line: *sin-cerely* instead of *sincere-ly.*
- Do not end a page or more than three consecutive lines with hyphens.
- Leave syllables consisting of a single vowel at the end of the first line (*impedi-ment* instead of *imped-iment*), except when the single vowel is part of a suffix such as *-able, -ible, -ical,* or *-ity* (*re-spons-ible* instead of *re-sponsi-ble*).
- Divide between double letters (*tomor-row*), except when the root word ends in double letters (*call-ing* instead of *cal-ling*).
- Wherever possible, divide hyphenated words at the hyphen only: instead of *anti-inde-pendence,* use *anti-independence.*

Practice Session: Mechanics

Circle the letter of the preferred choice in each of the following groups of sentences.

1. **a.** When you are in New York City for the sales meeting, be sure to visit the art deco Chrysler Building.
   b. When you are in New York city for the sales meeting, be sure to visit the Art Deco Chrysler building.
   c. When you are in New York City for the sales meeting, be sure to visit the Art Deco Chrysler Building.

2. **a.** We plan to expand our national operations to the west, as well as the south.
   b. We plan to expand our national operations to the West, as well as the South.
   c. We plan to expand our national operations to the west, as well as the South.

3. **a.** Lee Marrs, who is President of Lee Marrs Designs, has been chosen to revamp our website.
   b. Lee Marrs, who is president of Lee Marrs Designs, has been chosen to revamp our website.
   c. Lee Marrs, who is President of Lee Marrs Designs, has been chosen to revamp our Website.

4. **a.** There's one thing we know for sure: Having a good idea doesn't guarantee success.
   b. There's one thing we know for sure: having a good idea doesn't guarantee success.

5. **a.** Be sure to order manila envelopes in all sizes: 9″ × 12″, 11″, 14″, etc.
   b. Be sure to order manila envelopes in all sizes: 9″ × 12″, 11″, 14″ and etc.

6. **a.** The traditional trading period for U.S. stock exchanges is 9:30 A.M. to 4 o'clock P.M.
   b. The traditional trading period for U.S. stock exchanges is 9:30 A.M. to 4 P.M.
   c. The traditional trading period for U.S. stock exchanges is 9:30 A.M. to 4:00 P.M.

7. **a.** The number of members on the board of directors has been reduced from 13 to nine.
   b. The number of members on the board of directors has been reduced from 13 to 9.

8. **a.** The CDs are priced at $15, $12.95, and $11.00.
   b. The CDs are priced at $15.00, $12.95, and $11.00.
   c. The CDs are priced at $15, $12.95, and $11.

9. **a.** Twenty people have signed up for the spreadsheet software class, but there is room for 25.
   b. 20 people have signed up for the spreadsheet software class, but there is room for 25.

10. **a.** The best way to divide the word *sincerely* is "sin-cerely."
    b. The best way to divide the word *sincerely* is "sincere-ly."

4.0 Vocabulary

Using the right word in the right place is a crucial skill in business communication. However, many pitfalls await the unwary.

4.1 Frequently Confused Words

Because the following sets of words sound similar, be careful not to use one when you mean to use the other:

Word	Meaning
accede	to comply with
exceed	to go beyond
accept	to take
except	to exclude
access	admittance
excess	too much
advice	suggestion
advise	to suggest
affect	to influence
effect	the result
allot	to distribute
a lot	much or many
all ready	completely prepared
already	completed earlier
born	given birth to
borne	carried
capital	money; chief city
capitol	a government building
cite	to quote
sight	a view
site	a location
complement	complete amount; to go well with
compliment	expression of esteem; to flatter
corespondent	party in a divorce suit
correspondent	letter writer
council	a panel of people
counsel	advice; a lawyer
defer	to put off until later
differ	to be different
device	a mechanism
devise	to plan
die	to stop living; a tool
dye	to color
discreet	careful
discrete	separate
envelop	to surround
envelope	a covering for a letter
forth	forward
fourth	number four
holey	full of holes
holy	sacred
wholly	completely

Word	Meaning
human	of people
humane	kindly
incidence	frequency
incidents	events
instance	example
instants	moments

interstate	between states
intrastate	within a state
later	afterward
latter	the second of two
lead	a metal; to guide
led	guided
lean	to rest at an angle
lien	a claim
levee	embankment
levy	tax
loath	reluctant
loathe	to hate
loose	free; not tight
lose	to mislay
material	substance
materiel	equipment
miner	mineworker
minor	underage person
moral	virtuous; a lesson
morale	sense of well-being
ordinance	law
ordnance	weapons
overdo	to do in excess
overdue	past due
peace	lack of conflict
piece	a fragment
pedal	a foot lever
peddle	to sell
persecute	to torment
prosecute	to sue
personal	private
personnel	employees
precedence	priority
precedents	previous events
principal	sum of money; chief; main
principle	general rule
rap	to knock
wrap	to cover
residence	home
residents	inhabitants
right	correct
rite	ceremony
write	to form words on a surface

Word	**Meaning**
role	a part to play
roll	to tumble; a list
root	part of a plant
rout	to defeat
route	a traveler's way

shear	to cut
sheer	thin, steep
stationary	immovable
stationery	paper
than	as compared with
then	at that time
their	belonging to them
there	in that place
they're	they are
to	a preposition
too	excessively; also
two	the number
waive	to set aside
wave	a swell of water; a gesture
weather	atmospheric conditions
whether	if
who's	contraction of "who is" or "who has"
whose	possessive form of who

In the preceding list, only enough of each word's meaning is given to help you distinguish between the words in each group. Several meanings are left out entirely. For more complete definitions, consult a dictionary.

Practice Session: Confused Words
In the following sentences, underline the preferred choice within each set of parentheses.

1. If our bid is (*accepted, excepted*), we will begin the project in November.
2. This website offers some great (*advice, advise*) on setting up a new business.
3. How will the accounting scandal (*affect, effect*) Arthur Andersen's future?
4. Most of the costs of the project will be (*born, borne*) by the contractor.
5. In preparing the budget, we have to decide where best to invest our (*capital, capitol*).
6. Be sure to (*cite, site*) the sources for your data when you prepare your report.
7. The acquisition of LPC Group should (*compliment/ complement*) our other holdings.
8. Leo sought the (*council, counsel*) of his attorney before signing the contract.
9. I didn't have to be told to be (*discrete, discreet*) about the sexual harassment case.
10. When Jennings Hardware got behind in its debts, one of the creditors placed a (*lean, lien*) on its building.
11. Mr. Hathaway was (*loath, loathe*) to fire Elizabeth, but he had no choice.
12. To comply with local zoning (*ordinances, ordnances*), we had to replace our sign.
13. As a teenager, Gary Sassaman used to (*pedal, peddle*) newspapers in downtown Pittsburgh.
14. Business owners along El Cajon Boulevard have vowed to (*persecute, prosecute*) anyone caught painting graffiti on their buildings.

15. We don't know of any (*precedence, precedents*) for the exponential growth of sales for this kind of product.
16. The (*principle, principal*) reason for closing down operations was obsolete production equipment that was too expensive to replace.
17. It's hard to say what (*role, roll*) the downturn in the economy played in the failure of Seven Hills Distribution.
18. Sunbeam employees were shocked by new CEO Al Dunlap's (*shear, sheer*) ruthlessness in axing jobs and slashing costs.
19. Now that our area code has changed, we will need to order new (*stationary, stationery*).
20. The Rodriguez brothers couldn't decide (*weather, whether*) to form a partnership or establish a corporation.

4.2 Frequently Misused Words

The following words tend to be misused for reasons other than their sound. Reference books (including the *Random House College Dictionary,* revised edition; Follett's *Modern American Usage;* and Fowler's *Modern English Usage*) can help you with similar questions of usage.

a lot: When the writer means "many," *a lot* is always two separate words, never one.

correspond with: Use this phrase when you are talking about exchanging letters. Use *correspond to* when you mean "similar to." Use either *correspond with* or *correspond to* when you mean "relate to."

disinterested: This word means "fair, unbiased, having no favorites, impartial." If you mean "bored" or "not interested," use *uninterested.*

etc.: This abbreviated form of the Latin phrase *et cetera* means "and so on" or "and so forth." The current tendency among business writers is to use English rather than Latin.

imply/infer: Both refer to hints. Their great difference lies in who is acting. The writer implies; the reader infers, sees between the lines.

lay: This word is a transitive verb. Never use it for the intransitive *lie.* (See Section 1.3.3.)

less: Use *less* for uncountable quantities (such as amounts of water, air, sugar, and oil). Use *fewer* for countable quantities (such as numbers of jars, saws, words, pages, and humans). The same distinction applies to *much* and *little* (uncountable) versus *many* and *few* (countable).

like: Use *like* only when the word that follows is just a noun or a pronoun. Use *as* or *as if* when a phrase or clause follows:

> She looks like him.
>
> She did just as he had expected.
>
> It seems as if she had plenty of time.

many/much: See *less.*

regardless: The *less* ending is the negative part. No word needs two negative parts, so don't add *ir* (a negative prefix) to the beginning. There is no such word as *irregardless.*

to me/personally: Use these phrases only when personal reactions, apart from company policy, are being stated (not often the case in business writing).

try: Always follow with *to,* never *and.*

verbal: People in the business community who are careful with language frown on those who use *verbal* to mean "spoken" or "oral." Many others do say "verbal agreement." Strictly speaking, *verbal* means "of words" and therefore includes both spoken and written words. Follow company usage in this matter.

Practice Session: Misused Words

In the following sentences, underline the preferred choice within each set of parentheses.

1. My boss told me that I still have (*a lot, alot*) to learn.
2. The U.S. Congress corresponds (*to, with*) the British Parliament.
3. I tried to convince my co-workers to sign up for the stress-reduction program, but they all seemed (*uninterested, disinterested*).
4. When you say that the books have some discrepancies, are you (*inferring, implying*) that our accountant is embezzling from us?
5. From the auditor's silent stare, Margaret (*implied, inferred*) that the man was not amused by her jokes.
6. The report came out to (*less, fewer*) pages than we had originally anticipated.
7. Mr. Martens was treating Heather (*like, as if*) she had done something wrong.
8. You have to finish the job, (*irregardless, regardless*) of your loathing for it.
9. When talking to customers on the phone, try (*and, to*) be as pleasant as possible.
10. When making (*an oral, a verbal*) presentation, it's a good idea to make eye contact with your audience.

4.3 Frequently Misspelled Words

All of us, even the world's best spellers, sometimes have to check a dictionary for the spelling of some words. People who have never memorized the spelling of commonly used words must look up so many that they grow exasperated and give up on spelling words correctly.

Don't expect perfection, and don't surrender. If you can memorize the spelling of just the words listed here, you'll need the dictionary far less often, and you'll write with more confidence.

absence	comparative	fluctuation	necessary	rhythmical
absorption	competitor	forty	negligence	ridiculous
accessible	concede		negotiable	
accommodate	congratulations	gesture	newsstand	salable
accumulate	connoisseur	grievous	noticeable	secretary
achieve	consensus			seize
advantageous	convenient	haphazard	occurrence	separate
affiliated	convertible	harassment	omission	sincerely
aggressive	corroborate	holiday		succeed
alignment	criticism		parallel	suddenness
aluminum		illegible	pastime	superintendent
ambience	definitely	immigrant	peaceable	supersede
analyze	description	incidentally	permanent	surprise
apparent	desirable	indelible	perseverance	
appropriate	dilemma	independent	persistent	tangible
argument	disappear	indispensable	personnel	tariff
asphalt	disappoint	insistent	persuade	technique
assistant	disbursement	intermediary	possesses	tenant
asterisk	discrepancy	irresistible	precede	truly
auditor	dissatisfied		predictable	
	dissipate	jewelry	preferred	unanimous
bankruptcy		judgment	privilege	until
believable	eligible	judicial	procedure	
brilliant	embarrassing		proceed	vacillate
bulletin	endorsement	labeling	pronunciation	vacuum
	exaggerate	legitimate	psychology	vicious
calendar	exceed	leisure	pursue	
campaign	exhaust	license		
category	existence	litigation	questionnaire	
ceiling	extraordinary			
changeable		maintenance	receive	
clientele	fallacy	mathematics	recommend	
collateral	familiar	mediocre	repetition	
committee	flexible	minimum	rescind	

Practice Session: Misspelled Words

In the following sentences, underline the preferred choice within each set of parentheses.

1. We try to (*accomodate, accommodate*) any reasonable request from our customers.
2. You will need to (*analyse, analyze*) the sales data to determine which products to phase out.
3. Because the weather in Chicago is so (*changable, changeable*), the conference reception has a backup indoor venue.
4. The board reached a (*concensus, consensus*) on the new CEO.
5. It will be (*embarassing, embarrassing*) for the company if this information leaks out.
6. The auditors discovered the (*existance, existence*) of hidden accounts in foreign banks.
7. Every company should have a written sexual (*harassment, harrassment*) policy.
8. In today's book business, (*independant, independent*) publishers are having a tough time finding distribution.
9. Use your best (*judgment, judgement*) when choosing the paper for our new stationery.
10. The cost of a business (*licence, license, liscence*) varies from city to city.
11. With all the turmoil (*occuring, occurring*) in the stock market, we've decided to shift our investments toward real estate.
12. The marketing survey found that consumers (*prefered, preferred*) brand-name dog food over generic brands.
13. Because her cost-cutting measures saved the company millions of dollars, Carolyn Kelly (*received, recieved*) a raise and a promotion.
14. Please send (*separate, seperate*) invoices for the two projects.
15. My supervisor didn't need to be so (*vicious, viscious*) in his critique of my performance.

4.4 Transitional Words and Phrases

The following sentences don't communicate as well as they might because they lack a transitional word or phrase:

Production delays are inevitable. Our current lag time in filling orders is one month.

A semicolon between the two sentences would signal a close relationship between their meanings, but it wouldn't even hint at what that relationship is. Here are the sentences again, now linked by means of a semicolon, with a space for a transitional word or phrase:

Production delays are inevitable; _____, our current lag time in filling orders is one month.

Now read the sentence with *nevertheless* in the blank space. Now try *therefore, incidentally, in fact,* and *at any rate* in the blank. Each substitution changes the meaning of the sentence.

Here are some transitional words (called conjunctive adverbs) that will help you write more clearly:

accordingly	furthermore	moreover
anyway	however	otherwise
besides	incidentally	still
consequently	likewise	therefore
finally	meanwhile	

The following transitional phrases are used in the same way:

as a result	in other words
at any rate	in the second place
for example	on the other hand
in fact	to the contrary

When one of these words or phrases joins two independent clauses, it should be preceded by a semicolon and followed by a comma, as shown here:

The consultant recommended a complete reorganization; moreover, she suggested that we drop several products.

Practice Session Answers

Answers for Nouns: 1. City   2. Building / building   3. hotels   4. *t*'s / *i*'s   5. 1990s   6. shelves   7. specialties   8. cases   9. company's   10. editor-in-chief's   11. businesses'   12. passengers'   13. day's   14. Dallas's   15. Jones's

Answers for Pronouns: 1. me   2. she   3. him   4. We   5. me   6. its   7. his or her   8. Who   9. whom   10. Whom   11. her   12. him or her   13. her   14. its   15. Who   16. your   17. its   18. I   19. their   20. its

Answers for Verbs: 1. comes, want   2. knew   3. begun   4. lie   5. laid   6. sits   7. set   8. raise   9. was   10. is   11. is   12. are   13. is   14. is   15. represents   16. is   17. are   18. is   19. send   20. were

Answers for Adjectives and Adverbs: 1. least   2. better   3. worse   4. more competent   5. unique   6. well-written   7. well written   8. beautifully written   9. credit card   10. well   11. well   12. really   13. slowly   14. could hardly   15. more heavily

Answers for Prepositions, Conjunctions, and Articles: 1. a   2. b   3. a   4. b   5. b   6. a   7. b   8. a   9. b   10. a   11. b   12. b   13. a   14. a   15. a

Answers for Sentences: 1. a   2. b   3. b   4. c   5. c   6. b   7. c   8. c   9. a   10. c

Answers for Punctuation 1: 1. b   2. a   3. b   4. b   5. a   6. b   7. a   8. b   9. b   10. c

Answers for Punctuation 2: 1. b   2. a   3. a   4. b   5. a   6. b   7. b   8. a   9. b   10. a   11. b   12. c   13. a   14. b   15. b

Answers for Mechanics: 1. c   2. b   3. b   4. a   5. a   6. c   7. b   8. b   9. a   10. a

Answers for Confused Words: 1. accepted   2. advice   3. affect   4. borne   5. capital   6. cite   7. complement   8. counsel   9. discreet   10. lien   11. loath   12. ordinances   13. peddle   14. prosecute   15. precedents   16. principal   17. role   18. sheer   19. stationery   20. whether

Answers for Misused Words: 1. a lot   2. to   3. uninterested   4. implying   5. inferred   6. fewer   7. as if   8. regardless   9. to   10. an oral

Answers for Misspelled Words: 1. accommodate   2. analyze   3. changeable   4. consensus   5. embarrassing   6. existence   7. harassment   8. independent   9. judgment   10. license   11. occurring   12. preferred   13. received   14. separate   15. vicious

Chapter 1

1. Adapted from Doug Glass, "Escaping the Rut Is Good Idea for Hallmark Artists, Writers," Orange County Edition, *Los Angeles Times,* 6 June 1996, D-7; Gillian Flynn, "Sending a Quality of Life Message: Hallmark Cares," *Personnel Journal,* March 1996, 56; Karen Matthes, "Greetings from Hallmark," *HR Focus,* 70 (1 August 1993): 12.
2. "Interpersonal Skills Are Key in Office of the Future," *TMA Journal,* July–August 1999, 53.
3. Lillian H. Chaney and Jeanette S. Martin, *Intercultural Business Communications* (Upper Saddle River, N.J.: Prentice Hall, 2000), 1–2.
4. James M. Citrin and Thomas J. Neff, "Digital Leadership," *Strategy and Business,* First Quarter 2000, 42–50; Gary L. Neilson, Bruce A. Pasternack, and Albert J. Viscio, "Up the E-Organization," *Strategy and Business,* First Quarter 2000, 52–61.
5. Some material adapted from Courtland L. Bovée, John V. Thill, Marian Burk Wood, and George P. Dovel, *Management* (New York: McGraw-Hill, 1993), 537–538.
6. A. Thomas Young, "Ethics in Business: Business of Ethics," *Vital Speeches,* 15 September 1992, 725–730.
7. Philip C. Kolin, *Successful Writing at Work,* 6th ed. (Boston: Houghton Mifflin, 2001), 24–30.
8. David Grier, "Confronting Ethical Dilemmas: The View from Inside—A Practitioner's Perspective," *Vital Speeches,* 1 December 1989, 100–104.
9. Joseph L. Badaracco Jr., "Business Ethics: Four Spheres of Executive Responsibility," *California Management Review,* Spring 1992, 64–79; Kenneth Blanchard and Norman Vincent Peale, *The Power of Ethical Management* (1989; reprint, New York: Fawcett Crest, 1991), 7–17.
10. Blanchard and Peale, *The Power of Ethical Management,* 7–17; Badaracco, "Business Ethics: Four Spheres of Executive Responsibility," 64–79.
11. Larry A. Samovar and Richard E. Porter, "Basic Principles of Intercultural Communication," in *Intercultural Communication: A Reader,* 6th ed., edited by Larry A. Samovar and Richard E. Porter (Belmont, Calif.: Wadsworth, 1991), 12.
12. Gus Tyler, "Tokyo Signs the Paychecks," *New York Times Book Review,* 12 August 1990, 7.
13. Otto Kreisher, "Annapolis Has a New Attitude Toward Sexual Harassment," *San Diego Union,* 30 July 1990, A-6.
14. Linda Beamer, "Teaching English Business Writing to Chinese-Speaking Business Students," *Bulletin of the Association for Business Communication* 57, no. 1 (1994): 12–18.
15. Edward T. Hall, "Context and Meaning," in *Intercultural Communication,* edited by Samovar and Porter, 46–55.
16. Beamer, "Teaching English Business Writing to Chinese-Speaking Business Students."
17. Charley H. Dodd, *Dynamics of Intercultural Communication,* 3d ed. (Dubuque, Iowa: Brown, 1991), 69–70.
18. James Wilfong and Toni Seger, *Taking Your Business Global* (Franklin Lakes, N.J.: Career Press, 1997), 277–278.
19. Philip R. Harris and Robert T. Moran, *Managing Cultural Differences,* 3d ed. (Houston, Gulf, 1991), 260.
20. Guo-Ming Chen and William J. Starosta, *Foundations of Intercultural Communication* (Boston: Allyn & Bacon, 1998), 288–289.
21. Sharon Ruhly, *Intercultural Communication,* 2d ed., MOD-COM (Modules in Speech Communication) (Chicago: Science Research Associates, 1982), 14.
22. Chen and Starosta, *Foundations of Intercultural Communication,* 39–40.
23. Richard W. Brislin, "Prejudice in Intercultural Communication," in *Intercultural Communication,* edited by Samovar and Porter, 366–370.
24. Mona Casady and Lynn Wasson, "Written Communication Skills of International Business Persons," *Bulletin of the Association for Business Communication* 57, no. 4 (1994): 36–40.
25. Jensen J. Zhao and Calvin Parks, "Self-Assessment of Communication Behavior: An Experiential Learning Exercise for Intercultural Business Success," *Business Communication Quarterly* 58, no. 1 (1995): 20–26; Dodd, *Dynamics of Intercultural Communication,* 142–143, 297–299; Stephen P. Robbins, *Organizational Behavior,* 6th ed. (Paramus, N.J.: Prentice Hall, 1993), 345.
26. "When Rumors Disrupt Your Staff," *Working Woman,* October 1992, 36.

Chapter 2

1. Michael H. Mescon, Courtland L. Bovée, and John V. Thill, *Business Today* (Upper Saddle River, N.J.: Prentice Hall, 1999), 203.

2. Stephen P. Robbins, *Essentials of Organizational Behavior,* 6th ed. (Upper Saddle River, N.J.: Prentice Hall, 2000), 98.

3. Larry Cole and Michael Cole, "Why Is the Teamwork Buzz Word Not Working?" *Communication World,* February/March 1999, 29; Patricia Buhler, "Managing in the 90s: Creating Flexibility in Today's Workplace," *Supervision,* January 1997, 24+; Allison W. Amason, Allen C. Hochwarter, Wayne A. Thompson, and Kenneth R. Harrison, "Conflict: An Important Dimension in Successful Management Teams," *Organizational Dynamics,* Autumn 1995, 20+.

4. "Better Meetings Benefit Everyone: How to Make Yours More Productive," *Working Communicator Bonus Report,* July 1998.

5. William C. Waddell and Thomas A. Rosko, "Conducting an Effective Off-Site Meeting," *Management Review,* February 1993, 40–44.

6. "Better Meetings Benefit Everyone."

7. Kathy E. Gill, "Board Primer: Parliamentary Procedure," *Association Management,* 1993, L-39.

8. Bob Lamons, "Good Listeners Are Better Communicators," *Marketing News,* 11 September 1995, 13+; Phillip Morgan and H. Kent Baker, "Building a Professional Image: Improving Listening Behavior," *Supervisory Management,* November 1985, 35–36.

9. Robyn D. Clarke, "Do You Hear What I Hear?" *Black Enterprise,* May 1998, 129; Dot Yandle, "Listening to Understand," *Pryor Report Management Newsletter Supplement* 15, no. 8 (August 1998): 13.

10. Sherwyn P. Morreale and Courtland L. Bovée, *Excellence in Public Speaking* (Orlando, Fla.: Harcourt Brace, 1998), 72–76; Lyman K. Steil, Larry L. Barker, and Kittie W. Watson, *Effective Listening: Key to Your Success* (Reading, Mass.: Addison-Wesley, 1983), 21–22.

11. Patrick J. Collins, *Say It with Power and Confidence* (Upper Saddle River, N.J.: Prentice Hall, 1997), 40–45.

12. Collins, *Say It with Power and Confidence,* 40–45.

13. Augusta M. Simon, "Effective Listening: Barriers to Listening in a Diverse Business Environment," *Bulletin of the Association for Business Communication* 54, no. 3 (September 1991): 73–74.

14. Jo Ind, "Hanging on the Telephone," *Birmingham Post,* 28 July 1999, PS10.

15. Lin Walker, *Telephone Techniques,* (New York: Amacom, 1998), 46–47.

16. Ind, "Hanging on the Telephone"; Dorothy Neal, *Telephone Techniques,* 2d ed. (New York: Glencoe McGraw-Hill, 1998), 31; Walker, *Telephone Techniques,* 46–47.

17. Ind, "Hanging on the Telephone"; Neal, *Telephone Techniques*; Walker, *Telephone Techniques*; Jeannie Davis, *Beyond "Hello"* (Aurora, Colo.: Now Hear This, Inc., 2000), 2–3.

18. Susan Ford, "Voice Messaging Systems," *Toledo Business Journal,* 1 November 2001, 26.

19. Mike Bransby, "Voice Mail Makes a Difference," *Journal of Business Strategy,* January–February 1990, 7–10.

20. Bransby, "Voice Mail Makes a Difference."

21. "Ten Steps to Caller-Friendly Voice Mail," *Managing Office Technology,* January 1995, 25; Rhonda Finniss, "Voice Mail: Tips for a Positive Impression," *Administrative Assistant's Update,* August 2001, 5; "How to Get the Most out of Voice Mail," *CPA Journal,* February 2000, 11.

22. Ruth Davidhizar and Ruth Shearer, "The Effective Voice Mail Message," *Hospital Material Management Quarterly,* 45–49; "How to Get the Most out of Voice Mail."

23. Davidhizar and Shearer, "The Effective Voice Mail Message."

24. Adapted from David A. Victor, *International Business Communication* (New York: HarperCollins, 1992); David Wallace, "Mind Your Manners," *World Trade,* October 1992, 52, 54–55; Hannele Duvfa, "Innocents Abroad: The Politics of Cross-Cultural Communication," *Communication and Discourse Across Cultures and Languages,* 1991, 73–89; M. Katherine Glover, "Do's & Taboos: Cultural Aspects of International Business," *Business America,* 13 August 1990, 2–6; C. Barnum and N. Woniansky, "Taking Cues from Body Language," *Management Review,* June 1989, 59–60.

25. Dale G. Leathers, *Successful Nonverbal Communication: Principles and Applications* (New York: Macmillan, 1986), 19.

26. Gerald H. Graham, Jeanne Unrue, and Paul Jennings, "The Impact of Nonverbal Communication in Organizations: A Survey of Perceptions," *Journal of Business Communication* 28, no. 1 (Winter 1991): 45–62.

27. Graham, Unrue, and Jennings, "The Impact of Nonverbal Communication in Organizations: A Survey of Perceptions."

Chapter 3

1. Adapted from Home Depot's website [accessed 8 March 2000] www.homedepot.com; Bernie Marcus and Arthur Blank with Bob Andelman, *Built from Scratch* (New York: Random House, 1999), 105, 110, 125, 135–137, 142, 149, 155–161, 178, 205, 216, 240–241, 255–258, 280, 287–289, 313; Carlton P. McNamara, "Making Human Capital More Productive," *Business and Economic Review,* October–December 1999, 10–13; Sarah Rose, "Building a Powerhouse," *Money,* December 1999, 62–64; Chris Roush, *Inside Home Depot* (New York: McGraw-Hill, 1999), 5–6, 12, 29, 31–35; 89, 101–108, 115, 141, 213–215, 221; Robert S. Salomon Jr., "Reinventing Retail," *Forbes,* 19 October 1998, 171; and Bruce Upin, "Profit in a Big Orange Box," *Forbes,* 24 January 2000, 122–127.

2. Sanford Kaye, "Writing Under Pressure," *Soundview Executive Book Summaries* 10, no. 12, part 2 (December 1988): 1–8.

3. Peter Bracher, "Process, Pedagogy, and Business Writing," *Journal of Business Communication* 24, no. 1 (Winter 1987): 43–50.

4. Mahalingam Subbiah, "Adding a New Dimension to the Teaching of Audience Analysis: Cultural Awareness," *IEEE Transactions on Professional Communication* 35, no. 1 (March 1992): 14–19; Ronald E. Dulek, John S. Fielden,

and John S. Hill, "International Communication: An Executive Primer," *Business Horizons*, January–February 1991, 20–25; Dwight W. Stevenson, "Audience Analysis Across Cultures," *Journal of Technical Writing and Communication* 13, no. 4 (1983): 319–330.

5. Laurey Berk and Phillip G. Clampitt, "Finding the Right Path in the Communication Maze," *IABC Communication World*, October 1991, 28–32.

6. Berk and Clampitt, "Finding the Right Path in the Communication Maze."

7. Raymond M. Olderman, *10 Minute Guide to Business Communication* (New York: Alpha Books, 1997), 19–20.

8. Mohan R. Limaye and David A. Victor, "Cross-Cultural Business Communication Research: State of the Art and Hypotheses for the 1990s," *Journal of Business Communication* 28, no. 3 (Summer 1991): 277–299.

9. Elizabeth Blackburn and Kelly Belanger, "You-Attitude and Positive Emphasis: Testing Received Wisdom in Business Communication," *Bulletin of the Association for Business Communication* 56, no. 2 (June 1993): 1–9.

10. Annette N. Shelby and N. Lamar Reinsch Jr., "Positive Emphasis and You Attitude: An Empirical Study," *Journal of Business Communication* 32, no. 4 (1995): 303–322.

11. Lisa Taylor, "Communicating About People with Disabilities: Does the Language We Use Make a Difference?" *Bulletin of the Association for Business Communication* 53, no. 3 (September 1990): 65–67.

Chapter 4

1. Court Bovée, John Thill, and Barbara Schatzman, "Communication Close-Up," in *Business Communication Today*, 7th ed. (Upper Saddle River, N.J.: Prentice Hall, 2002), 106.

2. Susan Hall and Theresa Tiggeman, "Getting the Big Picture: Writing to Learn in a Finance Class," *Business Communication Quarterly* 58, no. 1 (1995): 12–15.

3. Carol S. Mull, "Orchestrate Your Ideas," *Toastmaster*, February 1987, 19.

4. Ernest Thompson, "Some Effects of Message Structure on Listener's Comprehension," *Speech Monographs* 34 (March 1967): 51–57.

5. Mary A. DeVries, *Internationally Yours* (Boston: Houghton Mifflin, 1994), 61.

6. Randolph H. Hudson, Gertrude M. McGuire, and Bernard J. Selzler, *Business Writing: Concepts and Applications* (Los Angeles: Roxbury, 1983), 79–82.

7. Peter Crow, "Plain English: What Counts Besides Readability?" *Journal of Business Communication* 25, no. 1 (Winter 1988): 87–95.

8. Portions of this section are adapted from Courtland L. Bovée, *Techniques of Writing Business Letters, Memos, and Reports* (Sherman Oaks, Calif.: Banner Books International, 1978), 13–90.

9. Robert Hartwell Fiske, *Thesaurus of Alternatives to Worn-Out Words and Phrases* (Cincinnati: Writer's Digest Books, 1994), 171.

10. Alinda Drury, "Evaluating Readability," *IEEE Transactions on Professional Communication* PC-28 (December 1985): 12.

Chapter 5

1. Courtland L. Bovée, John V. Thill, Barbara E. Schatzman, *Business Communication Today* (Upper Saddle River, N.J., 2003), 140.

2. William Zinsser, *On Writing Well*, 5th ed. (New York: HarperCollins, 1994), 126.

3. Zinsser, *On Writing Well*, 9.

4. "Message Lost in Some Memos," *USA Today*, 25 March 1987, 1A.

5. Zinsser, *On Writing Well*, 7, 17.

6. Mary A. DeVries, *Internationally Yours* (Boston: Houghton Mifflin, 1994), 160.

7. Patsy Nichols, "Desktop Packaging," *Bulletin of the Association for Business Communication* 54, no. 1 (March 1991): 43-45; Raymond W. Beswick, "Designing Documents for Legibility," *Bulletin of the Association for Business Communication* 50, no. 4 (December 1987): 34–35.

8. "The Process Model of Document Design," *IEEE Transactions on Professional Communication* PC-24, no. 4 (December 1981): 176–178.

9. William Wresch, Donald Pattow, and James Gifford, *Writing for the Twenty-First Century: Computers and Research Writing* (New York: McGraw-Hill, 1988), 192–211; Melissa E. Barth, *Strategies for Writing with the Computer* (New York: McGraw-Hill 1988), 108–109, 140, 172–177.

Chapter 6

1. Courtland L. Bovée and John V. Thill, *Business Communication Today*, 6th ed. (Upper Saddle River, N.J., Prentice Hall, 2003), 90–91.

2. Mary A. DeVries, *Internationally Yours* (Boston: Houghton Mifflin, 1994), 168; Susan Benjamin, *Words at Work* (Reading, Mass.: Addison-Wesley, 1997), 61, 140–141.

3. Jill H. Ellsworth and Matthew V. Ellsworth, *The Internet Business Book* (New York: Wiley, 1994), 91.

4. Lance Cohen, "How to Improve Your E-Mail Messages," [accessed 25 July 2002] http://galaxy.einet/galaxy/Business-and-Commerce/Management/Communications/How_to_Improve_Your_Email.html.

5. Renee Bo Horowitz and Marion G. Barchilon, "Stylistic Guidelines for E-Mail," *IEEE Transactions on Professional Communication* 37, no. 4 (December 1994): 207–212; Cohen, "How to Improve Your E-Mail Messages."

6. David Angell and Brent Heslop, *The Elements of E-Mail Style* (Reading, Mass: Addison-Wesley, 1994), 20.

7. Horowitz and Barchilon, "Stylistic Guidelines for E-Mail"; Angell and Heslop, *The Elements of E-Mail Style*, 22.

8. Benjamin, *Words at Work*, 61, 140–141.

9. Adapted from "How Microsoft Reviews Suppliers," *Fast Company*, Issue 17 [accessed 3 September 2003] http://fastcompany.com/online/17/msoftreviews.html.

10. Adapted from Carl Quintanilla, "Work Week: Pizza, Pizza," *Wall Street Journal,* 18 August 1998, A1.

11. Adapted from Davide Dukcevich, "Instant Business: Retailer Lands' End Profits from Online Chat," Forbes.com, Special to ABCNEWS.com, 29 July 2002 [accessed 21 July 2003] abcnews.go.com/sections/business/DailyNews/forbes_landsend.com; Lands' End website [accessed 5 December 2003] www.landsend.com; Forbes.com staff, "Instant Messaging at Work," Forbes.com, 26 July 2002 [accessed 21 July 2003] www.forbes.com/2002/07/23/0723im/html; Tischelle George and Sandra Swanson with Christopher T. Heun, "Not Just Kid Stuff," *InformationWeek,* 3 September 2001 [accessed 21 July 2003] www.informationweek.com /story/IWK20010830S0030.

Chapter 7

1. Courtland L. Bovée, John V. Thill, and Barbara E. Schatzman, *Business Communication Today* (Upper Saddle River, N.J.: Prentice Hall, 2003), 184.

2. Daniel P. Finkelman and Anthony R. Goland, "Customers Once Can Be Customers for Life," *Information Strategy: The Executive's Journal,* Summer 1990, 5–9.

3. Donna Larcen, "Authors Share the Words of Condolence," *Los Angeles Times,* December 20, 1991, E11.

4. Adapted from Bruce Frankel and Alex Tresniowski, "Stormy Skies," *People Weekly,* 31 July 2000, 112–115.

5. Adapted from Keith H. Hammonds, "Difference Is Power," *Fast Company,* 36, 258 [accessed 11 July 2000] www.fastcompany.com/online/36/power.html; Terri Morrison, Wayne Conaway, and George A. Borden, *Kiss, Bow, or Shake Hands* (Avon, Mass.: Adams Media Corp., 1994, 1–5.

6. Adapted from Floorgraphics website [accessed 18 June 2001] www.floorgraphics.com; John Grossman, "It's an Ad, Ad, Ad, Ad World," *Inc.,* March 2000, 23–26; David Wellman, "Floor 'Toons," *Supermarket Business,* 15 November 1999, 47; "Floorshow," *Dallas Morning News,* 4 September 1998, 11D.

7. Adapted from Jamba Juice website [accessed 19 July 2001] www.jambacareers.com/benefits.html; Brenda Paik Sunoo, "Blending a Successful Workforce," *Workforce,* March 2000, 44–48; Michael Adams, "Kirk Perron: Jamba Juice," *Restaurant Business,* 15 March 1999, 38; "Live in a Blender," *Restaurant Business,* 1 December 2000, 48–50; David Goll, "Jamba Juices Up 24-Hour Fitness Clubs," *East Bay Business Times,* 30 June 2000, 6.

8. Adapted from George Anders, "Voyage to the New Economy," *Fast Company,* 36, 142 [accessed 11 July 2000] www.fastcompany.com/online/36/migration2.html; Pamela Druger, "Stop the Insanity!" *Fast Company,* 36, 240 [accessed 11 July 2000] www.fastcompany.com/online/36/stopinsanity.html; Anna Muoio, "Should I Go .Com?" *Fast Company,* 36, 164 [accessed 11 July 2000] www.fastcompany.com/online/36/stein.html.

9. Adapted from Dylan Tweney, "The Defogger: Slim Down That Homepage," *Business 2.0,* 13 July 2001 [accessed 1 August 2001] www.business2.com/articles/web/0,1653,16483,FF.html.

10. Adapted from Barbara Carton, "Farmers Begin Harvesting Satellite Data to Boost Yields," *Wall Street Journal,* 11 July 1996, B4.

11. Adapted from LifeSketch.com website [accessed 24 July 2000], www.lifesketch.com.

12. Adapted from Bernard Weinraub, "New Harry Potter Book Becoming a Publishing Phenomenon," *New York Times,* 3 July 2000 [accessed 12 July 2000] www.nytimes.com/library/books/070300potter-parties.html; Laura Miller, "Pottermania at Midnight," *Salon.com,* 8 July 2000 [accessed 12 July 2000] www.salon.com/books/features/2000/07/08/potter/; David D. Kirkpatrick, "Harry Potter Magic Halts Bedtime for Youngsters," *New York Times,* 9 July 2000 [accessed 12 July 2000] www.nytimes.com/library/books/070900potter-goblet.html; David D. Kirkpatrick, "Vanishing Off the Shelves," *New York Times,* 10 July 2000 [accessed 10 July 2000] www.nytimes.com/library/books/071000rowling-goblet.html.

13. Adapted from Carol Vinzant, "They Want You Back," *Fortune,* 2 October 2000, 271–272; Stephanie Armour, "Companies Recruiting Former Employees," *USA Today,* 2 February 2000, B1.

14. "Entrepreneurs Across America," *Entrepreneur Magazine Online* [accessed 12 June 1997] www.entrepreneurmag.com/entmag/50states5.hts#top.

15. Adapted from Lisa DiCarlo, "IBM Gets the Message—Instantly," Forbes.com, 7 July 2002 [accessed 22 July 2003] www.forbes.com/home/2002/07/0723ibm.html; "IBM Introduces Breakthrough Messaging Technology for Customers and Business Partners," M2 Presswire, 19 February 2003 [accessed 24 July 2003] www.proquest.com; "IBM and America Online Team for Instant Messaging Pilot," M2Presswire, 4 February 2003 [accessed 24 July 2003] www.proquest.com.

Chapter 8

1. Courtland Bovée, John Thill, and Barbara Schatzman, "Communication Close-Up," in *Business Communication Today,* 7th ed. (Upper Saddle River, N.J.: Prentice Hall, 2002), 226.

2. Mark H. McCormack, *On Communicating* (Los Angeles: Dove Books, 1998), 87.

3. Curtis Sittenfeld, "Good Ways to Deliver Bad News," *Fast Company,* April 1999, 58–60.

4. Ram Subramanian, Robert G. Insley, and Rodney D. Blackwell, "Performance and Readability: A Comparison of Annual Reports of Profitable and Unprofitable Corporations," *Journal of Business Communication* 30, no. 2 (1993): 49–61.

5. *Techniques for Communicators* (Chicago: Lawrence Ragan Communication, 1995), 18.

6. Maura Dolan and Stuart Silverstein, "Court Broadens Liability for Job References," *Los Angeles Times,* 28 January 1997, A1, A11; Frances A. McMorris, "Ex-Bosses Face Less

Peril Giving Honest Job References," *Wall Street Journal,* 8 July 1996, B1, B8.

7. Thomas S. Brice and Marie Waung, "Applicant Rejection Letters: Are Businesses Sending the Wrong Message?" *Business Horizons,* March–April 1995, 59–62.

8. Gwendolyn N. Smith, Rebecca F. Nolan, and Yong Dai, "Job-Refusal Letters: Readers' Affective Responses to Direct and Indirect Organizational Plans," *Business Communication Quarterly* 59, no. 1 (1996): 67–73; Brice and Waung, "Applicant Rejection Letters."

9. Korey A. Wilson, "Put Rejection Up-Front," *Black Enterprise,* November 1999, 69.

10. Judi Brownell, "The Performance Appraisal Interviews: A Multipurpose Communication Assignment," *Bulletin of the Association for Business Communication* 57, no. 2 (1994): 11–21.

11. Brownell, "The Performance Appraisal Interviews."

12. Stephanie Gruner, "Feedback from Everyone," *Inc.,* February 1997, 102–103.

13. Howard M. Bloom, "Performance Evaluations," *New England Business,* December 1991, 14.

14. David I. Rosen, "Appraisals Can Make—or Break—Your Court Case," *Personnel Journal,* November 1992, 113.

15. Patricia A. McLagan, "Advice for Bad-News Bearers: How to Tell Employees They're Not Hacking It and Get Results," *Industry Week,* 15 February 1993, 42; Michael Lee Smith, "Give Feedback, Not Criticism," *Supervisory Management,* February 1993, 4; "A Checklist for Conducting Problem Performer Appraisals," *Supervisory Management,* December 1993, 7–9.

16. Jane R. Goodson, Gail W. McGee, and Anson Seers, "Giving Appropriate Performance Feedback to Managers: An Empirical Test of Content and Outcomes," *Journal of Business Communication* 29, no. 4 (1992): 329–342.

17. Peter Fritsch, "It's Lighter Than Glass and Hurts Less When Thrown, But Can Plastic Stack Up?" *Wall Street Journal,* 24 July 1996, B1.

18. Adapted from the Disclosure Project website [accessed 20 August 2001] www.disclosureproject.org; Katelynn Raymer and David Ruppe, "UFOs, Aliens and Secrets," *ABCNews.com,* 10 May 2001 [accessed 20 August 2001] http://more.abcnews.go.com/sections/scitech/DailyNews/ufo010509.html; Rachael Myer, "UFO Probe Sought," *Las Vegas Review-Journal,* 11 May 2001 [accessed 20 August 2001] www.lvrj.com/cgi-bin/printable.cgi?/lvrj_home/2001/May-11-Fri-2001/news/16064080. html.

19. Adapted from Craftopia.com print advertisement, 31 July 2000; Craftopia.com website [accessed 24 August 2000] www.craftopia.com/shop/promo/martha3.asp; Claire Furia Smith, "West Chester Start-up Tries to Become a Crafters' Utopia," *Philadelphia Inquirer,* 26 June 2000 [accessed 24 August 2000] www.craftopia.com/shop/features/about_us_mc_6_26_00_ inquirer. asp; Laura M. Naughton, "Crafting a Niche," *Daily Local News,* 8 March 2000 [accessed 24 August 2000] www.craftopia.com/shop/features/about_us_mc_3_8_00_dailylocal.asp.

20. Adapted from Wolf Blitzer, "More Employers Taking Advantages of New Cyber-Surveillance Software," *CNN.com,* 10 July 2000 [accessed 11 July 2000] www.cnn.com/2000/US/07/10/workplace.eprivacy/index.html.

21. Adapted from Union Bank of California teleservices, personal communication, 16 August 2001.

22. Adapted from Associated Press, "Children's Painkiller Recalled," *CNN.com/Health,* 16 August 2001 [accessed on 22 August 2001] www.cnn.com/2001/HEALTH/parenting/08/16/kids.drug.recalled.ap/index.html.

23. Adapted from Julie Vallese, "Motorized Scooter Injuries on the Rise," *CNN.com/U.S.,* 22 August 2001 [accessed 22 August 2001] www.cnn.com/2001/US/08/22/scooter.advisory/index.html; The Sports Authority website [accessed 28 August 2001] www.thesportsauthority. com.

24. Pascal Zachary, "Sun Microsystems Apologizes in Letter for Late Payments," *Wall Street Journal,* 11 October 1989, B4.

25. Adapted from Associated Press, "Employers Restricting Use of Cell Phones in Cars," *CNN.com/Sci-Tech,* 27 August 2001 [accessed 27 August 2001] www.cnn.com/2001/TECH/08/27/cellphones.cars.ap/index.html;

26. Adapted from Ty Holland, "Vision Quest," *TV Guide,* 22 July 2000, 3.

27. Adapted from United Airlines website [accessed 31 December 2003] www.united.com; "United Airlines First To Offer Inflight Email on Domestic Flights: Verizon Airfone Outfits UAL's Fleet with JetConnectsm," United Airlines press release [accessed 21 July 2003] www.ual.com/press/detail/o,1442,51106, 00.html; "Laptops Sprout Wings with Verizon Airfone JetConnect Service," *PR Newswire,* 24 September 2002 [accessed 21 July 2003] www.proquest.com; "Verizon Hopes Data Flies with Airfone JetConnect," *Wireless Data News,* 7 May 2003 [accessed 24 July 2003] www.proquest.com.

28. Adapted from Sean Doherty, "Dynamic Communications," *Network Computing,* 3 April 2003, 14, no. 6: 26 [accessed 24 July 2003] search.epnet. com/direct. asp?an=9463336&db=bsh&tg=AN; Todd Wasserman, "Post-Merger HP Invents New Image to Challenge Tech Foes IBM and Dell," *Brandweek,* 18 November 2002, [accessed 24 July 2003] search.epnet.com/direct.asp?an=8887152&db=bsh&tg=AN; R. P. Srikanth, "IM Tools Are Latest Tech Toys for Corporate Users," *Express Computer,* 1 July 2002 [accessed 21 July 2003] www.expresscomputeronline.com/20020701/indtrend1.shtml.

Chapter 9

1. Courtland L. Bovée, John V. Thill, and Barbara E. Schatzman, *Business Communication Today,* 7th ed. (Upper Saddle River, N.J., Prentice Hall, 2003), 264.

2. Jay A. Conger, "The Necessary Art of Persuasion," *Harvard Business Review,* May–June 1998, 84–95; Jeanette W. Gilsdorf, "Write Me Your Best Case for . . ." *Bulletin of the Association for Business Communication* 54, no. 1 (March 1991): 7–12.

3. "Vital Skill for Today's Managers: Persuading, Not Ordering Others," *Soundview Executive Book Summaries,* September 1998, 1.

4. Mary Cross, "Aristotle and Business Writing: Why We Need to Teach Persuasion," *Bulletin of the Association for Business Communication* 54, no. 1 (March 1991): 3–6.

5. Robert T. Moran, "Tips on Making Speeches to International Audiences," *International Management,* April 1980, 58–59.

6. Gilsdorf, "Write Me Your Best Case for . . ."

7. Raymond M. Olderman, *10-Minute Guide to Business Communication* (New York: Macmillan Spectrum/Alpha Books, 1997), 57–61.

8. Gilsdorf, "Write Me Your Best Case for . . ."

9. William North Jayme, quoted in Albert Haas Jr., "How to Sell Almost Anything by Direct Mail," *Across the Board,* November 1986, 50.

10. Teri Lammers, "The Elements of Perfect Pitch," *Inc.,* March 1992, 53–55.

11. Kimberly Paterson, "The Writing Process—Sales Letters That Work," *Rough Notes,* April 1998, 59–60.

12. Paterson, "The Writing Process."

13. Robert L. Hemmings, "Think Before You Write," *Fund Raising Management,* February 1990, 23–24.

14. Conrad Squires, "How to Write a Strong Letter, Part Two: Choosing a Theme," *Fund Raising Management,* November 1991, 65–66.

15. Constance L. Clark, "25 Steps to Better Direct Mail Fundraising," *Nonprofit World,* July–August, 1989, 11–13.

16. Adapted from Michael H. Mescon, Courtland L. Bovée, and John V. Thill, *Business Today,* 10th ed. (Upper Saddle River, N.J.: Prentice Hall, 2002), 272–274; Jason Roberson, "Rush-Hour Rebellion," *Dallas Business Journal,* 22 June 2001, 31; Carole Hawkins, "Ready, Set, Go Home," *Black Enterprise,* August 2001, 118–124; Wayne Tompkins, "Telecommuting in Transition," *Louisville (Ky.) Courier-Journal,* 9 July 2001, 01C.

17. Adapted from Mescon, Bovée, and Thill, *Business Today,* 10th ed, 269; Peter Baker, "Work: Have Fun. And That's an Order," *The Observer* (London) 3 January 1999, 011; "The Power of Laughter," *Oprah.com* [accessed on 29 September 2001] www.oprah.com/living/lifemake/experts/tracy/expert_tracy_laughter.html.

18. Kevin M. Savetz, "Preventive Medicine for the Computer User," *Multimedia Online* 2, no. 2 (June 1996): 58–60.

19. Adapted from the American Red Cross website [accessed 3 October 2001] www.redcross.org; American Red Cross San Diego Chapter website [accessed 3 October 2001] www.sdarc.org/blood.htm.

20. Adapted from Annelena Lobb, "Identity Theft Survival Guide," CNN.com [accessed 4 April 2002] money.cnn.com/2002/04/03/pf/q_identity/index.htm.

21. Adapted from Julian E. Barnes, "Fast-Food Giveaway Toys Face Rising Recalls," *New York Times,* 16 August 2001, A1; Shirley Leung, "Burger King Recalls 2.6 Million Kids Meal Toys," *Wall Street Journal,* 1 August 2001, B2.

22. Adapted from Hotel del Coronado website [accessed 7 September 2001] www.hoteldel.com; International Shark Attack Files, Florida Museum of Natural History website [accessed 2 September 2001] www.flmnh.ufl.edu/fish/Sharks/Statistics/statsus.htm; "Sharks Attack Three Off Florida's East Coast," *CNN.com,* 20 August 2001 [accessed 21 August 2001] www.cnn.com/2001/US/08/19/shark.attack/index.html; "Year of Shark 'Hype,' Says Expert," *CNN.com,* 4 September 2001 [accessed 4 September 2001] www.cnn.com/2001/US/09/03/shark.perspective/; "Boy Dies After Shark Attack," *CNN.com,* 2 September 2001 [accessed 2 September 2001] www.cnn.com/2001/US/09/02/shark.attack/index.html; "Labor Day Shark Attack Survivor Hanging On," *CNN.com,* 5 September 2001, [accessed 5 September 2001] www.cnn.com/2001/US/09/04/shark.attacks/index.html; Thurston Hatcher, "Florida Panel Embraces Ban on Shark Feeding," *CNN.com,* 7 September 2001 [accessed 7 September 2001] www.cnn.com/2001/US/09/06/shark.feeding/index.html.

23. Adapted from Michael S. James, "No Expiration on Recall Risk," *ABCNews.com,* 31 August 2001 [accessed on 31 August 2001] http://abcnews.go.com/sections/living/DailyNews/meat_recall010830.html; James F. Balch, M.D., and Phyllis A. Balch, C.N.C, *Prescription for Nutritional Healing,* 2d ed. (Garden City Park, N.Y.: Avery Publishing Group, 199), 277–282.

24. Adapted from *CNET Shopper.com* [accessed 1 October 2001] http://shopper.cnet.com/shopping/0-1257.html?tag=sh.

25. Adapted from Gateway website [accessed 2 October 2001] www.gateway.com; Gateway customer service sales representative, 1-800-GATEWAY, personal interview, 10 October 2001.

26. Adapted from Bruce Haring, "Trouble Getting up to Speed," *USA Today,* 27 December 1999, D3, D2; Mike Rogoway, "AT&T Seeks To Improve Internet Connections," *Vancouver (Wash.) Columbian,* 9 March 2001, E1.

27. Adapted from Sarah Plaskitt, "Case Study: Hilton Uses SMS With Success," *B&T Marketing & Media,* 27 June 2002 [accessed 22 July 2003] www.bandt.com.au/articles/ce/0c00eace.asp; "Wireless Messaging Briefs," *Instant Messaging Planet,* 4 October 2002 [accessed 22 July 2003] www.instantmessagingplanet.com/wireless/print.php/10766_1476111; Hilton Hotels Corporation, *Hoover's Company Capsules,* 1 July 2003 [accessed 24 July 2003] www.proquest.com; Matthew G. Nelson, "Hilton Takes Reservations Wireless," *InformationWeek,* 25 June 2001, p. 99 [accessed 24 July 2003] www.web22.epnet.com; Hilton Hotels website [accessed 15 January 2004] www.hilton.com.

28. Adapted from IBM website [accessed 15 January 2004] www.ibm.com/ibm/ibmgives; IBM website, "DAS faces an assured future with IBM" [accessed 16 January 2004] www-306.ibm.com/software/success/cssdb.nsf/CS/DNSD-5S6KTF; IBM website, "Sametime" [accessed

16 January 2004] www.lotus.com/products/
lotussametime.nsf/wdocs/homepage.

Chapter 10

1. Adapted from Dell Computer Corporation's website [accessed 1 September 2001] www.dell.com; Michael Dell with Catherine Fredman, *Direct from Dell* (New York: HarperCollins Publishers, 1999) 8–15, 36–38, 66–80, 92–101, 133, 144–145, 175–182, 186, 196–197, 208; Daniel Roth, "Dell's Big New Act," *Fortune*, 6 December 1999, 152–156; Louise Fickel, "Know Your Customer," *CIO*, 15 August 1999, 62–72; Neel Chowdhury, "Dell Cracks China," *Fortune*, 21 June 1999, 120–124; "Interview: E-commerce Drives Dell Computer's Success," *IT Cost Management Strategies*, June 1999, 4–6; Carla Johnson, "Moving at the Speed of Dell," *HRMagazine*, April 1999, 50–56.

2. Tom Sant, *Persuasive Business Proposals* (New York: American Management Association, 1992), summarized in *Soundview Executive Book Summaries* 14, no. 10, pt. 2 (October 1992): 3.

3. Information for this section was obtained from "Finding Industry Information" [accessed 3 November 1998] www.pitt.edu/~buslibry/industries.htm.; Thomas P. Bergman, Stephen M. Garrison, and Gregory M. Scott, *The Business Student Writer's Manual and Guide to the Internet* (Upper Saddle River, N.J.: Prentice Hall, 1998), 67–80; Ernest L. Maier, Anthony J. Faria, Peter Kaatrude, and Elizabeth Wood, *The Business Library and How to Use It* (Detroit: Omnigraphics, 1996), 53–76; Sherwyn P. Morreale and Courtland L. Bovée, *Excellence in Public Speaking* (Fort Worth, Tx.: Harcourt Brace College Publishers, 1998), 166–171.

4. Jason Zien, "Measuring the Internet," *About.com*, 13 July 1999 [accessed 17 July 1999] internet.about.com/library/weekly/1999/aa071399a.htm; "FAST Aims for Largest Index," *Search Engine Watch*, 4 May 1999 [accessed 17 July 1999] searchenginewatch.internet.com/sereport/99/05-fast.htm.

5. Maier, Faria, Kaatrude, and Wood, *The Business Library and How to Use It*, 84–97; Matt Lake, "Desperately Seeking Susan OR Suzie NOT Sushi," *New York Times*, 3 September 1998, D1, D7.

6. Adapted from Bob Smith, "The Evolution of Pinkerton," *Management Review*, September 1993, 54–58.

Chapter 11

1. Courtland L. Bovée, John V. Thill, and Barbara E. Schatzman, *Business Communication Today*, 7th ed. (Upper Saddle River, N.J.: Prentice Hall, 2003), 442.

2. David A. Hayes, "Helping Students GRASP the Knack of Writing Summaries," *Journal of Reading* (November 1989): 96–101.

3. Philip C. Kolin, *Successful Writing at Work*, 6th ed. (Boston: Houghton Mifflin, 2001), 552–555.

4. A. S. C. Ehrenberg, "Report Writing—Six Simple Rules for Better Business Documents," *Admap*, June 1992, 39–42.

5. Michael Netzley and Craig Snow, *Guide to Report Writing* (Upper Saddle River, N.J.: Prentice Hall, 2001), 57.

6. Bickley Townsend, "Room at the Top," *American Demographics*, July 1996, 28–37.

Chapter 12

1. Courtland L. Bovée, John V. Thill, and Barbara E. Schatzman, *Business Communication Today* (Upper Saddle River, N.J.: Prentice Hall, 2003), 494; Leanne Anderson, "Speak Up," *Entrepreneur*, March 1997, 92–95.

2. Walter Kiechel III, "How to Give a Speech," *Fortune*, 8 June 1987, 180.

3. *Communication and Leadership Program* (Santa Ana, Calif.: Toastmasters International, 1980), 44, 45.

4. "Polishing Your Presentation," 3M Meeting Network [accessed 8 June 2001] www.mmm.com/meetingnetwork/readingroom/meetingguide_pres.html.

5. Kathleen K. Weigner, "Visual Persuasion," *Forbes*, 16 September 1991, 176; Kathleen K. Weigner, "Showtime!" *Forbes*, 13 May 1991, 118.

6. Kevan Albee, David L. Green, and Kari Woolf, "Pre-Show Business," *Presentations*, May 2001, 50–54.

7. Margo Halverson, "Choosing the Right Colors for Your Next Presentation," 3M Meeting Network [accessed 8 June 2001] www.mmm.com/meetingnetwork/readingroom/meetingguide_right_color.html.

8. Carol Klinger and Joel G. Siegel, "Computer Multimedia Presentations," *CPA Journal*, June 1996, 46.

9. Jon Hanke, "Five Tips for Better Visuals," 3M Meeting Network [accessed 8 June 2001] www.mmm.com/meetingnetwork/presentations/pmag_better_visuals.html.

10. Hanke, "Five Tips for Better Visuals."

11. Ted Simons, "Handouts that Won't Get Trashed," *Presentations*, February 1999, 47–50.

12. Sherwyn P. Morreale and Courtland L. Bovée, *Excellence in Public Speaking* (Fort Worth, Tx.: Harcourt Brace, 1998), 24–25.

13. Judy Linscott, "Getting On and Off the Podium," *Savvy*, October 1985, 44.

14. Iris R. Johnson, "Before You Approach the Podium," *MW*, January–February 1989, 7.

15. Edward P. Bailey, *Writing and Speaking at Work* (Upper Saddle River, N.J.: Prentice Hall, 1999), 138–145.

16. Patrick J. Collins, *Say It with Power and Confidence* (Upper Saddle River, N.J.: Prentice Hall, 1997), 122–124.

17. Sandra Moyer, "Braving No Woman's Land," *The Toastmaster*, August 1986, 13.

18. "Control the Question-and-Answer Session," *Soundview Executive Book Summaries* 20, no. 6, pt. 2 (June 1998): 4.

19. "Control the Question-and-Answer Session."

20. Teresa Brady, "Fielding Abrasive Questions During Presentations," *Supervisory Management*, February 1993, 6.

21. Adapted from Ronald L. Applebaum and Karl W. E. Anatol, *Effective Oral Communication: For Business and the Professions* (Chicago: Science Research Associates, 1982), 240–244.

Chapter 13

1. Courtland Bovée, John Thill, and Barbara Schatzman, "Communication Close-Up," in *Business Communication Today,* 7th ed. (Upper Saddle River, N.J.: Prentice Hall, 2002), 542.
2. Camille DeBell, "Ninety Years in the World of Work in America," *Career Development Quarterly* 50, no.1 (September 2001): 77–88.
3. John A. Challenger, "The Changing Workforce: Workplace Rules in the New Millenium," *Vital Speeches of the Day* 67, no. 23 (15 September 2001): 721–728.
4. Marvin J. Cetron and Owen Davies, "Trends Now Changing the World: Technology, the Workplace, Management, and Institutions," *Futurist* 35, no. 1 (March/April 2001): 27–42.
5. Amanda Bennett, "GE Redesigns Rungs of Career Ladder," *Wall Street Journal,* 15 March 1993, B1, B3.
6. Robin White Goode, "International and Foreign Language Skills Have an Edge," *Black Enterprise*, May 1995, 53.
7. Nancy M. Somerick, "Managing a Communication Internship Program," *Bulletin of the Association for Business Communication* 56, no. 3 (1993): 10–20.
8. Joan Lloyd, "Changing Workplace Requires You to Alter Your Career Outlook," *Milwaukee Journal Sentinel,* 4 July 1999, 1; DeBell, "Ninety Years in the World of Work in America."
9. Stephanie Armour, "Employers: Enough Already with the E-Résumés," *USA Today,* 15 July 1999, 1B.
10. Cheryl L. Noll, "Collaborating with the Career Planning and Placement Center in the Job-Search Project," *Business Communication Quarterly* 58, no. 3 (1995): 53–55.
11. Pam Stanley-Weigand, "Organizing the Writing of Your Resume," *Bulletin of the Association for Business Communication* 54, no. 3 (September 1991): 11–12.
12. Richard H. Beatty and Nicholas C. Burkholder, *The Executive Career Guide for MBAs* (New York: Wiley, 1996), 133.
13. Beatty and Burkholder, *The Executive Career Guide for MBAs,* 151.
14. Rockport Institute, "How to Write a Masterpiece of a Résumé" [accessed 16 October 1998] www.rockportinstitute. com/résumés.html.
15. Rockport Institute, "How to Write a Masterpiece of a Résumé."
16. Beverly Culwell-Block and Jean Anna Sellers, "Résumé Content and Format—Do the Authorities Agree?" *Bulletin of the Association for Business Communication* 57, no. 4 (1994): 27–30.
17. Ellen Joe Pollock, "Sir: Your Application for a Job Is Rejected; Sincerely, Hal 9000," *Wall Street Journal,* 30 July 1998, A1, A12.

18. "Scannable Resume Design," ResumeEdge.com [accessed 19 February 2004] www.resumeedge.com.
19. Kim Isaacs, "Tips for Creating a Scannable Resume," Monster.com [accessed 19 February 2004] www.monster.com.
20. Kim Isaacs, "Enhance Your Resume for Monster Upload," Monster.com [accessed 19 February 2004] www.monster.com.
21. "The Rogue's Gallery of 25 Awful Résumé Mistakes," CareerExplorer.net [accessed 19 February 2004] www.careerexplorer.net.
22. Pontow, "Electronic Résumé Writing Tips."
23. William J. Banis, "The Art of Writing Job-Search Letters," *CPC Annual,* 36th ed. (1992): 42–50.
24. Toni Logan, "The Perfect Cover Story," *Kinko's Impress* 2 (2000): 32, 34.

Chapter 14

1. Courtland Bovée, John Thill, and Barbara Schatzman, "Communication Close-Up," in *Business Communication Today,* 7th ed. (Upper Saddle River, N.J.: Prentice Hall, 2002) 580.
2. Sylvia Porter, "Your Money: How to Prepare for Job Interviews," *San Francisco Chronicle,* 3 November 1981, 54.
3. Stephanie Armour, "The New Interview Etiquette," *USA Today,* 23 November 1999, B1, B2.
4. Samuel Greengard, "Are You Well Armed to Screen Applicants?" *Personnel Journal,* December 1995, 84–95.
5. Charlene Marmer Solomon, "How Does Disney Do It?" *Personnel Journal,* December 1989, 53.
6. Marcia Vickers, "Don't Touch That Dial: Why Should I Hire You?" *New York Times,* 13 April 1997, F11.
7. Nancy K. Austin, "Goodbye Gimmicks," *Incentive,* May 1996, 241.
8. Robert Gifford, Cheuk Fan Ng, and Margaret Wilkinson, "Nonverbal Cues in the Employment Interview: Links Between Applicant Qualities and Interviewer Judgments," *Journal of Applied Psychology* 70, no. 4 (1985): 729.
9. Dale G. Leathers, *Successful Nonverbal Communication* (New York: Macmillan, 1986), 225.
10. Armour, "The New Interview Etiquette."
11. Shirley J. Shepherd, "How to Get That Job in 60 Minutes or Less," *Working Woman,* March 1986, 119.
12. Shepherd, "How to Get That Job in 60 Minutes or Less," 118.
13. H. Anthony Medley, *Sweaty Palms: The Neglected Art of Being Interviewed* (Berkeley, Calif.: Ten Speed Press, 1993), 179.
14. Gerald L. Wilson, "Preparing Students for Responding to Illegal Selection Interview Questions," *Bulletin of the Association for Business Communication* 54, no. 2 (1991): 44–49.
15. Jeff Springston and Joann Keyton, "Interview Response Training," *Bulletin of the Association for Business Communication* 54, no. 3 (1991): 28–30; Gerald L. Wilson, "An Analysis of Instructional Strategies for

Responding to Illegal Selection Interview Questions," *Bulletin of the Association for Business Communication* 54, no. 3 (1991): 31–35.

16. Stephen J. Pullum, "Illegal Questions in the Selection Process: Going Beyond Contemporary Business and Professional Communication Textbooks," *Bulletin of the Association for Business Communication* 54, no. 3 (1991): 36–43; Alicia Kitsuse, "Have You Ever Been Arrested?" *Across the Board,* November 1992, 46–49; Christina L. Greathouse, "10 Common Hiring Mistakes," *Industry Week,* 20 January 1992, 22–23, 26.

17. Marilyn Moats Kennedy, "Are You Getting Paid What You're Worth?" *New Woman,* November 1984, 110.

18. Harold H. Hellwig, "Job Interviewing: Process and Practice," *Bulletin of the Association for Business Communication* 55, no. 2 (1992): 8–14.

Appendix A

1. Mary A. De Vries, *Internationally Yours* (Boston: Houghton Mifflin, 1994), 9.

2. Patricia A. Dreyfus, "Paper That's Letter Perfect," *Money,* May 1985, 184.

3. "When Image Counts, Letterhead Says It All," *Stamford (Conn.) Advocate and Greenwich Times,* 10 January 1993, F4.

4. Mel Mandell, "Electronic Forms Are Cheap and Speedy," *D&B Reports,* July–August 1993, 44–45.

5. Linda Driskill, *Business and Managerial Communication: New Perspectives* (Orlando, Fla.: Harcourt Brace Jovanovich, 1992), 470.

6. Driskill, *Business and Managerial Communication,* 470.

7. Lennie Copeland and Lewis Griggs, *Going International: How to Make Friends and Deal Effectively in the Global Marketplace,* 2d ed. (New York: Random House, 1985), 24–27.

8. U.S. Postal Service, *Postal Addressing Standards* (Washington, D.C.: GPO, 1992).

9. Copeland and Griggs, *Going International,* 24–27.

10. Renee B. Horowitz and Marian G. Barchilon, "Stylistic Guidelines for E-Mail," *IEEE Transactions on Professional Communications,* 37, no. 4 (1994): 207–212.

11. William Eager, *Using the Internet* (Indianapolis: Que Corporation, 1994), 11.

12. Eager, *Using the Internet,* 10.

13. William Eager, Larry Donahue, David Forsyth, Kenneth Mitton, and Martin Waterhouse, *Net.Search* (Indianapolis: Que Corporation, 1995), 221.

14. Rosalind Resnick and Dave Taylor, *Internet Business Guide* (Indianapolis: Sams.net Publishing, 1995), 117.

15. James L. Clark and Lyn R. Clark, *How 7: A Handbook for Office Workers,* 7th ed. (Cincinnati: South-Western, 1995), 431–432.

SINGLE PC LICENSE AGREEMENT AND LIMITED WARRANTY

READ THIS CAREFULLY BEFORE OPENING THIS PACKAGE. BY OPENING THIS PACKAGE, YOU ARE AGREEING TO THE TERMS AND CONDITIONS OF THIS LICENSE. IF YOU DO NOT AGREE, DO NOT OPEN THE PACKAGE AND ALL ACCOMPANYING ITEMS TO THE PLACE YOU OBTAINED THEM. THESE TERMS APPLY **TO ALL LICENSED SOFTWARE ON THE DISK EXCEPT THAT THE TERMS FOR USE OF ANY SHAREWARE OR FREE-WARE ON THE DISKETTES ARE AS SET FORTH IN THE ELECTRONIC LICENSE LOCATED ON THE DISK**:

1. GRANT OF LICENSE and **OWNERSHIP**: The enclosed computer programs and data ("Software") are licensed, not sold, to you by Pearson Education, Inc. ("We of the "Company") and in consideration of your purchase or adoption of the accompanying Company textbooks and/or other materials, and you agreement to these terms. We reserve any rights not granted to you. You own only the disk(s) but we and/or our licensors own the Software itself. This license allows you to use and display your copy of the Software on a single computer (i.e., with a single CPU) at a single location for <u>academic</u> use only, so long as you comply with the terms of this Agreement. You may make one copy for back up, or transfer your copy to another CPU, provided that the Software is usable on only one computer.

2. **RESTRICTIONS**: You may <u>not</u> transfer or distribute the Software documentation to anyone else. Except for backup, you may <u>not</u> copy the documentation or the Software. You may <u>not</u> network the Software or otherwise use it on more than one computer or computer terminal at the same time. You may <u>not</u> reverse engineer, disassemble, decompile, modify, adapt, translate, or create derivative works based on the Software or the Documentation. You may be held legally responsible for any copying or copyright infringement which is caused by your failure to abide by the terms of these restrictions.

3. **TERMINATION**: This license is effective until terminated. This license will terminate automatically without notice from the Company if you fail to comply with any provisions or limitations of this license. Upon termination, you shall destroy the Documentation and all copies of the Software. All provisions of this Agreement as to limitation and disclaimer of warranties, limitation of liability, remedies or damages, and our ownership rights shall survive termination.

4. LIMITED WARRANTY AND DISCLAIMER OF WARRANTY: Company warrants that for a period of 60 days from the date you purchase this SOFTWARE (or purchase or adopt the accompanying textbook), the Software, when properly installed and used inaccordance with the Documentation, will operate in substantial conformity with the description of the Software set forth in the Documentation, and that for a period of 30 days the disk(s) on which the Software is delivered shall be free from defects in materials and workmanship under normal use. The Company does not warrant that the Software will meet your requirements or that the operation of the Software will be uninterrupted or error-free. Your only remedy the Company's only obligation under these limited warranties is, at the Company's option, return the disk for a refund of any amounts paid for it by you or replacement of the disk. THIS LIMITED WARRANTY IS THE ONLY WARRANTY PROVIDED BY THE COMPANY AND ITS LICENSORS DISCLAIM ALL OTHER WARRANTIES, EXPRESS OR IMPLIED, INCLUDING WITHOUT LIMITATION, THE IMPLIED WARRANTIES OF MERCHANTABILITY AND FITNESS FOR A PARTICULAR PURPOSE. THE COMPANY DOES NOT WARRANT, GUARANTEE OR MAKE ANY REPRESENTATION REGARDING THE ACCURACY, RELIABILITY, CURRENTNESS, USE, OR RESULTS OF USE, OF THE SOFTWARE.

5. LIMITATION OF REMEDIES AND DAMAGES: IN NO EVENT, SHALL THE COMPANY OR ITS EMPLOYEES, AGENTS, LICENSORS, OR CONTRACTORS BE LIABLE FOR ANY INCIDENTAL, INDIRECT, SPECIAL, OR CONSEQUENTIAL DAMAGES ARISING OUT OF OR IN CONNECTION WITH THIS LICENSE OR THE SOFTWARE, INCLUDING FOR LOSS OF USE, LOSS OF DATA, LOSS OF INCOME OR PROFIT, OR OTHER LOSSES, SUSTAINED AS A RESULT OF INJURY TO ANY PERSON, OR LOSS OF OR DAMAGE TO PROPERTY, OR CLAIMS OF THIRD PARTIES, EVEN IF THE COMPANY OR AN AUTHORIZED REPRESENTATIVE OF THE COMPANY HAS BEEN ADVISED OF THE POSSIBILITY OF SUCH DAMAGES. IN NO EVENT SHALL THE LIABILITY OF THE COMPANY FOR DAMAGES WITH RESPECT TO THE SOFTWARE EXCEED THE SOFTWARE OR THE ACCOMPANYING TEXTBOOK. BECAUSE SOME JURISDICTIONS DO NOT ALLOW THE LIMITATION OF LIABILITY IN CERTAIN CIRCUMSTANCES, THE ABOVE LIMITATIONS MAY NOT ALWAYS APPLY TO YOU.

6. GENERAL: THIS AGREEMENT SHALL BE CONSTRUED IN ACCORDANCE WITH THE LAWS OF THE UNITED STATES OF AMERICA AND THE STATE OF NEW YORK, APPLICABLE TO CONTRACTS MADE IN NEW YORK, AND SHALL BENEFIT THE COMPANY, ITS AFFILIATES AND ASSIGNEES. HIS AGREEMENT IS THE COMPLETE AND EXCLUSIVE STATEMENT OF THE AGREEMENT BETWEEN YOU AND THE COMPANY AND SUPERSEDES ALL PROPOSALS OR PRIOR AGREEMENTS, ORAL, OR WRITTEN, AND ANY OTHER COMMUNICATIONS BETWEEN YOU AND THE COMPANY OR ANY REPRESENTATIVE OR THE COMPANY RELATING TO THE SUBJECT MATTER OF THIS AGREEMENT. If you are a U.S. Government user, this Software is licensed with "restricted rights" as set forth in subparagraphs (a)-(d) of the Commercial Computer-Restricted Rights clause at FAR 52.227-19 or in subparagraphs (c) (1) (ii) of the Rights in the Technical Data and Computer Software clause at DFARS 252.227-7013, and similar clauses, as applicable.

Should you have any questions concerning this agreement or if you wish to contact the Company for any reason, please contact in writting: Prentice-Hall, New Media Department, One Lake Street, Upper Saddle River, NJ 07458.

Acknowledgments

Text

27 Business Communication Notebook, adapted from "Culture Quiz," *Workforce,* January 1998, 25; Valerie Frazee, "Establishing Relations in Germany," *Global Workforce,* April 1997, 16–17; James Wilfong and Toni Seger, *Taking Your Business Global* (Franklin Lakes, N.J.: Career Press, 1997), 282; Valerie Frazee, "Keeping Up on Chinese Culture," *Global Workforce,* October 1996, 16–17; David A. Ricks, "International Business Blunders: An Update," *Business & Economic Review,* January–March 1988, 11–14. **50** Business Communication Notebook, adapted from "Air Travel Fears to Drive Videoconferencing Market," *Electronic Commerce News,* 15 October 2001, 1+; "Amid Terrorism Fears, More Businesses Are Conducting Virtual Meetings," *Palm Beach Post,* 14 October 2001, 4F; Charles E. Ramirez, "Videoconference Demand Up: More Companies Seek Services After Attacks," *Detroit News,* 10 October 2001, 1; Fred O. Williams, "Reluctant Travelers: Videoconferencing Gets Boost from Businesses," *Buffalo News,* 7 October 2001, B11; Wayne Tompkins, "Face-to-Face Meetings Are Less Likely for Now," *Courier-Journal,* 1 October 2001, 05C; Benny Evangelista, "Meetings via Video: More Businesses Skipping Travel, Tuning Into Videoconferencing," *San Francisco Chronicle,* 1 October 2001, E1; James R. Healey, "Business Travelers Keep Their Feet on the Ground: Videoconferencing, Telecommuting Replace Good Old Face-to-Face," *USA Today,* 26 September 2001, B.01; Thomas E. Weber, "E-World: After Terrorist Attacks, Companies Rethink In-Person Meetings," *Wall Street Journal,* 24 September 2001, B1. **79** Business Communication Notebook, adapted from Mary Beth Currie and Daniel Black, "E-merging Issues in the Electronic Workplace," *Ivey Business Journal,* January–February 2001, 18–29; John J. DiGilio, "Electronic Mail: From Computer to Courtroom," *Information Management Journal,* April 2000, 32–44; Mike Elgan, "The Trouble with E-Mail," *Windows Magazine,* November 1998, 31; Jerry Adler, "When E-Mail Bites Back," *Newsweek,* 23 November 1998, 45–46; Amy Harmon, "Corporate Delete Keys Busy as E-Mail Turns Up in Court," *New York Times,* 12 November 1998, A1, C2. **136–137** Business Communication Notebook adapted from Reid Goldsborough, "Words for the Wise," *Link-Up,* September–October 1999, 25–26; John Morkes and Jakob Nielsen, *How to Write for the Web* [accessed 23 April 2000] www.useit.com/papers/webwriting/writing.html; Jakob Nielsen, *Reading on the Web* [accessed 23 April 2000] www.useit.com/alertbox/9710a.html; Jakob Nielsen, *Failure of Corporate Websites* [accessed online 23 April 2000] www.useit.com/alertbox/982028.html; Shel Holtz, "Writing for the Wired World," *International Association of Business Communicators,* 1999, 6–9; "Web Writing: How to Avoid Pitfalls," *Investor Relations Business,* 1 November 1999, 15; Michael Lerner, "Building Worldwide Websites," IBM [accessed 23 April 2000] www.4.ibm.com/software/developer/library/web-localization.html; Steve Outing, "Some Advice on Writing, Web-Style," *E&P Online* [accessed 23 April 2000] www.mediainfo.com/ephome/news/newshtm/stop/st061899.htm; *Good Documents Website* [accessed 15 July 2001], www.gooddocuments.com/techniques/techniqueshome.htm; Jakob Nielsen, *Microcontent: How to Write Headlines, Page Titles, and Subject Lines* [accessed online 23 April 2000] www.useit.com/alertbox/980906.html; Jakob Nielsen, P.J. Schemenaur, and Jonathan Fox, "Writing for the Web," Sun Microsystems website [accessed 23 April 2000] www.sun.com/980713/webwriting; Amy Gahran, "Writing for the Web and Creating Effective Online Content," *Webword.com* [accessed 31 May 2000] www.webword.com/interviews/gahran.html. **168–169** Business Communication Notebook, adapted from William Lutz, "Life Under the Chief Doublespeak Officer," *USA Today,* 17 October 1996, 15A; Toddi Gutner, "At Last, the Readable Prospectus," *Business Week,* 13 April 1998, 11; Philip Maher, "One for the Writers," *Investment Dealers' Digest,* 17 November 1997, 41; Ronald G. Shafer, "Government Bureaucrats to Learn a New Language: Simple English," *Wall Street Journal,* 2 June 1998, B1; Peder Zane, "For Investors, an Initial Public Offering of English," *New York Times,* 25 August 1996, 7; Dan Seligman, "The Gobbledygood Profession," *Forbes,* 7 September 1998, 174–175; Michael Weiss and James Hildebrandt, "Art of Clear Writing Lost in Sea of Legalese," *San Antonio Business Journal,* 28 October 1996 [accessed September 1998] www.amcity.com/ sanantonio/stories/102896/editorial2. htm. **207** Business Communication Notebook adapted from Mary A. DeVries, *Internationally Yours* (Boston: Houghton Mifflin, 1994), 195; Myron W. Lustig and Jolene Koester, *Intercultural Competence* (New York: HarperCollins, 1993), 66–72; Mary Munter, "Cross-Cultural Communication for Managers," *Business Horizons,* May–June 1993, 69–78; David A. Victor, *International Business Communication* (New York: HarperCollins, 1992), 137–168; Larry A. Samovar and Richard E. Porter, *Intercultural Communication: A Reader,* 6th ed. (Belmont, Calif.: Wadsworth, 1991), 109–110; Larry A. Samovar and Richard E. Porter, *Communication between Cultures* (Belmont, Calif.: Wadsworth, 1991), 235–244; Carley H. Dodd,

Dynamics of Intercultural Communication, 3d ed. (Dubuque, Iowa: Wm. C. Brown, 1989), 69–73. **243** Business Communication Workshop adapted from Stephanie Armour, "E-Mail Lets Companies Deliver Bad News from Afar," *USA Today,* 20 February 2001, B1; Cheryl Maday, "How to Break Bad News," *Psychology Today,* November– December 1999, 18; Nancy Flynn and Tom Flynn, *Writing Effective E-Mail* (Menlo Park, Calif: Crisp Learning, 1998), 4. **281** Business Communication Notebook adapted from Ronald A. Anderson, Ivan Fox, David P. Twomey, and Marianne M. Jennings, *Business Law and the Legal Environment* (Cincinnati: West Educational Publishing, 1999), 229–230, 237–240, 247, 524–526, 567; Sales Letter Tips [accessed 26 June 2000],www.smartbiz.com/sbs/arts/sbs47.htm; Instant Sales Letters [accessed 26 June 2000], instantsalesletters.com. **316** Business Communication Notebook, adapted from Paul Franson, *High Tech, High Hope* (New York: Wiley, 1998), 252; John R. L. Rizza, "Extranets: The Internet Gets Down to Business," *Entrepreneurial Edge* 3 (1998): 76–78; Samuel Greengard, "Extranets Linking Employees with Your Vendors," *Workforce,* November 1997, 28–34. **365** Business Communication Notebook adapted from Joan Minninger, *The Perfect Memo* (New York: Doubleday, 1990), 169–170. **394** Business Communication Notebook adapted from Sherwyn P. Morreale and Courtland L. Bovée, *Excellence in Public Speaking* (Fort Worth, Tx.: Harcourt Brace, 1998), 7; Leon Fletcher, "A Remedy for Stage Fright," *The Toastmaster,* June 1994, 8–10; Greg Dahl, "Fear of Fear," *The Toastmaster,* June 1994, 10–11; "A Survival Guide to Public Speaking," *Training & Development Journal,* September 1990, 15–16, 18–25; Arden K. Watson, "Ask an Expert," in Morreale and Bovée, *Excellence in Public Speaking,* 42. **437** Business Communication Notebook adapted from Richard N. Bolles, "Career Strategizing or, What Color Is Your Web Parachute?" *Yahoo! Internet Life,* May 1998, 116, 121; Tara Weingarten, "The All-Day, All-Night, Global, No-Trouble Job Search," *Newsweek,* 6 April 1998, 17; Michele Himmelberg, "Internet an Important Tool in Employment Search," *San Diego Union-Tribune,* 7 September 1998, D2; Gina Imperato, "35 Ways to Land a Job Online," *Fast Company,* August 1998, 192–197; Roberta Maynard, "Casting the Net for Job Seekers," *Nation's Business,* March 1997, 28–29. **462** Business Communications Notebook, adapted from "Career Strategies," *Black Enterprise,* February 1986, 122. Copyright ©1986, Black Enterprise Magazine, The Earl Graves Publishing Company, Inc., New York, NY. All rights reserved.

Figures and Tables

35 (Table 2.1) Madelyn Burley-Allen, *Listening: The Forgotten Skill,* (New York: Wiley, 1995), 70–71, 119–120; Judi Brownell, *Listening: Attitudes, Principles, and Skills* (Boston: Allyn and Bacon, 2002), 3, 9, 83, 89, 125; Larry Barker and Kittie Watson, *Listen Up* (New York: St. Martin's, 200), 8, 9, 64. **39** (Figure 2.3) Roger Axtell, *Gestures: The Do's and Taboos of Body Language Around the World,* (New York: Wiley, 1991), 117–119. **117** (Table 5.1) An original created by the authors of this text. **118** (Table 5.2) An original created by the authors of this text. **174** (Figure 7.2) Courtesy Ace Hardware 181 (Figure 7.6) Courtesy Herman Miller. **358** (Table 11.3) Catalyst, New York, cited in Bickley Townsend, "Room at the Top," *American Demographics,* July 1996, 31. **358** (Table 11.4) Catalyst, New York, cited in Bickley Townsend, "Room at the Top," *American Demographics,* July 1996, 31. **358** (Table 11.5) Catalyst, New York, cited in Bickley Townsend, "Room at the Top," *American Demographics,* July 1996, 33. **371** (Table 12.1) Adapted from Eric J. Adams, "Management Focus: User-Friendly Presentation Software," *World Trade,* March 1995, 92. **407** (Table 13.2) Rockport Institute, "How to Write a Masterpiece of a Résumé" [accessed 16 October 1998] www.rockportinstitute.com/ résumés.html. **411** (Table 13.3) Adapted from Anne Field, "Coach, Help Me Out with This Interview," *Business Week,* 22 October 2001, 134E4, 134E6; Joan E. Rigdon, "Deceptive Résumés Can Be Door-Openers but Can Become an Employee's Undoing," *Wall Street Journal,* 17 June 1992, B1; Diane Cole, "Ethics: Companies Crack Down on Dishonesty," *Managing Your Career,* Spring 1991, 8–11; Nancy Marx Better, "Résumé Liars," *Savvy,* December 1990–January 1991, 26–29. **442** (Table 14.2) Adapted from The Northwestern *Endicott Report* (Evanston, Ill.: Northwestern University Placement Center). **444** (Table 14.3) Adapted from H. Lee Rust, *Job Search: The Completion Manual for Jobseekers* (New York: American Management Association, 1979), 56. **445** (Figure 14.1) Adapted from *The Northwestern Endicott Report* (Evanston: Ill.: Northwestern University Placement Center). **447** (Table 14.4) "Dangerous Questions," *Nation's Business,* May 1999, 22.

Answer Key

Answer Key to the Level 1 Self-Assessment Exercises

Chapter 1: Self-Assessment—Nouns

1. Give the <u>balance sheet</u> to Melissa. (1.1.1)
2. We'd like to order <u>50</u> more <u>satchels</u> for Craigmont Stores , and <u>three</u> each for the other <u>stores</u> on our <u>list</u>. (1.1.1)
3. Tarnower Corporation donates a <u>portion</u> of its <u>profits</u> to <u>charity</u> every <u>year</u>. (1.1.1)
4. Which aluminum <u>bolts</u> are packaged? (1.1.1)
5. Please send the Joneses a <u>dozen</u> of the <u>following</u>: <u>stopwatches</u>, <u>canteens</u>, <u>headbands</u>, and <u>wristbands</u>. (1.1.1)
6. The <u>technician</u> has already repaired the machine for the client . (1.1.2)
7. An <u>attorney</u> will talk to the group about incorporation . (1.1.2)
8. After her vacation , the <u>buyer</u> prepared a third-quarter budget . (1.1.2)
9. The new flat <u>monitors</u> are serving our department very well. (1.1.2)
10. <u>Accuracy</u> overrides speed in importance . (1.1.2)
11. copies_____ Make sure that all <u>copys</u> include the new addresses. (1.1.2)
12. employees'_____ Ask Jennings to collect all <u>employee's</u> donations for the Red Cross drive. (1.1.4)
13. sons-in-law / businesses Charlie now has two <u>son-in-laws</u> to help him with his two online <u>business's</u>. (1.1.3, 1.1.4)
14. parentheses_____ Avoid using too many <u>parenthesises</u> when writing your reports. (1.1.3)
15. Ness's / week's_____ Follow President <u>Nesses</u> rules about what constitutes a <u>weeks</u> work. (1.1.4)

Chapter 2: Self-Assessment—Pronouns

1. whom_____ To <u>which retailer</u> will you send your merchandise? (1.2)
2. them_____ Have you given <u>John and Nancy</u> a list of parts? (1.2)
3. it/them_____ The <u>main office</u> sent the invoice to <u>Mr. and Mrs. Litvak</u> on December 5. (1.2)
4. its_____ The company settled <u>the company's</u> accounts before the end of the year (1.2)
5. whose_____ Which <u>person's</u> umbrella is this? (1.2)
6. The sales staff is preparing guidelines for ___its___ (*their, its*) clients. (1.2.5)

7. Few of the sales representatives turn in ___their___ (*their, its*) reports on time. (1.2.5)
8. The board of directors has chosen ___its___ (*their, its*) officers. (1.2.5)
9. Gomez and Archer have told ___their___ (*his, their*) clients about the new program. (1.2.1)
10. Each manager plans to expand __his or her__ (*his, their, his or her*) sphere of control next year. (1.2.3)
11. Has everyone supplied ___his or her___ (*his, their, his or her*) Social Security number? (1.2.3)
12. After giving every employee ___a___ (*his, their, a*) raise, George told ___them___ (*them, they, all*) about the increased work load. (1.2.3, 1.2.4)
13. Bob and Tim have opposite ideas about how to achieve company goals. ___Who___ (*Who, Whom*) do you think will win the debate? (1.2.4)
14. City Securities has just announced ___whom___ (*who, whom*) it will hire as CEO. (1.2.4)
15. Either of the new products would readily find ___its___ (*their, its*) niche in the marketplace. (1.2.5)

Chapter 3: Self-Assessment—Verbs

1. have become (1.3.1)
2. knew (1.3.1)
3. has moved (1.3.1)
4. will do (1.3.1)
5. will have taken (1.3.1)
6. Leslie Cartwright will write the report. (1.3.5)
7. No one ever recorded the transaction. (1.3.5)
8. Has the claims department notified you of your rights? (1.3.5)
9. We depend on their services for our operation. (1.3.5)
10. The customer returned the damaged equipment before we even located a repair facility. (1.3.5)
11. Everyone upstairs (*receive*/ receives) mail before we do. (1.3.4)
12. Neither the main office nor the branches (*is*/ are) blameless. (1.3.4)
13. C&B Sales (is /*are*) listed in the directory. (1.3.4)
14. When measuring shelves, 7 inches (is /*are*) significant. (1.3.4)
15. About 90 percent of the employees (plan /*plans*) to come to the company picnic. (1.3.4)

Chapter 4: Self-Assessment—Adjectives

1. greater (1.4.1)
2. most perfect (1.4.1)
3. most interesting (1.4.1)
4. better (1.4.1)
5. hardest (1.4.1)
6. A highly placed source revealed Dotson's last-ditch efforts to cover up the mistake. (1.4.2)
7. Please send an extra-large dust cover for my photocopier. (1.4.2)
8. A top-secret document was taken from the president's office last night. (1.4.2)
9. A 30-year-old person should know better. (1.4.2)
10. If I write a large-scale report, I want to know that it will be read by upper-level management. (1.4.2)
11. The two companies are engaged in an all-out, no-holds-barred struggle for dominance. (1.4)
12. A tiny metal shaving is responsible for the problem. (1.4)
13. She came to the office with a bruised, swollen knee. (1.4)
14. A chipped, cracked sheet of glass is useless to us. (1.4)
15. You'll receive our usual cheerful, prompt service. (1.4)

Chapter 5: Self-Assessment—Adverbs

1. good (1.5)
2. surely (1.5)
3. sick (1.5)
4. well (1.5)
5. good (1.5)
6. faster (1.5.2)
7. most recently (1.5.2)
8. more happily (1.5.2)
9. better (1.5.2)
10. most logically (1.5.2)
11. He doesn't seem to have any. *OR* He seems to have none. (1.5.1)
12. That machine is scarcely ever used. *OR* That machine is never used. (1.5.1)
13. They can't get any replacement parts until Thursday. *OR* They can get no replacement parts until Thursday. (1.5.1)
14. It wasn't any different from the first event we promoted. *OR* It was no different from . . . (1.5.1)
15. We've looked for it, and it doesn't seem to be anywhere. *OR* it seems to be nowhere (1.5.1)

Chapter 6: Self-Assessment—Prepositions and Conjunctions

1. Where was your argument leading ~~to~~? (1.6.1)
2. I wish he would get off ~~of~~ the phone. (1.6.1)
3. This is a project ~~into which~~ you can sink your teeth into. (1.6.1)
4. U.S. Mercantile must become aware <u>of</u> and sensitive to its customers' concerns. (1.6.1)
5. We are responsible for aircraft safety in the air, <u>in</u> the hangars, and <u>on</u> the runways. (1.6.1)
6. to (1.6.1)
7. among (1.6.1)
8. for (1.6.1)
9. to (1.6.1)
10. from (1.6.1)
11. She is active ~~in~~ not only <u>in</u> a civic group but also in an athletic organization. *OR* She is active in not only a civic group but ~~in~~ also an athletic organization. (1.6.2)
12. That is either a mistake or ~~was~~ an intentional omission. (1.6.2)
13. The question is whether to set up a booth at the convention or ~~be~~ <u>to</u> host a hospitality suite. (1.6.2)
14. We are doing better ~~in~~ both <u>in</u> overall sales and in profits. *OR* in both overall sales and ~~in~~ profits. (1.6.2)
15. She had neither the preferred educational background, nor ~~did she have~~ <u>the</u> suitable experience. (1.6.2)

Chapter 7: Self-Assessment—Periods, Question Marks, and Exclamation Points

1. Dr. Eleanor H. Hutton has requested information on TaskMasters, Inc. (2.1)
2. That qualifies us as a rapidly growing new company, don't you think? (2.2)
3. Our president, Daniel Gruber, is a CPA. On your behalf, I asked him why he started the company. (2.1)
4. In the past three years, we have experienced phenomenal growth of 800 percent. *OR* ! (2.1, 2.3)
5. Contact me at 1358 N. Parsons Avenue, Tulsa, OK 74204. (2.1)
6. Jack asked, "Why does he want to know? Maybe he plans to become a competitor." *OR* ! (2.1, 2.2, 2.3)
7. The debt load fluctuates with the movement of the U.S. prime rate. (2.1)
8. I can't believe we could have missed such a promising opportunity! (2.3)
9. Is consumer loyalty extinct? Yes and no. (2.2, 2.1)
10. Johnson and Kane, Inc., has gone out of business. What a surprise. *OR* ! (2.1, 2.3)
11. Will you please send us a check today so that we can settle your account. (2.1)
12. Mr. James R. Capp will be our new CEO, beginning January 20, 2003. (2.1)
13. The rag doll originally sold for $1,098, but we have lowered the price to a mere $599. (2.1)
14. Will you be able to make the presentation at the conference, or should we find someone else? (2.2)
15. So I ask you, "When will we admit defeat?" Never! (2.2, 2.3)

Chapter 8: Self-Assessment—Semicolons and Colons

1. This letter looks good; that one doesn't. (2.4)
2. I want to make one thing perfectly clear: neither of you will be promoted if sales figures don't improve. (2.5)
3. The Zurich airport has been snowed in; therefore, I won't be able to meet with you before January 4. (2.4)
4. His motivation was obvious: to get Meg fired. (2.5)
5. Only two firms have responded to our survey: J. J. Perkins and Tucker & Tucker. (2.5)
6. Send a copy to Mary Kent, Marketing Director; Robert Bache, Comptroller; and Dennis Mann, Sales Director. (2.4)
7. Please be sure to interview these employees next week: Henry Gold, Doris Hatch, and George Iosupovich. (2.5)

8. We have observed your hard work; because of it, we are promoting you to manager of your department. (2.4)
9. You shipped three items on June 7; however, we received only one of them. (2.4)
10. The convention kit includes the following response cards: giveaways, brochures, and a display rack. (2.5)
11. The workers wanted an immediate wage increase; they had not had a raise in nearly two years. (2.4)
12. This, then, is our goal for 2003: to increase sales 35 percent. (2.5)
13. His writing skills are excellent; however, he still needs to polish his management style. (2.4)
14. We would like to address three issues: efficiency, profitability, and market penetration. (2.5)
15. Remember this rule: When in doubt, leave it out. (2.5)

Chapter 9: Self-Assessment—Commas

1. Please send us four cases of filters, two cases of wing nuts, and a bale of rags. (2.6)
2. Your analysis, however, does not account for returns. (2.6)
3. As a matter of fact, she has seen the figures. (2.6)
4. Before May 7, 1999, they wouldn't have minded either. (2.6)
5. After Martha has gone, talk to me about promoting her. (2.6)
6. Stoneridge, Inc., will go public on September 9, 2003. (2.6)
7. We want the new copier, not the old model. (2.6)
8. "Talk to me," Sandra said, "before you change a thing." (2.6)
9. Because of a previous engagement, Dr. Stoeve will not be able to attend. (2.6)
10. The company started attracting attention during the long, hard recession of the mid-1970s. (2.6)
11. You can reach me at this address: 717 Darby Place, Scottsdale, Arizona 85251. (2.6)
12. Transfer the documents from Fargo, North Dakota, to Boise, Idaho. (2.6)
13. Sam O'Neill, the designated representative, is gone today. (2.6)
14. With your help, we will soon begin. (2.6)
15. She may hire two new representatives, or she may postpone filling those territories until spring. (2.6)

Chapter 10: Self-Assessment—Dashes and Hyphens

1. Three qualities—speed, accuracy, and reliability—are desirable in any applicant to the data entry department. (2.7)
2. A highly placed source explained the top-secret negotiations. (2.8)
3. The file on Marian Gephardt—yes, we finally found it—reveals a history of late payments. (2.7)
4. They're selling a well-designed machine. (2.8)
5. A bottle-green sports jacket is hard to find. (2.8)
6. Argentina, Brazil, Mexico—these are the countries we hope to concentrate on. (2.7)
7. Only two sites—maybe three—offer the things we need. (2.7)
8. How many owner-operators are in the industry? (2.8)
9. Your ever-faithful assistant deserves—without a doubt—a substantial raise. (2.8, 2.7)
10. Myrna Talefiero is this organization's president-elect. (2.8)

11. Stealth, secrecy, and surprise—those are the elements that will give us a competitive edge. (2.7)
12. The charts are well-placed on each page—unlike the running heads and footers. (2.8, 2.7)
13. We got our small-business loan—an enormous advantage. (2.8, 2.7)
14. Ron Franklin—do you remember him?—will be in town Monday. (2.7)
15. Your devil-may-care attitude affects everyone involved in the decision-making process (2.8)

Chapter 11: Self-Assessment—Quotation Marks, Parentheses, Ellipses, Underscores, and Italics

1. Be sure to read "How to Sell by Listening" in this month's issue of <u>Fortune.</u> (2.10, 3.2)
2. Her response (see the attached memo) is disturbing. (2.11)
3. <u>Contact</u> is an overused word. (3.2)
4. We will operate with a skeleton staff during the holiday break (December 21 through January 2). (2.11)
5. "The SBP's next conference," the bulletin noted, "will be held in Minneapolis." (2.10)
6. Sara O'Rourke (a reporter from <u>The Wall Street Journal</u>) will be here on Thursday. (2.11, 3.2)
7. I don't care <u>why</u> you didn't fill my order; I want to know <u>when</u> you'll fill it. (3.2)
8. The term <u>up in the air</u> means "undecided" (2.10, 3.2)
9. Her assistant (the one who just had the baby) won't be back for four weeks. (2.11)
10. "Ask not what your country can do for you . . ." is the beginning of a famous quotation from John F. Kennedy. (2.10, 2.12)
11. Whom do you think <u>Time</u> magazine will select as its Man of the Year? (3.2)
12. Do you remember who said "And away we go"? (2.10)
13. Refinements in robotics may prove profitable. (More detail about this technology appears in Appendix A.) (2.11)
14. The resignation letter begins, "Since I'll never regain your respect . . ." and goes on to explain why that's true. (2.10, 2.12)
15. You must help her distinguish between <u>i.e.</u> (which means "that is") and <u>e.g.</u> (which means "for example"). (2.10, 3.2)

Chapter 12: Self-Assessment—Capitals and Abbreviations

1. Dr. <u>P</u>aul <u>H</u>ansen is joining our staff. (3.1)
2. New <u>C</u>aressa skin cream should be in a position to dominate that market. (3.1)
3. Send this report to ~~mister~~Mr. <u>H</u>. <u>K</u>. <u>D</u>anforth, ~~rural route~~RR 1, <u>W</u>arrensburg, ~~new york~~NY 12885. (3.1, 3.3)
4. You are responsible for training my new assistant to operate the <u>X</u>erox machine. (3.1)
5. She received her ~~master of business administration~~MBA degree from the <u>U</u>niversity of <u>M</u>ichigan. (3.1, 3.3)
6. The building is located on the corner of <u>M</u>adison and <u>C</u>enter streets. (3.1)

7. Call me tomorrow at 8 <u>a.m.</u> ~~morning~~, ~~pacific standard time~~<u>PST</u>, and I'll have the information you need. (3.3)
8. When <u>J</u>ones becomes <u>CEO</u> next month, we'll need your input <u>ASAP</u>. (3.1, 3.3)
9. Address it to <u>A</u>rt <u>B</u>owers, <u>C</u>hief of <u>P</u>roduction. (3.1)
10. Please <u>RSVP</u> to <u>S</u>ony ~~corp.~~<u>Corporation</u> just as soon as you know your schedule. (3.1, 3.3)
11. The data-processing department will begin work on ~~feb.~~<u>February</u> 2, just one ~~wk.~~<u>week</u> from today. (3.3)
12. You are to meet him on <u>F</u>riday at the <u>UN</u> building in <u>NYC</u>. (3.3)
13. Whenever you can come, <u>P</u>rofessor, our employees will greatly enjoy your presentation. (3.1)
14. At 50 per box, our ~~std.~~<u>standard</u> contract forms are $9 a box, and our warranty forms are $7.95 a box. (3.3)
15. We plan to establish a sales office on the <u>W</u>est <u>C</u>oast. (3.1)

Chapter 13: Self-Assessment—Numbers

1. We need to hire ~~one~~<u>1</u> office manager, ~~four~~<u>4</u> bookkeepers, and ~~twelve~~<u>12</u> clerk-typists. (3.4)
2. The market for this product is nearly ~~six~~<u>6</u> million people in our region alone. (3.4)
3. Make sure that all 1<u>,</u>835 pages are on my desk no later than ~~nine o'clock~~<u>9:00</u> a.m. (or *nine o'clock in the morning*) (3.4)
4. <u>In</u> 2002<u>,</u> ~~was the year that~~José Guiterez sold more than $50,000 ~~thousand dollars~~worth of stock. (3.4)
5. Our deadline is ~~4/7~~<u>April 7</u>, but we won't be ready before ~~4/11~~<u>April 11</u>. (3.4)
6. ~~95~~<u>Ninety-five</u> percent of our customers are men. *OR* Of our customers, 95 percent are men. (3.4)
7. More than ~~1/2~~<u>half</u> the U.S. population is female. (3.4)
8. Cecile Simmons, thirty-eight, is the first woman in this company to be promoted to management. (3.4)
9. Last year, I wrote 20 ~~15-~~<u>fifteen</u>-page reports, and Michelle wrote 24 three-page reports. (3.4)
10. Of the 15 applicants, ~~seven~~<u>7</u> are qualified. (3.4)

11. Our blinds should measure 38 inches wide by 64-<u>8/16</u> ~~and one half~~ inches long by 7/16 inches deep. (3.4)
12. Deliver the couch to ~~seven eighty-three~~<u>783</u> Fountain Rd., Suite ~~three~~<u>3</u>, Procter Valley, CA 92074. (3.4)
13. Here are the corrected figures: 42.7<u>0</u>% agree, 23.25% disagree, 34.<u>00</u>% are undecided, and the error is <u>0</u>.05%. (3.4)
14. You have to agree that 50<u>,000,000</u> million U.S. citizens cannot be wrong. (3.4)
15. We need a set of shelves 10 feet<u>,</u> ~~eight~~<u>8</u> inches long. (3.4)

Chapter 14: Self-Assessment—Vocabulary

1. except (4.1)
2. device (4.1)
3. loath (4.1)
4. ordinance (4.1)
5. precedence (4.1)
6. than (4.1)
7. who's (4.1)
8. <u>a lot</u>   In this department, we see <u>alot</u> of mistakes like that. (4.2)
9. <u>judgment</u>   In my <u>judgement</u>, you'll need to redo the cover. (4.3)
10. <u>regardless</u>   He decided to reveal the information, <u>irregardless</u> of the consequences. (4.2)
11. <u>accommodate</u>   Why not go along when it is so easy to <u>accomodate</u> his demands? (4.3)
12. <u>imply</u>   When you say that, do you mean to <u>infer</u> that I'm being unfair? (4.2)
13. <u>embarrassing</u>   She says that she finds this sort of ceremony <u>embarassing</u>. (4.3)
14. <u>to</u>   All we have to do is try <u>and</u> get along with him for a few more days. (4.2)
15. <u>precede</u>   A friendly handshake should always <u>preceed</u> negotiations. (4.3)

Second Custom Edition

THINKING
MAKING
DOING

Course Reader
HUMANITIES
CORE COURSE

Julia Reinhard Lupton,
Course Director

Elizabeth M. Losh,
Writing Director

Custom Publishing

New York   Boston   San Francisco
London   Toronto   Sydney   Tokyo   Singapore   Madrid
Mexico City   Munich   Paris   Cape Town   Hong Kong   Montreal

Cover art: courtesy of Ellen Lupton

Printed in the United States of America

10 9 8 7 6 5 4 3 2 1

2008240441

JL/LS

Pearson
Custom Publishing
is a division of

www.pearsonhighered.com

ISBN 10: 0-555-03662-6
ISBN 13: 978-0-555-03662-4